Preface

The purpose of this text is to provide the reader with an introduction to the theory and practice related to the development and operation of information systems in organizations. Although the use of the computer in information systems is emphasized, the reader is reminded throughout the text that it is not essential that a computer be part of the overall design of an information system. Perhaps more importantly, the computer is not to be equated with the information system.

This textbook is intended to be used both by students pursuing a career in information systems and by those students desiring some exposure to information systems as part of their general background. For the potential information systems analyst, the subject matter presented in this text provides the basic foundation required for subsequent study in information system theory and practice. For students pursuing careers in accounting, management, statistics, computer science, and so forth, the material presented in this text provides a perspective for how they will interact with the information system during both its development and operation. We believe this approach is consistent with existing policies where, for example, management students take a basic accounting course in order to better understand the importance of accounting to management practice, but not to become accountants. Additionally, in the literature, management and information systems experts are identifying a need for greater participation of nonsystems and data-processing personnel during the design of the information system. Obviously, this participation will be enhanced as these individuals better understand the role they can play during the design process.

First and foremost, *Information Systems: Theory and Practice* is a textbook, not a book that one reads at leisure, but rather a book that one studies and labors over in order to gain a better insight into the problems and promises of information systems. In order to create a meaningful textbook the authors must not only concentrate on what material is presented, but also on how that material is presented. All of the material presented here has been class tested numerous times and the authors have made a conscientious effort to insure the teachability of this text. Overall, the text is divided into four major parts.

Part I gives a basic introduction and analysis of data and information processing concepts. This part begins with an overview; discusses terms such as data, information, and systems; examines the informational needs of management for functions such as planning, controlling, and decision

v

making; analyzes the information system concept itself; and presents some major methods of tailoring the information system to meet management's needs.

Part II is an in-depth treatment of data base concepts. This part also begins with an overview, but is for the most part, a somewhat technical discussion of subjects such as classifying and coding data, designing data files, and associating and manipulating data elements.

Part III is basically a discussion of systems work and is presented in the form of a methodology for the development of information systems. This part includes a presentation of systems analysis, general systems design, systems justification, specific systems design, and systems implementation activities. The part concludes with a presentation of considerations for managing both the development and operation of the information system.

Part IV is a set of Appendices which contains a discussion of ideas and topics important to information systems theory and practice, but which are usually discussed more comprehensively in other courses. We have included them in this text so that the student might have a convenient reference for a better understanding of some of the material discussed in the first three parts, and as a help in solving the exercises and problems presented throughout the text. Appendix A presents a variety of logico-mathematical models; Appendix B provides a concise discussion of computer and related technology; Appendix C explains the use of systems analysis tools and techniques such as interviewing, flowcharting, decision tables, and so forth.

The structure of each chapter is also intended to enhance the teachability of the text. Each chapter begins with an introduction and statement of objectives for that chapter. (In some chapters, where the material has an implied sequence, these statements of objectives are replaced by a flowchart.) Each chapter concludes with a summary which highlights those points presented in the chapter. At the end of each chapter we have included four work areas, which are: (1) *Questions for Review* which relate directly to the material presented in the chapter; (2) *Questions for Discussion* which also relate directly to the material presented but are intended to spark classroom (and other) discussion; (3) *Exercises* to allow the student to work in specific areas and to gain working knowledge of a particular technique or approach; and (4) *Problems* which are similar to exercises but broader in scope and not always as "cut and dried" in terms of their solutions.

Many instructors prefer to assign "real world" projects to their students to support lectures and readings. While this approach has much to offer and is encouraged, often it cannot be implemented successfully at a given school or with a specific class. We believe the questions, exercises, and problems included within this text will provide some feeling for the "real world."

The material included in the text was designed for use in a one semester course at the junior-senior-graduate level. It is suggested that the material in the first three parts be presented in sequence. Parts of the appendices might then be assigned as reading in support of these materials. For schools

Information Systems:

Theory and Practice

Information Systems:
Theory and Practice

JOHN G. BURCH, Jr.
University of Massachusetts
Amherst, Massachusetts

FELIX R. STRATER, Jr.
Vistron Corporation
Northampton, Massachusetts

 Hamilton Publishing Company
SANTA BARBARA, CALIFORNIA

to our wives,
GLENDA and JUDY

Copyright © 1974, by John Wiley & Sons, Inc.
Published by **Hamilton Publishing Company**
a Division of John Wiley & Sons, Inc.

Library of Congress Cataloging in Publication Data:

Burch, John G., Jr.
  Information systems: theory and practice.

  Includes bibliographies.
    1. Management information systems. I. Strater,
Felix R., Jr., joint author. II. Title.

T58.6.B87   658.4'03   73-9884

Printed in the United States of America

10 9 8 7 6 5 4

where quarters replace semesters, or where students have a minimum of data processing background, an instructor could elect to exclude Chapter 9 in Part II, or to minimize the amount of time allocated for class discussion of the problems. Additional suggestions for using the text can be found in the instructor's manual.

The authors wish to acknowledge their gratitude to the many colleagues, reviewers, and students who contributed to the completion of this book. For their criticisms and suggestions, we are indebted to the following reviewers: Elba Basken, University of North Carolina; William Charlton, Sr., Villanova University; J. Daniel Couger, University of Colorado; Arthur J. Francia, Pennsylvania State University; Ephraim R. McLean, University of California; Fred F. Newpeck, University of Massachusetts; Edward H. Rategan, College of San Mateo; J. D. Siebel, Louisiana State University; Alvin Stehling, San Antonio College; Gary T. Sundem, University of Washington; Harold M. Sollenberger, Michigan State University; B. A. Donelson and J. P. Lucey, Vistron Corporation; and C. R. Purdum of The Standard Oil Company (Ohio). We are also indebted to Wayne Leininger for using several revisions of this book in his classes at Virginia Polytechnic Institute; to Thomas Coppola and Gary Grudnitski of the University of Massachusetts for reviewing and editing the last revision; to Major James Capellman who contributed several good problems included in this book; and to Michael J. Turillo who prepared the MICDEB National Bank case, a case which we feel helps to summarize and put into proper perspective the major aspects of this book. Also, we express our appreciation to the many students at the University of Massachusetts who used various revisions of the manuscript in class and freely offered their helpful criticisms. Special thanks go to Mrs. Vesta Powers, Mrs. Ginger Donovan, and Miss Audrey Weatherill for their tireless typing and editing of several drafts of this book Special gratitude is also due them for their competency and cheerful attitude. Most importantly, we are grateful to our wives who provided daily inspiration throughout the preparation of this book and to whom it is dedicated. Otherwise, the authors accept full responsibility for any errors and flaws that may still exist.

Amherst, Massachusetts   *John G. Burch, Jr.*
Northampton, Massachusetts   *Felix R. Strater, Jr.*

About the Authors

John G. Burch, Jr. is assistant professor of accounting and information systems in the School of Business, University of Massachusetts, Amherst. He received his B.S. degree from Louisiana Tech University, his M.A. and Ph.D. degrees from the University of Alabama. He has done consulting work in food processing and worked with students on a number of special "hands-on" system projects in a variety of organizations such as hospitals, universities, and manufacturing concerns. Dr. Burch has presented several papers at computer and system conferences, and has written several articles on information systems. He has had the responsibility of coordinating the computer facilities and teaching of the basic computer course for the School of Business at the University of Massachusetts, where he also has responsibility for developing data processing and information system courses. He belongs to several organizations such as the Association for Computing Machinery, Association for Systems Management, and Society for Management Information Systems. Prior to his academic career, he worked in general accounting and managerial positions in the construction and oil industry.

Felix R. Strater, Jr. received his B.S. degree from John Carroll University and is presently Manager of Data Processing in the Fabricated Plastics Division, Vistron Corporation, a wholly owned subsidiary of The Standard Oil Company (Ohio). He is responsible for computer operations, as well as the design and programming of computer-based information systems. Prior to joining Vistron, Mr. Strater's activities in data processing and information systems development included systems analysis and design for The Standard Oil Company (Ohio), analysis and programming for The United States Steel Corporation, and independent EDP consulting services, in which the major project was the design and implementation of an inventory control and sales analysis system for a major distributor of hospital supplies. Mr. Strater has also lectured in the training program of the The Standard Oil Company (Ohio), and has been a guest lecturer at the University of Massachusetts on the development of information systems. While researching this text, he assisted Dr. Burch in conducting a course using this material.

Contents

I Introduction to Data and Information Processing Concepts

1 Data and Information Processing — An Overview   3

1.1 Introduction   3

1.2 A Historical Perspective on Data and Information Processing   4

1.3 An Introduction to Data and Information Processing Today   6

1.4 The Systems Approach and Systems Analysis   9

1.5 The Information Systems Analyst   13

2 Analysis of Basic Data and Information Concepts   22

2.1 Introduction   22

2.2 The Concepts of Data and Information   23

2.3 Producing Information from Data   26

2.4 Economics of Information   30

3 Analysis of Systems, Management, and Formal Information System Concepts   **45**

3.1   Introduction   45
3.2   Overview of Systems   46
3.3   Overview of Management   50
3.4   Overview of Formal Information Systems   56

4 Analysis of Information Systems   **70**

4.1   Introduction   70
4.2   General Discussion of Information Systems   71
4.3   Hierarchical Approach to Information Systems Design   74
4.4   Systems Approach to Information Systems Design   79
4.5   Applications   92

5 Tailoring the Information System to Meet Specific Informational Requirements   **110**

5.1   Introduction   110
5.2   Filtering Method   111
5.3   Monitoring Method   114
5.4   Modeling Method   117
5.5   Interrogative Method   123
5.6   External Method   123

II Introduction to Data Base Concepts

6 The Data Base—An Overview   133

6.1 Introduction   133
6.2 Definition of Data Base   134
6.3 Data Base Management   136
6.4 Analysis of Generalized Data Base
    Management Systems   141
6.5 Implementing a Sophisticated Data Base   143

7 Classifying and Coding Data   156

7.1 Introduction   156
7.2 Classification of Data Items   157
7.3 Coding Considerations   158
7.4 Types of Code Structures   160
7.5 Selected Coding Examples   165

8 General File Storage Considerations   175

8.1 Introduction   175
8.2 Computer Storage Media   176
8.3 Composition of Data Files   178
8.4 Classification of Data Files   181
8.5 Selection Considerations for File Media
    and File Organization Methods   184
8.6 File Design Considerations   188

9 Concepts of Data Structure, Association, and Manipulation   198

9.1   Introduction   198

9.2   Concepts of Data Structure   199

9.3   Concepts of Data Association   203

9.4   The Sorting Operation   209

9.5   Searching Techniques with Sorted Codes   213

9.6   Transformation Techniques for Direct Access   216

9.7   A Data Structure and Retrieval Application   218

III Introduction to Systems Work and the Information Systems Development Methodology

10 Systems Analysis   231

10.1   Introduction   231

10.2   Preparing to Conduct Systems Analysis   231

10.3   Sources of Study Facts for Systems Analysis   235

10.4   Frameworks for Fact Gathering   238

10.5   Techniques for Analyzing Study Facts   241

10.6   Communicating the Findings   242

11 General Systems Design   256

11.1   Introduction   256

11.2   The Design Process   257

11.3 Guidelines and Principles for
       Systems Design   264
11.4 Basic Design Alternatives and the
       Systems Design Proposal   266
11.5 Systems Design—An Example   269

12 System Evaluation and Justification   278

12.1 Introduction   278
12.2 General Systems Design Requirements   278
12.3 The Evaluation Process   283
12.4 Acquisition Considerations   286
12.5 Cost/Effectiveness Analysis   290

13 Detail Systems Design   306

13.1 Introduction   306
13.2 Control Points   307
13.3 Security Controls   318
13.4 Forms/Reports Design   324
13.5 Clerical Procedures   328
13.6 Program Specifications   330

14 Systems Implementation   344

14.1 Introduction   344
14.2 Training and Educating Personnel   345
14.3 Testing the System   347
14.4 Systems Conversion   349
14.5 Follow-Up to Implementation   355

15 Management Considerations of the Information System   360

15.1 Introduction   360

15.2 General Management Activities   360

15.3 Managing the Data Center   363

15.4 Managing Systems Work and Programming
      Development   365

15.5 Managing Maintenance   370

15.6 Auditing Considerations   374

15.7 Managing Change   378

IV Appendices

Introduction to Appendices

A Logico-Mathematical Models   392

Introduction   392

Traditional Accounting Models   393
  Bookkeeping Model   393
  Accounts   393
  Cost-Volume-Profit Model   394
  Budget and Performance Analysis Models   396
  Payoff Graph Analysis Model   397
  Net Present Value Model   398

Additional Models   398
  Contribution-By-Value Analysis Model   399
  Forecast Models   401
  The Least Squares Model   401
  The Exponential Smoothing Model   402
  Inventory Control Model   402
  Replenishment, Lead Time, and Safety Stock   402
  The Problem of How Much to Order   403
  Material Yield Analysis Model   404
  Quality Control Analysis and Reporting   405
  Network Model   406
  Expected Time   406
  Probability and Statistical Models   408

Probability Concepts 410
Statistical Concepts 411
Basic Queuing Models 412
Simulation Models 412
Linear Programming Model 413

B The Computer and Related Technology 418

Introduction 418

The Central Processor 418
  Overview of the Central Processor 419
  Size of the Central Processor 419
  Speed of the Processor 420
  Virtual Storage Technique 421
  Buffer Storage Technique 422
  Solid-State Storage 423
  Multiprocessors 423
  Types of Storage 424

Devices and Applications Peripheral to the CPU 424
  Analysis of Auxiliary Storage Devices 424
  Magnetic Tape 424
  Physical Characteristics 424
  Coding Scheme 426
  Density 426
  Transfer Rate 426
  Blocking Records 426
  Advantages/Disadvantages of Magnetic Tape 428
  Magnetic Disk 428
  Physical Characteristics 429
  Read Addressing 429
  Transfer Rate 430
  Simplified Example of Rating Disk Speeds 431
  Advantages/Disadvantages of Magnetic Disk 431
  Hybrid Systems 432
  Computer Output Microfilm (COM) 432
  Summary Characteristics of Auxiliary Storage Devices 432

Terminal Devices 434
  Telephone Terminals 434
  Intelligent Terminal 435
  Definition of Minicomputers 435
  Applications of Intelligent Terminals 435

Data Entry Techniques 436
  Keyboard-to-Storage 436
  Advantages/Disadvantages of Key-to-Storage Systems 436

Point of Sale (POS)   438
Optical Character Recognition (OCR)   438

Remote Computing Networks (RCN)   439
Classes of RCN   439
Advantages/Disadvantages of RCN   440

Word Processing   440
Definition of Word Processing   440
Application of Word Processing   440

Data Communications   441

Communication Channels   442

Data Transmission   442

Grade of Channels   443
Low-Speed Channels   443
Medium-Speed Channels   443
Comparison of Different Medium-Speed Services   444
High-Speed Channels   445

Modems   447
Modem Operation   447
Modem Types   447
Modulation Techniques   448

Multiplexers and Concentrators   448
Multiplexer   448
Concentrator   450

Programmable Communications Processors   450
Message-Switching   451
Front-End   451
Reasons for Using Programmable Communications
   Processors   452

Typical Front-End Configurations   452
Plug-for-Plug Replacements   453
Core-to-Core Systems   454
Psuedo-Device Systems   454
Data Link System   454
Inter-Computer Peripherals System   455

C Tools and Techniques of the Information Systems Analyst

                                                                458

Introduction   458

The Interview   458
Preparing to Interview   459
Conducting the Interview   459
Following Up the Interview   459

The Questionnaire   460
  Use of the Questionnaire in Systems Analysis   460
  Guidelines for Constructing a Questionnaire   460

Observation   460
  Types of Observation   461
  Preparing for Observation   461
  Conducting the Observation   461
  Following Up the Observation   461

Sampling and Document Gathering   461
  Sampling   462
  Document Gathering   462

Charting   463
  Organization Charts   464
  Physical Layout Charts   466
  Flowcharting   466
  The Template   471
  Other Charting Techniques   473
  Guidelines for Charting   475

Decision Tables and Matrices   476
  Decision Tables   476
  Structure of a Decision Table   477
  Decision Table Vocabulary   478
  Types of Decision Tables   479
  Constructing Decision Tables   479
  Matrices, Arrays and Value Tables   480

Glossary   483

Index   491

Introduction to Data and Information Processing Concepts

1 Data and Information Processing— An Overview

1.1 Introduction

Since the dawn of civilization people have required information to aid them in their personal battle for survival, as well as in their attempts to manage their organizations. The increasing complexity of society, particularly as it is manifested in social, political, and economic organizations, has concomitantly increased the requirement for more relevant information on a more timely basis. Before we analyze in some depth the informational requirements of modern organizations and the current approaches to processing data and information, we present in this chapter an overview to data and information processing. The specific objectives of this chapter are:

1. To provide a historical perspective on data and information processing.
2. To provide an introduction to modern data processing theory and technology.
3. To introduce the systems approach philosophy and its application in systems analysis.
4. To describe the role of the information systems analyst in modern organizations.

1.2 A Historical Perspective on Data and Information Processing

Historians have traced record keeping and data processing back to about 3500 B.C., where in Babylonia merchants were keeping records on clay tablets. Today, merchants still keep records and process data but clay tablets have been replaced by punched cards, magnetic tapes and disks, and other forms of recording media. In this section we briefly discuss (1) the significant events in the evolution of data and information processing and (2) the major pressures for producing still more information.

Significant Events

In recent years the terms "data processing" and "computer processing" have become somewhat synonymous in their usage. Certainly, in most organizations the computer is essential for a large part of the data processing requirement. However, from a historical viewpoint the computer can be viewed as simply the latest "revolution" in the evolution of data processing theory and technology. The first "revolution," and by far the most important, is the development of language and mathematical notation.

Although historians can not be sure when spoken languages originated, forms of ideographic writing can be traced back to the Babylonians of 3500 B.C. where records of wealth were imprinted on clay tablets (cuneiforms). However, it is not until 2,000 years later, that the Phoenicians can be credited with inventing the alphabet. Early systems of mathematics have also been traced to about 3500 B.C. Indeed, all subsequent developments in data and information processing are predicated upon these two achievements.

Through the use of language and mathematics people have continuously refined and expanded their knowledge and understanding of themselves and their environment. Moreover, the amount of available knowledge or information has become so vast that no one person is capable of obtaining all of it. As a result, we tend to pursue information in specialized areas such as physics, biology, economics, psychology, accounting, and so forth. While it is true that each new concept or idea discovered in one of these specialized areas directly affects what data are processed, how these data are processed, and what information is produced, a meaningful discussion of these contributions is obviously beyond the scope of this text. Our specialized interest lies in those accomplishments which affect the processing of data and information as a whole. For example, people have utilized many different media to record their thoughts and ideas since first using clay tablets. At one time or another records have been kept on stone, wood, metal, animal skins, papyrus, paper, and most recently, on magnetized surfaces.

Technology has consistently been developed in order to process quantitative data more efficiently. The abacus, perhaps the earliest known calculating device, has been in use since about 3000 B.C. In the seventeenth century there were three major advances in data processing technology: John Napier developed a set of numbered rods (Napier's Bones) which simplified multiplication and division operations; Blaise Pascal designed and built the first adding machine; and Gottfried Leibniz constructed a calculator that could add, subtract, multiply, and divide. In the nineteenth century, there were still further advances in data processing technology such as Joseph Jacquard's punched card loom, Charles Babbage's "difference engine" and "analytical engine," and Herman Hollerith's punched card machines which were used to process the 1890 census.

While each of these technological developments is important in the evolution of data and information processing, we must look to the fifteenth century for the second "revolution." This revolution resulted from the invention of the movable printing press. The printing press had an impact on humanity's ability to record, store, gain access to, report, and disseminate data and information, unlike any other achievement before it and for almost 500 years after it.

It is not until the twentieth century that we find our third "revolution" in data and information processing associated with a series of developments we can term collectively "mass-media." The impact of mass-media techniques such as radio and television are familiar to all of us although still not completely understood by any of us.

During this same century and even before the third "revolution" has subsided, data and information processing is experiencing a fourth "revolution" as a result of the digital computer. Similar to the impact of mass-media, the impact of the computer in our society is to a great degree an unknown quantity at this time. However, using the systems approach we seek to utilize the computer and its related technology, often in conjunction with mass-media techniques, to produce relevant information in modern organizations.

Pressures for More Information

In the previous section we discussed the evolution of data and information processing, primarily from the viewpoint of technological developments. Additional insights and understandings of this evolution can be obtained by examining briefly the pressures for producing more and more information.

Before the eighteenth century there were two primary reasons for processing data. First, there was a natural desire by men to provide an account of their possessions and wealth. As we previously cited, Babylonian merchants were keeping records back about 3500 B.C. Certainly as trade and commerce increased, people needed more and more aids to help keep track of details and state of affairs. In the fifteenth century, Luca Pacioli developed the double-entry bookkeeping system. This concept permitted economic events to be recorded in monetary terms by using a series of expense and equity accounts. This concept remains the foundation of our modern financial accounting systems today.

The second reason for processing data before the eighteenth century was governmental requirements. As tribes grew into nations, the authorities of these nations — Egypt, Israel, Greece, etc. — compiled administrative surveys to be used for raising taxes and conscripting soldiers.

In the mid-eighteenth century, there developed still more pressures for formally processing data. The Industrial Revolution had taken the basic tasks of production from the home and the small shop and put them into factories. The development of these large manufacturing organizations led to the development of other service industries such as marketing and transportation. Thus, the increased size and complexity of these organizations prohibited any one individual from effectively managing the organization without some data processing to provide additional information. Moreover, with the advent of the large factory system and mass production techniques, the need for more sophisticated capital goods necessitated large investments. These large capital needs forced the separation of investor from management. On one hand, management needed more information for internal decisions, while investors, on the other hand, needed information about the organization, and management's performance.

As new business policies emerged, the need to process data also increased. For example, the granting of credit created a need to maintain accounts receivable, accounts payable, and credit statistics. The concepts of financial accounting, which continued to be refined and expanded upon through the years, also required more data processing. In order to produce greater efficiency in production, the pioneers of "scientific management" identified the need for still more data and information processing.

The regulation, not only of corporations, but of society in general, by various government agencies has made a significant impact upon the data processing and reporting systems of many organizations by forcing these organizations to adopt up-to-date data processing practices. In the United States, government regulatory agencies include the several state regulatory commissions; the Interstate Commerce

Commission; the Federal Power Commission; the Securities and Exchange Commission; environmental control boards; the departments of Health, Education, and Welfare; and of Housing and Urban Development; and so on. All of these groups, in one form or another, require a variety of reports from many organizations and institutions throughout the country. Therefore, not only does the reporting organization have to maintain a sound data processing system, but the regulatory bodies must likewise maintain similar systems to handle large volumes of data. As a matter of fact, the United States government is by far the largest data processor in the country.

1.3 An Introduction to Data and Information Processing Today

As we have seen from our historical perspective on data and information processing, the information requirements of the modern organization are both vast and complex. In this section we will analyze both the role of logical and mathematical models and the digital computer in satisfying these requirements.

Logical and Mathematical Models

As the size, complexity, and specialization in organizations increase, it becomes increasingly difficult for decision makers to allocate available resources to various activities in a manner that is most effective and optimal for the organization as a whole. The design and implementation of logical and mathematical models can help to solve the problems of complexity in modern day organizations. Thus, in addition to developing reports and methods for historical record keeping and to satisfy operational and governmental requirements, modern information systems must include logico-mathematical models to provide alternative, predictive, optimative, and control information. (Refer to the Appendices for an in-depth discussion of several major logico-mathematical models.) The

development of such models is often referred to as the management science approach.

Some of the work done by people such as Frederick Taylor, H. L. Gantt, and Henri Fayol, anticipated the management science approach to decision making; however, the field of management science received its greatest impetus during and subsequent to World War II. There was a great need to allocate resources to the war effort in the most efficient manner and to help determine the most effective operations of warfare. Many of these endeavors were successful and it did not take long for many of these same techniques to find their way into helping management in industry after the war. Like military strategists, the managements of organizations must make decisions which deal with the future course of action for the organization over both the short run and long run. Managers are confronted with numerous decisions ranging from the routine to the highly complex. The latter includes such problems as: (1) sales promotion, (2) location of plant, (3) optimum product mix, (4) make or buy, (5) distribution of rolling stock, (6) production scheduling, (7) budgeting policies, (8) forecasting, (9) procurement policies, (10) financial planning, (11) selection of marketing channels, (12) personnel selection and control, (13) inventory control, (14) quality control, (15) scheduling and control, and so on.

The central theme of management science is to provide ACTION information, i.e., information from which management does take action. As Wagner[1] suggests, qualities of the management science approach are:

1. *A Primary Focus on Decision Making.* The principal results of the analysis must have direct and unambiguous implications for executive action.
2. *An Appraisal Resting on Economic Effectiveness Criteria.* A comparison of the various feasible actions must be based on measurable values that unequivocally reflect the fu-

[1] Harvey M. Wagner, *Principles of Management Science* (Englewood Cliffs, New Jersey: Prentice-Hall, Inc., 1970), p. 5. Used with permission of Prentice-Hall, Inc.

ture well-being of the organization. In a commercial firm, these measured quantities typically include variable costs, revenues, cash flow, and rate of return on incremental investment. A recommended solution must have evaluated the tradeoffs and have struck an optimum balance among these sometimes conflicting factors.

3. *Reliance on a Formal Mathematical Model.* The procedures for manipulating the data should be so explicit that they can be described to another analyst, who in turn would derive the same data.

4. *Dependence on an Electronic Computer.* This characteristic is not really a desideratum but rather a requirement necessitated by either the complexity of the mathematical model, the volume of data to be manipulated, or the magnitude of computations needed to implement the associated management operating and control systems.

The essence or key ingredient of management science is the formulation and manipulation of a model. This approach deals with logico-mathematical models which are used to study quantitatively treatable aspects of problems. The use of these models is based on a scientific attitude towards management phenomena. This attitude is normally called the scientific method which is based on a logical sequence of steps followed in any scientific research. These steps are:

1. *Observation.* The analyst makes a general examination of the situation to define the problem. In this phase, all the facts and relationships of the problem are identified.

2. *Formulation of Model.* The construction of the model is a direct result of the observation phase. It therefore expresses interrelationships of the variables and restrictions involved in the problem. In information systems work, the model can be a graph, a flowchart, an organizational chart, a statistical report, and, as so often is the case, it can be a model defined in symbolic and mathematical terms.

3. *Testing the Model.* The model is usually tested several times before it is used for the

basis of decision making. A key function of the model is its predictive ability, and data are gathered and manipulated via the model to test its effectiveness. Based on test results, modifications and refinements are made until it is perfected for application.

4. *Application.* The model is applied to give management the information needed for decision making.

It must be obvious to the student of information systems, that application of logico-mathematical models can never provide the basis for all decisions. Many informational needs of the organization can be met by establishing a well-designed data base and from it providing timely reports or online responses to the decision maker via remote terminals such as teletypes or cathode-ray tubes (CRT). Significant decisions, in many instances based on some rather fundamental reports, can be made effectively if the information contained in the reports is relevant and timely.

Although the use of logico-mathematical models is a vital component in providing information to management, by itself, it is not capable of meeting the total spectrum of informational needs. The context of the data processing and information system activities will, in most cases, encompass and utilize modeling techniques.

Digital Computer*

Although the computer affects all of our lives in one way or another, it remains today one of the most misunderstood tools of humanity's creative genius. If we were to ask at random a number of people passing on a street corner to provide us with their understanding of a computer, the responses would most likely be similar to the description of the elephant provided by the five blind men after each was given an opportunity to touch one part of the elephant's body before being queried. This situation exists today even though the computer has been used

---

* This section contains a very broad overview of the computer. For an in-depth discussion of the computer and its related technology, refer to the Appendices.

as an information processing tool in business and government for over twenty years.

Conceptually, a computer is composed of a processing unit having arithmetic and logical capabilities, a mechanism for placing data ("input") into the processing unit, a mechanism for storage of the data during processing, and a mechanism that allows the operator to obtain as "output" the information that has been processed. The computer's capabilities are limited to executing arithmetic calculations and executing decisions which are now limited to two alternatives. Figure 1.1 is a conceptual model of a computer.

Combining the computer's basic capabilities of arithmetic calculations and decision making power permits higher level activities such as the arranging, summarizing, calculating, retrieving, and storing of data to occur. Media for input to the computer, and output from the computer, are almost unlimited and depends on the computer in question. The normal media for input are punched cards, punched paper tape, magnetic tapes and disks, and magnetic markings on paper. Input can be entered into the computer through the use of dial settings, keyed directly into storage, or, even via the human voice. Output from the computer is normally recorded on printed paper, punched cards, magnetic tape or disk, and microfilm. Output can be achieved via recordings of human voices or electronic vibrations simulating the human voice. While the internal speed of the computer is measured in fractions of a second, the input-output data speeds are significantly slower, and are directly related to the input-output media being used.

One of the major themes of this chapter is the recognition of increasing size, complexity, and rapid change in our institutions and organizations. The computer, with the proper software, uniquely provides us with a tool for dealing with these complexities and changes. A conventional comment is that we have developed two kinds of tools: one is the physical tool which extends our muscle and handicraft power such as saws, hammers, motors, wheels, levers, etc., and the other is the intellectual tool which extends our minds. The computer obviously falls into the second category. It is only a tool, albeit a powerful tool, which will never control us but rather, will aid us in coping with complex organizations and a rapidly changing environment.

To deal with rapid change, the decision maker's effectiveness depends on a heterogeneous flow of information which is both relevant and timely. This kind of information will enable decision makers to operate under conditions of rapid change. The provision of this kind of information will require the design and implementation of fast response systems. Typical of online, fast response systems are airline reservation systems, banking systems, inventory control systems, stock price quotation services, and others.

The combination of computers with telecommunications media (telephone and microwave, for example) has provided us with powerful tools and techniques for implementing fast response systems, thus adding a new dimension to the information systems concept. As long as the data files are within reach of the telecommunications network, the decision maker can retrieve the information in these

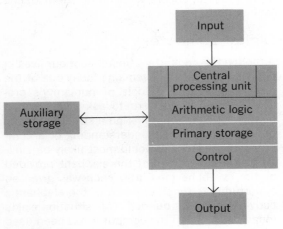

FIGURE 1.1. A conceptual model of a digital computer.

files and interact with the system. The effect of this interaction with the information system, on a fast response basis, is that time and space are compressed for the decision makers allowing them to manage their environment on a more timely basis.

1.4 The Systems Approach and Systems Analysis

The systems approach is a philosophy widely utilized today to direct the overall structuring of data processing activities necessary to satisfy the information requirements of modern organizations. In this section we provide an introduction to the systems philosophy and, an analysis of its practical application, systems analysis. Systems analysis is popular today, both as a general problem solving technique and, as a method for developing information systems.

The Systems Approach Philosophy

The systems approach is a philosophy or perception of structure which coordinates, in an efficient and optimum manner, the activities and operations within any organization or system. A system can be defined as any integrated assemblage of components or subsystems designed to achieve an objective. (The concept of a system is analyzed in depth in Chapter 3 of this part.) Defining what is to be a system is a logical distinction which may or may not relate to the actual distinctions found in reality. With the systems approach we are concerned with the individual component and we emphasize its role in the system, rather than its role as an individual entity. Using the systems approach to describe reality may provide an important benefit to the user. The effectiveness of components considered collectively as a system may be greater than the sum of the effectiveness of each component considered separately. This synergistic effect is often described as "the whole is greater than the sum of its parts." One of the tendencies of modern day organizations is increasing specialization. Components of an organization tend to evolve into relatively autonomous groups. Each group has its own objectives and value systems and can thus lose sight of how their activities and goals interrelate with those of the organization as a whole. Implementation of the systems approach cuts across traditional functional lines of the organization to gain optimization for the entire organization.

Normally, in most organizations there is an inherent conflict between different functions. Ideally, the problems of each functional area should be solved according to the objectives of the overall organization. Full optimization requirements include: (1) consideration of all alternatives, (2) consideration of all outside events, and (3) maximization of the objective functions of the entire organization. To illustrate this inherent conflict between functional areas, the problem of inventory control is used as an example.

The sales department, in general, wishes to have a large inventory of different products in order to achieve 100% customer service level. This objective of the sales department is impracticable and, consequently, clashes with the overall objective of the organization. On the contrary, the production department may wish to manufacture in large lot sizes to minimize production costs, but this reduction in production costs may give rise to increased in-process inventories and greater working capital requirements. The financial officer's objective is to cut the investment in inventory to a minimum. Still another point of view is that of the warehouse manager whose objective it is to establish routine methods of handling, receiving and shipping inventory and, thus, decrease special handling costs. It can, therefore, be seen that there are distinct and conflicting functions in an organization which need coordination to gain total optimization.

The function of management in today's large and complex organization is to coordinate and interrelate the activities of the various functional areas and optimize the objectives of the total organization. The systems approach philosophy is therefore the manner in which management views the interrelationship of the subsystems of the organization. The successful manager must bring these individual, often conflicting, subsystems into an integrated system with all subsystems working together to obtain the organizational goals. As pointed out earlier, with increasing size, specialization, complexity, and rapid change in most organizations, this problem of bringing together the subsystems of the organization into a viable whole will become even more acute in the future.

Although we will discuss how the systems approach is used for both problem solving and the development of information systems, there are a few guidelines which are applicable in general for utilizing this concept:

1. *Integration.* The various subsystems of the system must be integrated in such a manner to take advantage of the interrelatedness and interdependence between each element.

2. *Communication.* Channels of communication must be open between subsystems at all times.

3. *Scientific Method.* The scientific method must be applied by utilizing the various management science techniques.

4. *Decision Oriented.* In order to make the management function of planning and controlling more effective, programmed decision making is developed where appropriate. The objective is to program well defined decision systems, such as scheduling and logistics, to the point where they will be self-regulating. This approach will relieve management from much of the perfunctory, diversionary activities that he would otherwise be required to perform. The extra time which results will allow management to devote more attention to unstructured, nonprogrammed decision making.

5. *Technology.* The analyst should utilize modern technology wherever possible to aid in the implementation of techniques which develop from the above four guidelines, e.g., the computer significantly enhances integra-

tion, communication, the scientific method, and programmed decision making.

Systems Analysis and Problem Solving

Systems analysis utilizes both quantitative methods, where they are applicable, as well as qualitative factors such as judgment, creativeness, heuristics, common sense, and experience. When and where to begin systems analysis is somewhat arbitrary. Numerous think sessions and various empirical studies and experiences may precede the realization that systems analysis should be undertaken.

Within the framework of a problem solving approach, there are six basic steps to applying systems analysis:

1. Definition and formulation of the problem;
2. Development of alternative solutions;
3. Construction of models which formalize the alternatives;
4. Determination of the cost/effectiveness of the alternatives;
5. Presentation of recommendations;
6. Implementation of the chosen alternative.

Figure 1.2 illustrates these steps and highlights their iterative relationship.

A major task in performing systems analysis is to maximize the effectiveness of the solution at a minimum cost. To achieve this cost/effectiveness, alternative courses of action must be derived and compared. Any course of action requires a commitment of resources and produces an output at some level of effectiveness. An organization may take one approach to the exclusion of the other. For example:

1. *Effectiveness Approach.* For a specified level of effectiveness to be attained in the achievement of some objective, the analyst attempts to effect alternatives which will attain that level.

2. *Cost Approach.* For a specified level of resources, the analyst attempts to determine alternatives which will produce the highest level of effectiveness possible.

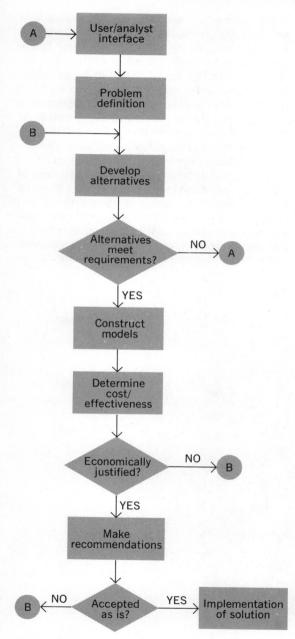

FIGURE 1.2. Schematic showing steps and iterative process of systems analysis used in problem solving.

Ideally, there has to be an optimum balance between the two approaches. There is some point where further effectiveness is insignificant when compared to cost. For example, if we can provide two alternative reports (A & B) for a decision making function and Report A can be provided twice per day and Report B can be provided once per day, is the additional effectiveness of getting Report A twice per day worth the extra cost? Suppose the cost to produce Report A is $100.00 per report and the cost for Report B is $130.00. On a per year basis, Report A costs $25,550 more than Report B (assuming 365 days). The additional decision making effectiveness represented by a quicker reporting cycle of Report A would have to be weighed against the added decision effectiveness which the same $25,550 would produce if applied to other purposes. Therefore, we have a tradeoff and opportunity cost phenomenon present in optimally minimizing cost while maximizing effectiveness. What this $25,550 would achieve, if it is not traded off to other alternatives, represents the opportunities foregone (or opportunity cost) of choosing a given course of action, which in this case would be Report A.

Systems Analysis and the Development of an Information System

The application of systems analysis to the development of an information system normally spans a greater time period than is associated with problem solving in general. Of course, this is not necessarily true in all cases. Moreover, the development of the information system from one viewpoint can be termed a solution to a problem, i.e., the need to know. However, to better describe the activities being performed during the development of a system we can identify three phases:

1. Systems Analysis
2. Systems Design
3. Systems Implementation

The activities performed in these phases closely parallel the six steps outlined previously. For example, *Systems Analysis* is similar to step 1—the definition and formulation of the problem. More appropriately it involves defining and describing the systems goals, objectives, and requirements. The *Systems Design* phase includes similar activities to steps 2–5. These activities may be restated as follows:

2. Develop alternative designs;
3. Build models which formalize the alternative designs;
4. Determine the cost/effectiveness of the design alternatives;
5. Make recommendations.

The activities comprising the phase labeled *Systems Implementation* would equate to step 6—implement the chosen alternative.

These three phases of systems development are depicted in Figure 1.3 as constituting the systems life cycle. In addition, the major activities of systems work related to each phase are also shown in this figure. (Each of these activities is discussed in depth in Part II and Part III.) Using the life cycle concept is an excellent way of illustrating the viable and dynamic nature of the information system itself. In addition, the life cycle concept provides us with an overview of the systems development methodology.

As with any dynamic entity, the usefulness of the information system's output, the efficiency of its operations, and the reliability of the overall system's performance can vary considerably over time. Consequently, the information system is subject to deterioration, obsolescence, and eventually, to replacement. How-

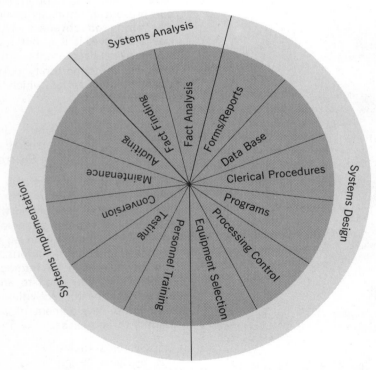

FIGURE 1.3. An illustration of the life cycle of an information system and the major activities associated with each life cycle phase.

ever, it is seldom that the information system in total is implemented at one point in time. Consequently, part of the information system, or a subsystem in the organization, is more than likely due to be repaired or rebuilt continuously.

At first glance, it would appear that the cycle time is equivalent to the rate at which the systems life cycle is repeated over and over again. Some authorities view the time cycle in terms of years. Many information systems experts project a normal information systems life cycle as being from two to ten years before a major redesign or overhaul is required. This judgment of the life cycle of an information system is subject to many conditions, and must be made for each individual information system or subsystem.

We feel, however, that the cycle time is really misleading in the sense that it connotes periodicity or a start-stop relationship. Generally, the application of the phases in the life cycle is a highly iterative and interactive ongoing operation, which is usually accomplished at the subsystem level and generally continues until the total system is modified and eventually supplanted. The situation where a systems analyst constructs a total system from scratch is rare, but if this is indeed the case, then the same phases as shown in Figure 1.3 would also be applicable.

1.5 The Information Systems Analyst

The catalyst and key person in the analysis, design, and implementation of the formal information system is the information systems analyst. This functional position is responsible for assisting the users of information in defining what information is required; how available data can be transformed into information; what technology is available to be utilized; and what is the best mix of money, men, machines, materials, and methods for implementing the information system. In this section we define the role of information systems analysts, analyze their activities within the context of the

systems life cycle, and speculate on their future roles in organizations.

Definition of the Information Systems Analyst

Basically, the systems analyst is a person who is an interface between the users of the information system and the technical persons, such as programmers, data base administrators, and machine operators, who work in the system. This function is a logical one, since information systems are developed to fulfill the requirements of a variety of users throughout organizations having (in most instances) a computer as a major, but certainly not the sole component of the system. The programming and computer operation functions that usually exist in information systems operations are mainly involved in the technical aspects of implementation and in maintenance activities.

Systems work has both a logical and physical nature. The logical aspects pertain to specifying the content and structure of the information system; the physical side is concerned with the specific software and hardware to be utilized. The systems analyst, therefore, to be effective, must: (1) be creative but pragmatic, (2) be a catalyst, and yet an arbiter, and (3) be organization-oriented, as well as technology-oriented.

The Analyst's Role in the Systems Life Cycle

During the *Systems Analysis* phase the analyst is involved with assisting the constituents, management, and other operating personnel of the organization with identifying what information is required, when it is required, how it is required, and for whom it is required. The problems during this phase are numerous but the analyst must give special attention to quantifying what is often expressed qualitatively or vaguely. Perhaps the most important value the analyst can add in this phase is to assist the information user in identifying what information is truly needed. This is often different from what users "think" they need, since their thoughts are based on some preconceived notion of what can be provided.

During the *Systems Design* phase the analyst is provided with an opportunity to be creative and original in determining how information may be processed. The main aspect of this phase is the translation of the information requirements specified in the investigation phase into a detailed plan. This phase may require interaction with certain technicians within the information system. The analyst should bring to bear their knowledge of what technology is available, what techniques are meaningful, and how resources can best be utilized.

Specific activities which require the analyst's attention during design include: (1) input and output forms, (2) logical and physical data base structure, (3) clerical procedures, (4) computer programs, and (5) processing controls. The criticalness of the analyst's function in this phase was made clear by a recent industry survey, which revealed that less than half of the new information systems undergoing design and development are ever completely developed and installed.

If an analyst's knowledge of processing techniques and tools is outdated or limited, it follows that any system he or she designs will reflect that knowledge. On the other hand, the analyst must guard against over designing. Today, in many organizations, much of the frustration which exists concerning the overall development of information systems can be traced to analysts who designed (or attempted to design) "superhighways" when all the organization required, or could afford, was a "hiking trail."

All of the analysis and design efforts come to a climax during the *Systems Implementation* phase of the life cycle. The analyst must identify cut off dates, train and coordinate user personnel, instruct computer personnel, install new procedures and forms, test the new system, and be on the alert for significant oversights or omissions from early phase endeavors. Unfortunately, more than one good information system has been scrapped due to poor conversion and implementation performance.

Systems maintenance, a seemingly unglamorous but necessary job, continues throughout the operation life of the system. The analyst will constantly be called upon to explain various aspects of the system to operating and management personnel. In addition, the analyst will have to identify systems malfunctions and prescribe remedies. The analyst should continuously monitor the system looking for ways to improve its performance, as well as to add new elements, as users' needs change. Finally, at some point in time, the analyst will again review the system in order to recommend a new, greatly improved, information system or subsystem for the organization.

The role of the information systems analyst just presented is, of course, a composite picture. In a large organization the information system is a vast, complex entity. There are many analysts involved in designing and implementing even one subsystem of the organization's information system. At a given point in time, an analyst might well be executing activities related to more than one phase of the system life cycle and these activities must be properly coordinated.

To make the system more effective, the systems analyst will be engaged in a wide spectrum of activities which will range from: (1) formal to informal, (2) quantitative to qualitative, (3) structured to unstructured, (4) specific to general, and (5) traditional to revolutionary. In performing these activities, the analyst will require the use of such tools and techniques as flow charts, decision tables, matrices, graphs, narrative reports, interviews, and management science techniques. The application of these tools and techniques reinforce one another and, when viewed in combination, provide the basis for systems work.

In Part III we analyze in depth the systems development methodology where the use of these tools and techniques is of utmost importance. However, because these aids are independent from the methodology itself and can be used in solving the exercises and problems

MAJOR ACTIVITIES OF SYSTEMS WORK

TECHNIQUES	Systems Analysis	Fact Finding	Fact Analysis	Systems Design	Forms/Reports	Data Base	Equipment Selection	Procedure Writing	Program Specifications	Systems Implementation	Personnel Training	Systems Testing	Auditing	Maintenance	General	Communication	Problem Definition
Interview	x				x	x				x		x	x			x	x
Observation	x									x		x	x			x	x
Charting	x	x		x	x	x	x	x		x	x	x	x			x	x
Questionnaire	x				x						x	x	x				x
Sampling	x	x		x							x	x	x				x
Document Gathering	x	x									x	x					x
Tables/Matrices	x	x			x	x	x	x		x	x	x	x			x	x
Models/Simulation	x	x		x	x	x		x		x	x	x	x			x	x

FIGURE 1.4.   A summary of the major tools and techniques, utilized by the analyst in the development of information systems, as related to the major activities of systems work.

presented throughout this text, we have provided complete descriptions of the major tools and techniques utilized by the systems analyst in the Appendices. Figure 1.4 summarizes these tools and techniques and relates them to the major systems development activities where they can be utilized.

The Future Role of the Systems Analyst

The role of the systems analyst continues to increase in importance. Certainly the costs of designing, developing, installing, and maintaining the complex information systems required today justify this special attention. But more importantly, the costs of providing inadequate or incomplete information versus the benefits of producing timely, relevant information cannot be left to chance.

Many individuals currently being hired . . . have an educational background inadequately suited to the job requirements. . . . This will not be sufficient for the future. . . .

Adequate preparation for positions in information systems requires an intensive educational background, one which provides concentration on both organizational and computer systems, as well as on the development process itself. Earlier analysis has led to the conclusion that such programs do not now exist in American universities.[2]

The importance of the information systems analyst is beginning to be reflected by the appearance of special curriculums in several colleges and universities across the country. Moreover, many large organizations have developed in-house formal training programs in order to develop competent information systems analysts. One of the problems that has prohibited both the universities and other organizations from providing this training earlier, has been the lack of agreement on what a program for developing systems analysts should include.

[2] R. L. Ashenhurst (ed.) "A Report of the ACM Curriculum Committee on Computer Education for Management," Volume 15, Number 5, May, 1972 *Communications of the ACM* (New York: Association For Computing Machinery, Inc.) p. 369. Copyright 1972, Association for Computing Machinery, Inc., By Permission.

Traditionally, commercial and public organizations developed their information systems personnel either from the ranks of computer programmers or from office methods departments. Managements of many organizations have begun to realize, however, that the function of a systems analyst is not necessarily a logical development from that of a computer programmer. Institutes of formal education, on the other hand, have traditionally offered special courses in computer technology, systems analysis, and management science techniques. With few exceptions, these course offerings have not been coordinated into an integrated program for developing information systems analysts as such. Much existing education for management deals with making decisions on the basis of available data and does not prepare the student for clinically analyzing information needs in a systematic fashion. Similarly, existing computer science education, usually emphasizing algorithmic problem solving rather than system dynamics, does not prepare the student for the discipline of evolving system specifications. The problem then is to make up for these deficiencies on both the organizational and the technological sides and to offer an integrated approach to information analysis and system design.[3]

SUMMARY

People have always had a need for information to aid them in the control of their environment. The evolution of data and information processing is characterized by

³ *Ibid*

advancements in both theory and technology. The most significant events in this evolution are: (1) the development of language and mathematical notation, (2) the invention of the printing press, (3) the emerging of mass-media, and (4) the development of the digital computer. The major pressures for more information are: (1) accountability; (2) government regulations; and (3) the size, growth, specialization, and complexity of organizations.

The two key factors impacting on modern data processing are: (1) logico-mathematical models and (2) the digital computer.

The Systems Approach is a philosophy or perception of structure which emphasizes the role of a component in a larger order or system of components. Systems Analysis is a term used to describe the practical application of the Systems Approach. Systems Analysis is widely utilized as (1) a general approach to problem solving and (2) an efficient approach to developing information systems.

As it relates to information systems, systems work contains three major phases: (1) Systems Analysis, (2) Systems Design, and (3) Systems Implementation. The application of these three phases to the information system, depicts the system as experiencing a life cycle. This life cycle concept reflects the dynamic nature of the information system.

The functions of the systems analyst are required in all organizations, although they are not necessarily performed exclusively by one individual. In performing systems work, the analyst uses a variety of tools and techniques. The function of the systems analyst promises to increase in importance in the foreseeable future.

REVIEW QUESTIONS

1.1 In general terms, trace the evolution of record keeping and data processing.

1.2 List and explain the major reasons for increased data processing demands.

1.3 Explain the role of logico-mathematical models in providing information to managements of organizations.

1.4 Compare and contrast the scientific method concept, and the management science concept.

1.5 List and define the computer hardware components installed at your school, or at some organization with which you are familiar.

1.6 Define computer memory. How does the concept of memory differ from the concept of storage?

1.7 Why not capture data in the precise form and media wanted for input to the central processing unit?

1.8 Define the term "Systems Approach." What benefits are associated with utilizing this approach? What might be some of the difficulties associated with utilizing this approach?

1.9 Describe at least three different practical situations utilizing the systems approach philosophy.

1.10 What is systems analysis? How does it differ from classical analysis?

1.11 Explain the basic steps in applying systems analysis in problem solving.

1.12 Define the term cost/effectiveness. Give at least two examples from recent government decisions where cost/effectiveness played a major role in determining the decision.

1.13 Explain what is meant by "systems life cycle." Referencing other systems texts, list two other synonyms for each phase named in the life cycle.

1.14 Compare, and contrast, the role of the systems analyst with that of an industrial engineer, a management consultant, an auditor, and an efficiency expert.

1.15 Define the term "systems work." Give five examples of what systems work entails.

1.16 List at least three tools and/or techniques which the systems analyst might use to do each of the following:

    (A) determine an individual's information requirements,

    (B) describe a complex decision making process,

    (C) describe the steps related to the use of a specific document,

    (D) explain an overall work proposal,

    (E) determine the volume or occurrence of a given event or transaction.

QUESTIONS FOR DISCUSSION

1.1 The emergence of large organizations, development of technology, and government regulation has created a need for sophisticated information systems. Discuss fully.

1.2 Discuss why management needs information. Is it possible for the management of an organization to make effective decisions without the aid of an information system? Discuss fully.

1.3 As President of General Motors what might your information needs be hourly? daily? weekly? monthly? annually? What might the information needs of the Governor of your state be for the same time periods?

1.4 Discuss the impact that technological changes have had on data processing techniques. Also discuss the impact of technological changes on the need for more information.

1.5 Why do modern organizations need more sophisticated information systems? Select one modern organization and list several of the users of the information system. What are their informational needs?

1.6 Identify and discuss the social, economic, and technological changes which are taking place today and determine what role, if any, the information systems analyst will play in aiding the proper control and management of these changes.

1.7 Elaborate on those organizations, institutions, and developments which have created an impetus for more timely and better information.

1.8 During the early part of this century, "barnstormers" could traverse the skies without the aid of sophisticated navigational and control systems. Why? Compare this situation with aviation today. Also, using an aviation and navigational system as an analogy, compare it with present day organizational information systems.

1.9 Discuss the positive and negative social consequences of technological development. Choose any subject you wish, e.g., computers, automobiles, television, space travel, jet planes.

1.10 "Instead of us controlling technology, it is controlling us." Discuss this statement.

1.11 Larger corporations have created a need for better information reporting for both managers of the corporation and various groups external to the corporation. Discuss this statement.

1.12 Discuss the statement, "Computers can make routine decisions."

1.13 Describe in general terms the information system in your school.

1.14 "The systems approach is more a philosophy than a way of doing things." Discuss.

1.15 "The way we handle our payroll system in this company is totally different than any other payroll system." Respond to this statement.

1.16 "Systems analysis is a new term for an old activity." Discuss.

1.17 "A systems analyst is a fancy term for what we called an efficiency expert." Why is this observation true or not true?

1.18 "The life cycle concept of an information system is inaccurate. In our organization the system is never complete." Explain.

1.19 What type of organization should you work for if you want to ensure your chances of participating in all phases of the systems life cycle?

1.20 If you were considering becoming a systems analyst as a stepping stone to general management, what phase of the life cycle provides the quickest orientation to all the organizational activities? The least?

1.21 "Systems analysts are programmers who don't or can't code." Discuss.

1.22 Cite examples of several types of systems where the Systems Implementation phase might be: (a) less than one month, (b) less than one year, (c) approximately five years, (d) greater than ten years.

1.23 "I don't care how much it costs. I want to know yesterday's sales by 8:00 A.M. the next day." Discuss the rationale behind this statement.

1.24 "We would like to have terminals on every manager's desk. However, we can't see how to justify doing it." Explain the rationale behind this comment.

1.25 "Systems analysis requires a great deal of creativity and, as such, you just can't teach a person how to conduct a systems analysis." Discuss the merit of this statement.

EXERCISES

1.1 Take one of the information conversion models of Appendix A and describe how it produces information for decision makers.

1.2 Outline in broad terms the approach you would take in order to conduct a systems analysis in the following situations:
- (A) customer complaints concerning poor quality merchandise,
- (B) inability of the shipping department to meet shipping schedules,
- (C) inaccurate invoices being sent to customers,
- (D) high level of obsolescence in raw materials,
- (E) excessive amount of returned goods from customers.

1.3 Select a development or individuals prominent in the evolution of data and information processing and prepare a brief report (2–3 pages) describing it or their impact in greater depth than discussed in this text.

PROBLEMS

1.1 A major manufacturer of cosmetic products is faced with a difficult decision. A recently completed study has revealed a new synthetic with properties similar to an existing raw material which is the prime ingredient in their inexpensive line of perfumes. This new synthetic will cost about 1/2 as much as what they currently spend. However, the new synthetic, when used in their product, has a tendency to produce a very red appearance in a product which traditionally has been light pink.

The company's market research group has concluded that the look of a perfume product, in that sales line, is almost as important as any other characteristic, including price and aroma. They estimate that using this new synthetic will result in a reduction in sales of between 20 and 50 %.

The company currently sells this perfume for $3.00 an ounce. $1.00 of this price is attributed to the raw material in question. Last year the sales for this product were approximately 1 million ounces. Gross profit attributed to this product was $500,000.

Using the Systems Analysis approach to problem solving, prepare a report to submit to the president concerning this decision.

1.2 A manufacturer of soap products in the midwest services over 20,000 retail establishments throughout the country. The company receives on an average about 800 customer orders per day. Finished goods are manufactured both to stock, and to order, at a ratio of about 70–30. Shipping papers are prepared by a computer daily. The shipping department maintains a file of orders to be shipped, since it is not always possible (or necessary) to ship an order the same day it is received.

The customer service department is responsible for handling customer inquiries concerning order status, availability of stock, and expediting orders through the shipping department. Presently, there is a computer based inventory reporting system which produces an inventory status report. This report is available each morning at 8 A.M. and includes production and shipping activity as of 5 P.M. yesterday. The report does not, however, recognize the demand for orders in house but not shipped. Consequently, request for product availability usually requires customer service expeditors to contact inventory and shipping personnel directly in order to determine availability of product for potential customers.

The sales department has indicated that sales amounting to $100,000 annually are lost, because of the company's inability to provide a firm shipping date on potential orders, and because of cancellations of orders due to their not being shipped as scheduled. The customer service department reports it is currently spending $20,000 annually on expediting.

A systems analyst has proposed a system be implemented which would provide inventory status on finished goods, which would also reflect the impact of the orders in house, and due to be shipped within one work week. This reference, it is felt, would provide an efficient source of product availability and reduce the present cost of expediting by 80%. In addition, an exception report would be produced daily for all orders scheduled to be shipped (but not shipped) as of yesterday.

The cost to develop and implement this system is estimated to be $60,000. The cost to operate the system is estimated at $1200 per week.

Would you recommend the company accept the analyst's proposal for the new system? Explain your recommendation both quantitatively and qualitatively.

BIBLIOGRAPHY

Ashenhurst (ed.), "A Report of the ACM Curriculum Cmmmittee on Computer Education for Management," *Communications of the ACM,* New York: Association for Computing Machinery, Inc., May, 1972.

Birkowitz and Munro, *Automatic Data Processing and Management,* Belmont, Calif.: Dickerson Publishing Co., Inc., 1969.

Bohl, *Computer Concepts,* Chicago: Science Research Associates, Inc., 1970.

Churchman, *The Systems Approach,* New York: Delacorte Press, 1968.

Cleland and King (eds.), *Systems, Organizations, Analysis, Management: A Book of Readings,* New York: McGraw-Hill Book Co., 1969.

Garner, *Evolution of Cost Accounting to 1925,* University, Alabama: University of Alabama Press, 1954.

Hendriksen, *Accounting Theory,* Homewood, Illinois: Richard D. Irwin, Inc., 1965.

Lott, *Basic Systems Analysis,* San Francisco: Canfield Press, 1971.

Wagner, *Principles of Management Science,* Englewood Cliffs, N.J.: Prentice-Hall, Inc., 1970.

2 Analysis of Basic Data and Information Concepts

2.1 Introduction

The tremendous growth of social institutions in both size and scope, necessitates the development of information systems of similar size, scope and complexity. The information required must reflect not only the internal activities of the organization, but competitive actions, environmental and sociological interests, and political and financial trends. This information must represent not only what has happened and what is happening, but, most important of all, what will happen. The information requirement includes all that is necessary to effectively plan, operate and control the activities of an organization. The information need exists equally in private industry, governmental agencies, the military, educational institutions, hospitals and various other organizations.

To achieve the information goals of a complex organization, a system must be designed to gather and process raw data in such a way as to produce the information required for all levels of decision making within and around the affected organization. We are no longer able to allow this information to be provided by happenchance, if we are to utilize all of our resources effectively.

In order to design and implement the sophisticated information systems that are required in today's complex world, it is first necessary to have a sound understanding of the basic concepts of data and information. The specific objectives of this chapter are:

1. To provide a descriptive and functional definition of the concepts: data and information.

2. To identify both the logical and physical ways in which data can be processed or manipulated to produce information.

3. To discuss the primary aspects of cost, value, and effectiveness as they relate to data and information processing.

2.2 The Concepts of Data and Information

In general usage the terms "data" and "information" are often used interchangeably when referring to two distinct concepts. Unfortunately, this ambiguous use of terminology often results in less than desirable communications concerning these two important ideas. Therefore, in order to assist the readers' understanding of the concepts presented, the nature of each term will be defined as used in this text.

Definition of Data

Data are raw facts in isolation which, when placed in a meaningful context by a data processing operation(s), allows inferences to be drawn. These inferences relate to the measurement and identification of people, events, and objects. Data representations act as surrogates for these items. For example, 12 engineers, $30.00 cash sales, or one office building are all data representations of people, events, and objects. The basic purpose of capturing and processing data is to produce information. The results of processing data can range from preparing payroll checks for employees to providing management with a report for planning

and control. Although data are the key ingredient used to inform the recipient, not all data produce relevant and timely information. Most organizations have an abundance of data but have been somewhat limited in their ability to extract and filter from these large pools of data the pertinent facts that decision makers need in order to make knowledgeable decisions. For example, a tray of cards representing sales invoices by itself means very little to the sales manager. However, manipulation of these data in accordance with certain procedures can provide meaningful sales information.

There is an unlimited amount of data from sources both internal and external to the organization. This wealth of data can be a burden if quantities of data are processed without an informational objective. In other words, an adequate data supply can exist with an inadequate information system. For example, reports produced by various data processing systems, and placed on managements' desks, have been compared to a daily newspaper printed without headlines or spacing between words—an avalanche of data but a paucity of information. The implication here, is that the volume of data has not been properly processed to meet the informational need of the recipient.

It is emphasized at this point that no data processing method—manual or computer—guarantees that data will be processed in accordance with the needs of the user. These needs must be determined in a context somewhat distinct from the data processing method used. Determining informational needs of the various users of information, among other aspects, is treated later in the text.

Definition of Information

Information is substantially different from data in that data are raw, unevaluated messages. Information is the increase in knowledge obtained by the recipient by matching proper data elements to the variables of a problem. Information is the aggregation or processing of data to provide knowledge or intelligence.

If everyone possessed perfect knowledge, then there would be no need for information. Anyone possessing less than perfect knowledge needs information as an aid to decision making. Information is the key ingredient in the decision making process for most individuals although it alone will not guarantee proper decision making. Within any data processing system large volumes of data can be stored or retrieved without a great deal of difficulty, but the objective is to harness this system to meet the information needs of users. If an information system is to be designed it is necessary to make explicit what is to be considered as information. And, once the users receive the information it is then their responsibility to match it with their present state of knowledge and take action accordingly.

Information is an occurrence or a set of occurrences which carry messages and, when perceived by the recipients via any of the senses, will increase their state of knowledge. The significance or value of information received can only be measured by the recipient.

> . . . To demonstrate a point . . . let's consider the implications to various people of a train whistle penetrating the evening dusk. To the saboteur crouching in a culvert it might signify the failure of his mission because the whistle indicates that the train has already passed over his detonating charge without causing an explosion. To the playboy, it might presage the imminent arrival of the transgressed husband. . . . To the lonely wife it means the return of her traveling husband. To the man with his foot caught in the switch down the track, it preshadows doom. . . . In brief, the nature and significance of any information is fundamentally and primarily functions of the attitudes, situations, and relevant responsibilities with respect thereto of the people involved with it. . . . Information is management information only to the extent to which the manager needs or wants it; and it is significant to him only in terms of its relation to his accumulation of relevant knowl-edge and plans and to his personal responsibility.[1]

For example, the orders received at a warehouse in a given time period have little meaning to an accountant and are considered merely data. Billable shipments from this warehouse during that time period, however, are indeed information to this same accountant. The Sales Manager requires both "pieces of information." The Employee Relations Manager ignores all order and shipment data.

Ideally, information communicates the state of a situation but the perception can differ markedly between users. Information containing the same message content and quantity communicated in the same way and at the same time does not mean that it will be used similarly by the receivers. Witness judges on a court reaching a 5 to 4 decision based on the same arguments, or investment analysts differing as to the financial condition of a company after having analyzed the same financial statements. Consequently, the way in which the information is used will depend to a great extent upon the perception, background, and prejudice of the user.

Function of Information

The primary function of information, and hence of an information system, is to increase the knowledge or reduce the uncertainty of the user. The information that is disseminated to the user may be the result of inputting data into, and processing, a decision model. However, in most complex decision making, information can only increase the probability of certainty or reduce the variety of choice. For example, in the model illustrated in Figure 2.1, the decision maker must decide whether to get in with an investment or get out.

---

[1] Edward D. Dwyer, "Some Observations on Management Information Systems," *Advances in EDP and Information Systems*, American Management Association, New York, 1961, pp. 16–17. Used with permission of American Management Association.

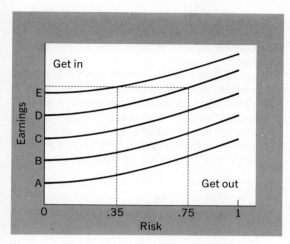

FIGURE 2.1. Chart showing degree of risk at different levels of earnings (Projects).

The information supplied to the decision maker provides a probability of the risk factor at different levels of earnings. For example, the probability of failure may be .75 on earnings level project D. The risk at this earnings level may be too great for this particular investment and the investor would get out. Conversely, for a different project E, the probability of failure is .35, which may be sufficiently low for the investor to get in. As shown in this simplistic model, the information can only provide probabilities and possibly a series of choices at different levels of earning. Therefore, the function of information is to reduce variety. Another example of how this function works is shown in Figure 2.2.

There is a 1000 dollar bill in one of these boxes (number 6 for total certainty). The question is to determine which one. With no information, the probability of successfully locating the correct box is 1/6. The probability of failure is 5/6 (i.e., 1 − 1/6). Therefore, through an intuitive process, one has 1/6 probability of earning $1000 (assuming one chance). But if the decision maker receives information that the $1000 is either in box 1 or box 6, then the probability of success has been increased to 1/2.

In both examples above, the function of information was to provide the decision maker with a probability basis for selection responses. It did not direct the decision maker as to what to do, however, it did reduce the variety and uncertainty to evoke a knowledgeable decision. Another major function of information is to provide a set of standards, measurement rules, and decision rules for the determination and dissemination of error signals and feedback for control purposes. In other words, assuming that the decision maker invests in a project, information is needed to help control the operations of the project.

Generally, there are many pieces of information which might be useful, and in one way or another influence the recipient's response in a given situation. Some information might arise from personal observation; some from conversations with others, and from committee meetings; some from external stimuli such as journals, news media, or government reports; and some might arise from the information system itself. We stress that the information system can only provide a part of the information that a decision maker uses and that this information is of a formal, quantifiable nature. In a general sense, an information system provides the user with formal information about a state of affairs which gives a greater degree of predictability, both of events, and of the results of activities (including the user's own) relating to the organization. Therefore, that information which can be handled, or produced, under a quantifiable organizing function is of interest.

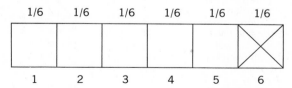

FIGURE 2.2. Row of boxes, one of which contains $1000.00.

Classifications of Information

There does not exist today one universally accepted classification scheme of information suitable for all situations. Each communicator provides a classification which is deemed appropriate for accomplishing the goal of achieving understanding. In fact, it is often difficult to obtain agreement as to what constitutes good and bad information.

We might, for example, wish to classify information according to its origin to a respective organization. Our classification might well be that it is either internal or external information. Moreover, this same distinction could be offered based on who is permitted to use the information.

Figure 2.3 is a table exemplifying many ways information can and is classified. This table is not intended to be all-encompassing or final. It is provided so that the reader recognizes the plurality of classifications and can appreciate that unless communication is quite clear there is always the possibility of misunderstanding.

Frame of Reference	1	2	3	4	5	6	7	8
Relationship to organization	x							
Time reference:								
Source of data		x						
Processing of data			x					
Reporting of information				x				
Nature of information					x			
Users' functional position						x		
Flow of information							x	
Quality of information								x

Information Classification	1	2	3	4	5	6	7	8
Internal	x							
External	x							
Batched		x						
Random		x						
Online			x	x				
Real time			x	x				
Periodic			x	x				
Descriptive—Historical					x			
Performance—Current					x			
Predictive—Future					x			
Simulated—What if (alternatives)					x			
Constituent of organization						x		
Strategic level						x		
Tactical level						x		
Technical level						x		
Horizontal							x	
Vertical							x	
Relevant								x
Timely								x
Useless								x

FIGURE 2.3.   Classification of information.

2.3 Producing Information from Data

Having discussed the concepts of data and information in the last section, it is proper at this time to examine the ways in which information can be produced from data. We can view this transformation both from a logical viewpoint, i.e., logical operations which are performed on data, and from a physical or technical viewpoint, i.e., the higher level methods within which data operations are performed.

Data Operations

Basically, data are raw material which must be manipulated and placed in a meaningful context before it is useful to the recipient. To bring order to data, and produce meaningful results, some combination of basic data operations must be performed. Ten basic operations which produce meaningful output can be identified in every information system. The role of these data operations in an information system is similar to the role of the simple machines described by the physical scientist. Just as all larger, more complex machines are composed of the simple machines, all complex information systems are composed of some combination of simple data operations. These operations are:

1. *Capturing.* This operation refers to the recording of data from an event or occurrence in some form such as sales slips, personnel forms, purchase orders, meters, gauges, and so forth.

2. *Verifying.* This operation refers to the checking or validating of data to ensure that it was captured and recorded correctly.

3. *Classifying.* This operation places data elements into specific categories which provide meaning for the user. For example, sales data can be classified by inventory type, size, customer, salesman, warehouse shipped from, or any other classification which will give the sales data more meaning.

4. *Arranging.* (Sorting) This operation places data elements in a specified or predetermined sequence. An inventory file, for example, can be arranged by product code, activity level, dollar value or by whatever other attribute is coded in the file and deemed desirable by a user.

5. *Summarizing.* This operation combines or aggregates data elements in either of two ways. First, it accumulates data in the mathematical sense; as when a balance sheet is prepared. The aggregate figure classified as current assets on the balance sheet more than likely represents several thousand specific and more detailed accounts. Second, it reduces data in the logical sense; as when the personnel manager wants a list of names of only the employees who are assigned to Department 13 in the organization.

6. *Calculating.* This operation entails the arithmetic and/or logical manipulation of data. For example, computations must be performed to derive employees' pay, customers' bills, students' grade point averages, and so forth. In many instances, very sophisticated calculations must be performed to manipulate the data in management science models such as PERT, linear programming, forecasting, and so on.

7. *Storing.* This operation places data onto some storage media such as paper, microfilm, and magnetizable devices, where it can be kept for access and retrieving when needed.

8. *Retrieving.* This operation entails searching out and gaining access to specific data elements from the medium where it is stored.

9. *Reproducing.* This operation duplicates data from one medium to another, or into another position in the same medium. For example, a file of data stored on a magnetic disk may be reproduced onto another magnetic disk

or onto a magnetic tape for further processing or for security reasons.

10. *Disseminating/communicating.* This operation transfers data from one place to another. It can take place at a number of junctures in the data processing cycle. For example, data can be transferred from a device to a user. The ultimate aim of all data processing is to disseminate information to the final user.

Data Processing Methods

As we noted in Chapter 1, advances in technology have resulted in many different devices that can be utilized to perform the ten basic data operations. The information system in most organizations is generally composed of a variety of technological and manual methods. In order to deal effectively with the vast variety of tools and techniques used to process data four broad categories, based on the level of automation represented, can be defined: (1) Manual, (2) Electromechanical, (3) Punched Card Equipment, and (4) Electronic Computer. These four methods of data processing, along with their relationship to the data operations, are illustrated in the operations/method matrix in Figure 2.4.

In the Manual Method, as depicted in the matrix, all of the data operations are performed by hand with the aid of basic devices such as pencil, paper, slide rule, pegboards, and so forth. The Electromechanical Method is actually a symbiosis of man and machine. Examples of this method would include an operator working at a posting machine, tub file, duplicating equipment, or cash register.

The Punched Card Equipment Method entails the use of all devices used in what is sometimes referred to as a unit record system. The principle of unit record is that data concerning a person, object, or event is normally recorded (punched) in a card. A number of cards which contain data about a similar subject are (e.g., payroll or inventory) combined together to form a tray of cards usually termed a file. A typical punched card system is comprised of any or all of the following devices: key punch, verifier, sorter, collator, reproducer, accounting ma-

Operations / Methods	Capturing and Initial Recording	Classifying	Arranging	Summarizing	Calculating	Storing	Retrieving	Reproducing	Disseminating and Communicating
Manual Method	Voice; observation; handwritten records; forms and checklists; writing boards; peg-boards	Hand-posting; coding; identifying; peg-boards	Alphabetizing; indexing; filing; edge-notched cards	Hand calculators	Human calculation; pencil and paper; abacus; slide rule	Columnar journals; ledgers; index cards; paper files	File clerks; stock clerks; book-keepers	Hand-copying; carbon paper	Hand-written reports; hand-carried or mailed
Electro-mechanical Method	Typewriter; cash register; autographic registers; time clocks	Posting machine; cash register; accounting machines	Semi-automatic (roto-matics; gather-matics)	Adding machines; calculators; cash registers; posting machines	Accounting machines; adding machines; calculators; cash registers; posting machines	Mechanical files (rotary or tub files); microfilm		Duplicating equipment (carbonization, hectograph, stencil, offset, photocopying thermograph); addressing equipment	Telephone; teletype; machine prepared reports; message conveyors; hand-carried or mailed reports
Punched Card Equipment Method	Key punch; verifier; mark-sensed cards; prepunched cards; machine readable tags	Sorter; collator		Accounting machine; calculator; summary punch		Card trays	Sorter; collator; hand selection	Reproducers; interpreter	Same as above
Electronic Computer Method	Key punch; verifier; paper tape punch; magnetic encoder; OCR en-scriber; collection devices; conversion devices; terminals	By systems design	Card sorter; internal computer sorting	Central processing unit		CPU, DASD; magnetic tape; paper tape; punched cards	Online inquiry into DASD; report generation	Same as above, plus on line copies from line printer; computer input/output; microfilm	Same as above, plus on line data transmission (telecommunication); visual display; voice output

FIGURE 2.4. Operation and methods of data processing.

chine, calculating punch, interpreter, and summary punch.

Several observations concerning data processing methods are appropriate at this time. First, it could be argued that the Punched Card Method is simply a sophisticated electromechanical method of processing data. However, because of the significant reduction in the level of manual intervention required in punched card processing as compared to other electromechanical devices, and the use of a recording media which permits a variety of processing to be performed on captured data, two categories seem justified. Second, advances in small computer technology are rapidly obsoleting punched card equipment as a primary alternative data processing method. However, a sufficient number of punched card machines are still used to make this method worthy of consideration for comparative purposes. Finally, it can readily be observed that both in the Electromechanical Method, and in the Punched Card Method, an individual machine seemed to be developed to perform each data operation separately. Not until the development of the electronic computer was one machine capable of performing most of the data operations without intermittent human intervention.

The computer, as we use the term in this text, means a configuration of input devices, a central processing unit (CPU), and output devices. The CPU is comprised of four basic components: (1) the arithmetic-logic unit, (2) the control unit, (3) the primary storage unit, and (4) the console.

A major innovation in the development of the CPU was the stored-program concept, which refers to the process by which instructions are stored within the primary storage unit of the CPU. Every CPU has a built-in repertoire of instructions which pertain to all of the operations that the computer is capable of performing. It is the task of the CPU to interpret the instructions supplied to it by the programmer and then to perform the functions called for in the instruction set. Basically, the stored-program performs the same function for the computer that the wired control panel does for punched card

equipment, but with much more sophistication and a great deal less human intervention during processing. The stored-program allows the computer to operate all devices in the configuration, and to perform all tasks, in accordance with the instructions provided by the programmer. A computer executes only the instructions given to it. Therefore, the results of its activities depend entirely upon how good or bad the program is, and/or on the accuracy and validity of the input data. Overall, however, the computer provides significantly greater data processing capabilities than the other three methods.

Selection Considerations

Selecting the proper data processing method for a specific application or organization requires the systems analyst to understand both the processing requirements and the performance capabilities of each data processing method.

Processing requirements can be viewed as being determined by the following considerations: (1) the *volume* of data elements involved, (2) the *complexity* of the required data processing operations, (3) processing *time* constraints, and (4) *computational* demands. Understanding that there are four elements in determining data processing requirements is essential, if the analyst is to select the correct data processing method for an organization. In many organizations one element is so dominant that the other three elements are not necessarily carefully defined. For example, a large bank processes so many checks that volume alone might justify selecting a computer. On the other hand, a small bank must consider the other aspects of their processing requirements before choosing a specific data processing method. Likewise a large engineering firm might choose a computer solely on the basis of massive computation requirements. However, a smaller engineering firm must consider volume, complexity, and timing before making such a choice.

The question of when does an organization select one method of data processing over an-

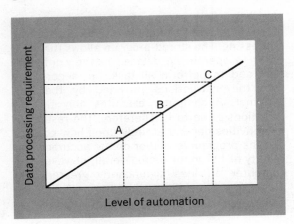

FIGURE 2.5. The relationship between data processing requirements and the level of automation. A: Theoretical point separating manual from electromechanical. B: Theoretical point separating electromechanical from punched card equipment. C: Theoretical point separating punched card equipment from computer.

other is largely an economic decision and will be discussed in more detail later in the text. However, in summary we can state that as the volume of data increases, as complexity increases, as time constraints become more severe, and as computational demands become more sophisticated, an increased level of automation is warranted. This relationship is illustrated in Figure 2.5.

Understanding performance capabilities is equally important when choosing a data processing method. While there are many dimensions of data processing to consider, fifteen basic performance factors are defined below.

1. *Initial Investment.* The expense of acquiring any materials or machines required for processing.

2. *Set Up.* The expense required to prepare initially captured data for subsequent processing.

3. *Conversion.* The one time expense of initially processing data with the new method.

4. *Skilled Personnel Requirement.* The education and training level of the individuals involved with processing data.

5. *Variable Cost.* The cost of a data unit as it relates to changes in volume.

6. *Modularity.* The ability to increase or decrease processing capability to match the requirements for processing. For example, if a machine can process 1000 transactions a day, and the requirement for processing is 1200 transactions per day, two machines would be required. This results in under-utilization of processing capability.

7. *Flexibility.* The ability to change the processing procedure to satisfy new or changing requirements.

8. *Versatility.* The ability to perform many different tasks.

9. *Processing Speed.* The time which is required to convert inputs to outputs.

10. *Computational Power.* The ability to perform complex mathematical operations.

11. *Processing Control.* The ability to verify that each data processing task is performed as planned.

12. *Automatic Error Detection.* The ability of the components of the method to identify processing errors.

13. *Decision Making Power.* The ability to choose among alternatives in order to continue processing.

14. *System Degradation.* The level to which the processing system is degraded because of the breakdown or unavailability of a component(s) of the system. For example, the breakdown of a CPU means total degradation of a computer system whereas an absent clerk in a manual system would only slightly degrade the processing capabilities of the manual system.

15. *Level of Automation.* Self-explanatory.

In Figure 2.6 we compare each of these performance factors for the four methods of data processing.

2.4 Economics of Information

Information is a valuable resource in any organization. Without formal information most organizations could not survive. In many

Factors	Manual	Electromechanical	Punched Card	Computer
Initial Investment	Low	Moderately low	Medium	High
Set Up	Low	Moderately low	Moderately high	High
Conversion	Low	Medium	Medium	High
Skilled Personnel	Low	Moderately low	Medium	High
Variable Cost	High	Medium	Moderately low	Low
Modularity	High	Low	Moderately low	Medium
Flexibility	High	Low	Medium	Low
Versatility	Low	Low	Medium	High
Processing Speed	Low	Moderately low	Medium	High
Computational Power	Low	Low	Medium	High
Processing Control	Low	Moderately low	Medium	High
Automatic Error Detection	Low	Medium	Medium	High
Decision Making	Moderately low	Low	Medium	High
Level of Degradation	Low	Moderately low	Medium	High
Level of Automation	Low	Moderately low	Medium	High

FIGURE 2.6. Comparison of the four data processing methods against fifteen basic performance factors.

organizations there is a growing tendency to expand the effectiveness and utilization of information beyond the meeting of mere legal requirements and routine problem solving. In order to accelerate the progress of their organizations, management and other constituents are actively seeking out new problems for solution. To meet these expanding needs, large investments are required. The question is: are the benefits received worth the investment?

The preparation of formal information is not free; it costs money. How much should an organization spend for information? Even if it were possible, it would be uneconomical to record every element of data and process it. Costs of recording and processing data to provide information must be weighed against the value of this information to the recipient. We have thus far alluded to the cost of producing information and the value of information; however, there is a strict dichotomy between measuring the cost of providing information and measuring the value of information. The cost of providing information (i.e., the cost of the information system with its methods, devices, and media) is tangible and fairly measurable. On the other

hand, information is conceptual in nature and has no tangible characteristics except in symbolic representations. It is basically distinct and separate from the physical methods and media which produce it; it has no physical embodiment, per se. The analyst, however, must come to grips with both the cost of providing information, and the effectiveness of the information, in order to optimize the information system function. In this section, an attempt will be made to give analysis and insight into the cost/value problem.

Cost of Information

In some organizations, the cost of processing data to meet legal and routine operations, and, also, for producing high level information will run between 5 and 15% of the entire cost of operating the organization. In certain financial organizations, the costs may run as high as 50%. The costs of operating the information system are identified as follows:[2]

[2] This section adapted from: Gordon B. Davis, *Computer Data Processing* (New York: McGraw-Hill Book Company, 1969) pp. 13–16. Used with permission of McGraw-Hill Book Company.

1. *Cost of the hardware.* This is normally a fixed or sunk cost over a relevant range. This cost would increase for higher levels of mechanization.

2. *Systems analysis, design, and implementation.* This is a sunk cost and would normally increase with higher levels of mechanization. This function includes formulating a methodology for overall data processing procedures. Using the computer method, it would also include the preparation of programs.

3. *Cost for space and environmental control factors.* This cost is semivariable. Examples of this cost are floor space, air conditioners and de-humidifier systems, power control units, security, and so on. Normally these costs increase with higher levels of mechanization.

4. *Cost of conversion.* This is a sunk cost and includes any kind of change from one method to another, e.g., electromechanical to computer.

5. *Cost of operation.* This is basically a variable cost and includes a variety of personnel, facilities and systems maintenance, supplies, utilities, and support facilities costs.

These costs are often classified as either vari-

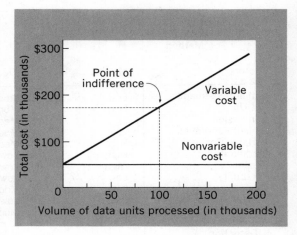

FIGURE 2.8 Cost chart with data volume as base for an electromechanical method.

able or nonvariable costs. The charts in Figures 2.7 and 2.8 help us visualize the characteristics and behavior of these costs and their relationship to volumes of data processed by two different data processing methods—computer and electromechanical (which can include punched card equipment).

The vertical scale is expressed in dollars and indicates the nonvariable and variable cost in relation to volume of data units processed. The volume is expressed on the horizontal scale. The nonvariable cost, or the investment for the computer system, is $150,000.00. The variable cost per unit of data processed is $0.15. Therefore at a volume of 100,000 data units processed, the total cost is $165,000.00 ($.15 × 100,000 + $150,000).

The costs for the electromechanical method shown in Figure 2.8 are $30,000.00 for nonvariable cost and $1.35 per unit of data processed. To compute the point of indifference, we let x equal the number of data units processed. Consequently we have:

$$\$.15x + \$150,000.00 = \$1.35x + \$30,000.00$$
$$\$1.20x = \$120,000.00$$
$$x = 100,000 \text{ data units}$$

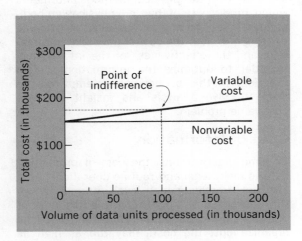

FIGURE 2.7 Cost chart with data volume as base for a computer method. A data unit might be customer orders, inventory transactions, invoices, and so forth.

In other words, at the volume level of 100,000 data units, it is a matter of indifference on a cost basis as to whether the computer method or the electromechanical method is used. If cost only is considered, with other things being equal, at a volume of less than 100,000 data units, it is more economical to use the electromechanical method. For example, the total cost at a volume of 90,000 data units for the electromechanical method is $151,500.00 ($1.35 × 90,000 + $30,000). The cost utilizing the computer method is $163,500.00 ($.15 × 90,000 + $150,000). Conversely, at a volume of data units greater than 100,000, the use of the computer method is economically justified.

With this general breakdown in cost factors, the cost curves in Figures 2.9 and 2.10 are an indication of the relative cost behavior of the different data processing methods. The general conclusion from these cost curves is that the manual method is most economical for low volumes of processing and that as volume becomes greater, an increased level of mechanization is justified. However, as indicated before, cost is not the only consideration, but it is a very important one.

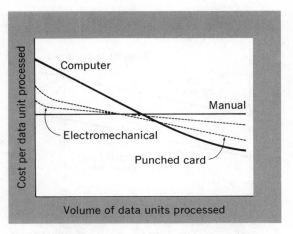

FIGURE 2.10 Average cost for different data processing methods.

Thus far our cost analysis has assumed static conditions. A dynamic assumption is that the cost of different methods does not remain constant over time due to technical developments, better mass production techniques, more computer sharing, greater equipment utilization, and increased wage levels. All of these factors, with the exception of increasing wages, has significantly improved the price/performance ratio of computers. In other words, it has become increasingly less expensive to process a unit of data using the computer method. Conversely, clerical costs have increased without a noticeable increase in performance and productivity. Therefore, as shown in Figure 2.11, an improvement in the price/performance ratio of computers makes this method of data processing competitive with manual and other less mechanized methods at lower volumes of processing. It can be concluded then that the impact of changing conditions has resulted in decreasing the cost of computer processing. It appears that this trend will continue. It must be emphasized that this analysis does not include more advanced processing needs due to complexities, time constraints, and extensive computational power, which less mechanized methods cannot normally handle.

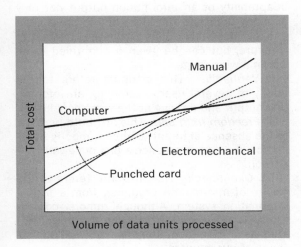

FIGURE 2.9 Total cost for different data processing methods.

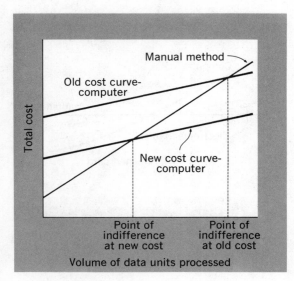

FIGURE 2.11. Effect of reduction in computer costs (improved price/performance ratio) on volume of processing at which the computer method is economical when compared to manual methods.

Value of Information

The value of information is based on ten attributes which are listed as follows:

1. *Accessibility.* This attribute refers to the ease and speed with which an information output can be obtained. The speed of access can be measured, e.g., one minute versus twenty-four hours. However, what is the information worth to the user? For example, is it worth $10.00 more per access over the old method?

2. *Comprehensiveness.* This attribute refers to the completeness of the information content. It does not necessarily mean volume but rather means the inclusive aspect of the information output. This attribute is quite intangible and, consequently, it's difficult to quantify.

3. *Accuracy.* This attribute pertains to the degree of freedom from error of the information output. In dealing with large volumes of data, two types of mistakes usually occur: errors of transcription and errors of computation. Many aspects of this attribute can be quantified. For

example, what is the error rate in every one thousand invoices prepared by a manually–oriented system versus a computer system? What is the value of less errors? For example, will a 10% decrease in errors in billing increase sales by one-half of one percent?

4. *Appropriateness.* This attribute refers to how well the information output relates to the users' request. The information content must be relevant to the matter in hand; all other output is superfluous, yet costly to prepare. This attribute is difficult to measure and, as with the other attributes, hopefully it will emanate from a better systems design.

5. *Timeliness.* This attribute is related to a shorter elapsed time of the access cycle: input, processing, and reporting of output to the users. Normally, for information to be timely, the duration of this cycle must be reduced. In some instances timeliness can be measured. For example, how much can sales be increased by providing online response to customer inquiries as to availability of inventory items?

6. *Clarity.* This attribute refers to the degree an information output is free from ambiguous terms. Revising a report can be costly. How much does it cost to revise this report? (A very accurate dollar value can be placed on clarity.)

7. *Flexibility.* This attribute pertains to the adaptability of an information output not only to more than one decision, but to more than one decision maker. This attribute is difficult to measure, but can be given a quantified value within a wide range.

8. *Verifiability.* This attribute refers to the ability of several users examining an information output and arriving at the same conclusion.

9. *Freedom from bias.* This attribute pertains to the absence of intent to alter or modify information in order to produce a preconceived conclusion.

10. *Quantifiable.* This attribute refers to the nature of information produced from a formal information system. Although rumors, conjectures, heresay, and so forth are often considered as information, they are outside of the scope of our concern.

Even though many aspects of these attributes are difficult to measure, the analyst must use them when determining the value of information versus its cost. The question is: how much is some portion of information worth to the recipient? Referring back to Figure 2.2, the recipient had a 1/6 probability of selecting the box with $1000.00 if the decision making were approached on an intuitive basis. The expected value in this example with zero information is $166.67. With some portion of information the probability of success was increased to 1/2, or to an expected value of $500.00. Is the portion of information received beneficial to the decision maker? We do not know unless we find out what it cost to get this information. If more than $333.33 were paid, the cost of the information exceeds its value. If $333.33 were paid, the recipient will break even on the average ($500.00–$166.67). What about enough information to give a probability of 1.0, or a level of certainty? Again, if more than $833.33 has to be payed for certainty, then the information has cost more than it is worth.

Cost Versus Value

The objective of the information system is to reach an optimum point where the marginal value of information equals marginal cost of providing that information. This relationship is shown in Figure 2.12. As can be noted in the illustration, an excess quantity of information

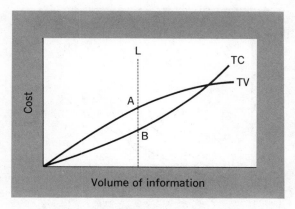

FIGURE 2.13 Relationship of total value and total cost of information.

with a relatively high cost can result in negative marginal value.

The optimal level of information processing is shown where the marginal cost of providing information equals the marginal value of this information. Concerning the level of output, we can state the following principles:

1. If marginal value > marginal cost: increase output.
2. If marginal value < marginal cost: decrease output.
3. If marginal value = marginal cost: output is optimum.

In gross terms, we can illustrate the optimum level in Figure 2.13.

The total cost of the information is represented by LB; the gross value of information is represented by LA; and the net value of the information is represented by AB. The optimum information level is located at L.

Assume three different methods can provide the organization with information (M_1, M_2, and M_3). Relative to cost, what is the most effective method? An interesting phenomenon can exist when choosing among methods and that is the cost/effectiveness relationship. This relationship is illustrated in Figure 2.14.

The analysis and design of the system has established a level designated by E. However, the analyst must assume a dynamic organization

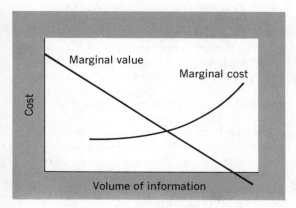

FIGURE 2.12 Relationship of marginal value and marginal cost of information.

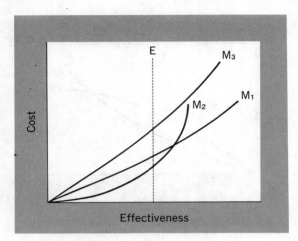

FIGURE 2.14 Cost/Effectiveness relationship of different information methods.

with changing needs resulting in changing demands on the information system. The analyst must therefore be aware of cost/effectiveness relationships of different methods. If he chooses M_1 an increase in demand of information by the organization can be accomplished by a relatively small increase in cost. The M_2 method will give a small increase in effectiveness with a concomitant large increase in cost. And, we will assume that M_3 represents a method beyond the organization's ability to support. However, there are many actual cases where organizations have attempted to acquire systems out of proportion to their resources. Clearly, the appropriate level will depend on the alternative methods available to provide the information and the ability of the organization to support a particular method.

SUMMARY

Data elements are the raw material for the production of information. Data are isolated facts which are converted into a meaningful context via decision models.

Information is the primary product of the information system. The nemesis to decision making is uncertainty. Since information decreases uncertainty it follows that information is a key aid to knowledgeable decision making. Information has two basic functions: to reduce variety and to provide feedback.

Information is a useful and valuable commodity, and, consequently, costs must be incurred to produce it. To be economically justified, the cost to produce it must match its value. It is obviously not economical to invest $10.00 for $1.00 worth of information. There are a number of attributes which help determine the value of information; however, in the final analysis, it is the user who must determine its real value.

Data operations are performed by any one of four basic methods: (1) manual, (2) electromechanical, (3) punched card, and (4) computer. Each method possesses certain advantages and disadvantages. The analyst, when selecting one method over the other, must be aware of tradeoffs between these advantages and disadvantages.

At lower levels of volume, less automated methods seem to have definite economic advantages over the computer. However, because of the ever-increasing improvement in the price/performance ratio of computer equipment, even this statement is no longer totally true. Also, increasing demands from management result in complexities, time constraints, and sophisticated computations. As these demands from management increase, it will become more difficult for less automated systems to cope with these demands. However, it must be pointed out that many computer systems can be economically justified on volume demands alone.

The cost factors of a computer system are: cost of hardware (CPU and its peripherals), cost of systems work (for convenience at this time, software is included in this category), cost of space and environmental control factors, cost of conversion, and cost of operations.

2.1 Define the terms data and information. Discuss fully the difference between data and information.

2.2 Why is it important to distinguish between formal and informal information?

2.3 What is the function of information?

2.4 Give an example for each classification of information presented in Figure 2.3.

2.5 Why is information considered a valuable resource of an organization?

2.6 Identify and describe the basic operations of data processing.

2.7 Describe the data processing methods which can be used to perform these operations. What are the main advantages and disadvantages of the different data processing methods? See if you can name some in addition to those listed in the chapter.

2.8 Can the computer be economically justified at low volume levels? Why? Why not?

2.9 List and discuss other demands on data processing systems in addition to volume demands.

2.10 What are data processing performance factors? How do they relate to processing requirements?

2.11 What are the cost factors in acquiring and operating a computer system?

2.12 Why is the value of information difficult to measure?

2.13 Do computers give efficacy to the attributes of information? Explain.

2.14 What are the limitations of the manual method? Describe three organizations where you would select a manual method.

2.15 In your own words, define price/performance ratio.

2.1 Discuss the statement: "Information is the cement that holds an organization together."

2.2 Discuss the statement: "Accounting is the language of business."

2.3 Many management science people criticize accountants for reporting historical information. Are accounting reports useful? Can we delete the accounting function? Why? Why not? If historical information is not needed, how could we redesign a system to cut costs?

2.4. Do managers need information that is Predictive? Simulated? Periodic? Explain.

2.5 What kinds of information do managers obtain outside the formal information system? Does the gathering of information outside the formal information system indicate that formal information systems should be eliminated or expanded? Could management function, if only formal information were available?

2.6 An in depth treatment of information systems has not yet been presented. As best you can, at this time, define an information system.

2.7 Assume that a particular data processing method, (e.g., computer method) meets all data processing considerations: (1) volume, (2) timing, (3) complexities, and (4) computational. Does this mean that all informational needs have been met? Discuss fully.

2.8 Discuss why magnetizeable storage media have a faster character transfer rate than punched cards. (Refer to Appendices for additional information.)

2.9 Some pundits have predicted that a computer or computer terminal will be in 70% of the households in this nation within the next decade. Do you agree? Why? Why not? Discuss the benefits derived, if any, from having a computer in your household.

2.10 "Computers have no morals or feeling." Discuss this statement.

2.11 As best you can, at this point, discuss the advantages/disadvantages that an organization might derive from the acquisition of a computer configuration.

2.12 Discuss a movie, magazine article, news report, etc., which dealt with computers. What was the general thrust of the content presented? Do you feel that it was accurate?

2.13 "Computers are nothing more than souped-up calculators and sophisticated clerks." Discuss this statement.

2.14 "Acquisition and installation of a computer will help to improve an organization's profit picture." Discuss.

EXERCISES   **2.1** List the attributes that add value to information and attempt to give a system of measurement for each attribute. See if you can list attributes that differ from those listed in the chapter.

2.2 Investigate an organization of your choice and describe the data processing method(s) used. Also, determine if this organization uses logico-mathematical models and the systems approach in developing the information system.

2.3 In your investigation of an organization of your choice, prepare a cost/effectiveness analysis on some aspect of the data processing system.

2.4 List and discuss ten uses of information.

2.5 Research the literature on any organization, with which you are familiar, for an application where a computer was installed to replace any other method of data processing. Why was the computer method chosen? Was it less costly? Did it replace personnel? If so, what kind of personnel? Were there any problems in converting to the computer method? Is the organization satisfied with the present method? Why? Why not?

2.6 "I'm the owner of two shoe stores in this city. I've heard a lot about computers and I've been wondering if some kind of a computer could help me run my business better." From the material presented in this chapter, prepare a response to this statement.

2.7 Select an organization that is familiar to you and design, in broad terms, an information system. Select a specific method of processing and discuss why you chose this particular method.

2.8 An organization has, on the average, two million arithmetic operations to perform per day plus handling five thousand sales transactions. Recommend a particular data processing method. State the reason(s) for your recommendation.

2.9 What combination of data processing operations would be required to: (1) prepare a payroll, (2) perform sales accounting, (3) prepare financial statements, (4) report sales statistics, and (5) determine quantity on hand of a specific item in inventory? (Use a flowchart, decision table, matrix, etc., to present your responses.)

2.10 Describe the basic data processing method that you would expect was being used in: (1) the corner drugstore, (2) a large department store, (3) a bank in your hometown, (4) a small medical clinic, and (5) a medium sized manufacturing company.

2.11 In the following hypothetical cases state a method of data processing that you would recommend, and the reasons why.

Case 1: A small supply company which handles 300 different inventory items, and processes most orders by mail. On the average 30 orders are processed daily. This company has 40 employees.

Case 2: A medium size medical clinic which has on its staff 25 physicians, 15 technicians, 46 nurses, and 30 administrative and clerical personnel. On the average, the clinic handles 450 patients per day who either pay for their treatment through an insurance program (government or private) or have a charge account. That is, few patients pay cash.

Case 3: A large, nationwide supply company which has in its warehouses from 20,000 to 30,000 different inventory items. Ninety percent of its orders are placed by telephone where most of the customers wish to know if the items requested are on hand for immediate delivery. Most customers will not accept backorders. The company employs 4000 people.

Case 4: A large motel organization has 300 motels scattered across the nation.

Case 5: A large manufacturing company has 16 plants and 175 warehouses throughout the country. In addition to general administrative data processing requirements (the company employs 26,000 people and has 40,000 customers) the company implements many management science techniques such as PERT, linear programming, forecasting, inventory control, and so forth.

State both the advantages and shortcomings of your recommended methods.

PROBLEMS   **2.1** Identify the information needed to properly manage a:
(1) hamburger stand,
(2) service station,
(3) university bookstore,
(4) large construction company,
(5) large manufacturing company.

2.2 Find a user of information in some organization (university, factory, business, hospital, etc.) and identify some information report that he or she receives. Ascertain the cost of this report and its value. Does the value exceed the cost? Explain fully.

2.3 Airline reservation systems are sophisticated online, real–time systems with elaborate computer and telecommunication capabilities. However, they are designed to answer simple inquiries, such as: "Is flight A on schedule?" "What is the fare, first class, from X to Y?" "Is there a seat available on flight B, and, if so, what is the time of departure?"

These questions help to accommodate, and make more efficient the travel plans of customers. However, airlines are also organizations managed by a variety of decision makers. Make some suggestions as to how such a system could also provide more information to these users. (Hint: the marketing manager may wish to know what type of customers they appeal to and what are their characteristics and occupations.)

2.4 From the library, obtain financial reports from *Standard and Poors* or *Moody's* on a particular company of your choice and try to decide whether or not you would invest in this company based on the information furnished by the financial reports. Using a scale from 0 to 9, (0 = very poor; 9 = excellent) weight these financial reports for: (1) accessibility, (2) comprehensiveness, (3) accuracy, (4) appropriateness, (5) timeliness, (6) clarity, and (7) flexibility. Give a brief reason why you assigned a particular weight to each attribute.

Did your state of knowledge increase after analyzing these financial reports? If so, by how much? Attempt to answer this question in quantitative terms.

2.5 Referring to the above problem, if your time is worth $50.00 per hour based on a 10 hour day, seven days per week and you have $10,000 to invest, assign a value to the information furnished you by the financial reports. Make any assumptions you wish. While analyzing the financial reports, were there any items in the reports you considered data? Information? For those items you considered data, did you have to perform any operations on these data before they were transformed into information? Explain fully.

2.6 Prepare a decision table for the selection of one of the methods of data processing. Base this table on specific needs of a hypothetical organization.

2.7 Two methods of processing data has been presented to Mr. Lee Roy Masterson, president of Bigload Trailer Company, by Tyrone Bedford, systems analyst. Consider the following fixed and variable costs:

	Method A	Method B
Variable cost per data unit	$ .21	$ .60
Fixed cost	$5,400	$2,400

   1. Calculate the point of indifference.

   2. What method would be best if units of data processed dropped to 5,200 units?

   3. What method would be more economical if units of data processed increased to 10,000?

   4. In your own words, define point of indifference.

2.8 Comfort Furniture, Inc., has two alternative methods of processing data proposed by its systems analyst, Judy Gooding. Method A is to purchase punched card equipment from another company which is going out of business. For all practicable purposes, assume this equipment is new. Method B recommends that a digital computer configuration be acquired. Comfort Furniture now has all their data processed by Numcruncher, Inc., a service bureau at a cost of $.30 per unit processed.

	Method A	Method B
Monthly fixed cost	$4,000	$10,000
Per unit variable cost	$ .20	$ .12

Required: The plant manager has requested the following information:

   1. For each method (A and B), the number of units processed where the monthly costs are equal to the costs of the service bureau.

   2. The most profitable method for 20,000 units processed monthly.

   3. The most profitable method for 80,000 units processed monthly.

   4. The volume level where there would be a point of indifference between Method A and Method B.

2.9 The total cost for processing data units using a manual method and a computer method is given as follows (this problem ignores the concept of diminishing returns).

Volume of Data Units	Manual Cost	Computer Cost
5,000	$ 4,800	$12,000
10,000	11,000	12,900
15,000	16,000	13,500
20,000	21,500	13,900
25,000	27,000	14,200

Plot graphs which show:

(1) Total cost to volume of data units and

(2) Cost per data unit to volume of data units. At what point would you recommend converting from a manual method to a computer method for processing data based on volume only?

2.10 The Rickshaw Cab Company serves a large metropolitan area and employs 500 drivers. The personnel manager is concerned over his lack of information concerning individual driver performance. He has requested that a "Drivers Incident Report" be compiled every six months. This report would list each driver, followed by the accidents he was involved in, the traffic violations he committed, the customer complaints directed against him, and the commendations he received. The personnel manager feels that the report could be used as a basis for decisions concerning raises, dismissal or remedial driver training. The company would benefit by a more equitable personnel program and more efficient usage of men and resources. In doing some research on the plan, the personnel manager read of a cab company on the West Coast that implemented a similar program and experienced a 5% decrease in accidents and an 8% decrease in traffic violations during the first year. He felt that roughly the same decreases would be applicable to Rickshaw. The top executives of the firm are only lukewarm to the idea, but will permit implementation of the plan, if there is a reasonable chance that the expected savings resulting from the report will at least offset the cost of generating it. Using the data below, compute the maximum cost that could be incurred by the generation of the report and still comply with the executive constraint for implementation. The information in Appendix A may aid you in arriving at a solution.

Historical Data

213 Accidents on the average per year.
298 Traffic violations on the average per year.

Distributions

Accidents		Traffic Violations	
Cost category in $	Percent	Cost category in $	Percent
1–100	30	1–10	15
101–500	40	11–15	35
501–1,000	25	16–25	35
1,001–2,000	2	26–50	10
2,001–5,000	1.5	51–100	4
5,001–10,000	1	101–200	1
10,001–20,000	.5		

2.11 The Wing Commander of a tactical fighter wing has requested the implementation of a formal information system to assist him in evaluating the quality of aircrew members. Although there are many factors related to determining an individual's quality level, it has been recommended that one source of objective data is from the testing process administered by the Standardization/Evaluation Section in the fighter wing. Each flightcrew member is tested periodically either by an instrument check or by a tactical/proficiency check to detect violations of standardized operating procedures or errors in judgment. The result of a test is either pass or fail and discrepancies such as single engine landing, dangerous pass, incorrect holding pattern, and so forth are noted where applicable. A general feeling exists in the Standardization/Evaluation Section that if these reports were prepared and disseminated in a timely fashion, the Wing Commander could take swift corrective action to prevent a hazardous practice or critical weakness from causing a decline in mission performance or even an accident from occurring. Further analysis indicates that such a report can be prepared daily, five days a week through out the year, at a cost of $14.10 per report. This time period for reporting is judged acceptable by the Standardization/Evaluation Section.

While there are many benefits anticipated from implementing such a system in terms of preventing the loss of aircrew member lives and the loss of aircraft property, as well as increasing the effectiveness of the fighter wing, the Wing Commander has requested that all new information systems be initially justified on pure economic grounds before other considerations are evaluated. As the systems analyst assigned to this project, you have decided to take the approach that the proposed system will help reduce the rate of major accidents from 2% to 1.5% as similar systems have done elsewhere, to economically justify implementation. From your investigation you have gathered the following statistics concerning major accidents:

Cost of Major Accident

Certain Costs:	
Aircraft	$1,600,000
Accident investigation	6,000
Property damage (impact point)	2,000
Total	$1,608,000
Possible Costs (both crewmembers are lost)	
Invested training in crewmembers	
2 @ $25,000	$ 50,000
Survivors benefits & mortuary costs	
2 @ $50,000	100,000
Total	$150,000
Probability of crew loss .25	

Can the proposed system be economically justified using this approach? Identify other economic factors not considered in this problem.

BIBLIOGRAPHY   Davis, *Computer Data Processing,* New York: McGraw-Hill Book Co., 1969. Dwyer, "Some Observations on Management Information Systems," *Advances in EDP and Information Systems,* New York: American Management Association, 1961.

McDonough, *Information Economics and Management Systems,* New York: McGraw-Hill Book Co., 1963.

Sanders, *Computers in Business: An Introduction,* Second Edition, New York: McGraw-Hill Book Co., 1972.

Sharpe, *The Economics of Computers,* New York: Columbia University Press, 1969.

Withington, F., *The Real Computer: Its Influence, Uses, and Effects,* Reading, Mass.: Addison-Wesley Publishing Co., 1969.

Withington, F., *The Use of Computers in Business Organizations,* Second Edition, Reading, Mass.: Addison-Wesley Publishing Co., 1971.

3
Analysis of Systems, Management, and Formal Information System Concepts

3.1 Introduction

Before we move into other parts of this text and more detailed discussions of computers and related technology, information systems and data bases, and systems analysis, it is appropriate at this time to develop a sound understanding of systems, management, and information system concepts. Anyone studying information systems should have a basic understanding of these concepts in order to build a framework from which to use information systems and/or to develop them. The specific objectives of this chapter are:

1. To present a detailed, conceptual analysis of systems using basically a classification and input-output approach.

2. To provide a basic understanding of the management function, especially in the context of the relationship between managements and their informational needs to properly run an organizational system.

3. To summarize the above two points by presenting a conceptualized model of a total system.

3.2 Overview of Systems

Systems is a ubiquitous term used to describe a number of things, objects, methods, or groups. An ordered group of facts, principles, philosophies, beliefs, and traditions such as, the democratic system of government, is described as a system. A respiratory system is a set of organs or parts in a living being which perform one or more vital functions. This system, in turn helps to support the being, which also can be considered a system. An organization of men, money, methods, material, and machines can form a business system. A computer configuration, which can contain a number of printers, card readers, memory units, control devices, tape drives, and other processing devices, is often referred to as a system, because it represents a group of interrelated objects which form a unified network.

There is a real need to understand and be able to work with systems in an intelligent manner. For this reason, the systems approach should be used to pick out the significant features of the system, which in turn will suggest what changes to make to improve the system. Moreover, utilization of the systems approach means that the components of the system are allocated and integrated in a way which optimizes the overall effectiveness of the system. That is, application of the systems approach helps to attain a synergistic effect wherein the united action of the different parts of the system produces a greater effect than the sum of the varied parts.

Classification of Systems

One conceptual way to classify systems[1] is based on two distinct criteria, which are as follows:

---

[1] The ideas for this section are adapted from: Stafford Beer, *Cybernetics and Management* (New York: John Wiley & Sons, Inc., 1966) Chapter II.

1. *Level of Predictability.* This criterion is based on a two-fold scheme: deterministic and probabilistic.

2. *Level of Complexity.* By adopting this criterion, it is possible to classify systems according to a three-fold scheme: simple, complex, and exceedingly complex.

When one can predict with certainty how a system will react, or perform in different situations, then the system is *deterministic.* There is never any doubt as to the outcome. Given the last state of the system and a present, determined, amount of information, it is always possible to predict, without any risk of error, the succeeding state of the system. Conversely, when one cannot predict with certainty the outcome of a particular system, the system is *probabilistic.* Some might observe that a probabilistic system is, in reality, a deterministic system which we do not fully understand. Such an observation has an element of truth which we will allude to later in this section. In any event, all managers and analysts must deal with probabilistic systems.

A *simple deterministic system* is one having few subsystems and interrelations, and which reveals completely predictable behavior. Steel balls placed in a track (as in a pinball machine) represent a simple deterministic system. However, once the balls have been thrust from the track, their paths become probabilistic. A row of machines on a production line can be studied and arranged to minimize the distance that materials must flow. When it is required to study what actually happens when materials begin to flow, the system at once becomes probabilistic.

Similar considerations apply when we study the *complex deterministic system.* A computer is a complex system, but it is deterministic in the sense that it will do what it is programmed to do. An automated warehouse is complex, but deterministic. When behavior of a complex deterministic system becomes less than fully predictable, it simply means that the system has developed a malfunction (or bug).

A *simple system* can also be *probabilistic.* For example, the tossing of a coin is a simple

Systems	Simple	Complex	Exceedingly Complex
D E T E R M I N I S T I C	Steel balls in track	Computer	No classification
	Production line layout	Automated warehouse	
P R O B A B I L I S T I C	Coin tossing	Small corporation	Large corporation
	Quality control system	Inventory system	National economy

FIGURE 3.1.   A table of systems classification.

system, but one which is notoriously probabilistic. A quality control system which predicts the number of defects in a population is a simple system, but also probabilistic.

A corporation is a *complex probabilistic system* that has as its objective to make a profit. Decisions are made, which affect a variety of subsystems in the system, and the influences of these decisions, to some degree, change the operations of the corporation to attain a level of profit, all of which is probabilistic.

So far four of the six possible categories that were set out for consideration have been considered. A system which is so complicated as to be virtually indescribable is *exceedingly complex*. Since this fifth category is so complex, it follows that it cannot be deterministic; therefore, there is no classification for an *exceedingly complex deterministic system*.

In the *exceedingly complex probabilistic* cate-

gory, however, the results are quite different. The nation's economy, for example, is so complex and so probabilistic that it does not seem likely that it will ever be fully described. In Chapter 1, we stated that organizations today have become more complex, to the point where many fall into the exceedingly complex probabilistic category. It is essential that techniques of information processing be developed which will aid management in handling this complexity.

A summary of the classification of systems is presented in Figure 3.1.

Cause-Effect Analysis

Systems can be analyzed in terms of inputs and outputs where the inputs are considered to be causes which interact to produce an output which, in turn, represents the effect. This cause-effect relationship is illustrated in Figure 3.2. The system acts as a function box which changes inputs to outputs.

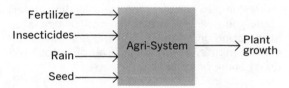

FIGURE 3.2.   A system illustrating a cause-effect relationship.

In the agri-system, a combination of different inputs such as fertilizer, insecticides, rain, and seed, often interact in complicated ways to produce an effect or output. In our system, of course, the output is plant growth.

Effect-Delay Analysis

In the agri-system, an input of causes will not result in a simultaneous output-effect of plant growth. The time gap after making the inputs, which lasts until the plants begin growth (and are ready for harvest) is called the effect-delay phenomenon. This circumstance can be more clearly understood by referring to Figure 3.3, which represents a simplistic throttle system in an airplane.

Notice that the speed of the airplane (the

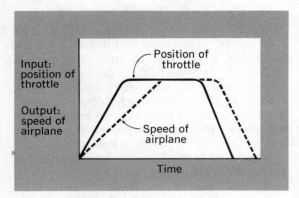

FIGURE 3.3. Illustration of the effect-delay phenomenon of a system.

output) remains fairly constant after the throttle (the input) has been pulled back. Also note that the speed decreases well after the throttle has been depressed to its original position. Projecting from this simple illustration to a more complex system one can readily understand the need for predictive and/or simulated information in order to determine, based on certain inputs, where some level of output will be, at some point in time.

Deterministic-Probabilistic Analysis

The classic example of a simple deterministic system is that of a heating system. The decision made to turn the heat on, or off, in most systems is well defined, and routine, in nature. When room temperature reaches the level at which the thermostat is set, it shuts off the heat; when the temperature drops, the thermostat turns the heat on again. The thermostat works both as the measurer of outputs and the controller of inputs. Contacts in the thermostat close the circuit which activates the fire in the furnace. The heat output from the furnace is fed back to the thermostat through the air, which, by heating a metallic element in the thermostat, opens the contacts again. The heated air links the furnace and thermostat in a closed feedback loop that ties together the action of the one with the other in an endless chain of cause and effect. The key idea in this

system is that output is attained by self-regulation, which is gained by having the recipient and measurer of the output be that which provides the input.

A complex probabilistic system will have many inputs which in turn will interact to produce many outputs. The input-output (cause-effect relationship) situation fall into three categories: (1) it is known with certainty that if certain inputs are made, certain outputs will occur; (2) uncertainty exists as to what inputs, or how much of certain inputs, to make in order to gain a variety of outputs; and (3) some of the inputs and outputs are totally unknown and/or uncontrollable. These three categories exist together in any complex probabilistic system. An illustration of this kind of system, with a great deal of simplification, is shown in Figure 3.4.

In the business system notice that the profit output (in a real world situation there would be many outputs) is not certain but is represented by some probability level. If the management of the business system knew with certainty the mix, number, and level of all the inputs shown in the example, and, if they had control over other unlisted inputs, such as natural disasters and strikes, then the output would be certain. Stating it another way, the probability of amount of profit would equal one. Alas, such a condition is not the case. Therefore, the probability level will always be something less than one. It is stressed that the result of information is to decrease uncertainty and by so doing the probability level can increase and approach one.

Another example of the probabilism inherent in some complex systems is illustrated by a

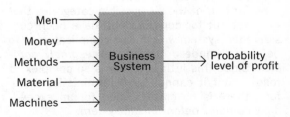

FIGURE 3.4. Complex probabilistic system.

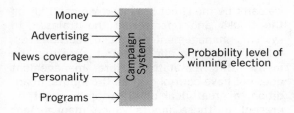

FIGURE 3.5. Campaign system with some probability of winning election.

political campaign. Such a system is shown in Figure 3.5.

In this complex probabilistic system, the final output is winning the election. But there is one thing for sure, no one knows for certain the final outcome. it can only be probabilized by pundits. Even the politician and his aides are uncertain as to what inputs to make, and when to make them, in order to increase the probability of winning.

Optimization Analysis

In any system, there are also opportunities to attain an optimum mix of inputs which in turn produces the desired output and by so doing optimizes the entire system. For example, suppose there is a project to paint a water tank and you have the responsibility of selecting the number of painters to work on the project. Would four men be better than two? Would eight men be better than four? Would twelve men be better than eight? It may seem that the greater number of painters you select for the project, the greater the efficiency. Such an assumption is normally not the case. In Figure 3.6 an illustration is made of the optimum number of painters selected to complete the project in the least time.

Notice that the time required to complete the project decreases as more painters are added, but after a certain point is reached (where the slope of the curve is zero) as still more painters are added, the time to completion begins to increase. The point of diminishing returns has been passed. Consequently, point $T_0 P_0$ represents the optimum number of painters for the project. One can observe many real world examples which clearly point out the applicability

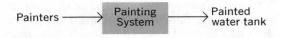

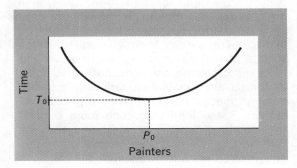

FIGURE 3.6. Optimization of a painting system.

of this analysis. In the selection and acquisition of data processing tools, one will often find the attitude that more and more equipment will, in some magical way, make the information system more responsive to management's needs. What often happens as a result of such a philosophy is that management is often inundated with reams of computer output (data pollution) with a distinct absence of information content.

Input-Output Subsystem Phenomenon

Normally in complex systems, whether they are deterministic or probabilistic, there are a number of subsystems which make up the total system. In such a situation the output of one subsystem becomes the input of another subsystem, and so on. In Figure 3.7 a simplified oil production system illustrates the input-output subsystem phenomenon.

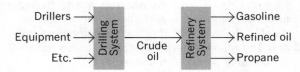

FIGURE 3.7. Sequence of input-output showing two subsystems in an oil production system.

This analysis can be related to an information system where data from the results of operations and transactions of a business enterprise, becomes the input for the information system. Information, the output of the information system, in turn becomes the input into the management system. The management system selects plans, makes decisions to solve conflicts and problems, and takes corrective action to control and manipulate various inputs (e.g. money, machines) into the organizational system. These inputs produce more outputs, the results of which are measured thus becoming data inputs to the information system. And, again, the cycle is repeated.

3.3 Overview of Management

What is the function of management and how does it perform this function? Some authorities have stated that the essential task of management is to deal with changing conditions. Others have said that the essential task is to recognize and assimilate technological changes in such a manner that practical values will be produced and disseminated to society in an orderly, timely, and economical way. Still others state that management is simply "getting things done through the efforts of others."

A survey of the literature identifies a multiplicity of tasks associated with the management function. These are: planning, scheduling, commanding, organizing, hiring, training, controlling, supervising, and so forth. Traditionally the management function has been described as planning, organizing, and controlling. We divide the management function into three basic tasks: (1) planning, (2) controlling, and (3) decision making. If systems analysts are to design effective information systems to serve management, it follows that they must understand not only the management function but also the informational needs of management.

As Hall states: "We may set the signals, operate some switches, and perhaps establish the minimum and maximum speed limits, but we can't be the Great Engineer. We can't lay all the tracks and operate all the trains."[2] In systems, management can make decisions, establish plans, and effect control by setting the inputs. But, as stated before, management does not have control over all the inputs. In addition, a great deal of uncertainty might be present in those inputs which management does have control over.

Planning

It should be stated at this point that all systems are goal-seeking. Planning provides, prior to any activities, the criteria that managers must meet in order to achieve prescribed goals. Planning is basic to controlling and decision making, although one could argue that one must first *decide* on a plan. Without planning, however, there would be no need to control, because planning is the foundation of management and controlling, as well as of other activities such as organizing and scheduling. Management needs information to establish goals and courses of action. It is impossible to provide all the information to cover all aspects and contingencies of a plan; however, information can help to reduce uncertainty, the nemesis of management.

Upon analyzing the planning activity further five basic tasks which the planner must perform can be identified:

1. Establish goals and/or objective(s).
2. Identify the events and activities which must be performed to achieve the objective(s).
3. Describe the resources and/or talents required to perform each activity.
4. Define the duration of each activity identified.
5. Determine in what sequence, if any, the identified activities must be performed.

It should be evident from the above description of the planning activity that it is continuing requirement of management in most, if not all, organizations. Moreover, in most organizations, the planning task is shared in varying degrees by all levels of management.

[2] D. M. Hall, *The Management of Human Systems* (Cleveland, Ohio: Association for Systems Management, 1971), p. 3.

Controlling

Very seldom, indeed, do things go according to plans. Deviations from plans are caused by happenings beyond the control of management, such as errors in estimates and mistakes by subordinates. In most systems something always goes wrong, thus necessitating the controlling activity. Controlling is a process consisting of three basic steps: (1) measuring the outputs of the system; (2) comparing these outputs with plans, and ascertaining the deviations, if any; and (3) correcting unfavorable deviations by taking corrective action. It is stressed here, that for the manager to take corrective action, it is assumed that he or she has the *power* to modify or change some input, a very important assumption.

As stated earlier, the planning function establishes goals and the control task ensures that these goals are attained via a feedback of information to management. This section, consequently, treats the analysis of the control activity in systems.

Elements of Feedback and Control. If a person sits in one place too long with his or her legs crossed, upon arising, the person may find to his or her dismay that it is quite difficult to stand according to plan. What has happened is that the feedback from the sensors at the base of the feet has all but disappeared. Consequently, control cannot be effected in order to bring the person to a planned position.

In throwing a football, quarterbacks rely on a feedback system which provides a continuous measurement of error between their position, the speed and position of their receivers, the position and speed of onrushing linemen, and their level of protection. To properly control the throw, they must reduce this error to zero or near zero.

The elements of a system which have been enumerated are input, output, and process. These elements represent parameters of the system, some portions of which can be measured and evaluated. To measure the overall effectiveness of the system in attaining its goals, we turn to the output parameter, which represents the focal point of control. Three ele-

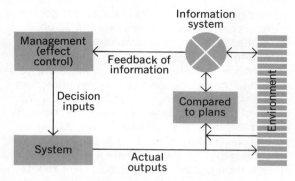

FIGURE 3.8. Elements of feedback and control.

ments of control are set up to use this parameter as a control point. These are:

1. Establishment of a standard output, i.e., the desired performance or goal of the system.
2. Design and implementation of a sensor which gathers data that relates to the output, evaluates and measures the performance of the output, and communicates the resulting information to management.
3. Employment of a manager(s), or a mechanism, which takes corrective action should the information indicate a need for such action. This corrective action results in the release of decisions, which act as inputs, back into the process of the system. A simple example of control is illustrated in Figure 3.8.

The information system measures and evaluates output from the process. This output can consist of sales, sales performance, earnings, quality control, purchases, level of production, performance of personnel, flow of funds, utilization of assets, and so on. These outputs emanate from the process of the system.

If it is a business (or many other types of) organization, the information system must disseminate information to external, as well as to internal, users. External users such as stockholders or government could have some impact upon what decisions the internal management group makes. The information system should also collect data from the environment about level of demand, price of material, availability of labor, price of labor, competitive action, government action, customer response, and so on.

To effect control, the decision maker expects a definite output representing a planned or desired value. Deviations from this value are reported to the decision maker via communicated information containing a control error E. This error is the difference between the desired output DO and the actual output AO, which results in a deviation of $E = DO - AO$. The smoothing out of this difference is the job of the decision maker. Proper action from the decision maker generates the decision inputs which activate the process. If the decision maker is successful, $DO - AO = 0$. If, for example, the output (amount of products, quality of products, sales, profit) of an organizational system is not what it is supposed to be, according to predetermined plans, information indicating these deviations from plans is fed back to managers who have the power to act to correct the deviations or to alter the plans.

The control of a system will be effective: (1) if the actual output is properly measured and compared to the desired output, (2) if the required action decisions are implemented, and (3) if both the feedback of information and the decision making activities are rapid enough to make corrections before the factors in the process become inconsistent with the corrections made.

Types of Control. There are two types of control systems: (1) open-loop and (2) closed-loop.

1. *Open-loop system.* This system is set up to achieve one purpose and there is no feedback of information. For example, a washing machine can be set by a timing control device to run through a wash cycle of a predetermined duration. One could start the machine, leave it and come back later, only to find that the machine had gone through the complete cycle without the use of water because the water valve was not turned on. If the control device was apprised of this situation by a feedback system, then measures could have been established to correct the fault in the system. One can also think of institutions in our society which fail to operate properly either because of a poor system of feedback or, because the control mechanism fails to take cognizance of the feedback information that is available.

On a larger and more complex scale, business systems which are managed on an open-loop basis can become involved in crisis situations which are beyond management's ability to correct. For example, the output of food products must be measured with care for detection of certain contaminants. In turn, this quality control information must be fed back to managers who have power to correct any deviations. Without such a feedback of information, management runs a real risk of becoming involved in a disastrous situation which cannot be corrected. On a more global scale, some historians have indicated that the results of the attack on Pearl Harbor could have been mitigated had our leadership received the necessary information.

2. *Closed-loop system.* This kind of a system is one where the control mechanism receives and uses feedback information. In our washing machine example, if the control mechanism is set up to begin the wash cycle only after an established volume of water has flowed into the tub, then washing can take place only if the tub contains a certain volume of water. The control mechanism is apprised of this condition by a feedback loop.

All of our institutions and organizations should have an information flow which utilizes the closed-loop system. The reason for having such a system becomes obvious when it is recognized that any system, if it is to attain its goals, must have available to its management system, on a timely basis, information which reveals its level of attainment. In general, then, we can state that every goal-seeking system should utilize a closed-loop system for proper control.

Decision Making

One of the basic activities of management is to understand the system enough to make proper judgments which will improve performance of the total system within certain prescribed constraints. Decision making, thus, is a process of selecting from among several alternatives, which may be either quantitative or qualitative, the best alternative in order to solve a problem or resolve a conflict.

Elements of Decision Making. The reason a manager must make a decision is because of a problem confrontation or a conflict situation. The act of deciding brings forth a solution to the problem or a resolution of the conflict. An orderly process of deriving a decision contains four elements:

1. *Model.* The model represents a quantitative or qualitative description of the problem.

2. *Criteria.* The stated criteria represent goals or objectives of the decision problem (e.g., to achieve maximum customer service). When there are several criteria which are in conflict (e.g., increase customer service *and* reduce inventory), the decision maker must compromise.

3. *Constraints.* There are added factors which must be considered in the solution of the decision problem. Lack of funds is an example of a constraint.

4. *Optimization.* Once the decision problem is fully described (the model), the manager determines what is needed (the criteria), and what is permissible (the constraints). At this point the decision maker is ready to select the best, or optimum, solution.

Types of Decision Making. Decision problems and conflicts are everywhere. Some are simple and deterministic in nature and result in minor ramifications. Others are quite complex and probabilistic in nature and can make a significant impact. Decision making can be routine and structured or it can be complex and ill-structured. Therefore, in broad terms, there are two types of decision making: (1) programmed and (2) nonprogrammed.

1. *Programmed.* This category of decision making involves an automatic response to previously established policies. All problems that are repetitive and routine in nature with well defined parameters readily lend themselves to programmed decision making. A great challenge to the analyst is to identify these kinds of decisions and to provide methods by which programmed decision making can be implemented wherever possible. In order to effect this kind of decision making a decision rule must be totally defined and clearly stated. Once this decision rule has been derived, it is simply a matter of developing an algorithm which will make the proper decision on a routine and automatic basis.

In many organizations there are opportunities to implement programmed decision making because many decisions are made in accordance with routine standard operating procedures. The payoff from implementing programmed decision making is that it frees management for more important tasks. Once implemented, the process of this kind of decision making is of the type illustrated in Figure 3.9.

An example of a programmed decision would be that of inventory control where the derivation of the economic order quantity, the reorder point, and the safety stock are all handled by the computer system on an online basis. When the stock falls to a predetermined level, an order is automatically initiated to reorder N number of items to replenish the stock.

2. *Nonprogrammed.* This category of decision making represents the process of dealing with ill-defined problems. They are normally complex, wherein only a portion of the parameters are known, and many of the known parameters possess a great deal of probabilism. It takes all the talent of a skilled decision maker

FIGURE 3.9. Schematic of the programmed decision making process.

plus the aid of the information system to make sound nonprogrammed decisions. Expansion of plant facilities, development of a new product, processing and advertising policies, personnel management, purchase versus lease, and mergers, are all examples of problems which require nonprogrammed decisions. The following section analyzes the decision makers and their role in this category of decision making.

The Decision Making Process. Decision makers have a rate at which they can assimilate information which determines their information processing efficiency. A person's past knowledge, coupled with their information processing efficiency, will determine their individual decision making capacity. Faced with alternatives, the decision maker identifies an objective and then attempts to attain this objective by choosing the best alternative based on the knowledge that they possess. If an inability to come to grips with the meaning of each alternative at the individual's present level of knowledge is recognized, additional information will be sought. Problems arise, and further decision making activity is required, when the decision maker acts without sufficient information. Insufficient information results from the inability of the sources of information to provide the needed information or from the inability of the decision maker to prescribe accurately his informational needs. An illustration of the decision making process is shown in Figure 3.10.

A significant amount of time is expended by business leaders, government officials, school administrators, and other organizational managers in solving problems and resolving conflicts. It follows that a large measure of their success in these activities will be directly related to the quality of information with which they work.

Our view of decision making is that it is a rational information-using process, not an emotional process. Thus, in this context, difficulties in decision making can be attributable to either:[3]

[3] Samuel B. Richmond, *Operations Research for Management Decisions* (New York: The Ronald Press Company, 1968), p. 16.

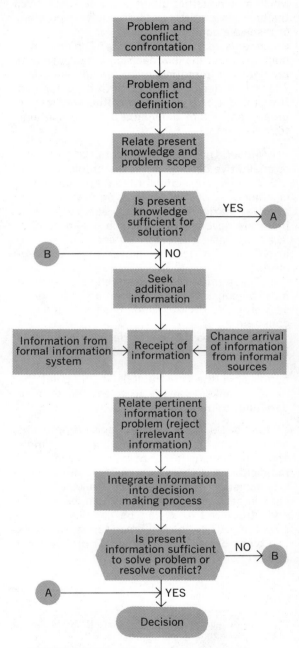

FIGURE 3.10. Flowchart of the use of information in a decision making process.

1. *Inadequate information;* incorrect or incomplete information about the various possible alternative courses of action and about their implications with respect to the ultimate outcome; or

2. *Inadequately specified objectives:* failure to specify which outcomes are more desirable than others.

Levels of Decision Making. Decision making can range from the very routine, perfunctory kind of decisions (programmed) to the complex ones which make a significant impact on the system (nonprogrammed). For classification, we place decision making at three levels: (1) strategic, (2) tactical, and (3) technical.

1. *Strategic level.* Strategic decisions are characterized by a great deal of uncertainty and are future oriented. These decisions establish long range plans which affect the entire organization. The goals of the organization are stated and a range of strategies are made which might entail, for example, plant expansion, determination of product lines, mergers, diversification, capital expenditures, or the sale of the organization. Strategy, therefore, is concerned with long range planning and includes establishing objectives, policy making, organizing, and attaining an overall effectiveness for the organization.

2. *Tactical level.* Tactical decision making pertains to short term activities and the allocation of resources for the attainment of the objectives. This kind of decision making relates to such areas as formulation of budgets, funds flow analysis, deciding on plant layout, personnel problems, product improvement, and research and development.

Whereas strategic decision making entails largely a planning activity, tactical decision making requires a fairly equal mix of planning and controlling activities. This kind of decision making has a small, if any, potential for programmed decision making. The decision rules in tactical decision making are, for the most part, ill-structured and not amenable to routine and self-regulation.

3. *Technical level.* At this level of decision making standards are fixed and the results of decisions are deterministic. Technical decision making is a process of ensuring that specific tasks are implemented in an effective and efficient manner. This kind of decision making requires specific commands to be given which control specific operations. The primary management function involved in this class of decision making is that of control, with planning performed on a rather limited scale. Examples of this kind of decision making involves acceptance or rejection of credit, process control, scheduling, receiving, shipping, inventory control, and allocating workers.

Informational Requirements for Decision Making. Different levels of decision making require different informational requirements. This statement can be illustrated in Figure 3.11.

The lines as depicted in Figure 3.11, cannot be precisely delineated because, in practicable situations, the lines between categories of decision making are blurred and tend to overlap. Analysts must, however, be aware of these

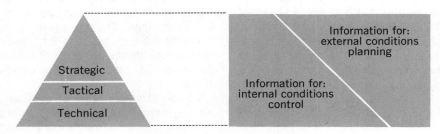

FIGURE 3.11. Kind of information required for various classifications of decision making.

Strategic information	1. External information
	  (a) Competitive actions
	  (b) Customer actions
	  (c) Availability of resources
	  (d) Demographic studies
	  (e) Government actions
	2. Predictive information
	  (long-term trends)
	3. Simulated-what if information

Tactical information	1. Descriptive-historical
	  information
	2. Performance-current
	  information
	3. Predictive-future information
	  (short-term)
	4. Simulated-what if information

Technical information	1. Descriptive-historical
	  information
	2. Performance-current
	  information

FIGURE 3.12.   Characteristics of information which meet requirements of different kinds of decision making.

types of decision making, and how the information system can be designed to meet differing requirements, because the information which is produced by the information system is dependent upon these requirements. The characteristics of information which meet these needs are listed in Figure 3.12.

3.4 Overview of Formal Information Systems

All organizations have one kind of an information system or another that is supposed to meet their informational requirements and thus reduce the probability of making poor decisions. However, many information systems are incapable of providing relevant information for strategic decision making, and to some degree, for tactical decision making. It is imperative that for strategic decision making, information systems will have to be designed to grasp the realities of the environment such as the actions of competitors; economical, social, and political

trends; situations in foreign countries; technological developments; and so forth, and to report this information to the persons involved in strategic decision making.

Please note that the term "formal" is used to describe the information system discussed in this text. This term simply means that we are only concerned with handling those information requirements which can be produced from objective, verifiable data. Such an information system, in other words, does not include rumors, grapevines, hearsay, or informal personal communications.

Effectiveness of the Information System for Different Levels of Decision Making

Because of the differences in requirements, the information system must be designed to satisfy all three levels of decision making. In many organizations many strategic and tactical decisions are made more on the basis of intuition, heuristics, and interpretation, than on relevant information from the formal information system. Implementation of strategic type information processed by the information system will prove of significant value to the persons who make these decisions. However, a formal information system is limited as to how effective it can be in producing relevant information for the three kinds of decision making. This phenomenon is based on the concepts illustrated in Figure 3.13.

Each of these schematics represent general concepts which are subject to modification. The purpose of these illustrations is to show not only the potential effectiveness of the formal information system but also the probable limitations. The literature is replete with grandiose promises of what the information system can do for management. Many of these promises are far beyond the current state of the art.

At the strategic level of decision making in any system, the range of problem variety reaches its peak. Often these problems are of a nonrecurring nature, of great importance, and must be handled by management under condi-

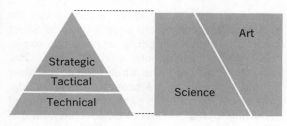

(a) Degree to which decision making is an art/science.

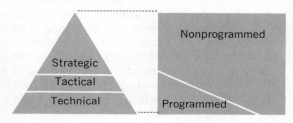

(b) Degree to which decision making can be programmed/nonprogrammed.

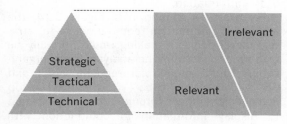

(c) Degree to which information produced by the formal information system is relevant/irrelevant.

FIGURE 3.13. Concepts which show the degree of effectiveness a formal information system can have on decision making.

tions of almost total uncertainty. Therefore, the belief that total information systems can be developed which will produce solutions to all problems (as in *2001: A Space Odyssey*) is simply infeasible. It requires a great deal of decision making art, wisdom, and experience to make rational decisions at this level; however, well designed information systems can provide information which will help to reduce variety and uncertainty at this level. Methods used to ac-

complish this objective are discussed in the next chapter.

Since tactical decision making deals mainly with determining the most efficient utilization of resources, the formal information systems have a real opportunity to help management at this level by implementation of modeling techniques which help to select, simplify, diagnose, and optimize. There is very little opportunity, if any, at this level to routinize any decision making process. At this level, there is still a great need for classical management skills.

Technical decision making is well defined, routine, and deterministic. Much of the "information" produced for this level emanates from the normal administrative data processing activities of any system to meet normal business needs such as payroll, and reporting requirements to stockholders and the government. For example, when a manufacturing or sales organization receives a customer order, this order triggers a chain of events which includes data processing, report generation, and physical material processing. In addition, payrolls must be prepared to pay employees, sales records must be kept, government and financial reports prepared, and so forth. If proper systems work is performed at this level while developing the information system, much of the raw data generated can be used to produce information for higher levels when needed. For example, if a logical scheme of classification and coding is developed, then the basic sales data can be used to generate a variety of information combinations such as sales forecasting, inventory control, and sales analysis (e.g., either by product, customer, salesman, or territory). Also, basic data items can be logically associated to provide information to a wide variety of managers at all levels.

It should not be assumed from the above discussion that this level of processing is unimportant. Conversely, a system which performs reliable administrative data processing is absolutely essential for the smooth operation of any organization. Should data processing procedures fail or become faulty at this level, the organization itself will immediately face a crisis.

Classification of Information	Technical	Tactical	Strategic
Dependence on External Information	Very low	Moderate	Very high
Dependence on Internal Information	Very high	High	Moderate
Information Online	Very high	High	Moderate
Information in Real Time	Very high	Very high	Very high
Information Reported Periodically	Very high	Very high	Very high
Information That Is Descriptive-Historical in Nature	High	Moderate	Low
Information That Is Performance-Current in Nature	Very high	High	Moderate
Information That Is Predictive-Future in Nature	Low	High	Very high
Information That Is Simulated-What If in Nature	Low	High	Very high

(Categories of Decision Making heading spans the top of the Technical/Tactical/Strategic columns)

FIGURE 3.14. Classification of information which meet the requirements of the three levels of decision making.

There is, however, a great potential for implementing programmed decision making at this level, thereby allowing managers to devote more of their time to the other two creative levels of decision making.

Relationship of Classifications of Information to Levels of Decision Making. The matrix in Figure 3.14 relates major classifications of information to the three levels of decision making.

The nature of the information requirements can, without a doubt, be related to the decision making process. For each decision making activity, a determination should be made

regarding the information desired by the responsible managers to enable them to effect their planning, controlling, organizing, implementing of assignments, and so forth. Consideration by both the analyst and the user should be given to the scope of coverage, degree of detail, contents of reports, frequency of reporting, period of time to be covered, and distribution and communication methods.

The user who is responsible for the decision making activity under analysis, and who will be the principal user of the information, should be given considerable leeway in determining their information requirements and the conditions of processing and communication. Because the information system is designed on the basis of information requirements which are to be met, it is important that each user (manager) guard against a natural tendency to request more information, or to have it communicated more frequently, and in a more elaborate manner, than is warranted by the cost/effectiveness ratio of the information.

For example, as shown in Figure 3.14, the amount of information required online for strategic level decision making would normally be moderate, if not nil. The analysts of an organization could install picturephone units and CRT's (cathode-ray tube—video display) in top management offices throughout an organization to display information in conjunction with normal voice communication. To gain access to and select information for display, the manager simply uses a touch-tone phone and inputs an access code based on an index of information available to him. This index might contain categories such as actual sales to date compared to objective sales, prior year's actual sales, income (after taxes) year to date of Division A, and so forth.

All of this information is vitally important, but in order for strategic decisions of any consequence to be made, days, weeks, or months of thought are normally required. Instantaneous decisions to complex problems probably do not allow enough time for the application of management's judgment. Secondly, even when online information, such as scheduled trips of top executives, stock exchange information, political news, foreign exchange rates, and so forth, is interesting and necessary, its cost via online facilities might far exceed the effectiveness of such a system. In addition, the same information is often available from other, less elaborate sources at lower costs.

Analysis of the Communication Process

The basic concept which deals with the flow of information and actually disseminating it to management is communication. Communication takes place when information is transmitted from a source to a receiver through a defined channel linking them.

Effective communication is important in all aspects of human pursuits. There is a wide spectrum of communication systems ranging from simple person to person communication to highly complex systems, such as the entire communications network of an organization. In this section, we are specifically concerned with that communication which relates to the formal information system and the formal information of the organization. Its purpose is to deliver objective, unbiased, and formal information to the receiver.

Communication Model. A communication model is shown in Figure 3.15.

The broad objectives of an effective information system are: (1) convey the information, and (2) ensure proper perception by the user. The information contains the messages which are transmitted via a channel to a receiver. Also included in the model is a noise source which interferes, at some level, with the information between the source and receiver. Noise is

sometimes manifested in inaccurate or biased reports. In a large, complex system having a series of senders and receivers, noise can emanate from a number of junctures. Cumulative noise results when the noise at one juncture is added on to the noise at another juncture.

The communication system as illustrated in Figure 3.15 can be no more effective than its least effective component—a chain is no stronger than its weakest link. If the source does not provide relevant and timely information; if the messages are distorted or delayed; if the recipient cannot use the messages; then, the entire system is degraded to the lowest common denominator. All of the steps must be accomplished on an equal basis if the system as a whole is to be effective.

Categories of Communication. Communication, as we deal with it in this section, and as it applies to the information system concept, falls into two categories: (1) personal communication, and (2) media communication. The essential characteristics of personal communication are: (1) a specific person communicating with another person, (2) a person communicating with a group, or (3) a group communicating with another group.

Communication media represent the impersonal means of conveying information to the receiver. These include: books, journals, television, radio, remote terminals, and various prepared reports. Remote terminals are connected to the CPU via telecommunication devices such as telephone lines, microwave, or communication satellites. The combination of computers and communication equipment can be, in some situations, a significant component in information systems. The modes of transmission of data and information in these systems are accomplished through: (1) time sharing, (2) teleprocessing, (3) computer to computer transmission, and (4) remote inquiry capabilities. Telecommunication allows the following interactions: man-to-machine, for extensive computational work done from a remote location; storage devices-to-machine, for remote transmission of voluminous data files; machine-to-machine, for satellite, master/slave, or backup systems; and man-to-machine, for interactive

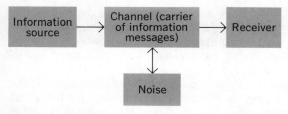

FIGURE 3.15. Schematic of a communication model.

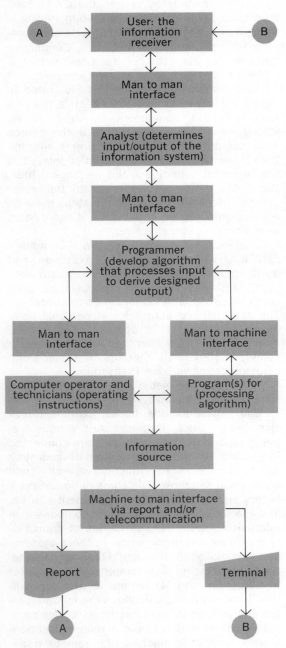

FIGURE 3.16. Schematic of communication interfaces between components of an information system.

processes of remote update of files and quick access of information from files. The growth in communication media has given us powerful tools and techniques that makes the computer a highly versatile tool. In addition to processing masses of data and preparing information reports, it is also an effective interactive device. By virtue of compressing time and space, communication technology makes information more pertinent and concise, since it can give specific responses to specific inquiries, and can reduce information delays.

Communication Cycle of Information Systems Work. There are many communication interfaces existing in the information system. In performing systems work, which is treated in greater detail later in the text, proper communication between the several components of the total system is vitally important. Assuming the use of the computer as the major processing tool, a schematic of these communication interfaces is illustrated in Figure 3.16.

A real barrier to effective investigation, problem definition, analysis, and problem solution is the lack of effective communication. If the analyst were the only one involved in systems work, then the only limit to the effectiveness of his or her work would be solely based on his or her degree of competency. Obviously, the analyst is not the only one involved; he or she must, therefore, establish a complete communication cycle which begins and ends with the user—the ultimate receiver of information.

General Model of the Formal Information System

Although many aspects of the formal information system will be discussed throughout the text, it is appropriate at this time to bring together, into a conceptual model, many of the points discussed thus far. A conceptual model of a business organization is illustrated in Figure 3.17.

As alluded to earlier, the formal information system is a necessary subsystem for the effective management of any total system, whether the total system is a business organization,

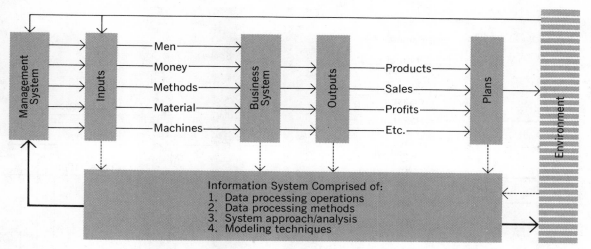

FIGURE 3.17. Illustration of the formal information system and its relation to the total business system. Legend: → inputs from management and outputs from business system. Also inputs from environment, e.g., natural disasters or government action; ⇢ data inputs into the information system; → information from the information system.

government agency, or institution. To emphasize this point, we also present, in Figure 3.18, a model of an ecological system. The legend for this illustration is the same as Figure 3.17 and is therefore not repeated.

In Figure 3.18, the output of the human population system is, of course, the amount of people. The amount and placement of these people, in turn, results in an impact on waste disposal, pollution, and conservation, all outputs of the ecosystem. Data from these systems must be collected, processed, and the results communicated to the management system (e.g., legislators, government officials). Notice that some of the inputs are not connected to the management system because these represent those inputs that are beyond the control of management. Also notice, however, that the impact of one input, disease, can be offset by effective implementation of health care. Moreover, observe that one controllable input such as health care will help to increase population growth while another input such as birth control education can help to decrease growth. This seemingly paradoxical situation only helps

to point out the complexities inherent in applying proper management skills.

The information systems in these two idealized models perform the following tasks: (1) handle all routine and administrative data processing; (2) perform programmed decision making where applicable; and (3) provide the necessary information to all levels of the management system for effective planning, controlling, and decision making.

As we shall see later in the text, there are several ways to view the information system, such as: (1) what its objectives are, (2) specific methods used to meet management's needs, (3) how it is structured in the overall system, (4) the technology that makes it operative, (5) the data base which is its foundation, and (6) the various ways information can flow throughout the system. For now, the formal information system can be viewed as a subsystem which processes data and, in turn, provides information to management and other constituent groups, such as the stockholders of a corporation. We should also appreciate the fact that the information system is a vital

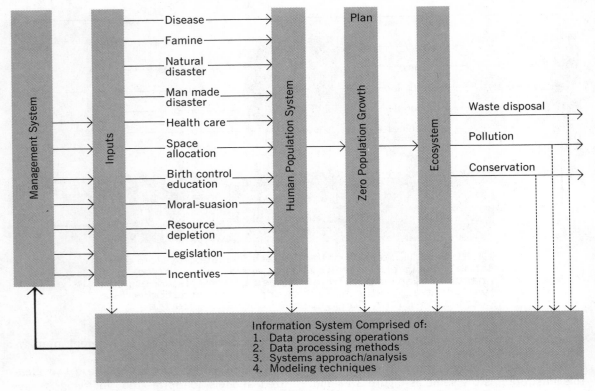

FIGURE 3.18. Illustration of the formal information system and
its relation to the total ecosystem.

key to the effective operation of any organizational system, business or otherwise.

SUMMARY

Systems can be very effectively described and analyzed. The classification of systems ranges from simple deterministic to exceedingly complex probabilistic systems. From an input-output analysis, systems are described with regard to: (1) cause-effect relationships, (2) the effect-delay phenomenon, (3) deterministic-probabilistic levels, (4) optimization, and (5) input-output subsystem phenomenon.

Primarily, it is the responsibility of management to effectively manage systems,

business or otherwise, to attain objectives. The activities of management to meet this responsibility are threefold: (1) planning—the foundation of management, which includes setting objectives, (2) controlling—keeping the system in line with the plans, and (3) decision making—solving problems and resolving conflicts.

Planning not only includes the setting of objectives, but the description of activities, methods, and benchmarks as to how these objectives will be achieved. Management needs information to aid it in selecting the best plans to achieve these objectives.

The activity of controlling is totally ineffective without information. To effect control, management must have a subsystem which measures the outputs of the system and compares this measurement with the planned objective. Then, and only then, can management take the necessary appropriate action to correct deviations from plans. Feedback of information is implemented if a closed-loop system is used.

Decision making is basically a problem solving activity. The elements of the decision making process are: (1) the derivation of a model which describes the problem, (2) selecting criteria which serve as standards, (3) finding constraints that act as limitations to various alternatives, and (4) an optimization, which results in the best solution. Some decision making activities are quite routine and can be set up on a self-regulating basis. Other, ill-defined, problems require the best skills of management plus a viable information system. The decision making process is described at three levels: (1) strategic—policies and long range plans, (2) tactical—implementation of plans, and (3) technical—day-to-day routine operations.

It is a real challenge to information system developers to design and implement information systems which will significantly aid decision makers at higher levels, especially at the strategic level.

The formal information system is made up of four basic components: (1) data processing operations, (2) data processing methods, such as computers and related technology, (3) systems analysis, and (4) modeling techniques. Once the information requirements have been ascertained through systems analysis, data from various areas are collected, operated upon, and communicated to the management system.

REVIEW QUESTIONS

3.1 Define the term system. Give at least three examples of a system.

3.2 In mathematics, a relationship can be defined as $Y = f(X)$, which can be described as:

$$X \longrightarrow \boxed{f(X)} \longrightarrow Y$$

Describe this mathematical relationship in terms of a system.

3.3 If a manager does not know all of the interaction and process that the inputs go through to produce outputs, will this prevent him from making sound decisions? Why? Why not?

3.4 When analyzing systems, what is the importance of identifying: (a) cause-effect relationships, (b) effect-delay phenomena, (c) deterministic-probabilistic behavior, and (d) optimization opportunities?

3.5 Define at least two major criteria which can be used to classify systems.

3.6 Provide an illustration of the input-output subsystem phenomenon. Why is it important to recognize this situation in systems?

3.7 What role does an information system play in a complex probabilistic system? Give an example of one and illustrate how the information system works in the system.

3.8 Define the term "planning." What major tasks are involved in the planning process?

3.9 Define control and feedback. Give an example of how one may control a system via feedback information.

3.10 List the two kinds of control. Discuss both and show their applicability to the control of different systems.

3.11 Are business type organizations the only organizations that need information systems? Explain.

3.12 Look up the terms "cybernetics" and "homeostasis" in the library. Relate them to our discussion on feedback.

3.13 Define decision making. Distinguish between programmed and non-programmed decision making.

3.14 Using a moon shot as a basis of decision making, give an example each of programmed and nonprogrammed decision making.

3.15 Discuss the decision making process. Classify the various difficulties related to decision making.

3.16 What are the major levels of decision making? Relate the relative importance of planning and controlling at each level. What kind of information is required at each level?

3.17 Why does it become increasingly difficult for the formal information system of the organization to meet the information needs of tactical and strategic decision makers?

3.18 What impact does the implementation of programmed decision making have on the management system of an organization?

3.19 Why do decision makers use a model? Why should they bother with criteria and constraints? Why don't they simply make decisions without regard to optimization?

3.20 What criteria would you use if selecting an automobile for yourself if money were not a constraint? Suppose you have $3,000.00 to invest in an automobile. Do the criteria remain the same? Are any relaxed, modified, or deleted?

3.21 Define communication. What role does it play in information systems? Discuss fully.

3.22 Explain the communication interfaces between components of an information system. Show how each aids in performing effective systems work.

QUESTIONS FOR DISCUSSION

3.1 Does the statement of objectives provide managers with clear goals toward which activities can be directed? How can managers determine whether or not the objectives are being met?

3.2 Can you relate an experience, of which you are aware, where the lack of objectives resulted in a crisis? Explain.

3.3 Comment on the following statement: "It takes more to manage than the mere statement of objectives."

3.4 Besides profitability, discuss several objectives that the following managers may state: (1) sales manager, (2) materials manager, (3) credit manager, and (4) personnel manager. Briefly list the information that each manager must have to effect these objectives? Can the formal information system provide all the information required? If not, where will the other information come from?

3.5 Discuss the following statement: "Management is the process of getting things done through people."

3.6 Discuss the following statement: "There is no need to perform planning. No one can predict the future."

3.7 A frequent complaint made by management is that cost reports arrive too late to be of any value. What do they mean by this complaint? How can this problem be alleviated?

3.8 Discuss the statement: "Management must not rely on intuition and judgment."

3.9 Discuss the following comment: "Many activities and processes are beginning to look almost unmanageable, owing to their vast size, their wide-flung networks of interdependent relationships among ever increasingly specialized functions, and their manifold aspects and ramifications that must be comprehended and unified. Surely one of the crucial sources of the improved management that is necessary in the face of the threatening complexity of our age is improved information." (From M. H. Schwartz, "Identifying Universal Principles in MIS Design," *Proceedings Third Annual Conference,* September 9 & 10, 1971 (Chicago, Illinois: The Society for Management Information Systems), p. 5.

3.10 What level of decision making is required for scientists in developing a particular moon exploration project? What level of decision making is required from lift-off to splash-down?

3.11 Do the scientist and space administrators need a great deal of online information? Do the controllers in charge of the flight and exploration phase of a moon shot need online information? Why? Explain.

3.12 "In the end, the information system must be recognized only as a foundation for human judgment, insight, and inventiveness." Discuss this statement.

3.13 "The computer is a vitalizing information foundation for the manager. In this setting, the manager, endowed with the capacities that education and experience have brought to maturity, stands as the enduring center of creative policy formation and decision." Discuss this statement.

3.14 If a great deal of technical decision making has a potential for programmed decision making techniques, then why don't tactical and strategic decision making have the same potential?

3.15 "Formal information can't do much to help top level decision makers." Discuss this comment.

3.16 Approximate the amount of programmed decision making in a typical moon shot. Do you believe that there is a higher percentage of programmed decision making in the management of a large metropolitan area or the management of the moon shot? Why? Why not? Explain.

EXERCISES

3.1 You have just been appointed sales manager for Big Reel Wirerope Company. The major objective of the organization is to establish markets throughout the nation. You have at your disposal competent systems analysts and data processing personnel and resources. In addition you have 126 qualified salesmen with at least seven who possess managerial talent. Outline how you would set up your new job indicating your management approach, your method of implementing the management function, the kind of information required for your particular functional area, how you want this information reported, and to whom you want it reported.

3.2 You have been assigned line manager in charge of the mixing department of the Cover Up Paint Company. You are to establish material usage standards and labor efficiency standards. Describe how you would develop these standards and ensure that you are maintaining control of material usage and labor efficiency. Make any assumptions you wish.

3.3 Establish a control system for a research and development department of a large manufacturing company. Does it appear that planning and control of research and development is more difficult than planning and control of the manufacturing function? Explain.

3.4 Analyze any system of your choice as to: (1) cause-effect, (2) effect-delay, (3) deterministic-probabilistic, (4) optimization, and (5) subsystem relationships.

3.5 You have been charged with the responsibility of designing an office system for a political campaign office. Describe this problem and the solution thereof in terms of: (1) model, (2) criteria, (3) constraints, and (4) optimization. Make your own assumptions.

3.6 Draw a control system for the quality control of Brand X product.

3.7 As best you can, draw a conceptual model of a university system and its information system.

3.8 Pick an organization of your choice and determine those people who are responsible for strategic, tactical, and technical decision making. Is there any individual who is involved in all three levels of decision making? Explain.

3.9 Select three or four decision makers in an organization of your choice and ask them about their experiences in decision making. Try to draw a schematic of the decision making process they go through to reach a decision. Relate this exercise especially to the informational aspect in their decision making.

PROBLEMS   **3.1** The yield in production is often expressed as the percentage actually obtained of the amount theoretically possible. (For a discussion about yield, refer to Appendix A.) The yield figure is, consequently, useful information for managerial control.

The standard, product-mix per gallon of Rust—O paint is:

Resin—3 lbs. @ $.30 per lb.
Fish oil—1 qt. @ $1.00 per qt.

During a recent production run, 50,000 gallons were produced from an input of:

Resin — 175,000 lbs. @ $.41 per lb.

Fish oil — 64,000 qts. @ $1.12 per qt.

Required: (1) Calculate the price and yield variances. (2) Are these variances significant? (3) If you were general manager, what corrective action would you take, if any? (4) Who would you hold responsible for the price variance? (5) Who would you hold responsible for the yield variance? (6) For better control, when would you want this information reported to you?

3.2 Select a company of your choice and gather as much information as you can about this company to provide yourself with a sufficient base to make a decision as to whether or not to invest $1,000 in common stock.

Required:

(1) Did you invest the $1,000? Why? Why not?

(2) Did you receive sufficient information from formal sources, e.g., financial statements, stock exchange reports, etc.? If not, what other sources did you use? Were there any sources which you know of that would provide information but which you have no access to? Elaborate. Would this information be important?

(3) Do you believe that the technique of programmed decision making be applied to making investments in the stock market? Why? Why not?

(4) What level(s) of decision making were you involved with in making your investment decision? Explain.

(5) Classify the kind of information you used to make your investment decision.

(6) Are investment decisions an art or a science? Elaborate.

3.3 Write a two-page report on a hypothetical decision concerning your future career. Direct your report to the kinds of information you utilized in order to reach your decision. Be specific. Solve this problem in terms of: (1) model, (2) criteria, (3) constraints, and (4) optimization.

3.4 Draw a schematic of a system with its management system, inputs-outputs, its relation to the environment, and its information system. Choose any organizational system with which you are familiar.

3.5 An air traffic control system is composed of 21 Air Traffic Control Centers, each of which is further subdivided into sectors. The actual control of aircraft is performed by human controllers, who are assigned to each sector and who are served by a computer at the center in which they're located. An aircraft enters the system by filing a flight plan at the departure airport. The flight plan is a coded message describing the pilot's intentions and includes: destination, route of flight, airspeed, requested altitudes, proposed takeoff time, estimated time enroute, and expected arrival time. This flight plan, which is filed two hours prior to takeoff, is initially transmitted to the ATC center in which the departure airport is located. It is stored in that computer until five minutes prior to the proposed takeoff time, when an abbreviated version is transmitted to the controllers in the first sector which will control the aircraft. As the flight continues, the abbreviated flight plan is transmitted to the controller of the affected sector five minutes before the aircraft enters that sector. Five minutes before the aircraft leaves the ATC center in which he departed, the flight plan is transmitted to the next ATC center computer and the communications procedure is duplicated as the aircraft progresses on its flight.

A chronic problem in the air traffic control system, is the bottle-necks that occur at high-density airports. Aircraft stack-up in holding patterns due to the inability of controllers to handle landing traffic as fast as it arrives. The information system notifies the ATC centers when landing delays are being experienced at specific airports, but only after the congestion occurs. Considering the basic description of the system and the communications network in existence between the centers, can you propose a systems improvement to make the feedback loop more responsive?

Two additional considerations are: (1) it is considered more favorable to have aircraft delay their takeoffs rather than aggravate the congested condition at a particular airport; and (2) the ATC centers have varying traffic loads and at least one center has excess computer capacity that could be further utilized.

BIBLIOGRAPHY   Anthony, Dearden, and Vancil, *Management Control Systems,* Homewood, Illinois: Richard D. Irwin, Inc., 1972.

Beer, *Cybernetics and Management,* New York: John Wiley & Sons, Inc., 1966.

David, Piel, and Truxal, *The Man-Made World,* New York: McGraw-Hill Book Co., 1971.

Dearden and McFarlan, *Management Information Systems,* Homewood, Illinois: Richard D. Irwin, Inc., 1966.

DeGreene (ed.), *Systems Psychology,* New York: McGraw-Hill Book Co., 1970.

Fuchs, *Cybernetics for the Modern Mind,* New York: The Macmillan Co., 1971.

Hall, *The Management of Human Systems,* Cleveland, Ohio: Association for Systems Management, 1971.

Hare, *Systems Analysis: A Diagnostic Approach,* New York: Harcourt, Brace, Jovanovich, 1967.

Koontz and O'Donnell, *Principles of Management,* New York: McGraw-Hill Book Co., 1968.

LeBreton, *Administrative Intelligence-Information Systems,* Boston: Houghton-Mifflin Co., 1969.

Nilsson, *Problem-Solving Methods in Artificial Intelligence,* New York: McGraw-Hill Book Co., 1971.

Richmond, *Operations Research for Management Decisions,* New York: The Ronald Press Company, 1968.

Schoderbek, *Management Systems,* New York: John Wiley & Sons, Inc., 1967.

Schwartz, M. H., "Identifying Universal Principles in MIS Design," *Proceedings Third Annual Conference,* Chicago, Illinois: The Society for Management Information Systems, 1971.

Terry, *Principles of Management,* Homewood, Illinois: Richard D. Irwin, Inc., 1968.

4 Analysis of Information Systems

4.1 Introduction

Thus far a variety of concepts and terms which are preliminary to a specific analysis of information systems have been dealt with. Although we have referred to the term information system throughout the previous chapters, such references were primarily related to a particular area being developed and did not pertain specifically to this term. In the previous chapter, for example, a perspective was gained on the information system, its support of the management function, and on its reporting responsibilities to constituents external to the organizational system.

The major objectives of this chapter are as follows:

1. To define more clearly the concept of information systems.

2. To consider the flow of information and the arrangement of the information system in the organizational system.

3. To provide some examples of information systems which will in turn spark the imagination for other applications.

4.2 General Discussion of Information Systems

The terms, "management information system" (MIS), "information system," "computer-based management information system" (CBMIS), and so on are ubiquitous terms used in much of the information systems literature.[1] These terms (and others) have received a great deal of attention in recent years, yet much confusion exists as to their true meaning and proper role in organizations. This confusion is shared not only by management personnel but by many systems people who are supposed to be implementors of information systems. There have been many definitions offered to give meaning to the information system concept, but none to the pleasure of everyone.

Since the introduction of the management information system approach (MIS) in the early sixties, there have been reactions to it, both for and against.[2] MIS has been used to denote any kind of application ranging from basic data processing for payrolls and billings, to accounting systems, library card catalogs, process control systems, and so on.

The original concept was either not clearly understood or purposely distorted in order to apply the new, buzz–word to systems that were really not in keeping with the concept.[3]

At the outset, we have used the term "information system," rather than "management information system," "computer-based management information system," or some other more restricted term.

The reasons for using "information system" are:

1. This term has a broader connotation; in that it implies a provision of information, not only to the management of the organizational system, but also information to external constituents as well.

2. It is quite feasible for some organizations with low volume, complexity, timing, and computational demands to develop a viable information system without computers and related technology. In other words, the information system does not have to be computer based.

3. In developing a textbook we believe that the authors should not take sides. Rather, a comprehensive presentation should be developed by discussing all facets of the subject matter. For example, an MIS normally denotes an integrated approach to the arrangement of the information system in the organization. As shown later in this chapter, there are other approaches. Also, we wish to impress upon the reader that concepts and techniques presented in this text are just as applicable to building information systems for non-profit or governmental organizations (e.g., school, city) as they are for business information systems.

Definition of Information Systems

All organizations have some kind of an information system even though some systems might be nothing more than filing cabinets and a limited chart of accounts in a ledger. But in order to have a viable information system that is responsive to a variety of informational requirements, all the measurable data pertaining to the organization must be organized in a manner where it can readily be recorded, stored, processed, retrieved, and communicated as required by a variety of users.

For our purpose, an information system is defined as follows: a systematic, formal assemblage of components that performs data processing operations to (a) meet legal and transactional data processing requirements, (b) provide information to management for support of planning, controlling, and decision making activities, and (c) provide a variety of reports, as required, to external constituents.

An information system is somewhat analogous to a production system that takes raw material and converts it into a product which is either utilized by an ultimate consumer, or becomes a raw product for another conversion phase. Likewise, an information system con-

---

[1] For respected opinions, see: "Management Information Systems," *ADP Newsletter,* January 10, 1972.
[2] "Information Systems," *Data Processing Digest,* March, 1972, p. 17.
[3] *Ibid.*

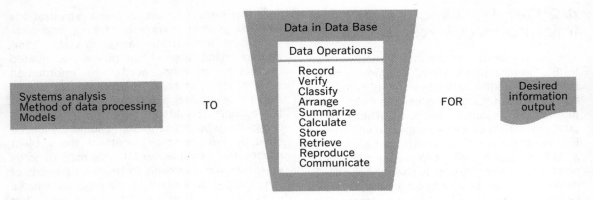

verts raw data either into a consumable report or an input for a later processing cycle.

Regardless of the particular manner in which information systems are designed, the components shown above are required.

The information system would include some, if not all, of the following items which give efficacy to the above illustrated components. These items are:

1. Data entry and preparation devices.
2. Data storage devices.
3. Telecommunications and equipment.
4. Data processing equipment.
5. Terminal devices.
6. Procedures, programs, methods, and documentation.
7. Data manipulation models such as accounting and budgeting models, standard costing techniques, cost-volume-profit models, linear programming, PERT, inventory models, statistical techniques, and so forth.
8. Decision rooms with graph display boards and charts.
9. Duplicating devices.
10. And, obviously, information systems analysts to implement and utilize these items.

Objectives of the Information System

In its most elemental form, an information system acts as a repository for transactional data and handles the routine data processing operations which pertain to: (1) order entry, (2) billing, (3) accounts receivable, (4) purchasing, (5) accounts payable, (6) payroll, (7) basic inventory reporting, and (8) the general ledger. At this basic level, there has not been a great deal of systems analysis in ascertaining the informational requirements of various managers, especially at the tactical and strategic levels. Consequently, managers will often fail to get information vital to effective functioning at these levels.

Higher level information must be produced as a by-product of basic data processing, by developing models and methods that present information tailored to each level of management, which takes into account the scope and nature of the information and the degree of interaction of each manager. In other words, the information system's output of information must meet the ten attributes of information as discussed in Chapter 2 and listed here for reference: (1) accessibility, (2) comprehensiveness, (3) accuracy, (4) appropriateness, (5) timeliness, (6) clarity, (7) flexibility, (8) verifiability, (9) freedom from bias, and (10) quantifiability. Therefore, the information system is more than a basic accounting and data processing system. It should not be viewed as an end in itself, but as being based on: (1) data flow and data processing operations, (2) determination of information requirements, (3) information flow, and (4) management and operational interactions throughout the organization which it helps to support.

In various organizations, the information

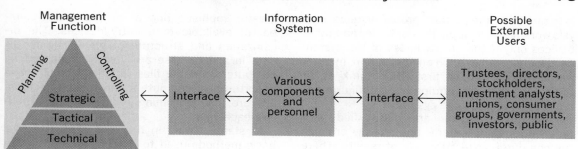

FIGURE 4.1. Internal and external interfaces with the information system.

system concept assumes that there is a necessary interface between the formal information system, the management function, the organizational structure, and the information users in the environment. This relationship is illustrated in Figure 4.1. Information interfaces connect the users with the dimensions of information that fulfill their informational needs.

Formal Versus Informal Information

If all managers in an organization could contain in their memory all of the information that they require, there would be no need for formal information systems. A basic data processing system to take care of payrolls, billings, and various other routine data processing activities would be sufficient. However, managers in today's larger organizations cannot retain in their memories all the information that they need. Given the variety and complexity of items to be examined and problems to be solved each day, it is imperative that they receive much formal information via performance reports, financial statements, sales analyses, evaluations, alternatives, or interrogative responses from an information system which is formally designed for this purpose. Since human memory is limited, the information system becomes a formal extension of it.

However, not all the information that managers receive emanates from the information system; they might, for example, receive valuable information outside of this system by making a phone call to a friend or colleague or

by conversing with a group of people. This latter kind of information comes from sources not specifically structured to provide the manager with information. Consequently, the information received from sources outside the information system is considered informal and is not considered in this text per se. Neither do we attempt to consider which kind of information has the most significance. On a day-to-day basis, the information system provides the formal information necessary for managing the organization. However, informal information might make the largest impact on the organization. It is conceivable that such information could change the whole course of the organization.

Role of the Computer and Its Related Technology

First, it should be understood that a computer system, per se, is not an information system. However, it can be the basic tool which increases the effectiveness of the system and provides the means for performing certain activities that would otherwise be impossible. It is stressed here that not all formal information systems need a computer and related technology, nor can a computer necessarily improve a system, nor do all reports produced by a computer qualify as information. Merely computerizing an existing system, or an old process, will not necessarily improve its effectiveness. Conversely, the installation of a computer in a poorly designed information system will normally result in a perpetuation of existing errors and flaws at an exponential rate. The main point is to formalize and perform proper systems analysis work first and apply the computer and other devices only if the effectiveness of the system can be improved by such an application. In other words, think systems first, then think about those devices and equipment configurations required to support the system.

Many managements are dissatisfied with their information systems and sharply criticize the computer system for lack of results. There are a number of reasons for this state of affairs. Commonly, however, three reasons are most pervasive: (1) great expectations which cannot be met, (2) lack of proper systems analysis, and (3) a computeritis syndrome which manifests itself in managements who acquire computers, and electronic gadgets, as a cure-all to management problems.

Often, there has been a tendency to overacquire costly configurations of blinking lights, CRT's, and OCR devices when all that was needed was getting information reports to managers when they needed them. In many systems, such activities can be adequately handled by a less automated method of data processing.

By the same token, computers and related technology do provide very sophisticated tools to the systems analyst. And if analyzed on a cost/effectiveness basis and utilized properly they can, in a number of situations, considerably enhance the effectiveness of some information systems, especially those with high volume, complexity, timing, and computational demands. There is no doubt that with the advent of computers, storage devices, terminals, and telecommunications, the systems analyst has been provided with an opportunity to formalize and systematize, to a level never before attained, the data processing and information activities of the organization. For example, telecommunications facilitated by multiprogramming, DASD, and data communication technology, has reduced to almost zero the dimensions of time and space and has, therefore, allowed any authorized remote manager to get information immediately. The accuracy and quickness in processing massive volumes of data are increased because of the greater sophistication of an increasing number of available data entry devices. The organization and structure of great volumes of data in a data base are greatly facilitated by computer readable files. In the face of these opportunities, computers and related technology are also becoming relatively less expensive each year.

As stated earlier in this text, there are four basic methods used to process data: (1) manual, (2) electromechanical, (3) punched card, and (4) computer. In the further analysis found in this chapter, and to a great extent throughout this text, the computer and its related technology will be used as a vehicle for illustrating certain techniques and concepts. In many cases the substitution of any of the other three methods would be appropriate. However, computer systems are used for these illustrations for two basic reasons: (1) admittedly, the computer and its related technology are quite dominant in many information systems today and will become even more dominant in the future; and (2) computers provide a more systematic method with which to illustrate many specific concepts.

4.3 Hierarchical Approach to Information Systems Design

The manner in which information flows within the organization depends basically on two things: (1) management philosophy and (2) the approach used to design information systems. Management philosophy concerns the degree of centralization or decentralization of management authority and responsibility in the organization. Our analysis will not relate specifically to this consideration, but only treat it in an ancillary fashion. As to the second consideration, i.e., the approach to the design or arrangement of the information system in the organization, there are basically two broad approaches. These are: (1) the hierarchical approach and (2) the systems approach. The hierarchical approach is further subdivided into two types: (1) with centralized data processing, or (2) with decentralized data processing, both of which will be discussed in this section. In the next section, the systems approach to information system structure is discussed.

Whether we refer to centralized or decentral- methods of data processing, the following are characteristics of the hierarchical ap- proach:

1. Activities of data processing are unrelated to information requirement analysis. That is, the data processing facilities are set up to process data (number crunchers) with little regard to the informational needs of specific users.

2. Segregated data bases are divided along functional, departmental, or divisional lines.

3. Subordinate-superior relationships exist in processing and flow of information. That is, requests for information flow down functional, departmental, or divisional lines and reporting information flows up these lines.

An example of information flow in a tradi- tional organization is illustrated in Figure 4.2. Notice that this example uses the departmental or functional areas of production, marketing, and finance. Such a selection is arbitrary, since other divisions such as school board, water and sewerage, fire department, police department, could be used in an example of a municipality. In a multidivisional organization, division A, di- vision B, division C, could be used in the ex- ample. Obviously, all of these examples have the same basic management functions as illus- trated.

Traditionally, a great number of organizations

utilize a hierarchical approach where data pro- cessing, and the consequent provision of infor- mation, is handled by each functional area in accordance with each area's own objectives. The basic level of each functional area captures data pertinent to its operations, has it pro- cessed, and passes reports up to the next level until a summarized report reaches the strategic level. In addition, an organization using such an approach has an accounting department which is either separate from the other functional areas or based in the finance area. Mostly, this department processes financial data for the en- tire organization and also maintains a chart of accounts. But, in addition to processing ac- counts receivable, accounts payable, and so forth, its role in the organization is that of stewardship and controllership. These roles traditionally provide little operating informa- tion for managers throughout the organization. In other words, the accounting department could be viewed as a financial information sys- tem which maintains a chart of accounts, per- forms routine data processing tasks, and pri- marily provides financial statements to both internal and external users.

Centralized Data Processing

With centralized data processing, the majority of data processing operations are performed by a separate facility. Normally, this is a separate department set up in the organization and re- ferred to as the Electronic Data Processing (EDP) Department. However, data processing can also be provided by: (1) a service bureau, which is a private company outside the organi- zation, that provides various data processing services, (2) timesharing facilities which are purchased or leased from some private com- pany, or (3) a facilities management (FM) arrangement whereby a private firm takes over running the organization's data processing operation.[4] However, organizations are certainly not limited to following a single approach in designing an information system. For example, an organization using decentralized data pro-

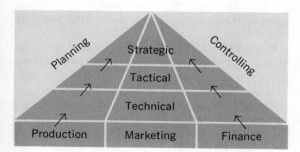

FIGURE 4.2. Information flow utilizing a hierarchical systems approach.

[4] For further treatment of facilities management, refer to: "Facilities Management is Here to Stay." *Administrative Man- agement,* July, 1972, pp. 16–17.

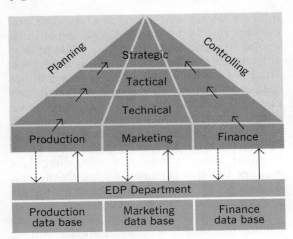

FIGURE 4.3. Hierarchical approach utilizing a centralized data processing method. Legend: ⇢ raw data to be processed; → processed data.

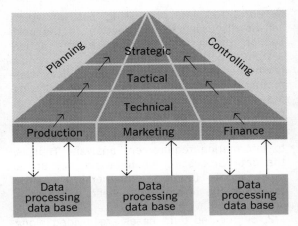

FIGURE 4.4. Hierarchical approach utilizing a decentralized data processing method. Legend: → raw data to be processed; → processed data.

cessing could just as easily have different functional areas, using different facilities for their individual data processing needs. For instance, the engineering, and research and development departments could acquire timesharing facilities, while the finance department could be using an in-house computer in addition to purchasing additional computer time from a service bureau. At the same time, the marketing people might be using the finance department's computer, while the manufacturing group is using a computer system operated by a facilities management (FM) firm, and so on.

An illustration of centralized data processing under the hierarchical approach is shown in Figure 4.3.

Decentralized Data Processing

The structure of the hierarchical approach for using decentralized data processing also involves, as does the hierarchical approach using centralized data processing, several rather autonomous functional areas or suborganizations within the total organization. The flow of information is still vertical within each functional area. However, the major difference is that each area has control over its own data processing activities whereas, in centralized data

processing, the EDP department is isolated from the other areas.

The data processing activities are submerged within traditional organizational areas. Accounting functions are handled in the finance or controller's department. Inventory control and manufacturing data processing are handled by some group in the production area, and so on. Data processing applications are categorized as part of one or another traditional functional areas of the organization. In Figure 4.4, a schematic illustrates decentralized data processing.

General Summary of the Hierarchical Approach

Using a traditional organizational chart, the two types of data processing are illustrated again in Figure 4.5.

Regardless of the type of data processing method employed, the general flow of information in the organization is the same. The major difference is that centralized data processing is controlled by a central authority whereas decentralized data processing is controlled exclusively by the area management which it serves. Also, even though previous examples tend to indicate otherwise, centralized data processing can disperse both personnel and equipment

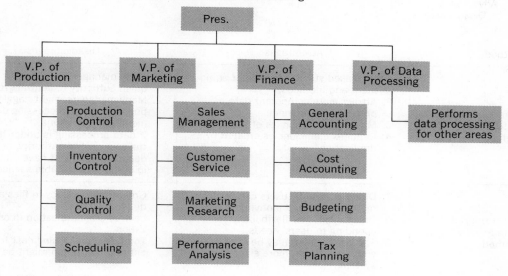

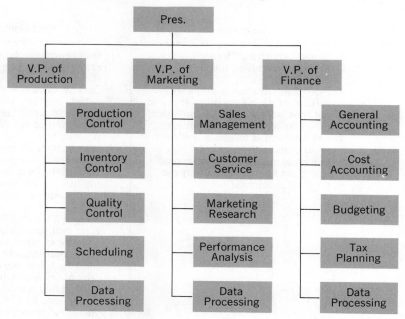

FIGURE 4.5. Traditional illustration of two types of data processing methods used in hierarchical approach.

Advantages/Disadvantages Method	Advantages	Disadvantages
Centralized Data Processing Method	1. Increased standardization of equipment and methods. 2. Attract more competent data processing personnel. 3. Might gain economies of scale. 4. Reduces inefficiencies created by duplication.	1. Many managers reluctant to relinquish authority to central group. 2. Many managers might haggle over budget for data processing development and operations. 3. If data processing is under the control of a central authority, other departments might have difficulty in obtaining equitable service.
Decentralized Data Processing Method	1. Direct control by users can result in more interest and motivation. 2. Probably greater flexibility in responding to users' needs. 3. The organization may be unable to support a larger, more elaborate system.	1. Greater redundancy in files and duplication of effort. 2. Lack of standardization in organization. 3. Total data processing cost for entire organization might be more.

FIGURE 4.6. Advantages and disadvantages of centralized/decentralized data processing.

Advantages/Disadvantages Method	Advantages	Disadvantages
Hierarchical Approach	1. Simple and straightforward. 2. Flow of information follows traditional lines. 3. Flow of information is primarily vertical which means other areas do not have access to this information (this may also be a disadvantage). 4. Any interaction follows a well defined scalar pattern. 5. Parochial objectives of many managers can be more effectively met (in some instances).	1. Great emphasis on data processing rather than on information production. 2. Data processing application oriented — payrolls, billings, etc. 3. Failure to recognize data as a valuable raw material resource of the organization. 4. When computer technology is applied, there is a great tendency to computerize existing data processing functions without regard to basic systems work being done first. 5. Many managers tend to suboptimize their own functional areas at the expense of other areas. 6. Little awareness that some data are used for input into other areas, i.e., lack of cross-communication and vertical and lateral integration of operations. 7. Basically ignores the SYSTEMS APPROACH.

FIGURE 4.7. Advantages and disadvantages of the hierarchical approach.

throughout the organization, especially in multidivisional organizations, to get the needed data processing methods close to where the work is, but all data processing is still under central control.

For further analysis, we present the basic advantages and disadvantages of centralized versus decentralized data processing. This analysis is summarized in Figure 4.6.

Lastly, the advantages and disadvantages of the hierarchical approach to information systems are presented disregarding either centralized or decentralized data processing. This analysis is shown in Figure 4.7.

4.4 Systems Approach to Information Systems Design

The basic objective of the systems approach to information systems design is to make available a broad base of comprehensive information, flowing on a timely basis, to those managers and others throughout the organization who, by receiving such information, can make effective decisions. The basic objective of this approach is to optimize the organization as a whole and thus overcome suboptimization.[5] As stated before, the key person involved in applying the systems approach is the systems analyst who maintains a total view of the organization, identifies information and data processing requirements, and formulates methods of meeting these requirements.

[5] For a detailed treatment of suboptimization, refer to: Charles Hitch, "Sub-optimization in Operations Problems," *Journal of Operations Research Society*, Volume 1, Number 3, May, 1953, pp. 87–99.

Even though the systems approach strictly recognizes the strategic, tactical, and technical levels of decision making, and the classic activities of planning and controlling, it views the organization as an interlocking, coordinated assemblage of subsystems whose connections look more like a network than a hierarchy. Moreover, the systems approach, to a great degree, separates the management system from the information system. That is, the management system performs planning, controlling, and decision making activities, whereas the information system provides information, of sufficient quality and quantity, to the management system.

Basically, there are two types of information systems which can be developed using the systems approach: (1) the integrated system and (2) the distributed system. In a number of ways the integrated system is similar to the centralized data processing method and, likewise, the distributed system is similar to the decentralized data processing method. In this section, the significant differences will be highlighted.

Before specifically discussing the two types of information systems, a broad illustration of the relationship between the management system and the information system will first be given in Figure 4.8.

Notice that the flow of information is directly to the user who needs, and is authorized, to receive it. There is also very little, or no, superior-subordinate reprocessing of data. It is also much easier with this approach to implement both a vertical and lateral flow of information which transcends traditional functional lines.

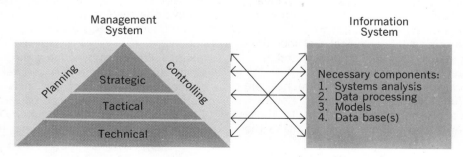

FIGURE 4.8. Information flow utilizing systems approach.

Integrated System

As stated in the previous section, with centralized data processing the emphasis is strictly on data processing activities. In such a situation, there is usually an EDP department, that includes a collection of machines managed by technicians, where decisions are made, based on factors revolving around internal conditions, with minimal regard to factors which affect the organization as a whole. That is, the data processing department is typically isolated from the mainstream operations of the organization.

It must be recognized that data, to one degree or another, are used by different subsystems in the organization and, consequently, the information system must be designed so that there are proper interfaces between these subsystems in order to benefit the total interdependent network.

On the other hand, the integrated information systems approach purports to channel all the data of an organization into a common data base and service all data processing and information functions for the entire organization. This approach is presently quite fashionable; however, it seems highly unlikely that all objectives of this approach will be attained in the foreseeable future. At present, collecting all the data and meeting all the information requirements of an organization is technically impossible and economically infeasible. However, even though full implementation of a totally integrated system appears to be impracticable at this time, many organizations are attempting to move toward a greater degree of integration. This progression toward more integration is based on two aspects: (1) dissatisfaction with the hierarchical approach because of fragmentation and noncoordination of the information function and (2) potential ability to effect more integration due to technological developments especially in the area of computers and telecommunications.

The integrated information system has the potential for providing many benefits. However, it can also present some problems to those managements who are not ready to make the commitment necessary in order to install such a system. Since an integrated system is somewhat monolithic in concept, anything less than a total commitment might result in chaos. The development of this kind of system requires: a total commitment from management (at all levels) based on a long-range master plan, the employment of highly skilled personnel, the acquisition of sophisticated equipment, and the expenditure of sufficient funds.

In addition to requiring a long-range commitment of time and resources, the integrated system also requires a change in traditional methods of handling data and information. Since the integrated system brings together all the functions of data collection, data processing, information production, and information communication, there is, consequently, a significant consolidation of both financial and operational data. Since this consolidation embraces the accounting function, there is no longer a need for a separate accounting department, per se. This occurs because it is also the responsibility of the information system, besides providing other operational information, to perform all the traditional accounting activities.

Other areas which are affected by the integrated systems approach include the individual staff groups set up for specific areas of operation such as production, and marketing. The major task of these groups is to supply information to different managements via the analysis of data based on the application of operations research and management science models. Again, since the objective of the integrated information system is to service users across the organization, it naturally follows that these staff functions will also be incorporated into the system, resulting in a more optimum and coordinated utilization of these staff functions.

In the following subsections, the integrated systems approach is analyzed in order to derive a better understanding of what it is and, also, to determine its advantages and disadvantages.

1. *Key Component—The Common Data Base.* The basic characteristics of the integrated

system are: (1) fast response to queries via remote terminals, (2) online mass storage, (3) instantaneous and simultaneous updating of files, and (4) centralized batch data processing in addition to online processing. Even though remote terminals and online processing are listed as characteristics of an integrated system, it is possible to design such a system without these characteristics, depending upon the accessing requirements. In other words, it is conceivable, for example, that all activities could be handled in batch mode. Notice, however, that all these characteristics imply the utilization of the common data base, the key component of an integrated information system. Inputs originate from events, and transactions are recorded, either directly into the common data base or, on to a source document that is batched for later input into the system.

Selection of the file media to be used in designing a common data base depends on the alternatives available and purpose of the different files. In analyzing the use of the files, the analyst must evaluate the major activities of each file. The following questions must be answered.

(1) Does redundancy exist in the present system of files? Can this redundancy be reduced? That is, can files be consolidated?

(2) How is the file used? Is it used as an intermediate file or is it used for final output? Does it have to be sorted or merged for further processing?

(3) How often is the file changed or updated?

(4) What concept for the retention of files is used?

(5) How is the file referenced? Can batch processing meet the demands on the system or are most demands in inquiry mode? What is the frequency of inquiries into the file?

(6) How volatile is the file? Are records constantly being added to and deleted from the file? What is the growth rate of the file?

Where the need is for periodic batch processing, file media such as magnetic tape or paper tape is acceptable. If the need, on the other hand, is for online inquiry into the file, a direct access storage device (DASD) is required. Although some theoreticians insist that the common data base should be contained in one readily accessible file, we contend that such an arrangement is technically and economically impracticable at this time. One main file would eliminate all duplication and redundancy but the record lengths would be horrendous. From a practicable standpoint, a common data base is, in actuality, made up of a number of files. These include files such as a customer and sales file, an inventory file, an accounting file, and a personnel file, all of which are coordinated in a manner which reduces storage redundancy, supports processing efficiency, and provides output to the user at the proper time. It is incumbent on the analyst to design the data base so that the users' requirements are satisfied, else the users will continue to maintain their own system and thereby subvert the purpose of the common data base. An illustration of the integrated system and its common data base is shown in Figure 4.9.

2. *A Typical Example.* As noted above, the common data base does not necessarily mean *one* file but rather a number of interrelated files which hold data for different applications. Regarding the consolidation of files in order to reduce duplication and redundancy, the systems analyst looks for commonalities of items and operations. Customer information is an example of an area where the systems analyst can often develop a common data base. Customer information in an organization is of importance to at least four different functional departments: (1) order entry/billing (O.E./B.), (2) sales accounting (S.A.), (3) accounts receivable/credit (A.R./C.), and (4) advertising and promotion (A./P.). The order entry/billing department requires information pertaining to a customer in order to prepare necessary shipping papers and invoices. This information includes items such as customer number, customer bill-to name and address, ship-to name and address, special shipping instructions, special handling instructions, salesman number and so forth. The sales accounting department requires similar information in order to prepare

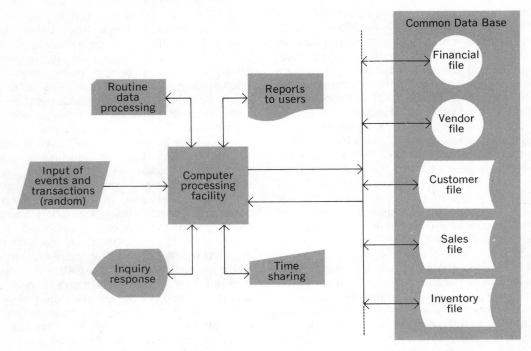

FIGURE 4.9.   An integrated information system with a common
data base.

a variety of sales analysis reports. In addition, special coding, refering to the customer's class of trade, salesman's division, territory, etc., is also often required. Accounts receivable, on the other hand, requires only that information necessary to prepare statements and dunning letters. The fourth functional department, advertising and promotion, requires name and address information, and any special kinds of coding which would permit selected mailings.

In a typical organization, when a new customer is approved for the firm, a new customer authorization of some sort is completed. Copies of this authorization are then forwarded to each affected department to be used to generate input for their customer master files. Using the common data base approach, one unit within the information system is responsible for supplying accurate and timely customer information to one file where it can be used for each application as approved and as necessary. In the areas such as accounts receivable and

sales accounting, where activity information is also maintained, this information can be maintained in files which are constructed to expedite actual processing.

By referring to Figure 4.10 the differences in file sizes required can be seen. On the top half, the traditional approach is depicted; on the bottom half the common data base approach is depicted. Notice that in the common data base approach elements common to all files are necessary in order to relate the file of static information to the file of dynamic information; however, minimum redundancy results. In Part II the structure of the data base will be discussed in more depth. Our purpose here is to simply illustrate one example of how a common data base can be constructed.

3. *Communication Network.* All users throughout the organization interact directly with the integrated system. Often this interaction is via telecommunication devices, but sometimes it might simply be through turning

Data Field	Size	Applications Using Fields			
		O.E./B.	S.A.	A.R./C.	A./P.
(1) Customer No.	10	X	X	X	X
(2) Billing name	30	X	X	X	X
(3) Billing address	60	X		X	X
(4) Shipping name	30	X	X		
(5) Shipping address	60	X			
(6) Special handling instructions	45	X			
(7) Sales division code	5	X	X	X	X
(8) Territory code	3	X	X		X
(9) Salesman code	2	X	X		X
(10) Dun's number	8		X		X
(11) Quota $	6		X		
(12) Credit limit	6	X	X		
(13) Class of trade	2		X		X
(14) Industry code	8		X		X
(15) Monthly sales dollars	72		X		
(16) Open items*	140			X	
Total characters of information per customer (total all applications is 806 characters per customer).		251	182	245	128
(1) Customer No.	10	X	X	X	**
(2) Billing name	30	X			
(3) Billing address	60	X			
(4) Shipping name	30	X			
(5) Shipping address	60	X			
(6) Special handling instructions	45	X			
(7) Sales division code	5	X			
(8) Territory code	3	X			
(9) Salesman code	2	X			
(10) Dun's number	8	X			
(11) Quota $	6	X			
(12) Credit limit	6	X			
(13) Class of trade	2	X			
(14) Industry code	8	X			
(15) Monthly sales dollars	72		X		
(16) Open items*	140			X	
Total characters of information per customer (total all applications is 507 characters per customer)		275	82	150	0

* Based on 35 characters per open item, average 4 open items per customer.
** Separate file for advertising and promotion not required.

FIGURE 4.10. Comparison of traditional file requirements approach to common data base approach.

in the request for a report and picking up the report in the next few days. To establish a communications network for six users in an integrated system, we would need N(six) channels, as shown in Figure 4.11.

4. *Manager of Information Systems.* The Manager of Information Systems has a different task from that normally thought of as Manager of the Computer or Manager of Data Processing. His or her responsibilities are much

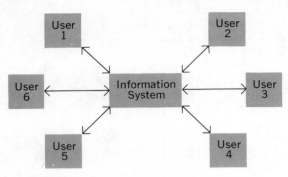

FIGURE 4.11. Communication network for six subsystems of an organization that utilizes the integrated systems approach.

wider in scope as this person must be well versed in all operations of the organization. This executive must be able to unify the diverse and suboptimizing components of the organization via an unbiased flow of information to all users. A generalist, rather than a technician, this person will have to be concerned with problem solving and optimization of the overall organizational goals. These activities should be neutral and independent of other executives in the organization. This executive should not be an advocate of any department and should be responsible only to the top management, owners, or directors, of the organization.

A Manager of Information Systems must possess a deep understanding of the functional areas of the organization. Using a manufacturing organization as an example, he or she should understand such functions as manufacturing, engineering, marketing, logistics, and finance. Without such an understanding, it is difficult to serve the needs of each user and to see how the diverse functions are interrelated.

Such a manager must also be talented in task-group or project management, because much of the systems work that is done is handled on a task-group basis. He or she should be familiar with planning, scheduling, and control techniques (such as PERT) as well as with cost/effectiveness. A sound understanding of computer technology, information processing techniques, and management and decision making principles is also necessary.

The responsibility of the Manager of Information Systems is to manage the information system that performs the data processing and information activities for all of the organization's major functional departments. The information system is an information producer; all the other functional areas and subsystems of the organization are information users.

Specifically, the duties of the Manager of Information Systems include:

(1) Planning and control of all activities included in the information system.

(2) Evaluation and selection of all information processing equipment and aids.

(3) A program of constant review of the system and development of design alternatives where appropriate.

(4) Selection of personnel. These include: (a) accountants, (b) systems analysts, (c) programmers, (d) market research analysts, (e) managers of data processing facilities, (f) budget analysts, (g) operations researchers, and so on.

(5) Establishing a training program for new information system employees. Also, the setting of performance criteria for all personnel.

(6) Setting up a system of processing priorities.

(7) Establishing the input-editing and data security requirements of the system.

(8) Defining and documenting all information system objectives and having these objectives approved by top management.

(9) Developing an educational and training program for users of the system.

5. *Position of the Integrated System in Organizations.* The position of the integrated information system is based on four criteria:

(1) *Kind of applications.* For example, an airline reservation information system requires almost exclusive online processing with a great deal of autonomy from its users.

(2) *Level of automation.* Greater use of sophisticated equipment requires high level people to manage such equipment. Such people are often more highly trained than those managers to whom they provide information.

(3) *Level of integration.* A totally integrated system inherently denotes an autonomous system independent from the control of functional management.

(4) *Level of resource commitment.* If top level management considers the information system to be an important function in the organization, the Manager of Information Systems and his staff will be at a high level in the organization. If this situation exists, the Manager of Information Systems would report to the president or chief executive officer of an organization.

With these assumptions Figure 4.12 offers the following organizational structure as the proper position of such a system in the organization.

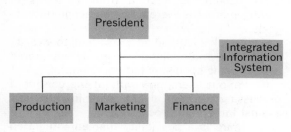

FIGURE 4.12. Proper location of an integrated information system in the organization.

At this level, the information system can perform its tasks without restraint and provide unbiased, objective, and timely information, at any level of detail, to all users across the organization. The personnel that work in this information system should consist of professional information specialists whose duty and responsibility it is to fully disclose and report all pertinent information to all users. This function should be performed in the manner they deem necessary, through systems investigation work and consultation with users, without being encumbered or restrained by any single group (or individual) either inside or outside of the organization. The personnel of the information system, since they are specialists, have the duty to search out information needs and recommend better methods whenever and wher-

ever the opportunity arises. All service to organizational units should be performed in an impartial, independent, and professional manner.

6. *Probable Advantages of the Integrated Information Systems Approach.* Advantages which can accrue from the implementation of an integrated information system are:

(1) Reduction of redundancy and duplication of files and programming work and increased standardization.

(2) More security, controls, and protection of the common data base against access by unauthorized users.

(3) Reduction in the amount of clerical intervention in the input, processing, and output operations, thereby minimizing the possibility of errors.

(4) Permits the instantaneous and simultaneous updating of files (those on DASD), thus providing current status information and identification of conditions requiring immediate attention and corrective action.

(5) Allows more than one user to concurrently retrieve, update, or delete data from the common data base (assuming the files are on DASD).

(6) Relieves management from routine data processing and decision making activities.

(7) Since the integrated system serves a variety of information needs and multiple data processing applications for the entire organization, there is a potential for economies of scale. With adequate processing volume, computer technology results in reduced operating cost. This reduction results from a lower unit cost for each data element processed for both equipment and personnel. There is a better utilization of equipment and skilled personnel in an integrated system and concomitantly a more formal and rapid implementation and application of new techniques and technology.

(8) Better opportunities exist for recruiting skilled, professional employees if the organization has a large integrated system with sophisticated equipment. Also, better training programs can be established and maintained.

(9) Better utilization of processing capabili-

ties. With a hierarchical approach, one division might have excess capacity while in another division there might be a processing overload.

(10) Increases in overall performance due to the provision of more timely, relevant, and accurate information. For example, cost savings result from better credit checking and more efficient inventory control. Also, an increase in revenue can result from a reduction in backlogs, and from better customer service.

(11) Freedom of the management system from an organization straitjacket by separating the information function from the management function. The management system can get at a broader scope of information and work under differing thresholds of detail without having to go through several levels of processing. Access to different levels of information is available to top management. This serves as a positive force to keep profit center managements more alert and effective, because the information about a profit center (or division) comes from the information system, not the profit center itself.

(12) A reduction of information bias, that might be inherent in other systems, because the decision making and operating activities are separated from the measurement and performance activities. Data are collected and information produced from a position (and point of view) that are detached and independent of the ones making the operating decisions. The separation of the information system leaves management free to manage, using the information reported to them as guides and benchmarks. The information system maintains objectivity and treats processing on an impersonal basis. This results in the dissemination of relevant, impartial information without detracting from an overall frame of reference which includes the entire organization.

(13) Ability to provide smaller or, remote divisions with access to a centralized computing system and files. Otherwise a single division might not be able to support a computer configuration on its own.

(14) An increased ability to implement and follow master plans for the system that are consistent with the long-range plans of the organization as a whole.

(15) A probable allowance for a better overall evaluation of projects for technical, economic, operational, and schedule feasibility.

7. *Probable Disadvantages of the Integrated Information Systems Approach.* The probable disadvantages are as follows:

(1) To attain maximum effectiveness, the information systems personnel, especially the systems analysts, must have the necessary level of authority and responsibility to execute their tasks properly. Otherwise, the system is doomed to failure.

(2) Without cooperation from all levels of management, the system will not accomplish its goals.

(3) A lack of qualified personnel to design, implement and maintain a highly integrated system using sophisticated equipment.

(4) Various users, now without the control of processing activities, might be inclined to rebel against integrated processing.

(5) There is a possibility that an integrated system might not be responsive to users' needs.

(6) Downtime in integrated systems can be catastrophic. For example, if the CPU goes down, the total system is completely degradated unless the information system has backup facilities. However, backup facilities are costly and of course redundant. This disadvantage cannot be overemphasized, because with all of the processing activities integrated into a single system, a breakdown of the system over a duration of time could result in a total collapse of the organization, especially in financial organizations such as banks, stock brokerage houses, or insurance companies where the processing of data is the lifeblood of the organization.

(7) Cost of development is very high.

(8) Modifications are difficult because of interdependencies.

(9) Unless management is willing to make long term commitments of time and resources, the attempted implementation cannot succeed.

(10) The attempted implementation of a totally integrated system is technically and financially risky, even for the largest organizations.

Distributed System

It would seem at this point that the integrated system has much to offer as a viable approach to information system development. Conversely, there are a number of authorities who feel that the integrated systems approach is a mistake and that it cannot effectively meet the variety of needs throughout the organization.

. . . experience has shown that the massive 'universal' system approach rapidly leads to substantial diseconomies in software overhead and administration. By analogy, the computer is not a universal machine, 'a truck, a motorcycle or a racing car—each has a different engine which is designed for high performance, and in the specific use intended.' The computer system and MIS that seeks to be all things to all people in one package is doomed to failure at the outset. The cost balance in configuration is between operating control over a fragmentation of diverse specialized systems which may be locally optimal but globally expensive and the universal system 'dinosaur.'[6]

The basic principle of the integrated systems approach is that there is a total concentration of all organizational data in one common data base and all processing is done from a central complex. Proponents of the integrated system think that it is only logical that informational needs of all users can be evenly satisfied whether the information is for marketing, finance, or production. However, Professor John Dearden[7] purports that there is a notable lack of success in implementing integrated systems and the lack of this success is dependent upon four fallacies.

Fallacy #1: Management information is sufficiently homogeneous to make it an area of specialization for an expert.

Fallacy #2: If the different information systems used by a company are developed separately, the resulting management information system will be necessarily uncoordinated and therefore inefficient and unsatisfactory.

Fallacy #3: The system approach is a new boon to business administration.

Fallacy #4: It is practical to centralize control over a company's entire management information system.

Professor Dearden further states that a company should strive to develop and coordinate individual systems which satisfy the information needs of individual areas of the organization. He believes this approach is necessary because an integrated system encompasses such a huge assortment of different types of activities that no person can possess a sufficiently broad set of skills to effectively integrate such a complex.

The alternative, then, to an integrated systems approach is a distributed systems approach. Whereas the integrated system is monolithic in nature, the distributed system is modular. The integrated system utilizes a central data processing facility with a common data base. The distributed system, on the other hand, employs a group or aggregation of information systems arranged in such a manner that a system of subsystems, or a system of islands of information, is formed.[8]

The basic aim of the distributed system is to establish relatively independent subsystems which are, however, tied together in the organization via communication interfaces. This

---

[6] Charles H. Kriebel, "The Future MIS," *Business Automation,* June, 1972, p. 44. Reprinted from *Infosystems* (formerly *Business Automation*), June, 1972, By Permission of the Publisher. © 1972 Hitchcock Publishing Company. All Rights Reserved.
[7] John Dearden, "MIS is a Mirage," *Harvard Business Review,* January-February, 1972, pp. 90–98. With permission.

[8] For example, Comdr. Grace Hopper supports the use of minicomputers as components of a "system of computers" rather than "computer systems." McFarlan, "Brainy Operations Staff Are an Asset," *Computerworld,* July 5, 1972, p. 4. With permission. Copyright by *Computerworld,* Newton, Massachusetts 02160.

system of systems is a network of subsystems located at, and customized to, areas of need. In such a network, three basic conditions will exist: (1) some of the subsystems will need to interact with other subsystems, (2) some will need to share files with others and even share data processing facilities, and (3) some subsystems will require very little interaction with other subsystems, and for all intents and purposes will be fairly isolated and self-sufficient.

As with the integrated systems approach, the distributed systems approach is analyzed in the following subsections in order to develop a greater understanding of this approach and, also, to determine its advantages and disadvantages.

1. *The Data Base.* To develop a common data base for an entire organization requires a vast amount of resources, skill, and time. Moreover, different functional areas of the organization might require different treatment and all data elements would not, consequently, be amenable to integration. Moreover, because of the inherent diversity in some organizations, only some portion of data would be applicable to all areas of the organization. In this case, these common data elements could be consolidated and stored in some central locality for ready access by other areas when and if they needed such data.

In anticipating the next ten years, my first prediction is the demise of the present–day data base orientation as the dominant user model image in MIS development. Instead, the development focus will shift back to an output orientation that is user dependent.[9]

For many organizations, it appears that a more rational approach to structuring the data base involves a network of data bases. One of these data bases (e.g., at the home office) would store general summary data, act as a store of data, and as a clearinghouse with the capability of interacting with some, if not all, of the other bases in the distributed system.

. . . Very few files really need be centralized. Airline reservations appear to justify central-

ization, but even here a single centralized file is not necessarily the best approach. Subsets of such files are needed only along specific routes. Many locations in the system will never access these subsets. The same is true of nationwide inventory involving many warehouses and depots. The incidence of a California dealer requesting a part from a Florida warehouse is rare.

Large files can become many small files, each located in the area of 'need to know.' If you can't find what you need locally, a human with a telephone can often be a cost/effective solution to the problem. If more 'sophistication' at higher cost is wanted, many small machines can call one another with simple requests; e.g., 'Do you have a part "X" in your inventory?' Control is not lost by distributing information; it is enhanced and the cost is less.[10]

2. *A Typical Example.* The distributed system disperses both the data base and processing facilities closer to users. A typical manufacturing company utilizing a distributed systems approach is shown in Figure 4.13.

In this example, there is a multiplicity of data files and data processing facilities. We will assume, for example, the following overall network of data processing devices.

(1) The marketing department has one minicomputer, two disks for local data storage, one CRT, and one teletypewriter. This subsystem can process most of its own data, especially that used for informational purposes such as sales analysis, market trends, competitive reaction, and performance comparisons. Much of the raw data it needs and processes are transmitted from transactional data collected in the general office data base. The marketing department requires little data from the finance area, but it does require a great deal of data from production especially concerning inventory and finished product schedules.

---

[9] Kriebel, *op. cit.* p. 42.

[10] Henry Oswald, "Maxi-empire, No! Mini-empire, Maybe?," *Business Automation,* June, 1972, pp. 35–36. Reprinted from *Infosystems* (formerly *Business Automation*), June, 1972, By Permission of the Publisher. © 1972 Hitchcock Publishing Company. All Rights Reserved.

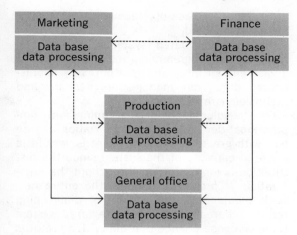

FIGURE 4.13. Example of a distributed system. Legend: ⇢ interaction between functional areas; → interaction with common data elements.

(2) The production department has an "intelligent terminal" (a terminal usually incorporating a stand-alone minicomputer processing capability) because it does not require a great deal of local data processing but does transmit a great deal of data to marketing, finance, and the general office. Production uses its subsystem, besides transmission of data throughout the network, for production scheduling, flow analysis, and variance control.

(3) The finance department has a fairly large computer system with several tape and disk drives, card readers, and printers. This department performs a great deal of analysis such as revenue performance, budget variances, cash flow, industry trends, monthly reconciliation work, asset management, cash planning, preparation of financial reports, and so on. It receives a large volume of data from the other areas.

(4) The general office is set up, both to take care of normal routine data processing and to make available, from time to time, any standard summary data required by other areas. This department has a general purpose computer system with card readers, printers, a number of magnetic tape drives, and some punched card equipment. This department prepares payrolls, invoices, purchase reports, and so forth. It also prepares data for transmission to all of the other areas.

3. *Communication Network.* Unlike all of the users in an organization who interact directly with an integrated system, users in a distributed system interact among and between each other. This kind of a system will, in most instances, require some amount of telecommunication equipment. Obviously, if the system is configured with computers and related equipment, it would require a fairly sophisticated telecommunication network. In any event, whether data are hand carried, shipped by truck or parcel post, or transmitted electronically, the network in a distributed system would need $N(N-1)/2$ channels of communication. Such a network is illustrated in Figure 4.14. The distributed system requires a greater number of channels of communications (either personal or media) than does an integrated system. In Figure 4.14, it is assumed that six subsystems need to communicate with one another in order to coordinate operations. It will require fifteen channels of communication to handle the dissemination of information, i.e., $N(N-1)/2$ or $6(6-1)/2 = 15$.

4. *Manager of Information Systems.* The Manager of Information Systems performs basically the same functions in a distributed system

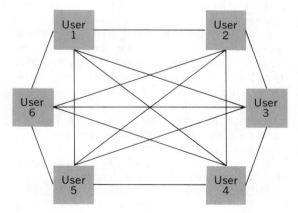

FIGURE 4.14. Communication network for six subsystems in an organization that utilizes the distributed systems approach.

as in an integrated system. His or her orientation would be more toward coordination than in an integrated system. In some organizations the manager would report to departmental, functional area, or divisional heads, rather than to the chief executive. In others, the manager might report to the chief executive officer in addition to departmental heads. Some would argue that a Manager of Information Systems is not necessary. We feel that the absence of this talent and coordinating force, implemented via the systems analysts, would cause the distributed system to revert to a hierarchical system with decentralized data processing.

5. *Position of the Distributed System in Organizations.* The distributed system is a network of subsystems which are customized to meet the informational needs of the user groups or departments and, in addition, each subsystem is physically located within the area which it serves.

6. *Probable Advantages of the Distributed Information Systems Approach.* Advantages which might accrue from the implementation of a distributed information system are:

(1) Their cost/effectiveness. The development in recent years of economical minicomputers that have significant computing power, and the ability to handle telecommunications efficiently, has considerably enhanced the cost/effectiveness of the distributed systems approach.

(2) Using a distributed system can reduce overall system costs by taking some of the processing burden from a central facility and also by reducing the amount of data that has to be transmitted. However, transmission of data might not be reduced if there is a great deal of interaction between users. The more interaction, the more likely that this aspect would become a disadvantage.

(3) This systems approach can be more easily modified to meet user requirements.

(4) Some attempts at integrated systems have been abandoned because of vacillating support from management. It seems that management has a greater propensity to support the distributed concept.

(5) Security, back-up, recovery, and control are easily handled.

(6) Most distributed systems require relatively simple programming and technology. To implement an integrated system, very sophisticated data base management systems and technology are required.

(7) The volume, complexity, timing, and computational demands of an organization can be met with greater precision. There is very little waste in capacity of the system since the distribution is more uniform throughout the organization. If properly balanced, the entire network should never hit a point of diminishing returns whereas in a large, integrated system there is a good chance that diminishing returns will set in.

(8) Much simpler and possibly less costly to process data where it is used or where it occurs and consolidate summaries at a central place. Distributing hardware and processing is much less expensive because hardware is cheaper, software is less complex, and it costs less to develop a simple program and distribute a thousand copies than to create a complex multiprogrammed version of the same thing, in one copy for a central complex.[11]

(9) A breakdown of one subsystem will not significantly degrade the entire network.

(10) New subsystems can be added without affecting other subsystems.

7. *Probable Disadvantages of the Distributed Information Systems Approach.* The probable disadvantages are as follows:

(1) There is a considerable reduction in online interrogations provided to all users for access to all parts of the system.

(2) Extracting corresponding data from different files may be difficult.

(3) Inconsistencies can creep into the system causing mismatches in editing, formats, and general data processing devices.

(4) Coordination of activities can be more difficult particularly in cases where the subsystems become loosely coupled and independent.

[11] *Ibid.,* p. 35.

(5) Oftentimes a distributed system requires, in total, more skilled personnel, such as computer programmers.

(6) Because of different data bases there will be more duplication of data. For example, in a typical situation a customer name may be in the sales department, finance department, and general office.

(7) A distributed system requires more channels of communications.

Further Evaluation of Integrated and Distributed Systems

There are a number of alternative philosophies for structuring information systems. These alternative philosophies range from a completely integrated system to completely independent, isolated information subsets, and include all combinations and gradations in between. For analytical purposes, four distinct approaches have been discussed. We do not favor the hierarchical approach, including either centralized or decentralized data processing, because; (1) the emphasis is on routine data processing activities; (2) there is a distinct absence of an informational requirements orientation; and (3) there is a limited use of the systems approach. These shortcomings lead to the obvious question: Which is better, the integrated or distributed system?

In reality, a distributed system is an information system with some degree of integration. Or looking at it another way, an integrated system is an information system with some degree of distribution. There is no absolute. Moreover, there are a number of functions which can be integrated in varying degrees and, in addition, combinations of functions can be integrated. As a result, there is an almost endless list of different varieties of integration. In order to simplify, general types of integration are presented below.[12]

(1) *Integrate the Data into Data Bases.* This means that instead of residing in a number of unrelated files, the data are stored in planned fashion in order to provide retrievals. The exact fashion the data are stored in depends on the results to be achieved. The data can be stored to reduce redundancy, facilitate maintenance, expedite access, reduce storage costs, etc.

The result of integrating the data into the data bases is that the outputs available to the user (retrievals) are integrated. This means that the user can get all of the necessary information about a task, or event, as a unit without having to get one piece of information from one place and another from somewhere else. Data for the user is arranged so that all of the information he or she needs to know about a particular topic is presented as a unit no matter where it originated.

(2) *Integrate Data Processing Functions.* With this approach, applications are no longer individual computer programs. The functions performed by these programs are now performed by a group of functionally oriented modules. For example, data capture is handled by a common input processor, regardless of the source of the data.

(3) *Integrate Data Flows.* In most companies, there is a natural flow of information. In a manufacturing company, for example, the start might be in engineering. Then, the mainstream flow of product information could be to manufacturing planning, manufacturing, and testing. Financial information would have a different natural flow. When we speak of integrating the data flows, this means to divide the company's system of information flows into modules, in a planned way, so that the outputs of a processing module can be used directly as the inputs to other modules. In addition, all data that are needed downstream in the processing are collected at the source.

(4) *Integrate the Data into Data Bases and Also Integrate Data Processing Functions.* This system is a combination of items 1 and 2.

(5) *Integrate the Data into Data Bases and Also Integrate Data Flows.*

(6). *Integrate Data Processing Functions and Also Integrate Data Flows.*

(7) *Integrate the Data into Data Bases, In-*

[12] J. C. Pendleton, "Integrated Information System," AFIPS *Conference Proceedings*, Volume 39 (Montvale, N.J.: AFIPS Press, 1971) p. 492–93. With permission from AFIPS Press.

tegrate the Data Processing Functions, and In-tegrate Data Flows.

(8) *Integrate the Outputs.* This alternative simulates an integrated data base from the users' standpoint, by giving them the same retrieval capacity that they would be likely to have in an integrated data base. This method can be accomplished by using integrating networks, by copying files, or by using various retrieval programs.

The problem is to decide whether one should lean toward a more distributed system with a minimum of integration or toward a highly integrated system. A fair evaluation of the two approaches (and combinations in between) can be based on the advantages and disadvantages already presented. However, the systems analyst must first determine the circumstances present, the kind of organization structure, and the objectives of management before weighing advantages and disadvantages.

Besides the advantages and disadvantages of the integrated system versus the distributed system, the two overriding considerations are: (1) the view of management as to how it wants to manage the organization, and (2) the level of diversity within the organization. If, for example, top management wishes to manage the organization as an integrated unit, then the information system should be integrated as much as possible. If, on the other hand, top management wishes the organization to operate on the basis of separate functional units, then the distributed approach is preferred.

The level of diversity inherent in some organizations also has a great deal to do with how the information system is structured. For example, in a large manufacturing organization, such as an aerospace company, there is inherently a diversity between the several functional areas. This situation exists not because these functional areas are really independent from a systems viewpoint, but rather, it is due to the links and interfaces being so complex and nebulous that an integrated information system which supports all areas would be beyond present system technology.[13] An information

[13] *Ibid.,* p. 495.

system designed for such an organization would have to be distributed with various subsets of integration.

Commercial airlines, on the other hand, are quite unified in their operations. All operations such as general administration, scheduling, and maintenance revolve around the reservation system. Therefore, it appears from the interdependencies and commonness that exist among these areas that a highly integrated system would be appropriate.

4.5 Applications

In this section, some examples of information systems are presented from the point of view as to how they are structured and what role they play in the support of a variety of organizations.

Migrant Student Information System

The critical needs of a child's health and educational development are usually attended to by the family doctor and the community school. In this country, however, there are more than 800,000 children who have never received this kind of attention. On an average these children move from school to school and state to state anywhere from three to fifteen times per year; and in most cases, both their health and education suffer significantly.[14]

These children are the offspring of migrant workers who follow the harvests to eke out a living to support their families. Today their health and educational development are being planned for on a coordinated basis by the use of an integrated information system supported by a central computer and integrated data base located in Little Rock, Arkansas. Connected to this system via Wide Area Telephone Lines (WATS) are 137 teletypewriters scattered throughout the United States. This system serves over 7000 schools.

Timing demands created the need for this

[14] Summarized from "Communication Network Keeps Tight Rein on Migrant Students," *Computerworld,* June 14, 1972, p. 12. With permission. Copyright by *Computerworld,* Newton, Massachusetts 02160.

kind of a system. A transfer record is maintained for each student including student-identifying data, inoculation data, urgent condition data, special interests and abilities data, health data, special test and academic status data. Essentially, this transfer record provides a profile of a child as he or she moves from school to school. Originally, these transfer records were mailed, but it became evident that this method would not be sufficient. In most cases, by the time the transfer record reached a school, the child had moved on to another. His record was lost; his whereabouts were unknown. Without the transfer record, educators had no accurate way to assess a child's capabilities, and the school doctors and nurses had no way of obtaining or knowing the child's health history.

Now, with the new integrated system, every time a migrant child arrives at a school, his identifying and enrollment data are collected and relayed to the nearest teletypewriter operator. The operator prepares a paper tape of this data and transmits it to the data base in Little Rock. The computer scans its files to determine if the child is currently registered in the data base. If so, the enrollment data updates the files. The computer then extracts information significant to the initial placement and care of the migrant student from the student's record. This information is transmitted back to the operator who, in turn, relays it to the proper school.

If the student is not registered in the data base, then the computer uses the new student's identifying and enrollment data to establish a record. This information will follow the child from school to school and will remain in the data base until the child is mature enough to leave the program or be graduated from it. Every time a student's status changes (new test scores, health data, program data, etc.), the computer updates its record. In this way, the current status of any student is available whenever and wherever needed.

Business Information System

Diversity, Inc. (a hypothetical company), is an organization made up of four plants, each with

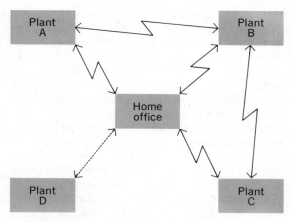

FIGURE 4.15. Total distributed information system.

its own information subsystem connected to a central home office. A general schematic of this distributed information system is illustrated in Figure 4.15.

Plant A manufactures ballpoint pens. It has an information subsystem which processes orders and shipments, inventory control, accounts receivable, accounts payable, transfer pricing, costing, general ledger, production scheduling, and, in addition, produces various reports which meet the informational requirements of plant management. Payroll data and summarized sales statistics are transmitted via telecommunication facilities to the home office. Also, inventory status and order requisitions are transmitted between Plant A and Plant B. The information subsystem at Plant A is supported by a minicomputer with disks, magnetic tapes, paper tapes, readers, printers, teletypewriters, and telecommunication devices.

Plant B manufactures various plastic moldings which are used for raw material primarily by Plants A and C. A portion of Plant B's output is also shipped to outside customers. The information subsystem for Plant B is quite similar to the one at Plant A in that information system personnel and equipment are located at the plant and the subsystem is customized to meet the specific needs of the plant's users. However, because of exceptional payroll processing requirements peculiar to this type of manufacturing, and specific union contracts, all payroll processing is handled by the subsystem rather than by transmitting each week's payroll data to the home office. Periodically, historical data and sales summaries are transmitted to the home office. Data processing equipment which supports this subsystem is very similar to that used at Plant A.

Plant C manufactures toys and its information subsystem is also similar to the one at Plant A. Once again, however it has been customized to meet the peculiar needs of the users at Plant C. A substantial portion of the computer system's capacity, in addition to normal data processing and information producing functions, is devoted to engineering research and development. The information subsystem is supported by a medium size central processing unit, magnetic tapes, magnetic disks, card readers, printers, plotters, CRT's and telecommunication equipment. In addition to transmitting production and inventory data back and forth from Plant B, the information subsystem also transmits historical data, sales summaries, and payroll data to the home office.

Plant D is a small manufacturer of grandfather clocks. Its information subsystem handles the normal routine data processing for purchases, orders, shipments, inventory control, and so on. However, this small plant is in no way related to the other plants. Its information system is supported solely by manual and electromechanical methods. It transmits weekly sales statistics and payroll time sheets to the home office by mail.

Top management and a large administrative staff are located at the home office. Much of the data transmitted to the home office are used in planning models which help management set long range policies and establish marketing strategies. Common data elements that are needed by any of the other three plants—A, B, and C—are stored in a common data base. All data for financial and other reports, which must be periodically furnished to stockholders and governmental agencies, are prepared at the home office. Payrolls are processed for plants A, C, and D. Historical data about payrolls, sales,

and general accounting statistics for all plants are maintained in a magnetic tape library. The home office information system is supported by a medium size computer configuration.

Hospital Information System

Thirteen Wisconsin hospitals, operating a shared computer center with the Wisconsin Blue Cross Plan, are getting advanced hospital information processing at a fraction of what it would cost them to install their own systems.[15] Remote terminals are located at each hospital. These terminals are connected to a central computer system and data base. The system receives patient and hospital data, and service charges, from each hospital. In turn, the system provides a wide variety of hospital accounting services. Through the terminals, each hospital can inquire into specific patient records, and receive a response within seconds.

The data base is comprised of a series of five comprehensive master files for each hospital. These include:

1. A hospital profile, containing some 3000 pieces of data to delineate the hospital's particular requirements and mode of operation. The data here includes patient and medical service classifications, details of accounting procedures, and report formats, billing cycles and final bill hold interval—in short, all of the guidance information the system needs to tailor its processing to hospital specifications.

2. A charge description master file, identifying every charge within the hospital and the pricing to be applied to each.

3. A room and bed master file, detailing each room and each bed within the room.

4. A doctor's master file, listing all physicians and surgeons on the hospital staff, along with their fields of specialization.

5. An approved medical insurance file, containing coded details for up to 3600 different medical insurance programs.

[15] Summarized from Harry L. Anderson, "13 Users, One Computer Center Diagnosed Healthy," *Computerworld*, June 21, 1972, p. 5. With permission. Copyright by *Computerworld*, Newton, Massachusetts 02160.

Each hospital pays an established fee per patient-day to the center. In return, each hospital receives virtually total automation of all patient-related accounting records, from admission to discharge and settlement of the bill. This procedure includes automatic preparation of the bill itself, with detailed insurance apportionments and full Medicare documentation.

Patient billing is a key application, both in eliminating a tremendous manual record-keeping chore and in providing a basis for many administrative control reports. As each patient is admitted, the computer creates a new patient record on the master file and sets up the entries on the room and bed master.

Once the patient is in the hospital, and the necessary records are established, per diem charges are automatically applied to the patient's record until the hospital transmits a notice of discharge. Service charges to the patient are recorded at the source (laboratory, X-ray, pharmacy, etc.) on a standard charge ticket.

The computer prices the charge item by referring to the master charge file, then posts the charge amount to the patient's record. At the same time the computer adds the charge transaction to the cumulative record, for service utilization statistics, and adds the dollar amount of the charge to revenue statistics.

When the patient is discharged, the computer initiates the patient billing routine. First, the system automatically makes the necessary record changes to update the room and bed master file, and then it breaks out patient-day statistics. Next, a fully detailed bill is printed out, ready for mailing to the patient. Drawing from the comprehensive medical insurance plan master file, the system makes all of the charge pro-rations and calculations and prints out any required commercial insurance bill, Blue Cross bill, and Medicare bills.

On a daily basis, working with patient admission, transfer, and discharge transaction data transmitted from the hospital, the computer prepares both a trial and a final patient census. The standard final census report lists patients by nursing station in room and bed number order and includes the patient's age, sex, religion, doctor, and medical program code.

Some of the participating hospitals request census data in a pre-established form to serve as the basis for temperature charts, day reports, pharmacy charge reports, and Medicare reports.

Regardless of the particular census format that a hospital requests, the full, daily patient census is transmitted from the computer and printed out at the hospital terminal in the early morning hours, before the start of the day's routine. In addition to the census, the computer transmits daily reports to the hospital for any accounting and administrative control functions. These daily reports include: a balancing of charge items by patient; detailed admission statistics; a listing of patient transfers and discharges; a summary of patient-day statistics, of bed occupancy by private, semi-private, and ward classifications; and many other reports tailored to the hospital's requirements.

The first objective of this system was to create a data communications network linking member hospitals to a central shared-system for hospital accounting and business office functions. Currently, systems work is being done to ascertain the feasibility of applying the combination of the computer and online terminals to patient care as well.

Court Information Systems

According to U.S. Senate sources,[16] the failure of criminal courts to take full advantage of computer technology is partly to blame for the breakdown of the criminal justice system, and for the weakened "deterrent effect." To correct this alleged failure, Senator Henry Jackson has introduced the Criminal Justice Reform Act of 1972. In support of his bill, Jackson states that it is

> not just a question of more prosecutors, more defense counsel, or more judges. It is a

[16] Based on: Ronald L. Baca, Michael G. Chambers, Walter L. Pringle, and Stayton C. Roehm, "Automated Court Systems," *AFIPS Conference Proceeding,* Volume 39 (Montvale, N.J., AFIPS Press, 1971) pp. 309–315. With permission from AFIPS Press.

matter of instituting new management techniques to control criminal dockets. It is a matter of changing archaic courtroom and appeals procedures that shackle our criminal courts.[17]

The American Bar Association special committee on crime prevention and control, proposed computer use in three of its twenty ideas. The ABA committee said that

computers should be utilized to assist the court in scheduling, routine paperwork, avoiding conflicts, and providing various types of judicial statistics needed for effective court operation and planning.[18]

Many court systems are overwhelmed by the volume and complexities of their court cases. In many metropolitan areas, it is not unusual to read about how someone was denied their freedom due to a simple clerical error or a breakdown in communications between the various departments that comprise the criminal justice system. The massive volumes of data that result from judicial proceedings are, in many instances, handled by outdated manual bookkeeping procedures.

In addition to the duplication of work and data records, there are errors in processing data and problems with keeping files current. Such difficulties create delays and inefficiencies in the operation of the total system.

However, information systems can be developed that will help to reduce basic data processing problems and, in addition, models can be derived which can provide information to those in positions of authority. In turn these authorities can set policies and establish control procedures which will help to deter crime. The court information system presented in this section shows how some of the problems that have arisen in the administration of criminal justice can be alleviated.

The court information system maintains all data concerning criminal cases and the defendants involved. All information is availale, via printed reports and remote terminals to the District Clerk, District Attorney, Sheriff, Probation Department, and to the various courts. Although many legal documents are still manually processed, the information system maintains such data in the files and can thereby provide an instant response to many questions concerning criminal cases.

As a litigant progresses from one step in the judicial process to the next, information regarding this progress is recorded in the information system. Any authorized inquirer will therefore always have current status information concerning any litigant. In the past, inquirers have often been transferred from one office to another as each office searched for, but failed to find, the requested information.

As the system monitors the progress of each case, it periodically prepares action reports. These action reports include lists of persons being held for no apparent reasons, cases that are ready for trial but have not been calendared, and persons whose probation periods have elapsed but have not been officially terminated. The system also provides numerous written reports which assist the criminal justice officials in preparing a case for trial, scheduling each event of the trial, and preparing local and state statistical reports.

Moreover, the system has the ability to use data to produce various statistical reports to aid in evaluating administrative procedures and to test hypothetical changes in these procedures. Additionally, quick access to accurate case load information is extremely useful for budget planning and evaluating future manpower and facility requirements.

Figure 4.16 is a schematic representation of the various departments that are connected to the integrated information system. The data in the common data base consists of files that are online, via telecommunication facilities, for fast response to remote inquirers. Other files are in batch processing mode for the preparation of various periodic reports.

The system's computer configuration is illus-

[17] Edward J. Bride, "Archaic Courtrooms—Need More DP to Deter Crime," *Computerworld*, June 21, 1972, p. 1. With permission. Copyright by *Computerworld*, Newton, Massachusetts 02160.
[18] *Ibid.*

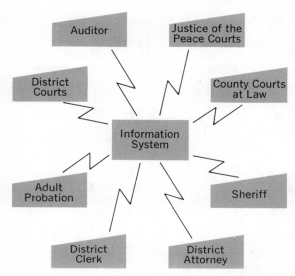

FIGURE 4.16. Schematic of the total court information system.

minal inquiries, and are briefly described as follows:

CAS: allows the user to search, retrieve, and update the Case History File, and to display all associated transaction records at the terminal.

NAM: allows the user to search, retrieve, and update the Name File, and to display the desired records at the terminal.

NUM: allows the user to search, retrieve, and update the Identification Number File, and to display the desired records at the terminal.

ANM: allows the user to display all available identification numbers associated with a defendant.

PER: allows the user to display all available personal descriptor information associated with a defendant.

JAC: allows the user to display the arrest/conviction history of a defendant.

CAL: allows the user to search, retrieve, and update the Calendar File, and to display the docket of a court.

All terminal inquiries are logged on the Log File to provide system backup. In the event of a system failure, all transactions can be reconstructed and the integrity of the basic data files ensured. The Log File also provides a data base for the analysis of user requests and overall terminal usage.

In every information system incorporating a large data base, security and privacy of information are important considerations. These considerations are especially applicable in court information systems. The two basic problems that exist are: (1) errors and (2) unauthorized access.

Errors usually result from mistakes that occur during the manual preparation of the input data. Errors on source documents, typographical or keypunching errors, and the inadvertent omission of pertinent data are typical examples. The input routines detect invalid input data (numeric value out of range, alphabetic character in a numeric field, unknown code, etc.) and all data input via cards is verified by being displayed and matched with the source document. As data are input, routines also check for incon-

trated in Figure 4.17. The various files and queues are shown in the center with the telecommunication facilities to the left and the batch processing facilities to the right.

The three basic data files are the Case History File, Name and Identification Number File, and the Calendar File. Each basic file is separated into an active and inactive file to augment the online and batch oriented functions.

The remote terminal user has nine basic teleprocessing functions available. These consist of Remote Batch Input (RBI), Batch Output Reporting (REP), and seven online functions: CAS, NAM, NUM, ANM, PER, JAC, and CAL. These functions aid the user in the interrogation, retrieval, and updating of the basic data files via the remote terminals.

RBI allows for the input of batch data (via the remote terminals) by placing the input in a queue to be processed by the Batch Input Subsystem. REP allows the user to request batch output (from the remote terminals) by placing the requests on a queue to be processed by the Batch Output Subsystem. The seven online functions give terminal displays in reply to ter-

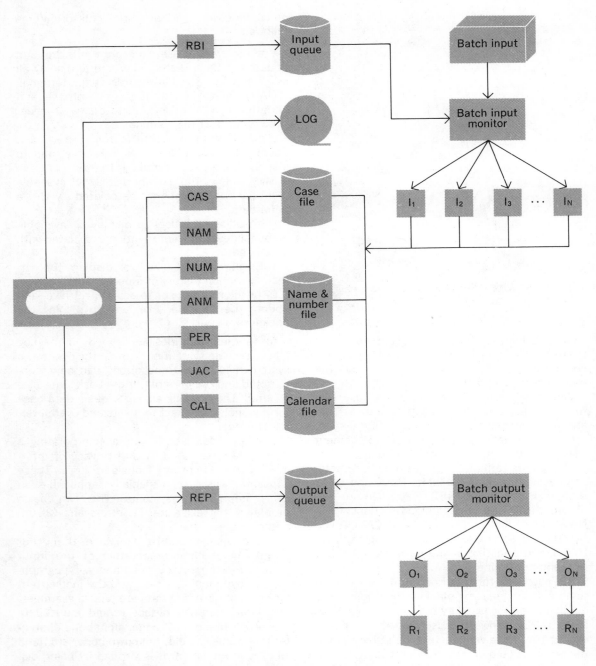

FIGURE 4.17. Computer configuration which supports the information system.

sistencies in data (such as a warrant for arrest that is shown as having been executed prior to its having been issued).

The second problem, that of unauthorized access to the data files, is particularly critical. The criminal records system deals with highly sensitive information. Destruction or modification of this information would severely cripple the effective performance of criminal justice. Therefore, a considerable amount of effort has been made to ensure the integrity of the information contained in the criminal records system.

The criminal records system allows for the updating of records from remote terminals. This provides up-to-the-minute information in the files but can be a source of problems if unauthorized personnel have access to the terminals. Several steps have to be taken to alleviate this problem.

1. Each person authorized to update the files is assigned an access code which is changed periodically. Without the code, modification of or additions to the files cannot occur. Furthermore, the access codes are valid only for a particular terminal.

2. Certain terminals are designated as display terminals only and allow no modifications or additions to occur. In addition, use of those terminals, through which modifications or additions can be made, can be restricted to those periods when authorized persons are on duty.

3. The system also provides file protection by terminals. Thus, modifications or additions can be made from a particular terminal to a record in the Name File, but *not* to one in the Case or Calendar File.

4. The system also has the ability to restrict the transactions allowed on a given terminal. Thus, a particular terminal can be used for an inquiry that is not allowed through some other terminal. This allows controls, via software, to be placed on the use of any terminal.

Periodically the information is transferred from disk storage to magnetic tape. Two copies of the files are made. One is stored locally and can be used to recreate the files in the event of an inadvertent, (hardware malfunction) or delib-erate, destruction of the files currently re-corded on disk storage. The other copy is kept at a remote location as protection against the destruction of both the files on disk storage and the magnetic tape copy.

While the above mentioned capabilities provide a means of protection, the ultimate success depends on the people involved and the extent to which the operating procedures are followed.

Brief Examples of Societal Information Systems

Although this text is concerned mainly with information systems pertinent to formal organizations, one can also perceive their great potential for providing information for helping to solve social problems and for allowing more effective social management. It is our opinion that if a systems analyst is competent in designing information systems for various organizations—e.g., universities, hospitals, businesses—he or she will also be competent in designing social information systems. The techniques learned as a systems analyst for typical organizations apply to any system, at every level of complexity, from the primary work group through large-scale formal organizations to an entire interacting social community. The proper integrated activities of large social groupings depends upon effecting communication of information to those who must make decisions about various problems in the same way as do the decision makers in formal organizations.

Many social scientists feel that we must design and implement information systems oriented to key social problems to help increase the decision making powers of an array of participants. It is beyond the scope of this text to list all of the information systems suggested, but a few which might help solve some societal problems are:

1. Systems to provide information about product ratings, production methods, social costs, and prices to consumers.

2. Financial information systems to maintain accounts and act as clearinghouses for transac-

tions between individuals and organizations. This system would considerably reduce the flood of paperwork and the amount of personal record keeping.

3. Information systems to provide information about pollutants in the environment. Sensors could gather data on the amount of pollutants being produced by offenders and determine the share of cost and level of abuse for each offender.

4. Medical information systems could be designed to make the latest medical information about the treatment of various illnesses accessible to physicians.

5. Information systems designed to help the unemployed worker find jobs. A perennial problem of society is to effectively match available jobs with the unemployed.

6. Criminal justice information systems designed to attain (1) a coordinated system of criminal justice and, (2) the effective apprehension, prosecution, adjudication, and rehabilitation of offenders.

7. Integrated municipal information systems with a multi-functional data base which could be shared by authorized users and/or generators of data. Frequently in municipalities, as in any large complex organization, there is a multiplicity of users for the same data, such as the tax assessor, clerks of courts, fire department, police department, building inspectors, etc. In most instances now, the requirements of these users are satisfied by each user independently collecting and storing the same data.

Information systems such as these, and others, offer a way to manage and help solve some of the problems of a complex and dynamic society. However, there is also a great potential for undermining human freedom and individuality. A fact which must be kept in mind is that some of these systems, and others not listed, require a detailed data base which might result in the identification, qualification, and monitoring of individual participants. Large dossiers including psychological ratings, crimi-

nal records, credit and insurance ratings, and other personal data for each individual will be maintained. Many feel that such data bases will result in an invasion of privacy, a problem which will far outweigh those problems that the social information systems purport to solve.

It is not our goal in this text to discuss the ramifications of an invasion of privacy, but we do feel that it *is* a possible problem in implementing social information systems and one which the citizens of any country must seriously consider. We have mentioned it here simply to call it to the readers' attention for their consideration.

SUMMARY

Information systems are those subsystems of an organization which handle all data processing activities and provide information to a variety of users, especially management and external constituents. Information systems can be developed using two approaches: (1) hierarchical and (2) systems. The hierarchical approach uses either centralized or decentralized data processing. With this approach, emphasis is on basic data processing functions with little regard for meeting informational requirements. The systems approach emphasizes a viable coordination of both data processing and information reporting. Information systems developed via the systems approach are either integrated or distributed.

The hierarchical approach is not recommended because of its obvious disadvantages. The systems approach, on the other hand, is recommended. In evaluating which type of system to apply, integrated or distributed, one must be aware of the advantages and disadvantages of each. Moreover, since no single system is correct for all applications, the systems designer must also consider the objectives of management and the kind of organization the information system will serve.

4.1 Formulate a definition of the term information system. Compare and contrast your definition with that one presented in the chapter.

4.2 List all of the techniques and devices you can think of which might be useful in data processing and information reporting.

4.3 Distinguish between a computer system and an information system.

4.4 What is the relationship of the accounting function to the information system? What is the relationship of market research to the information system?

4.5 Compare and contrast formal and informal information. Give three examples of each.

4.6 Contrast and compare the hierarchical information system with centralized data processing and the integrated information system. Give examples of each.

4.7 There are advantages and disadvantages to both the hierarchical system and the integrated system given in the chapter. See if you can add to this list.

4.8 List and explain the major differences between centralized and decentralized data processing.

4.9 What position should the integrated information system have in the organization? Explain.

4.10 What is meant by social information systems? Give an example of one not listed in the text.

4.11 What is meant by external users (constituents of the organization) of the information system? Give examples of at least three and describe what kind of information they might receive from the information system.

4.12 Without reading further in the text, try to give a definition of a common data base. What is its purpose? Give an example of the use of the common data base.

4.13 List the attributes requisite for the Manager of Information Systems. What are his or her duties?

4.14 Differentiate between the distributed system and the integrated system.

4.15 Discuss the major ways the information system can be integrated. Which do you consider the easiest to accomplish from a technical viewpoint? Most beneficial? Least beneficial?

4.1 Discuss fully the purpose of an information system.

4.2 Discuss fully the meaning of a common data base. Give an example of one.

4.3 Discuss both the problems solved and the problems created by social information systems.

4.4 "I get all my important information from Washington, D.C. and on the golf course." Is this comment referring to formal or informal information? Discuss the importance of such information.

4.5 Discuss the following statement: "The integrated information system permits instantaneous and simultaneous updating of files, thus providing current status information and identification of conditions to a multiplicity of users throughout the organization."

4.6 "Downtime of the computer configuration which supports the integrated information system can be catastrophic." Discuss this statement.

4.7 "In a hierarchical information system with decentralized data processing there is usually a great deal of redundancy in files and duplication of effort." Discuss this statement. Can the same be true for a distributed information system?

4.8 "The integrated information system means centralization of management." Discuss this statement.

4.9 "The manager who has the information also has the power." Discuss this statement.

4.10 Discuss the positive and negative social ramifications of social information systems.

4.11 What does "invasion of privacy" mean to you?

4.12 Discuss the pro's and con's of Professor Dearden's four fallacies concerning integrated information systems.

4.13 "Our organization can not afford to wait for the design and implementation of an integrated information system." Discuss this statement.

4.14 Discuss several organizations which in effect are information systems, i.e. their sole reason for existence is to provide information.

4.15 Cite several examples of where a higher degree of integration would result in benefits to various governmental organizations. What might be some of the disadvantages to this integration?

EXERCISES   **4.1** Assume some hypothetical organization and describe how the information may flow within this organization, based on: (1) the hierarchical approach, and (2) the systems approach.

4.2 Visit an organization of your choice and describe its information system. Is it based on the hierarchical or systems approach, or a variation thereof?

4.3 Construct a communication network with six subsystems using both integrated and distributed information systems.

4.4 Choose a governmental agency of your choice and describe their information system. Determine what data they store and how they use it.

4.5 Interview a variety of individuals (e.g. a businessman, a blue collar worker, professor of accounting, an officer in the military) and obtain their definitions of an information system. Prepare a presentation which compares and contrasts their definitions with the definition provided in this chapter.

4.6 Visit the local office(s) responsible for issuing licenses for both operating motor vehicles and registering a motor vehicle in your state. Evaluate the literature you obtain and determine the following:

(1) Are these two functions administered separately or as one department?

(2) How many information systems are operated to perform both functions? To what degree are the systems integrated if there are more than one?

(3) What commonalities exist, if any, between the data collected for each function?

(4) If more than one system exists, what technical difficulties might prevent the designing of a single system? What other difficulties might be encountered by integrating these systems?

PROBLEMS **4.1** Litigants in criminal cases, especially in large metropolitan centers, are experiencing delays of up to two or more years before their cases can be adjudicated. In the meantime, it is not uncommon to find that witnesses involved in a case have forgotten many of the details, moved away, or even died.

Many of these courts use manual bookkeeping procedures which cannot meet the complexities, volume, and timing demands. Also, backlogs and delays result from the lack of coordination in docketing cases. Such systems often result in: (1) unnecessary duplication of records among agencies and departments, (2) high number of clerical errors which can severely handicap the performance of justice, (3) lack of communication between the various departments that comprise the criminal system, (4) extension of the time that dangerous criminals are free on bond (assuming they can post bond), and (5) creation of long delays for innocent people who cannot post bond and must remain in jail until their case is brought to trial.

Objective of Proposed Judicial Information System:

To design and implement an information system which will provide an efficient means of monitoring the progress of criminal cases and to define methods of using such information to reduce the total time and effort required to process a case.

Requirements of Proposed Judicial Information System:

1. Provide periodic summary reports about impending cases.

2. Allow the user to search, retrieve, and update the files in the common data base.

3. Allow the user to retrieve the docket of a court.

Specific Examples of Information Retrieved:

1. Complaint Index via terminal:

Number	Defendant's Name	Offense Code	Offense Description
210002	DOE, JOE	2501	Forgery of checks
235271	HOOD, ROBIN	2270	Burglary and theft

2. Grand Jury Index via terminal:

Complaint Number	Date Filed	Defendant's Name	Offense Code	Offense Description
14296	01-12-73	DOE, JOE	2501	Forgery of checks
14298	04-17-73	HOOD, ROBIN	2270	Burglary and theft

3. Felony Index via terminal:

Case Number	Defendant's Name	Case Disposition
310157	CAPONE, AL	Guilty
310894	DILLINGER, JOHN	Guilty
314732	THOMPSON, SADIE	Not billed
317492	PERFECT, PETER	Not guilty

4. District Courts Index via terminal:

Case Number	Defendant's Name	Offense Code	Defendant Status
319777	BANANA, CHIQUITA	2607	In jail
319842	BATMAN, IRA	2734	Out on bond
319973	TERRIFIC, TERRY	2301	Wanted
319984	BOND, JAMESON	2007	In jail

Defense Status	Prosecution Status	In Process	Case Pending Status
Ready	Ready		Ready for trial
Ready	Not ready		Ready for arraignment
Not ready	Ready		Not ready to calendar
Ready	Ready	Trial	Calendared

Components of Proposed Judicial Information System:

1. The system will consist of telecommunication and batch processing components built around a nucleus of files which serve as a common data base.

2. The common base is made up of three files, which are: (a) Case History File, (b) Name and Identification File, and (c) Calendar File.

Users of Proposed Judicial Information System:

The users of the system are scattered throughout the city and include:

(1) County courts
(2) District courts
(3) Sheriff
(4) District clerk
(5) District attorney[19]

[19] Information for this problem based on: Ronald L. Baca, Michael G. Chambers, Walter L. Pringle, and Stayton C. Roehm, "Automated Court Systems," *AFIPS Conference Proceedings,* Volume 39 (Montvale, N.J.: AFIPS Press, 1971) pp. 309–315. With permission from AFIPS Press.

Requirements for Solution:

Using the material you have read thus far, plus the appendices, please: (1) Briefly design the overall system you believe necessary to meet the overall system objectives and requirements. (2) Sketch a computer configuration necessary to support your systems design. (3) Although we have not discussed security and privacy in systems yet, try to anticipate security and privacy problems that may arise in your system and outline methods you would implement to alleviate these problems. (4) Make suggestions as to additional benefits that could be implemented besides those outlined in the problem. Make any assumptions you feel necessary for the presentation of your problem solution.

4.2 The purpose of a city is to provide public services desired or demanded by its citizens. These services or functions, of which there are many, include such things as: (1) protection of the citizens from those who break the law, (2) provision of water and sanitary services, and (3) provision for the transportation of people and goods. The total of these functions can be broadly grouped into four sectors: (1) public safety, (2) human resources development, (3) public finance, and (4) physical and economical development.

Present Conditions:

In cities, as in any large complex organization, there is multiplicity of requirements for the same information. Too frequently, however, these requirements are satisfied by each user independently collecting and storing data for himself. The tax assessor, the fire department, and the building inspector, for example, all require similar information about buildings, including such things as: (1) address, (2) dimensions, (3) construction type, (4) number of access ways, etc. Frequently, in many cities, there are a vast number of people whose job it is to "massage" data, putting it into a form useful for managerial decisions ranging from "what are my budget requirements for next year" to "which of the traffic signals should have preventive maintenance performed."

There is a preponderance of the latter type inquiry which, in many instances, require routine decisions but which, at the same time, occupy so much of a manager's time. By way of example, such decisions include: (1) designation of which properties in the city should be reappraised, (2) scheduling vehicles and equipment for preventive maintenance, and (3) preparation of lists of those people who should be sent notifications of their failure to pay tickets.

Requirements for Proposed Municipal Information System:

1. Furnish information to top management, middle management, and other users necessary to carry out the day to day activities.

2. Provide a means to interface the system with outside organizations or special districts including: (a) independent school boards, (b) water districts, (c) citizen or civic organizations, and (d) economic development districts. In addition, the system must also be responsive to the many reporting demands of the Federal Government.[20]

[20] Information for this problem based on: Steven E. Gottlieb, "Integrated Municipal Information Systems: Benefits for Cities — Requirements for Vendors," *AFIPS* Conference Proceedings, Volume 39 (Montvale, N.J.: AFIPS Press, 1971) pp. 303–315. With permission from AFIPS Press.

Requirements for Solution:

Assume that you are a systems analyst for a consultant firm.

1. Conceptualize, in broad terms, the kind of Municipal Information System you propose. Draw any schematics and write all narratives which you feel are necessary in communicating your systems design. Be as specific as you can, but bear in mind that this design is introductory in nature. (This problem solution should be based on the material you have read thus far plus any material from the appendices that you deem pertinent.)

2. Prepare, in addition to your conceptual systems design, a complete report on some of the benefits that you envision will accrue to the city should the mayor and others commission you for the development and implementation of the information system. Be specific.

3. Prepare a list of questions that you intend to ask the mayor and divisional heads in your meeting with them.

4. Please enumerate the advantages as well as the disadvantages of your proposed system.

4.3 The Louisiana Yam Company has three plants for processing and canning yams. These plants are located in Louisiana, Mississippi, and Alabama. Each plant also has a warehouse where finished goods are stored and later shipped to food brokers and distributors throughout the nation. The home office of Louisiana Yam is located in Monroe, Louisiana. In addition to performing normal accounting and routine data processing (e.g. preparing bills and payroll) the home office also keeps inventory records for all three plants' warehouses.

The owner/manager has an office located in Monroe, but under his direction are three plant managers, one for each plant. By tradition each manager has his own "staff" who maintain inventory records, perform various clerical duties, and periodically prepare sales and production performance reports. Each plant manager is expected to purchase raw produce for the necessary production of their respective plants. Raw produce is supplied by a variety of growers throughout the Mis–Lou–Ala area.

Management of Louisiana Yam Company has had problems of production scheduling, quality control, inventory management, purchasing, and general reporting of performance information.

Assume that you work for Burstrater Consultants, Inc. of Shreveport and have been charged with the responsibility of spending several days with the management of Louisiana Yam Company to: (1) outline a broad information systems proposal, (2) present possible applications of management science techniques, and (3) sketch a computer configuration necessary to support your systems design.

The owner/manager of Louisiana Yam has requested that you submit at least two alternatives to your proposed information systems design and computer configurations, i.e., one from an integrated systems viewpoint and one from a distributed systems viewpoint. He also wants you to prepare a recommendation as to which system you consider better, and why.

In your recommendations, include the advantages and disadvantages you foresee in a particular systems design, plus any suggestions you have concerning overall management organization and philosophy.

Make any assumptions that you deem necessary.

4.4 Due to recent expansion at a large university in the midwest, the administration has identified a need for an improved information system to support the large maintenance force responsible for the physical plants. The campus data center has offered the use of their facilities if the information system includes a computer in its design. Moreover, the data center will install at no cost an input-output terminal in the maintenance departments control center for accessing computer files online. You have been commissioned to design and implement the required system. The following facts are given to you.

1. The maintenance budget is 1.5 million dollars annually.

2. The maintenance staff consists of: (a) laborers (20), (b) carpenters (10), (c) electricians (8), (d) plumbers (4); and (e) painters (6).

3. In addition to the above personnel, the maintenance department includes: (a) four job supervisors; (b) two job estimators/schedulars: (c) one work expediter; (d) two stockroom clerks; and (e) three clerical typists. All report to the manager of the department.

4. Work assignments are prepared each day for the following day. Each man in the department completes a time card and submits this card at the end of the day.

5. Each job is assigned to a job supervisor and the required skills report to that supervisor throughout the duration of the job.

6. Maintenance is classified as: (a) scheduled/preventive; (b) emergency; (c) minor improvements; and (d) major improvements. An estimated cost of $1000 separates minor from major improvements.

7. All major improvements are contracted to outside firms, and are not performed directly by the maintenance department, although a job supervisor is assigned to the job.

8. Maintenance requests, other than those termed emergency, which are estimated at $250 or more, must be individually approved by the treasurer under one of the various funds which make up the maintenance departments budget. Usually there are ten different funds available in any one year.

9. It is estimated that as many as 100 requests for maintenance are accepted and in process at any one time. The average number of maintenance requests in process during the last two years was 60.

Requirements for Solution:

Based on the above facts, and on any assumptions that you deem necessary, prepare a proposal for the design of the required information system. Your proposal should include the following:

(1) A flowchart describing the system.
(2) A brief narrative describing the system.
(3) A statement of all critical assumptions you used in arriving at your proposal.
(4) A brief justification of the data processing method that you chose.
(5) A decision table which illustrates the logical process in classifying maintenance requests.
(6) Illustrations and explanations of all source documents required.
(7) A brief description of what data will be stored and how it is to be stored.

(8) An illustration and explanation of each informational output that you recommend for the following: (a) treasurer; (b) manager of the maintenance department; (c) job supervisors; (d) job estimators/schedulars and expediter; and (e) any other person within or responsible for the maintenance department.

BIBLIOGRAPHY

Anderson, "13 Users, One Computer Center Diagnosed Healthy," *Computerworld,* June 21, 1972.

Baca, Chambers, Pringle, and Roehm, "Automated Court Systems," *AFIPS Conference Proceedings,* Montvale, N.J.: AFIPS Press, 1971.

Blumenthal, *Management Information Systems: A Framework for Planning and Development,* Englewood Cliffs, N.J.: Prentice-Hall, Inc., 1969.

Bower, Schlasser, and Zlatkovich, *Financial Information Systems—Theory and Practice,* Boston: Allyn and Bacon, Inc., 1969.

Bride, "Archaic Courtrooms—Need More DP to Deter Crime," *Computerworld,* June 21, 1972.

Brightman, *Information Systems for Modern Management,* New York: The Macmillan Co., 1971.

Burch, "An Independent Information System," *Journal of Systems Management,* March, 1972.

Carrithers and Weinwurm, *Business Information and Accounting Systems,* Columbus, Ohio: Charles E. Merrill Books, Inc., 1967.

"Communication Network Keeps Tight Rein on Migrant Students," *Computerworld,* June 14, 1972.

Cuadra (ed.), *Annual Review of Information Science and Technology, Vol. 2,* New York: John Wiley & Sons, Inc., 1967.

Custard, "Long-Range Systems Plan," *Proceedings Third Annual Conference,* Chicago, Illinois: The Society for Management Information Systems, 1971.

Dearden, "MIS is a Mirage," *Harvard Business Review,* January–February, 1972.

Dippel and House, *Information Systems,* Glenview, Illinois: Scott Foresman & Co., 1969.

Enger, *Putting MIS to Work,* New York: American Management Association, Inc., 1969.

"Facilities Management is Here to Stay," *Administrative Management,* July, 1972.

Ferguson, "A Corporate Level Information System," *Proceedings Third Annual Conference,* Chicago, Illinois: The Society for Management Information Systems, 1971.

Gottlieb, "Integrated Municipal Information Systems: Benefits for Cities—Requirements for Vendors," *AFIPS Conference Proceedings,* Montvale, N.J.: AFIPS Press, 1971.

Greenberger (ed.) *Computers, Communications, and the Public Interest,* Baltimore: The Johns Hopkins Press, 1971.

Hitch, "Sub-optimization in Operations Problems," *Journal of Operations Research Society,* May, 1953.

"Information Systems," *Data Processing Digest,* March, 1972.

Krauss, *Management Information Systems,* New York: American Management Association, Inc., 1970.

Kriebel, "The Future MIS," *Business Automation,* June, 1972.

Kuhn, *The Study of Society: A Unified Approach,* Homewood, Illinois: Richard D. Irwin, Inc., and The Dorsey Press, 1963.

MacKay, *Information, Mechanism and Meaning,* Cambridge, Mass: MIT Press, 1969.

"Management Information Systems," *ADP Newsletter,* January 10, 1972.

Matthews, *The Design of the Management Information System,* Philadelphia: Auerbach Publishers, 1971.

Maynard (ed.), *Handbook of Business Administration,* New York: McGraw-Hill Book Co., 1967.

McDonough, *Centralized Systems Planning and Control,* Wayne, Penn.: Thompson Book Co., 1969.

McFarlan, "Brainy Operations Staff are an Asset," *Computerworld,* July 5, 1972.

Murdick and Ross, *Information Systems for Modern Management,* Englewood Cliffs, N.J.: Prentice-Hall, Inc., 1971.

Oswald, "Maxi-empire, No! Mini-empire, Maybe?" *Business Automation,* June, 1972.

Pendleton, "Integrated Information System," *AFIPS Conference Proceedings,* Montvale, N.J.: AFIPS Press, 1971.

Prince, *Information Systems for Management Planning and Control,* Homewood, Illinois: Richard D. Irwin, Inc., 1970.

Rosove, *Developing Computer Based Information Systems,* New York: John Wiley & Sons, Inc., 1967.

Ross, *Management by Information System,* Englewood Cliffs, N.J.: Prentice-Hall, Inc., 1970.

Rothman and Mosmann, *Computers and Society,* Chicago: Science Research Associates, Inc., 1972.

Sackman, *Mass Information Utilities and Social Excellence,* Philadelphia: Auerbach Publishers, 1971.

Schwartz, "Identifying Universal Principles in MIS Designs," *Proceedings Third Annual Conference,* Chicago, Illinois: The Society for Management Information Systems, 1971.

5

Tailoring the Information System to Meet Specific Informational Requirements

5.1 Introduction

In the previous chapter the various general structures of information systems in organizations were identified and discussed. In this chapter several specific methods for tailoring the information system to the informational requirements of an organization are analyzed. The methods discussed at this time are useful regardless of the overall structure of the information system. Although each method will be analyzed independently, it should be noted that in practice some combination of methods is usually required to satisfy informational requirements. Selecting the appropriate method or combination of methods is also an essential part of the design process, and it is further described in Part III of this text. The objectives of this chapter are:

1. To explain how filtering data can provide information.
2. To identify and describe the major ways the monitoring method can be implemented.
3. To introduce the use of logico-mathematical models as a method for providing information to decision makers.

4. To illustrate, based on the interrogative method, how information is provided.

5. To develop an awareness for the use of information reflecting events and activities external to the organization.

5.2 Filtering Method

Organizational decision makers are subjected to an avalanche of data. Particularly where computers are utilized, great quantities of data are collected, processed, and reported. For a given decision maker, these reports might be meaningless, or some relevant information might be found, if the recipient is willing to spend the time searching for it. In the latter case, much of the recipient's available time is expended in searching for the information needed to make the decision rather than in evaluating it, and the alternatives available. One approach to providing decision makers with less data, but with more relevant information, is to filter the amount of detail data made available to each level of decision making.

Threshold of Detail

Filtering is a process of screening or extracting unwanted elements from some entity as it passes, or is communicated, from one point to another. Data can be filtered through summarizing and classifying operations that screen out detail unnecessary for a given level of decision making. The basic assumption supporting the filtering method is that persons at different levels of decision making require different levels of detail information for the performance of their duties. The relationship between levels of decision making and requirements for detail is illustrated in Figure 5.1.

FIGURE 5.1. Relationship between levels of decision making and requirements for detail information.

As a rule, strategic decision makers have a higher threshold for detail than either tactical or technical decision makers. For example, the president of a large manufacturing organization is certainly concerned with the sales of that organization; however, this concern does not necessarily require a daily listing of invoices; a monthly summary of total sales dollars might be satisfactory. However, it must be recognized that thresholds for detail can vary significantly within any one category of decision making. Ideally, an information system should be designed to permit the filtering of selected data elements from the data base so that each decision maker can obtain the level of detail appropriate to his or her individual needs. Traditionally, information has been filtered at each subordinate-superior level in the organization. However, in modern organizations, the systems analyst has an opportunity to design this filtering process as an essential element of the information system.

Examples of the Filtering Method

The filtering method has widespread applicability in most organizations. The reporting of costs and sales dollars are two examples which can be used to illustrate the filtering process.

In a construction company, an awareness of actual costs incurred is an important aspect of each manager's job regardless of his position in the organization. The president of the firm is likely to be concerned with the total costs incurred in a given time period.

The vice — president responsible for construction might require a further breakdown of total costs into prime costs and overhead costs. Each lower level of management would require a correspondingly higher level of detail concerning costs related to their activities only. In Figure 5.2 we illustrate how the filtering method can be used to report construction costs to the various levels of decision makers.

Reporting sales activity in a large organization is another area where the filtering method is effective. In Figure 5.3 a series of reports are shown which describe the sales effort of a company and the distribution of these reports.

President:

- Construction costs → 7,200,000
- Manufacturing costs   xxxx

V-P—Construction:

	Airport Projects	Highway Projects	Building Projects	Total
Prime costs	2,050,000	xxxx	xxxx	5,200,000 →
Overhead costs	700,000	xxxx	xxxx	2,000,000 →

Projects Mgr:

	Project-1	Project-2	Project-3	Total
Direct labor costs	250,000	xxx	xxx	850,000 →
Material costs	400,000	xxx	xxx	1,200,000 →
Overhead costs	220,000	xxx	xxx	700,000 →

Superintendent:

	Concrete Pipe	Excavation	Structures	Total
Direct labor costs	60,000	xxx	xxx	250,000
Material costs	100,000	xxx	xxx	400,000 →
Overhead costs	50,000	xxx	xxx	220,000 →

Pipe Foreman:

Direct labor costs

Names	Operators	Laborers	Total
J. Caldwell	xx		
H. Custer	xx		
J. Smith		xx	
A. Taylor	—	xx	
	xx	xx	60,000 →

Material costs

Item	36″	42″	Total
X	xx		
Z	—	xx	
	xx	xx	100,000 →

Overhead costs

Description	Controllable	Noncontrollable	Total
A	xx		
B		xx	
C	xx	—	
	xx	xx	50,000 →

(Note: All figures are in dollars.)

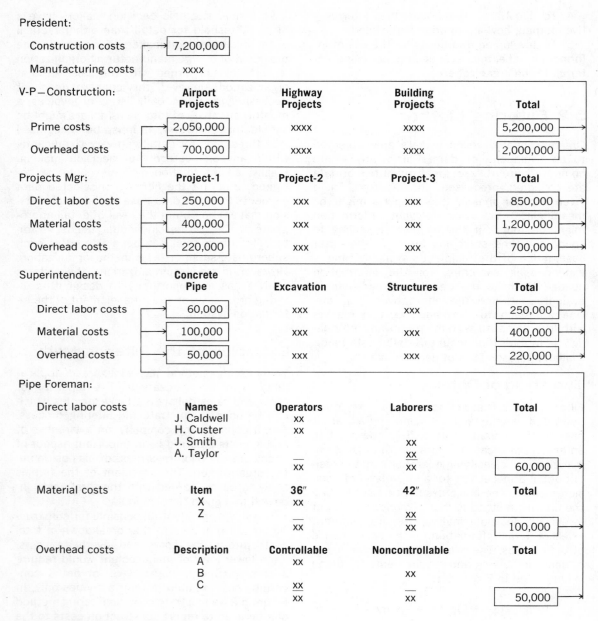

FIGURE 5.2.   Illustration of using Filtering Method to report construction costs.

Company Sales			
Division	Year to date	This month	
Eastern	$292,000	$ 76,650	← Sales dollars, shown by company division; produced for Vice-President of Marketing
Central	284,000	83,100	
Pacific	310,000	101,000	
Total Company	$886,000	$260,750	

Eastern Division			
Territory	Year to date	This month	
New England	$ 58,830	$ 11,250	
Mid-Atlantic	73,190	14,100	← Sales dollars, shown by territory, for each division; produced for each Division Manager
Seaboard	42,080	15,800	
Southeast	35,000	12,000	
Northeast	82,900	23,900	
Total Division	$292,000	$ 77,050	

New England Territory			
Salesman	Year to date	This month	
J. Dee	$ 19,010	$ 3,000	
M. Horish	12,190	4,200	← Sales dollars, shown by salesman, for each territory; produced for each Territory Manager
J. Michaels	11,480	2,300	
J. Lucey	16,190	1,750	
Total Territory	$ 58,870	$ 11,250	

Super Manufacturing			
Product	Year to date	This month	
1/4" Drills	$ 350	$ 75	
1/2" Drills	790	140	
Sanders	1,150	–	← Sales dollars, shown by product, for each customer; produced for each salesman
Jig Saws	4,580	1,150	
Rip Saws	290	–	
Others	1,375	75	
Total Sales	$ 8,535	$ 1,440	

FIGURE 5.3. Using the Filtering Method to report sales dollars.

Advantages and Disadvantages

Filtering, as a method for providing information to decision makers, represents a significant improvement over the production of voluminous listings. To summarize our analysis of this method we present the major advantages and disadvantages associated with filtering.

There are two major advantages to utilizing the filtering method: (1) the amount of useless data provided to each decision maker is re-duced considerably since the level of detail received is based on individual requirements, and (2) organizational resources are conserved. Eliminating the need to produce massive reports conserves data processing resources; minimizing the need to search for information conserves decision makers' time.

There are two major disadvantages to utilizing the filtering method: (1) implementation is difficult when the threshold of detail among decision makers at the same level varies considerably, and (2) in large and more complex organizations filtering alone does not provide adequate "action oriented" information to decision makers.

5.3 Monitoring Method

The monitoring method is another alternative for reducing the amount of data decision makers receive while still increasing the amount of relevant information at their disposal. Instead of producing streams of data to be handled by a decision maker, the information system monitors the data and provides informational outputs to the decision maker on an automatic basis. There are three basic ways to implement the monitoring method: (1) Variance Reporting, (2) Programmed Decision Making, and (3) Automatic Notification.

Variance Reporting

This form of the monitoring method requires that data representing actual events be compared against data representing expectations in order to establish a variance. The variance is then compared to a control value to determine whether or not the event is to be reported. The result of this procedure is that only those events or activities which significantly deviate from expectations are presented to the decision maker for action.

For example, the XYZ Company develops and maintains standard costs for each product manufactured. The product line includes 23,000 different products. A cost variance report including each product would require more than 1000 pages. Many of the entries in this report would show that the products were manufactured at, or very close to, the established standard. However, a much smaller report would be produced if it were assumed that only products varying more than ± 5% from a standard required management's attention. Moreover, each entry in the smaller report would represent a need either for further analysis, or action, on the part of a decision maker. In this example, it can be seen that the time spent by the human decision maker to identify every variance has been eliminated. Such monitoring is still accomplished, but now it is performed by the information system, and the system in turn reports to the decision maker only those variances which are significant.

Another example of variance reporting can be applied to sales reporting. In a sales organization where each salesman is assigned a sales quota, the sales manager reviews only those salesmen who are well above or below their quota in any given time period. The sales manager assumes that the salesmen are operating satisfactorily when sales are within 10% of the quota. In Figure 5.4, the sales performance of one salesman has been plotted for twelve months.

From this chart, it can be seen that our salesman exceeded the guidelines in the months

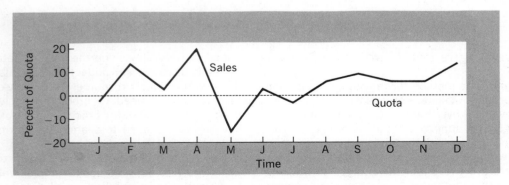

FIGURE 5.4. Chart which shows deviation from quota.

of February, April, May, and December. Using the variance reporting method, the sales manager receives detailed sales reports on this individual's sales performance only at these times. In the remaining months, the sales manager assumes that this particular salesman is making sales according to expectations. In effect, the sales manager has been freed from monitoring reports which contain little, if any, useful information; therefore, the manager can better utilize his time and energy where they are most needed.

To implement this form of the monitoring method, the analyst must execute the following procedure:

1. Establish the norm at which performance is anticipated (e.g. budget, plan, quota, schedule, standard, etc.).

2. Establish the amount of deviation from the norm which is considered acceptable. This deviation can be both above and below the norm, or only in one direction (the amount may be unequal, i.e., the deviation above the norm might be set at 30% and the deviation below might be set at 10%).

3. Establish a procedure for collecting actual performance data and comparing it to the norm.

4. Extrapolate past performance to see if trends can be highlighted (optional).

5. Disseminate the variances as they occur to the decision maker responsible for the performance.

Programmed Decision Making

A second application of the monitoring method involves the development and implementation of programmed decision making. A significant part of technical decision making, and a small part of tactical decision making activities, involve routine repetitive decisions. By designing the information system to execute these routine decisions, the systems analyst has provided the human decision makers with more time to spend on less structured decisions. There are many opportunities to implement programmed decision making in most organizations.

For example, credit checking customer orders is an important, but repetitive, decision making process that can be programmed. Figure 5.5 illustrates one approach to programming this process. Once the credit manager is relieved of checking each customer order processed, he or she is able to concentrate on those orders which have a problem, such as collection, or cash flow analysis, associated with them.

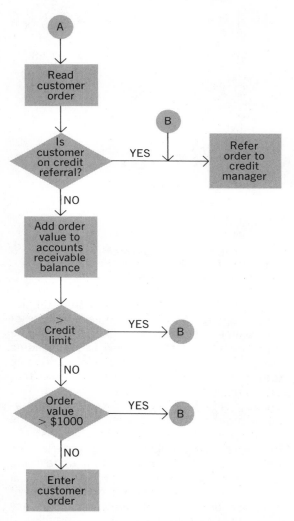

FIGURE 5.5. An example of programmed decision making in the credit checking process.

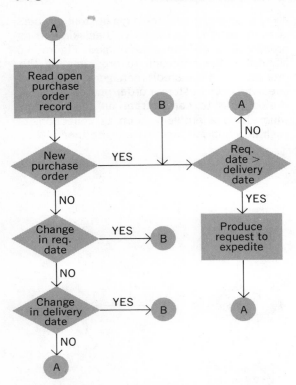

FIGURE 5.6. An illustration of programmed decision making in the purchasing function.

The purchasing function provides still another opportunity for the implementation of programmed decision making. Periodically, a purchasing agent must review all outstanding purchase orders in order to determine if some form of expediting is required to ensure that the purchase is delivered when needed. This process entails an examination of each purchase order and a comparison of the date the purchase is scheduled to arrive against the date when the purchase is required for use. Both dates are subject to continuous revision. In many organizations this process can be a tedious task since hundreds or thousands of purchase orders may be outstanding at any point in time. Obviously, if the system is allowed to monitor outstanding purchase orders, and the decision as to which orders are to be expedited

is programmed, much time and effort could be saved. Figure 5.6 illustrates one approach to programming this decision making process.

In many manufacturing operations, this method of providing information is used to automatically control the operation without manual intervention. Process control, as it is commonly termed, involves sensors which determine what is actually happening, and in turn, inputs this data into a programmed decision making structure. Based on the logic programmed, the output may cause a valve to open or close, a bell to ring, or the operation to cease.

In all of our examples, the principle is identical. The system monitors the flow of data, and when an activity "triggers" or reflects a condition inside the programmed decision making range, a decision is automatically made by the system based on predetermined conditions.

Automatic Notification

A third form of the monitoring method is termed automatic notification. In this approach the system does not make any decisions as such, but because it is monitoring the overall flow of data rather than being a decision maker, it can release information at a predetermined time where needed. With this method, the vast memory capabilities of computers are taken advantage of to keep track of large amounts of detail information.

For example, in a large hospital the patients in a given area might be the responsibility of many different doctors. Each doctor has prescribed a definite schedule for administering medication, therapy, tests, and diets to each patient. Generally, a head nurse is responsible for monitoring these instructions and seeing that they are performed as scheduled in each area. In a twenty-four hour operation there are at least three head nurses involved. Moreover, patients are always coming and going, and doctors are continuously changing schedules.

If the doctor's instructions are input in a computer based information system, specific information, in the form of instructions, can then be issued periodically to the head nurse via a CRT or teletype device. This automatic notification permits the nurse to spend time in other areas, providing patient service, rather than in keeping track of administrative details.

In an industrial organization, this method of providing information is used to present work assignments to individual workers. For example, when a worker completes his current assignment, he receives his next assignment notification automatically from the system. The allocation of other resources is also monitored. In a construction company, an inventory schedule of heavy equipment is monitored. Periodically, a notice is output which identifies machinery scheduled to be available for another project assignment.

In the above examples, the system merely monitors a large file of data. The automatic notifications are issued based on some predetermined criteria, but the individual decision makers must decide whether or not any action is required.

Advantages and Disadvantages

To summarize the discussion of the monitoring method, its major advantages and disadvantages are presented here. The major advantages are:

1. Widespread applicability.
2. Provides a high level of "action oriented" information.
3. Relieves decision makers from routine and tedious decision making activities.
4. Adaptable to most approaches to management (e.g. management by objectives, management by costs, management by budget, etc.).
5. Improves utilization of organizational resources.

The major disadvantages are:

1. Requires a high level of systems analysis and design.
2. Requires a clear definition of how things are or should be.
3. Requires a large amount of data collection, storage, and processing activity.
4. Requires sophisticated hardware and software development.

5.4 Modeling Method

In Chapter 1, the impact of logico-mathematical models on data, and on information processing in general, was cited. The use of models to transform data into information is becoming increasingly important as a means of providing needed information to tactical level decision makers. In many instances, modeling is the only method which is capable of providing this information. While some logico-mathematical models require the model builder to possess a high degree of proficiency in mathematics, the vast majority of these models require a minimum of mathematical expertise on the part of the builder. In this section, a general overview of logico-mathematical models is provided in order to ensure proper perspective of where these models apply in the development of information systems.

A Definition of Model

In the broadest sense, a model is simply a representation of something else. In order to produce information, a model is usually a verbal or mathematical expression describing a set of relationships in a precise manner. A model can be useful simply in explaining or describing something, or it can be used to predict actions and events. Models can be classified in many different ways. In Figure 5.7, five different approaches to classifying models are illustrated.[1] Certainly, other attributes of a model could be chosen to provide still more classification schemes. However, the point is that in most organizations logico-mathematical models have a widespread applicability for providing information.

Appendix A provides a brief description of a selection of logico-mathematical models. The purpose of these descriptions is not to give the reader the necessary expertise to build or implement the models, but rather to convey an understanding as to how these models are uti-

---

[1] Summarized and adapted from Robert G. Murdick and Joel F. Ross, *Information Systems for Modern Management* (Englewood Cliffs, N.J.: Prentice-Hall, Inc., 1971) pp. 379–381. With permission from Prentice-Hall, Inc.

Class I   Function

Type	Characteristics	Examples
1. Descriptive	Descriptive models simply provide a "picture" of a situation and do not predict or recommend.	(a) Organization chart. (b) Plant layout diagram.
2. Predictive	Predictive models indicate that "if this occurs, then that will follow." They relate dependent and independent variables and permit trying out "what if" questions.	(a) $BE = F/(1 - v)$ which says that if fixed costs (F) are given, and variable costs as a fraction of sales (v) are known, then breakeven sales (BE) are predicted (deterministically). (b) $S(t) = aS(t - 1) + (1 - a)S(t - 2)$, which says that predicted sales for period t depend on sales for the previous two periods and a represents a weighting factor.
3. Normative	Normative models are those that provide the "best" answer to a problem. They provide recommended courses of action.	(a) Advertising budget model (b) Economic lot size model. (c) Marketing mix model.

Class II   Structure

Type	Characteristics	Examples
1. Iconic	Iconic models retain some of the physical characteristics of the things they represent.	(a) Scaled 3-dimensional mockup of a factory layout. (b) Blueprints of a warehouse. (c) Scale model of next year's automobile.
2. Analog	Analog models are those for which there is a substitution of components or processes to provide a parallel with what is being modelled.	An analog computer, in which components and circuits parallel marketing institutions, facilities, and processes so that by varying electrical inputs, the electrical outputs provide simulation of the marketing system outputs.
3. Symbolic	Symbolic models use symbols to describe the real world.	(a) $R = a[ln(A)] + b$, which says in symbols that sales response (R) equals a constant (a) times the natural log of advertising expenditure (A), plus another constant (b). (b) $TC = PC + CC + IC$, which says in symbols that total inventory cost (TC) equals purchase cost (PC) plus carrying cost (CC) plus item cost (IC).

Class III   Time Reference

Type	Characteristics	Examples
1. Static	Static models do not account for changes over time.	(a) Organization chart. (b) $E = P_1 S_1 + P_2 S_2$, which states that the expected profit (E) equals the probability (P_1) of the occurrence of payoff (S_1) multiplied by the value of the payoff

Class III   Time Reference *Continued.*

Type	Characteristics	Examples
		(S_1), plus the probability (P_2) of payoff (S_2) multiplied by the value of (S_2).
2. Dynamic	Dynamic models have time as an independent variable	$dS/dt = rA(t)(m - S)/M - \lambda s$, which gives the change in sales rate as a function of a response constant r, advertising rate (as a function of time) $A(t)$, sales saturation (M), sales rate (S), and sales decay constant (T).

Class IV   Uncertainty Reference

Type	Characteristics	Examples
1. Deterministic	For a specific set of input values, there is a uniquely determined output that represents the solution of a model under conditions of certainty.	Profit = Revenue − costs
2. Probabilistic	Probabilistic models involve probability distributions for inputs (or processes) and provide a range of values of at least one output variable (having a probability associated with each value). These models assist with decisions made under conditions of risk.	(a) Actuarial tables that give the probability of death as a function of age. (b) Return on investment (ROI) is simulated by using a probability distribution for each of the various costs and revenues with values selected by the Monte Carlo (random) technique.
3. Game	Game theory models attempt to develop optimum solutions in the face of complete ignorance or uncertainty. Games against nature and games of competition are subclassifications.	Two gasoline stations are adjacent to each other. One owner wonders: "Shall I raise or lower my price? If I raise mine, my competitor may raise or lower his. If I lower mine, he may raise or lower his. I know the gain or loss in any situation, but once each of us sets the price, we must keep it for the week. We can't collude."

Class V   Generality

Type	Characteristics	Examples
1. General	General models for business are models that have applications in several functional areas of business.	(a) Linear programming algorithm for all functional areas. (b) Waiting line model. Applications appear in production, marketing, and personnel.
2. Specialized	Specialized models are those that have application to a single functional area of business.	(a) Sales response as a function of advertising might be based on a unique set of equations. (b) The probabilistic bidding model has a single application to one functional area.

FIGURE 5.7.   An illustration of the various ways models can be classified.

lized to produce information. However, the reader *is* encouraged to pursue a further understanding of various models and the model building process by using some of the many references indicated.

The Model Building Process

In Chapter 1, the major steps involved in the model building process were identified. These steps are illustrated for reference at this time in Figure 5.8.

The "real world" situation in step 1 represents the environment in which the analyst is working. At this point the problem to be solved must be defined and the essential variables related to the problem abstracted. In step 2, the analyst must sequence and quantify the identified variables. Testing the model requires that the analyst process some data through the model and compare his output with his expectations or actual results. If the model has pro-

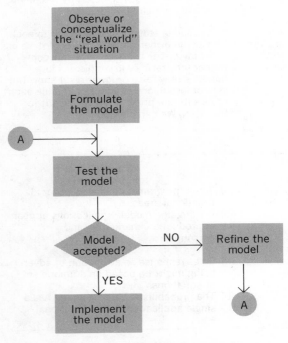

FIGURE 5.8.   An illustration of the modeling process.

duced acceptable output, the analyst may implement the model for use by organizational decision makers. On the other hand, if the outputs from the model are unacceptable, the analyst must continue to modify or add to the variables which comprise the model.

Advantages and Disadvantages

To summarize the discussion of the modeling method, the major advantages and disadvantages in using models are listed.

The major advantages to using models are that they:

1. Provide action oriented information.
2. Provide future oriented information.
3. Permit alternative courses of action to be evaluated before implementation.
4. Provide a formal, structured description of a complex problem situation.
5. Represent a scientific approach to replace intuition and speculation.

The major disadvantages are that:

1. Users of the model tend to lose sight of the fact that the model represents an abstraction of reality and not reality itself.
2. Qualitative factors such as experience and judgment are minimized or eliminated.
3. The model building process is often very difficult and expensive.
4. Potential users of the model often have a fear or resistance to change which results in difficulties implementing the model.
5. Many models assume linearity which is not applicable to most "real world" situations.

5.5 Interrogative Method

In all of the methods presented thus far in this chapter, the information system disseminates information without any action on the recipient's part. In the interrogation method, the decision maker is required to request needed information from the system. This method of providing information is extremely valuable since many decision makers are unable to identify what information is necessary to perform their duties until the situation confronts them.

Definition of the Interrogative Method

To interrogate means to question, and this is the basic premise underlying the interrogative method. The interrogative method is a micro, interactive concept applicable to any individual who requests a response based upon a specific interrogation of the data base. The essential elements of this method are: (1) the information requestor needs only to format or structure his inquiry and submit it to some access mechanism or interface, and (2) the information is presented to the requestor both in a relevant and usable format, and time period. To implement the interrogative method, it is necessary that an extensive data base exist, organized in a manner where a variety of users can access needed data elements.

While aspects of this method can be implemented within a manual or electromechanical environment, recent advancements in computer technology have significantly expanded the potential applications for implementing the interrogative method.

Examples of the Interrogative Method

The production or manufacturing environment in many organizations provides several opportunities to utilize the interrogative method. For example, employees can receive work assignments from a computer via a terminal device such as a teletype or CRT simply by identifying themselves, their work station, and requesting their next job assignment. A message is displayed giving the next job order number and operation, the location of the material, manufacturing information, and a list of necessary tools and their location.

In addition, employees can use these terminals to record their attendance and overtime, job requests, job completions, material and tool receipts and issues, the results of all inspec-tions, and their shift–end accomplishments as they leave for the day. In return, the plant (and other) managers can retrieve, via their own terminals, a broad spectrum of information including:[2]

1. Long-term backlog behind critical facilities.
2. Short-term backlog behind each facility and work station.
3. Up-to-the-minute status of every order-in-work.
4. Promised dates on all orders.
5. Location of all tools in the plant.
6. Status of all purchase orders.
7. Complete inspection and quality control information.
8. Status of work-in-process as to percentage completion.

An order entry system provides a second example of the applicability of the interrogative method.[3] In the order entry system, the salesman or desk clerk in a field location communicates with the system via a CRT linked to the computer and common data base by a telephone line. Users complete a telephone connection with the computer and enter their identifying authentication. A list of functions available to the user are then displayed. For example, the user may enter a customer order into the file, cancel an order, alter an order, reschedule an order, or obtain an inquiry response relative to sales performance items. An example of a gross transaction display is illustrated in Figure 5.9.

The user makes a selection by depressing the appropriate key. If key "2" is depressed, an order entry transaction is displayed upon the screen. An example of this response is shown in Figure 5.10.

Next, an order entry form can be displayed providing a background form which consists

[2] T. A. LaRoe, "A Manufacturing Plant Information System," *Proceedings Third Annual Conference* September 9 & 10, 1971 (Chicago, Illinois: The Society for Management Information Systems, 1971), p. 20. With permission.
[3] This example based on: Joseph F. Kelly, *Computerized Management Information Systems,* (New York: The Macmillan Company, 1970), Chapter 4. With permission.

CRT Screen

```
Gross Transaction Display
   1. Customer Record Control
   2. Order entry control/old customer
   3. Billing, taxes, and freight information
   4. Sales administration
   5. Inquiry
   6. Order entry control/new customer
   OPERATOR: MAKE A SELECTION
```

FIGURE 5.9.   CRT Display of Gross Transaction.

CRT Screen

```
Order Entry Transaction Display
   1. Order
   2. Alteration
   3. Cancellation
   4. Reschedule
   5. Special Request message
   6. Administration request message
   OPERATOR: MAKE A SELECTION
```

FIGURE 5.10.   CRT Display of Order Entry Transaction

CRT Screen

```
        Order Entry Form Display
Customer Name          Customer Number

Address                Date

Sales Location         Salesman

Purchase Plan

Item Number    Quantity   Price
```

FIGURE 5.11.   CRT Display of Order Entry Form.

CRT Screen

```
Display Customer Record
   1. Credit Status
   2. Sales History
   3. Payment History
   4. Billing Instruction
   ENTER LINE NUMBER/CUSTOMER
   NUMBER
```

FIGURE 5.12.   CRT Display of Customer Record.

of customer name, customer identification number, address, date, sales location, salesman, purchase plan (such as sale or lease), plus the items ordered. When the operator depresses the "1" key, the form shown in Figure 5.11 is displayed on the CRT screen and the clerk makes the proper entries.

When an entry has been completed, the order is checked against other constraints in the system such as credit status, inventory availability, and so on. If the final order is accepted by the system, then the order is processed in accordance with predetermined criteria. This process, incidentally, is an example of programmed decision making at the technical level. The order entry system is comprised basically of three files: the customer master file, inventory master file, and sales-performance file. All three are updated along with any others that are required. Also, all necessary documents are prepared for transactional data processing. This design concept reduces the amount of paper processing, especially in the branch office and warehouse locations. The inquiry capability into administrative areas replaces extensive file requirements and the need for operational and information clerical personnel in branch offices, various departments, and warehouses. For most organizations the order entry provides basic data because this event triggers an input into almost every functional area of the organization. It is possible to develop this method to fit the requirements of different decision makers by making it as complex (or simple) as can be economically justified.

These files must accommodate a series of transactions that can be accessed by users other than the sales department. For instance, the credit department needs the following information illustrated in Figure 5.12.

An interrogative method such as that described above requires a method of ensuring data security and integrity. Certain changes are initiated by various operators throughout the organization. Control is exercised, however, to ensure that a department or branch office changes only that part of the files over which it would normally exercise control. For example, a branch office could change address data for a given customer but could not, on the other hand, change the customer's credit status. The statistical data contained in the sales performance file could not be changed from a local branch office, and so on.

The sales department has normally received its information based on a weekly report with a month-end summary. However, for information to be effective it must not be only relevant but timely. Only the decision maker who knows what is happening in a department as soon as it happens can effectively adjust means to objectives. So, in addition to the periodic reports, action oriented information is needed. Periodic reports provide a useful means of making historical analyses and highlighting present status and trends. These reports also can be easily provided via the remote terminal. Inquiry information is supplied to the user who requires responses from the system on a non-routine basis. This type of information gives to the user a specific response based on a specific inquiry and usually results in some action being taken by the user.

The opportunities for implementing the interrogative method are restricted only by the imagination of the analyst. Financial data can be stored regarding closings and financial planning. Displays of orders entered for a specific time period, sales billed, and income-after-taxes to date, can all be made instantaneously. Sales managers can also interrogate sales statistics files for information pertaining to market participation, product performance, salesmen penetration, customer activity, and up-to-date forecasting information, to mention only a few possibilities.

Advantages and Disadvantages

To summarize the discussion of the interrogative method the major advantages and disadvantages related to its implementation and use are listed.

The major advantages of the interrogative method are:

1. Widespread applicability.
2. Permits each decision maker to obtain relevant, specific information when it is required.

3. Allows previously unanticipated inquiries to be entered and processed.
4. Reduces paper work and paper pollution.
5. Reduces the time required to disseminate information.
6. Supports other methods of producing information such as filtering, monitoring, and modeling.
7. Alleviates organizational controversy by allowing each decision maker independent access to a common data base.

The major disadvantages of the interrogative method are:

1. Requires an expensive investment in data processing resources. This includes not only hardware, but also systems analysts and programmers who must design, develop, and implement this method.
2. Although sound in concept, it has proved to be almost impossible to provide the necessary data base required to respond to more than a small percentage of requests that one or more decision makers can structure.

5.6 External Method

In Chapter 1, we indicated that in most organizations the automation of data and information processing was initially concentrated in traditional bookkeeping areas. Subsequent efforts were directed at providing relevant information concerning the organization's operations to technical and tactical decision makers. With rare exceptions, formal information systems have failed to provide information to assist strategic decision makers. This failure is due, mainly, to the very nature of strategic decision making. In general, strategic decision makers are concerned with decisions related to the overall development, growth, and plans of the organization. The forces which affect these decisions include political, social, economic, and competitive activities. Moreover, these decisions are usually of a once only nature and are arrived at within the framework of those organizational policies and objectives in effect at the time.

This type of information is often termed "intelligence" information and is gathered from sources such as newspapers, trade journals, government reports, demographic studies, marketing surveys, and so forth. Although there is a limited utility regarding the "intelligence" that can be provided by a computer based information system, the systems analyst can be effective in providing this information in the following manner:

1. By making publications available for quick dissemination through the use of collating, indexing, and document retrieval.

2. By gathering and summarizing documents from the government affecting the organization, e.g., truth in packaging, wage and price control, foreign trade, economic indicators, consumer affairs, foreign exchange rates, stock exchange information, and so forth.

3. By making studies to highlight: population trends, data on research activities, developments in the money market, general trading and stock trends, and developing technology.

This external information has come into many organizations, on a somewhat spasmodic and informal basis, through general reading and occasional studies by management personnel. This informal approach becomes inadequate when organizations grow larger and more complex. A point is reached where external information has to be communicated in a formal manner, rather than being acquired through the occasional collections and observations of the decision maker himself.

Presently, there are movements in many trade associations directed at providing economic and marketing data in a format which would allow participating companies to input this data into the formal information system for dissemination to strategic decision makers. This information could be reported on its own merit or in conjunction with internally generated information. For example, a strategic decision maker might be given a report showing his products' sales, the overall value of the market, and the percentage of the market captured. If capturing a certain percentage of the market is one of the organization's objectives, the actual share might be compared to the objective.

The Census Bureau is another source of external data which might lend itself to being incorporated in the formal information system.

Early in 1973, the Census Bureau will start collecting information for reports on economic activity in 1972 in areas such as manufacturing, mining and quarrying, construction industries, and others. These censuses are taken at 5-year intervals and are the primary source of facts about the structure and functioning of the economy.

Businesses will use the data to gauge potential markets, to make economic or sales forecasts, to analyze sales performance, to lay out sales territories, to allocate sums for advertising, to decide on locations for new plants, warehouses, or stores, and many other purposes. Trade and professional associations will use the information to study trends in the businesses of their members and of competitive businesses. Federal, state, and local governments, Chambers of Commerce, and other groups will use the data to better understand particular economic situations.[4]

Another approach to providing external information to decision makers in various organizations, in a more structured fashion, is to secure the services of organizations especially designed to provide this type of information.

When (and, some sceptics say, if) the information bank passes its in-house tests later this year, it will enable users to access and display on their video terminals information which has appeared in the *Times,* or in some 35 other periodicals, within the last three to five years. An invaluable marketing, investing or financial research tool, users will be able to search through the several million article abstracts using any of 11,000 subject terms. As evidenced by preliminary demonstrations of the system, a user can, within seconds, find out what has been printed on such diverse

---

[4] "Economic Census to Cover 1972 Activity," *Automation,* October, 1972, p. 8. With permission. Copyright 1972, The Penton Publishing Co., Cleveland, Ohio 44114.

topics as a foreign nation's investment policies, consumer attitudes toward specific corporations or specific products, or agricultural production in the midwest. And he can do it without complex or confusing codes.[5]

In essence, the systems analyst must be aware that if a formal information system is to serve all levels of decision making, information generated outside the organization must be collected, processed, and reported.

SUMMARY

Since there are different levels of decision making, it would seem to follow that there would also have to be different kinds of information to specifically serve these levels.

To a large extent, the strategic decision maker needs filtered, future-oriented, and external information. Formal information systems are severely limited as to how much relevant information it can provide this level of decision making. At the present time it appears that information systems are substantially more effective, and serve users better, at the tactical and technical decision making levels. However, there is still a great potential for analysts to serve strategic level decision makers better than in the past.

Informational requirements at all levels can

[5] Richard M. Laska, "All the News That's Fit to Retrieve," *Computer Decisions,* August 1972, pp. 18–22. With permission.

be met more effectively if the analyst and user will work together to tailor the information output to fit the user's needs. Systems producing and disseminating volumes of irrelevant data to users are good data processors, but poor information processors. The information systems analyst can improve the effectiveness of information output by the following five basic methods: (1) filtering method, (2) monitoring method, (3) modeling method, (4) interrogative method, and (5) external method.

The filtering method is based on the premise that various levels of decision makers require various levels of detail information to perform their duties. The higher the level of decision making, the less detail information required. The monitoring method allows the system to keep a close check on the flow of data and automatically reports information only when certain criteria are met. The three basic forms of the monitoring method are: (1) variance reporting, (2) programmed decision making, and (3) automatic notification. The modeling method utilizes various logico-mathematical models to transform data into information. This method provides information which is predictive in nature. The interrogative method relies on the decision maker to format a specific query to the data base to meet a specific but previously unanticipated need to know. The external method refers to gathering information which is generated outside of the organization. This method is directed toward providing relevant information for strategic decision makers.

REVIEW QUESTIONS

5.1 In your own words, prepare a definition of the Filtering Method. Give two examples of how this method is implemented.

5.2 Discuss fully the meaning of threshold of detail. Give at least one example where a strategic decision maker of your choice would need a greater degree of detail.

5.3 Compare and contrast the several ways of implementing the Monitoring Method. Give two examples of each type.

5.4 What is the major difficulty associated with implementing the Monitoring Method? Suggest two ways this difficulty can be minimized or overcome.

5.5 What is a model? Illustrate at least three different ways a systems analyst can utilize models.

5.6 List and define the major steps in the model building process.

5.7 Compare and contrast the Modeling Method to the Monitoring Method.

5.8 Define the Interrogative Method. Contrast this method to both the Filtering and Monitoring methods.

5.9 Using sales data as a reference, discuss the difficulties encountered in implementing the Interrogative Method.

5.10 What is external information? Explain the difference between external and informal information.

QUESTIONS
FOR
DISCUSSION

5.1 Why be concerned with tailoring information to management requirements? Discuss fully.

5.2 Former President Eisenhower had a high level of threshold for detail, whereas Secretary of Defense McNamara, in Johnson's administration had a low threshold level. Discuss.

5.3 "I'm sure I have all of the information I need in this situation. Unfortunately, I have too much." Discuss.

5.4 "The major difficulty in implementing programmed decision making with the computer is that a few decision makers truly understand the decision making process." Evaluate this comment as it relates to the systems analyst function.

5.5 "We don't worry about trying to tailor information to fit management's needs. We just store the data in the files and if management wants a report, we generate it." Discuss this comment.

5.6 "Decision makers must guard against the unconscious development of a narrow perspective when dealing with information on an exception basis only." Discuss.

5.7 "The use of models for assisting decision makers simply adds a scientific feeling to old fashion guessing." Evaluate.

5.8 "Interrogation is a great concept, but it is not much use to the small organization who cannot afford sophisticated computer systems." Prepare an answer to this comment.

5.9 "A true management information system has not yet been implemented." Discuss why this statement is both true and false.

5.10 List at least five sources of formal information that originates external to most commercial organizations and could be integrated into the formal information system of that organization.

5.11 "My responsibility is long range planning. I don't see how you (systems analyst) can help me directly." Provide some suggestions as to how this function can be assisted by a formal information system.

5.12 "We spend so much time designing and developing systems that by the time we implement the system, the decision makers have changed and so have the information requirements." Evaluate.

EXERCISES

5.1 As best you can, illustrate schematically a simple system, utilizing the interrogative method, from both centralization and decentralization of authority. Do you believe that the design of your system is dependent upon either approach? Discuss.

5.2 How can the implementation of the external method help the strategic level decision maker? Investigate the needs of this kind of a decision maker in an organization of your choice and attempt to define his other external informational needs.

5.3 Interview a technical decision maker associated with the administration of your school and identify at least one possibility for implementing programmed decision making. Illustrate the decision process with a flowchart or decision table.

5.4 Prepare a report describing the decision making process you used when selecting your school.

5.5 Assume that you are the owner-manager of a local discount department store. You have no computer facilities but you do employ several clerical persons for data processing. Reporting to you are the supervisors of three selling units, the credit department, security, purchasing, and customer service. What formal information would you desire for each departmental supervisor: (a) hourly; (b) daily; (c) weekly; and (d) monthly? What information would you require from these departments in the same time periods?

5.6 Life insurance agents are concerned not only with securing new policy holders but also with maintaining and upgrading existing policy holders. All large insurance companies are prominent in the use of computers for processing data and information. Focusing on the specific tailoring method of monitoring, and taking advantage of a large data base and sophisticated hardware, list several ways the information system can provide information to assist the agent in servicing existing policy holders.

PROBLEMS

5.1 Select an organization of your choice and, from the management group, interview at least one top level manager to determine if any one method or a combination of methods as outlined in this chapter would help in his other decision making process. Write a two page report disclosing the results of your interview.

5.2 From the material that you have read in the chapter, plus the material in the Appendices, discuss the computer hardware configuration required to support the interrogative method.

5.3 Prepare a series of reports, utilizing the Filtering Method, which might be implemented at your university to reflect student enrollments in individual classes, majors, schools, etc.

5.4 You are a systems analyst employed by a data processing service bureau. One of the specialties of your organization is to provide keypunch service to other organizations in the area in addition to supporting your own operations. Much of this special keypunch effort involves large jobs in short time periods. The goal of your organization is to provide a firm cost estimate for each job to the prospective customer. You employ approximately 100 punchers both full and part time. The manager of the service bureau has requested you to design an information system which will assist him to plan and control the keypunch operations. You have investigated the situation and determined the following:

1. A sampling of work indicates that there are three primary factors related to the time (and therefore cost) needed to complete a job: (a) the experience level of the puncher; (b) the number of strokes per card punched; and (c) the format of the source document from which the data is entered.

2. You have classified punchers as: (a) trainees; (b) juniors; and (c) seniors. A trainee is considered to have a productivity factor of 75%, a junior 100%, and a senior 125%.

3. Source documents are classified as: (a) formatted, or (b) mixed. A junior puncher can punch 10,000 strokes an hour from a formatted source document and 8000 strokes an hour from a mixed document.

4. The keypunch machine has a memory capability to keep track of the number of strokes punched in a job. When the operator indicates end of job, the machine will punch a card which contains the number of strokes punched in the job.

5. Approximately 40% of the keypunch work done by the service bureau is repetitive.

6. The service bureau has a computer with both card and magnetic tape, batch processing capabilities.

Requirements for Solution:

In your design proposal include the following:
    (1) A flow diagram, and narrative, describing the system.
    (2) An analysis of a simple planning model which could be used.
    (3) The informational outputs available for use in both planning and controlling activities.

5.5 Old New England Leather is a large manufacturer and marketer of quality leather goods. The product line ranges from wallets to saddles. Because of the prevailing management philosophy at Old New England Leather, the company will accept orders for almost any leather product to be custom made on demand. This is possible since the leather craftsmen employed by the company perform a job in its entirety, i.e. the company does not utilize production line techniques. Each leather craftsman is responsible for the complete manufacturing of a given product. Currently, the company employs about 150 leather craftsmen and has been growing at the rate of 20% the last three years. However, management does not anticipate this growth rate in the future, but instead sees a steady growth rate of 5% over the next ten years.

Old New England Leather markets a proprietary line of leather goods worldwide. However, these stock products compose only 50% of the output from the craftsmen. The remaining products are produced to special order. When a custom order is received, the specifications for the order are posted along with an expected shipping date. Each craftsman is then eligible to bid on the order or a part of it. Once the bids are evaluated, the company determines which individual has agreed upon the date, and accepts the lowest bid for production. It is this custom part of the business which has shown the greatest growth in recent years. During the last 12 months, there has been an average of 600 orders in process at any one time.

Along with growth, Old New England Leather management has incurred many problems related to providing consistent, on time delivery. It appears that the skill craftsmen often fail to report on a timely basis when a job is complete. In addition, management has never had a satisfactory control for ensuring that orders are worked on in a priority sequence. Other problems, such as a craftsman over committing himself in a given time period or simply losing an order, are also becoming serious.

The company leases a medium size computer for processing payroll, inventory, accounts receivable, accounts payable, and so forth. This computer has capabilities for online processing with as many as 20 terminals. Currently, there are ten terminals in operation throughout the plant.

Propose a system for controlling the production of orders which will benefit the craftsmen, management, and the company's customers.

BIBLIOGRAPHY

"Economic Census to Cover 1972 Activity," *Automation,* October, 1972.

Kelly, *Computerized Management Information Systems,* New York: The Macmillan Company, 1970.

LaRoe, "A Manufacturing Plant Information System," *Proceedings Third Annual Conference,* Chicago, Illinois: The Society for Management Information Systems, 1971.

Laska, "All the News That's Fit to Retrieve," *Computer Decisions,* August, 1972.

Murdick and Ross, *Information Systems for Modern Management,* Englewood Cliffs, N.J.: Prentice-Hall, Inc., 1971.

Ream, "On-Line Management Information," *Datamation,* March, 1964.

Introduction
to Data Base
Concepts

6 The Data Base—An Overview

6.1 Introduction

Throughout Part I, many of the major concepts related to data and information processing were identified and analyzed. It was emphasized repeatedly that modern organizations have a continuing need to collect, process, and store large quantities of data in order to obtain that information necessary for effective decision making. Moreover, in most organizations, for reasons of volume, complexity, timing, and computational demands, this collected data must be stored in a format capable of being processed by a computer. The purpose of Part II is to present and analyze the major concepts related to developing a computer accessible data base.

In this chapter a general discussion of the data base is presented in order to demonstrate its importance in overall information systems development, and to provide a perspective for the more specific subjects treated in the remaining chapters. Chapter 7 is devoted to the essential functions of classifying data and designing coding structures. Chapter 8 concentrates on the general considerations related to file storage. Chapter 9 analyzes the concepts of data structure and record association.

In order to attain a complete understanding of data base design and structure, it is necessary to consider both physical and logical aspects pertinent to the data base. In Part II the emphasis is placed on the logical concepts of the data base. The physical aspects of computer accessible data bases are noted only when they are necessary to explain more clearly the logical concepts. The reader is urged to refer to Appendix B for an in depth discussion or review of physical aspects as necessary.

The specific objectives of this chapter are:

1. To provide a basic understanding of the structure and function of the data base.
2. To present an explanation of data base management.
3. To identify the advantages and disadvantages of generalized data base management systems.
4. To explain the basic components necessary for implementing a sophisticated data base and data base management system.

6.2 Definition of Data Base

The term data has already been discussed extensively in Part I and at this point it should be fairly well established that information is knowledge derived from processes performed on data. However, the term "base" has not been discussed, nor has a great deal of time been spent on analyzing the data base concept.

In essence most dictionaries agree that the term base means the support, foundation, or key ingredient of anything. Therefore, base supports data and data are the raw material of information.

It would seem to follow that the data base must, therefore, be the foundation of the information system. As a matter of fact, any serious efforts made toward the development of a sophisticated information system will quickly indicate that the establishment of a data base is essential. And also that the primary function of the data base is the service and support of the information system which justifies its cost.

General Structure of the Data Base

A data base is composed of a logical scheme of elements which can be characterized as the structure of the data base. This structure is illustrated in Figure 6.1.

In a typical organization, data are stored in computer accessible media, and noncomputer accessible media such as filing cabinets, ledgers, tub files, and microfilm. In essence, all of this data belongs to that organization's data base. However, we are at this time directing our attention only to data that are computer accessible.

The smallest data element in the data base is usually termed a field. Some examples of data fields are shown in Figure 6.2.

A field is a meaningful data element to some user of that element. The data contained in a field can be either alphabetic, numeric, a special character, or some combination thereof. A field can contain, in theory, 1 or N number of characters; any restrictions imposed on a field are due to the specific hardware or software processing that field.

A collection of logically related fields forms a record. Some examples of records are illustrated in Figure 6.3. Any restriction on the size

Data Base

| Files |
| Records |
| Fields |

FIGURE 6.1.   Logical data structure of the data base.

Field Name	Field Contents
Customer name	Jack & John Supply Co.
Customer number	175483
Order quantity	1200
Record code	*
Unit of measure	DZ
Color	Lt. Rose
Credit limit	50,000

FIGURE 6.2.   Examples of data fields.

Customer Record

Field Name	Field Contents
Customer name	Ajax Mfg.
Street address	388 River St.
City, state, zip code	Port Tag, Oh 44113
Credit limit	100,000
Year to date sales	2,500,000
Accounts receivable balance	75,000

Product Record

Field Name	Field Contents
Product number	1753248
Description	Tape Dispenser
Quantity on hand	107,542
Unit of measure	Each
Cost per u/m	1.25
Location	AJ105

FIGURE 6.3.   Examples of data records.

Employee	Accounts receivable
Product	Inventory
Customer	Sales history
Vendor	Payroll
Assets	Accounts payable
Purchases	Open orders

FIGURE 6.4.   A partial listing of typical files in an organization.

of a record is imposed by the hardware and software utilized to process that record.

A collection of logically related records forms a file. Any restriction imposed on a file content or size is the result of the limitations of the hardware and/or software processing that file. A partial listing of files typically found in most organizations is shown in Figure 6.4.

The data base, then, is a consolidation of files. There may or may not exist a logical relationship among data files in the data base. For example, a customer name and address file has a logical relationship to an open order file, an accounts receivable file, and a sales file. On the other hand, the vendor file has no implied logical relationship to any of the above named files but does relate to the purchases file.

Whether or not this logical relationship is a real relationship depends upon the overall design of the information system in the organization. As discussed in Chapter 4 of Part I, the hierarchial approach to systems design does not necessarily relate one data file to another. The systems approach to information systems design does organize data files in a manner so that two or more processing functions can be performed with minimal repetition of data elements and processing activities. The advantages and disadvantages of integrating data files in the data base will be discussed in more detail in subsequent sections of this chapter.

Physical Versus Logical Files

Physically, a file is associated with DASD (direct access storage devices) computer storage media such as magnetic disk, magnetic drum, and data cells; or with sequential media such as magnetic tape, punched paper tape, or a tray of punched cards. It should be understood at this point that a logical file may extend across more than one physical file or a physical file may contain only one logical file or multiple logical files.

It is paramount that the designer clearly define and maintain the distinction between the physical world of data bases and the corresponding logical world.

It is unfortunate that the disagreement which exists today, concerning the role and definition of the data base in information processing, is due almost entirely to the failure to separate physical and logical concepts. The academic and research communities are tempted to ignore the physical, while the hardware salesman is prone to ignore the logical. The momentary stance of any given manufacturer of processors and peripherals or suppliers of software can be traced directly to their ability or inability to accommodate both worlds.[1]

Figure 6.5 illustrates the logical/physical file relationship. As mentioned earlier, a discussion

[1] John K. Lyon, *An Introduction to Data Base Design* (New York: Wiley–Interscience a Division of John Wiley & Sons, Inc., 1971), p. 5. With permission.

One Logical File Over Multiple Physical Files

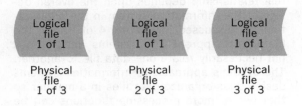

Physical file 1 of 3   Physical file 2 of 3   Physical file 3 of 3

One Physical File Containing Multiple Logical Files

Physical file 1

One Logical File Contained in One Physical File

Physical file 1

FIGURE 6.5. Illustration of logical/physical file relationship.

of the data base requires a separation of the physical concepts from the logical concepts even though there is obvious interaction between the two. Moreover, to a great degree, logical organization and storage considerations are guided by physical considerations.

Physical means of storing data have existed for thousands of years. Early data storage media include such things as clay tablets. However, clay tablets were clumsy and awkward to handle and, thus, to a great degree any manipulation of data was restricted. Later, large masses of data were stored in books, journals, ledgers, and so forth. Still later, data were stored in cards to allow the mechanization of data access and manipulation. Today we have devices which store data on magnetic surfaces so that these data are accessed and manipulated via electronic computers.

Relative to magnetic media, tape can quite adequately store large masses of data, but the variety of possible approaches to data organization and storage is limited. To provide direct retrieval of data elements, one must utilize DASD.

With the advent of DASD, telecommunication, terminals, and modulation/demodulation devices, the design, organization, and storage of data has, to a great degree, allowed the user to become independent of the hardware. This condition allows data to be organized in a manner that meets the users' requirements, rather than the requirements of the hardware.

The most sophisticated computer configuration containing online DASD and terminals is no better than the software which supports it. To implement a particular data base design, certain hardware constraints must be met, but, in addition, there must be software which supports the basic access methods to the data files.

Within an integrated data base, the logical organization of data is cross-referenced and interrelated with respect to particular functions for various informational requirements. This integration of related items is accomplished by chains, pointers, and indexes, etc., which are discussed in Chapter 9. It is the responsibility of the designer(s) of the software systems to organize the data to accommodate user requirements. This organization is effected by logical methods that can permit any combination of data elements to be retrieved from any number of different (or single) storage devices, in any manner or order desired.

6.3 Data Base Management

In the last section the structural aspects of the data base were emphasized in the discussion. Perhaps equally important for acquiring a basic understanding of the data base, is a consideration of the activities required to enter data into the data base, to control data stored in it, and to report information from it. Many terms are used to describe these activities collectively, such as "update and retrieval," "file management," "data management," "data administration," "data base management," and so

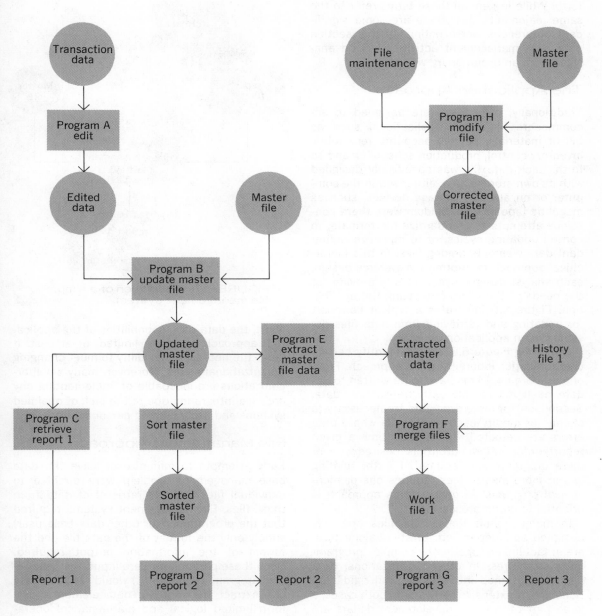

FIGURE 6.6. Illustration of updating and retrieving data files in an application approach.

forth. While in general these terms refer to the same major activities, there are some significant differences worth noting. In this section data base management activities will be analyzed from an evolutionary viewpoint.

The Application Approach

Traditionally, data files were designed to accommodate individual applications, such as bill of materials, payroll, accounts receivable, inventory control, production scheduling and so forth. Each data file was specifically designed with its own storage area, either within the computer or on auxiliary storage devices, such as magnetic tape or disk. Seldom were there conscious attempts to standardize file formats, to control updating cycles, or to minimize redundant data elements among files. In this hierarchical approach to information systems design, each analyst designed their files to provide for the needs of the users requesting the application. Figure 6.6 illustrates a typical flowchart for updating and retrieving from data files designed in an application approach.

Reviewing Figure 6.6, we can identify certain characteristics inherent in this approach. First, one or more programs have to be written to update each master file with transaction data. Second, one or more programs are necessary to change or modify each master file where data errors are detected. Third, each time a given report (information output) is desired one or more programs are required. Fourth, relating two or more master files requires one or more special programs. In general, this approach is oriented to batch processing.

In many organizations, data files originally designed as independent, or stand-alone files, are in fact linked together by complex programming structures. In other organizations, data files are designed into specific and rigid relationships by extensive software. In both cases, a large part of systems development dollars are spent on customizing programs to perform the data base management activities. In addition, each time a data file is modified or a reporting requirement is changed, a large investment is required to modify the customized software. In

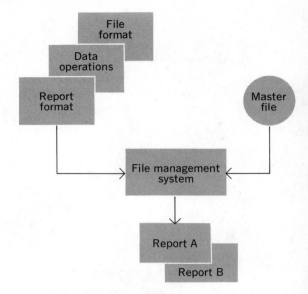

FIGURE 6.7. Illustration of a simple file management system.

short, the data base capabilities of the application approach are quite limited, or at best, it lacks the necessary flexibility to meet changing organizational needs. Moreover, many small organizations are incapable of implementing any data file integration due to the lack of qualified systems and programming personnel.

File Management Approach

Early attempts to minimize or solve the data base management problem were directed to individual files and the retrieval of data from these files. File management systems required that the programmer (or other data base user) supply only the format of the data file and the format of the information output required. Once these parameters were input, the generalized program (or programs) would read the data file, extract the required data elements, perform limited logical and mathematical operations, and format the informational output. Figure 6.7 illustrates this procedure.

As development efforts for file management systems progressed, the following improvements were implemented:

1. Capabilities for processing more than one file.

2. Capabilities for processing files organized in some manner other than sequentially.

3. Expanded logical and mathematical capabilities.

4. Capacity for more than one form of informational output.

5. Capability for processing with interactive devices such as CRT's and teletypes.

The terms "data management system" and "data base management system" began to replace "file management system" as further improvements were made in (1) the ability to update and perform maintenance, (2) the ability to access the same file with two or more programs simultaneously, and (3) the separation of the file format from the application programs accessing the file.

The Generalized Data Base Management Approach

The major purposes of the generalized data base management approach are:

1. To effect data independence.
2. To reduce data duplication.
3. To logically relate and make the data consistent with the functional aspects of the organization's users.
4. To reduce application, storage, and processing costs.

Data independence provides a capability that allows data to be used by more than one program concurrently. It also allows a change in data definition to occur without a concomitant change in programs. Traditionally, files have been established to accommodate a single program having a data description contained within it (e.g., DATA DIVISION of COBOL).

Data independence is a capability frequently identified as required for data base management systems. The term 'data independence' remains to achieve a widely accepted rigorous definition. It can be taken to imply some degree of insulation between a program and the data with which the program

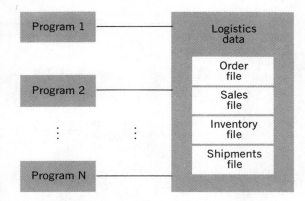

FIGURE 6.8. Data base approach to file structure and processing.

interacts. Depending on the extent of that insulation, programs can accommodate varying degrees of change in the definition and structure of that data, without it being necessary to modify the program or possibly recompile it.[2]

The generalized data base management approach attempts to alleviate these problems by combining data elements on the basis of logical relationships, commonalities, and also by separating the data description from the programming. For example, the data elements of the files illustrated in Figure 6.8, are integrated into one logical file accessible by several programs. The total number of these programs depends on the required retrieval, processing, and updating applications.

In the above approach data elements are organized and stored on the basis of logical relationships and the data description is contained within the file. No longer is the programming function dependent upon data description. Data redundancy has been reduced and the updating of each item in the data base occurs simultaneously.

The generalized data base management approach does not necessarily assume one massive data file with all data elements con-

[2] CODASYL Systems Committee Technical Report, *Feature Analysis of Generalized Data Base Management Systems* (New York: Association of Computing Machinery, May, 1971), p. 20.

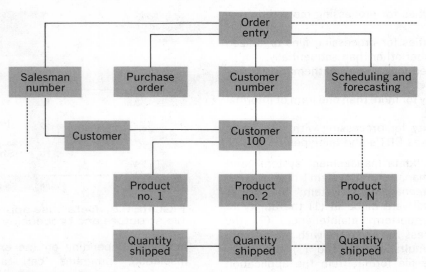

FIGURE 6.9. Partial illustration of data organized to meet the needs of a variety of users.

tained therein. However, as shown in Figure 6.9, it does assume a logically and functionally unified subsystem of files where data are accessed by a number of users to meet a variety of informational and data processing requirements.

As shown in Figure 6.9, the data elements are functionally related where a number of updates and retrievals can be made. For example, data elements are updated simultaneously as affected by transactions or events; forecasting and scheduling plans are kept current; general and specific sales performance information can be accessed at any time; quantity-on-hand of inventory items is kept current; analysis of customers' profitability can be obtained readily; and sales by product, customer, or salesman can be made available quickly.

The result of data independence is that the cost of application programming is reduced. With a more traditional approach, each time there is a request for a new information report, an application programmer must write a new program along with a full description of the data used.

There are many groups studying and developing techniques for the advancement of general-

ized data base management systems and data base design.[3] Moreover, there are a number of organizations involved in developing and marketing various types of generalized data base management systems.

Generalized data base management systems are developed and marketed today under various generic names. Such appellations as data management system, generalized information retrieval system, information management system, and file management system are the main terms in use. The more elementary systems search a sequential file having simple record facilities. More elaborate systems handle several files via indexes or links and function in an online mode. The number of ways in which these systems may vary is at least as numerous as the number of distinct features listed in the revised survey,

[3] Example: Data Base Task Group, operating under the CODASYL (Conference on Data Systems Languages) Programming Language Committee CODASYL is a voluntary group of interested persons, supported by their own organizations, who contribute their efforts toward the development of techniques and languages for data base development and administration.

and a user trying to select among the enormous variety of systems available faces a difficult evaluation problem.[4]

To fully implement an information system through the systems approach, some form of generalized data base management system is required. This system can either be developed by the organization or purchased as a package. In the next section some of the advantages and disadvantages of implementing an integrated data base with a generalized data base management system will be examined.

6.4 Analysis of Generalized Data Base Management Systems

There is a great possibility that not all organizations can afford or in fact need to implement a generalized data base management system. Many organizations can probably operate just as effectively using a simple batch system, with nonrelated sequential files, and a library of programs. The decision whether or not to implement the data base approach is based primarily on the requirements and objectives of the users. Some organizations have certain applications, objectives, and situations which lend themselves naturally to the use of the generalized data base management system.

Features of a Generalized Data Base Management System

The CODASYL Programming Language Committee Data Base Task Group is perhaps the leading group researching the problem of just what should be included in a generalized data base management system. Their recommendations are:[5]

1. Allow data to be structured in the manner most suitable to each application, regardless of

the fact that some or all of that data may be used by other applications—such flexibility to be achieved without requiring data redundancy.

2. Allow more than one run-unit to concurrently retrieve or update the data in the data base.

3. Provide and permit the use of a variety of search strategies against an entire data base or portions of a data base.

4. Provide protection of the data base against unauthorized access of data and from untoward interaction of programs.

5. Provide for centralized capability to control the physical placement of data.

6. Provide device independence for programs.

7. Allow the declaration of a variety of data structures ranging from those in which no connection exists between data–items to network structures.

8. Allow the user to interact with the data while being relieved of the mechanics of maintaining the structural associations which have been declared.

9. Allow programs to be as independent as possible of the data in the data base and of the data known to a program.

10. Provide for a description of the data base which is not restricted to any particular processing language.

11. Provide an architecture which permits the description of the data base, and the data base itself, to be interfaced by multiple processing languages.

Advantages and Disadvantages of Generalized Data Base Management Systems

The advantages of the generalized data base management system are:

1. Ability to organize data in a manner which is suitable and appropriate to the interrelated functions of the organization.

2. Data description is contained in the data base independent from programming functions, thus relieving programmers of data management.

---

[4] CODASYL Systems Committee Technical Report, *op. cit.,* p. 15.

[5] "Data Base Task Group Report," (New York: Association for Computing Machinery, April, 1971), pp. 6–7.

3. Ability to provide users with a direct interface with the data base.

4. Allows more integration of data elements to minimize redundancy.

5. Ability to grow without a major overhaul of the system.

6. Gives faster response to user needs.

7. Allows users to interrogate the data base and make inquiries that are basically unanticipated. For example, the personnel manager might interrogate the data base to determine how many electrical engineers the company has in its employ who are located in the midwest division, have ten years experience, are single, and speak French. The sales manager may wish to know the names and locations of customers who purchased over 100 cases of Product XYZ in the last thirty days. In a matter of minutes, or concurrently, other inquiries can be made which require a completely different response. The data base must be designed to respond to such inquiries.

8. Ability to meet changing needs of users over time. Users of the information system cannot anticipate all requirements that they might need nor can they guarantee that present requirements as stated will remain constant.

9. Ability to meet changes in management without major revision. If the data base is organized on the basis of functional relationships, thus modelling the operations and flow of activities, then a major change in users of the system should not create a need for significant changes in the general data base design. Theoretically, Manager B might replace Manager A, make many more requests than A, and have a higher (or lower) threshold for detail, and still be accommodated by the data base without major changes.

10. The updating of files occurs simultaneously, i.e., when a transaction occurs all files related to this transaction are updated to reflect this change.

11. Data errors and inconsistencies are reduced because duplication is reduced.

12. Broader, more coordinated, and more relevant information service can be provided users throughout the organization.

13. Cost savings are effected.

14. Direct interrogation of data is available, with a concomitant reduction in the output of voluminous reports.

15. Manual handling of data is reduced because much data re-entry and transfer is eliminated.

It is emphasized that, at the present time, these advantages can be achieved only to a certain level, beyond which it is technically impossible to go. Moreover, it is economically untenable to attempt to design a generalized data base management system which will contain anything and everything. However, the implementation of the generalized data base management system, with ancillary evolving technology, provides the users, systems analysts, and programmers with significant capabilities to truly challenge and exploit the information processing potential of the computer.

The disadvantages of the generalized data base management system are:

1. The design and implementation of the data base approach requires highly skilled professionals.

2. The initial investment is extremely high.

3. If single source data is in the system and the system "crashes," many operations of the organization might be halted until the system is restored.

4. A sophisticated level of hardware and software is necessary.

5. High level of security safeguards and backup is required.

6. Errors might develop throughout the data base because of a single error emanating from a source document.

Notice that the advantages and disadvantages of the generalized data base management approach are similar to the advantages and disadvantages of the information systems approaches discussed in Part I. This similarity is natural because an information system implemented with the systems approach requires, as its key component, a data base with relatively high degree of integration of common elements. Also, the more traditional approach to the organization of data files parallels the hierarchical

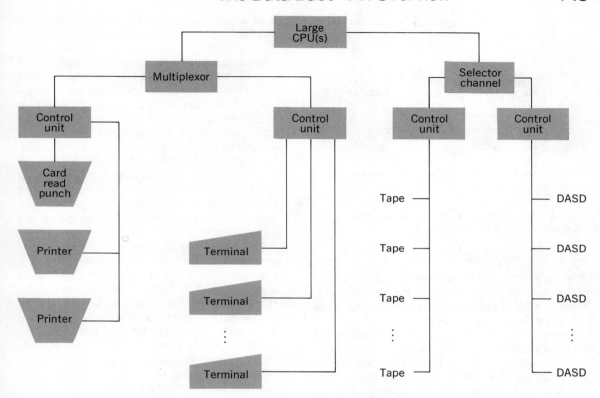

FIGURE 6.10.   Typical computer configuration required to
support a generalized data base management system.

information system. Again, this is only natural, because the hierarchical information system uses the nonrelated approach for file organization.

Hardware Considerations

When the systems analyst considers whether or not a generalized data base management system is appropriate for his organization, he must be aware of the hardware requirements necessary to support this type of system. As discussed previously, it is possible to implement some functions of a generalized data base management system and achieve immediate benefits, without implementing every desirable feature. However, certain hardware components are normally required. Figure 6.10 illustrates the typical computer configuration

required for supporting existing generalized data base management systems.

6.5 Implementing a Sophisticated Data Base

In this section the basic components necessary for implementing a sophisticated data base and its generalized data base management system are analyzed. These components are: (1) data base unit, (2) data base users and originators, (3) data base administrator, (4) file management language, (5) data description language, (6) data manipulation language, and (7) application programs. In addition, processors, assemblers, compilers, systems analysts, programmers, and so forth are also required. How-

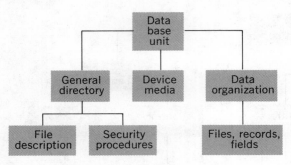

FIGURE 6.11. Schematic of the data base unit.

ever, in this section, only the seven numbered components will be discussed.

Data Base Unit

The data base unit is comprised of the various file device media as well as software elements. Figure 6.11 illustrates those elements that comprise this major component.

The general directory serves as a library of files which provides general file description, access key, and file location. File description elements provide the name of the file, a description of records and files contained in it, and a description of unused space, pointers, and indexes. The security element permits authorized access to files, or access only to predetermined levels within the file (record and field level). It also, in accordance with appropriate keys, allows the user to interrogate only, update only, or both. The device media are, of course, the physical media where the data are stored. Data organization represents the logical methods used to structure data elements so that data needs can be effectively met.

Data Base Users and Data Originators

Four levels of users may be identified—data base administrator, applications programmer, nonprogrammer, and parametric user.

. . . systems identify the role of an individual called the data base administrator. In a user environment in which an important data base is kept on-line for access by several individuals, there must be a single individual who carries responsibility for many facets of its use. Certainly he should be responsible for its initial creation and for instituting any structural modifications which may be required. In identifying specific features of the generalized data base management systems as restricted to privileged use by one individual, the Systems Committee is expressing a collective opinion on what such features should be. The use of the system features provided for the data administrator may call for considerably different levels of expertise in the different systems.

The next level of user is the applications programmer for whom the host language capabilities are specifically provided. He is well identified in terms of current practices. However, when programming to operate on data which is stored on-line under the management of a generalized data base management system, he may have to accept constraints and disciplines which have been noticeably absent in previous methods for handling business applications.

A third level of user is the nonprogrammer for whom the self-contained capabilities have been designed. Finally, is the other nonprogrammer level which is of importance only in an on-line environment. He may be called the parametric user, since his interface with the data base is one of invoking predefined transactions and possibly providing values to any parameters they may have.

A generalized data base management system is potentially capable of providing generalized processing facilities for either the programming user or the nonprogramming user, or both.

The *nonprogramming user* is not necessarily a nonprogrammer. This term is used to indicate that the user is not required to write a program in a conventional programming language in order to use the data base. In this sense, users are being described according to what they have to *do* as opposed to what they have to *be* (their skills, etc.). For the nonprogramming user, the system may provide facilities for performing such functions as data definition, file creation, interrogation, extraction, update, and data structuring. The user invokes the function and provides the input it requires which could be anything from a small set of parameters to a "program" written in some special purpose language. A self-contained system usually provides a special language for the user to specify high level operations oriented to the function to be performed.[6]

The ability of the nonprogrammer to interrogate the files directly and get immediate response considerably decreases the normal time lag inherent in report generation systems. Moreover, the direct linkage of the data entry clerks, who input transactional data into the data base, helps to ensure current status of files, as well as helping to decrease traditional data preparation activities.

Application programmers use what is referred to as a "host language" by the Data Base Task Group of the CODASYL Programming Language Committee. A few examples of host languages are COBOL, FORTRAN, and PL/1.

Thus far we have discussed the data base unit and the user and data originators, both of which are shown in Figure 6.12.

Those components that go in between these two areas are what link the users with the data base and, thus, make the data base concept operative. The complete data base system is illustrated in Figure 6.13.

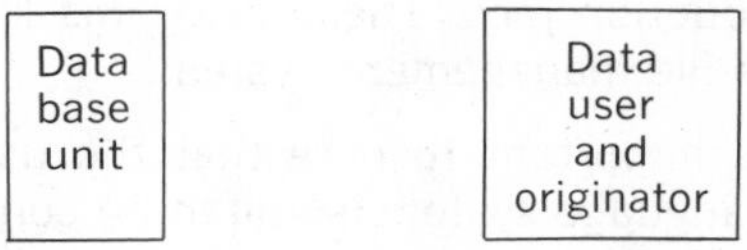

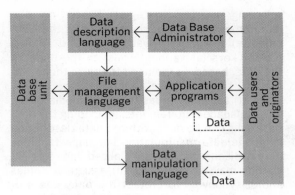

FIGURE 6.13. Components of the data base system.

Data Base Administrator

The data base administrator[7] function is a human activity requiring much mediation of conflicting needs among the various users. The Data Base Administrator is assumed to be a specialist acting in this capacity. The Data Base Administrator's major technical functions are data definition and file creation. In addition, other technical functions include:

> . . . monitoring system operation, preservation of system integrity and security, and providing for restructuring the data base to accommodate new record types or new items. Some of the the data administrator's functions may have to be performed with a programmer level language in some systems.[8]

This functional component of the data base system can be divided into three categories: (1) organizing, (2) monitoring, and (3) reorganizing.

1. *Organizing.* This category includes the following activities: (a) receiving data input from data users and originators where appropriate, (b) employing data structures that model the data requirements, (c) assigning names in such a manner as to assure their uniqueness, (d)

Data base unit

Data user and originator

FIGURE 6.12. Schematic of the data base unit and the data user and originator.

[6] CODASYL Systems Committee Technical Report, *op. cit.*, pp. 21, 23, 24, and 40.

[7] Description based on: "Data Base Task Group Report," *op. cit.*, p. 22–23.
[8] CODASYL Systems Committee Technical Report, *op. cit.*, p. 30.

selecting search strategies based on the requirements of the various users of the data base, (e) assigning privacy locks and issuing privacy keys (at various levels) to the users of the data, based on the need to utilize those portions of the data base affected by the privacy locks, (f) assigning areas to device media based on time/space requirements, (g) loading the data base (this can be done with the data description language/data manipulation language facilities herein discussed, but specialized facilities for loading may be provided), (h) assigning names and/or synonyms to protect the uniqueness of the names already assigned to the data base, (i) selecting and structuring the proper subset of the data base that must be available to the application programmer, and (j) where applicable, altering the privacy locks and assigning privacy keys to the application programmers.

2. *Monitoring.* It is also the Data Base Administrator's responsibility to monitor the data base for usage, response, privacy breach, and potential reorganization. He can use various logging facilities or sampling techniques to gather statistics.

3. *Reorganizing.* As a result of information gained through monitoring, or because of new information required in the data base, the Data Base Administrator might have to reorganize the data base. The administrator might reassign areas to different devices/media, remove "dead" records, and compact space by reorganization of files.

Data Description Language

The data description language (DDL) is the component that provides the data description within the data base and accommodates the proper interface with user programs. It defines records, sets of records, their interrelationship, and their area of storage. Its purpose is to describe the data used by each application program, which can involve different host languages.

The record description facilities of the DDL should include the ability to:

1. Retrieve the records and/or fields of data from the data base called by the host program.

2. Describe the structure, format, representation, and other general data characteristics of the data in the data base. This should be done in a manner that is consistent with the data description facilities of the host language

File Management Language

This component is used to assign data to particular physical storage devices/media and to provide a basic means of access to the data base files. In some applications, it can be contained in the data description language. The assignment of areas to devices, space to media, specifying and controlling buffering, paging, and overflow are also all handled by the file management language (FML). It can also provide the utility or service routines required to support a data base in day-to-day operations. Examples of such routines are load routines, dump and edit routines, statistical routines, and compare routines.

Data Manipulation Language

The data manipulation language (DML) is the component that provides the interface between the data base and nonprogrammer users. It provides the procedural capabilities required to manipulate specific data in a manner which will allow the user either to receive a specific response based on an inquiry, or to modify, delete, substitute, or add, certain data records or fields in the data base files.

Application Programmer

The application programs are written by programmers to generate specific reports and to run production jobs. These programs interface with the file management system.

It is important to note that the user of a host language system is still to be considered an applications programmer in the sense that he writes a set of statements to be executed sequentially as in COBOL. He exercises almost the same degree of procedural control over the machine in his program as if he were programming in COBOL, except that the facilities of the data base system handle his data transfers once he has initiated them. He has control over the logical flow of his program and may mix conditional statements, action statements and loops virtually as he wishes. The enhanced data structure allows him a facility in handling certain data structures more completely than he would be able to in the host language alone. He is, of course, insulated from the physical storage structure, although required to assign a media type and define the file level structure for data base storage.[9]

A General Example

The underlying difference between the functioning of the application programmer method and the nonprogrammer DML method (in query mode) can be shown by the following example.

During the week, the Sales Manager makes a number of information requests. A typical request is:

Provide Sales Information on Product 120 By Salesman, By Customer, In Market Area 3.

Assuming that the application programmers had time to honor such a request, they would either have to write a new program or rewrite an old one and then process the necessary data. Otherwise, the Sales Manager would have to wait for a periodic report, gather the necessary data, and reprocess it, in order to obtain a specific response to his initial inquiry. By this time the information would probably no longer be relevant.

If one assumes that the application programmer does write the necessary algorithm to provide a report for each inquiry (a somewhat far-fetched assumption), then the following activities would have to be gone through each time a program is written.

1. Describe output report
2. Define data input
3. Write procedure division
4. Test program
5. Debug

On the other hand, with the DML allowing a direct interface with the data base, the Sales Manager user can provide parameters in an interrogative mode to access the necessary information. For example, the interrogation instructions can be formulated as follows:

```
FILE = SALES
PROD = 120
AREA = 3
SORT KEY = SALESMAN-NO: CUST-NO
```

The Sales Manager could have an almost instantaneous response to the request for information. Such a system provides a mechanism for responding in a rapid manner to *ad hoc* interrogations and updates. Management information needs, especially at the tactical and strategic levels, are characterized by their changing nature. Often managers at these levels cannot foresee what they will need to know. What they need to know today will not necessarily help them next week. This situation means that one of the most important features of the data base must be its flexibility, and its ability to organize and disseminate data in accordance with a broad range of parameters.

SUMMARY

The data base is the foundation of the information system. In reality the data base is a collection of data files. A data file in turn is a collection of data records that are composed of data fields. A complete understanding of the structure and function of the data base includes logical as well as physical considerations.

The term "data base management" is used to describe all of the activities involved in entering data into the data base, controlling data stored in the data base, and retrieving data from the data base. Traditionally, individual programs have been written to perform each required data base management function. Currently, efforts are being expended to develop a generalized data base management system.

Although many so-called generalized data base management systems exist today, there is no

---

[9] *Ibid.,* p. 17.

universal agreement as to what functions these systems should perform or how these functions should be performed. When evaluating whether or not a generalized data base management system should be implemented, the systems analyst must consider both his data processing requirements and the computer resources available to perform this processing.

The basic components in a sophisticated data base are: (1) a data base unit, (2) the data base users and originators, (3) the data base administrator, (4) a file management language, (5) a data description language, (6) a data manipulation language, and (7) the application programs.

REVIEW QUESTIONS

6.1 Identify and define the elements comprising the data base. Explain the relationships among these elements.

6.2 Distinguish between logical and physical files.

6.3 What activities are described by the term data base management?

6.4 Discuss the major differences between the application approach and the generalized data base management system approach to data base development.

6.5 What are the major advantages and disadvantages to the development of a generalized data base management system?

6.6 List the computer hardware components essential for the support of a generalized data base management system.

6.7 Define the term "data base unit." Discuss at least two kinds of data base units.

6.8 What are the major levels of data base users? How do these users differ from one another?

6.9 Discuss the function of the data base administrator.

6.10 Explain the relationships among the file management language, the data description language, and the data manipulation language.

QUESTIONS FOR DISCUSSION

6.1 "Every organization maintains a large data base. The problem confronting both management and the systems analyst today is how to organize this data base so that it can be more effectively utilized." Discuss fully.

6.2 "Our data base is contained on 150 magnetic tapes." Explain.

6.3 "Today we design a data base; a few years ago we designed files. The activities are still the same, whatever you choose to call them." Discuss.

6.4 "The data base is the underlying and basic component of the integrated information system." Discuss fully.

6.5 "We spent nearly 3 years and $100,000 and have still not identified everything which should be in our data base." Discuss.

6.6 "Online processing and direct access to records requires sophisticated, elaborate, and expensive hardware and software." Discuss this statement.

6.7 "While current computer hardware is in the third generation and is moving into the fourth, information systems, per se, are still in the second generation. As a result, most current computer-based information systems are not meeting users' needs, particularly timely response and coordinated reporting." Discuss this comment.

6.8 "The substance of most of the systems on which we are working is file maintenance. At least 50–70% of the time is spent in updating files. Updating is an absolute necessity. There are no data bases that do not need changing. It is only a question of how often. Some of them every second or two. Others take weeks or maybe months between changes; but still there are changes and you have to handle them. There is a great variety of such changes. I will consider two extremes. One is the ability to change a piece of data anywhere in the data base at any time. The other extreme is handling batches of updating data, and it is also a case that we have to provide for in our generalized data base management systems." (From "The Large Data Base, Its Organization and User Interface," *Data Base* (New York: Association for Computing Machinery, Fall, 1969), pp. 11–12.) Discuss this statement.

6.9 "Most organizations operate under a great deal of pressure that emanates from competition. This pressure tends to limit the amount of time available for the planning and execution of plans. The pressure of competition forces quick decisions and quicker action. How does an organization meet its competition? By offering a good product at reasonable cost and by maintaining a high level of customer service. This last aspect can be achieved by providing answers to questions concerning a multiplicity of matters, such as order status, scheduled shipment date, method of transportation, inventory availability, pricing schedules, change orders, and so forth." Comment on this statement, especially as it relates to the design of the data base.

6.10 "A generalized data base management system which will satisfy the needs of every organization is a mirage. We don't read about engineers trying to build one manufacturing process to fit every organization." Discuss this rationale.

6.11 "The concepts related to retrieving data from a file are the same whether the file contains payroll data, purchasing data, or production data. It doesn't seem to make much sense, reinventing the wheel for each system designed in each organization." Discuss this rationale.

6.12 "The problem of security is the least understood and most difficult to solve when designing large, complex data bases." Explain.

6.13 "As manager of data processing and programming in our company, you might say I am also the data base administrator." Explain how this might be true.

6.14 "The implementation of a generalized data management system can be partially justified by a reduction in the number of systems analysts and programmers necessary to support the information system." Discuss the pros and cons of this statement.

6.15 "Before the average organization attempts to implement an integrated, online data base, they will have to acquire personnel with a greater understanding of communication hardware and software." Explain.

EXERCISES **6.1** Interview a manager from a local organization (preferably someone knowledgeable about data processing) which is large enough to utilize a computer for processing data and information; or, review the literature for a report or article which describes the data processing activities in a particular organization. The objectives of your efforts are: (a) to determine what data is contained in the computer accessible data base; (b) to what extent is this data base integrated; (c) what is the philosophy of the organization as it relates to the development of information systems; (d) what are the goals of management concerning future expansion of the data base; and (e) what is the present hardware configuration. Prepare a report describing your findings.

6.2 Using your own experiences and some minimal research, identify the types of data files and records which are likely to be found supporting the following organization's operations (ignore considerations such as payroll, inventory control, miscellaneous accounting, and so forth):
(1) A personnel recruiting agency
(2) An independent credit bureau
(3) A dating and escort service
(4) A dog breeders association
(5) A custom/antique jeweler

6.3 From recent journals and magazines, related to information and data processing, research one or more file management or data base management systems being offered for purchase. Evaluate these packages in terms of the capabilities and functions they propose to perform.

6.4 Below are listed a series of documents and reports prepared by various types of organizations. Evaluate these informational outputs and determine the following: (a) what type of data files must be maintained to produce the output; (b) what data could be entered once for many uses; (c) what data must be entered each time the document is produced; and (d) what relationships exist, if any, among the data files you have identified.
(1) An employee paycheck.
(2) A year to date sales report by customer.
(3) A purchase order for raw materials and miscellaneous supplies.
(4) An invoice to customers for purchases.
(5) An analysis of records performed, against a planned work schedule.
(6) A check to vendors.

PROBLEMS **6.1** Zoot Suit Tailors, Inc., make four models of men's suits. A customer initiates an order by mailing to Zoot Suit a document specifying the model suit chosen, with a specification of measurements, and the material necessary to make the suit. Upon receipt of the document, the receiving clerk assigns a particular tailor a copy of the specifications along with the material. The tailors are paid on a job basis.

Besides preparing payrolls for all employees of Zoot Suit, the information system must handle the following types of requests for information: (1) date order received, (2) status of work in process, (3) projected completion dates, (4) complete history of customer orders and measurement specifications for the past five years, and (5) various sales analyses.

In general terms, describe the data base you would recommend for Zoot Suit. Also, outline any hardware components you deem necessary.

6.2 Ark–La–Tex Airlines has recently incorporated and has been given permission to set up operations, transporting passengers and freight, in eight southern cities: Dallas, Houston, Lake Charles, Lafayette, Baton Rouge, New Orleans, Shreveport, and Little Rock.

Among other assets, they have twenty-four large commercial planes ready for service. They have leased storage and maintenance hangars at Dallas, Shreveport, and New Orleans. In addition, they have also leased ticket counter and baggage handling facilities at each of the eight airports.

You have been brought in as a consultant to present, in a broad outline to management, the kind of information system you recommend; plus the kind of data base, and hardware support, such a system will require. Assume you will be in another part of the country on a different job for the next week, which means that you will have to depend on a narrative and descriptive report for fully communicating to management your broad system design alternatives. In addition to this report, you feel that it is necessary to prepare a list of questions, that must be answered by management, before embarking on a more detailed study. For convenience, and for your reference, assume that the problems (e.g. scheduling, reservation, passenger service) of Ark–La–Tex will be similar to the problems of any other airline.

6.3 The capture of data and the dissemination of information is quite often the manufacturing organization's (as well as many other organizations) most difficult problem. Data are voluminous, scattered, and often difficult to obtain. Five general kinds of information dissemination exist: (1) replies to inquiries, (2) standard routine reports, (3) exception reports, (4) cost reports, and (5) special reports.

Implementation of an integrated data base, using the systems approach, normally can handle all the mainstream data needed for the operation of the organization. The data are stored on magnetic disk files and are, for the most part, online. Because of this structure, summary and detail information can be retrieved.

Each of the data base records is linked in a particular way wherein the user can make detail requests for reports and/or make specific interrogations. For example, a part number accessed from an item master record may lead to a bill of materials (or product structure), work-in-process and degree of completion, standard routing, an open purchase order status, cost data, and so forth. Figure 6.14 is an example of an item master record within the Item Master File.

The item master record layout represents a typical record design with its cross references which allow the integration of the mainstream data flow. This cross referencing, or linkage, is the key reason why information is accessible via multiple points throughout the organization. With this cross referencing, no longer is it necessary to spend hours or days in trying to

Product Item Number	Description	Unit of Measure	Inventory Value Code	Engineering Cross Reference	
				To standard routing	To product structure

Order Policy	Forecasting	Lead Times	Unit Costs	Unit Prices	Parts Usage History	Current Period Inventory	Inventory on Hand (Qty. and locations)

Gross Requirements	Planned and Released Orders	Purchasing Cross Reference				Open Job Order Control Cross Reference		
		Total qty.	Purchase master	Vendor master	Detail requisitions	Total qty.	Order summary	Operation detail

FIGURE 6.14. Item master record.

capture and bring together data scattered in files, file drawers, or ledger cards. Moreover, the files are updated simultaneously.

The item master record is stored in the Item Master File. Also, in this file module are the Work Center Master and the Tool Master. Three other file modules which are linked to the Item Master module include:

1. Purchase Order Control. This file module is composed of: (1) Purchase Master, (2) Vendor Master, (3) Purchase on Order, and (4) Open Purchase Requisition.

2. Open Job Order Control. This file module actually represents production planned, and on order, and is made up of: (1) Order Summary and Detail and (2) Operation Detail.

3. Engineering Indices. This file module is comprised of: (1) Standard Routing and (2) Product Structure (bill of materials).

Taking the above information, in broad terms, develop a schematic showing how these file modules should be linked for overall information access. Also, list the functional areas to which information from the data base will flow and examples of what kind of information it will be. Examples of functional areas and information flowing to these functional areas are:

1. Work Center Control: (1) labor reporting, (2) material movement and logistics, (3) work in process, (4) costing, and (5) reporting of variances.

2. Capacity Planning: (1) projected work center load report, (2) planned order load, (3) order start date, and (4) production leveling.

6.4 Production can be divided into two phases: (1) planning, and (2) execution. The data flow leads from an initial input of customer orders and statistical sales background data to the final shipment of an order.

Planning:

Planning begins with the preparation and projection of order forecasts. Stock availability and on-order status are screened across product inventory records. But component family characteristics of the product line must also be recognized. Product structure or bill of materials enter into these decisions.

After a determination of net requirements, an order quantity analysis takes place to ascertain lot sizes and lead times for two distinct groups:

1. Those raw material items which must be purchased from outside sources.

2. Those raw material items which are either assembled or fabricated internally.

Purchased items required, are placed on a purchase requisition. At this point, prices are ascertained, delivery dates are negotiated, selection of a vendor is made, and a purchase order is released. Scheduled receipt documents may be prepared simultaneously with the purchase order and forwarded to the inspection-receiving area of the warehouse. An open purchase order record is now established for follow-up procedures.

Internally made items are routed to production planning for assembly and fabrication. Some similarity exists in these two levels. An assembly order is generated for the assembly area, a shop order for the fabrication area. Material requisition and move tickets accompany both documents. Three basic types of records (standard routing, work center load, and open job order) permit assembly and fabrication to schedule, to load, and to level the line, or the shop, and to release the order paperwork.

Execution:

Execution begins at the purchasing level with the need for order follow-up and vendor expediting. The vendor ships material to the plant warehouse, accompanying his shipment with packing lists and an invoice.

Varied execution functions are performed at the assembly and fabrication levels. Orders are dispatched, rescheduled, and expedited between work centers. In the meantime, current production reporting updates work center and open job order records.

Purchased items, along with components from the assembly and fabrication areas, move to the inspection area. These finished products move from final processing to the final inspection and receiving areas. The final cycle in this flow is a shipment authorization requesting the warehouse to pack and ship to a branch warehouse or to the customer.

Develop a production model (flow diagram) from the above information.

One aspect of this problem is purchasing. Design record layouts of: (1) Item Master Record, (2) Open Purchase Requisition, (3) Open Purchase Order, (4) Vendor Master, and (5) Purchase Master. The Item Master Record would contain many fields such as product item number and description, unit of measure, material costs (both at standard and actual), lead time, quantity on hand, and so forth. However, only show that segment of the Item Master Record which links to:

1. The Open Purchase Requisition Record which is comprised of: (1) buyer code, (2) quantity, (3) a list of vendor numbers which supply the par-

ticular item, (4) date the item is required, (5) closing date of the requisition. (Closed requisitions remain on the file for one month, after which time they can be placed on magnetic tape for future access.)

2. The Open Purchase Order Record which contains: (1) date due-in, (2) price, and (3) closing data of the order. In addition, fields are set aside to record vendor promise dates, receipts, and rejects.

3. The Vendor Master Record is made up of: (1) vendor code, (2) name, (3) address, (4) telephone contact, (5) the last shipment made by the vendor, (6) price breaks, (7) terms, (8) a summary of deliveries, (9) rejected shipments, and (10) the dollar amount of business transacted over the last twelve months. Also, vendor delivery and quality ratings are provided to assist the buyer in vendor selection, and for reporting purposes. A delivery index composes lateness of current shipments with those of a prior base period; a quality index shows the trend in rejections.

4. The Purchase Master Record is an extension of the Item Master Record. It contains a history of the last five vendor quotations of the purchased item (with price and terms) and the last six buys of the item (providing order number, vendor, quantity, date, and price).

6.5 In a typical manufacturing organization, the data flow, to one degree or another, affect eleven major areas:

1. Sales analysis for decision making for management objectives, determination of product line, market, advertising, sales promotion, and production scheduling.

2. Management control based on reporting of costs and variances from standards.

3. Engineering which includes research and development, product design, specifications, catalogs and bill of materials.

4. Inventory control.

5. Manufacturing facilities which include plant and equipment personnel, maintenance, and machine loading schedule.

6. Purchasing, receiving, and shipping.

7. Payment to vendors.

8. Determination of income and preparation of reports to stockholders and governmental agencies.

9. Credit checking.

10. Handling customer orders.

11. Providing reports to management such as variance reports, sales statistics, market analysis, and income statements.

With these areas in mind, develop a flow diagram of how you visualize the mainstream flow of data and information would occur in this typical manufacturing organization. Make any assumptions that you deem necessary.

BIBLIOGRAPHY   *CODASYL Data Base Task Group April 71 Report,* New York: Association for Computing Machinery, 1971.

CODASYL System Committee Technical Report, *Feature Analysis of Generalized Data Base Management Systems,* New York: Association for Computing Machinery, 1971.

Data Description and Access, 1970 ACM SICFIDET Workshop, New York: Association for Computing Machinery, 1970.

Lyon, *An Introduction to Data Base Design,* New York: Wiley-Interscience, a Division of John Wiley & Sons, Inc. 1971.

Patterson, "Data Base Hazards," *Datamation,* July, 1972.

Prendergast, "Selecting a Data Management System," *Computer Decisions,* August, 1972.

Steig, "File Management Systems Revisited," *Datamation,* October, 1972.

"The Debate on Data Base Management," *EDP Analyzer,* March 1972.

"The Large Data Base, Its Organization and User Interface," *Data Base,* Fall, 1969.

The Production Information and Control System, IBM Data Processing Application, Third Edition, (White Plains, New York: IBM Technical Publications Department, 1969).

7 Classifying and Coding Data

7.1 Introduction

Data emanates from various transactions and events which occur in all organizations: a sale is made which must be recorded; a student enrolls in college and takes a variety of courses for which he receives credit; and a patient enters a hospital to receive certain treatment and medication that must be meticulously recorded. All of these transactions and events create voluminous amounts of scattered data which must be collected, processed, and retrieved from time to time.

Within an information system data can be stored in a myriad of devices such as library cards, file folders, documents, index cards, and computer accessible devices. Regardless of the devices used for storage, data are usually input into the system according to some predetermined structure which is based on future processing and retrieval requirements. It is fairly simple to collect data; however, the point is, if data items are not systematically classified and coded it may be difficult, if not impossible, to gain access to the data once it has been collected and stored.

In order to implement the sophisticated data bases necessary to support modern information systems, the systems analyst must understand thoroughly the data operation of classification and a related practice, the development of coding structures. The objectives of this chapter are as follows:

1. To provide a basic understanding of data classification.

2. To identify the major considerations related to coding structures and their design.

3. To identify and explain the primary types of code structures.

4. To provide several examples of classification and coding structures.

7.2 Classification of Data Items

The mere gathering of data without regard to organizing and classifying it into a meaningful pattern will seldom serve a useful purpose for those who ultimately will need these data. Classifying data was identified in Part I as being one of the basic operations performed on data to produce information. Classification is the intellectual process of identifying and placing data items into categories according to common characteristics and attributes. The scheme of classification utilized depends upon the subsequent uses to which the data items will be put. For instance, it is of little use to classify students as to their political preference, hospital patients as to the cars they own, or raw materials according to their color, if such classifications are of no significance and will not be used.

There are an unlimited number of ways to classify data items. The panelists on a TV show might classify a subject as animal, vegetable, or mineral. An item can be classified as a person, object, or process. Adam Smith in his *The Wealth of Nations,* classified the factors of production as being land, labor, capital, and entrepreneurship. The telephone company classifies subscribers in the white pages according to name. However, in the yellow pages, subscribers are classified by occupation, profession, service, or trade.

Many libraries use the Dewey Decimal Classification. This system of classification divides all knowledge into ten major classifications, as follows:

000–099	General Works List
100–199	Philosophy, Psychology, Ethics
200–299	Religion and Mythology
300–399	Social Sciences
400–499	Philology
500–599	Science
600–699	Applied Science
700–799	Fine Arts
800–899	Literature
900–999	History, Geography, Biography, Travel

During systems analysis the analyst attempts to identify and define required classifications of data which the system's users infer when stating their information requirements. For example, the statement, "I need daily orders and shipments, expressed both in quantity and dollars by product code," reflects a need for many different classification schemes. "I am accountable for inventory of bulk, raw material," or "I tally overtime dollars by labor grade, monthly," are further examples of a need for classification of data.

During systems design, the structure of the data base, as well as the sequence of processing steps, is directly related to two items. These are the classifications of data which have been identified as being able to satisfy users' needs, and the operational characteristics of the storage and processing devices utilized. A significant amount of time is spent by systems analysts in constructing coding structures to reflect the needed classifications of data.

No matter what the classification purpose is, the following basic guidelines should be noted:

1. The classification must coincide with the identified requirements of the users.

2. The classification should permit growth and expansion to handle newly identified items.

3. The classification into which a data item is placed must be logically apparent.

4. The classification scheme must anticipate a wide range of needs.

Once data have been classified, the structure of the classification can be readily codified. The use of codes and coding structures is the subject of the next section. At this point it is essential that the systems analyst understand the role of the classification operation and its importance in the design of the data base.

7.3 Coding Considerations

Codes provide an abbreviated structure for classifying items in order to record, communicate, process, and/or retrieve data. Codes can use letters, numbers, words, and special symbols, or any combination thereof; however, systems analysts are primarily concerned with code structures utilizing numbers and letters. The use of computers has provided a strong impetus to the utilization of codes, especially numerical codes in the processing of information. In this section the functions of codes, the available coding symbols, and some considerations of code design are discussed.

Function of Codes

The function of a code is twofold. It provides a brief, unambiguous identification for a data item, record, or file, and confers a special meaning to these data structures which will assist in retrieval and manipulation.

Considering the volume of data that already has to be processed in most organizations, lengthy definitions, descriptions, names, etc. adversely affect both processing efficiency and accuracy. Efficiency is affected since, as more characters are used in a name or description, more time must be spent in reporting, recording, acknowledging, and understanding. Moreover, the amount of space required to record and/or store the necessary characters or figures is important. This effect on efficiency occurs with manual operations and in machine execution. Accuracy, on the other hand, is almost impossible to achieve when a given name, description, or characteristic must be used by many different individuals in the processing of data. Standardization of data item identification is a must in computer processing.

The use of a properly designed coding structure helps to alleviate all of these problems. For example, a 3-digit code uniquely and concisely identifies 1000 different items and, obviously, requires much less space than a language description for each of these items.

In addition to using codes for enhancing processing efficiency and accuracy, coding structures can be established to provide special meaning for the data item. For example, an employee might be coded on an employee master file for sex, age, education level, skill, residence, benefit program participation, and so forth. Once the coding has been accomplished, data concerning this employee can be sorted, summarized, or statistically analyzed according to prescribed algorithms.

Codes are required for both routine batch processing and online inquiry systems. The use of coding systems in modern organizations varies widely from very crude, simplistic structures to quite sophisticated systems. A well planned coding structure is an essential component of any viable information processing system today.

Coding Symbols

In selecting a given code format, the character set available must be considered. Analysts have a large number of symbols at their disposal. They have numbers, letters, and special characters (e.g., dollar sign, colon, period, etc.). However, numbers are by far the most widely used symbols in coding systems, especially where electromechanical and electronic equipment are utilized. This is true today because most computers on the market can store two digits in the same storage location as one alphabetic character. Consequently storage requirements are reduced and processing efficiency is increased.

A numerical code provides up to ten classifications for each position in the code. These codes are quite amenable to machine processing; however, if manually processed by clerks, large numerical codes are difficult to remember accurately. Alphabetic codes provide up to 26 classifications for each position in the code. Codes which use both numbers and letters are called alphanumeric. Numbers and letters can be mnemonically structured to help the user remember what the code stands for. For example, 3 BR CV, may represent a three inch brass check valve.

While numeric, alphabetic, and alphanumeric codes comprise the majority of coding structures used in information processing today, future systems will most likely provide for data coded in special symbols which are understandable only by special scanning or sensing devices. Symbolic coding structures seem appropriate in many point-of-sale (POS) applications where vast amounts of data are available but quite costly to collect with present input methods and procedures.[1] Included later in this chapter is a discussion of one proposal for a symbolic coding structure.

Considerations of Code Design

There are many possible arrangements of digits, letters, and characters which can be designed into codes. However, a great deal of thought must go into the coding scheme if it is to satisfy a variety of users. The following considerations should be kept in mind when designing codes.

1. The coding scheme must logically fit the needs of the users and the processing method used.

2. Each code must be a unique representation for the item it identifies. For example, an inventory item number or employee identification code must identify one and only one inventory item or employee.

3. The code design must be flexible in order to accommodate changing requirements. It is

too costly and confusing to have to change the coding structure every few months or years. However, the coding structure should not be so extensive that part of it will not be used for a number of years. For example, if a sixteen digit code will handle all processing needs for three or four years, then it would be costly to set up a code larger than sixteen digits. There is a basic tradeoff in the length of the code. Normally, the shorter the code, the less is the cost of classification, preparation, storage, and transmission. On the other hand, the longer the code, the better the translation, and the more variety of data retrieval, statistical analysis, and information processing.

4. The code structure must be easily understood by various users in the organization. It should be as simple, practical, and meaningful as possible.

5. As discussed before in this text, the integrated concept means that a particular transaction affects a number of files in the information system. For example, an order from a customer triggers changes in inventory, sales, accounts receivable, purchasing, shipping, etc., and requires credit checks. Therefore, a code structure must be designed to be meaningful in all related situations. Codes must pertain to the overall functions of the organization. It might not be feasible to design one code structure that would take care of all requirements for each individual function or subdivision in the organization. However, the structure must be broad enough to encompass all functions and provide a basic cross reference for any additional special purpose codes for a variety of processing requirements.

6. Standardization procedures should be established to decrease confusion and misinterpretation for persons working with the code structure. Some of the procedures that can be easily standardized in most systems are: (1) Elimination of characters which are similar in appearance. The range of permissible characters to be used should be selected on the basis of their dissimilarity to other characters. For example, the letters O, Z, I, S, and V may be confused with the digits 0, 2, 1, 5, and the letter U

[1] Peter N. Budzilovich "Tomorrow's Supermarket—The Automated Checkout Counter," *Computer Decisions*, Sept., 1972, pp. 24–26. With permission.

respectively. (2) Gaps in code numbers should be avoided where possible. (3) Days and weeks should be numbered. For example, days are numbered one to seven and weeks numbered consecutively beginning with the start of the fiscal period. (4) The use of a twenty-four hour clock alleviates the AM/PM confusion. (5) Dates should be designated by digits using the Year Month Day format YYMMDD, (where September 18, 1972, becomes 720918); or through the use of the Julian Calendar dating system.

7. The layout of the code itself should be equal in length. For example, a chart of accounts code should read 001–199 (for assets) rather than 1–199.

Designing coding schemes is one of the most important tasks of the systems analyst. Any coding scheme should be designed for the organization as a whole. For example, a code for the chart of accounts should encompass all functions of the organization or at least provide a cross reference for more detailed, special purpose coding systems.

The coding system must be designed to accumulate and classify all data of the organization, in the most efficient and economical way, and respond to the informational requirements of a variety of users. In the manual systems of the past systems analysts were somewhat limited by the comprehensiveness of coding structures. However, with the advent of computers, opportunities now exist for designing and using codes of greater complexity.

7.4 Types of Code Structures

Codes can be formatted in a variety of ways and selecting a specific code structure is critical. In this section several code types used in a number of organizations are discussed and an attempt made to indicate the advantages and disadvantages of each.

Sequential Code

A sequential (or serial) code represents a one-for-one, consecutive assignment of numbers to such items as payroll checks, account numbers, inventory items, purchase orders, employees, and so on. Any list of items is simply numbered consecutively, usually starting with one. For example, a sequential coding scheme for inventory items might be structured as follows:

001	WRENCHES
002	HAMMERS
003	SAWS
.	.
.	.
.	.
678	VALVES

The advantages of a sequential coding scheme are:

1. It is most commonly used because of its simplicity.
2. It is short and unique.
3. It provides a simple way of locating records or documents on which the code appears. (This of course assumes that the requestor knows which number he is looking for.)
4. It is simple to administer.

The disadvantages are:

1. It has no basic scheme of classification.
2. It is inflexible because it cannot accommodate changes.
3. Additions can be made only at the end of the numerical sequence.
4. Vacant number codes must either remain open or wait for reassignment at a later date.
5. It contains no useful information about the item except its order in the list.

Block Code

The block code classifies items into certain groups where blocks of numbers (or letters) are assigned to particular classifications. The block representing a particular classification must be set up on the basis of an expected maximum utilization of that block.

A typical example of a block scheme is the ZIP Code (Zoning Improvement Plan) used by the United States Postal Service. This coding scheme uses a five digit code divided into blocks as follows:

ZIP Code: X XX XX

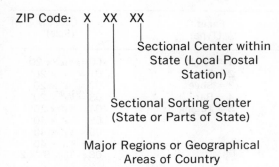

Sectional Center within
State (Local Postal
Station)

Sectional Sorting Center
(State or Parts of State)

Major Regions or Geographical
Areas of Country

Code Position / Code Number	1	2	3	4
1	Truck	Lease	Service contract	Airport division
2	Bulldozer	Purchase	No service contract	Highway division
3	Grader	Rent	–	–
4	Pile driver	–	–	–
5	Crane	–	–	–

FIGURE 7.2.   Block coding structure.

For another example of a block code, suppose that customers are classified into five groups; wholesale, retail, educational, military, and government. In addition there is a classification according to amount of purchases for credit analysis. This classification could be handled as illustrated in Figure 7.1.

A simple two-digit code could be used to classify type of customer and amount of purchase. For instance, the code 34 represents an educational customer with purchases of $50,000–$99,999.

The basic format of a simple block code is further illustrated in Figure 7.2.

The equipment is classified into meaningful categories so that a code number identifies certain attributes of a particular piece of equipment. For instance, in the equipment file those bulldozers, on a rental contract, and owned by the airport division can be determined by accessing all records with a "2" in position 1, a "3" in position 2, and a "1" in position 4. Or we can retrieve any information or make any statistical analysis desired just so long as the code contains the requisite classifications.

The advantages of a block code are:

1. The value and position of the numbers have meaning.

2. The coding structure is more amenable to information processing, in that data items can be easily retrieved, manipulated, analyzed, sorted, and so on.

3. A category of the code can easily be expanded unless that category has reached its maximum limit (e.g. our equipment example can handle only ten pieces of equipment, 0–9).

4. Whole categories can be added or deleted.

The disadvantages are:

1. The code length will depend upon the number of attributes classified. As a result codes can become quite lengthy.

2. In many instances the code will contain spare numbers (e.g. in our equipment example attributes 2, 3, and 4 have spare slots; however, this condition may not in reality always represent a disadvantage).

3. Block codes used as identifiers or record keys pose significant systems maintenance problems when they require modification.

Variations of Block Codes

Like the facets of a cut gem, many items handled by organizations possess different aspects.

Type of Customer		Amount of Purchases	
Code	Classification	Code	Classification
1	Wholesale	1	Up to $9,999
2	Retail	2	$10,000–$29,999
3	Educational	3	$30,000–$49,999
4	Military	4	$50,000–$99,999
5	Government	5	over $99,999

FIGURE 7.1.   An example of a block coding structure.

Facet A (Source)	Facet B (Method of Production)	Facet C (Type)	Facet D (Size)*
1 = Foreign 2 = Domestic	1 = Hot rolled 2 = Cold drawn 3 = Cast	1 = Angle 2 = Flat 3 = Sheet 4 = Bar 5 = Tubing	00 = $1/16'' \times 20'$ 01 = $1/8'' \times 20'$ 02 = $1/4'' \times 20'$ 03 = $1/2'' \times 20'$ 04 = $3/4'' \times 20'$ 05 = $1/4'' \times 40'$ 06 = $1/2'' \times 40'$ 07 = $3/4'' \times 40'$ 08 = $1'' \times 8'' \times 20'$

* Partial list of sizes.

FIGURE 7.3. A facet coding structure.

A code that describes each different facet of the item in question, is referred to by some authorities as a *faceted code.* With this method, items are classified in accordance with pertinent facets so that each facet of every item has a place. Each facet is further subdivided into its various parts. For example, consider the structure illustrated in Figure 7.3, which is designed to show the various facets available relative to an inventory of steel products.

With such a coding system, domestic hot-rolled flat iron of size $1'' \times 8'' \times 20'$ is coded 21208. This system, however, does create some redundancy because certain combinations of numbers are illogical. For example, angle iron is not cold drawn or cast and its size is meaningful only in terms of thickness, width of each flange, and length. (Angle iron sizes are not shown in the illustration.)

Hierarchical block codes are developed on the basis of ascending significance (usually from left to right), i.e., special significance is attached to the location of the numbers within the code. Conventionally, this structure starts with the most general, or most significant, aspect of the item as the left-most group of characters, and moves toward the right as subclasses or less significant aspects are classified.

For example, the clearing of checks through the Federal Reserve check clearing system uses a coding system developed by the American Bankers Association. This code uses a combination of standardized magnetic ink characters which includes ten digits (0–9) and four special symbols. These characters are printed at the bottom of the document in three specific areas as illustrated in Figure 7.4.

The transit number code is printed near the left edge of the document (or check). This classification uses eleven characters; four digits for the transit number, four digits for the American Bankers Association number, a separating dash symbol, and a beginning and ending transit number symbol. The next classification represents, in order, the transaction code (deposit or withdrawal) and the customer account number. The right-most characters, which are not part of the coding scheme per se, represent the dollar amount of the document. (Not shown in the illustration.)

The hierarchical scheme is also quite applicable to the area of accounting where the left-most digits represent the account classification. Subsequent digits represent the item identification, its location in the warehouse, user department, and so on.

Decimal codes, such as the Dewey Decimal coding system, are basically hierarchical block codes where the group of digits, left of the decimal point, represents the major classification and the digits to the right of the decimal point denote the subclassifications. As mentioned earlier, the Dewey Decimal System, a hierarchical decimal coding structure, classifies books by dividing them into ten main knowledge groups. Each of these ten main groups is broken up into more specialized areas. For ex-

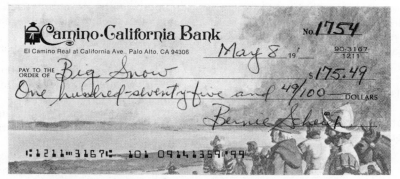

FIGURE 7.4. An illustration of hierarchical block codes.

ample, class 600–699, Applied Science, is subdivided into ten special classes. And, in turn, each of these divisions is further subdivided. The numbers 630–639, for example, represent Agriculture, and are subdivided into such classes as Field Crops, Garden Crops, Dairy Products, and so on.

Using the area of applied science as an example this system can be subdivided into meaningful relationships in the field of nursing, as shown in Figure 7.5.

In addition, two similar areas may be related by linking two separate code numbers. For instance, human anatomy in the area of teratogenesis, coded 611.012, can be linked to biochemistry under human physiology, coded 612.015, by use of a hyphen, resulting in 611.012–612.015, wherein these two linked codes signify that the designated book or article treats the first subject area from the viewpoint of the second.

Mnemonic Codes

These codes are primarily used in manual systems to aid clerks in identifying specifications of items. The characters used in the codes actually aid the memory of the user. For example, in our previous facet code for steel products, domestic hot-rolled flat iron of size $1'' \times 8'' \times 20'$ was coded 21208. However, a code such as this may be meaningless to the human requestor. It may, therefore, be necessary to derive a mnemonic code, e.g., DFI-1 $\times$ 8 $\times$ 20 for efficiency of reference. Of course, the major disadvantage of this coding scheme is that it is not conducive to computer processing.

Phonetic Code

A given name is analyzed according to certain rules (based on phonetic principles) and a code is derived which is supposed to represent this name in abbreviated form. These codes are frequently used in applications which require the retrieval of persons by name rather than by a number such as an account number. The code structure contains one letter followed by three digits, and has the form A123. Following is the "Soundex" code developed by Remington Rand.[2] The steps in deriving the code are:

Code	Field of Knowledge
600	Applied science
610.7	Health care
610.73	Nurses and nursing
610.732	Private duty nursing
610.733	Institutional nursing
610.734	Public health nursing
610.735	Industrial nursing
610.736	Special nursing
610.736.1	Psychological

FIGURE 7.5. An illustration of the use of decimal codes.

[2] Remington Rand Brochure LVB809, "Soundex: Foolproof Filing System for Finding Any Name in The File."

1. Given any name, retain the first letter.
2. Delete the following: A E I O U Y W & H.
3. Assign numbers, as shown by the following list, to the remaining letters. Perform this procedure from left to right until three numbers are obtained. If the name is short and has insufficient consonants to generate three numbers, then insert zeroes to fill. The code now contains one letter plus three digits, or a four position code.

Code Number	Letters to Be Included
1	B F P V
2	C G J K Q S X Z
3	D T
4	L
5	M N
6	R
0	Insufficient consonants

(Note: the digits 7, 8, and 9 are illegal in this scheme)

4. Example: By the rules above, the name BURCH is coded as B620, but the code also represents BIRCH. The code for STRATER is S363, as it is for STRAITER.

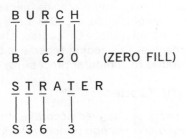

As another illustration, the name Darlington would become D645. By this technique, names that sound the same will be given the same code number, or very closely related code numbers, regardless of minor variations in spelling. When sorted in order, the names will be adjacent, or nearly so, in the file. If a name code identification has several names included in its category, each of those names is then examined in detail to obtain the exact match required. The purpose of the code is to provide

an approximate, if not an exact, location of the name even though slight differences in spelling may exist.

Advantages of this coding system are:

1. It provides a sound system for handling inquiries by phone or mail where only the name is known.
2. A reduction in the number of letters reduces the chance of spelling errors.
3. Similar sounding names are placed together.
4. It works well in jobs which require extensive name and address processing.
5. The codes can be derived by computer.
6. The codes are short in length.

The disadvantages are:

1. A particular code might not be unique, in that it can represent more than one name, resulting in a sequential search.
2. The codes are rather limited for general information processing application.

Use of the Check Digit in Coding Structures

In instances where a particular code is an essential element in processing information, particularly where financial control is involved or where humans are required to transcribe this code repeatedly, its accuracy is verified by using a check digit. The check digit is generated when the code is initially assigned to a data element, and, in fact, becomes part of the code itself. The check digit is determined by performing a prescribed arithmetic operation on the number itself. In subsequent processings, this same arithmetic operation can be performed to ensure that the number has not been incorrectly recorded.

A check digit guards against typical errors such as:[3]

1. Transcription errors, in which the wrong number is written, such as 1 instead of 7.
2. Transposition errors, in which the correct

[3] From SYSTEMS ALNALYSIS edited by Alan Daniels and Donald Yeates. © National Computing Centre 1969. Adapted by permission of Sir Isaac Pitman and Sons Limited. Reprinted by permission of Science Research Associates, Inc.

numbers are written but their positions are reversed, such as 2134 for 1234.

3. Double transposition errors, in which numbers are interchanged between columns, such as 21963 for 26913.

4. Random errors, which are a combination of two or more of the above, or any other error not listed.

The Modulus 11 check digit method is the most frequently used method to generate check digits.[4] Three different approaches to using Modulus 11 are illustrated below.

1. Arithmetic progression:

Account number:	1	2	3	4	5
	×	×	×	×	×
Multiply by:	6	5	4	3	2

Add result of multiplication:
$$6 + 10 + 12 + 12 + 10 = 50$$
Subtract 50 from next highest
multiple of 11: $55 - 50 = 5$
Check digit $= 5$
New account number: 12345–5

2. Geometric progression:

Account number:	1	2	3	4	5
	×	×	×	×	×
Multiply by:	32	16	8	4	2

Add result of multiplication:
$$32 + 32 + 24 + 16 + 10 = 114$$
Subtract 114 from next highest multiple
of 11: $121 - 114 = 7$
Check digit $= 7$
New account number: 12345-7

3. Prime number weighting:

Account number:	1	2	3	4	5
	×	×	×	×	×
Multiply by:	17	13	7	5	3

Add result of multiplication:
$$17 + 26 + 21 + 20 + 15 = 99$$
Subtract 99 from next higher multiple of
11: $99 - 99 = 0$
New account number: 12345-0

It has been determined from statistics that using Modulus 11 with prime number weight-

[4] Suggested by: Friden, Inc., subsidiary of Singer Corporation.

ing, a method developed by Friden, Inc., will actually detect the highest number of possible transposition and transcription errors. Consequently, this method will guarantee the most accurate result. Figure 7.6 illustrates the efficiency of the various methods used to establish check digits.

It should be pointed out that under any Modulus 11 system a percentage of all numbers will have the number "10" as a check digit. Since the check digit must consist of one digit only, all numbers that lead to a check digit equal to 10 must be discarded and cannot be assigned.

Although it is most common that the check digit becomes the last digit of an account number, such placement is not necessarily imperative. As long as the check digit is placed in a constant position, most pieces of equipment can verify the correctness of the account number whatever the position of the check digit. In a manual or semiautomatic operation there are many advantages to be gained by separating the check digit from the main number by means of a hyphen, since it is much easier to sort and read the account number. In the case of fully automatic equipment and computers, the placing of the check digit should be dependent upon the type of equipment used and the system to be employed.

7.5 Selected Coding Examples

To summarize the discussion of classification and coding several examples of typical coding situations, and the coding structures proposed for them, are provided.

The Chart of Accounts

Accountants classify data from transactions using what is termed a chart of accounts. The structure and content of the chart of accounts depends upon the types of information management and others wish to retrieve. Normally, charts of accounts contain two kinds of classification. They are a classification by the na-

Modulus	Range of Weights That May Be Used	Max. Length of Number without Repeating Weight	Weights Used	Percentage Errors Detected				
				Transcription	Single Transposition	Double Transposition	Other Transposition	Random
10	1–9	8	1–2–1–2–1	100	98.8	Nil	48.9	90.0
			1–3–1–3–1	100	88.9	Nil	44.5	90.0
			7–6–4–3–2	87.0	100	88.9	88.9	90.0
			9–8–7–4–3–2	94.4	100	88.9	74.1	90.0
			1–3–7–1–3–7	100	88.9	88.9	74.4	90.0
11	1–10	9	10–9–8 · · · 2	100	100	100	100	90.9
			1–2–4–8–16, etc.	100	100	100	100	90.9
13	1–12	11	Any	100	100	100	100	92.3
17	1–16	15	Any	100	100	100	100	94.1
19	1–18	17	Any	100	100	100	100	94.7
23	1–22	21	Any	100	100	100	100	95.6
27	1–26	25	Any	100	100	100	100	96.3
31	1–30	29	Any	100	100	100	100	96.8
37	1–36	35	Any	100	100	100	100	97.3

FIGURE 7.6.　Efficiency of check-digit methods.

ture of the data item, and a classification by organization function.

In the first kind of classification, it is a convention to group all the asset accounts together, followed by liabilities, equities, revenue, and expense accounts, respectively. A representative list is illustrated in Figure 7.7.

A comprehensive list of General Ledger Accounts, uniformly coded, has been presented by Lee.[5]

The Uniform Coded Chart of Accounts is designed to be used in coding the chart of accounts of any organization; the result being simplification of accounting and bookkeeping procedures.

. . . .

The Uniform Coded Chart of Accounts is

divided into nine basic divisions. Assets are numbered from 1000 to 1999, Liabilities from 2000 to 2999, Net Worth or Capital from 3000 to 3999. Income from 4000 to 4999, Cost of Income from 5000 to 5999, Burden Expenses from 6000 to 6999, Selling Expenses from 7000 to 7999, General and Administrative Expenses from 8000 to 8999. Nonoperating Income and Expenses from 9000 to 9999. Each of the basic divisions has account titles for almost every conceivable general ledger account; and these are presented in a sequence in accord with recommended financial statement presentation, with grouping of financial statement classifications within the basic divisions. There are over 6000 specific account titles including over 800 different expense titles, and there are additional unused numbers with each division for personalized or additional titles.

[5] Preface by W. E. Karrenbrock on: Alton Lee, Jr., The Uniform Coded Chart of Accounts, A Coding Dictionary (Newport Beach, California: Quintus Cyntania).

Customer Coding

To better understand their operations, more and more organizations are implementing extremely large coding structures to identify their customers. Although these codes are expensive to install and maintain, the information they provide is judged as justifying this cost. For example, the 33 position customer code in a hypothetical organization might look like this:

10814008500732191135004371655327 9

Examing this code in detail it is found to represent the following information:

1. The first 8 digits—10814008—is a random identification number assigned to each new customer account.

2. The next 2 digits—50—provide for identifying each geographical point related to a customer and to where goods might be shipped.

3. The next digit—0—indicates whether this location is the source of payment for this customer.

4. The next 3 digits—732—relate this account to a parent organization.

5. The next 2 digits—19—identify the customer's general classification of trade.

6. The next 7 digits—1135004—indicate the sales division (the first 2 digits), the sales territory (the next 2 digits), and the salesman for the account (the last 3 digits).

7. The next 5 digits—37165—indicate the zipcode.

8. The next 2 digits—53—equal the credit rating.

9. The final 3 digits—279—indicate the plant from which shipment is usually made and from where freight charges might be calculated.

While at first this code may seem somewhat complex and extended, more and more organizations are adopting similar codes for their accounts.

Data Universal Numbering System (D–U–N–S)®[6]

Dun & Bradstreet, Inc. has developed and markets a coding structure known as the Data Universal Numbering System (D–U–N–S®). This code is a nine digit number with the high order position (left-most) containing a check

---

BALANCE SHEET STATEMENT ACCOUNTS

Assets (100–299)

Current assets (100–199)
101   Cash
110   Accounts receivable
120   Inventory
126   Securities (marketable)
147   Supplies
158   Prepaid rent

Plant and equipment (200–289)
201   Land
231   Furniture and fixtures

Intangibles (290–299)
291   Goodwill
293   Organization cost

Liabilities and Stockholders' Equity (300–499)

Current liabilities (300–359)
301   Accounts payable
326   Notes payable

Long-term liabilities (360–399)
361   Long-term notes payable
376   Bonds payable

Stockholders' equity (400–499)
401   Capital stock
436   Retained earnings
499   Dividends

INCOME STATEMENT ACCOUNTS (500–999)

Revenue (500–529)
501   Sales store A
502   Sales store B

Expenses (530–989)
531   Salaries
537   Power and supplies
540   Rent

Summary Accounts (990–999)
991   Revenue and expense summary

FIGURE 7.7.   An illustration of a simple chart of accounts classification.

6 Dun & Bradstreet Brochures D-U-N-S® *Data Universal Numbering System, Dun's Market Identifiers.* With permission.

digit. Subscribers to this system have access to the financial and marketing data base maintained by Dun & Bradstreet, Inc. This data base has additional coding structures which identify the number of employees, dollar value of sales, net worth, state and city codes, and as many as six Standard Industrial Classifications (SIC) codes which relate to each establishment coded in the data base.

All maintenance of these coding structures is provided by Dun & Bradstreet, Inc., and for designated fees, a subscriber can obtain an extraction from this data base on a medium which permits further computer processing.

Other Coding Systems

A series of coding structures have been proposed recently in order to improve the communications among manufacturers, wholesalers, and retailers, as well as to improve their data processing efficiency.[7]

1. *National Drug Code (NDC).* This coding structure uses a nine character, three field identification code. The first three characters are the manufacturer's or labeler's identification number as assigned by the Federal Drug Administration (FDA). The next four characters represent the product and are assigned by the manufacturer. The last two characters are the trade package size and are also assigned by the manufacturer.

2. *National Health Related Items Code (NHRIC).* This coding system uses a ten character, two field identification code. The first four characters are the manufacturer's identification number as assigned by the FDA. The next six characters represent the product identification and are assigned by the manufacturer.

3. *Universal Product Code (UPC).* For several years, the Grocery Industry Ad Hoc Committee studied an overall method to optimize checkout procedures in grocery stores. Seven companies, plus IBM, National Cash Register, Litton Industries, and Singer, submitted proposals for a coding symbol. In April 1973, the Ad Hoc Committee rejected all symbols and came up with its

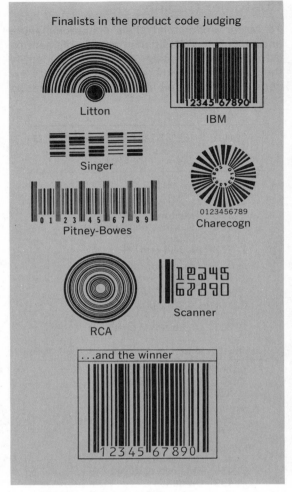

FIGURE 7.8. Illustration of seven finalists for the universal product code plus the winner adopted by the Grocery Industry Ad Hoc Committee.

own design. The finalists in the product coding symbols submitted plus the one finally adopted by the committee are shown[8] in Figure 7.8. This coding system uses a ten character, two field identification code. The first five digits are to identify the manufacturer and the last five identify the specific product. By labeling various

---

[7] Data Processor, Oct. 6, 1972, a newsletter published by the National Wholesale Druggists' Association. With permission.

[8] "A Standard Labeling Code For Food," *Business Week,* April 7, 1973, pp. 71–73.

kinds of food products according to a single industry standard, retailers, wholesalers, and manufacturers can increase efficiency and slim profit margins by conversion to a point-of-sale (POS) system using electronic cash registers and computers.

By changing the bar widths in the code and the spaces between the bars, all variations of products and sizes stocked by the user can be indicated. The code on the packages can be read either by a wand reader or by a fixed, automated scanner as each coded package passes by on a conveyor. In either event, this point-of-sale entry system enables users to decrease checkout time; increase inventory control; eliminate price marking and price changing every item (prices along with other data will be stored in the computer system); improve communications between store, warehouse, and manufacturer; improve resource and shelf allocation; and generally produce a broader range of more timely information to a variety of decision makers.

SUMMARY

Identifying meaningful classifications of data is an essential aspect of developing sophisticated data bases. The systems analyst guards against the extremes of narrow, specialized classifications and broad,

extensive, and expensive classifications.

The use of codes and the code structure is equally important when developing a system. Codes are used to identify data and to give meaning to it. There are three basic sets of coding symbols important to information processing: (1) numeric, (2) alphabetic, and (3) alphanumeric.

The two primary approaches to the development of code structures are sequential codes and block codes. Variations of block code structures include: (1) facet, (2) hierarchical, and (3) decimal. Special purpose codes include: (1) mnemonic, (2) phonetic, and (3) symbolic (e.g. UPC). Mnemonic codes are used extensively in manual systems for aiding memory of human users. Phonetic codes are used in systems where there is a great need for accessing names. Symbolic coding techniques for use in data collection promise to become more important in future information systems development.

The use of a check digit in code structures provides a standardized procedure for validating codes.

The Chart of Accounts and customer identification are two primary examples where classification and coding are important. Coding structures related to transactions or activities common to many different organizations exist and must be considered in the design of information systems.

REVIEW QUESTIONS

7.1 Define classification. Why are data classified?

7.2 Define coding. Relate classification to coding.

7.3 What are the functions of codes?

7.4 Briefly explain the considerations involved in code design.

7.5 What are the advantages and disadvantages of sequential codes? of block codes?

7.6 What is the key aspect that differentiates block codes from sequential codes?

7.7 What is the purpose of a mnemonic code?

7.8 What is the purpose of a phonetic code?

7.9 Describe a hierarchical block code. Give an example of one besides that given in the chapter.

7.10 Why should check digits be appended to code numbers? At the very minimum, how many times is the check digit calculated?

7.11 What are some of the major advantages and disadvantages related to implementing a standardized coding system for use by many different organizations?

QUESTIONS FOR DISCUSSION

7.1 Why are not all data items simply given a sequential code number?

7.2 "We don't worry about classifying data too much. We just store it in our files and retrieve when we need it." Comment on this statement.

7.3 "As far as we are concerned, as accountants, classification of data fall into five broad categories: assets, liabilities, equities, revenue, and expenses." Comment on this statement.

7.4 "Classification is an intellectual process, whereas coding is a mechanical process." Comment on this statement.

7.5 "What good are phonetic codes? You can't use them for basic data processing." Comment on this statement.

7.6 The importance of using check digits for important codes is increasing. Recent developments in data entry devices, e.g. buffered keypunches, permits the automatic verification of codes with certain check digits at the time they are recorded. This valuable control concept should be utilized in the design of all new systems. Discuss.

7.7 "With recent advancements in computer technology, there is less need for using codes to identify certain data than ever before. Although use of codes is still more efficient than descriptive data, codes tend to depersonalize individuals. The inefficiencies related to processing noncoded data should be balanced against the benefits of minimizing feelings of depersonalization which are associated with computer processing." Discuss this statement from both its technical and nontechnical implications.

7.8 "It seems no matter how many different ways we code a given element of data, someone in the organization needs still another aspect coded in order to produce his informational requirements." Discuss.

7.9 "If an individual would only examine the type of coding required to input data into the data base, he would understand the basic information available to him." Explain.

7.10 "Each new standardized coding system implemented in our society removes one more barrier to an individual's privacy." Evaluate.

EXERCISES

7.1 Using prime number weighting and Modulus 11, prepare a check digit for three account numbers of your choice. Then prepare the algorithm in a programming language of your choice which verifies the accuracy of these numbers as they are read into the computer.

7.2 Using the Soundex System, prepare a code for your name.

7.3 Examine the subscription label from any magazine or journal in terms of the coding printed on that label. Identify, as well as you can, what each part of this code represents. What characteristics might you expect that the publishers would desire to be codified to assist their operations?

7.4 Examine the statement from a credit card system of your choice. Prepare a report which analyzes the coding found on the statement. Include in your report some recommendations for additional coding schemes which might be implemented to provide additional information.

7.5 The increasing emphasis on automotive safety has resulted in Detroit automobile manufacturers having to recall millions of automobiles for real and potential safety defects. Oftentimes the potential safety problem is related to a certain part made in a specific plant or in a specific time period. Obviously, if the automobile manufacturer could determine which automobiles had which parts, needless expense could be eliminated in many recalls. Moreover, structural defects in older cars could also be addressed, as they are determined, after years of operations. One suggestion offered by safety experts is the development of an indentification number which could be imprinted on a metal plate and attached to each automobile. This number would be recorded by a dealer on all new sales and by the owner on all subsequent resells.

Using the above ideas and any additional assumptions or ideas of your own, prepare a proposal for a coding structure to be used by the automobile manufacturers.

PROBLEMS **7.1** Design a chart of accounts for Drs. U. Pullem and I. L. Fillem, partners in dentistry.

7.2 Design a chart of accounts for a small manufacturing company that produces BBs.

7.3 You are a systems analyst for the Bayon State Insurance Company of Ruston, Louisiana. Your job, among other things, is to design a coding structure for the Automobile Claims File. Following are items of the file which must be coded.

1. Identification of cities and towns in Louisiana.
2. Personal Injury Protection Deductible Coverage:
   Full coverage
   $250 Deductible Name Insured
   $500 Deductible Name Insured
   $1,000 Deductible Name Insured
   $2,000 Deductible Name Insured
   $250 Name Insured and Members of Household
   $500 Name Insured and Members of Household
   $1,000 Name Insured and Members of Household
   $2,000 Name Insured and Members of Household

3. Bodily Injury Limits:

5/10	50/100
10/20	20/50
15/30	100/300
20/40	Excess of 100/300
25/50	All other

4. Medical Payments Limits:

$500	$3,000
750	5,000 and over
1,000	All other
2,000	No Medical Payments

5. Property Damage:

$ 5,000	$ 50,000
10,000	100,000
15,000	300,000
25,000	All other
35,000	No Property Damage

6. Property Damage Coverage:
Full Coverage + Option 1
Full Coverage + Option 2
Full Coverage + Option 3
Deductible   + Option 1
Deductible   + Option 2
Deductible   + Option 3
Full Coverage
Straight Deductible

Design a coding scheme to properly classify and make the above items more manageable, meaningful, and amenable to processing.

7.4 A transaction code has been developed for the Ample Foundation Company as illustrated in Figure 7.9.

Following is a partial list of the transactions for September:

Acct. No.	Code	Quantity	Cost Code	Sales Price
400	23241301038	400	MRT	OFU
✓	43222102044	300	OPL	EFU
✓	55422307740	250	RTT	UFI
✓	45422124937	500	ROP	PET
✓	45422236783	275	ROP	PET
✓	44425173047	800	OFT	UPF
✓	43534407451	750	OIF	ULF
✓	75741380415	450	ETU	LFU
✓	53635407082	600	RTU	POF
✓	33422410121	950	OIU	ULU

Please answer the following questions based on the partial list of transactions for September.

Position	1	2	3	4	5	6	7–8 Market[1] region	9–10 Outlet[2]	11 Salesman	12–15 Quantity[3]
Digit	Size	Cup	Color	Style	Trim	Market				
1	30	A	White rain	Standard	Plain	South	Dallas	Neiman–Marcus	Larry Lovely	xxxx
2	32	B	Black velvet	Strapless	Lace	West	Little Rock	Godchaus	Bruce Bardot	
3	34	C	Pink cherry	Foundation	Color inset	Midwest	Memphis	Goldrings	Tyron LeRock	
4	36	D	Red amber	Long line	Zig–zag stitch	Northeast	New Orleans	Holmes	Geraldine Goodbody	
5	38	E	Blue ice	Other	Ribbon	–	Birmingham	Palais–Royale	Peter Perfecto	
6	40	–	Psycho-delic	–	–	–	Jackson	etc.	Prissy Galore	
7	42	–	Polka dot	–	–	–	Atlanta		Herman Hands	
8	–	–	–	–	–	–	Richmond		John deJohn	
9	–	–	–	–	–	–	Charlotte		U. R. Quicki	
0	–	–	–	. –	–	–	etc.		B. G. O'Toole	

[1] Market regions are sequence codes (00–99) within the market.
[2] Outlets are sequence codes (00–99) within the Market Region.
Example: Market: South; Market Region: Dallas; Outlet: Holmes is 10003.
[3] Represents actual quantity—cannot exceed 9999.
In addition, Dollar Code is: 1 2 3 4 5 6 7 8 9 0; last two letters in a code = cents.
MOREUPLIFT

FIGURE 7.9. Coding structure for Ample Foundation Company.

1. What is the most popular color nationwide? In the Northeast?
2. If the selling price of 23241 is $2.95 each, what is the income from the item?
3. What salesman produced largest dollar sales? What salesman sold the most quantity of item? What salesman produced the largest profit?
4. What market is the most profitable?
5. What market uses the most E cups?
6. How many 36 E cups did Herman Hands sell this period?
7. How many 36 C Blue Ice items were sold this period?

7.5 A bank data base contains several files, one of which contains a complete customer profile. This file is stored on a DASD and is accessible by bank tellers via online inquiry devices. One way to access this file is by an abbreviated alphanumeric code. The last name of the customer is abbreviated by a computer-generated key based on eliminating certain letters and replacing others with phonetic symbols. Using this method, as outlined in the text, code the following names: RODRIGUEZ, BROWN, JOHNSON, COHEN. Would you code the names, RODRIGEZ, JONSON, AND COHAN the same? If not, then how would you access, say, IZZY COHEN if you also have an IZZY COHAN in the files?

7.6 Old Briar Patch, Inc., is a major corporation which acts as a holding company for numerous smaller corporations engaged in the distillation, blending, bottling, and distribution of spirits. Old Briar Patch controls 45 corporations, sells six basic spirit types (Gin, Bourbon, Scotch, Canadian, etc.), sells under 60 different brand names, bottles 26 sizes (from small one-drink bottles to gallons in various increments), engages in both domestic and export business, offers many special packages (Christmas, Father's Day, etc., as well as wooden crate, cardboard carton, and similar variations), and distributes in up to 1000 subclassifications of geographical area. Develop a product/customer combination code.

The product code should uniquely identify each product sold, and, in addition, provide for statistical analysis by financial account, spirit type, brand, size, market, area sold, and so forth. Also, the combined customer code indicates at least three items, such as the major area within domestic and export class, subclass within major area, and customer serial within area subclass. (Adapted from: Van Court Hare, Jr., *Systems Analysis: A Diagnostic Approach* (New York: Harcourt, Brace, Jovanovich, 1967), pp. 501–503.)

BIBLIOGRAPHY   "A Standard Labeling Code for Food," *Business Week,* April 7, 1973.

Alan and Yeates, *Systems Analysis,* Palo Alto, California: Science Research Associates, Inc., College Division, 1971.

Budzilovich, "Tomorrow's Supermarket—The Automated Checkout Counter," *Computer Decisions,* September, 1972.

Classification and Coding Techniques to Facilitate Accounting Operations, N.A.A. Research Report 34, New York: National Association of Accountants, 1959.

Clifton, *Systems Analysis for Business Data Processing,* Philadelphia: Auerbach Publishers, 1970.

Data Processor, a newsletter published by the National Wholesale Druggists' Association, October 6, 1972.

Dun & Bradstreet Brochures, *D–U–N–S,®* *Data Universal Numbering System, Dun's Market Identifiers.*

Hare, *Systems Analysis: A Diagnostic Approach,* New York: Harcourt, Brace, Jovanovich, 1967.

Lee, Preface by W. E. Karrenbrock, *The Uniform Coded Coded Chart of Accounts, A Coding Dictionary,* Newport Beach, California: Quintris Cyntania.

Slavin, Reynolds, and Malchman, *Basic Accounting for Managerial and Financial Control,* New York: Holt, Rinehart, and Winston, Inc., 1968.

"Soundex: Foolproof Filing System for Finding Any Name in the File," Remington Rand Brochure LVB809.

8 General File Storage Considerations

8.1 Introduction

In Chapter 6 it was indicated that a data base could be defined as a collection of data files. A data file was identified as a physical and/or logical organization of data. The design of data files has always been an important part of information systems work, even in purely manual systems. However, with the development of computer technology and storage media, and the trend towards greater integration of data files, this activity may well be considered *the* most important systems activity. Consequently, in this chapter, a discussion of the concepts related to general file storage and design is presented and in Chapter 9 additional concepts related to data structure and record association are analyzed. The specific objectives of this chapter are:

1. To review the primary computer storage media for data files.
2. To analyze the composition of data files.
3. To present the most common classifications used to describe data files.

175

4. To identify the basic criteria used to select file media and file organization methods.

5. To summarize the primary considerations related to data file design.

8.2 Computer Storage Media

Data files can be stored on a variety of hardware storage media accessible during computer processing. For a given system the storage media selected depends upon the objectives and requirements of that system. The characteristics of the various types of file storage must first be understood before the systems analyst can make a logical determination as to how data files are to be selected, organized, and processed. One popular classification of storage media is based on the methods in which data can be accessed, and provides two broad categories: sequential and direct. Sequential access is merely serially searching through a file of records until the appropriate record has been found. On the other hand, records stored on a direct access storage device (DASD) have a unique address. Thus, records can be stored on a DASD in such a way that the location of any one record can be determined without extensive searching, so that records can be accessed directly rather than sequentially.

Figure 8.1 lists the basic storage media and

Media	Sequential Access	Direct Access
Punched Cards	X	
Punched Tape	X	
Magnetic Tape	X	
Magnetic Drum	X	X
Magnetic Disk	X	X
Data Cells	X	X
Core (Memory)	X	X

FIGURE 8.1. Basic file media with method of access.

indicates which access method is applicable. Note that while all storage media can be accessed sequentially, certain media cannot be accessed via the direct method.

Punched Cards and Punched Paper Tape

Two of the earliest developed and most widely used storage media are punched cards and punched paper tape. Although many small organizations still process their data via these storage media, they are seldom considered as desirable alternatives in more sophisticated data base applications. However, these media are still extremely valuable as alternatives for inputting data transactions, particularly in batch processing environments.

While there are many versions of punched cards (tab cards) utilized for data processing, by far the most widely used card is known as the Hollerith card, named after its inventor. The Hollerith card provides storage for as many as 80 characters of data. This data is entered into 80 vertical columns with twelve punching positions in each column. One or more punches in a single column represents a character. Figure 8.2 illustrates one coding structure for character designation. Data on a card might represent part of a record, one record, or more than one record. If a particular record contains more data than one card can hold, then two or more cards can be used. Continuity in the cards of one record is obtained by punching an identifying code in a specified column of each card.

Paper tape is a continuous storage medium. Consequently, paper tape can be used to store records of any length, limited only by the capacity of the buffer area of the equipment being used to process the tape. Paper tape can contain five or eight channels (punching positions) with which data can be represented. Certain combinations of punches in the channels provides a binary representation of characters which can subsequently be interpreted and processed.

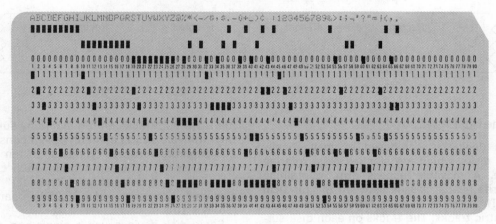

FIGURE 8.2. A Hollerith card showing how different characters are represented.

Magnetic Tape

Magnetic tape[1] is also a continuous storage medium similar to the tape used in sound recorders. Data are stored in magnetized bits, are permanent, and can be retained for an indefinite period. As data are stored, the previous data are destroyed, thus permitting repetitive use of the tape.

A typical tape segment is shown in Figure 8.3. Each record is separated from the adjoining record by a blank section of tape known as the interblock gap. The size of tape records may vary from a few characters to several thousand and is restricted only by the capacity of the equipment that processes the tape.

[1] Magnetic storage media is discussed in more depth in Appendix B.

Actually the term "record" can mean a logical unit or a physical unit of data. A logical record may be defined as a collection of data classified and identified by a code. A customer file, for example, would contain, among other things, a logical record for every customer number in the file. A physical record is comprised of one or more logical records. The term "block" is equivalent to the term "physical record."

Since the interblock gaps waste space, the logical records are usually "blocked" in groups of N physical records where N represents the blocking factor. For example, the tape of Figure 8.3 could be blocked using a blocking factor of 4 as illustrated in Figure 8.4.

Although blocking conserves storage space and decreases the processing time required for reading and writing the tape, it adds to the core requirement of the program processing the file.

I B G	Record 1	I B G	Record 2	I B G	Record 3	I B G	Record 4	I B G

FIGURE 8.3. Segment of magnetic tape.

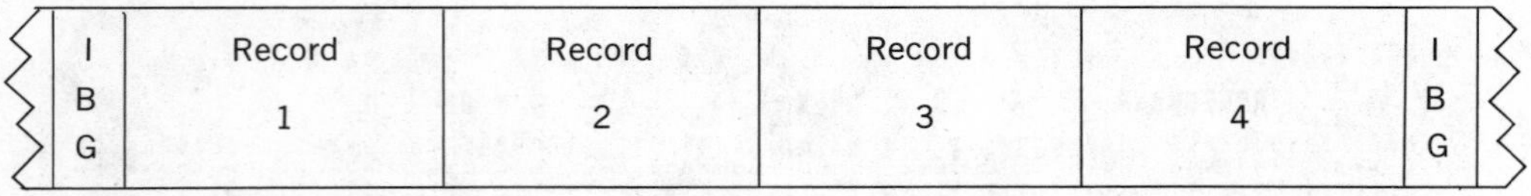

| I B G | Record 1 | Record 2 | Record 3 | Record 4 | I B G |

FIGURE 8.4.   Magnetic tape segment with blocked records.

Magnetic Disk

A disk device is composed of magnetically coated disks, which are stacked on a rotating spindle. A movable access arm, containing read/write heads, passes between the physical disks. The surface of each disk is divided into concentric tracks. The tracks on each disk surface are located physically one above the other forming a sort of series of concentric cylinders. A schematic of a disk device is shown in Figure 8.5.

A "cylinder" of data is the amount that is accessible with one positioning of the access mechanism. The concept of a "cylinder" is an important one because the movement of the access mechanism represents a significant portion of the time required to access and transfer data. A large amount of data can be stored in a single "cylinder," thus minimizing the movements of the access mechanism. For example, the magnetic disk system in Figure 8.5 consists of ten separate horizontal recording surfaces. If

there are 200 tracks on the recording surfaces, then from an access point of view, it consists of 200 separate vertical "cylinders" of ten tracks each. If each track can contain 3625 characters (bytes) of data, then a "cylinder" has a maximum capacity of 36,250 characters (3625×10).

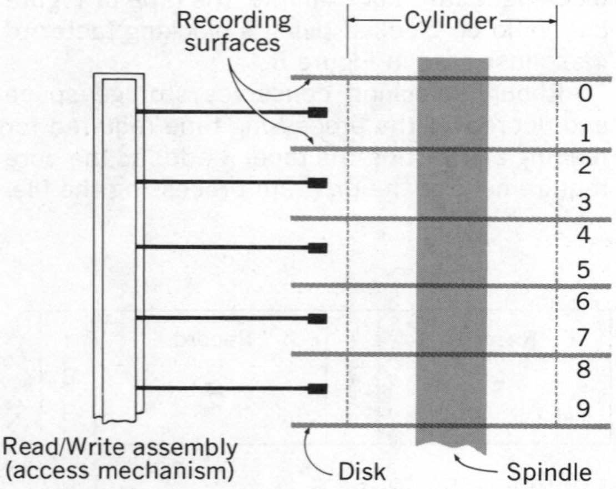

Some disk devices use a single-arm access mechanism, which moves both horizontally and vertically to access any track within the disk file. However, most disk devices are equipped with a comb-type access mechanism in which the arms are arranged like the teeth on a comb and move horizontally between the disks. The read/write heads are aligned vertically and all move together. Thus, for each position of the access mechanism one entire cylinder surface is accessible to the heads. There are also disk devices which contain read/write heads permanently located at all cylinders thereby eliminating any arm movement.

Data records stored on a DASD, are recorded in locations that are identified by unique addresses. A disk address is a number that represents a particular cylinder on which a desired data record has been written or is to be written. For example, if a particular record is located in cylinder 84 of disk surface 3, then the actual (sometimes called the relative address) hardware address of the record is 843. The read/write heads are "told" to go to this particular address, whereupon the fourth read/write head either reads from or writes on this location.

8.3 Composition of Data Files

A file in an information system is a collection of records. These records in turn contain specific

FIGURE 8.5.   Magnetic disk system.

fields of data. Each record, although it may contain common attributes with other records in the file, is a discrete, specific entity that is usually identified by a unique record code. There are a number of techniques for arranging records within the files to meet specific processing and reporting requirements.

Review of Records

A record is a collection of fields (data items) arranged in a defined format and related to a code (identifier, key, address, etc.). A record code such as a customer account number, an inventory item number, a student number, and so on, are used for data access, manipulation, etc., as discussed previously. There can be more than one code in a record for various information purposes. The relative position of a record in the hierarchical scheme of the data base itself is illustrated in Figure 8.6.

The term record can be used in reference to either its logical or physical structure. A logical record describes the limits of the related data without reference to the actual structure of the data on the storage media. A physical record, on the other hand, ignores related data struc-

ture and describes the physical limitations of the storage media.

Types of Records and Their Functions

Within a given data file, there are commonly three types of records each having its own function.

1. *Data Records.* The bulk of a file is comprised of data records which contain specific values about things, persons, or objects.

2. *Label Record.* This type of a record is used for file identification and control, and is usually generated by the operating system of the computer. The label record is normally the first record read in a file and contains information such as the name of the file, creation date, retention cycle, and so forth.

3. *Trailer Record.* This record is similar to the label record but is positioned at the end of a file. Its function is also to produce control and identification information pertaining to the data file.

Logical and Physical Record Relationships

There are four possible relationships between physical and logical data records within a data file.

1. *Fixed-Fixed.* In a fixed-fixed format, the number of logical records within a physical record (block) is constant throughout the file. The length of the logical record within each block is of the same length and the blocking factor is constant. A fixed-fixed format (i.e., each physical record containing the same number of logical records) is illustrated in Figure 8.7.

2. *Fixed-Variable.* In a fixed-variable format, the number of records within a block is constant, but the length of these logical records vary, as illustrated in Figure 8.8.

3. *Variable-Fixed.* In this format, a variable number of fixed-length logical records are contained within each physical record, i.e., the logical records are of equal length, but the blocks

FIGURE 8.6. Hierarchical system of the data base.

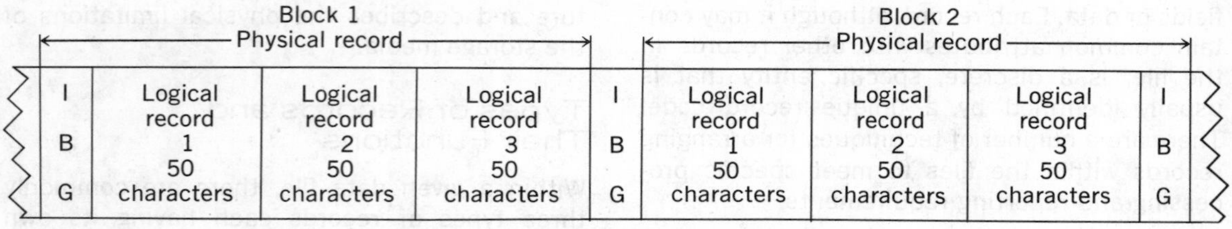

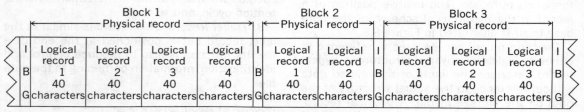

FIGURE 8.7. Fixed–fixed format.

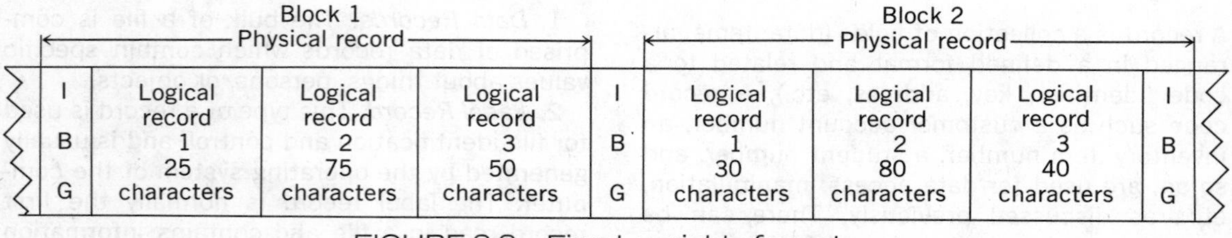

FIGURE 8.8. Fixed–variable format.

FIGURE 8.9. Variable–fixed format.

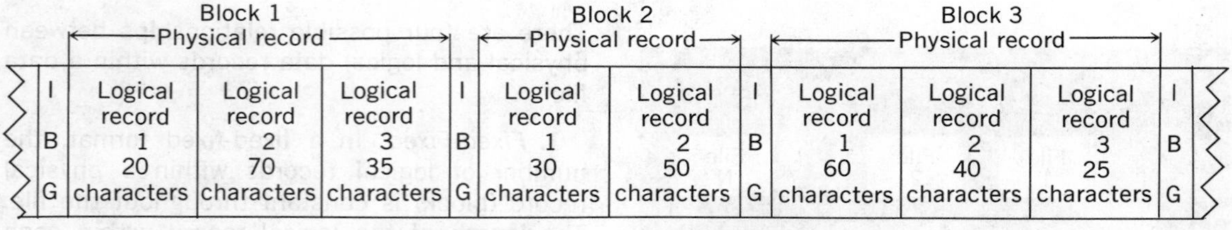

FIGURE 8.10. Variable–variable format.

are of different lengths, as represented in Figure 8.9.

4. *Variable-Variable.* In this format, both the length of the physical record and the logical record vary, as illustrated in Figure 8.10.

Determining the content, structure, and format of data records is an essential element of file design which the systems analyst must make during the design phase of a system. Unless an analyst is aware of the various types of record formats available for use in computer processing, and evaluates the appropriateness of each format as it relates to his or her other problems, the final design of the system may be less than optimum.

When evaluating the record format to be utilized, analysts should first consider the processing and storage problem they are attempting to solve. Additional considerations, which are also important, include the processing capabilities of the computer to be utilized, and the programming considerations as related to each type of record format. Obviously, any deviation from a fixed-fixed format creates a formidable programming challenge.

8.4 Classification of Data Files

The way data files are used in an information system, together with the available hardware device characteristics, will help guide us in considering and selecting storage media and file organization. Following are some of the ways files are used according to contents, mode of processing, and organization.

Classification According to Contents

In this classification files fall into seven basic categories: (1) master file, (2) transaction file, (3) index file, (4) table file, (5) summary file, (6) archival (historical) file, and (7) backup file.

1. *Master File.* This category of file contains data records for basic identification as well as an accumulation of certain statistical data. Examples of master files are: customer file, employee file, vendor file, stockholder file, product file and so forth. Descriptive data contained in these files might include: Customer file—name, address, credit rating, account number, billing and shipping instructions, etc.: Product file—product code, styles, components, packaging, weight, etc. Statistical data contained in these files is generally of the current status type, such as: outstanding balance owed, quantity on hand, purchases to date, shares owned, and so forth. Master files can be utilized effectively in both offline and online processing as required to satisfy the organization's requirements.

2. *Transaction File.* If the method of updating is batch, then a transaction file is necessary to accumulate activity records which will be used to update the master file. The records in this file are usually created from source documents such as receiving reports, invoices, purchase orders, time cards, etc.

3. *Index Files.* These files are used to indicate, via an index key or address, where specific records are located in other files, usually in some master file. This file is analogous to a card catalog in a library, where index records are retrieved first to indicate locations of particular books of interest.

4. *Table Files.* These files provide fairly static reference data, normally used during processing. For example, one may use a pay rate table for preparation of payrolls, a freight rate table for preparation of bills-of-lading, a premium table for insurance billing, and so forth.

5. *Summary File (Report File or Work File).* This file represents data extracted from other files or which has been compiled into a more concise or meaningful form. For example, once data has been extracted and summarized from several accounting ledger files, then accounting reports can be prepared.

6. *Archival Files (History Files).* These files are also often termed master files. They contain statistical data for noncurrent periods and are used to create comparative reports, plot trends, pay commission, and so forth. Archival files are normally updated periodically and involve large volumes of data. In an online mode, they can be utilized for reference purposes.

7. *Backup File.* These are simply noncurrent files of any type which are stored in a file library and are used as a link in a file creation process if a current master file is destroyed.

Classification According to Mode of Processing

There are three modes in which files can be processed: (1) input, (2) output, and (3) overlay.

1. *Input.* The data from the file is read into the CPU's storage and operated upon. An output that can be placed in another file results. For example, an old master tape file is read into storage, along with the transaction file.

2. *Output.* Data are processed and then written on another tape, resulting in a new master tape file.

3. *Overlay.* A record can be accessed from a file into main storage, updated and written back to its original location. The original value of the record is lost unless such updates are recorded (or logged) in another file. Only DASD can be

utilized in overlay mode. An obvious advantage using this mode of processing is that it is possible to deal with only a specific record of the file without having to process the entire file. Countervailing this advantage is the risk of destroying data which cannot be recreated easily.

Classification According to Organization of Files

For strictly card and tape-oriented systems, file organization is normally sequential. However, DASD, in addition to accommodating sequentially organized files, can also handle files where data records are organized as follows: indexed sequential, partitioned sequential, and direct.

Sequential Organization. With the use of sequential organization of data records, these records are placed on the file using a key or code for sequencing, e.g. inventory item sequence. Usually before changing or updating the sequential file, all new items are first batched and sorted into the same sequence. To access any data record in the sequential file, all records preceding the one in question must first be read. That is, in order to access record number 1000, the system must read past 999 records. An insertion of a data record means creating a new sequential file.

Sequential organization is an efficient method of storage if there is a large volume of records and a high percentage of the records are required during a processing run. If, on the other hand, only isolated data records are processed, the access time with this type of organization is sometimes too great to make this method efficient.

Indexed Sequential Organization. Data records are physically arranged in some prescribed sequence as in the sequential organization method. In addition to this sequence a table of addresses is established which equates to selected codes or keys in the data record. The keys are selected during programming. The actual addresses are assigned to data records as the file is created, or updated, and inserted in the table. In this method or organization, the computer operating system has control over the location of the individual records. The user, therefore, need do very little I/O programming, since the operating system does a large portion of it.

When the file is accessed, the desired data record key or code is matched against the index table. The actual address of that record (or one reasonably close) is secured, and used by the program, to locate and read the data record in the physical file. Such an arrangement provides the capability of locating a particular record without reading all preceding records. This approach is again similar to using the card index to locate a book in the library.

Figure 8.11 illustrates the principle of indexed sequential organization.

This example shows records that are recorded in cylinder 87, on disk surfaces 0 through 3. The first four data records in the file are accessed by read/write head 0. The value of the record codes in this particular track are 10,

Index Table Created by Computer Operating System			File	
Address of cylinder	Surface	Highest value of code in track	Actual disk address	Record codes
87	0	13	870	10,11,12,13
87	1	18	871	14,15,16,17,18
87	2	22	872	19,20,21,22
87	3	25	873	23,25

FIGURE 8.11. Example of indexed sequential file.

11, 12, and 13 respectively. The next five records are accessed by read/write head 1, and so on. The entire file of data records is stored between the two disk addresses 870 and 873. The addresses of the disk relate to both the cylinder and to the highest numbered record in a particular track.

In an access, the cylinder index first positions the read/write heads to the correct cylinder. Then the proper track index, in which the specific record in question is located, is determined. Once the proper track has been located, the proper read/write head is activated and the desired record is then read (or written assuming update).

Assume, for example, that we wish to locate record 16. Remember that a table with each code number and the address to which it is assigned on the disk has been established.[2] Therefore, to access a particular record, the requestor specifies the code number of the desired record, and the computer "looks up" its address and accesses it immediately, by the following steps. The computer searches the cylinder index and determines that record 16 is somewhere in cylinder 87. The access mechanism moves all read/write heads to this cylinder; the track index is searched and, since record 16 is greater than 13 and less than 18, it is determined that record 16 is on surface 1 of cylinder 87. Next, all of the data at 871 is read into CPU storage and searched sequentially for record 16.

Most file organization schemes set aside several tracks on each disk surface for storage of records which must be added later but still fit into the present file organization. For example, suppose that the records stored at address 873 completely fill that track and consist of records with codes of 23 and 25. If we wish to add a data record which has a code of 24 to the file, it would obviously belong at address 873 but we cannot insert it there as the file is presently set up. We might restructure the entire file by

dumping all data records on a backup file and then recreating the file with record 24 inserted between records 23 and 25. This operation takes a great deal of time and is quite inefficient. Moreover, the need to insert or add data records in a file may happen fairly frequently. Therefore, to avoid the necessity of restructuring the file each time a record is to be inserted, overflow tracks are set up to accommodate these records. Proper references are established in the index so that these new records can also be accessed. Over a period of time the overflow tracks also become full, therefore it may become necessary to restructure the entire file from time to time although not as often as would be required if overflow tracks were not set aside. Additionally, most organization schemes also provide for secondary overflow which can be utilized when any one or more track overflows are filled.

Partitioned Sequential. A partitioned sequential file is one divided into sections or members, each having an individual name in which the items are stored sequentially. In this kind of organization a directory containing the names and location of these members or sections within the file is searched to find the location of a particular member, i.e., the name and actual disk address of each member is listed in a member index established by the computer operating system.

The first item stored in any member is accessed directly, then the remaining items in that particular member or section are accessed sequentially. This type of organization is used mainly for the storage of programs, subroutines, libraries, or core dumps. Although magnetic tape can accommodate partitioned files, such as a library of programs or subroutines, direct access to a specific member is not possible because all preceding data have to be read in order to find the desired member.

Direct Organization. Direct organization (sometimes called random) stores and accesses data records using a scheme of converting the code of a record into an actual address to which the access mechanism positions itself. With direct organization, there is a definite rela-

---

[2] Although indexes can be established by individual programmers, the operating systems of many computers have this preprogrammed logic standardized and, for the most part, it is not reinvented for each application.

tionship between the code of a record and its actual address on the physical file. For example, a program may state that when a particular code is multiplied by 248 and then added to 70, the cylinder address of the record is determined, and when added to 12, the surface number is derived. Therefore, no index table or directory, as used with indexed sequential organization, is used for the actual address. Rather, a mathematical calculation or transformation technique is performed on the code which in turn provides the actual address of the record.

With direct organization, there are two ways to address the file:

1. *Direct addressing.* With direct addressing, every possible code in the file converts to a *unique* address. This condition makes it possible to access any record in the file with only one seek and one read. This method minimizes processing time when performing random processing, but in many instances there is a waste of storage, i.e., a location must be reserved for every code in the file's address range even though many of them are not used.

2. *Indirect addressing.* With this type of addressing, the range of codes for a file is reduced to a smaller desired range of addresses by using some transformation technique (also called randomizing technique) when the code is converted to an address. However, this method usually produces some level of "synonyms"—two or more records whose codes transform to the same address causing a conflict. (A brief discussion of transformation techniques is presented in Chapter 9.)

This discussion of ways to classify files was intended to provide an understanding of general file storage considerations. This understanding is particularly critical when choosing an approach to the organization of a file. There exist no hard and fast rules, based on contents alone, for the determination of whether a certain type of file should be placed on magnetic tape, disk, or data cell. The final decision, as to what media a file should be designed for, depends upon considerations presented in the next section.

8.5 Selection Considerations for File Media and File Organization Methods

Selecting the most appropriate storage media, and the best file organization methods, for a particular computer configuration depends on a number of considerations based on application requirements and available resources. A discussion of these considerations follows.

File Update

Figure 8.12 presents a schematic which represents the updating of a *sequential processing* system:

The major characteristic of the above updating procedure, using sequential file storage media, is that the old master is read into the computer each time it is updated and an entirely new master file is created. Since the entire old master file must be read during each updating cycle, it is normally desirable to accumulate transactions in large batches before processing them. This reduces the frequency of set up and processing operations.

Alternatively, the direct or *random processing* method processes transactions and inquiries as

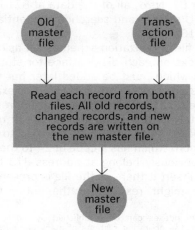

FIGURE 8.12. An illustration of sequential updating.

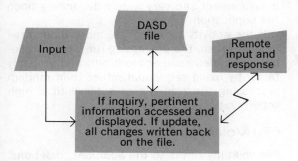

FIGURE 8.13. An illustration of online, random processing.

they occur. This processing method is the one most widely utilized for online processing via terminals. A schematic of online, random processing is shown in Figure 8.13.

In most organizations using this kind of a system, a number of I/O devices are scattered throughout the organization so that a variety of users can get access to the files concurrently for a variety of reasons. However, this method is also applicable in batch processing environments where it has been determined that a number of files are required online simultaneously for efficient processing. For example, Figure 8.14 depicts a processing step that is

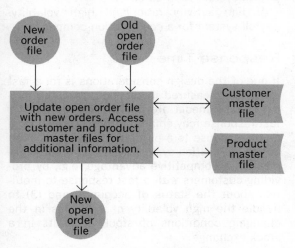

FIGURE 8.14. An illustration of random processing in a batch environment.

adding new customer records to an Open Order File. At the same time, the Customer Master File and Product Master File are used in processing. The new orders are placed in order number sequence to expedite updating of the Open Order File sequentially. Each order accesses the Customer Master File and Product Master File randomly in order to extract necessary information.

File Size

Magnetic tape, removable magnetic disk packs, and punched cards, can provide unlimited off-line storage. Small files can be combined on magnetic tape and disk or they may be stored on punched cards and paper tape.

Magnetic tape is normally used with larger files, if the type of processing is sequential or there is no need for online processing. There is no restriction on the volume of data if processing is sequential. Magnetic disk can also store large volumes of data but at a higher cost than magnetic tape. In random processing, the size of a file is limited to the amount of data that can be stored online.

The growth potential of the files is also an important consideration. Normally, the systems analyst should design files on the basis of their anticipated growth over a period of years.

File Interrogation

Interrogation is simply a referral to a specific record for a specific response without changing the record in any way. File interrogation can normally be handled more quickly and easily if a DASD is used. Normally, a teletype or CRT device is used to input an inquiry specifying the information required to the CPU. The data base management system determines the location of the applicable record in the file, accesses it, and transfers it to the CPU to be communicated to the requestor. Usually this whole sequence is accomplished within seconds after the inquiry is made.

Users of an information system have often found it necessary to obtain specific information from files during normal data processing activities. Before the development of direct access storage devices, the ability to retrieve information directly from storage devices was severely limited. Methods were developed to overcome these inherent limitations, but at best they resulted in time consuming interruptions, and often the information responses were outdated when received. The special ability of direct access storage systems to process data items online, as they occur, and for multiple applications, along with the ability to simultaneously update all affected files, makes it possible to interrogate the files and receive the information directly. This ability is important because it no longer makes it necessary to interrupt normal processing runs, nor does the user need to wait a long time for a response.

Examples which emphasize the significance of this interrogation ability are: (1) in banking, "What is the balance of account number 1385?"; (2) in airline transportation, "Is there a seat available on flight 27?"; (3) in inventory control, "What is the quantity on hand of inventory item number 91736?"; (4) in manufacturing, "What is the material price variance of product number 67641?", or "What is the level of completion of work in process of job lot 41?", or "What is the quantity on hand of subassemblies for assembly 734?"; (5) in financial control, "What is year to date profit of division 3?", or "What customers are 90 days overdue?"; and so forth. Any of these inquiries could eventually be answered using sequential storage media and batch processing. The question is, how long would it take and how many disruptions would it cause? Usually, a special interrogation would have to be handled at the end of a processing run. At that time the response for the inquiry might be outdated and, consequently, of no value.

File Activity

Activity is the measure of the proportion of records processed by an updating run. The activity ratio is equal to the number of records processed during a run compared to the number of records used during the run. This measurement can vary widely depending upon the application.

If the activity ratio is high, more than three records in ten, the processing run would probably be handled more economically and probably faster by using sequential rather than random processing. An example of a file with a high activity ratio is a payroll file.

File Volatility

File volatility refers to the additions, deletions, and/or changes in a file during some time period. Where files are accessed a number of times during a working day, such a file is said to have high volatility. For example, reservation systems, banks, and stock exchanges would by necessity, require highly volatile files. On the other hand, while a payroll file has a high activity ratio, it normally has low volatility.

With these two conditions in mind, some examples of files with different activity ratios and volatility are given in the following list.

1. Low activity ratio and low volatility: Insurance company's archival file.
2. Low activity ratio and high volatility: motel reservation system.
3. High activity ratio and low volatility: payroll system for a bank.
4. High activity ratio and high volatility: payroll system for a construction company.

Response Time

If one of the design considerations is for a fast response, measured in seconds, then the logical storage media are DASD. The reasons for fast response may emanate from: (1) need for a quick response to a particular inquiry, as in an airline reservation system; (2) to bring the organization a competitive advantage, e.g., by providing customers with a fast response to inquiries about the status of accounts; and (3) to handle the high volatility of a file, as in the changing conditions of stock accounts in a stock exchange.

In the past, many applications were rejected for online processing because of the excessive

| File Usage Considerations | File Update | | Large File Size* | File Interrogation | Large File Activity Ratio | High File Volatility | Response Time | Cost | Software Support | Implementation |
Methods of Organization and Media	Seq.	Direct								
Sequential (Tape and Cards)	Excellent	N.A.	Unlimited	Poor	Excellent	Poor	Poor	Modest	Low	Simple
Indexed Sequential (DASD)	Good	Good	Moderately unlimited	Good	Good	Good	Good	High	Medium	Difficult
Direct (DASD)	N.A.	Excellent	Limited	Excellent	Fair	Excellent	Excellent	Very high	High	Very difficult

* Theoretically, all methods would have unlimited capacity, but from a practicable viewpoint unlimited file size for direct access would be cost prohibitive.

FIGURE 8.15. Comparison of file usage considerations with methods of file organization and file storage media.

volume of data required to be accessible for a response, and the cost of DASD devices. Not only is the cost of DASD devices diminishing but technological advancements in magnetic tape devices continue to improve the speed with which magnetic tape files can be processed. Both of these situations require the systems analyst to consider carefully new requests for fast response systems.

The table in Figure 8.15 helps to spotlight some of the considerations one should be aware of when selecting the file organization methods and file storage media. However, in most cases, it is not a matter of selecting one method over another, but one of selecting a combination of methods to meet the variety of requirements imposed upon the information system. Note that sequential, indexed sequential, and direct organization are presented because partitioned sequential is to a great degree similar to indexed sequential and is normally used for special purposes as already mentioned.

Note that selections of hardware storage media, and of the organization of data records, should place records with high volatility or frequent use where they can be located quickly and easily. Through proper systems work, it might be discovered, for example, that ten percent of the inventory items may give rise to eighty or ninety percent of the references made. (A classic example of the application of contribution analysis, also called ABC analysis, as described in Appendix A). By the same token, the analyst could apply this same idea to ascertain those records which have the highest rate of access and organize them for direct access while organizing the remaining records sequentially or indexed sequentially.

8.6 File Design Considerations

The file design considerations discussed in this section should not be viewed separately from many of the items discussed throughout the text. Rather, these considerations should be viewed as a culmination and reinforcement of what has thus far transpired.

File Aspects

The basic approach to file design is to study the various specific aspects that relate to a particular file. On the basis of this study, findings should be recorded on a worksheet similar to the one illustrated in Figure 8.16.

Along with this worksheet, the analyst should also include a specimen of each record layout. In this way, the file design worksheet describes the file, and the record layout describes, in detail, the records contained in the file.

General File Considerations

The following general considerations should be observed when designing files:

1. There is a classic tradeoff between the current status of a file, the storage capacity of a file, and its cost. All master files should be maintained to some level of up-to-dateness depending upon the requirements. Periodically, out-of-date items must be deleted from the file, and restructuring may be necessary to meet changing applications and requirements. The frequency of processing for batch operations must be equated with the cost of processing a run against the current status of the data items within that file. In a batch processing system, the file is always out-of-date by some factor equal to the age of the items in the transaction file being accumulated. In many instances this condition is permissible, e.g., payroll file.

2. All applications and processing jobs that utilize the file must be doublechecked to ensure that no necessary data items have been omitted.

3. The analyst must anticipate future requirements of the present procedures. For example, it may be reasonable and less costly in the long run to include additional fields in a payroll file to handle changes in government requirements (e.g., deductions for Medicare and Medicaid). It is more efficient and less

File Design Worksheet

Date started _____

Date completed _____

File name _____   Analyst _____

File update	File organization	Process cycle	Activity ratio	Direct access	Volatility	Record characteristics		
Batch Direct	Sequential Indexed sequential Partitioned sequential Direct	On demand Hourly Daily Weekly Monthly Yearly	Low Medium High	Yes No Seldom	Low Moderate High	Type; fixed variable	Blocking factor	No. of characters

File dynamics					File size	File media
No. of records A	Yearly % add B	Yearly % drop C	3 year % growth D	Total no. records E	Total characters = E × Average Number Char. in Records.	General description of storage media file specifications (hardware).
$D = 3 \times (B - C)$		$E = A + AD$				

Source of data for processing	Type of information required and reported	General remarks

FIGURE 8.16. Analyst's file design worksheet.

costly in many instances to include additional space rather than to restructure a file. Moreover, it avoids reprogramming or a patched–up record layout at a later date.

4. The analyst should study the feasibility of combining existing data files, applicable to a broad functional area, into a single, integrated file in order to eliminate redundancy of common data items. As pointed out in Chapter 6, the traditional approach to file design has been to set up a separate file for each data processing job. The integrated data base approach helps to mitigate some of the disadvantages of the traditional approach. The integrated data base is highlighted again in the following quote, because of its importance.

The typical approach to file design has been to set up a separate file for each data processing application. This provides a satisfactory file for that application but leads to several files with similar data which must be separately maintained and which are not necessarily compatible. The payroll file and the personnel file have much data which is common, but where there are separate files, they may not be the same even for the same data items because of different delay factors for updating or because an updating entry may be initiated by the payroll department but not reported to the personnel department. This arrangement of data files makes it difficult to obtain an answer to any management inquiry which crosses the lines between applications. An alternative is an organization-wide data file or data base. A data base for a bank, for example, would store in a single file, suitably linked together, all information about an individual's dealings with the bank—as a depositor, saver, borrower, safety deposit box holder, endorser, etc. The objectives of data base systems are user-oriented. The files should be structured to increase user control over the creation of, maintenance of, and access to data. The information processing support should aid the decision making and creative investigation process. Data base systems require considerable software support which fortunately is becoming available with third-generation systems.[3]

5. Another consideration is that the analyst must determine that the data needed for particular applications, for which the proposed data file is intended, is not already available in another file.

6. The analyst should receive a verification from all designated users of the file that it meets the requirements of these different users in terms of content.

7. The analyst should establish a plan of security and audit control to ensure the integrity of the data items stored in the file in accordance with the degree of sensitivity and confidentiality of the data. There is no foolproof method of restricting access to unauthorized

[3] Gordon B. Davis, *Computer Data Processing,* (New York: McGraw-Hill Book Company, 1969), p. 377. Used with permission of McGraw-Hill Book Company.

users. Those safeguards which are established via programming, for example, can be changed the same way, and those persons in charge of controlling security procedures can themselves allow access at their discretion.

SUMMARY

Data files can be stored on a variety of hardware storage media, such as: (1) punched cards, (2) punched paper tape, (3) magnetic tape, (4) magnetic drum, (5) data cells, and (6) core memory. Data can be stored on these files either sequentially, directly, or by a combination thereof.

A data file is composed of records. A record can be defined either logically or physically. There are three basic types of records: (1) data records, (2) label records, and (3) trailer records. The relationship between logical and physical data records can take four forms: (1) fixed-fixed, (2) fixed-variable, (3) variable-fixed, and (4) variable-variable. When designing files, the analyst must be aware of the types of records that make up a file, their purpose, and how they may be formatted.

Files can be classified in three different ways, according to: (1) content, (2) mode of processing, and (3) organization. When selecting the media and organization to be used for a file, the systems analyst must measure the systems requirements against certain criteria, such as: (1) method of update, (2) size of file, (3) degree of interrogation, (4) activity and volatility rate, (5) file operations, and (6) response time.

REVIEW QUESTIONS

8.1 What is the basic classification of storage media as it relates to accessing data?

8.2 Which physical storage devices support direct access?

8.3 Can punched cards be used where the requirements for the data record exceed 80 characters? How?

8.4 What is the function of the interblock gap? Is this a real or logical space on a magnetic tape?

8.5 What does the term "record" refer to? Give at least two examples of a record.

8.6 What is blocking? Why are logical records blocked? Why are printed materials not blocked? If blocked records are more efficient for processing than unblocked records, why not combine all logical records into one superblock? What determines the maximum block length?

8.7 Distinguish between a track and a cylinder on a magnetic disk.

8.8 What is the purpose of a record code? Distinguish between a record code and a record address.

8.9 Define the various types of records found in most data files. Give an example of what each type contains.

8.10 List and define the relationships that can exist between logical and physical records. What is the importance of selecting a given record relationship when designing data files?

8.11 What are the various classifications of data files based on their contents? Give at least two examples of each.

8.12 List two advantages and two disadvantages of (1) sequential file organization, (2) indexed sequential file organization, and (3) direct file organization.

8.13 List the general characteristics of: (1) sequential file organization, (2) indexed sequential file organization, (3) partitioned sequential file organization, and (4) direct file organization.

8.14 What is overlay? Is it feasible to use the overlay concept on a sequential file such as magnetic tape?

8.15 Differentiate between activity ratio and volatility. Give examples of both.

8.16 What is the basic difference between updating a payroll and an inventory file? Explain. What kind of file storage media would you use for each process?

8.17 Explain how the following factors affect the selection of file storage media and file organization methods: (1) file update, (2) file size, (3) interrogation, (4) activity ratio, (5) volatility, (6) response time, (7) cost, (8) software support, and (9) implementation.

8.18 What is the relationship of a magnetic disk to magnetic tape in terms of speed, capacity, and functions within an information system?

8.19 Describe some of the principal uses of a direct access system.

8.20 Why might a combination of storage media be used in an information system instead of only one type throughout? (For example, part magnetic tape and part magnetic disk, along with a card reader.)

QUESTIONS FOR DISCUSSION

8.1 "Direct access systems have advantages not found in sequential processing systems. Direct access systems also require programming and systems considerations that are not required by sequential systems." Comment on this statement.

8.2 "Under program control, the computer system can, in milliseconds, access particular data from a DASD and display the results on an output device. In contrast, in a sequential system, much preprocessing and sorting must be done before producing the desired information. Thus interrogation becomes somewhat impracticable using a sequential system. By use of interrogation capability, the direct access system makes possible a completely different kind of information system." Comment on this statement.

8.3 "To sift out the information wanted from a sequentially organized file, a great deal of sorting (arranging) of data is normally required, and if only a small percentage of the records are affected in a processing run, then many records are read unnecessarily." Comment on this statement.

8.4 "I can furnish any information you want from my batch processing system. It may take me a little longer, but I can still perform any information processing tasks that they can perform in those fancy direct access systems." Comment on this statement.

8.5 "Punched cards and tape no longer seem meaningful as storage media in the information system of large organizations." Discuss the validity of this statement.

8.6 "The widespread use of label records and trailer records on data files did not take place until computer manufacturers forced their use by restrictions in manufacturer supplied operating systems." Explain.

8.7 "An analyst who requires anything other than fixed length records in a systems design is asking for a lengthy and difficult implementation process with most business programmers." Discuss the possible rationale behind this statement.

8.8 "Although data files with direct organization are applicable in many situations, most organizations do not use this technique to organize their data files." Discuss fully.

8.9 "The benefits of random processing should not be restricted to online processing only." Explain this comment.

8.10 "Many data files are organized sequentially because the analyst who designs the file does not understand what factors must be evaluated when choosing a file organization approach." Discuss why this statement may be true.

EXERCISES   **8.1** Prepare a list of questions a systems analyst might use to determine the type of file organization that should be used in a particular application. Provide answers for this checklist of questions and, based upon these answers, indicate the appropriate file organization method. Give supporting reasons for choosing the particular method (e.g. of typical questions: "What is the expected activity ratio?," or, "What is the time limit from initiation of a particular operation to its completion?").

8.2 The file dynamics are stated as follows: (1) number of records is 180,000, (2) yearly percent add is 26, and (3) yearly percent drop is 10.

Calculate, on the average, two year percent growth and total number records.

8.3 In designing a file, it has been determined that there will be 15,000 records and that each record is 200 bytes. Calculate: (1) records per track, (2) number of tracks required, and (3) number of cylinders required. Assume the model disk pack available has 200 cylinders, each cylinder has ten tracks, and each track has a maximum capacity of 7294 bytes.

8.4 Access motion time is negligible if a file is being processed in sequence. The significant times, in this case, are rotational delay and data transfer. If the full rotational delay is 25 milliseconds per track and the data transfer is 312KB (thousands of bytes per second) or 0.0032051 milliseconds per byte, using exercise 8.3, calculate the time required to read all the records.

8.5 A disk pack has 200 cylinders. There are 10 recording surfaces or tracks and each track can store a maximum of 3625 bytes (characters). What is the maximum capacity of each cylinder? What is the maximum capacity of the disk pack?

8.6 There are 200 cylinders in a disk pack. Each cylinder has a maximum capacity of 145,880 data bytes. If there are 20 recording surfaces, what is the maximum capacity of each track?

8.7 Assume that a tape drive has a transfer rate of 75,000 bytes per second and a start/stop time at each IBG of 10 milliseconds. If this tape drive is to read 15,000 blocks and each block is 50 characters in length, how long will it take? This exercise, so far, represents 15,000 unblocked records. Suppose, however, that the 15,000 records to be read were blocked, 10 to a block. How would this blocking affect the total time to read the records from the tape?

8.8 A seven track tape has 556 CPI density and a tape unit speed of 60 inches per second. The number of blocks on the tape is 6000, the blocking factor is 4, and each logical record contains 25 bytes. The size of the IBG is .75 inch and the time to pass an IBG is .012 seconds. Calculate: (1) stated transfer rate, (2) size of each block, (3) total number of bytes, (4) total start/stop time, and (5) total time for reading data.

8.9 Assume the availability of 2400 foot magnetic tape reels with 800 bytes per inch density. Further assume 200 byte logical records, blocked 5, .00125 inches per character, and .60 inch IBG. On a 2400 reel, there is 28,440 inches available for storing working records (2400 foot reel minus 30 feet of combined header and trailer records). Calculate the physical and logical records per reel.

8.10 Sketch and identify the record formats for the following specifications: (1) 4 records, blocking factor 1, record length 25 bytes; (2) 4 records, blocking factor 4, record length 25 bytes; (3) maximum record length 25 bytes, block size 100 bytes, (4) blocking factor 1, maximum record length 25 bytes; and (5) maximum record length 50 bytes, variable blocking factor. Make any necessary assumptions.

PROBLEMS   **8.1** Select a configuration of file storage media for the following applications. State your reasons for choosing a particular configuration.
    (1) School library.
    (2) Inventory system.
    (3) Police department.
    (4) Motel reservation system.
    (5) Payroll system for a university.

8.2 Red River Data Service handles the billing operations for a number of businesses in the local community. There are 150,000 customer master records maintained and about 70,000–80,000 of these are updated nightly. That is, at the end of the working day, credit sales slips are transported to Red River from the various businesses where these source documents are keypunched for further processing. Client managers of Red River each want a print out of previous day's sales with various sales statistics, credit exceptions, aging of accounts receivable, income statements, and so forth. The management of Red River have been handling their data processing with unit record equipment. You have been commissioned to outline to Red River management a new data processing system for their consideration. In your proposal, be sure to suggest the type of file media and data organization method(s) that should be utilized.

8.3 Pitts Foundry, Inc., a new business developed to fabricate sheet piling and concrete forms has hired you as one of their systems analysts. Your job is to set up a filing system for storing over 800 programs for a variety of programming procedures. Nearly all of the data will be processed online, regardless of the type of record accessed or updated. For example, when a job order is released, several programs are retrieved to process various cost and inventory calculations, billing procedures access other routines, bills of material interrogations trigger still other routines, and so forth. A tape program library has been considered to maintain these various programs. Do you agree that a tape library should be used? Why? Why not? Outline your proposal and state its advantages.

8.4 MoParts, an automotive parts dealer, maintains six warehouses scattered throughout the southwest. MoParts carries an inventory of 30,000 different items, each of these items identified by a twelve-digit part number. MoParts management wants to record each transaction affecting each item, as it occurs, so that if any one item in inventory reached or exceeded the reorder point, the buyer(s) would receive an out-of-stock notification. In broad terms, provide a sketch of the computer configuration and description of the system you could suggest to the management of MoParts for implementation. Specify type of file media and data organization to be implemented in addition to the possible application of management science techniques.

8.5 Consider a basic data processing system which performs order processing, invoicing, inventory, and accounts receivable applications. Sales orders are received and a combined invoice and shipping-order form is prepared on the printer. Inventory and accounts receivable master records, on magnetic tape, are updated. The first step is keypunching and key verifying; there are at least five more steps in the computer processing run to maintain this system. Flowchart these six steps and list the requisite hardware. Assume the same system, except, instead of using tapes, the files have been converted to magnetic disk. Flowchart this system. How many steps are required?

8.6 A large manufacturer of children's toys is considering the implementation of a marketing information system to assist its sales force. There are approximately 300 salesmen working out of 15 branch offices throughout the continental U.S. and Canada. The goal of the system will be to have customer sales history files on line at central headquarters, in St. Louis, which can be accessed by remote terminals at each branch office during normal business hours. New customer orders, and shipments which are received from each branch office nightly, will update the sales history file that same night.

There are approximately 30,000 customers on the file at any one time. Approximately 50 customers are added, and 20 customers deleted, daily. History will be maintained for 13 months by product for each customer. Each customer is expected to have a master record with descriptive data equal to 100 characters. The average number of product records per customer is expected to be 20, each leaving 70 characters of information. Finally, projections indicate that the volume of order and shipment records updating the history file will be 3000 nightly.

Prepare a brief report describing the structure of the required data base you would propose.

8.7 A car manufacturer has implemented a system whereby its customers can call a district representative toll-free to lodge any complaints, or dissatisfactions, which they feel were not adequately handled by their dealer. The district representative then attempts to aid the customer by coordination with the dealer, the manufacturer, or both. Phase I of this program was launched by a national advertising campaign. The major objectives of Phase I were to fortify the company's image, in the area of customer service, and to increase customer confidence in the reliability of their product.

The objective of Phase II has been formulated, but the detailed modifications to the original system have not been firmed up. The basic goal of Phase II is to create a feedback from the customers to the manufacturer. The data flowing through the feedback loop would be stored in a data base, where it would be available to various functional areas within the corporation. Two obvious users would be the design engineers and quality control people. It is apparent that information from the field would be valuable in quickly replacing defective parts and improving the design of parts and components. The corporation executives see the network of district representatives as a skeletal framework which could be expanded to handle the demands of Phase II.

Bearing in mind the extensive resources available to a major automobile producer, present your ideas about the following aspects of the proposed Phase II system:

(1) Specific description of the data which should be collected.
(2) How it should be collected, and by whom.

(3) How it should be transmitted to the manufacturer.

(4) How it should be stored at the corporation's main office in order to facilitate retrieval by numerous users.

Additional Background Information

In addition to handling customer complaints, the district representative also serves as a watchdog on the dealers in his zone. In this role, he must ascertain that the individual dealers, franchised by the company, are complying with the service standards imposed by the corporation. The office staff and facilities of the representatives are presently limited to those needed in the performance of Phase I duties.

Two coding structures, utilized by the corporation, may be useful in this problem. The first is the serial number affixed to each auto. A sample serial number and its interpretation is given below.

$$2\ G\ 2\ 9\ R\ 4\ G\ 1\ 0\ 6\ 1\ 1\ 3$$

2 G	Brand name (major manufacturers produce several brands)
2 9	Body style (station wagon, convertible)
R	Engine (code representing engine model)
4	Year (last digit of year)
G	Factory (factory where produced)
1 0 6 1 1 3	Car's serial number (discrete code depicting one particular car)

A second code structure is used for identifying parts. Each individual part of an automobile is coded with a nonintelligent, 7-digit number. The problems associated with locating a particular part number from the thousands incorporated in one car are obvious. To facilitate the retrieval of part numbers, all the part numbers are structured within a directory code. The directory code is composed of five digits. The first two run from 00 to 15 and identify the major subsystems, i.e., 01 represents Engine Cooling, Oiling and Ventilating systems. The last three digits are a serial code representing the individual parts incorporated in the major subsystem. An example may provide clarity. Let us assume that we're trying to locate the part number for the oil pump cover gasket for a 1973 6-cylinder Bassethound. The Bassethound is one of the brands produced by the major manufacturer, Dogs, Inc. Searching the directory we find that 01.724 is the directory number for oil pump cover gaskets. This number is the general part number for all oil pump cover gaskets produced by Dogs, Inc. Looking in the parts manual under 01.724 we find the specific part numbers for this particular gasket for the individual years and models. Searching this list we find that the gasket for a 1973 Bassethound 6-cylinder has a part number of 3789970. This number identifies the exact part.

In concluding the background information, one point should be emphasized. Under the present system, the district representative only receives information concerned with customer complaints. The details and financial arrangements of warranty service, performed by the dealer in a satisfactory manner, are communicated directly between manufacturer and dealer, bypassing the district representative. You may desire to alter this information flow in your solution.

8.8 A systems analysis study has been completed in a large company which manufactures and markets various types of paper for the printing industry. This study initially was intended to identify the informational requirements related to the purchasing function, but was subsequently expanded to include the accounts payable function as well. The justification for expanding the study was based on the similarity of the data required in the data base to support each function.

The study identified the need for purchasing to maintain three files: (1) a customer master file which contain name, address, purchasing terms, and miscellaneous descriptive data, (2) an open purchase order file which contained all of the data related to purchase orders placed but not yet completed, and (3) a history file of purchases made in a two year period, by product, within customer. At the time of the study, these files were maintained in a manual system.

The accounts payable department on the other hand required the following files: (1) a customer master file which contains the descriptive data necessary to produce and mail a check for purchases received, (2) a file of invoices from vendors received but not yet paid, and (3) a one year history file of paid vendor invoices. Currently, accounts payable maintains a manual customer master and open invoice file. A tab system was used to create checks to vendors and to maintain paid invoice history.

The company leases a medium sized computer with both magnetic tape and disk storage available in a batch processing mode. Approximately 20% of all purchases are considered re-buys from an existing vendor. At any point in time there are 3000 active vendors; 5000 open purchase orders; 1500 open invoices; and annually, the company places 40,000 purchase orders.

From the above facts, your assignment is to determine the following:
  (1) How many data files are necessary in the required data base?
  (2) What data fields will be required in each data file? (Prepare a table or matrix which illustrates the relationship of data fields among files.)
  (3) What storage media should be used for each data file?
  (4) How should each file be updated, and which department is responsible for keeping the file current?

BIBLIOGRAPHY   Becker and Hayes, *Information Storage and Retrieval* (*tools, elements, theories*), New York: John Wiley & Sons, Inc., 1964.

Data File Handbook (C20–1638–Z), White Plains, New York: IBM Corporation, Technical Publication Department, September, 1969.

Davis, *Computer Data Processing,* New York: McGraw-Hill Book Co., 1969.

Gregory and Van Horn, *Automatic Data Processing Systems,* Belmont, Calif.: Wadsworth Publishing Co., Inc., 1963.

Sanders, *Computers in Business: An Introduction,* New York: McGraw-Hill Book Co., 1972.

Thierauf, *Data Processing for Business and Management,* New York: John Wiley & Sons, Inc., 1973.

Concepts of Data Structure, Association, and Manipulation

9.1 Introduction

Throughout this part concepts related to the data base have been discussed. In Chapter 6, an overview of the data base was presented; in Chapter 7, the classification and coding of data elements was analyzed; and in Chapter 8, the concept of file emphasizing basic storage considerations was analyzed. In this final chapter of Part II, the major concepts related to the logical structuring and manipulation of data will be presented. Because of the very nature of the concepts presented, the discussion is somewhat more technical than in previous chapters. However, when designing a sophisticated data base, the importance of these ideas must be understood clearly by the systems analyst. The specific objectives of this chapter are:

1. To present and analyze the basic concepts of data structure.
2. To present and analyze the basic concepts of data association.
3. To provide a general understanding of the sorting operation.

4. To introduce several techniques applicable to searching sorted codes.

5. To provide a basic appreciation for the transformation techniques utilized in direct access applications.

6. To present an example of data structure.

9.2 Concepts of Data Structure

There are several different approaches to analyzing the logical structure of data in complex data bases.[1] One common approach is to view data structure as having three basic representations: (1) lists, (2) trees, and (3) networks.

Lists

A list is nothing more than a sequential data structure made up of data records where the Nth record is related to record $N - 1$ and $N + 1$ simply because of positioning. This structure is illustrated in Figure 9.1.

The records in Figure 9.1 might represent customers, employees, products, vendors, and so forth. The records might be related to each other by customer number, employee number, product number, or vendor number. This format is commonly termed a simple list. There are many variations of list structure which are extremely valuable in data base design. One such variation is a list of grouped or related

[1] See Richard F. Schubert, "Basic Concepts in Data Base Management Systems," *Datamation,* July, 1972, pp. 42–47, for an analysis of data structure using set mechanisms.

records. Figure 9.2 illustrates this form of a list.

In this variation, one record is termed "owner" in the group, and the remaining records are termed "member." There may be N owner records within a file and there is a one-to-N relationship between each owner record and its member records. This structure is appropriate where technical documents such as purchase orders, customer orders, and invoices make up the file. For example, in a purchase order file, the owner record might contain the vendor name, address, and purchase terms. Each member record contains the details associated with each line item on the purchase order. Obviously, a purchase order can contain from one-to-N number of line items. The data file would be a list in sequence by purchase order number, with each purchase order represented by at least one owner record and one or more member records. Figure 9.3 illustrates a purchase order file using this data structure.

With most lists, processing begins at the first record in the file and continues until an end-of-file condition is sensed. However, there are situations where a list is processed to a point, and rather than continuing to the end of the file, processing is returned to a previous record. Lists processed in this manner are termed circular lists. An illustration of processing with circular lists is shown in Figure 9.4.

Using a personnel information system as an example, records A, B, and C in Figure 9.4 represent employee records which contain only general descriptive information concerning the employee. Records D and G are data records in a different list and contain job information for

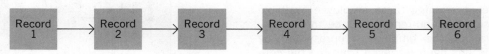

FIGURE 9.1. Example of a simple list structure.

FIGURE 9.2. Example of owner/member relationship.

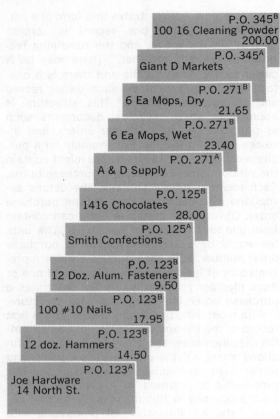

FIGURE 9.3. A purchase order file with a list structure using owner/member relationships.

each year the employee has worked. Records E and F contain data in a third list which represents individual job skills attained by the employee. Individual files are maintained because it is not always necessary to have all information pertaining to an employee available for processing requirements. Once the historical data for the employee, represented by record B, has been retrieved from the file containing records D and G, processing is returned to record B. The same logic is applied to the data file which contains records E and F. In Figure 9.4, two examples of processing circular lists have been shown, one nested within the other.

Another variation of list processing is referred to as "inverted" lists. The inverted list is particularly applicable where one's requirements include a great deal of interrogation, such as: "How many salesmen do we have in sales region 3, who have sold 20% over quota?" or "How many rooms in Fletcher Hall do we have available between 7:30 P.M.–8:30 P.M. March 15, with a seating capacity of between 30–40?"

Before illustrating the inverted file structure, an example of a typical formatted file is shown in Figure 9.5. As presently structured, this formatted file is not very amenable to interrogation procedures.

The formatted file illustrated in Figure 9.5, is quite applicable to conventional data processing, such as report generation, but our objective is to create a file which can respond to a variety of specific inquiries. In order to accomplish this objective, we establish an inverted file made up of attribute sublists, wherein all values belonging to a particular file are linked or cross–referenced to other values in the file. In Figure 9.6, the results of inverting the formatted file illustrated in Figure 9.5 are shown.

The advantage of using the inverted list structure is that the retrieval process is faster and more logical than with the formatted struc-

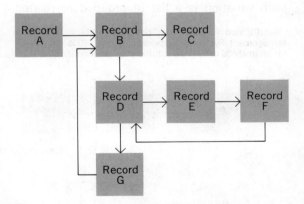

FIGURE 9.4. An illustration of processing with circular lists.

Address	Name	Job	Education	Computer Language	Marital Status
150	Larance	Analyst	MS	FORTRAN	Married
110	Rabb	Programmer	MS	FORTRAN	Single
120	Andrews	Analyst	BS	*	Married
160	Gooding	Programmer	BS	COBOL	Married
270	Nugent	Programmer	HS	APL	Single
480	Woodall	Operator	HS	*	Married
330	Widener	Supervisor	PHD	COBOL	Married
280	Stevens	Operator	HS	*	Single
340	Ferrand	Operator	BS	*	Divorced

FIGURE 9.5. Example of a typical formatted file.

Name		Job		Education		Computer Language		Marital Status	
Value	Address	Value	Address	Value	Address	Value	Address	Value	Address
Larance	150	Operator	280	HS	280	COBOL	270	Single	110
			340		480		160		270
Rabb	110		480		270		330		280
Andrews	120	Programmer	270	BS	340	FORTRAN	110	Married	150
			160		160		150		120
Gooding	160		110		120	APL	270		160
Nugent	270	Analyst	150	MS	110				480
Woodall	480		120		150				330
Widener	330	Supervisor	330	PHD	330			Divorced	340
Stevens	280								
Ferrand	340								

FIGURE 9.6. Example of inverted list structure.

ture. The disadvantage is that all values must be cross-referenced, and indexed, in order to meet a variety of specific inquiries into the file. For example, several typical inquiries into our inverted file are:

INQUIRY: How many COBOL programmers do we have and what is their educational background?

RESPONSE: TOTAL OF 3: 1 HS, 1 BS, 1 PHD

INQUIRY: State the name(s) of the programmer(s) we have in our employ who are single.

RESPONSE: RABB
NUGENT

INQUIRY: List the name of our FORTRAN programmer(s).

RESPONSE: RABB
LARANCE

INQUIRY: List the names of all employees who have an MS degree.

RESPONSE: RABB
LARANCE

INQUIRY: List the programmers who have a high school degree only.

RESPONSE: NUGENT

INQUIRY: List the systems analysts who have a high school degree only.

RESPONSE: NONE

INQUIRY: Who are the married employees and what are their job classifications?

RESPONSE: LARANCE   ANALYST
          ANDREWS   ANALYST
          GOODING   PROGRAMMER
          WOODALL   OPERATOR
          WIDENER   SUPERVISOR

Tree Structures

A tree structure is a nonlinear multilevel hierarchical structure in which each node may be related to *N* nodes at any level below it, but to only one node above it in the hierarchy. That is, entry is from the top, and the direction of the search or processing is downward, and no branches on the tree touch. Figure 9.7 illustrates a tree structure.

It should be pointed out that a few authors depict the tree as a real tree grows. We have chosen to illustrate our tree structure as most authors do, which is upside down relative to how real trees grow. Consequently, node *A*, which represents the root, is at level 1. For a full explanation of the tree structure illustrated in Figure 9.7, node *A* is the root and has as its two subtrees *BDEFIJK* and *CGHLMNO*. Node *B*, at level 2, is the root for tree *DEFIJK*, and with the respect to the entire tree, it has three subtrees, *DIJ, EK,* and *F*. Node *C* is the root for tree *GHLMNO* or with respect to the whole tree structure, it has three subtrees *GLM* and *HNO*, and so forth. Nodes *IJKFLMO* represent the terminal nodes of the entire tree structure.

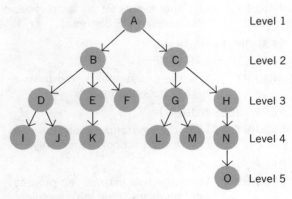

FIGURE 9.7. Example of a tree structure.

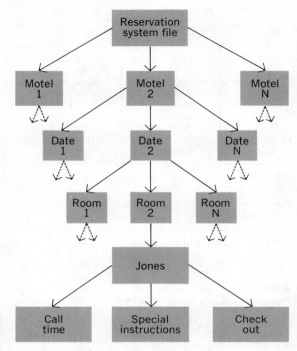

FIGURE 9.8. Illustration of a reservation system represented by a tree structure.

In order to traverse a tree, pointers and chaining procedures must be established, and algorithms created accessing specific nodes (records) of the tree structure. For example, in order to establish a reservation system for a large motel organization, a system of data structure, as depicted in Figure 9.8, would have to be designed.

Network Structures

The network structure, another form of hierarchical structure, allows the file designer to structure the data logically in the file so that the storage and access algorithm can start with any record in the file and traverse the file in a multidirectional manner throughout the hierarchy. Therefore, whereas tree structures do not have branches that connect, the network structure does. In network structures, any record may be related to any other record in the file.

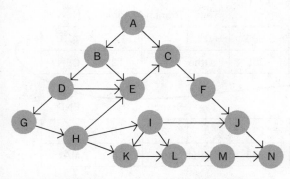

FIGURE 9.9.   Example of a network structure.

Figure 9.9 depicts a network structure in which, for example, node *C* has two branches into it and node *E* has three.

Figure 9.10 illustrates part of an order entry data system where there are records with more than one branch entering them. In this network structure, there are records which are owner-records of other records and, at the same time, a member of other records. For example, the Product Statistical Record is a member of three owner records: General Customer Record, General Product Record, and In Process Record. At the same time it is also an owner record of the Backorders Record. Consequently, the fact that a record may participate as a member in more than one record set and, at the same time, be an owner of another record(s), permits the structure of networks.

9.3 Concepts of Data Association

As has already been discussed, data in a file are divided into records (called entities or nodes by some authors); each record consists of a contiguous string of data divided into fields. If one is going to associate a record with other records (or fields), then there must be a logical system to achieve this linkage. In discussing the concepts of data structure in the previous section, by implication, the concepts of data association have already been explored. However, we need

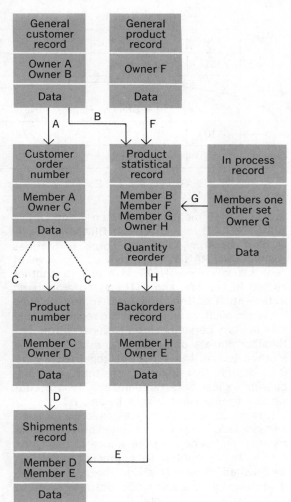

FIGURE 9.10.   Example of an order system (partial) using a network structure.

to be more specific as to the technique used to achieve this association. The major portion of this section, therefore, is devoted to chaining and pointers, the technique of data association.

Illustration of Data Association

The objective in this illustration is to represent records of military personnel. The conditions

	Tag	Branch	Rank	Next		Tag	Branch	Rank	Next
TOP →	300	1	1	2	385 →	385	0	4	12	110
	301	Other data	2	CORP		386	Other data	12	GEN

	Tag	Branch	Rank	Next		Tag	Branch	Rank	END
→	110	1	3	3	272 →	272	1	2	10	*
	111	Other data	3	SGT		273	Other data	10	MAJ

FIGURE 9.11. Example of record linkage in a military personnel file.

are: TAG = 1 means the person is on active duty; TAG = 0 means retired; BRANCH = 1, 2, 3, or 4 for Army, Navy, Air Force, or Marines respectively; RANK = 1, 2, . . . , 12 for level of rank classification; NEXT is a *link* to another record in the file; and TITLE is an alphabetic abbreviation of the rank used in the display.

For simplicity, assume that the records of only four military personnel are contained within the file. Our primary objective is to establish some method to link these records together. Figure 9.11 depicts this linkage. Note that when discussing logical data relationships, it is a convention to represent linkage by arrows.

Now we come to the critical objective for such an association, which is a method of relating the records, and accessing the values of the fields within the records. This procedure is accomplished by simply giving the name of the field followed by a link to the desired record in parenthesis. For example:[2]

$$TITLE \ (TOP) = 2 \ which \ is \ Corporal$$
$$BRANCH \ (TOP) = 1 \ which \ is \ Army$$
$$RANK \ (273) = 10 \ which \ is \ Major$$
$$TAG \ (385) = 0 \ which \ is \ Retired$$
$$RANK \ (NEXT(TOP)) = 12 \ which \ is \ General$$

To make this example more meaningful, we will now state a simple, hypothetical algorithm for placing a new record as a first record,

[2] Reprinted by special permission from: Donald E. Knuth, *The Art of Computer Programming: Fundamental Algorithms*, (Reading, Massachusetts: Addison-Wesley Publishing Company, 1969), pp. 230–31.

assuming NEWREC is a link variable whose value is a link to the new record:

1. Set NEXT (NEWREC) ← TOP. (This statement sets the appropriate link in the new record).
2. Set TOP ← NEWREC. (This statement keeps TOP as the beginning of the file).

Another example is an algorithm which simply counts the number of records currently in the file.

1. Set $N = 0$, $X =$ TOP. (N is an integer variable, X is a link variable).
2. If $X = *$, stop; N is the number of records in the file.
3. Set $N = N + 1$, $X =$ NEXT (X), and go back to Step 2.

Chains and Pointers

Chains are used logically, not physically, to link records together based on commonalities and functional interrelationships. A pointer represents the address of a particular record. The chaining operation is achieved by using pointers, which may or may not be embedded in the records themselves. Regardless of whether or not a chain has embedded or nonembedded pointers, the essential aspect of a chaining operation is that there are pointers directly or indirectly associating one record in the chain to the next record in the chain. This technique will be discussed assuming embedded pointers.

Chaining, as a logical technique, allows users to leap-frog from one record to another without being concerned with those records that are physically stored in between. It is a technique that allows direct access to specific data elements and in any order.

. . . In most cases, the need for chaining arises when information is stored in a sequence other than the one that facilitates the type of retrieval we would like to make. As a result, from a practical standpoint, we have four options for accomplishing our objective: (1) we could have the computer look at every record on file and select only those in which we are interested; (2) we could establish and maintain a duplicate file containing only those records that meet our selection criteria; (3) we could maintain an index; (4) we could use a chaining technique, which obviates the need to either examine all records sequentially or maintain indexes or a separate file of duplicates.

On the surface, chaining is the most attractive of the four. That does not mean that its use is always advised . . . there are trade-offs to be considered. Unlike the other three, chaining requires additional and sometimes more complex program logic. . . .[3]

Chaining alleviates the need to examine all records sequentially, provides faster access, and reduces redundancy of data items. However, it requires a great deal of logic and software support, a sophisticated I/O system, use

[3] Leonard I. Krauss, *Computer-Based Management Information Systems* (New York: American Management Association, Inc., 1970), pp. 169–70. With permission of AMA.

N	Social Security Number	Name	Title	Pointer
1	436449084	Custer H. L.	Systems Analyst	
2	435779921	Tinsley W. A.	Programmer	7
3	237124444	Hamlin B. A.	Operator	
4	761234581	Pesnell B. R.	Programmer	5
5	477810020	Pesnell Glenda	Programmer	*
6	423871422	Powers Vesta	Scheduler	
7	400471748	Cranford H. L.	Programmer	4

FIGURE 9.12. Simple chain structure which associates programmers in an employee file.

of DASD, additional storage for pointers, and a high degree of maintenance (changing and keeping track) of pointers. Moreover, deletion of records causes wasted space, which means that the entire file must be restructured from time to time. Obviously, the major advantage of using chains and pointers is that flexibility of information retrieval is substantially increased. Three types of chaining structures are discussed below.

1. *Simple Chain.* Assume that we have employee records stored on a DASD and that we wish to access all programmers. As illustrated in Figure 9.12, there are a total of seven employee records in the file. N gives the physical address of each employee's record in the file and the pointer provides the ability for the

algorithm to retrieve only those employees who are programmers. We will assume that the starting location is at Record 2. Note that the pointer containing an asterisk indicates end of chain.

Suppose that we wish to add another criterion which would give us only those programmers with five or more years' experience. This situation being the case, we would have to have the number-of-years'-experience field added to the records, and also pointers to relate this back to the appropriate records. This file structure is shown in Figure 9.13.

2. *Ring Structure.* The ring structure (also called a circular structure) allows the end of the last record to point back to the head record (also called starter record or master record). This particular chain structure provides for the

N	Social Security Number	Name	Title	Years Experience	Pointer$_1$	Pointer$_2$
1	436449084	Custer H. L.	Systems Analyst	4		
2	435779921	Tinsley W. A.	Programmer	6	7	5
3	23712444	Hamlin B. A.	Operator	2		
4	761234581	Pesnell B. R.	Programmer	5	5	*
5	477810020	Pesnell Glenda	Programmer	8	*	4
6	423871422	Powers Vesta	Scheduler	7		
7	400471748	Cranford H. L.	Programmer	3	4	

FIGURE 9.13.   Simple chain structure which associates programmers with five or more years' experience in an employee file.

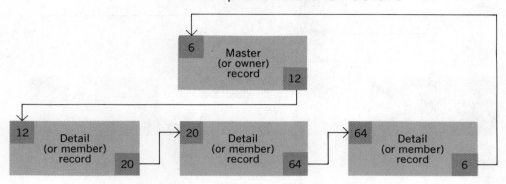

FIGURE 9.14 Illustration of a ring structure.

association of master records with a number of detail records. Figure 9.14 represents a ring structure.

Note that the final record in the ring structure contains the address of the master record instead of an asterisk which would represent end of chain. In utilizing a ring structure, one can enter the file at any record and access all other associated (linked) records and always, if desired, return to the master record regardless of the entry point.

3. *Modified Ring Structure.* The modified ring structure requires that all records in the chain contain some combination of NEXT, PRIOR, and MASTER pointers. Figure 9.15 illustrates three combinations of structures, which include: NEXT/MASTER, NEXT/PRIOR, and NEXT/PRIOR/MASTER. Note that instead of using numbers, the letters N, P, and M are used to designate NEXT, PRIOR, and MASTER pointers respectively.

These multidirectional chain structures significantly increase the ability to associate records and thus substantially enhance the accessibility of a variety of items. However, it must be pointed out again that there is a price to pay for this ability, in additional space for pointers, sophisticated algorithms, time required to traverse the chain, and maintenance of the pointers.

An example of the multichain structure, as discussed above, is where detail records are related to more than one master record, that is, where a detail record is linked by two or more separate chains. In Figure 9.16, the objective is to relate detail sales statistics records to master records contained in a customer file, and a salesman file. The simple request is to determine the quantity of items sold by salesman one, to customer ten.

Directories

The pointer in a directory is the functional equivalent of a chain which accesses a particular record within a file. However, records contained in the data file do not contain pointers for chaining to each other. The pointers which access particular records are contained in the directory and are not embedded in the records themselves. An example of this structure is illustrated in Figure 9.17.

The directory is in fact a physical file itself. An advantage in using a directory, instead of embedded pointers, is that in many data associations the number of relationships may vary from one type of record to another. As new associations are desired, it is simply a case of determining the new addresses and recording these in the directory. With embedded pointers, it might be necessary to enlarge record sizes in the affected files, which is a time consuming, tedious, and expensive ordeal. The alternative is to design records with sufficient space to add

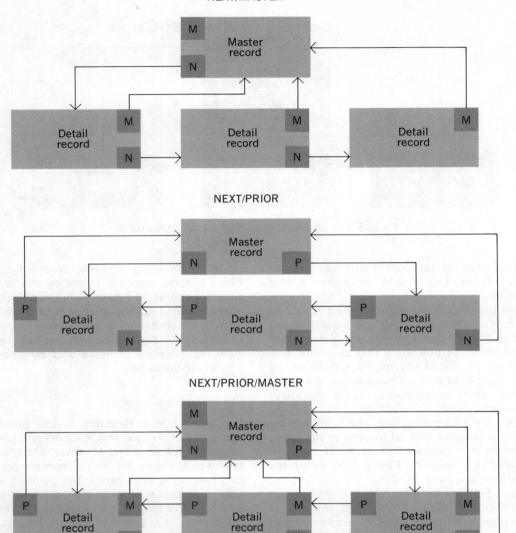

NEXT/MASTER

NEXT/PRIOR

NEXT/PRIOR/MASTER

FIGURE 9.15. Examples of modified ring structures.

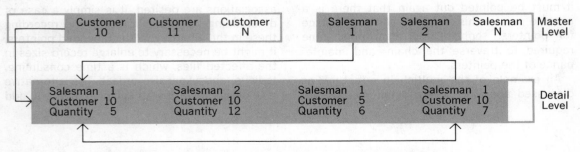

FIGURE 9.16. Illustration of a multichain structure.

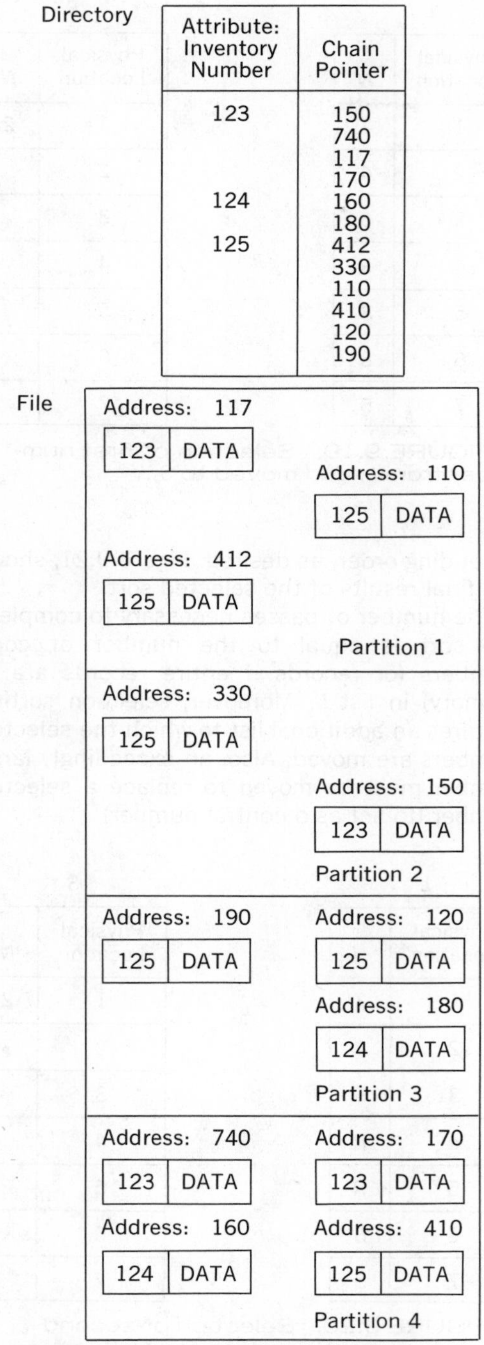

Directory

Attribute: Inventory Number	Chain Pointer
123	150
	740
	117
	170
124	160
	180
125	412
	330
	110
	410
	120
	190

File

Address: 117

123	DATA

Address: 110

125	DATA

Address: 412

125	DATA

Partition 1

Address: 330

125	DATA

Address: 150

123	DATA

Partition 2

Address: 190

125	DATA

Address: 120

125	DATA

Address: 180

124	DATA

Partition 3

Address: 740

123	DATA

Address: 170

123	DATA

Address: 160

124	DATA

Address: 410

125	DATA

Partition 4

FIGURE 9.17. Illustration of a directory chain structure.

additional pointers, when they are identified as necessary. This results in large amounts of storage being unused for some period of time, an equally undesirable situation.

9.4 The Sorting Operation

Throughout the first sections in this chapter, the important concepts related to data structure and association have been presented. Closely related to these ideas, are concepts related to manipulating data and accessing specific data records in a predetermined sequence for reporting. In the next sections, therefore, the manipulation of data, by the data operation of sorting, is discussed.

Purpose of Sorting

One of the major activities performed in processing a list (file) of data records is, the arranging of these data records into some predetermined order, using a field (or fields) in the record as a sorting key. If, for example, the list is an inventory file, it might be desirable to arrange it according to a sequence of largest-to-smallest selling items, by quantity-on-hand, or dollar value of product classes. In an employee file, on the other hand, the records might be arranged in alphabetical order using employees' last names as the sorting key; or sequencing by age, skill type, and years of employment. The need to sort data records is universal in all organizations including manufacturers, banks, insurance companies, universities, public agencies, and so forth. There are many ways to sort records, depending upon the file media and equipment used.

Although most computer manufacturers provide software packages for sorting data, many organizations choose to build their own sorting routines for specific processing tasks. The systems analyst must, therefore, be aware of different methods and, in particular, of which ones will help to reduce sorting time.

Internal Sorting

Internal sorting by computers has made it almost routine to sort voluminous files of data records efficiently and quickly relative to other data processing methods. However, the major constraints to the sorting of large files are: (1) the instruction repertoire of the computer, (2) the capacity of main storage, (3) the type of auxiliary storage devices used, and (4) the size of the data records to be sorted. In this section, specific constraints are ignored and two ways to perform an internal sort on a data file are discussed.

1. *The Selection Technique.* In Figure 9.18, a list *L* with *N* numbers is to be sorted in ascending order. There is also another list, *S*, which will eventually contain the sorted numbers, but which is presently either empty (as in our example) or contains extraneous data which will be destroyed as the selected numbers are moved to their proper locations.

The method of selection sorting is the simplest and most straight-forward. List *L* is examined, wherein the smallest element, $N = 2$, is selected and sorted in list *S* at S_1 and replaced by an arbitrarily large number *R*, as illustrated in Figure 9.19.

List *L* is again examined for the smallest number and this number is then moved to S_2 and again replaced by *R* as illustrated in Figure 9.20. This process is repeated until all the numbers have been selected and moved to *S* in

L			S	
Physical Location	N		Physical Location	N
1	7		1	2
2	4		2	
3	6		3	
4	R		4	
5	3		5	
6	8		6	
7	5		7	

FIGURE 9.19. Selection of first number from *L*; and moved to S_1.

ascending order, as desired. Figure 9.21, shows the final results of the selected sort.

The number of passes necessary to complete the sort is equal to the number of code numbers (or records if entire records are in memory) in list *L*. Moreover, selection sorting requires an additional list to which the selected numbers are moved. Also, an exceedingly large number must be moved to replace a selected number (to act as a control number).

L			S	
Physical Location	N		Physical Location	N
1	7		1	
2	4		2	
3	6		3	
4	2		4	
5	3		5	
6	8		6	
7	5		7	

FIGURE 9.18. List to be sorted, *L*, with list *S*, which will eventually contain the sorted numbers.

L			S	
Physical Location	N		Physical Location	N
1	7		1	2
2	4		2	3
3	6		3	
4	R		4	
5	R		5	
6	8		6	
7	5		7	

FIGURE 9.20. Selection of second number from *L*; and moved to S_2.

L

Physical Location	N
1	R
2	R
3	R
4	R
5	R
6	R
7	R

S

Physical Location	N
1	2
2	3
3	4
4	5
5	6
6	7
7	8

FIGURE 9.21. Lists L and S after selection sort.

Original List			Sort Stages			
L	L_1	L_2	L_3	L_4	L_5	L_6
7	2	2	2	2	2	2
4	4	3	3	3	3	3
6	6	6	4	4	4	4
2	7	7	7	5	5	5
3	3	4	6	6	6	6
8	8	8	8	8	8	7
5	5	5	5	7	7	8

FIGURE 9.22. Sorting using selection with interchange.

2. *Selection with Interchange Technique.* The main objective in using selection with interchange sorting is to perform the sorting task by using only one area, as opposed to the two areas necessary with selection sorting. When one considers the amount of data that must be sorted in real world applications during a sorting project, in addition to the storage required for the sorting algorithm, the concern for storage in many large applications can be critical.

With this method of sorting, the list L still must be searched to find its smallest number. But, when it is found, instead of moving it to another list, this smallest element is interchanged with the first element at list L_1. After this interchange, the first element in L_1 is the smallest; consequently, there is a new sublist to search. That is, the next search is made on the list excluding the first element in L_1. After the smallest element in this sublist is found, it is interchanged with the second element in L_2. Next, the list excluding element one and element two is examined to determine the smallest number, and so forth. For an example of this operation refer to Figure 9.22.

This sorting technique involves, at most, one interchange at each stage. In stage 1, during the first pass where the number of items = N, the position of the smallest element is deter-

mined by $N - 1$ comparisons. At stage 2, during the second pass, $N - 2$ comparisons are required. At stage 3, $N - 3$ comparisons are required, and so forth. Therefore, the total number of comparisons necessary in list L with dimension N is $N(N - 1)/2$ comparisons, or one-half the number of comparisons required in the selection method. The number of passes required to sort list L is equal to $N - 1$ because the Nth element is positioned by exclusion.

Sorting and Merging Using Auxiliary Devices

In practice, a data file is normally too large for its contents to be input into main storage at one time. Therefore, a sort/merge technique is required to perform the sorting operation. This technique normally includes two phases: (1) from the original file to be sorted, small strings of data are input in main storage, sorted, and output on other devices; and (2) these strings are repeatedly merged with other strings until, finally, the entire original list is sorted.

What is called a two-way sort/merge will be used here to illustrate the concept of sorting with auxiliary devices. This method usually uses four devices and builds up a sorted file by merging strings of sorted records. With a simple two-way sort/merge, the original list of records are read from one file in strings, or sublists, of a predetermined size (in our example, two records to the string); sorted into ascending order, using an internal sorting routine (some of which we have already discussed); and output on alternate files.

In our example, it is assumed that there are four tape drives available, designated Tape 1, Tape 2, Tape 3, and Tape 4. It is further assumed that the original, unordered, tape file to be sorted is stored on Tape 1.

In Figure 9.23 a string of two records from Tape 1 is read into the input buffer area. These records are sorted and then written as a sorted string, S_1, onto Tape 2. Next, a second string of two records is read in the same way, sorted and output on Tape 3 as string S_2. This process is continued in the same way, writing alternate sorted strings on Tapes 2 and 3, until all the records on Tape 1 have been read, sorted, and written onto Tapes 2 and 3.

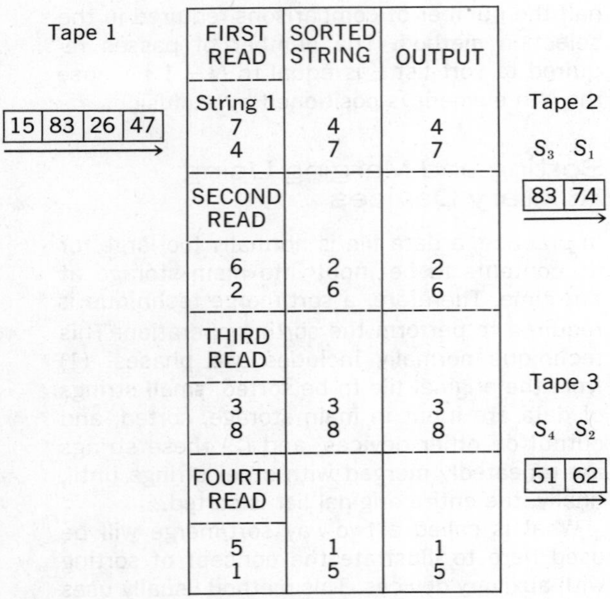

Now, we rewind Tapes 1, 2, and 3 and reverse their positions as shown in Figure 9.24. One

Tape 2: S_3 S_1 — 83 | 74
Tape 1: SS_1 — 7 6 4 2

	FIRST READ	SORT AND MERGE	OUTPUT
String 1	4 2	4 2	2
SECOND READ	6	4 6	4
THIRD READ	7	6 7	6 7
FOURTH READ	3 1	3 1	1
FIFTH READ	5	5 3	3
SIXTH READ	8	5 8	5 8

Tape 3: S_4 S_2 — 51 | 62
Tape 4: SS_2 — 8 5 3 1

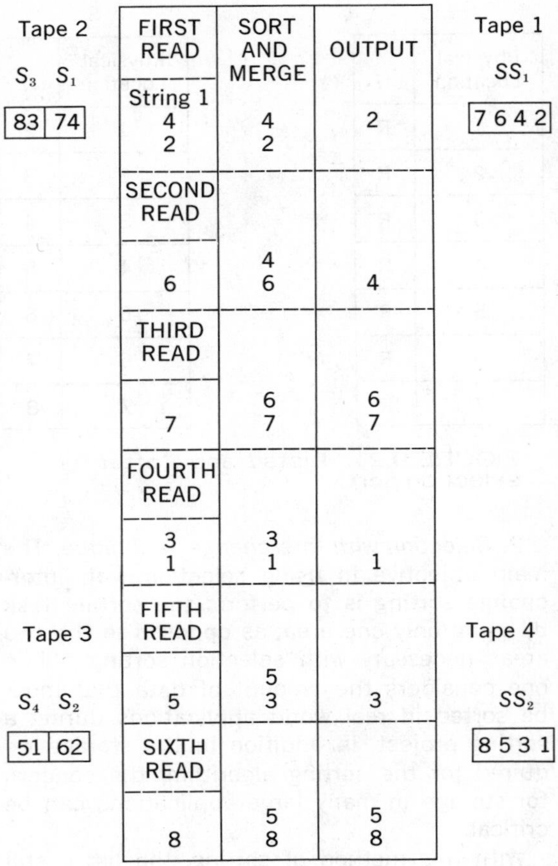

FIGURE 9.24. Sort/merge of Tapes 2 and 3.

record from Tape 2, string S_1 is read, and one record from Tape 3, string S_2 is read. The record with the smaller code (key) is written on Tape 1 and, then, another record is read from the tape that furnished the smaller code. This is compared with the larger of the first two codes and, again, the smaller code is written on Tape 1. This process is repeated until all records from strings S_1 and S_2 have been written on Tape 1 as a sorted string SS_1. Then, this process is repeated on strings S_3 and S_4, writing the results this time on Tape 4, which produces string SS_2.

Again, the tapes are rewound, and their positions reversed. Tapes 1 and 4 become input

Tape 1: 15 | 83 | 26 | 47

	FIRST READ	SORTED STRING	OUTPUT
String 1	7 4	4 7	4 7
SECOND READ	6 2	2 6	2 6
THIRD READ	3 8	3 8	3 8
FOURTH READ	5 1	1 5	1 5

Tape 2: S_3 S_1 — 83 | 74
Tape 3: S_4 S_2 — 51 | 62

FIGURE 9.23. Reading and sorting strings from original file and outputting on alternate tapes.

Tape 1

SS₁

	FIRST READ	SORT AND MERGE	OUTPUT
7 6 4 2	2	1	1
	1	2	2
	SECOND READ		
	4	3	3
	3	4	4
	THIRD READ		
	6	5	5
	5	6	6
	FOURTH READ		
	7	7	7
	8	8	8

Tape 4

SS₂

8 5 3 1

Tape 2
(Sorted File)

87654321

FIGURE 9.25. Final sort/merge.

which are merged either on Tapes 2 or 3 (depending on where our final sorted list is to be stored), because with this operation our file will be fully sorted. For illustrative purposes, it is assumed that Tape 2 will hold the sorted file. The final sort/merge is shown in Figure 9.25.

Sorting data files is a time consuming, expensive operation, but in the absence of more sophisticated chaining structures, sorting is an effective way to bring about necessary data associations. In many data processing operations, sorting data files consumes the largest percentage of processing time on the computer. This fact must be acknowledged by the systems analyst when he or she considers the various structures and associations required to achieve their informational outputs.

9.5 Searching Techniques with Sorted Codes

Searching techniques are utilized to give the user access to specified data elements, to delete or modify this data, or to use it to answer a query. This section investigates how such access can be made when data are organized as a sorted linear list.

Sequential Search

With a sequential search the access of any item starts at the beginning of the list. In Figure 9.26, there are twelve entries and in this example if we wanted to access item 88, nine entries must be read before the one we want is found.

Sequential search is simple, and is ideally suited for routine sequential requests or normal sequential processing. On the other hand, where requests are of a random nature and the file is large, a sequential search is cumbersome and inefficient.

Binary Search

The binary search technique provides a way to process a sequential list in somewhat of a random fashion. The middle of the list is located first to determine if the requested item is above or below the accessed record. In other words, a high/low comparison is made to determine if the requested record is in the top half or lower half. The proper half of the list is then divided by two. Another check is made to determine if the requested record is above or below this list. By continuing this searching pattern of halving the number of records to be read, the requested record is eventually located. An example of the binary search is shown in Figure

Number of Entries	1	2	3	4	5	6	7	8	9	10	11	12
Data Elements	8	10	14	16	25	34	78	80	82	88	89	94

FIGURE 9.26. Linear list of data items showing code (or key) only.

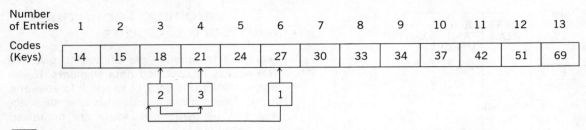

Number of Entries	1	2	3	4	5	6	7	8	9	10	11	12	13
Codes (Keys)	14	15	18	21	24	27	30	33	34	37	42	51	69

1   Compare requested record's code with midpoint code 21 < 27; therefore divide lower sublist by two.

2   21 > 18

3   Sublist cannot be divided, requested record next record.

FIGURE 9.27.   Example of binary search.

9.27. The requested record is identified with Code 21.

Directory Method

There are three basic approaches using the directory method:[4] (1) one-for-one directory structure, (2) linked directory, and (3) directory for sublists.

1. *One-for-one directory.* This method provides one directory entry for each record in the list, as shown in Figure 9.28. The list itself contains the records in the order of their arrival, often random. The directory is ordered so that succeeding entries correspond to a serial key of increasing magnitude. In this way, the list itself is unordered, yet the records which make up the file are ordered for the user via the use of the directory. The advantages of this method are: (1) the list need not be kept in order; (2) since the directory is ordered, search is expedited; (3) records in the list file can be large and of variable length, whereas the directory contains small entries; and (4) it is easier to add a record to the file, because it is placed at the end of the file, and the directory is reshuffled moving entries down (or up) to make room for the new entry.

[4] Based on: Ivan Flores, *Data Structure and Management* (Englewood Cliffs, N.J.: Prentice-Hall, Inc., 1970), pp. 125–132. With permission of Prentice-Hall, Inc.

2. *Linked directory.* The linked directory file structure, illustrated in Figure 9.29, is a total directory stored as a linked list. This method has the advantages of the linked list structure, and the one-for-one directory structure, making it easy to add or delete records without lengthy revision of the directory, since the latter is kept in linked list form.

Figure 9.29, illustrates only the directory part of the structure when it is started with the beginning entry called VENDOR. This entry points to the first directory-entry 734 ACME wherein there is a pointer, 801, which points to the ALLEN record, and so forth.

To add a record to the file, it is inserted in the next free space in the list, where an entry is made which also contains the record key and a pointer connected to another entry. The search is made in the linked list directory to determine the proper place for the entry. The advantages to this method are: (1) it is easy to manage variable length records, (2) the linked directory area can be much smaller than if the full size records were kept there, and (3) it provides a sound system to handle inquiries.

3. *Directory for sublists.* With this method, the original list is partitioned into sublists and a directory is prepared wherein each sublist has an entry designated by a key. To devise this system an ordered, contiguous list is divided into a number of sublists. Then a directory is

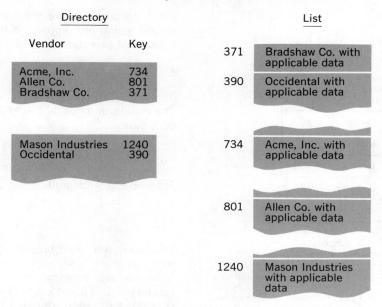

Directory			List
Vendor	Key		

Acme, Inc.   734
Allen Co.   801
Bradshaw Co.   371

Mason Industries   1240
Occidental   390

371   Bradshaw Co. with applicable data

390   Occidental with applicable data

734   Acme, Inc. with applicable data

801   Allen Co. with applicable data

1240   Mason Industries with applicable data

FIGURE 9.28. Example of one-for-one directory structure.

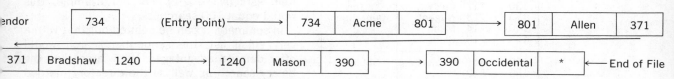

| Vendor | 734 | (Entry Point) ⟶ | 734 | Acme | 801 | ⟶ | 801 | Allen | 371 |

| 371 | Bradshaw | 1240 | ⟶ | 1240 | Mason | 390 | ⟶ | 390 | Occidental | * | ← End of File |

FIGURE 9.29. Example of a linked directory file structure.

formed wherein there is a directory entry for each sublist, as illustrated in Figure 9.30.

The appropriate key in the directory directs us to the proper sublist or neighborhood ("neighborhood locatability" a term coined by Ivan Flores). With a very large list, the directory is also large and in this case we might want to build a master directory for the directory. The master directory directs us to a subdirectory which directs us to a particular sublist. In either case, the directory method takes us immediately to the proper sublist in the list and localizes our search to this sublist. However, once arriving at the appropriate sublist, it still must be searched, to access the requested record, using one of the searching techniques already described.

One way to compare the various methods of searching is to examine estimates of how many searches must be performed before the item we are seeking is found. For a good size file—say 10,000 items—we have on the average 5000 searches ($N/2$), using a sequential search technique. Using the binary search method, the number of searches on that same file can be reduced to about 13, ($\log_2 N - 1$). To calculate the number of searches needed using the directory method we first must decide on how many sublists are to be considered. Flores[5] has shown that given N items, the best distribution results when we have $\sqrt{N}$ sublists, each with $\sqrt{N}$ items. For optimum division of sublists, assume there

[5] *Ibid.*

Directory

Employee Key		Pointer
111	Custer	100
211	Rabb	125
311	Barker	150
411	Sweeney	175
511	Hudnall	200

Employee
File

Location	Employee Key		
100	111	Custer	Sublist 1
105	112	French	for
110	113	Andrews	Department
115	114	Whitman	1
120	115	Crawford	
125	211	Rabb	Sublist 2
130	212	Caldwell	for
135	213	Nugent	Department
140	214	Mann	2
145	215	Clark	
150	311	Barker	Sublist 3
155	312	Wilson	for
160	313	Larance	Department
165	314	Rives	3
170	315	Flowers	
175	411	Sweeney	Sublist 4
180	412	Penz	for
185	413	Garner	Department
190	414	Rheaume	4
195	415	Konowski	
200	511	Hudnall	Sublist 5
205	512	Ford	for
210	513	Pesnell	Department
215	514	Coates	5
220	515	Lee	

FIGURE 9.30. Example of a directory and a list of five sublists of an employee file.

are N records and we store X records in each sublist giving N/X entries in the directory. The number of searches, S, is given as

$$S = \frac{N}{2X} + \frac{X}{2}$$

The optimum value is found by differentiating both sides:

$$O = \frac{N}{-2X^2} + \frac{1}{2}$$

Transposing and multiplying by $2X^2$, we have:

$$X^2 = N$$
$$X = \sqrt{N}$$

The optimum distribution, therefore results when we have $\sqrt{N}$ sublists each with $\sqrt{N}$ entries. For our example, this would mean 100 sublists of 100 items each. Once the number of sublists has been decided, the number of searches necessary to find a particular item equals the average length of our sublists and item lists ($N/2 + N/2$). For our example, this would equal 100 searches.

In summary, it can be pointed out that with a very small list, the sequential search would offer definite advantages. With large files the binary search as well as the directory method offer certain advantages. However, note that the binary search requires a great number of calculations. On the other hand, with the directory, maintenance of the directory entries can present a problem.

9.6 Transformation Techniques for Direct Access

In files where there is high volatility, the records can be stored and accessed in a direct rather than a sequential manner. To map these records to unique addresses, and to later access a particular record, the actual addresses of the records must be derived. Such a process requires sophisticated software support which includes code-to-address transformation techniques (sometimes called address generation or randomizing techniques). The advantages and disadvantages of this type of processing have been alluded to before, and are now summarized below.

The advantages of direct access are:

1. Records can be input and retrieved directly, in a random manner, thus eliminating the need for sorting.

2. No directory or index is required because calculation of the direct address is derived. This method also provides faster access to a particular record.

The advantages are particularly applicable in those situations where the file is used for online systems with high volatility.

The disadvantages of direct access are:

1. The method requires a great deal of both hardware and software support.

2. It can create waste in storage because of empty storage space.

3. Some records overflow, causing a need for an overflow area to be set aside and a method derived to link to this overflow area.

4. If the file has a high activity ratio, processing is much more expensive than with sequential files.

The key to implementing this kind of processing is the use of techniques which calculate the address by converting the code of the record to a particular address in storage. In this section the considerations important to evaluating transformation techniques are discussed and two such techniques are presented.

Transformation Technique Considerations

The dominant parameters affecting performance of the code-to-address transformation techniques are: (1) loading factor and (2) distribution of digits within the codes. The loading factor is the ratio of the number of records to the number of record locations. The distribution of digits in a code is simply the number of times each digit occurs in a code position. A decrease in the loading factor reduces the number of synonyms. In other words, the amount of records which are mapped to the same location are reduced. The more uniform the code distribution, the more uniform the calculated addresses.[6]

Two main objectives must be considered when selecting a transformation technique: (1) every possible code in the file must map to an address in the allotted storage space, and (2) the addresses should be distributed in such a manner to minimize the number of synonyms. There are a large number of transformation techniques, and selecting the best one for a particular file will often require some trial and error. Usually any transformation technique which produces less than twenty percent synonyms is acceptable.

Prime Division Technique

The prime division technique, or the simple division method, is suggested as the best technique in the majority of the cases. With prime division technique, the code is divided by a prime number[7] that is approximately equal to the number of allotted addresses in the file. The remainder from the division of the prime number into the code is used as the address.

If, for example, 6000, 120 byte records are to be mapped onto a DASD (containing 6000 bytes per track) and an eighty percent loading factor is assumed, 7500 record locations are required. Since we can load fifty records to the track, 150 tracks are required. A prime number close to but less than 150 is 149. Therefore, we divide the codes by 149 and the remainders (000–148) equal the track addresses.

This technique automatically guarantees that every possible code in the file will be mapped to the allotted storage space. The number of synonyms that this technique produces can only be determined empirically.

[6] V. Y. Lum, P. S. T. Yuen, and M. Dodd, "Key-to-address Transform Techniques: A Fundamental Performance Study on Large Existing Formatted Files," *Communications of the ACM*, Volume 14, Number 4, April, 1971, p. 229. Copyright 1971, Association for Computing Machinery, Inc., By Permission.

[7] A prime number is a whole number that cannot be divided, without a remainder, by any whole number except itself and one; 2, 3, 5, 7, 11, and 13 are examples of prime numbers.

Distribution (Frequency) Analysis

Since the major objective of a transformation technique is to derive addresses spread evenly across a range, it might be possible to utilize any existing evenness of distribution of digits within the codes.

The objective of using distribution analysis is to determine the frequency of digits in each position of the code. In other words, the number of times any one digit (0–9) appears in each position is determined. For example, if there are 15,000 records in a file, 0 might occur in the fourth code position for 3500 different records, a 1 might occur in this same position 2000 times, a 2 might occur 6000 times, a 3 might occur 400 times, a 4 might occur 3100, and the digits 5–9 would not appear in this position in any of the records. This count provides the actual distribution of digits occurring in each code position. If there were a perfect distribution, each digit would occur an equal number of times. With 15,000 records, each digit, therefore, should occur 1500 times in any one code position. Obviously, this situation is an ideal which is unlikely to occur.

We, therefore, establish a method by which to determine the deviation from the ideal distribution. For example, if 2 actually occurs in the fourth position 6000 times, the absolute deviation from ideal would be 4500 ($|6000 - 1500|$). This analysis is performed for each digit that occurs in this code position and then all the results are totaled to derive the total deviation for the code position. The total deviation is then expressed as a percentage of the total number of records. Those positions containing the most skewed distributions (highest deviation) are deleted from the code until the number of remaining digits is equal to the desired address length, which is the number of digits in the highest location number. Thus, those positions having the smallest deviations are used for deriving addresses. In Figure 9.31, an example of distribution analysis is illustrated.

If three positions can be used to generate the address numbers, then positions two, three, and five of the code would be the most obvious

Digits \\ Position	1	2	3	4	5
0	10000	1000	1800	3500	2100
1	2000	1800	100	2000	1700
2	3000	1900	1300	6000	3100
3	0	1400	1200	400	1000
4	0	1000	1600	3100	1200
5	0	1600	1200	0	900
6	0	1500	1700	0	1500
7	0	1700	1800	0	600
8	0	1600	1400	0	1800
9	0	1200	1000	0	1100
Total Variance	21000	2500	2900	17200	5400
Percent of File	140.0	16.7	19.3	114.7	36.0

FIGURE 9.31. Example of distribution analysis.

candidates and would therefore be extracted for this purpose. Even though this method is used in some systems, in a recent study, it was found to be the least desirable.

> Transformation by digit analysis (same as distribution or frequency analysis—author) is not recommended. Even with the additional processing required to analyze the distribution of the digits, the results were not satisfactory. . . . Uniformity in the distribution of addresses is not synonymous with the mapping of a key into addresses with equal probability.[8]

9.7 A Data Structure and Retrieval Application

To summarize our presentations of data structure, association, and manipulation, a detailed example of a familiar but complex data base application is presented.

Introduction

Most fabrication and assembly manufacturing organizations must maintain voluminous files of records within which are recorded the attributes of all the parts handled by the organi-

[8] *Ibid.,* pp. 238–39.

zation. These attributes consist of conventional information such as part number, description, cost, quantity on hand, and so forth. To retrieve specific data from these files, they must be sorted, summarized, and oftentimes reformatted to meet individual requirements.

In many organizations, each functional area of the organization—engineering, manufacturing, marketing, accounting—maintain parts files, for their own processing, to meet their particular requirements. This situation results in redundancy of data in storage and duplication of processing and file maintenance tasks. In addition, quite often there are inconsistencies and gaps among, and between, files maintained by each area.

The purpose of this section is to give an example of how a system may be established to provide an integrated data base and processing system using a computer configuration and DASD.

In order to maintain and retrieve current and accurate parts data, an integrated data base, which can serve all of the organization's functional areas concurrently, must be established. Specifically, such a system in a typical manufacturing organization would provide the following aspects:

1. Online retrieval of parts data, such as part structure (also called bill of materials and parts lists).

2. Online retrieval of where particular parts are used in the assembly process.

3. Data for routine, periodic, processing activities, such as: cost data for accounting, for transfer pricing, or for billing purposes.

4. Up-to-date information for scheduling or for marketing.

5. A system whereby various management science techniques, such as forecasting and inventory control models, can be implemented.

6. A single source for all users throughout the organization, thus allowing a uniformity of data.

Part Structure

The term part can be classified into three groups:

FIGURE 9.32.   Part structure tree.

1. *Top-level assembly* is a finished part that requires no further fabrication. It is considered a finished good in the organization that manufactures it even though it may be a subassembly in another organization which purchases it. In other instances, it is a consumer good.

2. *A subassembly* represents a major part of a top-level assembly.

3. *Components* are elementary parts which represent the basic parts of subassemblies and top-level assemblies.

Figure 9.32 shows a part structure tree for a top-level assembly *A*, made up of components *B*, and *D*, and subassembly *C*. Subassembly *C*, in turn, is made up of components *D* and *E*.

Initial Loading of Files

Data are recorded for these various parts, and loaded on DASD files, both in assembly sequence and in where-used sequence. These records are online for concurrent retrieval and processing. This scheme is displayed in Figure 9.33.

Note the symbols P,*, and ·, which represent pointers, end of chain, and top-level assembly indicator, respectively. These symbols are established during initial loading to effect certain retrievals and will be explained later in this section.

The master records are used as a master inventory type file. Each record contains the conventional descriptive data such as cost, quantity on hand, safety stock, reorder points, economic order quantities (EOQ's), and other data. The part structure data records are organized as a single file that allows retrieval in both assembly structure, and where-used sequence. The file organization–maintenance-retrieval program(s) establishes one record on magnetic disk storage for each part number regardless of

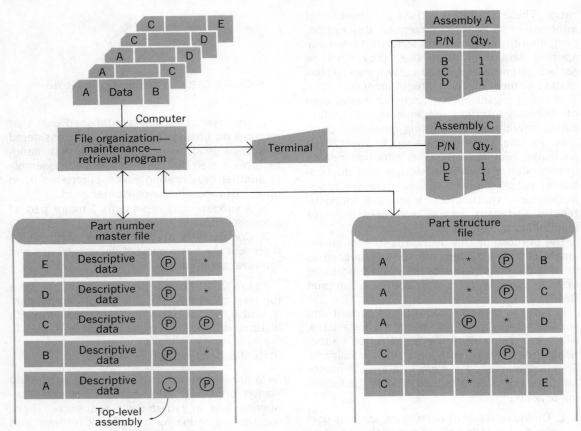

FIGURE 9.33. Loading of master and part structure files.

whether it is a top–level assembly, subassembly, or component. The part number master file is organized to permit an efficient method of directly accessing a particular part record, given the applicable part number.

Basic Retrieval for Assembly Part Structure

To determine the structure of a particular part, the pertinent part number is accessed through the master file. The chaining and pointer structure is built into the records and is properly accessed via a program which traverses the chain, determines the location, and makes the proper cross-references. As depicted in Figure 9.33, the chaining and pointer structure is es-

tablished during initial loading of the records. Figure 9.34, gives an example of the chaining and pointer structure for accessing information on assembly part structure for top-level assembly A and subassembly C.

The sequence of activities to access a part structure response are:

1. Access assemblies A and C from the master file (note that either one could be accessed individually).

2. The master records of A and C contain pointers which are the addresses of the first assembly component (or subassembly and components for A). This first component is B which is a part that goes in to make up top-level assembly A.

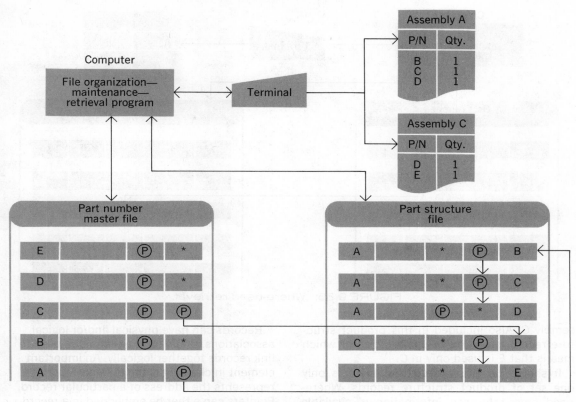

FIGURE 9.34. Part structure retrieval.

3. In each part structure record there is a pointer which gives the address of the next assembly component or subassembly.

Notice that if a user were to access a component such as *B*, the response would indicate an end of chain, *, which means that *B* is an elementary item and cannot be further subdivided as far as the organization is concerned.

Basic Retrieval for Where-Used

The programming algorithm to handle where-used inquiries operates on the basis of a chaining and pointer structure. However, the information requested is somewhat different from that requested in the part structure inquiries. In the where-used inquiry, we are attempting to determine where a particular part

is used throughout the part structure file. To accomplish this accessing, a second set of chains and pointers must also be created during initial loading to link all the direct usages for a part number together. Figure 9.35 depicts an inquiry of where component *D* is used.

In order to determine usage of part number *D*, the master record of *D* is accessed. This contains a pointer which addresses top-level assembly *A*. In the product structure record *A* there is a pointer linking another direct usage of part number *D* in another assembly, in this case subassembly *C*. In *C*, there is an end of chain indicator. If there is a where-used inquiry made on component *E*, for example, the pointer in the master record *E* would link to the last record in the part structure file and the response would be that *E* is used in subas-

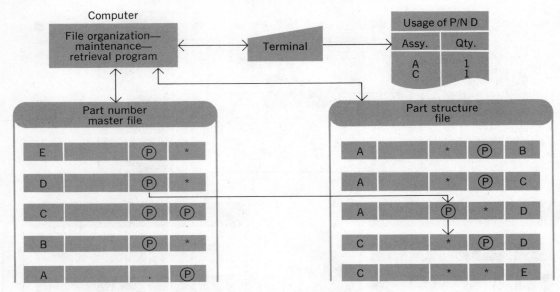

FIGURE 9.35.   Where-used retrieval.

sembly *C*. Also included in this product structure record is an end of chain indicator which means that *E* is used only in *C*.

It should be emphasized that there is only one set of product structure records. Where-used cross-reference information is available by using chains and pointers. This technique eliminates the need to maintain a separate where-used file, or to periodically sort the part structure file (which is arranged in assembly sequence) into a where-used sequence.

SUMMARY

The structure of data has three basic representations: (1) lists, (2) trees, and (3) networks. A list structure is a sequential arrangement of data records whose relationship is the result of the record's position. A tree structure is a nonlinear multilevel hierarchical structure in which each node can be related to *N* nodes at any level below it, but to only one node above it in the hierarchy. The network structure is another form of hierarchical structure where records can be related to other records regardless of their position in the hierarchy.

Records can have physical and/or logical associations. Chaining is a technique used to link records together logically. An important element in chaining is the pointer. A pointer represents the address of a particular record. Pointers can either be embedded in a record, or contained in a separate file called a directory.

Sorting is a major data operation used to structure data files in a predetermined sequence. Sorting can be accomplished either internally in storage, or via the use of auxiliary devices such as tapes or disks.

Searching a file with sorted codes can be done easily in a sequential fashion. Although simple in operation, this approach is not always the most efficient method. The binary search, or some form of a directory approach, is normally recommended for large data files.

To support many types of sophisticated file structures, it is often necessary to determine the physical location of each data record and to record this address either, in another related record or, in a directory of addresses. The mathematical algorithms used to determine an address are collectively termed transformation techniques.

9.1 What is the difference between a list and a file?

9.2 Explain the owner-member relationship between data records. Give at least two examples of such a relationship.

9.3 What are circular lists? In what kinds of situations is it meaningful to use circular list processing? Give an example of this technique.

9.4 What is an inverted list? What is the primary advantage of using inverted lists?

9.5 Distinguish between a tree structure and a network structure. Give an example of each type of structure.

9.6 What are chains and pointers? What relationship exists between them?

9.7 Distinguish between embedded and nonembedded pointers.

9.8 What are the basic types of chaining? Illustrate each type.

9.9 In your own words, what is the purpose of using chains and pointers within a data base?

9.10 What are the primary advantages and disadvantages associated with using chains and pointers in a data base?

9.11 What are the major constraints to internally sorting files via a CPU?

9.12 List and give a brief description of each of the sorting techniques.

9.13 Why is it often necessary to use a sort/merge technique when sorting large files?

9.14 What is the purpose and advantage of (a) a sequential search? (b) a binary search? and, (c) using the directory method?

9.15 What is the purpose of a transformation technique?

9.16 What are the parameters affecting performance of transformation techniques?

9.17 What are the two major objectives that one must consider when selecting a transformation technique?

9.18 What is the purpose of distribution analysis?

9.19 What is a synonym, as the term relates to transformation techniques? What is considered a normal percentage occurrence of synonyms?

9.1 "The progression from sequential, through list, to random, indicates a progression from simple data structures to complex data structures. Today's data management systems offer varying degrees of capability along this scale." Comment on this statement.

9.2 There are many applications for chaining techniques besides bill of materials applications. Discuss several.

9.3 "A major part in the design of any information system must be the study of how the data should be organized and structured." Discuss this statement.

9.4 Why should a systems analyst be familiar with the contents of this chapter?

9.5 "Binary search is efficient because successive searches each cut in half the number of records to be considered. However, it is more useful for large files." Comment on this statement.

9.6 "The amount of sorting needed to be done is an important factor in the design of the basic system of data processing." Comment on this statement.

9.7 "A random file is one in which incoming records are stored where they bear no simple relationship between the codes of the adjacent records. In order to gain access to a particular record it is, therefore, necessary to calculate its address. Can this be done?" Comment on this statement.

9.8 "It is inconceivable to me how modern day systems analysts can design highly integrated systems without understanding the restrictions of technology on data association." Discuss fully.

9.9 "The establishment of efficient directories is the key to implementing the interrogation approach for producing information." Explain this comment.

9.10 "A generalized data base management system must be able to process data in a variety of structures to be meaningful." Discuss.

EXERCISES

9.1 An N room motel system is planning to install an information system for handling room reservations. You have been hired to design the data file for this system. Some parameters which you should consider are:
(1) Number of beds and type (single, double) in each room.
(2) Cost of room.
(3) Location of room (e.g. next to swimming pool, next to highway, etc.).
(4) Special requests.
(5) Checkout times (assume that a room can be rented when it is empty and has been cleaned, even though this condition may occur before the time of checkout designated by the patron during signin).
(6) Advance room reservations are permitted.

9.2 Design an information retrieval system for physicians in a hospital. By entering a physician's code number, a display will be made listing his or her patients, their room number, and present health condition.

9.3 Referring to Figure 9.10, write an algorithm, which counts the number of records in the file. Write an algorithm that will display all personnel who are on active duty.

9.4 Using a simple chain structure, design a file for a banking institution which will allow the user to access all depositors with average balances amounting to $10,000.00 or more.

9.5 The code for just one record is as follows:

Salesman	Item	Cust.	Loc.
2	12	1	4

Group all combinations for the following reports: (1) by salesman, within item, within customer, within location; (2) by item within salesman, within customer, within location; and (3) by customer within item, within location, within salesman.

9.6 An inventory contains 25,000 different items. Information about quantity on hand, of each item, is stored in a sequential list. A user may determine the quantity on hand of a particular item by keying in the item number via a terminal which is connected to the computer. The requested number is accessed via a sequential search. Can you suggest a better way?

9.7 If there are 5000 entries in a file and 10,000 accesses per week (assume uniform distribution) and each search costs $.02; how much will it cost on the average to make these lookups if: (1) a sequential search is used, (2) a binary search is used, and (3) a directory search is used?

9.8 We have 1600 records to store and search via a directory method. What is the optimum division for sublists?

9.9 A DASD has a capacity of 7200 bytes per track. There are 3400 180 byte records to be mapped with an 85% loading tractor. How many record locations are required? How many tracks are required? Select a prime number for division.

PROBLEMS

9.1 Design a logical file to be used in simulating the movements of salesmen who spend 3 days in town A, 5 days in B, 1 day in C, 3 days in D, 4 days in E, and 6 days in F, before starting over at A again. Weekends are not included in the above counts and must be added to the length of his stay if they fall during or at the end of his stay in town. How would you include holidays in your program?

9.2 Design a file structure for an employment agency. It must be able to provide the following kinds of responses:
(1) How many male civil engineers do we have who are single, speak French, and have over five years' experience?
(2) Give me the name of a systems analyst who has an MS degree and belongs to a minority group.

9.3 Design a data file for a large nationwide construction company using a linked linear list structure to maintain all employees alphabetically. This file, on the average, contains 5000 employees, but because of the nature of the work, there are, on the average, 200 employees quitting and 200 new employees being hired each week. Use only 10–20 entries to illustrate your data structure. Would it be more efficient to maintain a simple sequential list? Explain.

9.4 Design a vehicle registry file for the state registry which will contain the following attributes: (1) name of owner, (2) make of vehicle, (3) year, (4) model or type, (5) color, and (6) license number.

Types of inquiries:
    (1) Given a license number, display owner's name.
    (2) Given the owner's name, display make, year, model, color, and license number of vehicle.

    Would you recommend sequential linear lists to meet the above requirements? Why? Why not?

9.5 Design a chaining and pointer structure for part structure and where-used information for the following list of parts:

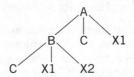

9.6 Design a personnel file, by employee number, to answer the following inquiries:
    (1) Those employees who are married.
    (2) Those who have more than four dependents.
    (3) Those who make over $12,000 per year.

    Use a structure other than an inverted file. For example, one solution to this problem is the application of a directory method.

9.7 Note the following schematic:

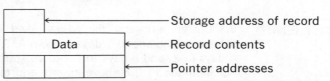

Using this schematic, as a guide, and the following records:

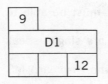

please work the following exercises:

    1. Assuming that $D1$ is the master record for construction division one, what projects are assigned to this division? $P1$, $P2$, and $P3$ represent projects 1, 2, and 3, respectively?

2. What superintendents (*S*1, *S*2, *S*3, and *S*4) are working out of division two (*D*2)?

3. Inserting the proper pointers, illustrate how you would accommodate an inquiry concerning the projects handled by division two.

4. Suppose a listing is required indicating location of all projects (*P*1 and *P*2 is in the north, and *P*3 is in the south) add required chains to give this information.

9.8 Using the sort/merge technique described, sort the following list of numbers in high to low sequence. Assume a 6-way sort/merge, blocked 2.
17, 105, 34, 28, 1, 7, 45, 16, 88, 34, 29, 87, 112, 119, 145, 35, 71

9.9 Using both the sequential search technique and the binary search technique find the following numbers in list A: [3−35−87−49−98−17]. Compare the actual average searches needed for each technique to the average searches indicated by formulas given in the chapter.

List A: 1, 3, 4, 8, 10, 12, 17, 20, 24, 29, 31, 35, 38, 43, 49, 54, 57, 63, 69, 71, 74, 78, 83, 86, 87, 92, 98, 100.

BIBLIOGRAPHY

Automated Manufacturing Planning, White Plains, New York: IBM Corporation, Technical Publications Department, January, 1970.

Barrodale, Roberts, and Ehle, *Elementary Computer Applications in Science, Engineering, and Business,* New York: John Wiley & Sons, Inc., 1971.

Bill of Material Processor—A Maintenance and Retrieval System, Second Edition, White Plains, New York: IBM Corporation, Technical Publications Department, September, 1969.

Clifton, *Data Processing Systems Design,* Philadelphia: Auerbach Publishers, 1971.

Desmonde, *Computers and Their Uses,* Englewood Cliffs, N.J.: Prentice-Hall, Inc., 1971.

File Organization, Selected Papers from File 68−An I.A.G. Conference Occasional Publication No. 3, Amsterdam: Swets & Zeitlinger N.V., 1969.

Flores, *Computer Sorting,* Englewood Cliffs, N.J.: Prentice-Hall, Inc., 1969.

Flores, *Data Structure and Management,* Englewood Cliffs, N.J.: Prentice-Hall, Inc. 1970.

Harrison, *Data Structures and Programming,* New York: Courant Institute of Mathematical Sciences, 1971.

IBM System/360 Disk Operating System Data Management Concepts, (Order Number GC24–3427–6) White Plains, New York: IBM Corporation, Technical Publications Department, October, 1970.

Information Management System/360 for the IBM System/360 Program Description, (Program Number 5736–CX3) White Plains, New York: IBM Corporation, Technical Publications Department, July, 1970.

Introduction to IBM System/360 Direct Access Storage Devices and Organi-

zation Methods, White Plains, New York: IBM Corporation, Technical Publications Department, October, 1967.

Johnson, *System Structure in Data, Programs, and Computers,* Englewood Cliffs, N.J.: Prentice-Hall, Inc., 1970.

Knuth, *The Art of Computer Programming: Fundamental Algorithms,* Vol. 1, Reading, Mass., Addison-Wesley Publishing Co., 1969.

Krauss, *Computer-Based Management Information Systems,* New York: American Management Association, Inc., 1970.

Lefkovitz, *File Structures for Online Systems,* New York: Spartan Books, 1969.

Lum, Yuen, and Dodd, "Key-to-address Transform Techniques: A Fundamental Performance Study on Large Existing Formatted Files," *Communications of the ACM,* April, 1971.

Schubert, "Basic Concepts in Data Base Management Systems," *Datamation,* July, 1972.

Stone, *Introduction to Computer Organization and Data Structures,* New York: McGraw-Hill Book Co., 1972.

The Production Information and Control System, White Plains, New York: IBM Corporation, Technical Publications Department, December, 1969.

Introduction to Systems Work and the Information Systems Development Methodology

10

Systems Analysis

10.1 Introduction

Systems analysis is the separation of anything into its constituent parts, and the study and evaluation of these parts to see if there are better ways of meeting the needs of management. In the previous chapters of this text objectives were presented in the introduction of each chapter. However, since systems work is step-oriented, objectives are not included in the introduction sections of some of the systems work chapters. Instead a flowchart of the significant steps involved is presented. A flowchart relating to systems analysis, the first phase in systems work is shown on p. 232.

10.2 Preparing to Conduct Systems Analysis

In this section, some of the reasons why systems analysis is initiated are discussed, as well as some of the difficulties of defining the scope of the analysis. Guidelines for preparing a Proposal to Conduct Systems Analysis are also given.

231

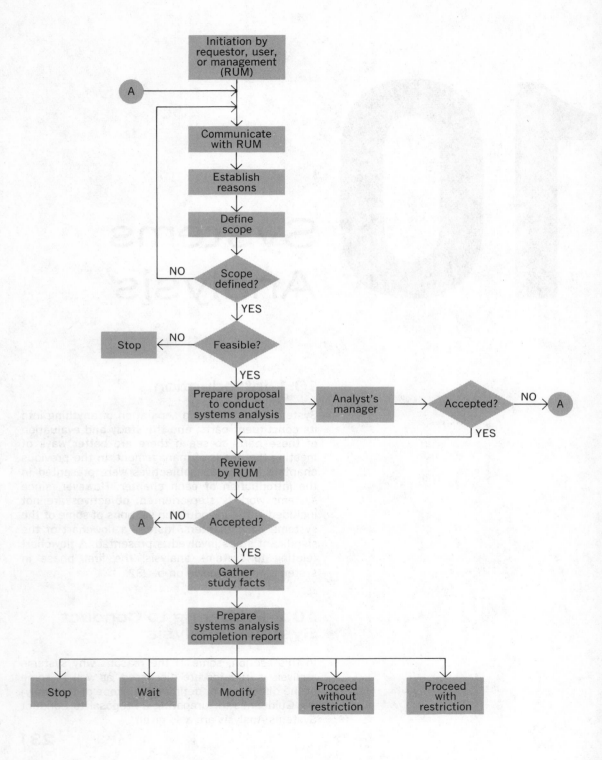

Reasons for Initiating Systems Analysis

Certainly, the first step in any systems analysis is for the analyst to acquire an understanding of the reason (or purpose) for which the analysis is being undertaken. A basic understanding can usually be attained through preliminary interviews with the persons requesting, or authorizing, the systems analysis. The basic reasons for initiating systems analysis are:

1. *Problem-solving.* It might be that the present system is not functioning as required and the analyst is called upon to correct this malfunction. Or, for example, it might be that some department in the organization has a scheduling, forecasting, or inventory control problem which must be corrected or improved upon.

2. *New Requirement.* A second reason for conducting systems analysis might be that a new requirement or regulation has been imposed upon the organization. This requirement might well be a new law, accounting practice, organizational service, or product, or even a new management practice. Regardless of what generates the new requirement, systems analysis will identify the necessary modifications or additions to the information system which are necessary to support the organization in satisfying this requirement.

3. *Implement New Idea/Technology.* A third reason for conducting systems analysis might arise from a desire to implement a new idea, piece of technology, or technique. For example, starting to use OCR (Optical Character Recognition) equipment for entering customers' orders will more than likely result in a new subsystem being designed to fully utilize this equipment.

4. *Broad Systems Improvement.* Finally, systems analysis might be initiated simply because of a desire to find a better way to do what is currently being done. Many of the data processing and information systems now operating in organizations were designed and implemented many years ago. In many instances, the reasons for designing these systems in a particular way are no longer valid. General objectives of systems improvement can be stated in such

terms as cost reduction, increased customer service, and faster reporting.

Initially, in many instances, these reasons are vague and poorly defined. However, the analyst must be careful to identify any specific objectives stated by the user or requestor of systems analysis. Frequently, there are specific objectives given to the analyst concerning elements of cost, quality, and timing, as related to conducting systems analysis, and effecting any recommendations that result. These stated objectives are a major part of what determines the scope of the investigation.

Defining the Scope of Systems Analysis

The activities and events comprising systems analysis are for the most part directed toward answering the question: What is the new system to include? In many cases this question can be more accurately phrased as: What more is the existing system to include? In answering these general questions, the analyst must address many specific questions concerning: What information is needed? by whom? when? where? in what form? how? where does it originate? when? how can it be collected? and so forth.

An overriding criterion, which to a great extent dictates the scope of systems analysis, is the systems philosophy adopted by the organization. In Chapter 4 four broad approaches were established as being used to develop information systems. These are the (1) hierarchical approach with centralized data processing, (2) the hierarchical approach with decentralized data processing, (3) the systems approach with an integrated information system, and (4) the systems approach with a distributed information system. If the systems analyst, in an attempt to develop a sales reporting system for marketing, relates data gathering and reporting to inventory control, purchasing, and accounting in an organization with a hierarchical philosophy, then the scope of the system is beyond that expected and required by the requestor. Any attempt to exceed the scope dictated by the systems philosophy of a particular organization will probably meet with resistance from management. Such a situation does not prevent the systems analyst from making suggestions as to how the total system might be improved. But the analyst still must work within the systems context dictated by top management for some duration of time.

Moreover, the scope of systems analysis can vary widely in terms of duration, complexity, and expense. Consequently, the scope of systems analysis must be defined somewhat arbitrarily at times to meet constraints such as time and cost. The primary problem for both the novice analyst (or skilled professional) is unconciously converting an instruction such as, "I want to know what yesterday's sales were by 8:00 A.M. today" into "Develop a new sales reporting system."

Often, in practice, an analyst who fails to properly define the scope of systems analysis, either fails to achieve objectives, or achieves them at a great loss of both time and money. However, it must be understood that the presence of limiting objectives (or constraints) on the scope of the analysis, limit the potential solutions and/or the recommendations that result from the analysis. As a rule, the initial definition of purpose and scope, as well as any given objectives and constraints, are subject to redefinition at a later date, based on early findings in the analysis.

Preparation of a Proposal to Conduct Systems Analysis

Once the systems analyst has conducted the initial interviews, and determines that systems analysis should be conducted, an understanding of what must be accomplished and the general approach toward this goal must be communicated formally to both the requestor and the systems analyst's own management. This communication is termed the Proposal to Conduct Systems Analysis. This proposal: (1) provides a checkpoint at which the requestor can evaluate whether or not the analyst clearly understands what is desired, and (2) provides the analyst's management with an opportunity to evaluate the approach and amount of resources to be utilized during the analysis.

The content of the proposal should initially facilitate an indepth understanding, as well as providing accessible reference points when actual performance of the analysis is periodically reported. The content of the proposal should include the following:

1. A clear but concise definition of the reason of the analysis.
2. A definition of the scope of the analysis.
3. An identification of the facts that will most likely have to be collected during the analysis.
4. An identification of potential sources where the facts will be obtained.
5. A statement of any given objectives or constraints imposed on the analysis.
6. A projection of any potential problems that might occur during the analysis.
7. A tentative schedule for conducting the analysis.

While the analyst should exercise a great deal of care in preparing his proposal, it should be remembered that the proposal itself is intended only to be a guideline. As the investigation progresses, the analyst might modify, add, or delete from his original plan. Thus, accuracy in preparing the proposal must be balanced with expediency in providing it. An example of how the proposal can change is illustrated below:

Michael Jay, a systems analyst for a large west coast electronics manufacturer, was charged with the responsibility to develop a corporate payroll system. Although Michael had been receiving paychecks from companies for many years, he had not before been involved with the payroll function in any previous assignments. In his Proposal to Conduct Systems Analysis he listed the following sources of facts in order to begin defining what a payroll system should include:

1. Manager, Corporate Payroll Department.
2. Supervisor, Salary Payroll.
3. Supervisor, Union Payroll.
4. The payroll check and other documents maintained in the Payroll Department.

5. J. D. Brown, the analyst who developed and installed the present payroll system.

Upon discussing the proposed payroll system with the Manager, Corporate Payroll Department, Michael added the following items to his list to be investigated:

6. The new union contract.
7. Manager, Corporate Benefits.
8. Manager, Corporate Work Scheduling.
9. State Law #107352.
10. Director, Corporate Planning.
11. Corporate file of requests for information from the National Labor Relations Board.

Next, Michael interviewed the Supervisor, Salary Payroll, and, again, added additional sources of facts to his list. And so it went. After each interview or document review, Michael added and subtracted potential sources of facts from his check list.

10.3 Sources of Study Facts for Systems Analysis

In this section, we discuss the various sources of study facts in and around the organization that are available to the analyst during systems analysis. There are three sources of study facts: (1) the existing system, (2) other internal sources, and (3) external sources.

Studying the Existing System

It is rare indeed when an analyst is provided with an opportunity to develop an information system from scratch. In most cases there is an existing system or subsystem which serves the organization. As a result, the analyst is confronted with decisions such as: What role does the old system have with regard to the new system? Should I analyze the old system? If so, what subsystems in the old system should I analyze?

Often a great deal of time and money is spent investigating, analyzing, and documenting the old system, but the results seem to have little,

if any, benefit in designing the new system. It is not uncommon to have experienced managers comment, "We spent $20,000 studying the old system only to have them tell us that we were correct in asking for a new system." At the other end of the spectrum, there are those who state emphatically that the first step in all systems studies is to analyze the old system. Again, many managers who have experienced new systems conversions comment, "I will never consent to implementing another new system before I have thoroughly analyzed my present system."

While it may be impossible to fully reconcile these two extreme positions cited, an examination of the advantages and disadvantages of studying the old system will shed some light on when the old system should be studied and to what extent it should be studied.

The primary advantages of analyzing the old system are:

1. *Effectiveness of Present System.* Studying the old system provides an opportunity to determine whether that system is satisfactory, in need of minor repair, requires a major overhaul, or should be replaced. To design a new system without this consideration might be comparable to purchasing a new car because your present car is out of gas.

2. *Design Ideas.* Analyzing the old system can provide the analyst with an immediate source of design ideas. These ideas include what is presently being done and how, as well as what additional needs or capabilities have been requested over the years. The analyst is able to gain an insight into how the present information system serves the decision making function as well as to ascertain key relationships.

3. *Resource Recognition.* Examining the present system allows the analyst to identify the resources available for the new system or subsystem. These resources might include: the management talent, the clerical talent, and the equipment currently owned and operational.

4. *Conversion Knowledge.* When the new system is implemented the analyst is responsi-

ble for having identified what tasks and activities are necessary to begin operating the new system and to phase out the old system. In order to identify these conversion requirements, he or she must know not only what activities will be performed but also what activities were performed. Studying the present system provides the analyst with the "What was."

5. *Common Starting Point.* When communicating with management, the systems analyst is an agent of change. As such, the analyst will often be confronted with resistance to new techniques, ideas and methods, a lack of understanding of new concepts, procrastination in obtaining decisions, lack of commitment to making the new system work, and other similar manifestations of human beings asked to change familiar work habits and activities. To minimize these reactions, it is helpful to be able to relate "newness" to "oldness." Having analyzed the old system, the analyst can contrast the new system to the old system and demonstrate that it is not entirely new, and specifically show points of similarity and differences.

The primary disadvantages of analyzing the old system are:

1. *Expensive.* Studying the old system requires time, and in all organizations time can be converted to money.

2. *Unnecessary Barriers.* An extensive analysis of an existing system can result in unnecessary or artificial constraints being included in the design of the new system. For example, in an existing system, if there is a document flow in a given department, and a series of actions are taken with that document, the analyst can become so involved with improving those actions that he or she fails to question whether that department should be involved at all. The more familiar an analyst becomes with a given system, the more likely it is that some perspective or objectivity concerning it will be lost. One may logically argue that an ideal systems approach should be used in performing systems work. That is, the analyst formulates an *ideal system* and proceeds with his or her systems work in this ideal framework.

Internal Sources

The single most important source of study facts available to the analyst is people. This includes not only the formal management and constituents of the organization, but the clerical and production workers as well. Information requirements can best be stated by the users of the information. However, the analyst can help the users define their requirements by explaining what can be provided. It is important to note that most individuals are guided in formulating their needs by arbitrary and often antiquated notions of what they "think" can be provided. The analyst's function, then, is to remove or expand these attitudes in order to obtain the real information requirements.

A secondary source of study facts for the analyst is the existing paperwork utilized and stored within the organization. The paperwork found in most organizations can be classified as: (1) that which describes how the organization is structured, (2) that which describes what the organization plans to do, and (3) that which describes what the organization is or has been doing. Figure 10.1 provides a partial list, by types, of some of the documents found in most organizations.

One word of caution is in order when organizational documents are utilized as sources of study facts in systems analysis. The documents identified as describing how an organization is structured, and what it plans to do, *do not* necessarily reflect what is actually happening. At best, these documents serve to give the analyst an understanding of what management thought of its structure and direction at one point in time. It is not uncommon for organizations and plans to change while their documentation remains unchanged.

A third source of study facts important to the analyst can be termed relationships. Defining the relationships that are observed between people, departments, or functions can provide the analyst with information and insights not known to the individuals involved nor documented anywhere within the organization.

Throughout his analysis, the analyst must

Documents Describing How the Organization Is Organized	Documents Describing What the Organization Plans to Do	Documents Describing What the Organization Does
Policy statements: Methods and procedure manuals Organizational charts Job descriptions Performance standards Delegations of authority Chart of accounts (All other coding structure references)	Statement of goals and objectives: Budgets Schedules Forecasts Plans (long and short range)	Financial statements: Performance reports Staff studies Historical reports Transactional files (including: purchase orders, customer orders, invoices, time sheets, expense records, customer correspondence, etc.) Legal papers (including: copyrights, patents, franchises, trademarks, judgments, etc.) Master reference files (including: customers, employees, products, vendors, etc.)

FIGURE 10.1. Illustration of the various types of documents available to the analyst in an organization from which he may obtain information pertaining to systems analysis.

guard against overlooking the obvious. It is not uncommon for an analyst to be questioning an individual and to be given some excellent ideas that management has previously been unwilling to take action upon. Similarly, a brief analysis of something as simple as counting the occurrence of some event, can result in a finding about that activity not realized or understood by management. In essence, the analyst provides an opportunity to present to management, at a time when their attention is strongly focused on a subject, not only personal revelations and discoveries, but the ideas, suggestions, and recommendations from various levels of operating personnel.

External Sources

The systems analyst's work can take him outside the boundaries of the segment of the organization for which the analysis is being conducted. Exploring other information subsystems within the organization can be a useful source of data collection, data processing, or information reporting ideas and techniques useful in the analyst's present study. Moreover, reviewing other systems provides an opportunity to identify potential interface points when the

analyst is involved in a limited or subsystem analysis.

Just as meaningful, but often overlooked, is the review of similar information systems in other organizations. Not only can this be a source of new ideas but it can provide the analyst with an opportunity to actually see a system, subsystem, concept, technique or mechanism in operation. While many organizations zealously guard manufacturing and marketing techniques, information processing exchanges are common. In fact, there are many societies and organizations in existence whose sole purpose is the exchange of information and data processing experiences, both good and bad.

Textbooks and professional journals provide still another source of study facts for the analyst. Studying this material may entail simply reviewing known theory and practice, or searching for new ideas, theories, and proposals. Along the same lines, the analyst can profit from attendance at professional seminars, workshops, and conferences held throughout the country.

Sales brochures from equipment and computer software vendors are an excellent source of concepts and ideas. When we consider that products and services are developed and marketed to satisfy needs, it follows that the brochures and proposals of the vendors offering the products attempt to clearly define the needs being satisfied.

The sources of study facts available to an analyst during systems analysis are varied and plentiful. What sources are exploited will differ from analysis to analysis as time and cost constraints are considered. The size and complexity of the system or subsystem under study will also help to determine which sources are utilized. Common sense is often the most compelling factor as to what sources of study facts the analyst actually employs. However, it is important to recognize what the overall choice of sources can be.

10.4 Frameworks for Fact Gathering

Many of the frameworks are dictated by the reason and scope of the study. Others are personal preferences of each analyst. A discussion of the more widely used frameworks for study fact gathering will not only demonstrate their usefulness but might also provide a basis for even more techniques to be conceived by the reader.

Decision Level Analysis

Using this approach, the analyst interviews the key managers to categorize the major resources of the organization. In this context, resources include both tangible and intangible assets such as inventories, plant and equipment, employee skills, and so forth. The major argument for this approach is that managers at all levels need an information system that provides information about resource use and not a system which provides information only by organizational function.[1] For example, one resource area is inventory. As shown in Figure 10.2, this resource (raw material and finished goods only) is broken

[1] Dr. Germain Boer, "A Decision Oriented Information System," *Journal of Systems Management,* October, 1972, pp. 36–39. With permission.

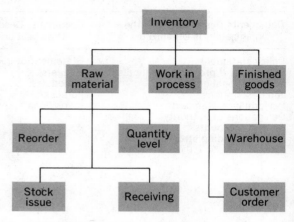

FIGURE 10.2. Decision points based on resource breakdown.

down into major types of decisions concerned with it.

Once the organization's resources are defined and categorized, the systems analyst breaks each one down into its decision levels so as to identify the information required for each decision level. After the information requirements are fully described, the analyst ascertains the sources of data (e.g., customer order) which generate this information, as shown in Figure 10.3.

Identifying the sources of data is useful for illustrating to managers the kinds of decisions that must be made before given subsystems can be developed. For example, before rules for inventory reorder decisions can be incorporated into an inventory control system, a decision rule must first be formulated.[2]

Moreover, this form of analysis graphically illustrates the many interrelationships among the decisions made in separate segments of the organization. For example, production scheduling decisions affect stock issue and stock level decisions, and stock level decisions in turn affect reorder decisions. These decision interfaces must be properly designed into the information system so that data can flow smoothly from one decision point to the other.[3]

[2] *Ibid.*
[3] *Ibid.,* p. 39.

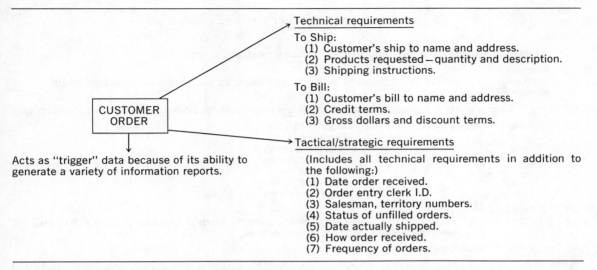

Technical requirements

To Ship:
    (1) Customer's ship to name and address.
    (2) Products requested—quantity and description.
    (3) Shipping instructions.

To Bill:
    (1) Customer's bill to name and address.
    (2) Credit terms.
    (3) Gross dollars and discount terms.

Tactical/strategic requirements

(Includes all technical requirements in addition to the following:)
    (1) Date order received.
    (2) Order entry clerk I.D.
    (3) Salesman, territory numbers.
    (4) Status of unfilled orders.
    (5) Date actually shipped.
    (6) How order received.
    (7) Frequency of orders.

CUSTOMER ORDER

Acts as "trigger" data because of its ability to generate a variety of information reports.

FIGURE 10.3.   Illustration of the information requirements from a customer's order as required to fulfill the order and as a potential source of management information to be used later in planning, controlling, and decision making activities.

Information Flow Analysis

A popular method utilized by systems analysts when attempting to identify what information is required, by whom, and from where it is obtained, is called the information flow analysis. Figure 10.4 illustrates the flow analysis approach as a framework for gathering study facts. As can be seen from this illustration, the analyst is concerned with what information the individual needs from others (supervisors, peers, and subordinates), and what information is required of him from others.

Input/Output Analysis

When the analyst is investigating the old system to gain an understanding of what is being done, particularly the mechanized or computerized portion of the system, facts can be collected in terms of inputs and outputs to the system. Figure 10.5 illustrates this approach as a framework for gathering study facts. If the example is studied, it will be seen that each input and each output is described.

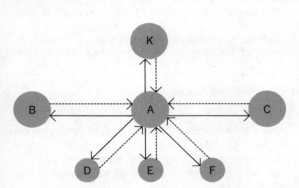

FIGURE 10.4.   The information need framework for collecting study facts. The solid lines represent what is given to others. The hyphenated lines represent what is required from others. A represents the individual being queried. B and C represent peers (other departments). D, E, and F are subordinates. K represents superiors or upper management.

Input/Output Analysis: Plant A, Inventory System

Inputs:

(1) Production.   (Quantity, product code, product number, batch no., operator no.)

Machine X
Machine Y   (Production ticket prepared by machine operator for each batch of completed goods.)
Machine Z

(2) Scrap.   A scrap ticket is prepared as necessary—same information as production ticket but coded scrap.

(3) Receiving.   All receipts are noted with: Product number
Receipt codes
Receiver's number
Product quantity
Date received
Purchase order
Authorization number

(4) Shipments
Finished Goods.   Received from billing computer system by product number, including date shipped, quantity shipped, customer order number.

(5) Transfers.   Transfers within company recorded with transfer code.

(6) Inventory Adjustments.   Inventory adjustments entered by auditors. The correct amount of product is entered with date of physical count.

Outputs:

(1) Input Listing.   A listing of all inputs is prepared daily with errors in coding. This report is received by the supervisors of manufacturing, shipping, receiving, and accounting.

(2) Daily Inventory Status.   A daily report is prepared indicating the status of all products. Report includes opening inventory, production, shipments, transfers, adjustments and closing inventory. Report is distributed to production scheduler, shipping foreman, auditor, and inventory analyst.

(3) Monthly Inventory Status.   A monthly report is prepared with same format as daily report, only reflecting that months activity. This report is issued to Plant Manager and Plant Accountant, in addition to daily distribution.

(4) Monthly Scrap Report.   A monthly scrap report is issued showing all scrap reported lost, by product, by machine operation. This report is issued to Plant Manager, Plant Accountant, Supervisor of Quality Control, Supervisor of Operations.

FIGURE 10.5. An example of the input/output framework for gathering study facts.

Hazards During Fact Gathering

There are three basic hazards which the analyst must constantly be on guard against while gathering study facts:

1. *Using incorrect or misdirected facts.* Often the analyst will be given facts concerning potential systems requirements which are misleading. This problem can result from the comments of a well meaning but unknowing manager or supervisor. It could well result from an erroneous chart, casual observation, or poor sample. The analyst can guard against this hazard by using many sources, or a number of different techniques, to acquire his study facts.

2. *Making conscious or unconscious assumptions.* It must be remembered that the analyst possesses some degree of knowledge concerning the organizational function being investigated. With experienced analysts in particular, the notion that, "I know what is needed, or being done, in that function" can replace doing the fact finding chores, and often results in erroneous facts being analyzed. This hazard

can usually be minimized by the analyst identifying his study assumptions in writing and having various users or other analysts review them.

3. *Checking and verifying every potential source.* Just the opposite of using unverified assumptions results from the analyst's checking and verifying every study fact which the analyst feels might have some importance. Obviously, this can result in an excessively expensive and time-consuming analysis which never seems to be concluded. This hazard can be minimized by establishing time objectives for each fact finding task, and applying some common sense.

10.5 Techniques for Analyzing Study Facts

Nearing the completion of systems analysis, the analyst has assembled a large quantity of raw facts, observations, insights and, perhaps, some basic understanding as to what the information system should be, and do. To attain a more complete understanding of this assemblage of study facts, the analyst must conduct a further level of analysis.

There are many different dimensions of a study fact or group of study facts which, when considered, offer a deeper understanding of the systems analysis phase. Figure 10.6 lists a few of the major dimensions within which a study fact(s) can be analyzed. All techniques noted are not valid or usable in each instance. Many times, two or more techniques used in tandem provide meaningful insights.

Figures 10.7 through 10.9 illustrate several different techniques used for analyzing the in-

Function	Pres.	V. P. Marketing	Sales Mgr.	Adv. Mgr.
General Sales Budget	S	S T_e	S T_a	A
Setting Sales Quotas		S	S T_e	A
Advertising Plans		S	A	S T_a
Salesmen Performance			S T_a T_e	
Advertising Performance				S T_a T_e

FIGURE 10.7. Example of analyzing four important positions in the company ascertaining responsibilities concerning marketing activities. Code: S: Strategic; T_a: Tactical; A: Advisory; T_e: Technical.

Information Content	Pres.	V. P. Marketing	Sales Mgr.	Adv. Mgr.
Sales Forecasts	S	S	S	D
Production Schedules	S			
Material Reports	S			
Marketing Information	S	S	D	D
Sales Reports	S	D	D	D
Inventory Reports	S	S	D	D
Personnel Needs		S	D	D

FIGURE 10.8. Illustration of the level of detail required by each manager related to specific activities within the organization. Code: S: Summarized (filtered); D: Detailed.

Time	Source/use
Cost	Necessary/desirable
Space	Mechanical/manual
Accuracy	Summary/detail
Trends	Ideal/acceptable
Frequency	Real time/delayed
Whole/part	

FIGURE 10.6 Illustration of a few of the techniques that can be used when analyzing study facts.

Management Level Sales Report Breakdown	Pres.	V. P. Marketing	Sales Mgr.	Adv. Mgr.
By Product	P	P	I S_i	P
By Territory	P	P	I S_i	P
By Customer	P	P	I S_i	P
By Salesman	P	P	I S_i	P
Percent of Total Market	E_x	S_i E_x E_n	P E_n	P E_x
Quotas	E_x	P	I	I
Profit on Sales	I	P		
Sales to Advertising		P		
Sales to Salesmen Cost		P	P I	

FIGURE 10.9. Example represents sales reporting and correlates these reports with time considerations as well as aspects pertaining to the base used to develop the information.
Code: P: Periodic; I: Inquiry; S_i: Simulation; E_x: Exception; E_n: External.

formation needs of an organization's President, Vice President Marketing, Sales Manager, and Advertising Manager.

Figure 10.7 indicates the various functions each individual is responsible for in an organization. In many instances, there can be overlapping responsibilities of a different nature, i.e., the President might have the responsibility of planning for next year's sales, among other responsibilities; the Vice President of Marketing might also be responsible for planning, but have additional responsibilities as well; and the Sales Manager might be involved in planning for next year's sales, but again, would have other responsibilities, and so forth.

Figure 10.8 represents these same functional positions but now is concerned with the level of detail each manager requires. A normal pattern in large organizations is that the higher the management level, the higher the level of summarization desired. Obviously, there are numerous incidents where top management personnel request a low level of detail.

Figure 10.9 represents an analysis of these four key management positions as related to sales reporting. In this example, the analyst attempts to show whether the information need is of a periodic nature or whether it must be satisfied by inquiry capabilities. Moreover, the analyst also attempts to represent whether the reporting is of actual occurrences or of simulated, "what if" occurrences.

10.6 Communicating the Findings

Throughout the systems analysis phase, the analyst should maintain extensive communications with the requestor, users, management, and other project personnel. This communication begins with the Proposal to Conduct Systems Analysis described previously. On a continuing basis this communication effort includes feedback to persons interviewed, or observed, as to what the analyst understands; verification with user personnel as to the findings in other, but related, functions or activities that the analyst identifies; and periodic status meetings to inform management and other project personnel about progress, status, and adherence to schedule.

Preparing the Systems Analysis Completion Report

Perhaps the most important communication of all, however, is the Systems Analysis Completion Report which describes findings of systems analysis. The format and content of this report include the following:

1. A restatement of the reason and scope of the analysis.

2. A brief description of the present system and its operations, if applicable, and any present problems not identified at the outset.

3. A restatement of all given objectives and

constraints, followed by any study findings which support or refute them.

4. A description of any unresolved or potential problems.

5. A statement of any critical assumptions made by the analyst during the analysis.

6. Any recommendations concerning the proposed system or its requirements, which actually equates to a preliminary design.

7. A projection of the required resources and expected costs involved in designing any new system or modification to a system. This projection includes the feasibility of continuing further systems work.

This report is backed up by, and prepared from the use of, a variety of techniques used during systems analysis. These techniques include, for example, questionnaires, interviews, PERT, flowcharts, decision tables, and grid charts. In addition, as the analysis is performed, investigation into the feasibility of applying computers and related technology, and models, may also be part of the requestor's reason for initiating the systems analysis. All of these basic techniques are described and discussed in the Appendices.

In general, the Systems Analysis Completion Report is directed to two different parties. First, the report is used by the analyst's management to determine if the analyst has done a competent job in identifying systems requirements and ascertaining how these requirements fit into any overall or master plan for systems development in the organization. Second, this report provides general and user managements with an opportunity to determine whether or not the analyst has considered all of the organization's requirements or needs.

In order to provide a meaningful report to both of these interested parties, the analyst should strive to be concise but thorough in preparing the report. Requirements should be quantified and explained specifically rather than in generalities. The analyst should avoid the use of technical jargon and acronyms in the report. Exhibits and supporting working papers used in the systems analysis phase should be attached or an indication given as to where they are available.

Throughout the text the importance of good communications between the analyst and the users has been emphasized as a key ingredient to successful information systems development. Achieving and maintaining good communications throughout systems analysis goes far to eliminate two real problems that have plagued practitioners in the development of systems to date. These are:

1. The failure to obtain user agreement for developing an improved information system because the proposed system is not clearly understood by the potential users of the system.

2. The need to "sell" the analyst's system to the user.

If the analyst has established an effective communications channel between himself and the users of the system, there won't be any difficulty in obtaining approval to design a new system due to the user's not understanding what that system will be. Moreover, there will not be a need to "sell" anything since the proposed system was "sold" each time the analyst obtained an agreement pertaining to a user's requirement.

The Feasibility Aspect

Systems work is a continuous cycle, but within this cycle it is also quite iterative. For example, the systems analyst might have to retrace his steps repeatedly and prepare several Proposal to Conduct Systems Analysis Reports before total agreement between the requestor and analyst is reached. This situation should be understood when one refers to the feasibility aspects of systems work. The systems analyst must continually ask whether something is feasible or not. For example, at the very outset, a requestor might indicate that some problem situation "should be investigated" by the analyst. Evaluating the situation quickly, the analyst might decide that it is infeasible to pursue the matter further at that particular time. Or it may be that the analyst begins the analysis in earnest only to find out later that it is infeasible to continue. Moreover, an entire systems analysis can be conducted for the sole purpose of proving or disproving the feasibility of something. For convenience, however, feasibility analysis is discussed along with the Systems Analysis Completion Report. As a matter of fact, the aspects of feasibility are discussed at two places in this text, here and in a different context in the next chapter. Again, however, the idea of feasibility is applicable throughout all systems work.

Feasibility analysis helps determine the likelihood that the recommendations proposed in the completion report can be carried out. In other words, these recommendations although still at a general, if not conceptual level, are capable of: (1) being specifically designed in terms of input/output, data base, models, processing controls, hardware/software, etc.; (2) attaining desired goals, user requirements, and system objectives; and (3) being successfully implemented at a later date.

The feasibility aspect is categorized into four areas abbreviated (TEOS).

1. *Technical Feasibility.* The technical area can be divided into two sections: hardware and software. Hardware simply means (in computer and related technology) the processor, peripherals, data communications equipment, and other related equipment. Software includes methods and techniques, as well as computer programs, and operating systems. Therefore, with technical feasibility, the analyst simply determines if the preliminary design can be developed and implemented using existing technology. Usually this determination includes technological expertise that presently exists in-house, but it may from time to time include the technological state of the art which can be acquired from outside the organization.

2. *Economical Feasibility.* With this category, the analyst determines if the benefits estimated as derivable from the systems recommendation are worth the time, money, and other resources required to achieve the recommendation. This aspect of feasibility is often referred to as cost/effectiveness analysis and includes the weighing of costs against the effectiveness of the recommendation. Cost/effectiveness is illustrated in the table. In Chapter 11, we will present a detailed cost/effectiveness

Estimating Costs	Assessing Effectiveness
Equipment costs Personnel costs Development costs Operating costs Etc.	*Direct benefits.* These are a direct result of the recommended system. These include reduction in errors, reduction of personnel, etc. *Indirect benefits.* These do not necessarily arise automatically from the system and they are difficult to measure except with the aid of probabilities. Examples of these benefits include increased efficiency, better decision making, more profit, increased customer service, etc.

analysis of a computer configuration.

3. *Operational Feasibility.* This aspect implies that the system will be able to perform the designated functions within the existing organizational environment with its current personnel and existing procedures. If not, and changes are required, the analyst must point out these changes and indicate the level of probability of such changes being successfully achieved. The operational aspect is really a human relations problem because the proposed system design will never be successful operationally unless the people problem is recognized. The Do's of the systems analyst are indicated by Ross and Schuster:[4]

Do begin in the initial stages to gather information on the workings of the emergent social system and the constraints it imposes. Pay particular attention to work group norms (i.e., expected standard of behavior) and emergent status relationships, both of which will be key factors in the acceptance or rejection of the system. *Do* design the information system within the emergent social system constraints, just as you design it within technical or physical constraints. *Do* consider the social and behavioral aspects of systems design to be as equally important as the technical or physical aspects. In addition to these Do's the analyst must also: (1) develop a tentative work force plan which indicates the

[4] Dr. Joel Ross and Dr. Fred Schuster, "Selling the System," *Journal of Systems Management,* October, 1972, p. 10. With permission.

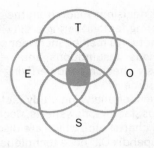

FIGURE 10.10. Schematic which illustrates total feasibility of a recommended design proposal.

probable need for orienting and training employees who will be performing the functions of the new system or subsystem if it is designed and implemented; (2) develop a list of required new skills which will be needed; and (3) develop a tentative placement plan which indicates how displaced employees are to be handled; possible changes in overall organizational structure; and changes in levels of responsibility, authority, and accountability.

4. *Schedule Feasibility.* This category means that the analyst must estimate when the proposed recommendation will be operative, assuming that it or alternatives are eventually accepted. The use of PERT and Gantt charts are helpful to the analyst in this area.

All of these categories must be feasible before any systems work can continue, as shown in Figure 10.10. Note that all aspects must be considered simultaneously for a total feasibility determination. This situation is indicated by the shaded area. For example, a preliminary design proposal may be feasible based on technical, operational, and schedule analysis, but not feasible based on economic analysis. In this case, such a design proposal would not be *totally* feasible.

Final Results of Systems Analysis

There are five alternative outcomes for any particular systems analysis. These are:

1. *Stop Work.* This result means that no further work is to be performed and systems work and resources should be directed toward other projects. The reasons for this outcome are, that a proposal(s) does not meet TEOS feasibility considerations, a change in management's or requestor's decision, or a reshuffling of systems priorities which results in the present project being scrapped.

2. *Wait State.* This result is quite common and can usually be ascribed to lack of funds or to the conservative attitude of management. Also, for example, costs may not be acceptable at present but expected forthcoming events will make the cost/effectiveness ratio acceptable sometime in the future.

3. *Modify.* This result means that management has decided that some aspects of the proposal must either be changed or combined with another subsystem.

4. *Conditional Proceed.* This outcome means that systems work will proceed as proposed, but that the final design proposal prior to implementation will have to be justified on a TEOS feasibility basis.

5. *Unconditional Proceed.* Many system or subsystem proposals are authorized by management with full knowledge that costs will exceed measurable benefits. For example, severe constraints imposed upon the organization by legislative and judicial action might require the development of a system regardless of cost. Or it may be that broader organizational objectives dictate the development of a system which is not cost/effective in a systems context. For example, management may be attempting to expand in a market area which will not be profitable for a number of years. A subsystem to support this venture would not be cost/effective within the foreseeable future.

SUMMARY

There are four possible reasons for the initiation of systems analysis: (1) to solve a problem; (2) to take care of a new requirement imposed upon the organization; (3) to implement a new method, technique, or idea; and (4) to make general system improvements or overhaul. In performing systems analysis the analyst must first define the scope or boundaries he or she will be working in. A Proposal to Conduct Systems Analysis is then prepared. This proposal is a communication device which allows both the requestor or future user of the system and the analyst's manager to know what is entailed during the systems analysis phase.

The study facts come from three major sources: (1) the existing system; (2) internal sources, which include people, documents, and relationships; and (3) external sources, which include other interface points outside the present system, user groups or societies to which the organization belongs, textbooks and periodicals, seminars, and vendors.

There are three major frameworks for fact gathering: (1) Decision level analysis breaks a system down based on resources. Decision points which control these resources are defined and appropriate decision rules formulated by management. The analyst then determines how the information will be produced to meet the requirements of these decision rules. (2) Information flow analysis shows what information is required, by whom, and from where it is obtained. (3) Input/output analysis simply shows the data inputs and information outputs of a system without

concern for decisions made from the outputs. Hazards during fact gathering are: (1) using incorrect facts; (2) making incorrect conscious, or unconscious, assumptions; and (3) needlessly checking and verifying every potential source.

Techniques for analyzing study facts include relationships, factors, flowcharts, decision tables, grid charts, etc., which are discussed in detail in Appendix C. These techniques are also used to communicate the findings to various persons and also to prepare the Systems Analysis Completion Report. The two major areas of the completion report are: (1) preliminary design recommendations and (2) the feasibility of continuing further systems work. Feasibility concerns four areas (TEOS): (1) technical feasibility, (2) economical feasibility, (3) operational feasibility, and (4) schedule feasibility.

The final results of systems analysis will be one of the following decisions: (1) stop any further systems work on present project; (2) wait for a period of time until some other events occur, at which time, it will be appropriate to continue; (3) modify present systems work and/or combine it into another systems project; (4) proceed with systems work based on further considerations, mainly cost/effectiveness; and (5) proceed with systems work without further restriction.

REVIEW QUESTIONS

10.1 What is systems analysis? What are the basic reasons for initiating systems analysis?

10.2 What are the purposes for preparing a Proposal to Conduct Systems Analysis? List and explain the major items included in this proposal.

10.3 Compare and contrast the sources of study facts available during a systems analysis, related to information systems development.

10.4 Distinguish between developing a framework for fact gathering, and performing analysis. Give an example of each.

10.5 Compare and contrast the use of the various types of study fact gathering frameworks discussed in this chapter.

10.6 Discuss how the following factors are used to perform analysis: (1) time, (2) cost, (3) whole/part, and (4) necessary/desirable.

10.7 Describe the Systems Analysis Completion Report. How does this report relate to the Proposal to Conduct Systems Analysis?

10.8 What does the term "feasible" mean? With what major aspects of feasibility is the systems analyst concerned? Explain.

10.9 What are the five possible outcomes of any systems analysis?

10.10 List and explain the major activities involved in conducting systems analysis in an organization.

10.11 Develop a check list of sources of study facts which could be used by any systems analyst.

QUESTIONS FOR DISCUSSION

10.1 "The systems investigation is a feasibility study." Evaluate this comment.

10.2 "All systems studies are directed to cutting costs." Evaluate this comment.

10.3 "The only thing wrong with the study Jim conducted was that it wasn't what management requested." Comment.

10.4 "The reason we cannot manage inventories any better today, than we could five years ago, is that we have the same inventory recording system now as we had then. The only difference is that a computer prepares the reports rather than some inventory clerk." Discuss.

10.5 "Don't ask clerks whether something is necessary or not. They only do what they are told. Management decides what is needed." Evaluate this statement.

10.6 "I never thought to define what was needed if the system utilized online terminals. I guess I assumed we were not going to have that kind of capability." Discuss.

10.7 "I have found that systems investigations are performed much faster when you fit the pieces together as you receive them." Comment.

10.8 "Just analyzing the entries in a pay stub indicates there is much more to a payroll system than calculating the correct pay." Evaluate.

10.9 "We just couldn't sell management that our study findings reflected the actual situation." Evaluate.

10.10 "The demands for systems analysts' efforts in this company are unending. It seems no sooner do we have a project completed when somebody wants us to take a look at the activity in a different perspective. It seems each new manager is looking for a better way to do things." Comment on this statement.

10.11 "I just returned from discussing the reporting requirements of the Government Wage/Price Control Program with the Vice President of Marketing. It appears that we have got some extensive modifications to make to our Marketing Information System in order to meet the government's reporting requirements. Unfortunately, we are going to have to postpone work on the new budget system to provide the government with the required information." Evaluate this comment.

10.12 "Although we only budgeted three man months to analyze the requirements on the new Personnel System, we executed fourteen man months before personnel cancelled the project." How could this situation be avoided in future systems' efforts in the organization?

10.13 "As a result of considering only the activities in the previous manual order entry system, we missed an opportunity to provide many new benefits to the organization when we designed the new system." Discuss how this situation could arise in any organization.

10.14 "The failure of the systems analyst to challenge outdated corporate policies results in many new systems being designed to satisfy nonsensical requirements." Fully discuss.

10.15 "As we progress from designing data processing systems to designing information systems, the emphases in the analysis must be changed from what must be produced, to what should be produced as informational outputs." Evaluate this comment.

EXERCISES

10.1 Choose an individual, responsible for a large number of decision making activities in an organization, and conduct an interview for the purpose of identifying the types of information presently received by this person; as well as any additional information this person might require to better perform his or her duties. In preparation for your interview, sketch a rough outline of the questions you will be asking. When you complete the interview, prepare a completion report which summarizes the proceedings. Lastly, write a brief summary comparing and contrasting what you anticipated in the interview versus what actually was said and done.

Note. The subject that you interview may be part of the administration of your school (e.g. registrar, a dean or department head, student housing director, etc.). Additional ideas for interviewing include a management person in the organization where you are employed, or someone in a local business establishment, or government agency. Employed friends and associates provide a third choice for interviewing, although this alternative should be used only as a last resort.

10.2 Select an individual involved at the technical level of an organization whose prime responsibility is to process data and observe his or her activities. Prepare a brief outline of what it is that you plan to observe. Take notes as you observe, and prepare a report summarizing what you have observed. Lastly, prepare a brief recommendation for any improvements or alternatives concerning the activity you observed.

10.3 The Tricor Manufacturing Company produces and sells several lines of bicycles, tricycles, scooters, and so forth, worldwide. Recently the company President, Jim Williams, announced a major reorganization that will affect all facets of Tricor's operations. Jim has decided to implement the relatively new concept of Materials Management in Tricor.

The Materials Management concept places the responsibility for the movement of all products in the company under one man. This involves combining the traditional functions of purchasing, production scheduling, inventory control, traffic and product estimating.

Ed Bishop has been appointed Vice President of Materials Management for Tricor. Presently, Tricor's headquarters are in Cincinnati, Ohio. All orders are entered in a centralized order entry system at Cincinnati. There are four manufacturing plants located in Rhode Island, Virginia, Colorado and Oregon.

Ed has decided to maintain a centralized purchasing staff consisting of six purchasing agents and a clerical staff of ten persons including the Supervisor at Cincinnati. J. Brown has been named Manager of Central Purchasing and will report to Bishop.

Virginia and Colorado contain relatively large plants, whereas Rhode Island and Oregon house smaller operations. Although Bishop is unsettled on the actual persons to appoint, he has decided on the following organizational structure. Each plant will be headed by a Manager of Materials Management who will report directly to the Vice President. The larger plants will have supervisors over each of the functional areas being consolidated. These supervisors will report directly to the manager at that location, although the Supervisor of Purchasing will have an indirect responsibility to the Manager of Central Purchasing.

The smaller plants will consolidate the functions of purchasing and traffic under one supervisor and the functions of production scheduling and inventory control under one supervisor. Supervising product estimating will be the direct responsibility of the manager at these smaller locations.

Each Manager of Materials Management at Tricor will be assigned a secretary, as will the Vice President. A field coordinator for Materials Management will report directly to Bishop. Before Bishop assigns specific persons to these positions and designates the size of each staff involved, he would like to review his preliminary thoughts with Jim Williams.

Ed has asked you to draw up an organizational chart according to the above facts.

10.4 The order entry system in most commercial organizations provide for shipping products on a pay-later basis assuming the customer has a proven credit record. However, a new customer, in many instances, is subject to credit approval. Consequently, most order entry systems are designed to also contain a credit checking operation as a standard procedure. The Tricor Company is no exception.

The centralized order entry system is computerized. A customer master file is used to process all orders. This file contains a record for each approved Tricor customer. Among the many fields of data in each customer record there exists a customer code, a class of trade code, a credit limit field, a current accounts receivable dollar field, a pass due accounts receivable dollar field, and a credit referral field. Currently, all orders must pass through the Credit Manager before they can be processed on the computer. A sampling has shown that less than 5% of all orders are held up by the Credit Manager. You have suggested that the credit check might be performed on the computer and only forward problem orders to the Credit Manager before shipment. This eliminates the Credit Manager having to handle all the orders, as well as decreasing the overall order processing time. The Credit Manager has agreed to try this approach.

The following narrative represents the Credit Manager's thoughts on how the credit checking procedure should operate in Tricor.

All orders entered at Tricor will have a credit check performed. All orders received from new customers must be forwarded to the Credit Manager. All orders exceeding $1000 must be forwarded to the Credit Manager. If the dollar amount of an order plus the present accounts receivable balance for that customer exceeds the credit limit assigned to the customer, the order must be sent to the Credit Manager. All orders from customers with pass due accounts receivable balances must be forwarded to the Credit Manager. All orders from customers on "credit referral" are forwarded to the Credit Manager. Orders from customers coded to class of trade 100 are not rejected unless the account is on "credit referral" or the order exceeds $10,000, or the present accounts receivable balance is greater than $50,000. Orders which pass the credit check are sent directly to the shipping department.

As the systems analyst you have three concerns with the above narrative:

(1) You must understand fully what is required,
(2) You want to ensure that the Credit Manager has not forgotten or misrepresented any concern,
(3) You want to communicate this credit checking logic to the programmer as clearly as possible.

You have decided to develop a decision table to satisfy these requirements (decision tables—Appendix C).

10.5 The processing of sales adjustments is an essential aspect of processing in the integrated system of The Magic Gadget Company. Potentially, sales adjustments can effect five different data files.

Goods returned to Magic Gadget require an adjustment to be processed to the sales statistics file, the accounts receivable file, the salesman's commission file, the inventory file and the financial file.

Invoice pricing errors result in an adjustment to the sales statistic file, and the accounts receivable file, the commission file and the financial file.

Invoice quantity errors result in adjustments similar to pricing errors in addition to an adjustment of the inventory file.

Transfers of goods between customers result in sales adjustments being processed to the sales statistics file and the accounts receivable file only.

Errors in recording the freight charges for shipments result in adjustments to the accounts receivable file and the financial file.

As the systems analyst responsible for this area, you are requested to make a presentation to the Sales Department explaining the processing of sales adjustments.

(1) Prepare a decision table representing this procedure.
(2) Prepare a flowchart(s) representing this procedure.
(3) Prepare a matrix (or array) representing this procedure.

Which method would you recommend for presentation to the Sales Department? Why?

10.6 Assume that you are a systems analyst for a data processing service bureau. Your organization has decided to offer a computerized dating service. You have been given the assignment to develop this proposed system.

    (1) Conduct a survey among your classmates to determine what characteristics are most important when choosing a date.

    (2) Develop a questionnaire which can be used for gathering the data necessary both for describing a participant in your dating service, and for evaluating potential dates to be assigned to the participant.

10.7 Identify the fact finding framework you would most likely use when investigating each of the following activities:

    (1) Customer order processing.
    (2) Expense account reporting.
    (3) The sales manager's budget.
    (4) Inventory scrap reporting.
    (5) Developing market strategy.

10.8 List at least five different sources of facts for each assignment described below.

    (1) Payroll system.
    (2) Accounts receivables.
    (3) Inventory management.
    (4) Sales forecasting.
    (5) Employee skill bank.

10.9 For each of the activities listed below, note two tools (or techniques) which you, as an analyst, might use in your study of these activities in order to gain a better understanding of them.

    (1) Preparation of the sales budget.
    (2) Classroom assignments.
    (3) Recording absences from work/class.
    (4) Preparing a customer order.
    (5) Recording inventory movements.
    (6) Ordering raw materials.
    (7) Recruiting new employees.
    (8) Recording birth certificates.
    (9) Planning for new facilities.
    (10) Calculating net pay.

10.10 Listed below are several potential systems assignments. For each assignment, indicate whether or not you would study the operations of the existing system. Explain your decision.

    (1) Computerize the company's manual accounts payable system.
    (2) Develop a real time online system for police officers requesting information concerning suspected stolen automobiles.
    (3) Develop a system for the first lottery in your state.
    (4) Develop a centralized order entry system for 12 subsidiaries, each presently having their own system.

PROBLEMS   **10.1** Based on facts in the following letter, prepare a Proposal to Conduct Systems Analysis.

James D. Student
Systems Analyst
Southwest Oil Co.

Dear Jim,

I enjoyed talking with you yesterday and am looking forward to seeing you again next week. I cannot tell you how pleased I am to hear that you are the analyst who will conduct the investigation for developing a forecasting system to assist in operating our lines. I thought I might take this time to provide you with some background to our needs.

As you are aware, we operate 3600 miles of pipeline throughout the Southwest. We are a contract carrier for petroleum products for ten major oil companies in addition to Southwest, our parent firm.

Petroleum products enter our lines from five different refineries, from 40 different storage tanks, and from four pipeline interface points in batches (we call them tenders). We deliver these products to 174 different bulk stations in addition to the above mentioned storage tanks and interface points.

Currently we employ over 1000 deliverymen whose sole responsibility is to open a valve to withdraw or input product and close that valve when the proper amount of product has been transferred. In a significant number of instances a deliveryman will not have any activity during his shift.

It is our opinion that if we could better forecast when products will be available at a given valve, we could reduce the number of deliverymen required through consolidation of assignments.

A few years ago we installed about three hundred meters in strategic locations throughout the lines which measure the product flow and report this information back to our central dispatching station via teletypewriter on demand.

Maybe we could feed this information into one of those computers you all have and predict arrivals of our tenders at selected valves.

I know you will need more facts than this before you decide what we need, but I do hope I have given you some idea of what it is we want to do.

If I can be of any further help, please do not hesitate to call on me.

Until next week,

R. G. Sherman

R. G. Sherman
Director,
Southwest Pipeline Co.

10.2 The selling and exchanging of mailing lists has become a profitable undertaking for many firms, particularly those lists which are computer accessible. The data processing service bureau that you work for has decided to construct a generalized mailing list for the metropolitan areas of Pittsburgh, Pennsylvania; Akron, Ohio; and Cleveland, Ohio.

The potential customers for this list will be small to medium retail establishments as well as local direct mail companies. Your president feels there will be an improved opportunity to market this mailing list if a potential customer can select the type of individual he or she wishes to reach on criteria other than solely geographical considerations.

Your assignment is to conduct an investigation to determine what data will be included in this generalized mailing list, and submit your findings and recommendations to the president. Based on the above facts and any assumptions you deem necessary, prepare a Systems Analysis Completion Report.

10.3 Scheduling the work for professional, semi-professional, and clerical workers, is a modern management practice gaining wide acceptance in government and industry. This technique is usually called work measurement or work scheduling.

The basic idea behind this mechanism is the establishment of standard times for performing specific tasks and measuring actual performance against these standards.

One approach to using this technique is to actually give a person some quantity of measured work and periodically check (e.g. every 2 hours) their progress. Another approach is simply to assign daily or routine tasks on a longer time period such as weekly or monthly, and check progress at some interval.

The key factor which makes this technique attractive to many managements is that a task can be estimated and, depending on the expected volume and time constraint, an approximate staffing level can be projected. Whether or not a person progresses on schedule, the supervisor can evaluate the impact of their progress according to the plan. Where work standards are proven to be loose, they can be tightened, and vice versa.

Additional advantages, such as following individual performance trends, evaluating fluctuating volumes, and costing specific activities regardless of who performs them, increase the attractiveness of this technique.

A significant disadvantage is that a seemingly high degree of clerical support is required to calculate performance ratios for each time period (usually every 2 hours), to perform maintenance to schedules of work standards, and to provide periodic summary reporting for middle and upper management.

You are a systems consultant who has been requested to install a work scheduling system in a mail order firm which employs 270 persons to merely open correspondence and forward it to the shipping or production departments. This firm, however, has access to a computer which supports online terminals for access. Based on the above facts, your assignment is to prepare a Proposal to Conduct Systems Analysis.

10.4 A systems analyst for a West Coast cosmetic manufacturer called a meeting of the various functional managers to solicit their ideas, experiences and information requirements as he was about to initiate a systems investigation project related to sales statistics. The participants of the meeting included the following: Manager, Accounting; Manager, Credit; Manager, Customer Service; Vice-President of Sales; Manager, Market Research; Manager, Budgets; Manager, Manufacturing; and Manager, New Product Developments.

The following notes were recorded by the analyst.

Manager, Accounting—Sales statistics provide the financial entry each month—(dollar figure for all sales); basis for paying monthly commissions; basis for paying quarterly bonuses; input to selected analysis and profitability studies; basis for paying state sales taxes.

Manager, Customer Service—Sales statistics used to resolve disputed shipping problems and/or invoicing problems; to assist customer in understanding what was purchased and when; to provide special analyses for salesmen, customers, and sales management.

Manager, Credit—sales statistics per se not essential, however, accounts receivable, current and past due balances, important; customers payment history provides analytical insight.

Vice-President, Sales—Historical record of customers' purchases for each product; basis for developing future quotas; routine summary reports of different dimensions of performance (i.e. product by customer, total product class, product within territory, actual versus budget, this year versus last year, etc.).

Manager, New Products Development—provides favorable/unfavorable trends; orders placed for new products; test market results of specific products, advertisements, promotions, etc.

Manager, Budgets—Historical sales provides part of input for preparing new budget, as well as measuring old budget, both at the salesman level and product level.

Manager, Manufacturing—A history of orders and shipments provides a comparison of supply and demand; potential inventory problems; provides an input to production forecast; reflects prior periods' performance.

Manager, Market Research—Provides a measurement to evaluate other competitor sales as reported in journals, studies, etc.

Analyze the above facts and prepare Systems Analysis Completion Report.

10.5 A large fabricator and marketer of customized aluminum products has a sales force of 400 men throughout the continental USA and Canada. A traditional problem in the company has been the delay of entering orders (via mail) from each of these salesmen to a centralized data processing center in St. Louis, Missouri. In addition, the salesmen are unable to respond to a customer's inquiry concerning the status of an in-process order in less than two days. A marketing study has estimated that delays in order entry costs the company $200,000 in lost sales annually. Moreover, customer frustration with late shipments resulted in a loss of $300,000 from cancelled orders in each of the last two years. The average profit margin for the company is 20%.

A recently completed systems analysis has revealed the following facts:

    (1) Each salesman can be assigned a small portable terminal to access the corporate computers directly at an initial cost of $500 per terminal.

    (2) Special communication networks to permit tollfree calls to be installed at a cost of $20,000 initially and $3500 per month.

    (3) Maintenance for all the terminals is estimated to cost $10,000 annually.

    (4) System development and implementation costs are estimated to be $250,000.

    (5) To operate the system with the centralized computer is estimated to cost $20,000 annually.

    (6) Corporate guidelines require new projects to have a pay out period of five years or less.

Analyze the above facts and prepare a report describing the feasibility of implementing the new system.

BIBLIOGRAPHY

Boer, "A Decision Oriented Information System," *Journal of Systems Management,* October, 1972.

Cleland and King, *Systems Analysis and Project Management,* New York: McGraw-Hill Book Co., 1968.

Glans, Grad, Holstein, Meyers, and Schmidt, *Management Systems,* New York: Holt, Rinehart, and Winston, 1968.

"New Training in System Analysis/Design," *EDP Analyzer,* August, 1972.

Optner, *Systems Analysis for Business Management,* Englewood Cliffs, N.J.: Prentice-Hall, Inc., 1968.

Ross and Schuster, "Selling the System," *Journal of Systems Management,* October, 1972.

11 General Systems Design

11.1 Introduction

Systems design is concerned with the development of specifications for a proposed new system or subsystem which achieves the requirements detailed during the systems analysis phase. Eventually therefore, the systems design becomes a detailed elaboration of the Systems Analysis Completion Report. In this chapter broad principles of systems design are presented, whereas in Chapter 13 detailed design considerations are dealt with. The flowchart of steps applicable to general systems design are shown as follows:

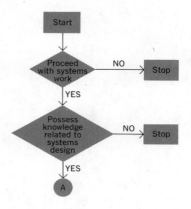

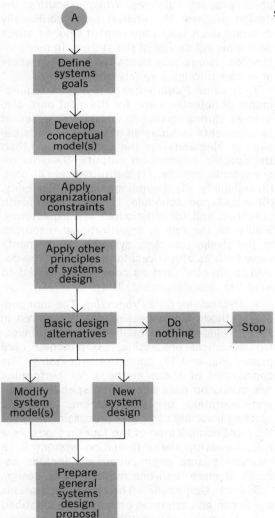

A

Define
systems
goals

Develop
conceptual
model(s)

Apply
organizational
constraints

Apply other
principles
of systems
design

Basic design
alternatives → Do
nothing → Stop

Modify
system
model(s)

New
system
design

Prepare
general
systems
design
proposal

11.2 The Design Process

In analyzing the design process we will: (1) define what it means to design, (2) summarize the elements of knowledge the systems analyst requires for designing a system, and (3) describe the basic steps in the design process.

Definition of Design

Systems design can be defined as the drawing, planning, sketching, or arranging of many separate elements into a viable, unified whole. Whereas the systems analysis phase answers the questions *what* the system is doing and *what* it should be doing to meet user requirements, the systems design phase is concerned with *how* the system is developed to meet these requirements. In the design process, the analyst develops alternative solutions and eventually ascertains the best design solution. The design phase is technically oriented to the extent that the analyst must answer the question: "How do we do it?" On the other hand, design is an art, and creatively oriented, to the extent that the analyst continually asks: "What if?" and "Why not?" questions.

At a broad systems design level, conceptual specifications are prepared which outline a complete systems design proposal. At this point, the design is reviewed against its user requirements and feasibility aspects (TEOS) and can be cancelled, modified, or continued. If the systems work continues, the next level of design is concerned with more detailed, technical design specifications such as, selection of I/O media, file size, controls, programs, and so forth. Once again, based on further systems work and additional information, a decision is made by management to cancel, modify, or continue the project. If the project is continued or modified, the next step in systems work is implementation, a subject which is discussed later in Chapter 14.

The Elements of Knowledge Related to the Design Process

In order to design a system the analyst must possess knowledge related to the following subjects: (1) organizational resources, (2) user information requirements, (3) other systems requirements, (4) methods of data processing, (5) data operations, and (6) design tools. To produce a systems design, the analyst must apply reason and creativity to these elements of knowledge.

1. *Organizational Resources.* The five basic resources of any organization are referred to as the five M's: men, machines, material, money, and methods. One of the objectives of systems design is to utilize these resources as effectively as possible. The level of resources available to the analyst for use in the system will vary considerably from organization to organization. Generally the analyst identifies the majority of resources available for use during systems analysis. However, as the design effort progresses, the analyst must constantly be alert for opportunities to utilize new or additional resources which were not previously being considered.

While the analyst seeks to attain optimum utilization of available resources, these resources in turn are constraints on potential alternatives for achieving a completely satisfactory design solution. Consequently, the final design proposal for a system acquires a unique form reflecting the resource environment in which the system must operate.

2. *User Information Requirements.* During the systems analysis phase, the information requirements of potential users of a system are identified and described. The primary purpose of the system is to provide information to satisfy these requirements. Seldom is a system designed and implemented, however, which satisfies all users' requirements completely. This lack of complete satisfaction usually results from the analyst's incorporation into the systems design the additional systems requirements, organization constraints and reality. For example, one user of inventory information identifies a need to know specific product balances on demand. In most organizations, this requirement demands an online terminal with interrogative capabilities. Due to lack of resources, or to the existence of other systems requirements, the system designed might be able to meet this need only with a daily printout of all product balances. While executing the design process, the analyst must continually evaluate each user requirement and its effect on the overall design of the system. In many instances, user requirements can be met in whole or in part through a variety of approaches.

3. *Systems Requirements.* Systems requirements or objectives are, for the most part, also defined during systems analysis. This set of requirements includes all of management's desires or demands on the system other than the specific information outputs. Systems requirements include: (1) performance, (2) cost, (3) reliability, (4) maintainability, (5) flexibility, (6) installation schedule, (7) expected growth potential, and (8) anticipated life expectancy. Similar to the role of organizational resources in the design process, systems requirements serve both as objectives, towards which the design is directed, and as constraints related to what the final design entails.

4. *Methods for Data Processing.* The four general methods for processing data discussed in Part I included: (1) manual processing, (2) electromechanical processing, (3) punched card processing, and (4) computer processing. The capabilities of these methods for performing operations on data affects the specific design and operation of each system. Designing systems involving computer processing is by far the most complicated of the four methods. As a rule, however, the information system in a medium-to-large organization will include aspects of more than one method in its design.

5. *Data Operations.* The basic operations which can be performed on data were identified in Part I as: (1) capture, (2) classify, (3) arrange, (4) summarize, (5) calculate, (6) store, (7) retrieve, (8) reproduce, and (9) disseminate. All systems are composed of some combination of these operations. Many of the data operations required in a given system are identified in systems analysis as a result of identifying spe-

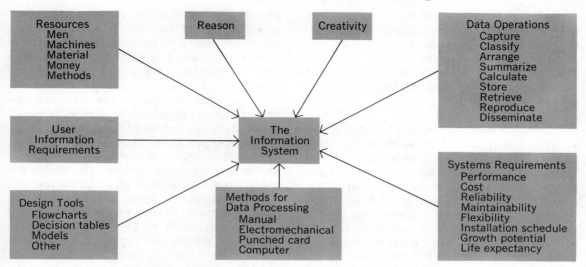

FIGURE 11.1. An illustration of the elements comprising the design process for an information system.

cific user information requirements. To produce a balance sheet, for example, we can list the required data to be captured, identify a means for classifying the data, and describe the summary and calculating operations which must be performed to attain the final product. However, depending on what data processing method is used, or what resources are involved, many additional data operations will be required. Thus, each decision leading to what the final design will entail, will affect both the number of data operations included in the system and the sequence in which they are executed.

6. *Design Tools.* In the Appendices, a series of tools and techniques utilized by the analyst in the overall development of a system are described. During the design process the analyst is greatly assisted by the use of flowcharts, decision tables, and modeling techniques. Flowcharting is of utmost importance in developing segments of the system which are heavily flow or movement oriented. Technical data processing for example, lends itself to being designed efficiently through the analyst's use of flowcharting. Decision tables are oriented to the efficient design of tactical and strategic requirements. The use of models provides the

analyst with an opportunity to experiment with different design alternatives. While it is possible to effect a systems design without using any of these tools and techniques, usually the analyst finds that they are not only beneficial but, in many instances, necessary.

Analysts apply their powers of reason and creativity to these six elements of knowledge to produce the systems design. Figure 11.1 illustrates all of the elements required in the design process.

The Basic Steps in the Design Process

In practice, the application of the design process is an iterative endeavor. As each of the design process elements is addressed by the analyst, he or she is usually forced to re-examine whatever structure or relationship had been developed to date, and modify it to satisfy the new requirement. This repetitive activity continues until each dimension of the proposed system has been considered and a final design proposal is formulated. The basic steps in the design process can be termed: (1) defining the systems goal, (2) developing a conceptual model, (3) applying organizational constraints, (4) defining data processing activities, and (5) preparing the Systems Design Proposal. The first three steps noted will be discussed next. The remaining steps will be discussed in the following sections.

1. *Defining the Systems Goal.* Defining the systems goal results from reviewing and evaluating the requirements described in the Systems Analysis Completion Report. It is important to note that the systems goal is not always equated with a specific user information requirement. The goal of a system can usually be defined by abstracting certain characteristics from all of the information requirements. Using an accounts payable system as an example, the difference between the systems goal and specific user requirements can be illustrated. The goals of an accounts payable system can be stated as: (1) to efficiently maintain an accurate and timely account of monies owed by the organization to its vendors; (2) to

provide internal systems control mechanisms which ensure the reliability of the system performance; and (3) to produce a variety of technical, tactical and strategic information to support the organization's overall objectives and operations.

By definition, the goal of the accounts payable system is not subject to change. However, the content and format of each specific input, output, and processing requirement is subject to change as organizational needs change. Let us examine briefly the various alternatives the analyst might consider when designing the specific organizational inputs, outputs, and processing elements to support the systems goals.

The basic inputs to the accounts payable system are identified in Figure 11.2 as the purchase order, the receiving report and the vendor's invoice. Purchase order data can be input to the system directly from a computer based purchase order system or it can be input via a hard copy of the purchase order, and some type of keying function, either in an online or offline mode. The receiving report can

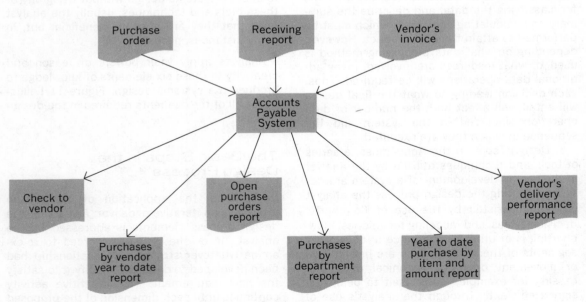

FIGURE 11.2. A conceptual design model of an accounts payable system.

also be input via a hard copy document or from an online terminal at the receiving depot. Finally, the vendor's invoice can also be input either online or offline. The specific data content can also vary in two different ways. First, the purchase order can contain all descriptive input data, while the receiving report and invoice could contain only variable data, such as actual quantity received and actual dollars owed. Second, the quantity of descriptive data associated with the payables function can vary from that required to satisfy basic technical requirements (e.g. a check to vendor, financial entry) to that used to produce related tactical and strategic information.

The basic technical information produced by the system includes the check to vendor and the accounts payable financial entry for the balance sheet. The number and composition of control reports (e.g. input registers, error reports) is dependent on both the stated needs of the users as well as the type of data processing logic included in the system. Finally, tactical and strategic information outputs (e.g. vendor performance, departmental usage) will vary continuously with the operating environment and demands of the organization as a whole.

When a system is designed to attain a goal, it generally provides some flexibility as to how this goal can be reached. This built-in flexibility results in the system being able to absorb continuous modifications from changing user requirements. On the other hand, when a system is designed to produce specific output(s), it is more than likely that it will have to be redesigned each time there is a significant change in the format, or the content, of that output.

2. *Develop a Conceptual Model.* Developing a conceptual design model of a system is the second step in the design process. Oftentimes, if the analyst is experiencing difficulty in identifying a system's goal, an attempt to develop a conceptual design model will aid in defining the system's goal. Figure 11.2 represents a conceptual design model of an accounts payable system.

To construct this conceptual model of the payables function does not necessarily require the analyst to review any specific organizational requirements unless, however, the classical accounts payable function is not understood. When the analyst considers the specific information requirements of an organization, the organization's structure, and the various organizational constraints an even more specific design model is produced. Figure 11.3 illustrates a more detailed form of an accounts payable design.

Once the analyst establishes a conceptual model of the proposed system, he or she begins to pragmatize it by applying the additional systems requirements and considering the available organizational resources.

3. *Applying Organizational Constraints.* Developing and operating information systems requires the extensive use of organizational resources. Many activities are pursued within the organization which also require use of organizational resources. Thus, the information system must vie with these other activities to obtain necessary resources. Organizational resources are usually allocated to those activities which will provide the greatest cost/effectiveness to the organization.

Applying systems objectives to the development, performance, or operation of the information system is management's technique for attempting to obtain the optimum cost/effectiveness from the information system. This fact is also applicable when the analyst must utilize data processing methods which are less than what available technology allows.

The task of obtaining a good or optimum mix of resources and objectives is an extremely significant problem confronting the analyst in the systems design phase. The overall requirements of a particular systems design are usually quite complex, vary widely, and depend on specific objectives.

Some of the factors which must be considered in the final selection of a systems design are: installation schedule, maintainability, flexibility, growth potential, and life expectancy. The short-term view normally considers cost, performance, and reliability. The long-term view, on the other hand, considers the installa-

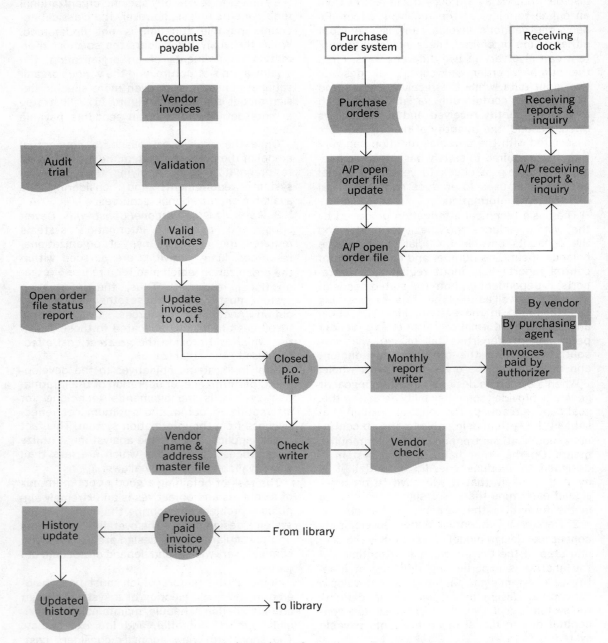

FIGURE 11.3. A detail design of an accounts payable system.

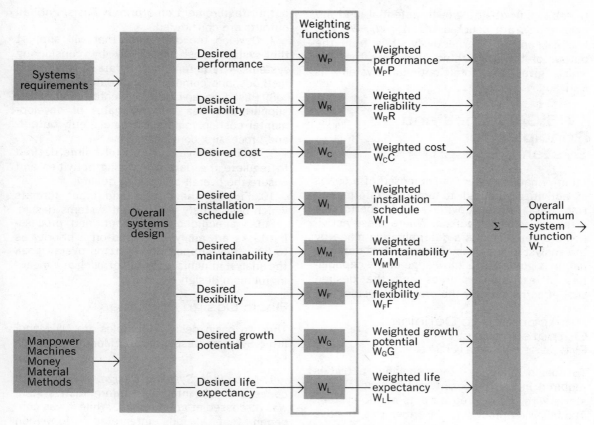

FIGURE 11.4. Model for optimum system design.

tion schedule, the developmental and operational resources, the flexibility of the system to accommodate changing user demands, the growth rate of the organization, and the life expectancy of the system.

All of the above mentioned systems objectives are interrelated. For example, performance and reliability can normally be achieved if the cost factors are increased. Conversely, the cost of the system can be decreased at the expense of poorer performance and reliability. Depending upon the application and management needs, some systems may stress performance, others reliability, others flexibility, and so on. Because of these different emphases, it is necessary to consider each system separately and to evaluate the relative importance of the various objectives in their proper perspective.

Models from other organizations, manuals, and texts can serve as guides, but the major part of every system has to be designed to meet the particular requirements of each individual organization and its managers. An illustration of how the different factors are related to provide optimization of a system is shown in Figure 11.4.

The inputs to the information system model illustrated are: (1) the system's requirements; and (2) resources in the form of manpower, machines, money, material, and methods. A weighting factor is applied to each objective, giving a set of weighted system objectives, which results in the criteria for an optimum system for the particular organization. The derived weighting factors for performance, reliability, cost, installation schedules, maintainability, flexibility, growth potential, and life expectancy, are denoted W_P, W_R, W_C, W_I, W_M, W_F, W_G, and W_L, respectively. It is from the output of these weighted objectives that W_T, which gives the total optimum system, is derived[1].

11.3 Guidelines and Principles for Systems Design

An information system is composed of a series of activities directed to produce information from data. These activities can be performed manually or by a machine. Where these activities are performed is a determination made by the analyst in the design process. This determination is guided by a knowledge of the capabilities of existing resources and the desired cost/effectiveness for the proposed system.

An Approach to Defining Outputs, Inputs, and Processing Activities

To begin defining the specific activities required in the proposed system, the analyst starts with the desired outputs of the system. The following procedure describes this iterative process.

1. Identify the most important output in support of the system's goal.
2. List the specific information fields required to prepare that output.
3. Identify the specific input data required to develop the information fields.
4. Describe the data processing operations, particularly the logical or calculating algorithms, which must be applied to the input data to produce the desired information.
5. Identify those input elements which can be input once and stored for use in subsequent processing.
6. Continue executing steps 1–5, for each

output requirement on a priority basis, until all outputs are considered.
7. Develop the data base that will support the system most effectively by considering systems requirements, data processing methods, and commonality of data.
8. Based on any developmental constraints, support priorities, and estimates of developmental cost, eliminate extreme input, output, and processing considerations.
9. Define the various control points desired to regulate the data processing activities and ensure the overall processing quality.
10. Finalize the output and input formats which best satisfy the current systems design.

When specific output, input, and processing tasks are analyzed, based on a priority as to how they support the systems overall goal, the analyst minimizes time in arriving at a meaningful main design structure.

Basic Design Principles

The two basic design principles are (1) Monolithic Systems Design and (2) Modular Systems Design.

1. *Monolithic Systems Design.* In Part I the concept of the integrated information system was discussed at great length. While it was conceded that a fully integrated information system might not be feasible in most organizations at this time, a trend towards integration of subsystems is prevalent.

During systems design the analyst must consider two basic forms of systems integration. First, the analyst must determine if integration of common data processing facilities is a viable method of accomplishing the objective. Integration of data processing facilities is a common practice in most organizations. Second, the analyst must address the potential integration of organizational data (e.g. common data base). Recent technological advances have resulted in this form of integration becoming highly desirable. In either case, the analyst bases his decision on the anticipated cost/effectiveness of systems integration.

2. *Modular Systems Design.* The principle of design modularity is understood to mean the

---

[1] Adapted from: Stanley M. Shinners, *Techniques of System Engineering* (New York: McGraw-Hill Book Company, 1967), Chapter 1. Used with permission of McGraw-Hill Book Company.

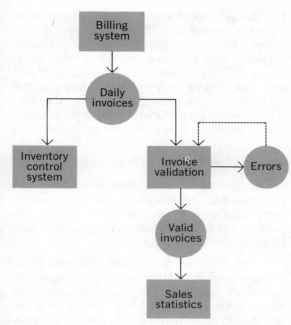

FIGURE 11.5. An illustration of the use of both the principle of monolithic design and the principle of modular design in systems design.

arranging of systems elements or subsystems in such a manner as to reduce the dependency of each element or subsystem on each other. Theoretically, the principle of monolithic design and the principle of modular design are opposed to one another. In practice, however, both principles can be effectively utilized in systems design. The following example illustrates this use of both principles in systems design.

Figure 11.5 illustrates the integration of three organizational data processing systems: a billing system, a sales statistics system, and an inventory control system. Invoicing information, produced in the billing system, flows into both the sales statistics system as well as the inventory control system.

The billing system has a control scheme, which is acceptable to the inventory system, and thus the billing data "passes" directly into the inventory system and provides the input to relieve finished goods. On the other hand, the sales statistics system, which is the basis for calculating salesmen's commissions, requires greater control, and thus has a validation procedure which must be executed before billing data is accepted into the system.

In our example, it can be seen that systems integration is achieved by using the output of one system as input for two other systems. Moreover, modularity exists in the systems design because the increased control required in the sales statistics system, in no way affects either the billing system or the inventory control system.

Specific Guidelines for Designing the Functional Subsystem in the System

Every information system can be viewed as being composed of seven functional subsystems: (1) data collection, (2) data processing, (3) file update, (4) data storage, (5) data retrieval, (6) information reporting, and (7) data processing controls. At this time some guidelines are stated as to how these activities are to be considered in the overall systems design phase.

1. Source data should be collected once, and only once, for input to the information system, regardless of the number of different ways it must be processed.

2. The accuracy of source data is directly related to the number of steps required to record, collect, and prepare the data for processing. The fewer the steps, the greater the degree of accuracy.

3. Data associated with transaction output from a computer based system should not have to be re-entered into other systems in the same organization at a later time for subsequent processing.

4. The timing requirement for collecting source data should never be greater than the timing requirement of the information it is required to produce. In other words, a daily information requirement requires at least a daily collection activity.

5. The cost of a new method or machine for

data collection should be compared to any existing method or machine in terms of the sum of the activities it effects, e.g., verifications, rate of error, and ease of correcting errors.

6. It is usually not justifiable to collect data online, when there is no requirement to report information, produced from that data, online.

7. All source data should be thoroughly edited and validated immediately after it has been collected.

8. Data previously validated when entered into the system should not require subsequent validation, of the same type, in further processing.

9. Control totals should be maintained and checked before and after a major processing activity.

10. Control totals during processing should be evaluated by programming logic rather than by manual checking.

11. Data should be stored in only one place in the data base unless this is prohibited by resource constraints.

12. All data files should have an entry procedure in case file maintenance is required.

13. All data files should be capable of being printed in a meaningful format for audit purposes.

14. Transaction files should be maintained for a minimum of one cycle when used to update the data base.

15. Backup and security procedures should be provided for all data files.

16. Every nonsequential file should have a procedure for periodic reorganization of that file.

17. All data files should have specific retention dates.

11.4 Basic Design Alternatives and the Systems Design Proposal

Thus far it has been assumed that the identified systems requirements, and users' information needs, must be met by the design of a new system. However, this is not always true.

The analyst should also be aware of the other available alternatives. Moreover, when a new systems design is required, there are additional decisions required concerning the manner in which the new system is to be developed and operated. In this section we will examine the basic design alternatives available to the analyst as well as some major guidelines for preparing the General Systems Design Proposal.

Basic Design Alternatives

The analyst has at least three basic design alternatives each time he or she evaluates a set of systems and user requirements: (1) to do nothing, (2) to modify an existing system, and (3) to design a new system.

1. *The Do Nothing Alternative.* In every systems decision as to how to satisfy users information requirements, or requests for systems improvements, the analyst has an opportunity to do nothing. This alternative does not mean that the analyst actually does nothing, but rather that he or she recommends no action be taken at this time. The reasons for choosing this alternative include: (1) a poor identification and definition of requirements or needs; (2) a determination that it is infeasible to develop a meaningful system or solution to the user's needs; (3) other systems requests have higher priorities, and developmental resources are fully allocated; or (4) the user's needs as stated are not real needs.

2. *Modify an Existing Systems Alternative.* The majority of all systems investigations conducted in organizations include some consideration of existing systems and subsystems. To effectively satisfy new or revised user requirements, the analyst often recommends modifying existing systems rather than designing new systems. Depending on the size of the organization and the particular subsystem being evaluated, systems modifications can have a larger impact on an organization than the development of an entirely new subsystem. This impact can result from either the size of the systems effort expended or from the change resulting in the organization.

When systems support is applied to solving an organizational problem, the emphasis is on immediate results. Thus changes are often implemented to existing systems until a new system can be defined and developed. In addition, the level of information systems development which exists today in many medium to large organizations has reached such a point that new user demands often require relatively small changes to data collection and storage elements. The emphasis appears to be placed on accessing available data in a new format or on a more timely basis.

3. *Design a New System Alternative.* The final alternative available to the analyst for recommendation is to design a new system to satisfy users' requirements. This last alternative is obviously the most complex and difficult solution to implement. This alternative can be viewed as a combination of two further choices of action. When an analyst recommends that a new system be implemented, a decision must be made whether this system is to be developed from scratch, or whether an acceptable system can be purchased from other sources, to satisfy user requirements. Traditionally, this decision is termed "Make or Buy."

Summary Points of Basic Design Alternatives

Figure 11.6 is a chart which demonstrates the various decision points that analysts must address themselves to when recommending the best use of organization resources to satisfy user information requirements.

Analysis of Make or Buy Decision

Make or buy decisions are not new to the management process. Manufacturing management continually review their operations to determine

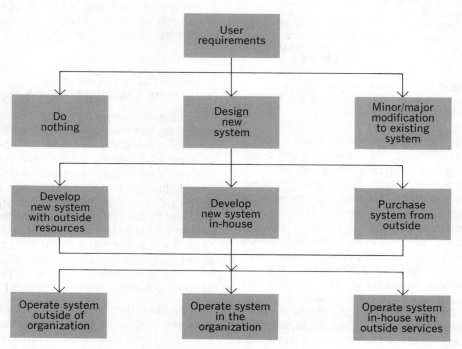

FIGURE 11.6. A chart showing the major design alternatives available to the analyst.

In-House Development	Purchase System
Advantages	
1. System tailored to requirements.	1. System tested and proven.
2. High degree of design integration possible.	2. Implementation time reduced.
3. Optimum use of organizational resources possible.	3. Advantages/disadvantages known.
4. Advanced state of the art techniques utilized.	4. Developmental resources freed for other efforts.
	5. Usually less cost.
Disadvantages	
1. Lengthy developmental time.	1. Does not meet all requirements.
2. Costs and benefits uncertain.	2. Inefficient use of resources.
3. Developmental talents are scarce and not always available.	3. Maintenance and modification are a greater problem.
4. Debugging and other problems occur long after implementation.	4. Less integration with other systems.
5. Usually more expensive.	5. Demoralizing on developmental staff.
	6. Generally, not latest state of the art.

FIGURE 11.7. Advantages and disadvantages related to the systems make or buy decision.

if a certain product or assembly can be manufactured as efficiently as it can be purchased. However, in the area of information systems, the make or buy decision is becoming increasingly more important. The development of computer based information systems is an expensive proposition in any organization, when it is compared to the resources available to that organization. Until recently, only very large organizations could afford extensive computer based systems development. As a result, many consulting firms and service bureaus were established that provide data processing systems for implementation in an organization. In many cases, these firms actually assume responsibility for operating a selected portion of an organization's data processing requirements.

As the manufacturers of data processing equipment, particularly computers, achieved drastic reductions in the initial cost of equipment, many smaller organizations acquired the necessary equipment to process their own data. However, the cost of reinventing the payroll or accounts payable wheel in each and every organization became even more expensive. Consequently, organizations began to purchase their basic data processing systems from consultants, computer manufacturers, and software houses whose primary function is to design, develop, and/or operate data processing systems for universal application.

The make or buy decision is less important in large organizations or where there is an information requirement somewhat unique or unusual. In most medium to small size organizations, however, the choice between making or buying, at least the basic data processing systems, represents a meaningful decision of which the analyst must be cognizant.

The advantages and disadvantages of purchasing or building a specific data processing system or subsystem are illustrated in Figure 11.7.

Preparing the General Systems Design Proposal

The General Systems Design Proposal is prepared to communicate to management and users in the organization *how*, at a broad level, the designed system will satisfy their information and data processing requirements. Assuming, at this point, that management authorizes continuation of the project it is the forerunner of the Final Systems Design Report. Otherwise, the project is modified to the extent that the analyst must once again retrace some steps, or it is abandoned. The following guidelines are offered as being of assistance to the analyst in preparing the General Systems Design Proposal:

1. Restate the reason(s) for initiating systems work, including specific objectives, and relate all original user requirements and objectives to the present systems design proposal.

2. Prepare a concise but thorough model of

the proposed system design. Moreover, always try to include design alternatives from which management can make choices, rather than presenting only one approach. Not only does the presentation of alternatives allow management to choose, but often it can be shown that a different alternative will make a significantly different impact on the organization. For example, a design proposal B may meet ninety percent of the requirements of design proposal A, but B may cost only forty percent of A. The point here is, never get into a situation where it's all one particular design or nothing.

3. Show all of the resources required to implement and maintain the system.

4. Identify any critical assumptions or unresolved problems which may affect the final systems design.

Certainly, the format of the General Systems Design Proposal is subject to wide variation from organization to organization. However, the main point to remember when preparing a design proposal, is that the person(s) who must authorize the development of the general systems design alternatives must have sufficient facts on which to make a decision.

11.5 Systems Design — An Example

Throughout this chapter the general guidelines and methodology to be used in designing systems have been discussed. In this section the design of a system that is required in almost all organizations, the Accounts Receivable/Credit system, is examined.

Accounts Receivable/Credit System — An Overview

From a financial viewpoint, the accounts receivable system is designed to maintain a permanent record of monies owed the organization by its customers. The credit function may or may not be performed in conjunction with the accounts receivable operation. The purpose of the credit function is to control the issuance of credit to customers as well as to follow up the collection of monies owed. As a rule, the credit function is the primary user of technical and tactical information produced from the data accumulated by accounts receivable.

The cash flow analysis concept is utilized by many organizations for the development of both short and long range planning. As such, this strategic information can, at least in part, be obtained from an Accounts Receivable/Credit system.

Accounts Receivable/Credit — Data Collection

The two primary inputs to the Accounts Receivable/Credit system are the customer payments for goods and the organization's invoices to its customers. Figure 11.8 illustrates how these data are collected and input to the system.

Customer payments are entered to the accounts receivable Open Item File via online key-

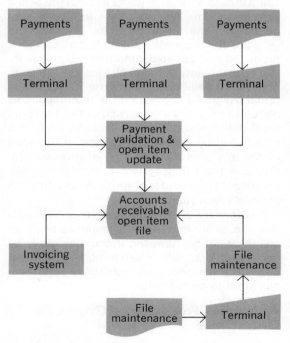

FIGURE 11.8. Illustration of the accounts receivable data collection operations.

board devices. At this time the operator enters the account number, payment amount, and the document number of the item being paid. If a problem occurs, such as input with an invalid account number, an error message is produced for the operator and the transaction is voided. The operator can verify the account number or place the payment document in a manually maintained file of problem payments. A second level of reconciliation would have to occur before that payment could be entered into the system.

At the completion of inputting specified batches of payments, the operator requests a control total from the system and to this total adds any error documents. This combined total must equal the batch control total given to the operator by another function, e.g., accounting.

The second primary input to the system is the organization's invoice. In our systems design, note that this input is a direct update to the accounts receivable Open Item File from the billing system. In other words, as an invoice is produced for the customer, the invoice data required for accounts receivable processing is produced and updated simultaneously. This integration of data flow eliminates the need to produce an additional copy of the invoice for internal use and a subsequent re-entering of this data into the computer portion of the accounts receivable system. Absolute financial control is maintained by a daily comparison of the total (dollar and quantity amounts) of invoices produced in the billing system to the total (dollar and quantity amounts) of invoices updating the accounts receivable system.

A secondary input to the system is file maintenance. In our design this is shown as being an online operation, however, it could as easily be performed in an offline batch mode. This input allows any file discrepancies caused by erroneous input to be corrected.

Accounts Receivable/Credit— Data Base

In Figures 11.8 through 11.10 note that there are three basic files in the data base: (1) Open Item File, (2) Closed Item File, and (3) Customer Master File.

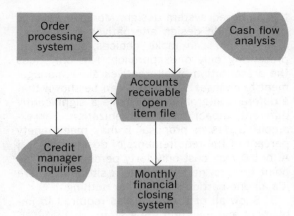

FIGURE 11.9. Illustration of the online status of the accounts receivable open item file which provides management with significant tactical information for short term planning and control.

The Open Item File is designed for online processing which includes random updating and access. All three figures show this file as being resident on a DASD. The Closed Item File, however, is shown as being a tape file which is primarily oriented to sequential or offline batch processing. Figure 11.10 shows the ability to interrogate the Closed Item File from a remote terminal. The difference in how the two files are shown is reflected in the fact that the Open Item File is used for technical requirements, whereas the Closed Item File is used to produce tactical and/or strategic information requirements as needed.

The Customer Master File is a source of reference data for our system. Thus, it is shown here only as a source of information with no updating or maintenance requirements. Again, this systems design demonstrates an integration of systems as being desirable since duplicate data processing operations pertaining to customer data have been eliminated.

Accounts Receivable/Credit— Output

In our systems design, examples of the various types of information that can be produced, as

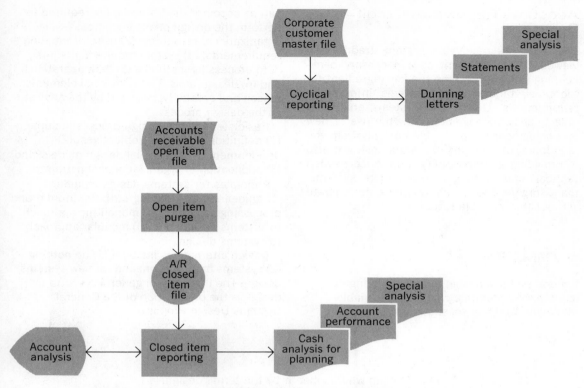

11.10. Illustration of A/R which provides strategic oriented
information as well as normal technical requirements.

well as the different ways in which it can be represented, have been provided.

Technical information is provided to the order processing system (Figure 11.9). Thus, when a customer order is entered, the order processing system uses the accounts receivable Open Item File to determine the customer's account balance. The account balance in conjunction with a pre-established credit limit on the Customer Master File, for example, permits automatic credit checking on every order processed. Additionally, the credit manager has the capability of interrogating the Open Item File for a more indepth analysis of one or more customer accounts. Routine technical requirements such as dunning letters and customer statements are also produced by the system. In these latter cases, however, the processing is accomplished offline.

Tactical and strategic information, representing cash flow and payment performance, is also produced both offline and online for management's use. One example of how this information might be used, is sales management can see what effect the establishment of a service charge would have on cash flow. Another example might be to see what effect a special marketing promotion for smaller accounts would have. The payment performance of small accounts might adversely affect short-term cash flow, in which case management might have to plan a source for short-term funding.

Additional strategic information of a what-if nature can be produced by the system. For example, what effect on the business would there be if payments were collected one day faster, or two days slower?

Accounts Receivable/Credit— Summary

The accounts receivable system, traditionally viewed by management as a necessary book-keeping evil, can become the key ingredient for technical, tactical, and strategic information requirements. Unless the systems analyst is able to show management how the use of new technology can be profitable not only from the standpoint of reducing operating cost, but also in providing an opportunity to produce needed tactical and strategic information systems, many organizations will continue to operate without this valuable resource.

SUMMARY

General systems design entails the bringing together of separate elements into a viable whole and by doing so, shows how something can be accomplished. Knowledge required to perform the design phase encompasses: (1) organizational resources, (2) user information requirements, (3) system requirements, (4) data processing methods, (5) data operations, and (6) design tools. Two additional elements, reason and creativity, are used by the analyst in the design process.

Basic steps in the design process include: (1) definition of systems objectives, (2) development of conceptual design models, and (3) application of organizational constraints.

Principles for systems design include: (1) guidelines for defining outputs, inputs, and processing activities; (2) monolithic approach to systems design; and (3) modular approach to systems design.

Design alternatives include: (1) do nothing, (2) systems modification, and (3) new systems design. The final step in general systems design is the preparation of the General Systems Design Proposal.

REVIEW QUESTIONS

11.1 Explain what is meant by the term "design."

11.2 What types of knowledge must a systems analyst possess in order to successfully design information systems?

11.3 Distinguish between user requirements and systems requirements.

11.4 List and explain the basic steps in the design process.

11.5 Compare and contrast systems requirements with organizational constraints.

11.6 What is the first step in specific systems design? Why? What is the signficance of step five in specific design as listed in this text?

11.7 Explain the major considerations related to the principle of Monolithic Systems Design.

11.8 Distinguish between the principle of Monolithic Systems Design and Modular Systems Design. Give at least one example where these two principles can be used to compliment one another.

11.9 Explain the relationship between data operations and the functional subsystems, and the functional subsystems and the information system.

11.10 List and explain the basic design alternatives.

11.11 Describe the logic behind the "make or buy" decision, as it pertains to the development of information systems.

11.12 What is the primary purpose of the General Systems Design Proposal? In your own words, what should this proposal include?

11.1 Compare and contrast the design of an information system with the design of an automobile. With a political system.

11.2 "There is only one real resource, and that is money." Discuss this comment.

11.3 Identify at least one major difficulty an analyst might experience with using conceptual design models. With not using conceptual design models.

11.4 Following, is a comment from a middle manager: "I just attended a presentation by systems regarding our new sales reporting system. They are 'blue skying' again." Discuss fully.

11.5 "We will have a new system within five months of starting work and the president will be pleased and satisfied; that is, until he understands what it costs to operate the system." Based on this comment, what design criteria were given priority in selecting the final design?

11.6 After having viewed a series of flow charts reflecting segments of a new system proposal, the following comment was overheard: "The design of the system is basically the same as the existing system but with up-to-date technology." Comment on this remark.

11.7 "We have had computers for over 20 years. We have only begun designing systems in the last two or three years." Explain this statement. Do you agree or disagree?

11.8 "We no longer design any new systems in our shop. We have found that we can buy a completely developed system for a much lower cost than if we designed and built it ourself." Discuss fully.

11.9 "Information systems should be designed by management, not by technicians." What, most likely, has prompted this comment?

11.10 "You can't teach someone how to design a system. Design is a creative act. You can't teach creativity." Discuss.

11.11 Discuss the design of one information system with which you are familiar. In particular, point out its good and bad points.

11.12 "The costs of operating the payroll system are somewhat deceiving. Each small change in either law or management's informational needs, requires extensive programming modifications." Discuss.

11.13 Discuss the probability of a large organization having an information system utilizing only one data processing method.

11.14 "Before you begin programming a new system, it is important to 'lock' the users in on what format the output reports will take." Do you agree or disagree with this statement?

11.15 "Implementation schedules do not directly affect systems design." Discuss.

11.16 "Eighty percent of the effort required to implement the new system resulted from the requirements of less than ten percent of the informational outputs." Evaluate this comment.

11.17 Discuss the probable reasons why systems analysts would not offer purchased systems as alternatives to management.

11.18 Define the terms: turn-key operation, facilities management, and proprietary system.

11.19 Discuss the importance of identifying critical assumptions in any systems design proposal.

11.20 Does it follow that a person who excels at analytical activities will excel in design activities?

EXERCISES

11.1 Prepare a conceptual design model showing the relationships between an inventory control system, purchasing system, and accounts payable system in a manufacturing organization.

11.2 Design a form, to be filled out by students, for entering personal data into a skills bank for matching part time job opportunities.

11.3 From the library, research information systems literature which describes at least two generalized data base management systems. Based on your readings, prepare a report describing how these systems will affect the design of a system such as payroll, or sales reporting.

11.4 There are many software packages available in the market for the express purpose of providing documentation for computer programs. Routinely, many of the data and information processing magazines publish articles which evaluate these packages. Select one such article and prepare a report describing how the analysis was performed.

11.5 Design a data record(s) which could be used in a data base to record the activity performed by the following types of persons:
  (1) An automobile mechanic in a large garage,
  (2) An intern or resident in a large hospital,
  (3) A tax specialist who prepares individual income tax forms,
  (4) A typewriter salesman,
  (5) A trainer of dogs to assist the blind.

PROBLEMS

11.1 Visit a local company and prepare a report for presentation in class which describes one or more of the major subsystems in their information system.

11.2 You have been hired by a large country club to design an information system for its golfing activities. This system is to accept golf scores from members and their guests and automatically update the members handicap. In addition, the system is to have the capability of providing a member with a complete analysis of all matches he or she participated in for a given year showing his or her strokes per hole. Finally, the club's management would like to have the ability to analyze activity on the course by day.

  You are given the following information: The course has a teletype tied in to a large timesharing computer system. The teletype is operable from 6 A.M. to 10 P.M. The course uses a handicap system which assigns a golfer handicap equal to 80% of the difference between actual scores and par based on the last ten rounds played. There are 18 holes on the course. The respective pars and difficulties are as follows:

Hole	Par	Difficulty Factor
1	4	14
2	3	7
3	4	9
4	5	8
5	3	12
6	4	14
7	4	10
8	4	4
9	5	11
10	4	13
11	3	15
12	4	17
13	3	18
14	5	2
15	4	6
16	4	5
17	4	3
18	5	1

(Handicap strokes are assigned to holes in order of difficulty. 1 = most difficult.)

Prepare a General Systems Design Proposal for your proposed system.

11.3 Prepare a complete General Systems Design Proposal for a budget and expense system to service middle and upper income families. Each family will be expected to lease a small CRT terminal for about $45 per month. Each family will enter the total amount of money it wishes to budget for appropriate elements annually. Each day, week, or month the family will be responsible for entering actual expenses incurred. The system should provide various analyses of expenses versus budget, as well as preparing a worksheet to be used for income tax preparation. You are to make any assumptions you feel are necessary concerning what data should be in the system and what the computer configuration must be to support this type of system. It is expected that your system will service as many as 20,000 families.

11.4 In many small and medium sized organizations, telephone expenses are a significant part of the total business expense. Although the telephone company provides a detail list of charges each month, this data as presented on the bill is not readily adaptable for controlling individual telephone users. In many organizations, a company telephone operator places all long distance calls and accepts all incoming collect calls. In each case, the operator is able to log which extension user in the company placed or received the call.

The telephone bill each month shows the total cost of all installed equipment, e.g. extension phones, switchboard, multiple lines on phones, etc. A separate inventory list is provided monthly which details equipment costs. Long distance, collect, third party calls, and credit card charges are shown in detail on the monthly bill. However, often these charges are a month or two late in being billed. Credit card numbers are issued by the telephone company and are usually logged by a clerk in the accounting department. The monthly telephone bill shows detail fields for each line item as follows: (1) date call placed or received, (2) number called or number called from, (3) code for type of call, (4) city called or called from, (5) credit card number if applicable, (6) length of call, and (7) charge for call.

Analyze the above facts and provide the following:

(1) A detailed design of an information system which collects, processes, and reports telephone expenses. Assume the organization has a computer which operates in batch processing mode utilizing punched cards, magnetic tape, and magnetic disk.
(2) The forms and procedures required to collect input data,
(3) The records and files to be contained in the data base,
(4) Your recommendations for the informational outputs to be received by each department manager and the company controller.

11.5 A small mid-western state plans to experiment with a new way of dispensing drugs required by doctors' prescriptions. In general, each hospital, doctor's office, and pharmacy will be required to purchase or lease a small terminal which is capable of accessing a large centralized computer. Rather than write prescriptions in the traditional sense, the doctor will enter the prescription into the terminal and forward the data to the computer. A large data base maintained at the central computer will contain inventory records for each pharmacy in the state. The patient can request that the prescription be filled at a pharmacy of his or her choice or at one of several pharmacies in a specified geographical area based on some criteria such as price, availability, etc.

The goals of this system are to reduce the mishandling and misinterpretation of patients' prescriptions, reduce the costs related to obtaining prescriptions, and provide a method for exercising control over illegal drug dispensing.

Prepare a General Systems Design Proposal for this system as you visualize it operating. Prepare a two or three page report discussing the advantages and disadvantages to this type of information system.

11.6 A food manufacturer has traditionally relied on "money back coupons" for promoting its products. This means that when a consumer purchases one of the manufacturer's products, he or she simply sends the label from the product with his or her name and address to the manufacturer who returns 25 or 50 cents to the consumer depending on the rules of the promotion. However, as business has grown, the Vice President of Marketing has had two concerns: (1) this type of promotion is not very successful in many parts of the country and (2) the cost of operating the promotion is nearing $1,000,000 annually.

This cost includes approximately $150,000 for manually processing refunds and $850,000 in payments. The firm has a large computer with online processing capabilities via teletypes or CRT's. The Vice President believes processing costs can be reduced by 50% if the computer is used to replace manual processing.

Analyze the above facts and make any assumptions you deem necessary in order to prepare a General Systems Design Proposal. Your design should include not only the processing of consumer claims but considerations for informing management as to the success/failure of the promotion through specific analytical reports.

BIBLIOGRAPHY Laden and Gildersleeve, *System Design for Computer Applications,* New York: John Wiley & Sons, Inc., 1967.

Matthews, *The Design of the Management Information System,* Philadelphia: Auerbach Publishers, 1971.

Shinners, *Techniques of System Engineering,* New York: McGraw-Hill Book Co., 1967.

12 System Evaluation and Justification

12.1 Introduction

In this chapter, the process the analyst must go through to prepare a Final Systems Design Report is discussed. This report is the basic document which management uses to make its decision as to whether or not the proposed systems design should be implemented. A computer configuration is used as the vehicle for our discussion in this chapter. However, the same kind of process should be followed for any kind of system evaluation and justification. The flowchart for the steps in this process is outlined on page 279.

12.2 General Systems Design Requirements

Not all systems designs call for computer equipment selection and acquisition. Assume, however, that it has been concluded at this point that some kind of a computer configuration is necessary to meet the general systems requirements. These requirements fall into three categories: (1) inherent

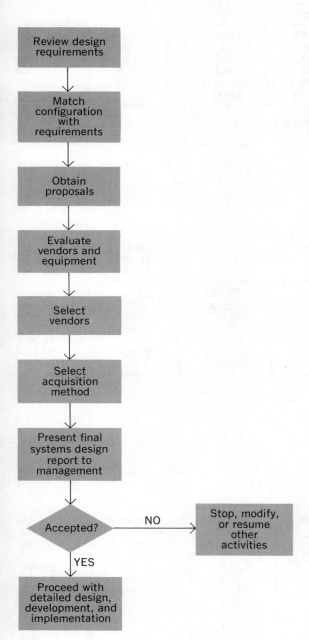

organizational requirements, (2) functional requirements, and (3) tailoring requirements.

Within categories two and three, there are certain aspects which are either imperative or desirable. The imperatives are essential to the implementation and operation of the new system and, no matter how one changes the overall systems design, these imperatives are always present and must be adhered to. For example, an imperative might be: that the system must process X number of payroll checks, produce a payroll register, and update all employee files, by noon each Friday, fifty-two weeks per year. Or that there must be instantaneous response to all inquiries made about inventory status. Desirables, on the other hand, aid and enhance the system but are not absolutely necessary for the system to become operative. For example, while it might be desirable to enter data via keyboard-to-storage devices, it may be determined that, because of a variety of circumstances, data must be prepared by keypunches, and entered via a card reader.

It is the job of the analyst to select from a wide range and class of equipment a specific computer configuration which will meet all of the imperatives and as many of the desirables as possible, at the lowest possible cost.

Inherent Organizational Requirements

The inherent requirements due to the nature of the organization which the information system serves can dictate, to a great degree, the kind of data processing method used. These requirements were discussed in Part I, and are restated here only for reference. They are: (1) volume requirements, (2) timing requirements, (3) complexity requirements, and (4) computational requirements.

Volume pertains to the number of data units processed during some time period. Timing refers to the degree of quickness with which the system must react to users' requests or to changing events. Complexity relates to the degree of intricate, interrelated, and complicated details which must be handled by the system.

Measurements Transactions	Characters Per Transaction	Number of Transactions Per Month	Total Characters	Growth Factor	Capacity Required
Sales order	50	25,000	1,250,000	+20%	1,500,000
Time card	60	3,000	180,000	+10%	198,000
Requisition	70	2,000	140,000	+15%	161,000
Job completion	30	22,000	660,000	+15%	759,000
Move ticket	20	30,000	600,000	+15%	690,000
Total			2,830,000		3,308,000

FIGURE 12.1.   Input requirements.

Measurements Output	Number of Forms Per Month	Lines Per Form	Total Lines	Growth Factor	Capacity Required
Customer invoice	5,000	15	75,000	+15%	86,250
Sales analysis	50	500	25,000	+10%	27,500
Inventory status	20	1,000	20,000	+20%	24,000
Payroll register	10	1,000	10,000	+15%	11,500
Payroll checks	4,000	10	40,000	+15%	46,000
Purchase orders	2,000	15	30,000	+15%	34,500
Total			200,000		229,750

FIGURE 12.2.   Output requirements.

Measurements File	Number of Records	Characters Per Record	Growth Factor	Overflow for Direct Access	Capacity Required
Customer (I)	1,000	200	+30%		260,000
Sales history (S)	1,200	20	+30%		31,200
Product master (D)	8,000	250	+15%	+20%	2,760,000
Work in process (I)	2,000	50	+20%		120,000
Vendor (I)	200	200	+10%		44,000
Payroll (S)	500	250	+20%		150,000
Total					3,365,200

FIGURE 12.3.   Data base requirements. Legend: S: sequential; I:
indexed sequential; D: direct.

Computational requirements simply means that the system must handle complex computations, such as are dictated by the application of a variety of models, e.g., linear programming.

Functional Requirements

The functional requirements pertain to specific operations in four areas: (1) input, (2) output, (3) processing, and (4) data base.[1]

In Figure 12.1, an input matrix shows a composite overview of input requirements which will be used for equipment specification.

In Figure 12.2, the output requirements are indicated. The various reports, documents, and the volumes for each are listed. For example, 4000 payroll checks requiring ten lines per document must be prepared each month. A 15% growth factor is used to arrive at a total of 46,000 lines of output. This output total is then added to the other output requirements for a grand total.

Figure 12.3 represents a compilation of the systems data base requirements. For example, the customer file contains 1000 customer records, each record of which contains 200 characters. A growth factor of 30% indicates a total storage requirement of 260,000 characters. Because there is need for routine processing, as well as for access of specific records, the requirements are listed under indexed sequential. On the other hand, because it has been determined that the payroll file has a high processing activity ratio, and little need for direct access of records, its requirements are listed under sequential. The product master requires direct access and, consequently, often needs an overflow area.

Tailoring Requirements

These requirements are instituted to enhance the system's information producing capabilities for the tactical and strategic levels in the management system. Such requirements that exist

at these levels, as pointed out in Chapter 5, are met by the: (1) Filtering Method, (2) Monitoring Method, (3) Interrogative Method, (4) Modeling Method, and (5) External Method. The implementation of these methods will normally require sophisticated equipment and advanced data base management systems.

Not only do the requirements imposed upon the system by these methods dictate the type of equipment selected, but they also restrain the degree of flexibility with which the analyst can work. For example, if the interrogative method is deemed necessary for better reporting to users, but it is decided to wait awhile before implementing this method, it is advisable to select the current computer configuration so that this method can be added at a later time. Conversely, if only the present routine data processing needs are considered, a major redesign job will be necessary when the interrogative method is added.

Matching Computer Configuration to Systems Requirements

In a dynamic, growing organization, an optimum match of a proposed computer configuration to information systems requirements means that the power and capabilities of the computer configuration should exceed by some margin the present information system requirements. This margin allows the growing information system requirements to be adequately met during the useful life of the computer configuration. Otherwise, growing system requirements will soon produce processing demands which cannot be met by a computer configuration precisely matched to today's requirements. This condition is illustrated in Figure 12.4.

In this illustration, there are two curves. The computer configuration capabilities curve rises rapidly as initial efficiency is achieved, but levels off as the limits of the configuration are ultimately approached. The systems requirements curve rises rather slowly at first, but more rapidly as systems requirements grow. This curve crosses the computer configuration

---

[1] Adapted from: Jerome Kanter, *Management Guide to Computer System Selection and Use*. (Englewood Cliffs, N.J.: Prentice-Hall, Inc., 1970), pp. 130–31. Used with permission from Prentice-Hall, Inc.

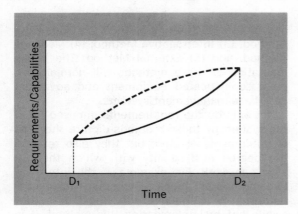

FIGURE 12.4. Optimum match of computer configuration capabilities with systems requirements.

curve at the replacement point, where another major decision must be made, at D_2.

Predicting the useful life of the computer configuration is a critical factor in optimum matching and must be coupled with a clear understanding of the systems requirements. Otherwise, one of two conditions will exist: (1) overmatching, where the two curves are widely separated and the organization is paying excessively for capabilities not needed; or (2) undermatching, where the computer configuration curve is below the requirements curve and the organization is paying for inadequate capabilities, and the system is growth-restricted.

Approaches to Obtaining Equipment Proposals

The various requirements of the systems design help to determine the computer configuration needed, e.g., processor, peripherals, and data communication devices. Although there are other ways to obtain computer processing, such as service bureaus and remote computing networks (RCN), it is assumed that the final computer configuration will be acquired (rented, leased, or purchased) from one of several general-purpose computer vendors. However, the selection methods outlined in this chapter have universal application.

There are three basic approaches which the analyst may choose in order to obtain equipment proposals. These are:

1. *Proposal for a Specific Configuration.* With this method, the analyst specifies a particular computer configuration and requests that the vendors submit proposals based on these particular specifications. One advantage of this approach is that it tends to reduce the complexity of evaluating different vendors' proposals. Secondly, it reduces the time period required by the vendor to prepare a proposal. The primary disadvantage is that this approach generally rules out a vendor's offering a new or different equipment configuration which the analyst was not aware of.

2. *Proposal for Performance Objectives.* In this second approach, the analyst translates the systems requirements into performance objectives and submits them to several vendors requesting a proposal for the type of equipment which they feel can best satisfy these objectives. For example, instead of stipulating that a computer must be able to support 12 online terminals, the analyst indicates that online information will be required by 12 different physical departments, and list the types of information required, expected frequency, volume of inquiries, etc. The advantages to this approach are: (1) it minimizes the analyst's lack of equipment knowledge, (2) it permits the most knowledgeable persons to configure the equipment, and (3) it provides further alternatives for performing an activity or satisfying an objective. The disadvantages include: (1) the vendor usually requires a longer time period to prepare a proposal, (2) the evaluation process of vendors' proposals is more complicated, and (3) the organization might not possess the expertise to implement a given proposal.

3. *Proposal from One Vendor.* A third approach which has widespread popularity, especially in smaller organizations, is to pick one respectable vendor and allow this vendor to propose one or two alternatives for meeting the systems requirements, based on the vendor's available technology. The advantage to this approach is that an organization spends very little

time and money choosing and evaluating equipment and is thus able to concentrate its resources on other developmental activities. The obvious disadvantage is that a particular equipment manufacturer will seldom (never?) recommend utilizing another vendor's equipment, in whole or in part.

12.3 The Evaluation Process

For our evaluation analysis, it is assumed that bids, based on a specific configuration, have been submitted to several vendors. The general process one goes through to evaluate these proposals follows.

First Level Evaluation

At this level, the analyst simply determines which vendors have met imperative requirements. Figure 12.5 is an example in the form of a decision table of how this evaluation is made.

	Vendor A	Vendor B	Vendor C	Vendor D
Imperative conditions:				
1. Cost less than X dollars per month	Y	Y	Y	Y
2. Offers family series of computers	Y	Y	Y	N
3. Offers COBOL compiler	Y	Y	Y	N
4. Printer speed equal to or greater 1200 LPM	Y	Y	Y	N
5. Handle DASD of X characters online	Y	Y	Y	Y
Actions:				
1. Accept for further analysis	X	X	X	
2. Reject				X

FIGURE 12.5. First level evaluation of vendors.

In our example, vendors A, B, and C meet the imperatives and are, consequently, included for further evaluation. Vendor D fails to meet at least one of the imperatives and is rejected from further consideration. Bear in mind that the list in Figure 12.5 is not all-inclusive, but is intended simply to be used for illustrative purposes.

Criteria Comparisons

The easiest way to make a broad comparison of selected vendors is to place basic criteria side–by–side in a matrix, as shown in Figure 12.6. Not all possible criteria are listed, but enough of the significant ones are listed to indicate how such a comparison is made.

Methods for Testing Equipment

Besides reading literature published by vendors and independent services, and querying users about vendors' equipment, there are two primary methods of testing equipment performance. These are: (1) benchmark method and (2) simulation method.

1. *Benchmark Method.* Test problems are prepared and run on the same equipment configuration proposed by the vendor. Overall, the benchmark programs test: (1) anticipated workload, (2) compilers, (3) operating system, and (4) application and utility packages. To apply benchmark programs, the systems analyst can obtain an agreement with the vendor to run the programs at their location, run the programs on some other user's computer system (assuming it is the same as the one proposed), or hire a consulting firm to perform the benchmark testing. The elapsed operating time required to run the test problem is the main determinant. If the test problems are representative of the future processing workload then required times for future operations can be extrapolated. This method is usually effective for evaluating operating time for typical batch processing configurations but is not particularly applicable to analyzing large total systems in an integrated environment.

2. *Simulation Method.* This method utilizes mathematical models which accept a number

Criteria \ Vendors	Vendor A	Vendor B	Vendor C
Processor Monthly Rental	$52,000 (1,536 K–char memory)	$86,000 (1,310 K–char memory)	$85,000 (1,573 K–char memory)
Processor Purchase Price	$2,500,000	$3,900,000	$3,600,000
Processor Monthly Maintenance	$5,600	$7,800	$2,500
Equipment Maintenance	Bundled	Unbundled	Bundled
Software	Unbundled	Bundled	Bundled
System Engineering Services	Unbundled	Bundled	Unbundled
Training Courses	Unbundled	Unbundled	Bundled
Cycle Time (μsec.)	0.080	0.100	0.600
Characters Per Access Cycle	2	4	6
Max. Memory Capacity (K–char.)	3,072	1,310	3,145
Extended Core Storage	No	Yes	Yes
Max. I/O Channels	12	36	18
Disk Capacity (M–char.)	800	838	2,000
Transfer Rate (K–char./sec.)	806	418	248
Average Access Time (msec.)	30	60	60
Max. Magnetic Tape Transfer Rate (K–char./sec.)	320	240	240
Max. Printer Speed (lines/min.)	2,000	1,500	1,200
Max. Card Reader Speed (cards/min.)	1,000	1,200	1,400

FIGURE 12.6.   Criteria comparison of vendors.

of measurements such as: sizes and structures of files, frequency of access to files, transaction volume, etc. These models are then run on computers to predict all kinds of time considerations such as turnaround time, clock time, response time, and so forth. In addition, simulation models help to predict systems capacity (used and unused), and define an optimal equipment configuration. Simulation packages can be purchased or leased from various suppliers of software. To effect a meaningful simulation requires an extremely detailed description of what the system is designed to do.[2]

[2] For further analysis, see: Salvatore C. Catania, "Computer System Models," *Computers and Automation,* March, 1972, pp. 14–18.

Other Criteria for Equipment Evaluation

There are a number of other standards and constraints which the systems analyst must be aware of when selecting equipment. These include: (1) modularity, (2) compatibility, (3) reliability, (4) maintainability, and (5) general vendor support.

1. *Modularity.* The concept of modularity allows the addition of components to the configuration thereby letting it change and grow to meet changing systems needs. This concept allows the organization to start with an initial installation of a less expensive, slower system and then increase the size of the CPU (e.g., more primary storage), and add peripherals, as the need arises. Also, substitution of a disk unit for a tape unit can be effected without the need to make major program changes except in I/O commands.

2. *Compatibility.* In some instances, the installation of one computer system to replace the old system meant major program rewrites, (i.e., two different computers are incompatible if they cannot operate together and/or handle the same input data and programs). Compatibility involves three considerations, which are: (1) computers are designed for a variety of purposes which allow them to be used for business data processing applications, communications and time–sharing, and scientific applications, with equal facility; (2) the design concept of a family of computers which allows a small "child" (e.g., IBM 360 model 30) to grow into an "adult" (e.g., IBM 360 model 65) without necessitating major software changes; and (3) the concept of machine-independent languages, such as COBOL, which permits programs written in this language to be run on a variety of computers. COBOL is a language that has a national standard, which alleviates most of the problems of compatibility one would encounter with a nonstandard language.

In selecting a computer configuration, the concept of modularity and compatibility plays an important role. Some models on the market are considered to be "dead end" machines, i.e.,

they are not part of a standard product series (e.g., computer family) and cannot, therefore, be upgraded to a larger compatible model, nor are their compilers compatible with other computers. In a standard product line the compilers are compatible all the way up the line, the peripherals are interchangeable throughout the line, and primary storage can expand. Because of these features, upward transition from a small computer to a larger computer is rather simple and worry-free. Selection of a "dead end" computer can, on the other hand, significantly increase conversion costs and transition time. In other words, money, time, and effort must be spent to convert from a "dead end" computer once it becomes too small to meet systems requirements.

3. *Reliability.* All computer configurations must be reliable, especially integrated configurations. If the configuration breaks down ("crashes"), not only do all processing operations come to a halt, but re-starting an integrated configuration requires an involved, complicated process. High reliability is based on the type of production control and testing methods used by the vendor. This area is difficult to measure, but any change in production methods, production facilities, and new technologies should be closely observed by the prospective computer user. The measure of reliability used by engineers is MTBF (Mean Time Between Failure). To minimize the probability of failure, the concept of redundancy is used. This concept utilizes two parallel components to decrease the probability of failure. For example, if the probability of failure of one component over a given period of time is .04, then the probability of failure of two parallel components is $(.04)^2$, or .0016.

4. *Maintainability.* MTTR (Mean Time To Repair), is the basic measure of maintainability. The MTTR consists of the time required to accomplish the following: detect the failure; isolate the malfunctioning element; remove the malfunctioning element; obtain a replacement for it; replace it; verify its operability; initialize the replacement; proceed to an operable state. The accomplishment of these actions is in-

Criteria	Value	Vendor A		Vendor B		Vendor C	
		Weight	Score	Weight	Score	Weight	Score
Modularity	10	6	60	7	70	5	50
Compatibility	10	7	70	7	70	5	50
Reliability	30	8	240	6	180	7	210
Maintainability	30	5	150	4	120	5	150
Vendor Support	20	2	40	5	100	7	140
Total	100		560		540		600

FIGURE 12.7.   Rating matrix.

fluenced by the physical construction, the level at which replacements can be made, the training of the maintenance technicians, the ability to detect and isolate malfunctions, the extent and quality of diagnostic tools, the built-in test and diagnostic facilities of the system, and the repair facilities of the complex.[3]

5. *General Vendor Support.* The support of the vendor is of primary importance when making a decision of the selection of equipment. In the long run, the equipment is no better than the general support from the vendor. This support includes such things as: (1) availability of training facilities; (2) installation support; (3) system development, conversion, and testing assistance; (4) experience level and competency of vendor's personnel; (5) duration of time any support is available after installation of equipment; (6) availability of a user group; and (7) availability of specialized software systems such as generalized data base management systems.

The concept of "bundling" has come to the fore in the past several years. This term simply means the degree to which vendors offer educational programs, compilers, application programs, and system engineers to the user "free of charge." Some manufacturers are completely "bundled" which means that they do not charge separately for these services. Others are "semi-bundled" which means that certain services are provided without charge relative to the amount of rental payments, i.e., the greater the amount

of payments, the more services the organization receives. Still other companies are totally "unbundled" which means that they charge for education, application programs, compilers, and system engineers as required.

It may be that the resulting quantitative measurements derived from criteria comparisons, benchmarks, and simulations are, within a prescribed cost range, quite similar. In such situations, qualitative criteria of modularity, compatibility, reliability, maintainability, and general vendor support, may, in the final analysis, dictate the selection of a particular vendor. To make a proper selection, the analyst uses a rating matrix as shown in Figure 12.7.

To prepare the rating matrix, the analyst first determines the relative value of each criterion using a base of one hundred. Next, based on the best information about the criteria applicable to each vendor, the analyst assigns a weight to each value. The weights are then multiplied times the criteria values. Each resulting score is finally summed to give a total score for each vendor. In our example, it appears that Vendor C has the highest score.

12.4 Acquisition Considerations

There are financial and legal considerations involved in acquiring computer equipment of which the analyst must be aware. The four financial alternatives for acquiring computer equipment are: (1) rent from vendor, (2) purchase from vendor, (3) lease from third party, or

[3] Dr. Boris Beizer, "The Viability of Computer Complexes—Reliability and Maintainability," *Modern Data,* December, 1969, pp. 60–63. Used with permission.

(4) a combination. Legal considerations involve the negotiation of a "risk free" contract.

Methods of Acquiring Computer Equipment

The method of acquisition is considered an economic question related to the cost of money to a particular organization and the useful life of the acquired equipment. The method of acquisition should be determined independent of the selection of the equipment itself. The four methods are defined as follows:

1. *Rent from Vendor.* Usually, rental is on a month-to-month basis. The rental rates are such that the basic purchase cost of the computer is recovered by the vendor within forty-five to sixty months. The user can also receive purchase credits which can range from ten percent to as much as fifty percent, depending on the vendor. The vendor offers two types of rental contracts: (1) unlimited use rental contract, and (2) prime shift rental contract. The first type provides for a fixed monthly price regardless of the number of computer hours used. The prime shift rental contract establishes a fixed monthly rental for one predetermined eight hour period each day. The rental is proportionately increased by the number of additional eight hour shifts used during the month. For example, the prime shift (first eight hour shift) is charged at $100 per hour; additional hours of usage beyond the prime shift are charged at 10%, or $10 per hour.

2. *Purchase from Vendor.* With this method the computer equipment becomes the property of the user. This method is usually the most popular where the equipment is kept over five years. Over 50% of Federal Government equipment is purchased and this percentage is expected to increase substantially in the future.

3. *Leasing from Third Party.* There are two types of third party leases: (1) operating and (2) financial. The operating lease is usually of relatively short-term duration (two to five years) and is cancellable, or it terminates, before the lease payments have equalled or exceeded the equivalent purchase price. The principle underlying the operating lease is that the third party com-panies assume a longer leasable life for the equipment than does the vendor. Consequently, third parties can offer lower rates than the vendor rental rates and still realize a profit. The financial lease (analyzed later) is of longer duration, is noncancellable, and obligates the lessee to lease payments which in total may equal or exceed the purchase price of the equipment leased. This method guarantees the leasing company a full return on its equipment. Obviously, many leasing companies prefer this method over the operating lease.

4. *Combination.* This method allows the user additional flexibility. A user can purchase those components of the computer configuration that have the longest useful life (over five years) and rent or lease the remainder. For example, an organization can purchase its central processor and rent or lease the peripheral devices. Or if cash flow is a problem, the organization might lease a central processor and rent peripherals.

Analysis of the Financial Lease

The financial lease decision is complicated because each rental payment is comprised of two components: (1) the implicit interest charged by the lessor and (2) the amortization of the principal sum. In effect, the lessor is a seller of an asset and a lender of money. The rental payment, therefore, provides the vendor with a recovery of the selling price of the equipment plus interest on the money advanced.

In actuality, the decision is not whether to "lease or purchase," despite the fact that most of the literature states it this way. But rather, the basic decision boils down to two points: (1) whether to acquire the equipment or not to acquire the equipment (at this point the decision is to acquire); and (2) whether to actually lease or borrow.[4]

Since the lease is presumed to require a contractually predetermined set of payments, it is reasonable to compare the lease with an alternative type of financing available

[4] Charles T. Horngren, *Cost Accounting: A Managerial Emphasis,* Second Edition. (Englewood Cliffs, N.J.: Prentice-Hall, Inc., 1967), pp. 516–17.

... that also requires a contractually pre-determined set of payments, i.e., a loan. It follows that the interest rate at which the firm would actually borrow, if it chose to acquire the asset by buying and borrowing, is an appropriate discount rate to use in this analysis. The recommendation holds even if the firm chooses to use some other discount rate for ordinary capital budgeting decisions.[5]

An Illustration: The ABC Company has chosen a computer configuration which will provide benefits in its information system operations measured at $980,000.00 per year over the equipment's useful life of five years. The equipment has zero resale value. The purchase price of the equipment is $2,700,000.00; it is also available on a five year, noncancellable lease at $720,000.00 annually. ABC's cost of capital is 12%. Should ABC lease or purchase? Disregard taxes.

1. Investment Decision:
   a. Discount future cash flow:
      Which is $980,000 at 12% for five years,
      $980,000 × 3.037 = $2,976,260.00
   b. Net present value of system:
      $2,976,260 − $2,700,000 = $276,260
   Therefore, continue analysis.
2. Financing Decision:
   Equivalent purchase price is $720,000 at cost of borrowing money (assume 8%) for five years: $720,000 × 3.993 = $2,874,960, which exceeds the purchase price by $174,960. Therefore, it seems that the decision would be: do not lease. However there are other considerations which are discussed in other sections.

Advantages/Disadvantages of Acquisition Methods

The advantages and disadvantages of the four acquisition methods are summarized in Figure 12.8.

[5] Harold Bierman, Jr. and Seymour Smidt, *The Capital Budgeting Decision,* Second Edition. (New York: The Macmillan Company, 1966), p. 220. Used with permission from The Macmillan Company.

Legal Considerations

Managements of organizations must establish more effective policies than those used in the past for negotiating contracts pertaining to the acquisition of computer equipment. Many organizations cannot afford the potential losses resulting from poor contract compliance, delays in delivery dates, component failures, and so forth. To guard against such losses, management must establish basic principles of contract procurement. The establishment of such principles may or may not be met by the vendor's "standard" contract. Normally, these standard contracts are drawn up more in favor of the vendor than in the interest of the user.

Most organizations sign standard contracts provided by the vendors when acquiring computer equipment. When delivery schedules are missed, and promised performance never materializes, very little is done by either party except to trade accusations and develop bitter feelings. Today, the analyst acquiring equipment is urged to utilize the services of professional purchasing agents and attorneys when negotiating the final contract. The contract should spell out very clearly the duties, rights, and responsibilities for each party as well as any appropriate penalty clauses to be assessed.[6]

Two important points which should be included in every contract are: (1) an acceptance test, and (2) a delivery date. The installation of equipment begins with the signing of a contract and ends with an acceptance test. Some 60–90 days prior to the delivery date, the analyst should furnish the vendor with the acceptance test required by the contract, it is in the vendor's interest to see that the computer configuration passes the test before it is shipped.

The focal point in the contract is the scheduled delivery date. Usually the vendor will offer a choice of two or more dates for delivery. However, before choosing a date, the analyst must consider what his or her organization has to do in order to accept delivery in a meaningful and systematic fashion. While awaiting delivery,

[6] For those details which a contract should contain, refer to: Dick Brandon, "Does Your Contract Really Protect You?," *Computer Decisions,* December, 1971, pp. 22–25.

Methods	Advantages	Disadvantages
Rent	1. Helpful to user who is uncertain as to proper equipment application. 2. Normally psychologically more amenable to management. 3. High flexibility. 4. If an organization does not have past experience with computers, this may be the safest method. 5. Maintenance charges included in rental payments. 6. Allows a favorable working relation with the vendor. 7. No long-term commitment. 8. Avoids technological obsolescence.	1. Over approximately five years, this is the most expensive method. 2. Rental payments increase by some factor less than one if usage exceeds a specified number of hours per month, assuming prime shift contract.
Purchase	1. The more mature users no longer need to depend on the security of renting. 2. Stabilization of computer industry means that changes in technology are not as disruptive as they once were. 3. Less costs for an organization with a fairly stable growth pattern which will keep the equipment relatively longer than a growth company (i.e., not subject to operational obsolescence). 4. Investment credit offers certain tax advantages. 5. All other advantages accruing to ownership.	1. Organization has all the responsibilities and risk of ownership. 2. Usually if equipment is purchased, separate arrangements must be made for maintenance. 3. In a growth company, there is a high probability of being locked in a computer configuration that fails to meet the changing requirements of the system. 4. Must pay taxes and insurance on equipment. 5. If the organization has better alternative investment opportunities, it would be more profitable for it to use the funds for these alternatives. 6. Ties up capital thereby impinging upon cash flow. 7. Increased risk of technological obsolescence. 8. Low resale value.
Lease	1. In long-run, can save 10–20% over the rental method. 2. Tax benefits. 3. Conservation of working capital because of low monthly payments. 4. Allows a user to select their equipment, have it purchased for them and then leased to them.	1. Lessee is obligated to pay a contracted charge if lease is terminated before end of of lease period. 2. Little support and consulting service. 3. Lessee loses a great deal of negotiating leverage. 4. For maintenance, the lessee must depend upon a service contract from the vendor, not from the leasing company.
Combination	1. Optimize the best advantages of other methods. 2. Flexible.	1. More recordkeeping. 2. Might have to deal with several vendors in case of breakdown.

FIGURE 12.8. A list of advantages and disadvantages of the four methods of equipment acquisition.

the analyst must make sure that all interface equipment is ready for connection. Test programs and data must also be prepared for use when the configuration is delivered.

12.5 Cost/Effectiveness Analysis

Justification of a proposed computer configuration, or anything else requiring a capital investment, should always be stated in terms of cost/effectiveness analysis. This analysis weighs the effectiveness derived from the direct and indirect benefits of a proposed system against resource constraints which, in this analysis, equate to costs. In short, this analysis determines if the proposed system produces benefits which outweigh costs. Normally, this analysis is performed on a number of desirable alternative systems and by simple comparison shows which one is the best. However, the aim in this section is to show how to conduct a cost/effectiveness analysis and not to confuse the reader with excessive detail. Again, it is stressed here that one of the keys to successful decision making is for management to be able to select from a number of alternatives.

Consideration of Cost and Effectiveness

Earlier, when the feasibility analysis based on TEOS considerations was performed, preliminary computer cost figures were estimated. However, after the analyst has proceeded further with the systems work and made equipment evaluations, these cost figures are much more precise. The next task is to identify all costs, including equipment costs, classify them, and estimate effectiveness over the useful life of the proposed system. First, these costs are defined: by type, by behavior, by function, and by time. Secondly, effectiveness is discussed. Lastly, methods of estimating both cost and effectiveness, and of comparing same, are discussed.

Definition of Costs by Type

1. *Direct Costs.* These costs represent expenditures which can be identified as resulting from the proposed system.

2. *Indirect Costs.* These are overhead costs which cannot be easily identified with the proposed system and are, thus, portioned out to each area in the organization. Examples are rent, insurance, taxes, management salaries, and employee benefits.

Definition of Costs by Behavior

1. *Variable Costs.* These costs fluctuate with volume changes in a direct manner. Examples are electrical power and supplies, (i.e., if the volume of work increases, the use of electrical power and supplies will also increase).

2. *Nonvariable Costs.* These costs might vary from period to period, but this fluctuation is not in response to volume changes in a particular period. Examples are depreciation, rent, taxes, and management salaries.

Definition of Costs by Function

1. *Development Costs.* These are costs incurred to bring something into being and making it better, more useful, etc. Examples are those costs expended to develop information systems; such as, systems work, programming, training, and so forth.

2. *Operational Costs.* These are costs which must be expended to make something work or perform. The employment of a computer operator involves operational costs.

3. *Maintenance Costs.* These costs are expended toward the support, upkeep, and repair of the system. Examples are computer parts and components, and the wages paid to maintenance technicians.

Definition of Costs by Time

1. *Recurring Costs.* These costs are repeated at regular intervals; such as, payroll costs, or computer rental payments.

2. *Nonrecurring Costs.* These costs will end

at some specific point in time. The cost of computer program development is a nonrecurring cost. (The cost of maintaining computer programs is recurring.)

Measurement of Effectiveness

The effectiveness of any proposed system is measured in terms of two kinds of benefits: (1) direct benefits, sometimes called tangible benefits; and (2) indirect benefits, sometimes called intangible benefits. These benefits occur over the useful life of the system which runs, from the point of start-up, to the point of operational obsolescence (the time at which the system is due for an overhaul).

1. *Direct Benefits.* These benefits are cost savings resulting from the elimination of an operation, or from the increased efficiency of some process. For example, in the present system it costs $2.00 to process each transaction whereas the proposed system will process the same transaction for $1.50. If there are 300,000 transactions processed per year, the cost savings resulting from the new system equals $150,000.00 [(2.00 − 1.50) × 300,000]. Since direct benefits are traceable to, and are a direct result of, the proposed system; they are consequently relatively easy to measure.

2. *Indirect Benefits.* Many benefits are often of an intangible nature, and cannot be easily traced to the system per se. However, an attempt should be made to express, in quantitative terms, those which can be identified. For example, an analysis of customer sales might show that the organization is losing 5% of its gross sales annually due to stockouts. The present system has an 85% customer service level whereas the new system, because of the implementation of better inventory control methods, will achieve a 95% customer service level. It is estimated that this expected increase in customer service will increase annual sales by 3% due to less stockouts.

Examples of benefits which increase the effectiveness of a system are: (1) increased labor productivity; (2) better work scheduling;

(3) better quality control; (4) better accounts receivable control, reduction in bad debts, and increased cash flow; (5) better inventory control and less stockouts; (6) quicker response to customer inquiries; (7) reduced clerical costs; (8) reduced data processing costs; and so forth. All these benefits, direct or indirect, can be reduced to quantitative measurements, though some of these measurements result from estimations. In all cases, benefits eventually increase profits or decrease costs. The analyst can always relate benefits to one or the other of these parameters showing, in quantifiable terms, how a particular benefit either increases profit, or decreases costs.

There are two basic methods used in estimating costs and effectiveness. These are:

1. *Objective Calculations.* These calculations simply result from a compilation of those costs, in bids and price lists, submitted by vendors. For example, a card reader might rent for $300.00 per month; and, we can process 300 orders per day with the new system versus 200 orders per day with the old. Such costs or benefits are simply compiled and verified.

2. *Estimations.* As we move from the objective measurement of costs and benefits side of the picture, to the development and intangible side, calculations become increasingly difficult. For example, we may know the wage rate of a programmer but not precisely how long it will take to prepare a particular program. Or, we cannot tell for sure how much time and effort it will take to convert from the old system to the new. It is also just as difficult to place a value on much of the informational output of the system. Historically, people have tended to grossly underestimate the development type costs and overestimate the value of output. The underestimation of costs results in budget overruns and the overestimation of benefits to users results in disappointment and dissatisfaction.

In those organizations where complete and accurate records are kept of standard tasks, the analyst can make fairly accurate cost estimates. However, the analyst must be careful not to rely too much on these records because in many instances he or she may be comparing apples with oranges. Whether one is trying to estimate costs or benefits, the use of expected values and probabilities can be used for effective results (refer to Appendix A).

Preparation of Cost and Effectiveness Summaries

Management is normally interested in direct costs, i.e., those add-on costs which relate directly to the proposal. For example, rental of the home office building in which the computer configuration will be housed is an indirect cost, and might not be considered. However, the rental charges of the computer configuration are a direct cost which is obviously relevant to the cost/effectiveness analysis. If, however, the installation of the computer in the office building caused another group to move to other quarters which resulted in additional costs, then such costs would be considered. Also, the opportunity for using a certain part of the building that the computer configuration requires might also be considered; however, opportunity cost considerations are beyond the scope of our analysis and, thus, are not included. The major aim here is to define those costs that will be different because of the implementation of the proposal. In other words, we are answering the question: "What difference will the development, implementation, and operation of the proposed system make?"

Many people make the mistake of thinking that the cost of a computer configuration itself is the major cost of the information system. There are many other costs incurred to support the computer configuration which, in total, amount to much more than the equipment. Computer configuration costs, and then all these additional costs, are discussed next.

Computer Configuration Costs. First, for an overview of possible computer configurations, we once again suggest that the reader review Appendix B. As discussed earlier, a computer configuration can be acquired by one or a com-

bination of the following financial methods: rental, purchase, and lease. We will assume for illustrative purposes that the configuration is rented, and that we have an unlimited use rental contract rather than a prime shift rental contract. This means that the hourly utilization of the system has no impact on the rental price. Therefore, the cost is nonvariable and recurring. Also, we include an "other equipment" category for miscellaneous equipment which does not fall into the computer category.

Environment Costs. These costs include all aspects involved in preparing the site not only for the equipment, but for offices, storage space, and conference rooms. The cost in preparing this site can range anywhere from the minor renovation of an existing site to the construction of a new building. Precautions should be taken in the design of structures to protect the system from dust, water, electrical interference, and outside factors. If public relations is a consideration, then provisions for visitors and special viewing facilities should be provided to eliminate interruptions within the system. In addition to the site itself, other features are needed such as:

1. Power Requirements: Different system configurations require different power requirements. However, the power parameters for any system would be measured in KVAs, Volts, and Kilowatts. For an approximate cost for power the total average KVA per month would be computed, based on the number of hours of use per day.

2. Air Conditioning: The newer computer systems have reduced to some extent the total need for air conditioning, but even with the newer generation of equipment, the need for air conditioning is still a major consideration. The temperature operational limits for typical equipment may range between 60 and 90° Fahrenheit, with relative humidity between 30 and 85%. Not only does air conditioning ensure proper functioning of equipment, but it provides comfortable working conditions for operating personnel.

3. Furniture and Fixtures: Proper equipment

must be provided for personnel operating the system.

4. Miscellaneous Features: Other features that may be included in the environment costs are: false flooring, special lighting, fire prevention equipment, lead-lined walls, and off-premises storage.

Physical Installation. In some cases the physical installation may present a real problem that can be solved by the use of special equipment such as cranes. Installing a system on the tenth floor of a building is not an easy task, but one often overlooked. Also, another charge not contemplated in some cost estimates is freight. It should be determined whether the vendor prepays freight. The freight charges for a very small system ($3500 — processor, and four or five peripherals) can run as high as $1500.

Training Costs. The training costs are normally high at the beginning and level off to a fairly constant rate. Training costs, if not provided "free" by the vendor, can range from $200 for a five-day introduction to programming, to over $1000 for a ten-day seminar course. This cost includes payment for the course only, which means that a company also might spend $600, or more, to send one employee to a five-day introductory course.

Program and Program Testing Costs. As different systems design applications are made, programming is initiated for proper application to the computer. The implementation of a new system will require a great deal of programming, but the need for programming does not stop after implementation. Changes are constantly being made to old programs and new design applications are being developed. Total programming time can sometimes be reduced by the use of application and utility programs, but of course these packages cost money and, in many instances, they require major modification before they can be applied to a specific system.

Cost of Conversion. The cost of conversion depends upon the degree of conversion. The degree of conversion depends on how many applications of the total system design, included in the first system are to be changed, and how much is to be handled as in the past. Several aspects are included in the estimate of cost of conversion:

1. Preparing and editing records for completeness and accuracy as, for example, when they are converted from a manual system to magnetic disk.
2. Setting up file library procedures.
3. Preparing and running parallel operations.

Cost of Operation. The cost factors discussed above are basically set-up costs. Most of the costs do not recur until another major systems conversion is made. Obviously, an exception is the recurring rental charge of the computer equipment. However, cost of operation includes all factors necessary to keep the system working. These factors are listed below:

1. Staff Costs: These costs include the payroll for all employees in the information system and for occasional consulting fees. This staff consists of: information systems manager, systems analysts, accountants, programmers, systems engineers, computer operators, data preparers, data base administrator, security officer, and general clerks.
2. Cost of Supplies: As the system operates, it consumes supplies. These supplies are in the form of punched cards, printer paper, ribbons, paper tape, magnetic tape, and so forth. These items are an inventory similar to other inventories, and as such should be subject to management control procedures. As is so often the case, control on these supplies is inadequate, consequently causing waste, and increasing costs.
3. Maintenance: Maintenance of a system may include one of three methods: maintenance performed by the organization's own engineers and technicians, maintenance performed by the manufacturer's personnel, or a combination of the two. In any event, maintenance is, in one form or another, a recurring expense.
4. Power and Light: After the initial equipment for servicing the system is installed there is a recurring charge, based on amount of use, for power and light.

Cost Items	Classification	Period (years)				
		1	2	3	4	5
Computer Configuration	D–NV–R	850	850	850	850	850
Other Equipment	D–NV–NR	100	–	–	–	–
Environment	D–SV–R	130	10	12	14	14
Physical Installation	D–NV–NR	80	–	–	–	–
Training	D–SV–R	40	10	30	20	10
Programming	D–SV–R	190	100	80	90	70
Conversion	D–NV–NR	800	–	–	–	–
Operation	D–V–R	1,500	2,000	2,100	2,900	2,800
Systems Work	D–NV–NR	250	–	–	–	–
Total (in thousands)		3,940	2,970	3,072	3,874	3,744

FIGURE 12.9. Cost summary. Classification—D: Direct; V: Variable; NV: Nonvariable; R: Recurring; NR: Nonrecurring; SV: Semivariable.

5. Insurance: For equipment purchased, it is sound policy to obtain insurance for fire, extended coverage, and vandalism. For equipment rented, it is advisable to determine whether or not to obtain similar insurance while the equipment is in your possession. To safeguard against disgruntled employees who are inclined to do injury to the system, it is advisable to obtain a DDD (disappearance, dishonesty, destruction) bond.

Further Systems Work. If it is decided, after the cost/effectiveness analysis has been performed, that the proposed system is to be implemented, additional systems work will be required. This work includes detailed systems design, control specification, procedure writing, and so forth.

In accordance with empirical data collected from a variety of sources, a hypothetical cost estimate is listed in Figure 12.9. These costs represent a medium-size configuration with on-line peripherals and batch processing capabilities. These costs are compiled and classified. Then, they will be compared to the benefits emanating from the proposed system.

Depending on the size and cost of the computer configuration, there is usually a direct relation to the additional costs required to support the configuration. These support costs can range anywhere from a factor of 1–4 times the

purchase price of the computer configuration. The factor decreases as the size, power, and cost of the configuration increases. For example, a small configuration rents for $6000 per month. By a rule of thumb, this rental price is multiplied by 45 to give the approximate purchase price of $270,000. Then, when this price is multiplied by a factor of 4, a total support cost of $1,080,000 results, spread over a period of about four and one-half to five years.

In Figure 12.9, typical cost data for a medium-size configuration have been used. The total cost of support, less other equipment and systems work, is $11,000,000. Dividing the support costs by the purchase price we get a factor of over 2.8, which is fairly close to what usually holds true for medium-size configurations (between 2.2 and 2.9). For large-scale configurations, the factor is usually close to 1.

Another aspect of computer size, power, and cost is that a configuration can be substantially upgraded with a relatively small increase in cost. For example, one can go from a 64K CPU to a 128K CPU which is double the capacity but not double in price. To be more specific, a vendor, not named here, offers a central processor with a maximum capacity of 262K for $15,000 per month. This same vendor offers a central processor with faster access time and maximum capacity of 562K for $22,000 per month.

	Period (years)			
	2	3	4	5
Direct Benefits (in thousands):				
1. Reduction in Employee Costs	930	940	970	990
2. Reduction in Rental of Old Equipment	470	750	800	900
3. Reduction in Service Bureau Costs	300	500	750	–
4. Reduction in Other Data Processing Costs	500	700	800	800
5. Reduction in Inventory Costs	200	400	500	300
6. Increased Production	200	600	700	900
7. Reduction in Bad Debts	200	450	800	960
8. Reduction in Outside Clerical Work	400	700	700	900
9. Reduction in Overtime	–	400	600	640
Total Direct Benefits	3,200	5,440	6,620	6,390
Indirect Benefits:				
1. Customer Service	400	700	900	900
2. Better Marketing and Logistics	200	400	500	500
3. More Effective Management	500	800	900	800
Total Indirect Benefits	1,100	1,900	2,300	2,200
Total Effectiveness	4,300	7,340	8,920	8,590

FIGURE 12.10.   Effectiveness summary.

These phenomena discussed are applicable to a variety of capital equipment. For example, compare earthmoving machine Model 1, with a capacity of X cubic yards of dirt, and a cost of $6000 to Model 2, which with a capacity of X^2 cubic yards costs $12,000. Moreover, both models require one operator whose wages are the same whether he or she operates Model 1 or Model 2. Maintenance, supplies, and parts might also cost only slightly more for Model 2 than Model 1.

The reason why vendors can offer more powerful machines, at relatively small increases in cost, is that larger machines require less material per unit of output for their construction than do smaller machines. Likewise they require less labor per unit of product for their construction, since it takes little or no additional time to assemble the parts of a machine designed to produce 100 units a day than to assemble the parts of a similar machine designed to produce 50 units. For example, looking at this phenomenon another way, a 5 hp. diesel engine cannot be built for 1% of the cost of a 500 hp. diesel.[7]

The effectiveness side of the coin, as stated earlier, is based on both the direct and indirect benefits which are estimated to emanate from the proposed system. In Figure 12.10, the estimated benefits are listed in an effectiveness summary. Notice that the benefits do not start until the beginning of the second year, the projected time for the start-up of the proposed system.

In Figure 12.11, we present a cost/effectiveness summary based on accumulated direct benefits to accumulated costs, accumulated indirect benefits to accumulated costs, and total accumulated benefits to accumulated cost. With this presentation, management can make a go/no-go decision, based on one category of benefits against the cost of deriving these benefits.

In the example, direct benefits outweigh costs in the fourth period, or three years after implementation, and have exceeded costs by $6000 at the end of the fifth period. The system obviously cannot be supported on indirect benefits alone. Taking into account both direct and indirect benefits, the costs of the system are recovered in the second period of operation.

The question now is: "Should authorization be given for acquisition of the computer configuration, further development work, and implementation of the proposed system?" From a purely financial viewpoint, it might be wiser to pay attention only to the direct benefits weighed against costs, because the indirect

[7] John F. Due and Robert W. Clower, *Intermediate Economic Analysis* Fourth Edition, (Homewood, Illinois: Richard D. Irwin, Inc., 1961), p. 137.

Comparisons	Period (years)				
	1	2	3	4	5
Accumulated Direct Benefits to Accumulated Costs	0	3,200	8,640	15,260	21,650
	3,940	6,910	9,982	12,856	15,600
Direct Benefits (+, −)	−3,940	−3,710	−1,342	+2,404	+6,000
Accumulated Indirect Benefits to Accumulated Costs	0	1,100	3,000	5,300	7,500
	3,940	6,910	9,982	12,856	15,600
Indirect Benefits (+, −)	−3,940	−5,810	−6,982	−7,556	−8,100
Total Accumulated Benefits to Accumulated Costs	0	4,300	11,640	20,560	29,150
	3,940	6,910	9,982	12,856	15,600
Effectiveness (+, −)	−3,940	−2,610	+1,658	+7,704	+13,550

FIGURE 12.11.   Cost/effectiveness summary.

benefits might never materialize. If direct benefits far outweigh costs then any risk of financial failure is reduced, if not completely eliminated. But, as alluded to before, projected costs for items such as programming, conversion, operation, and systems work can be grossly underestimated. Therefore, management must decide if there is enough cushion remaining in direct benefits to absorb any substantial budget overruns. If management determines that the answer is "no" or "possibly" then the proposed system probably is not justified. That is, unless management still wishes the system installed for reasons based on the potential indirect benefits, especially if these benefits contribute to the achievement of broad organizational goals.

In our above analysis, we have ignored the time value of money which is discussed in Appendix A. Also, we have not given an example of a project having to compete with other projects for a finite amount of available capital funds. Neither have we considered the impact of income tax factors relating to cash inflows and outflows. We consider, these aspects to be beyond the scope of this text and therefore recommend any good cost accounting text to those who wish to pursue these areas in greater detail.

Preparation of Final Systems Design Report

Prior to considering further detailed systems work and implementation work, management must make a final decision as to whether or not the proposed system is accepted for implementation. The document upon which management makes its decision is the Final Systems Design Report that includes, among other things, the cost/effectiveness analysis which is the key to management's go/no-go decision. This report should be prepared in a form similar to the following outline.

Final Systems Design Report
I. Introduction
   A. Purpose of Report
   B. Scope of Report
II. Statement of Improvements
   A. Interpretation of Improvements Based on Requirements of Users
   B. Written Description of Users' Requests
III. Management Summary
   A. Clear Documentation of Systems Design
   B. Employee Impact Study
      1. Development of work force plan

for orienting and training employees who will be performing the
functions of the new system.
2. Determination of ways and means
of acquiring necessary skills, i.e.,
retrain, reassign, or recruit.
3. Development of placement plan:
   a. Placement of displaced personnel
   b. Location of new system in
   organizational structure
   c. Potential changes in areas of
   responsibility and accountability
C. Recommendations Based on Conclusions
D. Implementation Plan and Schedule
IV. Justification of System
A. Details of Recommendations Made in
Management Summary
B. Cost/Effectiveness Analysis
C. Alternatives
V. Appendices

SUMMARY

The general systems design requirements will
dictate what kind of system is finally
implemented. In this chapter, we have
assumed that a computer configuration will
considerably enhance our systems design
proposal. The requirements which help to
dictate such a conclusion are: (1) inherent
organizational requirements, (2) functional
requirements, and (3) tailoring requirements.

After requirements have been determined, it
is necessary to select configurations which
optimally match these requirements.

Undermatching results in the organization
paying for inadequate service and, in addition,
the potential growth of applications is
prohibited. Overmatching results in the
organization paying too much for services
which are underutilized.

After proposals have been received from
vendors, each vendor is evaluated on the basis
of imperatives. Any vendors not meeting all
imperatives are automatically eliminated from
further evaluation. Next, in order to gain
further insight into what the remaining vendors
have to offer, criteria comparisons are made.
Performance of equipment can be determined
by two methods: (1) benchmarks and (2)
simulation. Having evaluated the vendors, the
analyst grades each vendor using certain
selected criteria.

There are four methods of acquiring a
computer configuration. These are: rent,
purchase, lease, and combination.
Management selects a particular method
based on advantages applicable to the
organization. If a computer configuration is
acquired, management should strive to sign a
"risk-free" contract.

The major consideration as to whether or not
an organization acquires a computer
configuration, or undertakes any project,
should always be stated in cost/effectiveness
terms. If the effectiveness of a proposed
system sufficiently outweighs costs of that
system then it is likely that the proposed
system will be implemented. To receive a
go/no-go decision from management, the
analyst should prepare a Final Systems Design
Report which should contain, among other
things, the results of the cost/effectiveness
analysis.

**REVIEW
QUESTIONS**
12.1 Draw a flowchart of the steps one must take to evaluate and justify
any general system design proposal.
12.2 List and explain general systems design requirements.
12.3 Explain the meaning of imperatives and desirables.

12.4 What represents an optimum match of a proposed computer configuration to designated systems requirements? Draw a chart to support your answer.

12.5 What conditions can exist if an optimum match between computer capabilities and systems requirements is not achieved?

12.6 List and briefly discuss the methods used in obtaining computer equipment proposals. Which do you consider the best? Make any assumptions you deem necessary to support your response.

12.7 Explain how a first level evaluation of vendors is made. Why is it made?

12.8 Do you believe that it is beneficial, to the systems analyst, to place the many criteria values of different vendors in a comparison matrix? Why? Why not?

12.9 What are the methods used to evaluate computer equipment? What are the advantages/disadvantages of these methods?

12.10 Select eight criteria of computer selection and rank them, in order of priority, from one to eight, one being the most important. You are not restricted only to those mentioned in the text.

12.11 Give a brief definition of: (1) modularity, (2) compatibility, (3) reliability, (4) maintainability, and (5) general vendor support.

12.12 List and explain the four methods of acquiring computer equipment.

12.13 Define costs by type, behavior, function, and time. Give an example of each.

12.14 Effectiveness can be equated to two types of benefits. Discuss and give an example of each.

12.15 Discuss the basic methods of estimating costs and effectiveness.

12.16 A computer configuration rents for $20,000 (a medium-size system) per month. What is the approximate purchase price of this configuration? Approximately, what are the support costs for this system?

QUESTIONS FOR DISCUSSION

12.1 "The problem of quantifying benefits, especially indirect benefits, is normally quite difficult. Nevertheless, to perform meaningful cost/effectiveness analysis, all aspects should be quantified." Discuss.

12.2 The Department of Transportation evaluates alternative highway safety measures by "cost per reduced fatality." How would you quantify the benefits?

12.3 If the amount of research funds to be allocated to various diseases can be approximately analyzed in terms of cost related to reduction in mortality, how, then, would you compare these costs to benefits?

12.4 Discuss the comment, "a reasonable, educated approximation is better than nothing at all."

12.5 "There is a propensity, by even the most competent people, to underestimate the cost of doing something new and overestimating the benefits derived therefrom." Do you agree? Disagree? Why?

12.6 "There is a tendency to place a great deal of confidence in anything that is quantified and printed on paper. Therefore, we constantly remind our managers to be skeptical about any quantifications about the future and assume a large margin of error." Discuss.

12.7 "Regardless of uncertainties, decisions must be made. If we have done a conscientious job in our cost/effectiveness analysis, we do not hesitate to make a decision; because, we feel that postponing action is in reality a decision to continue business as usual, which in many instances may be the worst decision of all." Discuss.

12.8 The relevant costs in any decision are those costs that are incurred if a system is implemented, but that would not be incurred if it is not undertaken. Elaborate on this statement and give several examples for illustrative purposes.

12.9 Discuss the statement, "cost calculations are only half the picture in cost/effectiveness analysis."

12.10 A basic principle in preparing cost/effectiveness analysis for management is to provide alternatives. Explain.

12.11 We may look at costs as being disadvantages and benefits as advantages. Therefore, for proper decision making, there must be a systematic attempt to determine, quantify, and weigh the advantages and disadvantages of each alternative proposal. Discuss.

12.12 Some authorities believe that not all factors involved in cost/effectiveness analysis can be measured and quantified. Do you agree? Why? Why not? If a factor is material, the analyst either quantifies or not. If he or she chooses not to quantify it, then how is it utilized in the decision making process?

12.13 "Measurement of the system is far more significant and meaningful in the long run than measurement of the CPU." Comment on this statement.

12.14 "You can't design a system until you know what kind of computer you are going to have." Discuss the merits of this statement.

12.15 "The most important consideration in choosing a vendor is, 'what level of support will you be provided with after you install the machine.'" Evaluate.

12.16 "The manufacturer apologized for failing to install the new machine on time. But in the meantime, we were stuck with renting outside computer time for six weeks." Discuss the implications of this comment.

EXERCISES

12.1 A sequential customer file will contain 500 records with 300 characters per record and a 20% annual growth factor. A direct access inventory file with a projected 25% overflow and an annual growth factor of 10% presently will require storage space for 10,000 records of 200 characters each. Calculate the capacity required for each file for a two year period.

12.2 Barry Bright, systems analyst for Graphics, Incorporated, has just completed his systems design proposal. Included in this proposal is some information concerning the acquisition of a computer configuration. This information is listed as follows:

(1) The purchase price of the computer is $800,000. Maintenance expenses are expected to run $50,000 per year. If the computer is rented, the monthly rental price will be $16,500, based on an unlimited use rental contract with "free" maintenance.

(2) Mr. Bright believes it will be necessary to replace the configuration at the end of five years. It is estimated that the computer will have a resale value of $100,000 at the end of the five years.

(3) The estimated gross annual savings derived from this particular alternagive computer configuration are $450,000 the first year, $500,000 the second, and $550,000 each of the third, fourth, and fifth years. The estimated annual expense of total operation expenses is $190,000 in addition to the expenses mentioned above. Additional nonrecurring costs are $70,000.

(4) If Graphics decides to rent the computer, the purchase price of $800,000 can be otherwise invested at an 18% rate of return. The present value of $1.00 at the end of each year, and discounted at 18% is:

End of Year	Present Value
1	.847
2	.718
3	.609
4	.516
5	.437

Based strictly on the above financial considerations, ignoring tax impact, which method of acquisition do you recommend?

12.3 Jobstream profiles are shown for Computer A (which you are now renting), and Computer B, which you are considering for acquisition to replace Computer A. These profiles are the result of 100 hours of similar workloads. What is your decision based strictly on these profiles? (Ignore all other considerations. Hint: Think in terms of total system throughput.)

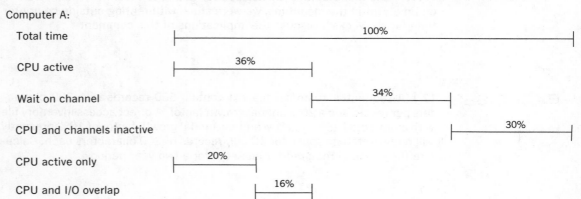

Computer A:

Total time	100%
CPU active	36%
Wait on channel	34%
CPU and channels inactive	30%
CPU active only	20%
CPU and I/O overlap	16%

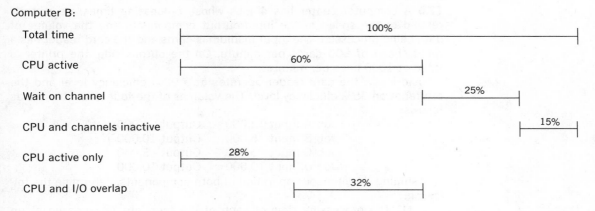

Computer B:

Total time	100%
CPU active	60%
Wait on channel	25%
CPU and channels inactive	15%
CPU active only	28%
CPU and I/O overlap	32%

12.4 The main objective of a benchmark study is to evaluate the relative throughput of similar computer configurations which fall within a predetermined cost range. The benchmark problems run on each configuration are based on well defined workloads which should test both the I/O and internal processing performance of each configuration. Based on the condensed and simplified measurements below, indicate which computer you would select. Explain why. Make any assumptions you deem necessary.

Criteria Comparison of Vendors

Criteria \ Vendor	A	B	C
Monthly rental	$30,000	$34,000	$36,000
Processor size	136K, 1.5μ, 48 bit words	196K, 36 bit words	768K bytes
Disk capacity	496M bytes	84M words	600M characters
Tapes	Six drives (same)	Six drives (same)	Six drives (same)

Benchmark Results: CPU Times (in Seconds) for Compilation and Execution of Different Programs

Vendor \ Type of Problem	Process Bound Problem	Input/Output Bound Problem	Hybrid Problem
A	400.5	1964.0	1147.5
B	104.9	720.4	340.4
C	175.4	404.8	296.8

12.5 A computer center has 4 jobs whose processing times are directly related to the speed of the input/output components and the volume of data being processed. The input medium is cards and the card reader has a rated speed of 800 cards per minute. On the output side, the printer is rated at 1000 lines per minute.

Historically, the card reader operates at a 92% efficiency level and the printer at an 85% efficiency level. The volumes of the four jobs cited are as follows:

Job A Input	3,000	Output 4,000
Job B Input	5,000	Output 10,000
Job C Input	5,000	Output 3,000
Job D Input	10,000	Output 10,000

Assuming simultaneous operation of both components, determine the following:

(1) The processing time of each of the four jobs (assume no setup time).

(2) Which component is the primary constraint for each job.

PROBLEMS **12.1** Tidex Manufacturing is planning on acquiring a computer system. The costs for such an undertaking are projected over a five year period. The first year is prior to the computer installation, while the remaining four years represent the life of the system. These costs and savings are estimated as follows:

Analyze these costs and benefits and make proper recommendations to management. Use any graphs you deem necessary to highlight cost versus benefits.

	0	1	2	3	4
1. Initial systems and programming	70,000				
2. Environment preparation	12,000				
3. Conversion	15,000	14,000			
4. Parallel operations		7,000	1,000		
5. Equipment rental		73,000	81,000	85,000	105,000
6. Systems and programming		70,000	79,000	70,000	70,000
7. Operations		60,000	64,000	70,000	72,000
8. Reduction in Service Bureau		65,000	120,000	125,000	130,000
9. Reduction in clerical costs		12,000	18,000	24,000	55,000
10. Reduction in inventory costs		35,000	130,000	160,000	160,000
11. Reduction in rental of old equipment		10,000	12,000	20,000	40,000

	0	1	2	3	4
12. Reduction in over- time			6,000	30,000	40,000
13. Increased customer service level		6,000	58,000	95,000	100,000
14. Improved manage- ment planning		8,000	45,000	50,000	50,000
15. Improved manage- ment control		9,000	50,000	50,000	50,000

12.2 Historically, computer power has been measured by CPU add and cycle times. These measurements were used extensively during the time when most programming was done in machine language. During this time raw speed was an adequate measure of relative efficiency, and power of equipment, since manufacturer supplied software systems were almost nonexistent, and the variety of computer architecture was limited. However, today this method is insufficient for measuring computer systems because it ignores: (1) the machine architecture; (2) the number of addresses included in an instruction; and, (3) differences in software, e.g., efficiency of compilers.

For example, a byte addressable computer might perform serial characters manipulation more efficiently than a word addressable computer, but the latter may perform parallel arithmetic operations more efficiently than a byte addressable computer. The data path of a particular computer may be different from that of a comparable configuration, making cycle times virtually incomparable. The comparison of computers having single address instructions with those having multiple address instructions is almost meaningless, since add times reflect instruction access times. Computer A with only one accumulator and one multiply register cannot be compared, with this method, to Computer B having multiple accumulators. Also, the predominance of nonarithmetic instruction executions such as loads, stores, branches, look–ahead features, input/output, and other special features is not considered by this method.

A much better method to use when measuring basic internal performance is Kernel problem comparison. A Kernel problem is a typical program which has been partially (or completely) coded and timed. Thus, it derives its name from the fact that the essential part, or Kernel, of the application under study is evaluated. The timings are based on the manufacturer's stated execution times for the instructions that comprise the Kernel program for a given computer. The *Auerbach EDP Standards* includes a compendium of such programs.

Hypothesize at least two imperatives (one of these imperatives will be maximum cost) and select three possible manufacturers. Taking some typical data processing application, such as a payroll system, evaluate the particular configurations you have chosen via the Kernel problem method. Prepare a complete report based on your evaluations. Make any assumptions you deem necessary. Also, try to make an evaluation of the different systems by using the add and cycle times method or any other method you feel appropriate.

12.3 Based on the problem above, prepare a criteria matrix as shown in Figure 12.6. Does this matrix help you get a valuable overview of the different computer systems you are evaluating? Why? Why not?

12.4 Let your Kernel problem take the form of a process bound problem versus an input/output bound problem.* Using the same assumptions and instructions as given in problem 12.2, prepare an evaluation report. Does this report differ from the one in 12.2? Explain.

12.5 In most cases, Kernel problems reflect a calculation of internal power. They usually do not consider a wide range of problems to accurately show differences in different computer systems. The final power of a computer configuration is not necessarily how fast it is internally, but how fast it can perform the complete job. That is, the efficient interaction of internal performance with input/output speeds and peripherals, as well as programming systems must be considered when evaluating a total configuration. A comprehensive series of benchmark problems run on different equipment can evince differences in machine architecture, input/output and peripheral performance, multiprogramming, and general throughput.

Synthetic programs are used where the job stream is less certain, or where standardized tasks exist. Such a program is coded and executed like a benchmark; however, like a Kernel, it is not representative of any existing piece of code. However, unlike a Kernel, it is coded and includes consideration of input/output, peripherals, and the environment provided by the operating system.

Research the literature, and any real world systems that you have access to, and prepare a report which compares and contrasts benchmarks with synthetic programs. Be sure to include in your report both the advantages and disadvantages of each. To get yourself started, read: Bucholz, "A Synthetic Job for Measuring System Performance," *IBM Systems Journal,* Volume 8, Number 4, 1969.

12.6 Simulation is the most powerful, and flexible, of the evaluation techniques as it provides a testing ground for (and insight into) the functions of the system. Simulation involves building information models of the system structures and then using these models with assumed models of programs and data. Two basic types of simulation have been used to evaluate computer performance: (1) the event-oriented unit step model, and (2) the empirically derived model which uses actual data distributions to represent the specific configuration and job load.

Prepare a report on the simulation method. To get yourself started, read: Calingaert, "System Performance Evaluation: Survey and Appraisal," *Communications of the ACM,* January, 1967; Campbell and Heffner, "Measurement and Analysis of Large Operating Systems During System Development," *AFIPS Conference Proceedings,* Montvale, N.J.: AFIPS Press, 1968; and Johnson, "Needed: A Measure for Measure," *Datamation,* December 15, 1970.

---

* Process bound means the problem requires a relatively large amount of internal processing while I/O bound means the problem requires a great deal of input and output with a relatively small amount of internal processing.

BIBLIOGRAPHY

Beizer, "The Viability of Computer Complexes—Reliability and Maintainability," *Modern Data,* December, 1969.

Bierman and Smidt, *The Capital Budgeting Decision,* Second Edition, New York: The Macmillan Co., 1966.

Brandon, "Does Your Contract Really Protect You,?" *Computer Decisions,* December, 1971.

Cantania, "Computer System Models," *Computers and Automation,* March, 1972.

Due and Clower, *Intermediate Economic Analysis,* Fourth Edition, Homewood, Illinois: Richard D. Irwin, Inc., 1961.

Horngren, *Cost Accounting: A Managerial Emphasis,* Second Edition, Englewood Cliffs, N.J.: Prentice-Hall, Inc., 1967.

Joslin, *Analysis, Design and Selection of Computer Systems,* Arlington, Va.: College Readings, 1971.

Kanter, *Management Guide to Computer Systems Selection and Use,* Englewood Cliffs, N.J.: Prentice-Hall, Inc., 1970.

13 Detail Systems Design

13.1 Introduction

Earlier in this part, the design of an information system was discussed at a conceptual level. In order to transform a general or conceptual design into a unified system of people and machines who collect and process data, and produce information, the systems analyst must perform some additional activities. Many of these activities were discussed in Part II as they related to the development of a data base. In this chapter, then, a variety of activities required to effect a detail systems design are discussed. The specific objectives of this chapter are:

1. To identify and explain the control points necessary to ensure reliable processing of data.

2. To identify the important aspects of security which must be considered during systems design.

3. To present the considerations important to designing efficient forms and reports for use in the information system.

4. To establish the need and importance of preparing formal, written procedures which describe the activities of individuals operating the system

5. To provide basic guidelines for preparing program specifications which serve to communicate the ideas of the systems analyst to the programmer in a formal manner.

13.2 Control Points

As discussed previously, the information system is a large and valuable resource to the organization. Ensuring that this resource is performing as required, and protecting its operation from both internal and external misuse, begins in the design phase. For effective administration and control of an information system, an overall framework of organizational and procedural controls must be designed and implemented. Such a framework helps to ensure the stewardship of assets, reliability of operations, and general integrity of the system. Figure 13.1 is a schematic of the information system showing the major control points.

All of these major control points can be grouped into five general categories and defined as follows:

1. *External Control.* These control functions emanate from, and are performed by, such groups as independent auditors and consultants, user departments, top management, special staff control groups, and/or various constituents of the organization. They establish an independent check on the overall activities of the system through observation and feedback.

2. *Administrative Control.* These controls emanate directly from the management of the information system and are traditional management functions, such as selection and assignment of personnel, delineation of responsibilities, preparation of job descriptions, establishment of performance standards, and so forth.

3. *Documentation Control.* Documentation control refers to all of the communications prepared by the analyst and his or her coworkers during the developmental phases of the system, and to the formal procedures which describe each and every activity required in the information system's operations.

4. *Processing Control.* Processing controls ensure that data are accurately and reliably transformed into information. These controls include input controls, programming controls, hardware controls, data base controls, and output controls.

5. *Security Control.* Security controls include all of the physical and logical preparations taken to ensure that the system is not intentionally or unintentionally disrupted during operations.

During the design of a system, the systems analyst must consider aspects from each of these major categories of control in determining the final design. However, because of the extensive nature of each of these control points, we will discuss each of them indepth as follows: (1) auditing, the major part of external control, is discussed in Chapter 15; (2) administrative controls, are also discussed in Chapter 15; (3) the various types of communication documentation related to developing a system (e.g., Proposal to Conduct Systems Analysis) are discussed when the activities in that specific phase of the life cycle are analyzed; (4) guidelines for preparing clerical procedures, and computer programs, are presented in this chapter; (5) processing controls are presented in this chapter; and, (6) security control is also discussed in this chapter.

The remaining discussion of control points in this section will focus on the specific types of processing controls. One of the major objectives of processing controls is to minimize or eliminate what are often termed clerical errors. The importance of designing an effective network of processing controls cannot be emphasized strongly enough. In addition to the direct costs incurred to identify and correct clerical errors, these errors are responsible indirectly for costs or losses in at least seven ways:

1. Delays—often with serious consequences—that are due to error.
2. Dispersion of the attention of higher priced personnel, supervisors, managers, etc., from their basic responsibilities.
3. Distracting, disturbing effects, emotional upsets, strain, etc., often caused by the discov-

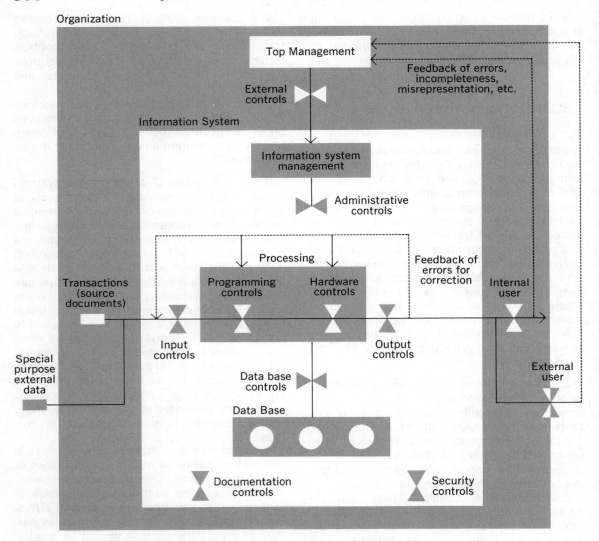

FIGURE 13.1. Control points relative to the information system.

ery of error, allocation of blame, fixing responsibility, attempting to prevent repetition, etc.

4. Demoralizing local, internal effects of the loss of confidence in the quality of work and the reliability of figures, data, records and other clerical work.

5. Cost of extra, precautionary, preventive, quality control and other special procedures and practices necessitated or required because of the incidence and effects of error.

6. Loss of goodwill and the deterioration of company image when errors affect customers, other departments, top management or any others outside the unit where the error is made.

7. The undeterminable loss of business that results when errors annoy customers suf-

ficiently to make them prefer to do business elsewhere.[1]

Input Controls

Data collection activities represent a vital subsystem in the overall information system operations. Figure 13.2 illustrates the four basic ways data can be collected and entered into a computer for subsequent processing.

The first schematic in Figure 13.2 shows the traditional and most widely used method for collecting data. This method has the source data initially recorded on a document, which must then be input to an operation such as keypunch or keytape in order to be converted into a format readable by a computer. The second schematic depicts the data initially recorded on a device which prepares a computer readable output. The third schematic depicts source data being input by a device in a computer readable format; but, as a by product of another operation. The fourth schematic shows source data being entered directly into a computer via an online device. Schematics 2, 3, and 4 are illustrations of what is generally termed Source Data Automation (SDA) or Point of Sale (POS) applications. With SDA or POS, the systems analyst can design elaborate input controls with programming logic, as discussed in the next section. However, the following input controls are useful in all four methods of data collection.

1. *Forms Design.* When a source document is required for the collection of data, this form can be designed to force more legible entries by the use of individual blocks for each character to be recorded. Figure 13.3 is an example of a source document which shows explicitly where each data item is to be entered.

2. *Verification.* Source documents prepared by one clerk can be verified or proof-read by another clerk in order to improve accuracy. In a data conversion operation such as keypunch, keytape, or keydisk, each document can be verified by a second operator. The verifying operator goes through the same keying operation as the original operator, but his or her keying efforts are compared by the logic of the machine to the entries previously made, and discrepancies are indicated by lights on the machine. Verification is a duplication operation and, therefore, doubles the cost of data conversion. To reduce this cost, it may be possible to: (1) verify only critical data fields such as dollar amounts and account numbers while ignoring such fields as addresses, names, etc.; (2) prepunch or machine duplicate constant data fields while keypunching only the variable field; and (3) use programming logic to provide verification.

3. *Control Totals.* In order to minimize the loss of data when it is transported from one location to another and/or to check on the results of different processes, control totals are prepared for specific batches of data. For example, a batch of source documents, such as time cards from a division of a plant, are sent to a control clerk in the information system. The control clerk runs a tape on employee numbers (a hash total) and a total of hours. These control totals are recorded on a control sheet. The source documents are then transferred to keypunch for conversion to cards. These cards, along with other batches, are converted to payroll magnetic tape. After each step in the processing is completed, the control totals input to that step can be compared to the control totals generated in that step. This ensures that all data can be accounted for through to the completion of processing, and the issuing of outputs. By establishing control totals at input time, the remaining processing controls, either manual or programmed, can be implemented on the same basis.

4. *Other Controls.* During the design of input collection, the systems analyst should also evaluate the use of check digits for important codes; such as, customer account number, product number, employee number, and so forth. (The use of check digits was discussed in Chapter 7.) The labeling of data files is another important control point. Labels contain information such as: file name, date created, date updated, retention, etc.

---

[1] William Exton, Jr., "Clerical Errors: Their Cost and Cure," *The Office,* December, 1970, p. 37. Used with permission.

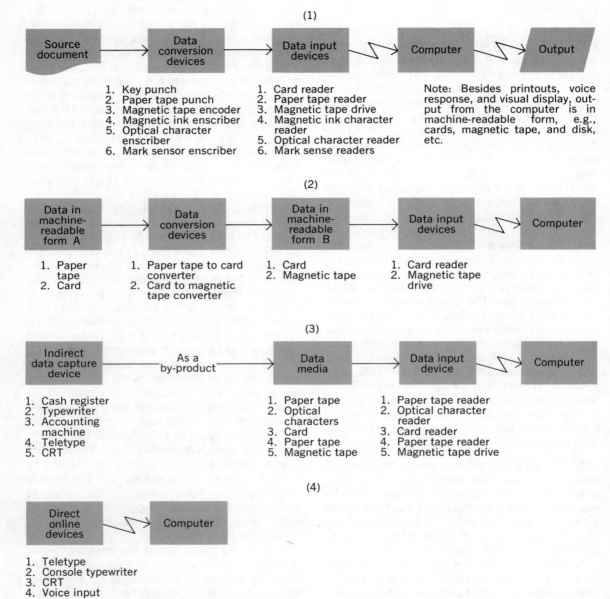

(1)

Source document → Data conversion devices → Data input devices ⟶ Computer ⟶ Output

Data conversion devices	Data input devices	Note
1. Key punch	1. Card reader	Note: Besides printouts, voice response, and visual display, output from the computer is in machine-readable form, e.g., cards, magnetic tape, and disk, etc.
2. Paper tape punch	2. Paper tape reader	
3. Magnetic tape encoder	3. Magnetic tape drive	
4. Magnetic ink enscriber	4. Magnetic ink character reader	
5. Optical character enscriber	5. Optical character reader	
6. Mark sensor enscriber	6. Mark sense readers	

(2)

Data in machine-readable form A → Data conversion devices → Data in machine-readable form B → Data input devices ⟶ Computer

Data in machine-readable form A	Data conversion devices	Data in machine-readable form B	Data input devices
1. Paper tape	1. Paper tape to card converter	1. Card	1. Card reader
2. Card	2. Card to magnetic tape converter	2. Magnetic tape	2. Magnetic tape drive

(3)

Indirect data capture device — As a by-product → Data media → Data input device ⟶ Computer

Indirect data capture device	Data media	Data input device
1. Cash register	1. Paper tape	1. Paper tape reader
2. Typewriter	2. Optical characters	2. Optical character reader
3. Accounting machine	3. Card	3. Card reader
4. Teletype	4. Paper tape	4. Paper tape reader
5. CRT	5. Magnetic tape	5. Magnetic tape drive

(4)

Direct online devices ⟶ Computer

1. Teletype
2. Console typewriter
3. CRT
4. Voice input

FIGURE 13.2. Methods of collecting data for computer processing.

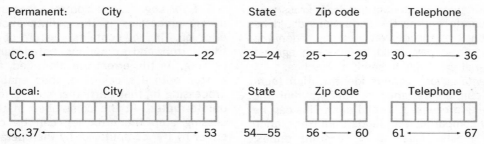

FIGURE 13.3. Example of source document layout for keypunch operator.

Programming Controls

Input controls are established primarily to prevent errors from entering into subsequent processing activities. Using programming controls, the computer can also be used to help detect input errors, as well as to detect error conditions which occur from processing the input. There are various ways that the computer can be programmed to provide control:

1. *Limit or Reasonableness Check.* This control is used to identify data having a value higher or lower than a predetermined amount. These standard high/low limits are ascertained and established from research performed by the systems analyst. This control technique detects only those data elements which fall outside the limits. Examples of how this technique can be used are:

a. If the highest account number in a customer file is 6000, but CUSTOMER-NUMBER 7018 is read then CUSTOMER-NUMBER of this particular record is in error.

b. If the minimum/maximum hourly rate for employees is $2.50/$10.50, any rate read which falls outside this range is in error.

c. A supply company handles parts for internal combustion engines numbered 0001–5999, and parts for electric motors numbered 6000–8999. If the parts file for electric motors is being processed and a part number is read that is greater than 8999 or less than 6000, then this part number is in error.

d. Employee hours worked in any single pay period cannot be greater than 60 hours. In ad-dition no gross pay amount can be greater than $735.00 or less than $2.50.

e. All customers with code A cannot purchase any order over $1000 on credit.

f. All B coded purchase orders are authorized for purchases, none of which can exceed $100.

g. An exception notice is printed or displayed if a customer order exceeds twice their average order.

2. *Arithmetic Proof.* Various computational routines can be designed to validate the result of other computations, or the value of selected data fields. One method of arithmetic proof is called crossfooting which means adding or subtracting two or more fields and zero balancing the result against the original result. This control method is applicable where total debits, total credits, and a balance forward amount are maintained for each account. For example, in the cash account, if the total debits equal $5000 and the total credits equal $4000, then the balance of cash should equal $1000. Other examples of the use of arithmetic proof are:

a. If fairly homogeneous items such as steel or grain are shipped to a customer, the billable amount can be checked for approximate accuracy. The average price for all steel stock may be $0.08 per pound. This rate is multiplied by the total weight of the shipment to derive an approximated billable amount. If this amount is say, not within four percent of the billed amount, then a message is displayed for subsequent investigation to determine if the billed amount is actually in error.

b. Net pay for employees is determined by

subtracting certain deductions from gross pay. In a separate routine the deductions could be added back to the derived net pay. Then the resulting gross pay could be checked against the original gross pay to see if it matches.

3. *Identification.* Various identification techniques can be designed to validate that the data being processed is valid data. This can be done by comparing data fields from transaction files to master files, or to constant tables, stored either internal to the program or on a peripheral device. Some examples of this technique are:

a. In a library, those books with code letters HD are maintained only on the fifth floor, which is the social science section. The computer can be programmed to test the identifying field to ensure that the processing of any social science book must contain the letters HD.

b. A chart of accounts may designate Current Assets with a number range of 100–199, where Cash is 100. If the cash register is being processed, all cash credits or debits must contain the identifier number 100.

c. The warehouse which handles steel stock and pipe is coded with a 1. If all issue and receipt transactions of steel and pipe inventory does not have the warehouse coded with a 1, then the transaction is either being entered in the wrong location or there is a keying error.

d. Each customer number entered in the order transaction file is compared to the customer master file. If a customer master record is not found, the order record is rejected.

4. *Sequence Check.* Files are often arranged in ascending or descending sequence, e.g., by employee number, account number, part number, etc. Instructions written in the processing program compare the sequenced field in each record or transaction with the sequenced field of the preceding record or transaction. With this technique, any out of sequence record can be detected and prevent the file from being processed incorrectly. Typical reasons for an occurrence of an out of sequence error are: (1) use of an incorrect file, (2) failure to perform a required sorting operation, (3) hardware malfunctions, and (4) incorrect merge operation.

5. *Error Log.* A vital control technique used during processing is the maintenance of an error log. This log contains a record of all identified errors and exceptions, noted during processing. As the errors are identified, they are written onto a special file, thus enabling the processing of that particular step to continue uninterrupted. At the completion of that processing step the error log can be checked, either by the computer or by the operator, and a decision made whether or not to continue processing.

The error log is then forwarded to either the department or group who prepared the original input or to a specially designated control group within the information system where the entries are corrected, reconciled, and resubmitted for processing.

6. *Other Programming Controls.* As noted previously, the computer can be programmed to read, write, and validate labels for each data file processed. Codes using check digits can be generated and validated with programming controls. Finally, control totals can be maintained and referenced at each step in the processing using programmed logic.

Data Base Controls

The raw material and lifeblood of the information system are its data files and programs. Because these items are so vital to the effective operations of the total system, procedures should be established and followed to safeguard them from loss or destruction. If loss or destruction does occur, then pre-planned procedures should be implemented to recreate these data files and programs. Through the use of programming controls, the systems analyst can help ensure, to some extent, that these files and programs are not destroyed during normal processing. However, the analyst, in conjunction with the management of the information system and the data base administrator, must also effect additional control over the physical and operational aspects related to processing and storing data files and programs.

Normally, files and programs are stored in a library while awaiting processing. It is here that physical safeguards should be implemented to ensure that the items will not be damaged or misused. These safeguards are:

1. The storage location should be constructed to help guard against fires.

The U.S. Air Force Statistical Office in the Pentagon once suffered the effects of a fire that damaged or destroyed three computers and more than 7000 reels of magnetic tape. The loss in magnetic tape alone, assuming a cost of $40 per reel, is $280,000. One expert estimates that the total loss in terms of data and the cost of reconstruction may have been as much as $30 million.

The lesson of this fire is that vital records and documents should be stored in fireproof areas. If they are not so stored, they can be totally destroyed by fire.[2]

2. Environmental factors such as temperature, humidity, and air should be properly controlled.

3. The storage site should be secure.

. . . vital files and documents should be stored in a secure area. Unless they are thus stored, they can be copied and returned without detection. Magnetic files can also be damaged or distorted by magnets and other devices. Magnets can change the data on a magnetic tape. This fact increases the need for secure storage of vital files.[3]

4. File-protect rings should be utilized. This plastic or metal ring acts as a safeguard against the accidental destruction of data. For example, if a tape file is to be written on, the operator places a file-protect ring on the back of the tape before mounting it on the tape drive. If a program attempts to write on a tape that does not have a file-protect ring, a writing error occurs and no writing takes place.

5. Off premises storage can be constructed by the organization, or rented, to provide further safeguards for vital files and programs.

[2] Norman L. Enger, *Putting MIS to Work,* (New York: American Management Association, Inc., 1969) p. 74. Used with permission from American Management Association, Inc.

[3] *Ibid.*

Operation control procedures are followed by the operating staff of the computer center, and personnel in the library, to ensure that data files and programs are handled properly and that if, by chance, an item is destroyed or lost, there will be specified methods to reconstruct such items. These procedures are enumerated below:

1. All items should be clearly labeled and indexed for proper identification.

2. Access to the storage areas should be restricted to authorized personnel only.

3. All files, programs, and other vital documents should be issued only to personnel authorized to receive those items. That is, there should be a systematic procedure installed to issue and receive vital documents stored in the library.

Regardless of the procedures implemented, files do occasionally get destroyed; or for various other reasons, the data becomes unreadable. To solve this problem, the systems analyst plans for backup or file reconstruction, i.e., a method of recreating records that have been lost. The most common method used for magnetic tape files is to keep the old master and transaction files when a new master file is updated. This method is referred to as the grandfather-father-son method since three versions of a file are available at any one time. This method of file control is illustrated in Figure 13.4.

In the first schematic, the original master file is established (e.g., payroll file, inventory file). By the end of the second update run we have the following: Tape 1 with transactions has become the grandfather, Tape 2 with transactions has become the father, and Tape 3 is the son which becomes the father in the third update run. In addition, the third update uses the original Tape 1 for output. At this point the transaction cards for the first update run are stored in some warehouse or possibly destroyed.

With the use of this method, recreation of lost files is possible. For example, if during the second update run, Tape 2 and Tape 3 were destroyed, then Tape 1 with the first period's transactions would be used to create an up-

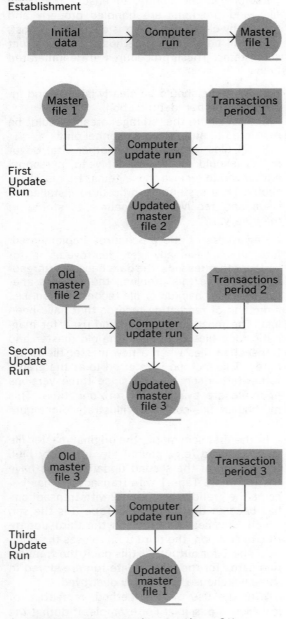

Initial File Establishment

First Update Run

Second Update Run

Third Update Run

FIGURE 13.4. An illustration of the Grandfather–Father–Son file backup procedure.

dated master file (Tape 2) and this file with the second period's transactions would be used to create an updated file for the second update run (Tape 3).

For direct access storage devices, the basic method for a file reconstruction procedure is to periodically dump the file contents onto another file medium, usually a magnetic tape. The frequency of file dumps depends upon the activity ratio and volatility of the file. For example, a master file would probably be dumped with greater frequency than a typical archival file.

With typical direct access master files, a daily dump or a backup file is usually implemented. With a daily dump, file reconstruction is simplified in that yesterday's dumped file can be processed with today's transactions, thus recreating a current file. Of course, this same procedure is followed whether or not the file is dumped daily; however, the greater the frequency of dumping, the higher the cost. Also, as the number of direct access storage devices increase, a daily dump of all devices will become less desirable because of the amount of CPU time required for dumps.

It should also be understood that methods of reconstruction applicable to data files are also applicable to reconstruction plans for programs. For instance, each time a program change is made, it should be documented and stored on a backup medium such as tape, should reconstruction become necessary.

There are, however, a number of approaches used to implement backup files or other media in different organizations.

Most of the installations that we visited used somewhat different methods for providing both daily and disaster backup; there seemed to be no 'standard' system. One life insurance company stores the grandfather generation of files in a locked safe in the basement. In addition, every quarter specified files are sent to a safe storage area at a distant location; printouts containing updating information and program changes are sent to this remote storage location daily. However, this company has found it difficult to get the complete documentation of program changes on a daily basis, so as to send this information along with the program change printouts.

A large bank makes duplicate copies of the updated master files and transaction files and these are sent to a remote site daily, some 25 miles from the computer center. Grandfather generation files are kept on site, for daily backup. Monthly, the program library is duplicated and sent to the remote site, as are duplicated copies of the operations documentation.

Still another company, which is research oriented, uses data transmission for sending copies of files and programs to a remote site. In this case, the remote site is another of the company's computer installations. Because of the nature of their processing, the volume of files and programs is suitable for this type of transmission. One advantage of this procedure is that the backup files could be transmitted to still another company site for processing, if this step were needed. On one test run, retrieval of the backup files commenced within a few minutes of the request. A fully operational set of records, programs, and documentation was received within five hours.[4]

Output Controls

Output control procedures are established as final checks on the accuracy and completeness of the processed information. These procedures are:

1. An initial screening should be conducted to detect obvious errors.

2. The dissemination of output should be controlled to ensure that only authorized users receive it.

3. Output control totals should be reconciled back to input control totals for agreement to ensure that no data has been lost or added during processing or transmission. For example, the number of records delivered for proces-

sing should equal the number of records that are processed, or hash totals should agree, or financial totals, such as net pay, should agree.

4. All vital forms (e.g., paycheck, stockholder registry forms, etc.) should be prenumbered and accounted for.

5. In spite of all the precautions taken, errors do slip through. The major detection control point for detecting such errors is, of course, the user. Therefore, procedures should be established by the systems analyst to set up a communication channel between the user and the control group for the systematic reporting of occurrences of errors or improprieties. Such a system design would employ a feedback loop where users would report all errors to the control group, and the control group, in turn, would take action to correct any inaccuracies or inconsistencies which might be revealed.

There are other output controls, such as systematic manual checks, statistical sampling, physical counts of inventories, and analysis of reports. Many methods can be devised for output controls, but the level of control should depend on the sensitivity of the output. For example, payroll checks should be tightly controlled, whereas departmental statistical reports require little control.

Hardware Controls

Although the analyst is not responsible for building equipment controls per se, they do enter into the overall design considerations of the system. Therefore, he or she must be aware of the types of equipment controls that are available and how they perform. In general, equipment controls are installed to detect electrical and mechanical failures in the computer and peripheral devices. These control checks are of two types: (1) preventive maintenance checks and procedures, and (2) built-in automatic equipment checks.

Preventive Maintenance Checks. Preventive maintenance accomplishes two things: (1) it ensures a continuation of proper control of such environmental factors as heat, humidity, and electricity and (2) it helps to forestall a deterio-

---

[4] "Computer Security: Backup and Recovery Methods," *EDP Analyzer,* January, 1972, p. 7. Used with permission.

ration in performance, or a failure of the various computer components, by an on-going system of detection, adjustment, and repairs.

Environmental specifications for the components which comprise a computer configuration are normally within close tolerances. When conditions exceed these tolerances, unpredictable errors can occur. In addition, the deterioration or destruction of various components within the system can occur. For example, a high percentage of humidity will damage such storage media as paper tape, punched cards, and magnetic tape; excess moisture will rust the metal parts of various devices; excess heat and dust will cause mysterious errors to occur during processing; and, if proper power control devices are not installed to guard against power surges or brownouts, there is a potential risk of having to repair or replace some parts (especially in the CPU) if either of these events occur.

Preventive maintenance procedures should be followed on a prescribed schedule wherein some of the more critical components are checked daily. The objective of this scheme is to detect impending failures and make proper adjustments or repairs before they occur. For example, the mechanical mechanism of such devices as card readers, printers, and card punches should be checked regularly to determine if any part needs changing. Any part that is worn or faulty should be replaced before it can cause trouble, such as card jams. On occasion the entire system may be shut down for a thorough testing of each segment of the system, whereupon any faltering part is immediately replaced. Therefore, it can clearly be seen that the aim of preventive maintenance procedures is to reduce the probability of error occurrences.

Built-in Equipment Checks. Inside the computer there must be a number of automatic checking features to ensure proper operation, just as there are various controls in any other electrical system. Such features are built into the circuitry for the detection of errors that might result from the manipulation, calculation, or transmission of data by the various components. These equipment checks are required to

make sure that only one electronic pulse is transmitted through a channel during any single phase, that specific devices are activated, and that the data received in one location are the same as were transmitted from another location.

Internal checking features are standard in many computers; where they are not, management should require that they be incorporated in the hardware by the vendor before it is installed. Examples of some of these internal equipment checking features follow:

1. *Parity Checks.* Data are calculated, and moved in the computer, based on a coded scheme of binary digits. When performing a number of operations, it is necessary to move data from one location to another. To ensure that the data initially read into the system have been transmitted correctly, an internal self-checking feature is incorporated in most computer systems. In addition to the set of bits used to represent data, the computer uses one additional bit (or a redundant bit) for each storage position. These bits are called parity bits, or check bits, and are used to detect errors in the circuitry which would result in the loss, addition, or destruction of a bit due to an equipment malfunction.

The parity bit makes the number of bits in a binary code either even or odd, depending on whether the computer uses even parity or odd parity. Either system requires an additional bit location associated with each coded set.

In an even parity machine, the coded set will always contain an even number of on bits, unless there is an error, i.e., unless the coded set has lost, or possibly gained, a bit because of a malfunction. Conversely, in an odd parity machine (most computers use odd parity), the coded set will always contain an odd number of on bits unless, of course, there is again a malfunction. Examples (using the letter J) of both even and odd parity using an Extended Binary Coded Decimal Interchange Code (EBCDIC) scheme are shown in Figure 13.5.

2. *Validity Checks.* Numbers and characters are represented by specified combinations of

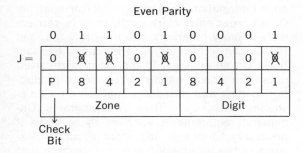

Even Parity

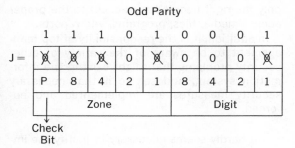

Odd Parity

FIGURE 13.5. Examples of the use of parity bits.

binary digits. Representation of these data symbols is accomplished by various coding schemes handled by the circuitry of the computer system.

In a single computer system several different coding schemes can be used to represent data at various stages of processing. Input to the computer may be represented by characters of one coding scheme and then converted to another before the input is entered in memory. In addition, once the input is in the computer it may go through another conversion phase for computational purposes. Then again on the output side, the data may have to go through still another conversion phase.

When input data are received from punched-cards, representation is usually in Hollerith code. The Hollerith characters of the input card are converted to Binary Coded Decimal (BCD), or Extended Binary Coded Decimal Interchange Code (EBCDIC), or to U.S.A. Standard Code for Information Interchange (USASCII). An example of code conversion phases is presented in Figure 13.6.

If output is written on an output device such as a printer or a card punch, the data will have to be converted to yet another code, one that is acceptable to these devices; i.e., a coding configuration which activates the mechanism to output the data either in human readable form, or in a Hollerith code data interpretation.

An interactive device such as a teletype may work off the basis of a Teletype Code (Baudot Code); if so, again a message either being transmitted or received will have to go through an encoding and decoding operation to make the message acceptable to the device in question.

3. *Duplication Check.* This check requires that two independent devices perform the same operation and compare the results. If there is any deviation between the two operations it is indicated as an error. For example, cards being read by a card reader would pass through two read stations. If the two readings do not equal, an error is indicated. This same principle of duplication (remember verification presented earlier in this chapter) is used in many other, both input and output, devices. For example, after a card is punched by a card punch, it

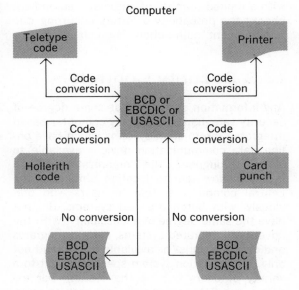

FIGURE 13.6. An example of code conversion procedures.

passes through a read station. The results are then read and compared with the original data. Again, if the results are not the same, the system would halt and/or the operator would be alerted via the console typewriter.

4. *Echo Check.* An echo check simply verifies that a proper device has been activated to perform a particular operation. The CPU transmits a message to an input or output device (e.g., card reader or card punch) to perform an operation. The receiving device sends a message back to the CPU where it is automatically checked to see if the correct device has been activated.

5. *Miscellaneous Error Checks.* In addition to those checks mentioned above, the computer system should also contain checks to detect various invalid computer instructions, on size or overflow checks, zero division checks, and defective storage media.

Unfortunately, not all computer devices that are installed today have a total complement of equipment checking features. In making equipment selection, the one charged with this responsibility must evaluate the completness of the error detection features incorporated in a particular component. If equipment is selected with a limited number of automatic equipment checks the probability of errors occurring due to equipment malfunctions is much greater.

13.3 Security Controls

Any information system needs some degree of security safeguards, especially computer based integrated information systems which have online data communication devices available to users throughout the organization. Such systems allow remote location entry into the central computer system by users who previously, with batch oriented systems, did not have the same degree of accessibility. With the advent of integrated systems, certain programs and data files must be available on demand not only to information system specialists, but to a variety of users outside the system. For example, the Sales Manager might wish to interrogate the sales statistics file for sales perform-

ance information via a remote CRT or teletype. Or, an order entry clerk might need to retrieve online library programs, the inventory file, and the customer file, for updating sales transactions. Or, an engineer in the plant might need data from a combination of files to run production loading and schedules analyses on a time-sharing basis, using their own programs. On-demand requirements such as these make it necessary to design additional security measures in the information system to ensure that only the right people have access to the proper access media, files, programs, and reports.

In addition, it is the responsibility of top management to be aware of the variety of other security problems that might exist in the information system, and see to it that necessary security measures are implemented and enforced.

It hardly seems necessary to justify the importance of this subject—the security of the computer center. Data processing managers are all too aware of the number of times in the past few years that articles have appeared describing such events as: the destruction of a computer by militants; operator errors that resulted in the erasure of the last backup copies of critical files; or programmers who altered production programs as part of a fraud scheme. If there is any doubt that these are actual problems, consider some of the statistics reported at a recent conference, sponsored by the American Management Association, on computer security problems:

- There were 4300 bombings in the U.S. in a recent 15 month period; only a part of these involved computers, however.
- There were 70,000 people arrested for actual or attempted fraud in 1970—but no one knows how many *weren't* caught.
- An "underground newspaper" published an instruction list for destroying computers. Highlights of the article were picked up by other publications.
- A university in New York offered students a 3-unit course on disruption of computers.

The course stressed that the most important asset of a company is its data. . . .[5]

Management must measure the information system's susceptibility to security risks, and potential disaster, and balance the cost of systems disruption and loss of information against alternative security control levels. Not only is it management's responsibility to implement security controls, but it is required legally.

. . . management may be held personally liable by stockholders if losses are due to negligence or improper security and control management. Managers may be personally liable to reimburse the losses. . . .[6]

Security Group

In larger, more complex information systems, it may be necessary either for part of the systems group or an independent group of skilled security specialists to be formed and charged with the responsibility of setting up, implementing, monitoring, and enforcing various security procedures. Such a group would be responsible for user access, controlled access, data transmission security, program integrity, and disaster recovery procedures. However, in many installations, the systems analyst is responsible for the security control points related to the system he or she is installing. Security control points

[5] "Security of the Computer Center," *EDP Analyzer,* December, 1971, pp. 2–3. Used with permission.
[6] "Computer Security: Backup and Recovery Methods," *op. cit.,* p. 10.

should be evaluated when the system is being designed.

User Access

A conventional method of allowing file and program access to a central computer system using online terminals, is to assign each authorized user a unique number and code. This number/code is then input from a remote terminal to allow certain prescribed entries into, and usage of, the central system. Similarly, an employee is permitted the use of the computer system on a batch mode basis through the issuance of a job card. Both the user number/code and the job card act as passwords or keys to various designated files, programs, and other items in the system.

Different user numbers can represent levels and kinds of access, based on the authority and areas of responsibility, of the user to whom it is assigned. Examples of these levels are:

1. Duration of time that a user number is operative, e.g., R numbers might be active on a thirty day basis, whereas S numbers might be active on a 60 day basis.
2. Kind of usage and access, e.g., timesharing only on 8K of storage, timesharing only with unlimited storage, job entry only, file establishment, file interrogation, file updating, file revision, program change, use of library programs, and so forth.

Each user, according to authority, rank, or some other criteria, can be given a specific level of access priority as shown, for example, in Figure 13.7.

User Numbers \ Access Allowed	Timeshare Only (8K)	Timeshare Only (Unlimited Storage)	Library Program Usage	Interrogate Sales File	Update Customer File	– –
R numbers	X		X			–
S numbers		X	X	X		–
P numbers			X		X	–

FIGURE 13.7. Usage and access matrix.

Controlled Access

Some degree of controlled access is imperative, whether one is talking about a terminal system or a batch oriented system. The following are true stories which help to emphasize this point:[7]

A large insurance company in an East Coast city recently gave a ladies' garden club a tour of its EDP facilities. The spinning tapes and blinking lights impressed one visitor so much that she felt she had to have a souvenir of the occasion. She later said, "I hope I didn't do anything wrong. There were all those boxes of cards on the table, and I just reached into the middle of a box and took one." Perhaps this lady only caused a program to be rerun. A more serious possibility is that the card may not have been missed at all, and the center is still trying to correct the resulting confusion.

A more frightening example:[8]

One dissatisfied EDP employee used magnets to destroy virtually every file and program that his company possessed. He accomplished this in practically no time at all, but reconstructing the data will take a very long time indeed. At last report, in fact, the auditors were not sure whether they could reconstruct enough information to keep the company in business. In this particular case, the consequences of poor security in the EDP area may have been not merely serious, but fatal.

Damage and disruption can emanate from a number of sources; from casual vistors innocently tampering with the system, to insiders or outsiders, bent upon fraud, sabotage, or deception. Controlled access to the computer center itself can be effected by certain precautions such as the deployment of guards and the implementation of entrance procedures (such as name tags, badges, and tour guides).

One of the first steps taken for facilities protection was to make access to the entire building more restrictive. Access to the operations room was made especially restrictive. A 24-hour-a-day guard service was instituted, located in the lobby at the main building entrance. The one other entrance to the building is now monitored by a closed circuit TV, with the viewing screen at the guard office. All other exterior doors are equipped as emergency exits only. Opening the doors will sound an alarm and notify the guard station. Visitors to the building are required to sign in and out, and none are allowed in after working hours. At the guard station (and also in the operations room) there are "hot line" telephones connected directly to local fire and police stations.

Access to the data processing department, and operations room in particular, has been restricted through the use of both a color-coded badge system and a master-sub-master key system. There are four different sets of sub-master keys, allowing employees to enter only one of the four data processing work areas (operations, keypunch, etc.). Supervisory personnel have master keys allowing access to all areas. Within operations, color coded badges note three different access authorizations—permanent operations employees, systems personnel who have need to access certain areas of the operations room, and visitors (who must be accompanied by an operations employee). Visitors and systems people are required to sign in and out of the operations room.

Both the badges and keys are registered to personnel, and are issued and retrieved on a shift basis at the guard station. The guard has an access authorization list and pictures of authorized employees. The lists are updated and are closely watched for employees recently terminated.[9]

The problem becomes a little more complex, if we are also concerned with controlled access to remote terminals and the development of control procedures that will ensure that access

---

[7] Brandt Allen, "Danger Ahead! Safeguard Your Computer." *Harvard Business Review,* November–December, 1968, pp. 97–101. Used with permission.

[8] *Ibid.*

[9] "Security of the Computer Center," *op. cit.,* pp. 1–2.

is limited only to those individuals authorized to use the facilities. Many terminals are scattered throughout the organization in locations that are not easily monitored and, in addition, are physically accessible to a variety of people. Moreover, some terminals are portable wherein a user with an acoustic coupler can gain access to the central computer via a telephone dial-up system.

The following guidelines can be used to prevent unauthorized access to a system with a variety of remote terminals:

1. Establish a procedure for issuing new user numbers on a frequent basis.

2. Through programming logic, establish restricted time periods for designated terminals.

3. Design monitoring systems to register erroneous attempts to access the system in part or whole.

4. Establish a procedure to automatically terminate a terminal hookup which has indicated no activity for a specified period of time.

Transmission Security

The central computer, communication lines, and terminals are all electronic devices that transmit signals which can be tapped by any person who possesses the proper equipment. Such tapping, particularly of the communication lines, falls into one of two categories: (1) passive or (2) active.

Passive tapping is accomplished through wiretapping or electromagnetic pickup, and limits the unauthorized user to data either being retrieved or transmitted by an authorized user. Active tapping consists of the actual connection of a terminal to the line. This unauthorized terminal may not be detected by the computer, and messages from it will appear as though they were transmitted by the authorized terminal. The active tapper can interrogate the data being transmitted as well as changing data, if they so desire.[10]

Both active and passive tapping can be guarded against through use of cryptographic codes. This means that a person with the key to the code is supposedly the only one who can read a transmitted message, or string of data. Putting data or messages into code is called cryptography, a word based on Greek terms meaning "hidden" and "writing." Cryptanalysis is the act of breaking codes without the key.

Common cryptographic systems involve transposition, substitution, transformation, or a combination of all three. A useful data transformation system[11] is one where the encoding and decoding processes are the inverse of one another. This system involves adding a bit to each bit transmitted. The same bit string is then subtracted from the transmitted text to get back to the original message.

To make this technique useful, a long sequence of bits to be added must exist. If transmissions are from computer to computer, identical random number generators can be programmed, and the priming number for the generator can be transmitted at the beginning of the message. Extremely long sequences of bits for coding purposes can be obtained in this manner, and the amount of work to encode such a message is substantial.

This transformation method can be used equally well for securing data files. If data are encoded with this method prior to being placed in a file, then the file can be updated or interrogated by only those who have access to the library program that accesses and manipulates these data. The decoding of the data would be handled by the program, thus no user would have to know the key. The encoding/decoding key must appear as an integral part of each record of the file; whenever the file is updated, the entire record must be rewritten. This transformation method is particularly appealing when file space is allocated on shared devices and the deliberate or inadvertent reading of the data by unauthorized persons is a severe potential problem.[12]

Even the best access control can be circumvented by a sophisticated and determined infiltrator; hence the system must be

---

[10] Martin L. Rubin, (ed.) *Advanced Technology-Systems Concepts,* Volume 5 of *Handbook of Data Processing Management* (Philadelphia: Auerbach Publishers, 1971), pp. 81–82. Adapted and reprinted by permission of the publisher. Copyright © Auerbach Publishers Inc. 1971.

[11] *Ibid.*
[12] *Ibid.*

protected from within also. Processing restrictions must be placed upon all sensitive files to ensure they are not read or altered by unauthorized persons. The degree of threat monitoring required by a system depends upon the criticalness of the information being processed.

As previously mentioned, the weakest link in our computer system is the communications link between the terminals and the processors. Here we must deal with not only the overt or active infiltrator, but also the covert or passive infiltrator, with his wiretapping methods or listening devices for electromagnetic radiation. An effective method of dealing with this threat, if not the most effective method at present, is cryptography. A good crytographic system, properly installed and maintained, will substantially reduce the threat against the communications system.

Briefly, this cryptographic system should contain three basic elements. First, there must be a set of codes which are sufficiently difficult to interpret. The system should also contain a mechanism for encoding and decoding at each end of the communications channel. This mechanism may be either manual or automated, depending upon the needs of the user. Finally the cryptographic system must contain its own built-in security procedures to protect the code sets and the encoding/decoding mechanism.

A very probable target of a sophisticated infiltrator is the system monitor, since the monitor is usually the primary key to the correct operation of security measures. Since the primary threat to the monitor will come from system personnel, protection will rely on adequate physical and personnel integrity of the system. A suggested method is for the monitor to be housed in read-only memory which can only be altered physically. . . .[13]

The amount of time and cost one expends to protect against tapping is a function of the vul-

nerability of communication lines, the potential threat of tapping, and the kind of data being transmitted. There are many coding systems which can be used, from simple substitution (e.g., THANKSLORD for 1234567890, where KR equals 59) to more sophisticated systems. These latter include digraphic substitution, polyalphabetic substitution, and combined substitution-transposition ciphers. Constructing codes and ciphers or breaking or solving codes and ciphers make up an area of study called cyptology which is beyond the scope of this text.

Program Modification

Procedures should be established to note the changes to programs in the library.[14] This process is adequate when changes are made through normal channels. However, if the change is not submitted through normal channels, the security group must establish a means to detect this. The detection can be achieved by having the system loader pass control to a security program after loading, but prior to passing control to the loaded program. The security program then computes a check-sum of the bits comprising the loaded program. This check-sum is compared to a previously stored table of valid check-sums. The check-sum table is accessible only by the security program. If the check-sum comparison fails, the program is aborted and the security officer notified.

After successfully passing the check-sum process described above, the program may begin execution, but might afterward be modified. Because of other safeguards, the major program modification of concern is the one which will change classified data already on file. This is considered the major problem because it must be assumed that the person making the change has already gained access to the program and the data which can be displayed as a result of its operation; otherwise, the modification could not be accomplished, or the program run. The problem is best controlled through

[13] William S. Bates, "Security of Computer-based Information Systems," *Datamation*, May, 1970, p. 64. Reprinted with permission of *Datamation*, Copyright 1970 by Technical Publishing Company, Greenwich, Connecticut 06830.

[14] This section adapted from: Rubin, *op. cit.*, p. 82.

tight control of the times and situations under which in-core modifications are to be permitted. All access to system information, such as where the program is loaded in memory, must be made difficult to obtain. Access to write in restricted files can be forbidden until a program is checked out, entered on the library file, and loaded from there.

Disaster Recovery Procedures

Planning based on common sense and the establishment of simple control procedures can guard against the occurrence of many obvious disasters. We know of one computer system that is housed in the same building as a radio station, an experimental wind tunnel, and a carpentry shop. No wonder the system is in constant trouble due to "mysterious" power lapses and surges. Other computer systems have been installed in close proximity to radar towers. Still other systems have been installed on sites immediately adjacent to large power plants. Poor site planning can be a major cause of some disasters, which, with a little more forethought, could have been avoided.

However, the potential occurrence of some types of disasters cannot always be precisely forecasted. For instance, natural disasters such as flood, fire, and wind can destroy an entire computer facility. Such events are unpredictable; however, precautions such as back-up facilities and off-site storage of duplicate items can be implemented to safeguard against such events.

Following are the types of data records that we have found included in the backup planning, at companies that have developed computer security programs:

Backup Copies Needed

1. System documentation.
2. Program documentation.
3. Operating procedures documentation.
4. Program source decks or tapes.
5. Program object decks or tapes.
6. Job control language cards or tapes, for production programs.
7. Data table card decks or tapes.
8. Operating system tapes or disk packs.
9. Data master files.
10. Data transaction files.
11. Data report files.
12. Forms masters.
13. Supply of key preprinted forms.
14. Masters of company manuals.
15. Printer carriage tapes (if used).
16. Control panel wiring diagrams (if used).
17. Documentation of duties of key personnel.
18. Description of the hardware, including all peripherals and all options.

In other words, if the computer center is destroyed by fire, by a flood, by a hurricane, or such, the company may well need all of these types of records in order to reestablish the data processing.[15]

Downtime of short duration can occur due to malfunctions such as inadequate air conditioning, faulty humidifying systems, and various equipment malfunctions. Failures of either long or short duration cannot be tolerated in most installations. Consequently, planning for backup facilities is necessary. There are basically two kinds of backup: (1) off site backup and (2) system components backup.

In the event of a natural disaster or any other occurrence causing total systems failure, a complete backup facility based in another organization is required. For backup off site, a provision should be negotiated to establish a reciprocal user agreement from a nearby organization. Again, off site backup requires proper planning, as witnessed in the following quote:[16]

Current thinking has it that the executive responsible ought to be sure that his company has a backup facility available. However, when a senior executive of a major New England corporation was asked about the company's contingency plan, should its com-

---

[15] Computer Security: Back up and Recovery Methods," *op. cit.,* p. 5.
[16] Allen, *op. cit.*

puter go down, he immediately replied that a nearby center could and would be used. A later interview with the manager of the center in question revealed that his center's equipment is not compatible with the company's; the nearest compatible equipment is located several hundred miles away; and that equipment is busy 24 hours a day, 7 days a week!

However, the location of an alternate configuration is a difficult problem because of many variations in equipment, peripherals, and operating systems.

Where do you start looking for a compatible alternate site, to be used as backup? Following are several suggestions that we came across:

Alternate Site Prospects

1. For companies with multiple installations, consider one or more of the other sites for backup. This solution is aided if the company has standardized on equipment, operating system, maximum program sizes, etc. Also, this is one argument for such a company having multiple installations rather than one large, centralized installation.

2. Check with other companies in the same industry as yours.

3. Check with companies in other types of business that are in your geographical area.

4. Check with your computer manufacturer.

5. Check with the service bureaus in your geographical area.[17]

On the other hand, reduction or prevention of downtime caused by various isolated malfunctions would call for backup from redundant components located in the system (e.g., redundant air conditioning, power control units, humidifiers, readers, printers, CPU, etc.). Obviously, most organizations cannot afford a 100% redundant system. However, some of the vital hardware components should be selected with sufficient backup to minimize the consequence of a hardware failure.

[17] "Computer Security: Back up and Recovery Methods," *op. cit.,* p. 9.

13.4 Forms/Reports Design

In every information system, the systems analyst must design a number of forms and reports for the purpose of recording source data and communicating information. Moreover, in highly sophisticated systems where much of the input is collected via some type of terminal and output is produced via a terminal, the format used by these terminals to collect or present data, demands the same design considerations as more traditional paper forms. The purpose of any form or report is to communicate from one person to another. The importance of good forms design can not be over emphasized. The true cost of a form is difficult to determine, but some form experts indicate that, in addition to any EDP processing costs related to the form, $20 worth of clerical expense is incurred gathering, entering, and reviewing data for each dollar actually spent purchasing the form.[18] In this section we will discuss the various types of forms and some basic guidelines in performing a forms analysis.

Types of Forms

There are many types of forms in a large information system. For example, there are paychecks, invoices, shipping papers, work assignments, budget worksheets, checks to vendors, purchase orders, sales reports, customer lists, routing files, and so forth. In order to deal with this multiplicity of forms and reports it is common to categorize each form as it relates to the information system. A form is either an input or an output. Inputs are generally termed forms, while outputs are called reports. There are cases, however, where this terminology is not strictly adhered to. A special type of form that is used both as input and output to the system is termed a turnaround form.

Input Forms. The primary purpose of this classification of forms is to record data for subsequent processing. The first determination the analyst must make is what data must be re-

[18] Ian Synders, "Forms Design Shapes Data Costs," *Business Automation,* December, 1968, p. 44. Used with permission.

corded. It is suggested that the analyst compose a list which includes, the purpose for collecting data related to this activity, the specific data fields required, and the anticipated length of each field.

Secondly the analyst must then consider how the data are to be recorded. By an employee of the organization? By one person or many different people? Will it be written or typed? Will it be recorded inside or outside of a building? Once the analyst has answered these questions he or she is in a position to design a form which will aid the recording process.

Since this type of form will require subsequent processing, the analyst must next consider the data processing method that will be used to process the data. A manual method? An electromechanical method? Punched card? Computer? If the analyst can design a form that captures all of the necessary data efficiently, and can be processed subsequently without being reformatted, or reproduced into another media, most likely, the ideal form has been designed.

In most cases the analyst chooses a final forms design through a series of tradeoffs between the ease of recording the data and the efficiency of processing it. Most of the forms used to record data are designed first, to aid the recorder and second, to facilitate processing. Moreover, the majority of forms designed today are recognized as requiring either further reformatting or reproduction into another media (such as punched cards or magnetic tape) before the data are processed. Thus, tradeoffs occur between ease of recording and ease of reproducing.

The analyst should be mindful of newer and more efficient ways of capturing and recording input data due to advances in technology. Source Data Automation (SDA), for example, allows data to be recorded on two different media simultaneously. One medium is clearly understood by a human recorder and the second medium is available for processing on a computer.

Source data which are entered on paper forms can also be readily processed when op-

tical scanning equipment is utilized. Optical scanning is often termed OCR (Optical Character Recognition). The use of special inks and character construction provide still another alternative for designing better forms.

Additional design considerations which affect the final form of an input document might be: (1) number of copies required, (2) loose or padded forms, (3) multicolored, (4) type of carbons desirable, and (5) number of forms required. We will consider these ideas and many others in the Guidelines for Forms Analysis section.

Output Forms. The design of output documents can be further subdivided into designing operational or legal documents, or designing information outputs. The design of legal or operational documents such as paychecks, invoices, shipping documents, etc., involves a reasoning process similar to that applied in the design of input documents. However, the design of information outputs such as budgets, performance summaries, trends, and the like is not as concerned with the quality of paper and type of print font. Information outputs must (1) contain meaningful content, and (2) display this content in a format which assists the reader in obtaining an understanding of what is contained therein.

When designing information outputs, the analyst must choose between using preprinted forms or stock paper. The current trend is to utilize preprinted forms only when a document is prepared for use by persons outside of the organization. The performance capabilities of modern printing devices allows columnar headings of every description to be produced. However, preprinted forms do permit more characters to be printed horizontally on a line than does stock paper. This occurs because a preprinted form may contain vertical lines to separate the information whereas spaces must be used to separate information on stock paper.

Some additional guidelines for designing information outputs are:

1. Each page should have a brief, descriptive report title.

2. Report pages should be numbered. A report which is prepared for functional use should begin each function's section with page 1.

3. Reports should contain a report number. Many different number schemes can be used which represent a specific production cycle (e.g., ACC, MFG., SAL, etc.), or a specific production cycle (e.g., day, week, month, etc.) or the computer program number which produced the report. Although the first two number schemes cited may seem more relevant, in a large organization the latter numbering scheme is more practical.

4. Reports should contain two dates in the heading. The first date reflects the time period included in the report and the second date reflects the day the report was produced.

5. Columnar headings should be brief but descriptive. Usually they should appear at the top of each page in the report. The exception to this rule is when a report is extremely voluminous, produced often, and used by the same individuals.

6. Reports to upper management should always include very descriptive headings.

7. Multiple formatted lines can be utilized in a report. Columnar headings can be included once at the top of each page in a group, or printed each time the line format changes. Readability for the former approach can be enhanced by carefully utilizing report spacing techniques.

8. Forms which will contain similar output should be placed side-by-side to the limit of printer capacity to increase printing efficiency. For example, if a printer can accommodate three payroll checks abreast, then printing time is decreased by two-thirds.

Turnaround Forms. The third classification of forms contains both input and output aspects, and is called a turnaround form. The cards we receive with our utility bills or charge accounts are examples of turnaround forms. Turnaround forms are produced as output from the processing of one system, and when returned to the organization which created them, they are used as input for processing in another system.

The turnaround form can be used in various ways. For example, many organizations produce these documents when a product is received and recorded in an inventory system. As the product is removed from inventory, the forms are input to record the depletion transaction. Other organizations produce checks to employees and vendors which are in reality punched cards that are later used as input for cash reconciliations.

Guidelines for Forms Analysis

In the discussion of types of forms some of the considerations the analyst must include when designing a form or report were indicated. In this section some additional guidelines that are helpful in analyzing and designing forms are provided.

1. *Forms Functions.* Perhaps the first step in analyzing a form is to determine its function. The eighteen basic forms functions are:[19]

to acknowledge	to identify
to agree	to instruct
to apply	to notify
to authorize	to order
to cancel	to record
to certify	to report
to claim	to request
to estimate	to route
to followup	to schedule

2. *Forms Distribution.* The distribution of a form can be either a sequential or a parallel flow. These distributions are illustrated in Figure 13.8. The approach used to distribute a form is important since it determines: (1) the number of forms required, (2) the total throughput time, (3) preparation time and costs, and (4) filing and retention procedures.

3. *Physical Considerations.* A complete discussion of the physical aspects of forms design is beyond the scope of this text. However, we can provide a list of the elements to be considered. They include:

form width	form length
horizontal spacing	vertical spacing

[19] Belden Menkus, "Designing a Useful Form," *Business Graphics,* September, 1972, p. 32. Used with permission.

Form X is sequentially passed from one department to the other:

Copies of form X are made and passed simultaneously to the several departments:

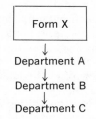

FIGURE 13.8.   An illustration of the two approaches to form distribution.

field size   marginal perforations
bindings   carbons
colors   font type
paper weight   special features

To summarize our presentation of forms analysis we present a number of suggestions for analyzing, designing, and implementing efficient forms.[20]

First, in the design of the component parts:

1. Determine the proper size, consistent with printing production standards, and be certain the form is reduced to the minimum practical size.

2. Determine the necessary number of copies to be included in the form. (Unneeded copies represent extra cost.)

3. Eliminate or reduce costly part-to-part composition changes within the form.

4. Guarantee that spacing on the form will be adequate for handwriting and properly arranged for the machines on which the form will be processed.

5. Assure an arrangement of items in the same sequence as the source, or the subsequent form arrangement.

6. Pre-print repetitive items to eliminate typing operations.

7. Design for use in window envelopes whenever practical.

8. Streamline the copy for use of tab stops.

9. Give consideration as to how the form will be filed, for how long, and what information on it will act as reference for retrieval.

10. Determine the need for a new form. Examine the possibility of using a substitute form before designing or approving any new form.

Second, in the materials specifications and construction of the form:

11. Specify the correct grade, weight and color of papers to be used. All of these factors affect the ultimate cost.

12. Determine the carbon specifications necessary to supply the needed number of legible copies. Weight, color, grade, size, striped, pattern, finish, all can affect the cost of the form.

13. Keep to a minimum, or eliminate completely, colored inks, matching colors, two or more colors, or special nonstandard colors.

14. Select the best type of binding, to hold the form together, for processing through various machine operations, and for the ultimate separation of parts, and removal of carbons. This requires careful consideration of types of gluing, stapling, crimping, perforations, and sizes both of margins and stubs.

[20] Albert F. Tiede, "21 Ways to Save Money on Forms," *Information and Records Management*, June/July, 1968, pp. 24–26. Used with permission.

Third, in the cost of the forms:

15. Set up the proper reordering points and quantities to assure a continual stream of supplies requisitioned in quantities that should result in the lowest price of each item.

16. Combine requisitions for forms of like size and construction for group purchasing to secure maximum savings.

17. Furnish "Guide Line Prices" to Purchasing, on new forms, as a reference against bids submitted.

18. Determine where a form can best be produced; at an outside vendor through Purchasing, or in an in-plant print shop. This assures the proper type of orders flowing to the internal print shops and eliminates the so called "bootleg" forms.

Finally:

19. Insure that normal quantities of existing forms will be reordered only when there are no contemplated changes in a system which may result in the obsolescence of one or more forms.

20. Enable the systems man to concentrate on his systems work assured that the forms designed will carry the full load regarding forms construction and layout.

21. Keep abreast of new developments in the business forms and business machines industries.

13.5 Clerical Procedures

Earlier in this chapter, documentation was identified as a form of control. Documentation was also classified as: (1) the communication prepared by the systems analyst throughout the developmental cycle of the information system (e.g., Proposal to Conduct Systems Analysis, Systems Analysis Completion Report, various project status reports, and so forth); (2) the formal description of the many clerical activities required in the information system; and (3) the formal description of the logical processing required, in each computer program, in the information system.

The first category of documentation has been discussed as required in each step of the systems development. In this section, the writing of clerical procedures is specifically discussed. This type of documentation formally describes what each person, who is part of the information systems operations, is to perform. The next section, discusses the design of program specifications, i.e., the documentation which formally describes the logic performed by a computer program.

We have included the writing of clerical procedures, and the preparation of program specifications, in our discussion of specific systems design topics, because the authors are strongly committed to the belief that these two activities are basically design activities essential to the successful development of the information system. As previously stated, the term design implies planning or arranging. The activities performed by persons operating the information system must be identified by the systems analyst. As such, there is no better way to ensure that these activities are clearly understood by the analyst, and by the individuals assigned to perform them, than to formally describe the activities. In this section we will: (1) analyze the purpose and use of clerical procedures, (2) describe guidelines related to the format and content of procedures, and (3) discuss general considerations for compiling a procedures manual.

The Purpose and Use of Written Procedures

The purpose of written procedures is to uniformly communicate management's desires as to what activities are to be performed, when, how, and by whom. In short, written procedures are one way for management to exercise control over the activities of the organization.

Once the systems analyst understands the purpose of written procedures, it is also important to understand the various ways in which written procedures are used. First, written procedures are used to achieve standardization where an activity or set of activities must be performed by more than one person. When an individual performs the same activities time and time again, there is no need for a written procedure except when an unknown or unexpected event occurs. Thus, a written procedure must lend itself to quick reference by the persons performing the activities described.

Secondly, written procedures are used to assist in the training of new persons. When used for training purposes, written procedures should be supplemented by other methods. These can include observing the activities being performed by another person, special training manuals and films, and so forth. Some additional approaches to personnel training are discussed in the next chapter.

A third use for written procedures is as a guideline and reference for auditors and analysts of the activities described therein.

Guidelines for the Format and Content of Written Procedures

Ideally, a written procedure should be provided for each distinct activity which must be performed in the operation of the information system. Some examples of the diverse activities which should be described in a written procedure include: (1) adding a new customer to a Customer Master File, (2) entering a customer remittance for Accounts Receivable, (3) modifying a product sales record, (4) balancing the Daily Labor Distribution Report, (5) issuing a Credit Memo for defective merchandise, (6) setting up the computer to process payroll, (7) distributing salesmen's commission checks, (8) preparing a request for processing a special profit analysis, (9) recording the inter-plant transfer of raw material, and (10) entering annual departmental budgets.

There are two major uses of written procedures: (1) for reference material and (2) for a communication link between personnel. Furthermore, while the specific content of each procedure depends on the activity it describes, in general the procedure should supply the answers to the following questions:

1. *What* activity is being described?
2. *Who* must perform the activity?
3. *Where* is the activity performed?

4. *When* is the activity performed?
5. *Why* is the activity performed?
6. *How* is the activity performed?

Figure 13.9 illustrates one approach to preparing written procedures. As can be seen from the illustration, the format is directed to an individual with a specific question or problem, rather than to be read as a novel at one sitting. Each section of the procedure answers one or more of the above questions concisely but clearly. The terminology used in each section is somewhat arbitrary, for example, the section labeled "Title" might also be termed "Subject," or "Purpose."

Considerations in Compiling a Procedures Manual

A system may include hundreds of individual procedures. It is not necessary, nor even desirable, to give each person involved with the system a complete set of procedures. As a rule procedures are combined into manuals which represent specific jobs, activities, or department responsibilities. A master procedures manual for the system is usually maintained in a special library within the information system and is readily accessible to both the systems analyst and other authorized users. However, each departmental level procedures manual should contain an index which identifies all procedures included within the system.

When procedures are written, compiled into manuals, and implemented in the organization, they will quickly be discarded or rendered obsolete if the analyst has not identified a simple method for modifying the contents of the manual. Although the written procedure represents management's desires, and therefore requires some level of management approval to become official, many changes will normally be identified at the user's level. Consequently, each procedures manual should include within itself a simple maintenance procedure for updating the system's procedures.

Assigning identification codes to procedures is a common practice in many organizations. This identification code not only helps to minimize ambiguity among similar or related proce-

Title	Procedure No.	175
Cash Discounts	Effective Date	MM–DD–YY

Policy Statement: All customers are entitled to a cash discount of 2% on purchases as follows:

    a. The order exceeds $1000, or
    b. The order is paid in full within 10 days of shipment, or
    c. The order is received as part of a special promotion which grants the cash discount as part of the promotion.

Locations Effected: All sales divisions.

Authorization: Vice-President, Marketing.

Specific Instructions:
  Salesman

    1. Enter the words "Cash Discount Due" on all orders eligible for cash discount.
    2. If only selected items are eligible for cash discount on an order, circle the line item number and place the letters "C.D.D." next to that line item.

  Order Entry Clerk

    1. If an order contains the words "Cash Discount Due," enter an "X" in column 7 of the order total line.
    2. If an order contains the letters "C.D.D." and the appropriate line item number is circled, enter an "X" in column 17 of the line item line.
    3. All other orders are to be left blank in these columns.

FIGURE 13.9. Illustration of a clerical procedure.

dures but it also helps to expedite modifications to the manual.

13.6 Program Specifications

Describing the activities to be performed manually in a system was treated in the last section on writing procedures. Describing the activities to be performed on a computer in a system is referred to as preparing program specifications, and is discussed in this section. The formal preparation of program specifications by the analyst provides three distinct benefits: (1) an opportunity for the analyst to rethink the systems design logic at a low level of detail, (2) a vehicle for communicating, with one or more programmers, that which is required of the programmer, and (3) a permanent record which describes or documents the activities performed by each program in the system. The importance of having complete and accurate

program specifications increases as systems become large, complex, and/or integrated.

Programming – A Definition

The writing of computer programs is normally the largest single activity in the development phase of a system. Programming can be defined as the preparing of procedures to be executed on the computer. The actual tasks performed by a programmer today differ little from what they were when computers were first introduced for the processing of data. What has changed in the relative emphasis that a programmer gives each of these tasks as a program is developed. We can define the tasks which constitute writing a program as follows:

  1. The first task in writing a program is to identify the purpose and scope of the logic which is to be executed by the computer within the boundaries of the program. This step can be accomplished by reviewing the program specifications.

2. Defining the sequence in which the logic is to be executed is the second task in writing a program. Various techniques such as flowcharts, decision trees, and decision tables can be of immense value to the programmer at this time.

3. Task three involves the translation of the identified logic into a coding structure which can be executed by the computer. To perform this task a programmer must possess a working knowledge concerning one of the many programming languages, or coding structures, available for execution by the computer.

4. The fourth task is related to checking out the written program to determine if all the rules of the programming language have been adhered to. This task is normally termed compiling or assembling the program. That is, the computer translates the source program written by the programmer to an object program of machine language instructions which are used by the computer during processing. As a rule, a programmer will require two or three attempts to compile before a "clean" (no detectable syntax errors) status is achieved for processing.

5. Testing is the task where the programmer attempts to validate that the logic written in the program equates to what was identified in the program specifications. The programmer submits simulated input and attempts to perform all of the related processing steps to produce the required output. The number of test attempts required is a function of both the programmer's ability and the specific complexity of the program. The process of resolving and reconciling errors detected during testing is termed "debugging" the program.

6. The sixth task performed by the programmer is the preparation of special instructions which will link this one program to the other software (i.e., operating system, master program, monitor, etc.) which must be utilized during program execution time. These special linkage instructions are termed Job Control Language (JCL) instructions. In practice, the programmer must prepare JCL instructions in order to compile or test the program. However, the composition of the JCL's differ from the operating mode to the test mode. A "debugging" process is also required to achieve the proper JCL instructions for processing.

7. The final task performed by the programmer before the program is installed is to prepare the necessary written procedures which describe the activities to be performed by data center personnel (e.g. computer operators) in order to execute the program.

With this basic understanding of the programming function, we will now discuss the major form of communication between the systems analyst and the programmer, i.e., the program specifications. Figure 13.10 is an illustration of a table of contents for a program specification which also serves as a guide to our presentation.

Program Control Sheet

Figure 13.11 is an illustration of what we have chosen to call the Program Control Sheet. This part of the specifications package presents the programmer with all of the administrative information related to the program. This includes:

1. A program name and program identification number are provided. This might be completed as:

"Daily Update"   SA 1234
"Monthly Master File Purge"   093-B
"Check Printer"   Pay 110

2. In large organizations the system is also given an identification number in addition to a name. This number would then be used to allocate costs, for example.

3. The testing authorization number might also be used to assess charges or as a security measure.

4. "Completion Date Scheduled," and "Man-hours Scheduled" gives the programmer an idea of the schedule within which he or she is expected to complete the assignment.

5. "Assigned to" and "Approval" signatures are both control and security measures.

6. The remaining entries on the form are self-explanatory and are required for general administrative and security purposes.

Table of Contents

Specifications for Program _____

　　　　　Prepared by _____ Date _____

_____ Program Control Sheet
_____ Procedural Overview
_____ Systems Flow Chart
_____ File Descriptions
_____ Record Formats
_____ Report Formats
_____ Specific Record Logic
_____ General Logic
_____ Reference Tables
_____ Users Variables
_____ Processing Controls
_____ Test Data
_____ _____
_____ _____

FIGURE 13.10. Table of contents for a program specification package.

Program Control Sheet

Program Name _____ I.D. _____

Systems Name _____ I.D. _____

Testing Authorization Number _____

Completion Date Scheduled _____ Actual _____

Manhours Scheduled _____ Actual _____

Assigned to _____ Date _____

Approval _____ Date _____

Analysts Acceptance _____ Date _____

Operations Acceptance _____ Date _____

Modifications/Revisions

Date	Programmer Initials	Approval Initials	Revision Code
_____	_____	_____	_____
_____	_____	_____	_____
_____	_____	_____	_____
_____	_____	_____	_____
_____	_____	_____	_____

FIGURE 13.11. An illustration of a program control sheet.

Procedural Overview

Systems
Identification

Program
Identification

Procedural Flowchart

The Purpose of This Program

File Assignments

File I.D.	Status	Log Assg.	Phy Assg.	File I.D.	Status	Log Assg.	Phy Assg.

FIGURE 13.12.   An illustration of a program considered as a procedure.

Record Format

Record Name   Record I.D.   Record Length

File Name   File I.D.   Organization   Blocking Factor

Record Created in Program _____

Record Used in Programs _____

Field Description	Field Mnemonic	Field Position	Value/Comments

Latest Revision Date _____/_____/_____

FIGURE 13.13. An illustration of a vertical record format

Procedural Overview/Systems Flowchart

Figure 13.12 is an illustration of a form which gives the programmer an overview and quick understanding of a specific program's purpose and scope. "File Assignments" information is required as part of the program logic itself.

A systems flowchart may or may not be included in every package of specifications given to a programmer. It is desirable that this flowchart be available in at least one specification package for each system with which the programmer is involved.

Record Formats/Report Formats

Figure 13.13 illustrates one approach to formatting record layouts. Traditionally, record layouts have been provided in a horizontal format oftentimes resembling the media which is being used (e.g. 80 column cards, magnetic disks, and tapes). The vertical format illustrated here is more desirable for many reasons: (1) this layout does not require a special form; (2) this layout lends itself to being typed, which is desirable from a documentation viewpoint; and, (3) a change in field sizes or positions can be penciled in and given to a typist for correction, thus eliminating programmers having to spend exorbitant amounts of time redoing outdated documentation.

Logic, Tables, and User Variables

Up to this point we have been able to make use of special forms in order to describe the type of information that must be contained in program specifications. However, the narrative is probably the most universal method of describing the processing logic to be performed in a program, although, many analysts have begun describing complex logic via techniques such as decision tables, or even with specific flowcharts, where a particular sequence of logic is critical. (Refer to Appendix C.)

Reference tables refer to variable information that must be used at program execution time, and which is subject to a high level of modifications. Consequently, it is desirable that the table entries not be included within the program structure itself. Reference tables may or may not be loaded into core storage at execution time. Where constant data is required in many different programs, it can also be accessed from reference tables rather than coded into each program.

User variables are similar to reference tables, in that it is desirable not to include them within the program logic. Examples of user variables might be instructions as to what reports to prepare, what fields are to be used, and in what sequence reports are to be printed. This type of entry is important where programs have multiple processing and reporting capabilities.

Processing Controls

The analyst should always provide the programmer with a list of the controls which are to be implemented within the program. Many of the different controls which can be implemented into each program were discussed earlier in this chapter.

Test Data

Many analysts find it highly effective to provide a programmer with prepared test data. Test data is a series of system inputs which is used to ascertain whether or not the program is performing as planned. Using test data prepared by the analyst, or under the analyst's guidance, reduces the time a programmer must spend in achieving an error free program. It also minimizes the amount of time the analyst must spend reviewing test results in preparation for accepting a completed program.

SUMMARY

An important part of the overall design of an information system is the establishment of effective controls. During the specific design phase, the systems analyst must identify and implement a series of processing controls to ensure the integrity and reliability of the information system. These processing controls can be categorized as follows: (1) Input Controls, (2) Programming Controls, (3) Data Base Controls, (4) Output Controls, and (5) Hardware Controls.

Security, another form of control, must also be considered during the design of an information system. In large information systems there might be a group responsible for establishing security. More often, the systems analyst must implement many security controls into the system. Some security considerations include: (1) access to data files, (2) access to physical components, (3) transmission intervention, and (4) software disruption.

Procedures for recovery after intentional or unintentional disasters must be designed and implemented.

A third important activity during detail design is the design of all the forms and reports required in the information system. Forms can be categorized as inputs, outputs, or turnarounds. In order to design effective and economical forms, the analyst must perform an analysis of the form, identifying its purpose, distribution, and physical attributes.

Clerical procedures are formal descriptions of the activities to be performed by the human elements of the system. Program specifications are formal descriptions of the activities to be performed by the computer.

REVIEW QUESTIONS

13.1 List and describe the major categories of control, as related to the information system.

13.2 What are the costs attributable both directly and indirectly to clerical errors?

13.3 Give an example of four different input controls.

13.4 Give an example of at least five different programming controls.

13.5 List several control techniques related to the data base and describe how they operate.

13.6 What is the final control point in the information system? Explain.

13.7 What are hardware controls? What is their purpose? List and explain three different types of hardware controls used in computers. Can you identify at least one type of hardware control not discussed in this chapter?

13.8 In your own words, do you expect the concern for security related to data and information processing to increase/decrease in the future? Why?

13.9 What are the special security problems posed by the capability for teleprocessing as compared to conventional batch processing?

13.10 Describe the major types of forms which an analyst must design during the development of an information system.

13.11 What is forms analysis? What are the basic goals of forms analysis? List at least ten points to be considered during forms design.

13.12 Distinguish between documentation in general and clerical procedures.

13.13 What are the three main reasons for preparing formal clerical procedures?

13.14 What is a procedure manual? What is the overall consideration related to the construction of a procedure manual?

13.15 In your own words, prepare a definition of program specifications.

13.16 List and explain the steps involved in writing a computer program.

13.17 What is the primary purpose of a program control sheet in a package of program specifications?

QUESTIONS FOR DISCUSSION

13.1 Give examples of control totals that can be used in the preparation of a payroll.

13.2 A master inventory file was destroyed by inadvertently writing over it by another processing run. What elementary control procedure was not used to prevent incorrect mounting of the file? What elementary item was not used to prevent the computer from writing on the wrong file? What method can the system use to recreate the file?

13.3 As long as the operator can mount the correct tape reel or disk pack by referring to its external label, why should it be necessary to also have internal header and trailer labels written on the files?

13.4 List at least 10 different types of processing controls which might be included in an inventory control system.

13.5 List some advantages of key-tape and key-disk devices as compared to a keypunch (refer to any journal related to data processing, programming, or systems in the library) from the aspect of improved control.

13.6 Describe how a master file of customer information can be used to provide control when processing orders.

13.7 List the advantages, from a control perspective, on the use of CRT's for input devices.

13.8 "We write the manual procedures after the programs have been implemented, if there is any time, that is." Comment.

13.9 "We never bother documenting our clerical procedures. In the past we have found this a quite expensive and one month after you are done, the documentation is obsolete." Evaluate.

13.10 "Yes, we have written procedures, books of them in fact. But what good are they? You can never find what you want anyway." Discuss fully.

13.11 "Program specifications? No we don't bother writing them. We find we can get our programmers working quicker if the analyst shows them the overall systems design and gives them the report formats. If a programmer has any questions about the logic, he can always ask the analyst." Comment on this statement.

13.12 "Equipment checks are more effective in ensuring the accuracy of processing than programmed control checks." Discuss the merits of this statement.

13.13 "Many control procedures in the information system are based on the principle of duplication." Discuss this comment.

13.14 "The extent and cost of implementing control procedures should be proportional to the vulnerability and risk of loss in the absence of such control procedures." Discuss the merits of this statement.

13.15 "Improved data entry devices must be evaluated not only according to what they do, but rather, according to how much less the computer will have to do in order to ensure accurate data." Evaluate this comment.

13.16 Discuss how most operating systems include various types of file protection controls.

13.17 "We verify everything that is input to our computer. Keypunching is cheap compared to rerunning jobs because of bad input." Evaluate this comment.

13.18 "Many users have become disenchanted with the computer because systems designers often fail to ensure the reliability of the systems performance with adequate control procedures." Discuss fully.

13.19 "Today, it is infrequent that we hear a programmer blame a systems problem on the hardware failing, and not detecting this failure. While this situation reflects a tremendous improvement in hardware today, it also indicates that most systems failures can be prevented during systems design." Explain.

13.20 "One sign that the computer has become an important resource in many organizations is the absence of viewing windows." Discuss.

13.21 "We document all programs after they are written and before they are accepted by the operations people." Discuss.

13.22 There appears to be a tendency among programmers (both student and professional) to consider themselves "almost done" when a compile is obtained. Based on our discussion of programming, comment on the validity of this feeling.

13.23 Give an example where security control procedures should be implemented in an information system.

13.24 List the procedures you might expect to find in a procedure manual describing a payroll system.

EXERCISES

13.1 In reviewing Appendix A, what management science techniques can be utilized by the programmer to provide processing control? Give an example for each technique identified.

13.2 Prepare a code using a check digit for each of five account numbers. Use a different modulus for each.

13.3 Write program instructions in any language of your choice (e.g. COBOL, FORTRAN) for each programmed control check listed in the chapter, with the exception of label checks.

13.4 From a current systems journal, describe what is meant by "Facsimile Transmission." How will this technique affect systems control considerations during the design phase?

13.5 During the past few years many states have implemented lottery systems as an alternative to raising or levying new taxes. The results from these lotteries have run the gamut from very disappointing to very good.

However, it appears that in states where the computer was utilized extensively in the lottery system, the results have been generally good. One of the most important advantages accruing from utilizing the computer is that the administrator of the lottery can implement extensive control procedures to minimize fraud and deception.

You are a systems analyst employed by a state which has decided to implement a lottery. Your assignment is to analyze the controls in the lottery system considered most successful to date. Below are three tickets which were purchased from the same lottery terminal. The only additional facts that you have at this time is that these tickets were printed on a central computer and manually distributed to the terminals.

Based on this information only, prepare a report describing the *possible* controls in the lottery systems operations.

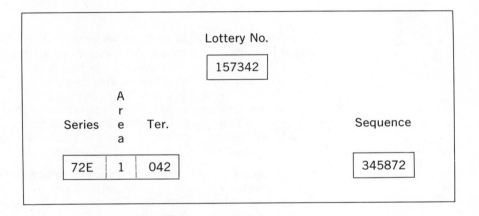

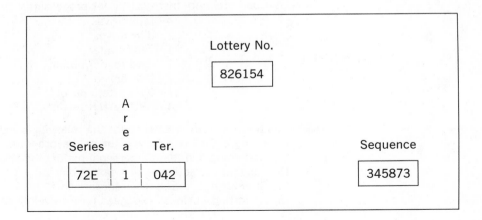

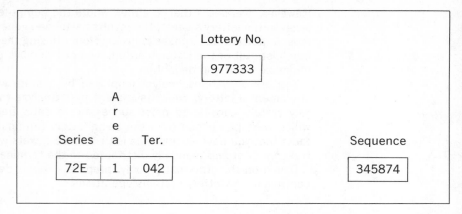

13.6 Secure copies of procedures for several of the following activities and prepare a critique of how each procedure was written.
  (1) Your state's requirements for reporting an automobile accident.
  (2) Registering for classes at your college.
  (3) Purchasing a house in your community.
  (4) Seeking unemployment compensation in your state.
  (5) Seeking university supported housing.
  (6) Obtaining a marriage license, automobile license, or fishing license.

13.7 To process a program on a computer correctly, requires that the computer operator be given specific instructions as to what peripherals are to be used, where input data are placed, and where output data are placed. These instructions are normally prepared by the programmer.

Assuming the following computer configuration, prepare a general procedure (with forms if desirable) to be used by any programmer in providing a computer operator with instructions for processing a program.

        4   tape drives
        2   disk drives
        1   card reader
        1   card reader/punch
        1   printer
        1   typewriter console
        4   CPU switch settings

13.8 Prepare a written procedure for the following situations:
  (1) Using a CRT or teletype for online programming at your school.
  (2) Recording a student's personal history for college entrance.
  (3) Logging the activities of a taxi cab.
  (4) Submitting a purchase order in a small manufacturing plant.
  (5) Reporting business expenses for a traveling salesman.

PROBLEMS **13.1** A bank in Pittsburgh, Pa. must relocate its data processing facilities, within the next 2 years, due to anticipated growth and the concomitant need for more physical space. Four possible sites for the new computer center are being evaluated: (1) the ground floor of the main office in the center of town which has recently been renovated with exterior walls of plate glass; (2) the basement of the same building cited in alternative (1) above; (3) the twelfth floor of the same building described in alternative (1); and (4) an old, converted warehouse about 2 miles from the main office at the edge of the business district.

Considering the aspect of overall security, evaluate each of the alternatives described and rank them in order of most desirable to least desirable. Support your conclusions.

13.2 Investigate the security procedure(s) for accessing the computer at your school. After completing your study, either describe the strengths and weaknesses of the procedure or suggest a possible improvement or elimination to the overall procedure. Support and document your position.

13.3 A steel products fabricator in the midwest is in the process of installing a computer based order entry system. Upon receipt, customers' orders will be coded and batched for processing on an hourly basis. The orders will be maintained on a magnetic tape, where it will provide the means for producing shipping papers, invoices, and, later, sales statistics. Because of this significant impact on all stages of the company's operations, the analyst has designed an extensive validation process early in the processing of customer orders. A customer master file exists on magnetic tape which contains a customer code, name and address, salesman identification, credit limit, and special shipping instructions for all approved customers. Similarly, a product master file exists on magnetic disk which contains the product number, market price, cost, unit of measure, current inventory amount, and miscellaneous information concerning weight, size, volume, etc., for all approved products.

Identify a control scheme which could be implemented through programming to ensure only valid orders were processed through the order entry system.

13.4 A bank has decided to utilize a check digit, on checking account numbers, to minimize the possibility of errors in posting account activity. The present code structure is composed of six numeric digits. Develop the procedure for arriving at a check digit, using two different moduli.

13.5 An inventory control system servicing 10 auto parts stores is operated in an online mode. As supplies are received the status of the inventory is updated. In addition, as various stores request the withdrawal of items their status is reduced. The inventory status is maintained on a magnetic disk. The file is accessible from 6 A.M. to Midnight seven days a week. Define a file backup procedure as part of the overall security program for this system.

13.6 The marketing department is planning a special sales promotion for the Fall. This program involves a certain trade class of customers who will be given a special 1% discount on all products they purchase if they purchase a certain group of products, and promote them with advertisements in newspapers or magazines. The promotion will last one year. However, the special discount will be paid each quarter for sales which qualify in that quarter. Each customer in the designated trade class will be given an opportunity to participate in the promotion. The company, through its salesmen, must verify that the customer advertised the required products each quarter before the special discount will be paid.

The information system maintains sales history by product for each customer in time increments of a month for a total of two years. In addition, this file contains customer account number, trade class, name, and address. A check writing system is also available to prepare checks from data stored in the data base.

The sales manager has expressed a desire to have a complete control reporting package for this promotion. Your assignment is to analyze the above notes and prepare a proposal for a series of control reports to present to the sales manager. (Note: The earliest control report could show all the customers who are eligible for the promotion. Another control report might show the customers who have received their special discount as evidenced by a cancelled check being returned.)

13.7 Prepare the program specifications required to produce at least one of the control reports identified in Problem 13.6 above.

13.8 You are called in as a systems consultant for a small enterprise. This enterprise is concerned with manufacturing a small line of women's bath accessories. They purchase about 500 different raw materials, labels, and cartons. They produce approximately 70 different items for sale. In general, their manufacturing operations include the following: (1) pouring the contents of specific gallon bottles into 4, 6, 10, and 12 oz. bottles; (2) labeling the filled bottles; and (3) packaging various types of liquids, soaps, and brushes into designated containers. As a rule, the enterprise orders raw materials upon receipt of a customer's order.

They have requested you to design, develop, and implement a simple inventory control system which would have the following attributes: (1) keep track of customer orders received, (2) keep track of inventory on hand, and (3) keep track of purchase orders issued

Although they have no formal inventory system today, they have been offered the use of a small computer in a local service bureau if they desire to implement a computer based inventory system. This computer has 16,000 bytes of primary memory, a card reader, a card punch, a 300 LPM (lines per minute) printer, and four tape drives.

First, design a system to meet the stated needs. Second, write the manual procedures required in this system. Third, prepare the program specifications to satisfy the system design.

BIBLIOGRAPHY

Allen, "Danger Ahead! Safeguard Your Computer," *Harvard Business Review,* November–December, 1968.

Bates, "Security of Computer-based Information Systems," *Datamation,* May, 1970.

"Computer Security: Backup and Recovery Methods," *EDP Analyzer,* January, 1972.

Enger, *Putting MIS to Work,* New York: American Management Association, Inc., 1969.

Exton, "Clerical Errors: Their Cost and Cure," *The Office,* December, 1970.

Gray and London, *Documentation Standards,* Philadelphia: Auerbach Publishers, 1969.

Menkus, "Designing a Useful Form," *Business Graphics,* September, 1972.

Reider, "Safeguarding Computer Records," *Management Controls,* October, 1972.

Rubin (ed.), *Advanced Technology—System Concepts,* Volume 5, Philadelphia: Auerbach Publishers, 1971.

"Security of the Computer Center," *EDP Analyzer,* December, 1971.

Synders, "Forms Design Shapes Data Costs," *Business Automation,* December, 1968.

Tiede, "21 Ways to Save Money on Forms," *Information and Records Management,* June–July, 1968.

14

Systems Implementation

14.1 Introduction

In the previous chapter, many of the specific design activities necessary for the development of an information system were discussed. In order to implement the new system successfully, there are a few activities which must be performed by the systems analyst which are not generally classified as design work, per se. These activities involve the training and educating of personnel, and the testing of the system. Moreover, because a new system must be implemented into the dynamic environment of an organization, there is a special consideration, termed systems conversion, required to achieve this implementation. Finally, the efforts of the systems analyst do not end with the implementation of the system. An implementation follow-up is often vital to the eventual acceptance of the system. Each of these subjects is discussed in this chapter.

The final activities required to implement a new system are illustrated on page 345.

344

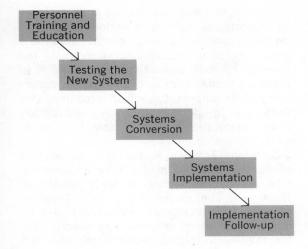

Personnel
Training and
Education

Testing the
New System

Systems
Conversion

Systems
Implementation

Implementation
Follow-up

14.2 Training and Educating Personnel

It has been emphasized repeatedly throughout this text that the key ingredient in every system is people. People design, develop, operate, and maintain the system, and they utilize the output generated by the system. If a new information system is to be implemented successfully, then everyone who is affected by the system must be made aware first, of their individual responsibilities to the system, and second, what the system provides to that person. The prime responsibility for effecting this educational process rests with the systems analyst.

In our analysis of the training and education of personnel we will discuss: (1) the types of personnel requiring training or education, (2) the various approaches to educating and training, and (3) some general considerations in choosing a training approach.

Training and Educating Categories

We can identify two broad categories of personnel who must receive some type of education and/or training concerning the new system.

Users of Information. This category of personnel includes general management, staff specialists, and the operating personnel in the various functional areas. These personnel include salesmen, accountants, production schedulers, and so forth. In addition, this category might also include customers, vendors, government officials, and the constituents of the organization. It is generally termed "education" when the information users are informed of what the system requires and provides. The educational process for many members of this group actually begins in the analysis phase when they identified their informational requirements. The emphasis at this later point in development is directed toward explaining how these requirements are to be met by the system.

Providing this kind of education is often minimized or overlooked during the implementation of a system for many different reasons. The systems analyst who has spent nearly every day for several months thinking about and working with the new system, fails to realize that most of the potential users of the system have spent relatively little time thinking about the new system. On the other hand, when plans are presented to management by systems personnel for what appears to be massive educational efforts, they are often reduced or eliminated on the grounds of being too expensive. Although it is fairly easy to calculate the costs of providing education, it is often quite difficult to identify the benefits of such education; or, the costs incurred when resources, such as information, are not utilized due to lack of understanding. The first problem identified can be corrected by systems analysts who recognize the need, and plan for, user education as part of the system's implementation process. The systems analyst can also overcome the second problem by the preparation of well thought out educational plans that are presented to management as part and parcel of the systems implementation process.

Operating Personnel. This category of personnel includes all of the individuals involved in preparing input, processing data, and in operating and maintaining both the logical and physical components. It also includes those persons responsible for direct control over the system. Generally, we call their educational process "training." Training operating personnel has two dimensions which must be considered by the analyst. First, operating personnel must be trained initially to run the new system. Second, training must be provided to this general category of personnel on a continual basis as the system is modified, or as new personnel are required. The importance of recognizing this second aspect of training will become better understood as we discuss the various methods which might be used to provide acceptable training when the system is initially implemented.

Approaches to Educating and Training Personnel

Psychologists and educators have demonstrated that different educational and training objectives call for a variety of educational and training approaches. A lecture is appropriate to generally explain to a group of users how the new system operates whereas a "learn-by-doing approach" might be used to train new operations personnel. On the other hand, a large number of people can perform any given job satisfactorily after they have performed that job once or a relatively few number of times. Consequently, to successfully provide people with education and training regarding the use and operations of a new system, the analyst must utilize many different approaches. These approaches include:

1. *Seminars and Group Instruction.* The use of this approach allows the analyst to reach many people at one time. This approach is particularly useful when the analyst is presenting an overview of the system. Additionally, this approach is worthwhile in large organizations where many people perform the same tasks.

2. *Procedural Training.* This approach provides an individual with the written procedures, describing his or her activities, as the primary

method of learning. Usually the individual has an opportunity to ask questions and pose problems concerning the procedure, either in a group session or individually, to complete the training. An extension of this technique is to provide a formal write-up of the system, particularly of the outputs, to each affected user. Use of the mail to inform information users outside of the organization is another example of procedural instruction.

3. *Tutorial Training.* As the term implies, this approach to training is of a more personal nature and, consequently, is fairly expensive. However, in conjunction with other training approaches, this technique can eliminate any remaining void which prevents a satisfactory understanding. In systems where certain tasks are highly complex or particularly vital to successful operations, tutorial training may be necessary to achieve the desired results. In practice, the analyst provides personal training or education not only to operating personnel, but also to users of the system's outputs.

4. *Simulation.* An important training technique for operating personnel is to use a simulated work environment. This can be achieved relatively easily by reproducing data, procedures and any required equipment, and allowing the individual to perform the proposed activities until an acceptable level of performance is achieved. Although simulation seems to be an expensive method to establish, actual performances usually result in less errors and rework when the individual is later placed in an operating environment.

5. *On the Job Training.* Perhaps the most widely used approach to training operating personnel is to simply put them to work. Usually the individual is assigned simple tasks and given specific instructions as to what is to be done and how it is to be done. As these initial tasks are mastered, additional tasks are assigned. The learning curve in this approach can be quite lengthy and, in many cases, what appears to be immediate results or production can be very expensive. Moreover, if a particular operation is highly complex, the individual may become frustrated and resign.

General Considerations when Choosing Training Approaches

The analyst's primary objective during the systems development is to provide training to existing personnel in order to implement the new system. However, careful planning at this time, can result in a meaningful training mechanism which can be utilized by the organization on a continual basis. This is important since employee turnover is expensive and affects all levels in the organization. When a training approach is chosen with both objectives in mind, the analyst will not hesitate to construct more expensive aids and programs for this initial requirement. For example, full scale training sessions, simulated facilities, and learning manuals such as Programmed Instruction courses, can rarely be justified for a one time effort. The real benefit to constructing these mechanisms lies in their use on a continual basis.

A second consideration along the same lines might be termed direct versus indirect training. Once a system is implemented, the systems analyst is often reassigned to an entirely new area of the organization. Consequently the analyst is not available to assist with the systems day-to-day problems with either operating personnel or users. In order to ensure that these problems can be satisfactorily addressed and resolved, the analyst can take a more indirect role during initial training. In other words, a select group of supervisors might be trained in the areas of data preparation and operations and allowed to conduct individual training for both clerical workers and user personnel. With this approach the analyst is rapidly removed from all but the exceptional problems related to the system. In most organizations this approach is highly desirable. The failure of many analysts in using this technique seems to be related to what we might term "pride of ownership." Having spent many long hours during the developmental phases, the analyst is quite often reluctant to give up this last minute control over the new system.

One final note is in order concerning the training activity. Oftentimes, without thinking, an analyst will begin to provide training starting with a single task and moving from task to task until the whole job has been presented. However, it is generally recognized that if individuals are provided with an initial overview, they can better relate to the significance of each task and activity which is required of them. Regardless of which approach is finally selected to accomplish the education and training of personnel, the effort should begin with the presentation of an overview.

14.3 Testing the System

As developmental efforts near completion, it is normal for individuals closely associated with the new system to have a strong desire to implement part or all of the system into the mainstream of the organization's operations. In order to attain this implementation successfully, however, the analyst must ensure that the system will perform as designed. Testing the system is an implementation activity that, similar to training personnel, requires careful planning on the part of the systems analyst. In this section, we will identify the various levels at which testing can occur, the different types of testing that can be performed, and the growing importance of testing new information systems.

Levels of Testing

The proper testing of a newly developed information system must be done at several levels within the system. Figure 14.1 illustrates the various levels of testing which should be conducted before a system is implemented.

Testing a logic module is usually the responsibility of a programmer. This activity is the most specific level of testing. Examples of testing a logic module are: checking to see if all input transactions are accounted for, checking to see if a specific transaction updates a master file correctly, checking to see if the page header prints on each page, and checking to

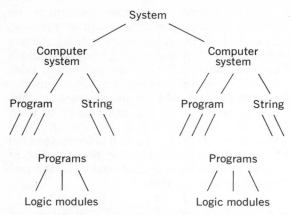

FIGURE 14.1. An illustration of the various levels of testing.

see if all files are closed at the end of processing.

Program testing is also usually the responsibility of the programmer. Similar to the testing of a logic module, the programmer checks to see if the desired output is produced accurately by the program and that all housekeeping chores (e.g., opening, closing files) are executed as planned.

String testing refers to testing two or more programs which process sequentially to one another and, therefore, are contingent on each other for successful operation. A string of programs might include the validation pass, the file maintenance programs or the file updating programs. The responsibility for string testing might fall to one individual, such as the systems analyst, or it might be shared by the programmers affected.

Testing the computer system means testing all of the programs to be implemented in support of the system. All of the various computer inputs are prepared and processed in order to produce the desired outputs. The outputs are checked for accuracy and reliability. This level of testing, again, is usually a shared responsibility, but is coordinated by the systems analyst or a lead programmer.

Systems testing differs from the previous level of testing because all of the supporting clerical procedures are included. An event

occurs and it is recorded, prepared for processing, processed, errors are resolved, master file maintenance is prepared and submitted, the data base is updated, and reports are prepared. Any discrepancies noted in the outputs or in the data base are tracked back through the processing steps until the problem is defined and resolved. It is as likely that a clerical procedure is in error as it is that a computer program is in error.

Types of Testing

There are five broad categories of testing the system which can be performed at each level of testing. Figure 14.2 identifies these categories and indicates their positions relative to cost of preparation and level of reliability.

Simulated logical testing refers to the programmer or analyst testing the system by tracing through the program(s) or system with a mental representation of a transaction. Programmers refer to this method as "desk checking." The systems analyst is continually using this approach as the system is being designed. Its primary advantage is that it is accomplished at almost no cost. The largest disadvantage is that it provides a relatively low level of reliability.

The use of random data refers to the analyst or programmer preparing a series of transactions with the primary intent of seeing if a program will execute, or go to the end of the job. Again, this method is relatively inexpensive but also provides a low degree of reliability.

The third type of testing uses "live" data,

Considerations Type of Testing	Cost of Preparation	Level of Reliability
Simulated Logical	Very low	Low
Random	Low	Low
Live	Medium	Medium
Production	High	Medium-high
Controlled	High	High

FIGURE 14.2. Comparison of types of testing.

that is, actual transactions are selected for processing. Usually, the programmer or analyst will ask the clerical group to submit a few transactions of each type of input. Since the input clerk is not likely to know at this point what the new system accepts and rejects, the input represents a random sampling but on a much larger scale. The advantage to using "live" data is its relatively inexpensive preparation cost, although this cost is usually greater than either of the previous methods cited. The degree of reliability associated with this method approaches the medium point, but still must be considered as a disadvantage.

The fourth method of testing is termed production testing. In this method all of the input is submitted for processing into the system. When the output is checked, if there are any errors in the system, they are corrected and the production test is rerun. If there are no errors identified in the system, the output is distributed to organizational users. The advantage is that this method of testing provides a medium to high degree of reliability and, at some point in time, actually provides the required outputs. The disadvantages are that preparing the input is expensive, checking the output is expensive, tracking the errors is expensive, and reruns of the system are expensive.

The fifth method of testing is called controlled testing. Controlled testing refers to the manner in which the input is prepared. Each type of input transaction is prepared for all of the permutations its data fields can include. This is done to ensure that the system works not only for the major valid processing steps but for the invalid and erroneous transactions also. As a rule, systems malfunction not because they cannot perform what they are designed to do but because they cannot handle invalid and extraordinary situations. The obvious advantage of controlled testing is that it provides a high degree of reliability to the installed system. A second advantage, which is not quite as obvious, is that the check out procedure is relatively quick and inexpensive. This results from the programmer or analyst knowing what they have input; therefore, they can then quickly check to see that the proper output is produced. The disadvantages to this method include a high cost of preparing input, and in most instances, it is impossible to test every permutation of every input transaction.

The Growing Importance of Testing

Testing, as a major development activity, is increasing in importance for a number of reasons.

1. The trend towards a higher degree of integration of systems within an organization requires each new system implemented to perform successfully initially, not only for its own purposes, but so as not to degrade other existing systems.

2. The increased dependency upon computer generated information, by all levels of users within the organization in their decision making and problem solving activities, relates the organization's performance directly to the systems performance.

3. Increased usage and familiarity with computer based systems has resulted in higher expectations by organizational users of the system.

4. The inflationary trend in the cost of other development activities can be reversed with improved testing procedures.

5. The investment in systems maintenance resources can be reduced with improved testing procedures before the system is installed.

In an attempt to improve the testing procedure for a system, the analyst must exercise a great deal of creativity. The involvement of user personnel during testing is one method being utilized in many organizations. Other organizations have developed, or have purchased, testing aids which, during systems testing, utilize the computer itself to detect potential shortcomings (or flaws) in the system.

14.4 Systems Conversion

The term conversion is used to describe the process of changing from one way of doing things to another way of doing things. When this term is applied to the information system in an organization, it describes the changing of specific activities related to collecting, storing, retrieving, and processing data, and the reporting of information. As we analyze this systems conversion process we can identify various types of conversions, different approaches to accomplishing the conversion, the special considerations required for the data base, and the importance of planning the conversion.

Types of Conversion

We can identify three general types of conversions with which the analyst should be familiar: (1) the equipment conversion, (2) the data processing method conversion, and (3) the procedural conversion.

The Equipment Conversion. This type of conversion involves replacing one piece of equipment with another; also included in this category might be the replacement of such equipment as typewriters, copiers, teletypes, and accounting machines. In the past, converting from one computer to another usually implied the rewriting or recompiling of existing programs which had to be processed on the new computer. This conversion did not necessarily mean changing the logic of the programs, although the logic could be affected; it was directed more toward putting the logic in a coding structure which was processable on the new computer. Today, however, computer conversions rarely require reprogramming. In many situations, the new computer or peripheral device is "plug to plug compatible" with the old equipment. In other words, the physical structure and operation of the new equipment has no effect on the logical operations of the programs. In other situations, the new equipment can be made to emulate the operations of the old equipment. These two improvements in equipment design have often resulted in an ability to obtain a faster or less expensive piece of equipment without the need to incur extensive conversion expense.

Manual Processing to:	Electromechanical Punched Card Computer
Electromechanical to:	Manual Punched Card Computer
Punched Card Processing to:	Manual Electromechanical Computer

FIGURE 14.3.   An illustration of the conversions which can occur among data processing methods.

The Data Processing Method Conversion. This type of conversion describes the changing from one method of processing data to another method of processing data. The possible conversions included in this classification are illustrated in Figure 14.3. As we discussed in Part I, early developments in data processing automation were directed toward replacing certain activities or groups of activities on a one-for-one basis. They were not intended to alter the overall design of the system. The initial approach to utilizing the computer was also to "automate" or "computerize" specific activities. Today, by utilizing the systems approach, the design of the information system requires much more than a simple data processing method conversion in most organizations. Usually there are extensive procedural changes also required with a data processing method conversion.

The Procedural Conversion. A procedural conversion can involve changing both the kinds of activities and the sequence in which the activities are performed. The procedures being converted can either be manual or automated (computer programs) procedures. A procedural conversion can be accomplished on its own or in conjunction with an equipment conversion or a data processing method conversion. For example, implementing a new input collection form or modifying and rewriting a computer program are simply procedural changes. Using a CRT device to input customer orders that were previously input through a keypunch, would probably involve both an equipment conversion and a procedural conversion.

With the implementation of a major subsystem of the information system, the analyst will more than likely be concerned with effecting all three types of conversions. Being able to logically relate the conversion activities according to the type of conversion it represents, can provide the analyst with valuable insights as to what approach must be taken with the organization's overall systems conversion.

Approaches to Systems Conversions

There are four basic approaches toward accomplishing the conversion of a new system: (1) Direct, (2) Parallel, (3) Modular, and (4) Phase-In. Figure 14.4 is a graphic representation of the four approaches to conversion.

1. *Direct Conversion.* A direct conversion is the implementation of the new system and the immediate discontinuance of the old system, sometimes called the "cold turkey" approach. This conversion approach is meaningful: (1) when the system is not replacing any other system, (2) when the old system is judged absolutely without value, (3) when the new system is either very small or simple, and (4) when the

design of the new system is drastically different from the old system and comparisons between systems would be meaningless. The primary advantage to this approach is that it is relatively inexpensive. The primary disadvantage to this approach is that it involves a high risk of failure. When direct conversion is to be utilized, the systems testing activity discussed in the previous section takes on even greater importance.

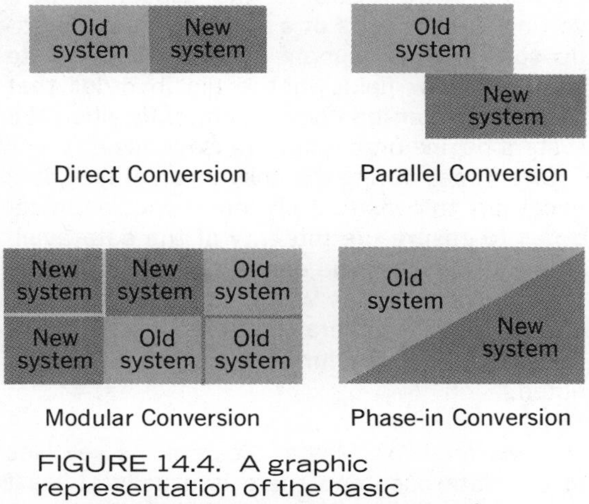

2. *Parallel Conversion.* Parallel conversion describes an approach which operates both the old and the new system simultaneously for some period of time. The outputs from each system are compared and differences reconciled. The advantage to this approach is that it provides a high degree of protection to the organization from a failure in the new system. The obvious disadvantages to this approach are the costs associated with duplicating the facilities and personnel to maintain the dual systems. Due to the high fatality rate experienced by organizations in the past when a new system was implemented, this approach to conversion has gained widespread popularity and usage. When the conversion process of a system includes parallel operations, the analyst should plan for periodic reviews with operating personnel and users concerning the performance of the new system and designate a reasonable expectant date for acceptance of the new system and discontinuance of the old system.

3. *Modular Conversion.* Modular conversion, sometimes termed the "pilot approach," refers to the implementation of a system into the organization on a piecemeal basis. For example, an order entry system could be installed in one sales region where it is proved out, and then installed in a second sales region, etc. An inventory system might be another example. The inventory system might be converted with only a selected product grouping; or with all products, but in only one location of a multiple location organization. The advantages to this approach are: (1) the risk of a system's failure is localized, (2) the problems identified in the system can be corrected before further implementation is attempted, and (3) other operating

FIGURE 14.4. A graphic representation of the basic approaches to systems conversion.

personnel can be trained in a "live" environment before the system is implemented at their location. One disadvantage to this approach is that the conversion period for the organization can be extremely lengthy. More importantly, this approach is not always feasible for a particular system or organization.

4. *Phase-in Conversion.* The phase-in approach is similar to the modular approach. However, this approach differs from the modular conversion in that the system itself is segmented, and not the organization. For example, the new data collection activities are implemented and an interface mechanism with the old system is developed. This interface allows the old system to operate with the new input data. Later, the new data base access, storage, and retrieval activities are implemented. Once again, an interface mechanism with the old system is developed. Each segment of the new system is installed until the entire system is implemented. Each time a new segment is added an interface with the old system must be developed. The advantages to this approach are: (1) the rate of change in a given organization can be minimized, (2) an integrated information system can be implemented over a lengthy time period and within a minimum budget, and (3) data processing resources can be acquired gradually over an extended period of time. The disadvantages to this approach include: (1) the costs incurred to develop temporary interfaces with old systems, (2) limited applicability, and (3) a demoralizing atmosphere in the organization of "never completing a system."

Data Base Considerations During Systems Conversion

The success of a system conversion depends to a great degree upon how well the systems analyst prepares for the creation and conversion of the data files required for the new system. This preparation is of particular importance in an organization where the information system has a high degree of integration through its data base. In some large organizations where an integrated information system exists, the analyst may work closely with the data base administrator to prepare for file creation and conversion. However, for our purposes, we will assume that the systems analyst must make all preparations for the systems conversion.

By creating a file, we mean simply that data is collected and organized in some recognizable format on a given storage medium. By converting a file, we mean that an existing file must be modified in at least one of three ways: (1) in the format of the file, (2) in the content of the file, and (3) in the storage medium where the file is located. It is quite likely in a systems conversion that some files can experience all three aspects of conversion simultaneously.

When creating a file which is to be processed on the computer, it is sometimes necessary to provide special start-up software which defines and labels a specific physical or logical storage location for the file. This process is referred to as creating a "dummy" file. Once the "dummy" file is created, the new system will process and store the designated data in this file.

When converting a file which must be processed on the computer, special start-up software is also required. This software contains logic which permits existing data to be input in the old format, or on the old medium; and output in the new format, or on the new medium. With regard to the aspect of converting the contents of a file, the special start-up software may simply initialize (e.g., set to zero) the new fields in the file in order that these fields can be updated correctly when the system begins processing transactions.

Oftentimes during the conversion of files, it is necessary to construct elaborate control procedures to ensure the integrity of the data available for use after the conversion. Utilizing the classification of files which was introduced in Part II, several general observations pertinent to each type of file during a conversion can be noted:

1. *Master Files.* Master files are the key files in the data base and there is usually at least one master file to be created or converted in

every system conversion. When an existing master file must be converted for the new system, the analyst should arrange for a series of hash and control totals to be matched between all the fields in the old file, and all the same fields in the converted file, to ensure that the conversion was executed properly. Special file backup procedures should be implemented for each separate processing step. This precaution is to prevent having to unnecessarily restart the conversion, from the beginning, in the event an error is discovered in the conversion logic at a later date. Timing considerations, when converting master files, are extremely important, particularly in online systems. If the converted file is not to be implemented immediately after conversion, special provisions must be made to keep track of any update activity occurring between the time of conversion and the time of implementation. In systems where data management functions are performed by individual application programs, the analyst must assure that each program that accesses the converted file has also been modified to accept the new format and/or medium.

2. *Transaction Files.* Transaction files are usually created by the processing of an individual subsystem within the information system, and can consequently be thoroughly checked during systems testing. However, the transaction files generated in areas of the information system other than the new subsystem may have to be converted, if the master files they update have been converted in format or media.

3. *Index Files.* Index files contain the keys or addresses which link various master files. Therefore, new index files must be created when their related master files have undergone a conversion which has invalidated the keys and addresses in the index files.

4. *Table Files.* Table files can also be created and converted during the systems conversion. The same considerations required of master files are applicable to table files.

5. *Summary Files.* Summary files are created during the processing of the new system in a manner similar to transaction files. Summary files created in other areas of the information system, however, do not usually have to be converted when a new subsystem is implemented.

6. *Archival Files.* Archival files are another category of files similar to master files. The considerations which apply to master files during the system conversion are applicable to archival files with two exceptions: (1) the timing considerations are not as severe with archival files as they are with master files, even in an online mode of processing; and (2) the volume of data records in archival files are usually far greater than that contained in master files.

7. *Backup Files.* The purpose for backup files is to provide security for the information system in the event of a processing error, or a disaster in the data center. Therefore, when a file is converted, or created, it is necessary also to create a backup file. The backup procedures for the converted file will more than likely be the same as the procedures which existed for the original file. The one exception to this statement might be where a change in file media was accomplished. For example, a card file which was previously backed up by another card file, when converted to magnetic disk or tape would probably be backed up on disk or tape also.

Determining which files are to be created or converted when a new system is implemented, and how these files will be created and converted, are part of the thinking process which is required to prepare a conversion plan.

Planning the Conversion

Although a system may be well designed and properly developed, a major part of its success is contingent on how well the conversion is executed. When a new system produces information that is inaccurate, or untimely, due to certain activities within the system not being performed as designed, it can create a stigma which remains long after the problems have been resolved. To avoid the creation of a "credibility gap" between a new system and the users of the system's outputs, the systems analyst must plan the systems conversion carefully.

In practice, the conversion plan is usually developed in two stages, which we can term simply: a broad plan, and a specific plan. As we indicated previously, the broad conversion plan dictates the scheduling of the systems work performed during the systems development phase. The specific conversion plan, prepared during the last stages of testing, identifies any special start-up procedures for personnel, the plan and schedule for file creation and conversion, establishment of acceptance criteria, and any special start-up control procedures. Figure 14.5 illustrates the relationship of the conversion plans to the developmental and implementation activities.

Preparing formal plans for executing the systems conversion is another vital communication task for the systems analyst. It is important that the management of the organization fully understand the approach that is to be taken for systems conversion. As a rule, the analyst's recommendations to the approach will be carefully weighed with other organizational commitments, and activities, which are also due, or planned, during the same time period. The preparation of carefully thoughtout conversion plans that are communicated to (and understood by) all affected personnel in the organization, will help to ensure a successful systems implementation.

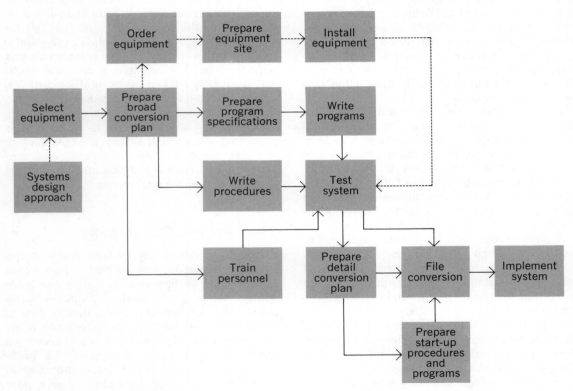

FIGURE 14.5 A scheduling chart illustrating the relative position of the conversion planning activities as they relate to the systems development and implementation activities.

14.5 Follow-Up to Implementation

Once the new system has been implemented, the systems analyst's participation does not necessarily end. In Chapter 15, many of the continuing activities performed by systems analysts during the life of a system are discussed. At this time, we will simply highlight the many different tasks the systems analyst must perform in the time period immediately following the implementation.

At first, he or she should check regularly that input, processing, and output schedules are being met. After it appears that a routine has been established, these checks can become less regular and directed only towards any trouble spots which can be identified.

Input preparation personnel (e.g., key punchers, order entry clerks) activities should be reviewed periodically. There is a high probability that some manual procedures will need additional clarification. A programming bug might be identified which requires immediate resolution. On occasion, certain procedures, manual or computer, might be identified as being somewhat inefficient, and a minor change will eliminate a bottleneck situation in the systems operations.

Perhaps the most important follow-up activity the analyst performs is to verify that the systems controls are functioning properly. In some instances where a large system is implemented, many input errors are initially processed into the system without detection. Usually, an efficient file maintenance mechanism for large quantities of errors does not exist. During the learning period, the analyst can assist the operations of the system either by providing a quick method for the reconciliation of errors, or by recommending to the appropriate supervisors where additional clerical support is required.

One problem the analyst will have during the follow-up period is distinguishing between suggestions for improvements and additional "niceties" in the system, and the identification of actual systems problems. During the education of systems users, the analyst should explain that when the information outputs are initially reviewed, the primary emphasis at that time will be placed on correcting errors. Other suggestions for improvements to the system are welcomed and encouraged; however, these suggestions will be compiled and evaluated after implementation is completed. In this way, all output users will be given an opportunity to be heard and further improvements to the system can be effectively implemented in total, as they relate to specific subsystems (or modules) of the new system. Without this distinction, the implementation activity of the system will continue indefinitely.

A final activity that the analyst might perform during the follow-up period is to remove all out-dated and start up procedures, programs, forms, etc., which were part of the old system or conversion effort. This action will eliminate the possibility of someone ever inadvertently referring to (or using) the wrong procedure or program.

An acceptance meeting should be held by the systems analyst, systems operating management, and user personnel, at which time there is an official termination of the developmental project. At this point, the systems analyst becomes available for a new developmental assignment.

SUMMARY

People are the key ingredient in any system. Providing adequate education and training both initially, and on a continual basis, is absolutely essential if a system is to achieve its objective.

Testing the system is the final activity before implementation. In reality, testing occurs at many levels within a system, with the highest level being systems testing. There are many different approaches available for testing. These approaches reflect a trade-off between the cost of preparing a test and the reliability obtained from the testing activity. Testing is becoming a more important activity in the implementation of a new system.

The implementation of many new systems involves a conversion process from an existing system. The conversion process can include one or more considerations: (1) an equipment conversion, (2) a data processing method conversion, or (3) a procedural conversion. There are four basic approaches to conversion: (1) direct, (2) parallel, (3) modular, and (4) phase in. The data base requires special considerations during the conversion process.

Planning is an important aspect of conversion. Generally, a broad conversion plan is prepared before specific design and developmental activities begin. A specific conversion plan is prepared shortly before the actual implementation of the new system.

Once the system has been implemented, the systems analyst serves in a consultant role. Immediately after implementation the analyst is available to assist operations and user personnel in understanding the new system, and in the solving of any identified problems.

REVIEW QUESTIONS

14.1 For whom must the systems analyst provide training and education before implementing a new or modified system? Give at least two practical examples of each personnel category as they relate to: (a) an inventory control system, (b) a manufacturing budget system, (c) a payroll system, and (d) an order entry/billing system.

14.2 List and explain the major considerations related to choosing a training approach.

14.3 Compare and contrast the major approaches to the education and training of systems users and operations personnel.

14.4 What is the purpose of testing in the development of a system? Distinguish the various levels at which testing can be performed.

14.5 Compare and contrast the various types of testing the analyst can utilize.

14.6 Why does the testing of newly developed information systems promise to be more important in the future?

14.7 What is the systems conversion? What are the basic types of conversion?

14.8 Compare and contrast the four approaches to systems conversion.

14.9 How is the data base affected during systems conversion? Be specific.

14.10 What is the primary importance for preparing a broad systems conversion plan? A specific plan? In which plan is the conversion approach selected?

14.11 Describe the major activities performed by the systems analyst as a follow-up to the implementation of a new system.

14.12 What is the importance of an acceptance meeting?

QUESTIONS FOR DISCUSSION

14.1 Discuss the merit of using operating procedures as training manuals.

14.2 Explain how you would prepare for training personnel in a department which annually experiences a turnover rate of over 10%; 40%; 80%.

14.3 "We spend about $20,000 annually preparing formal presentations for management to explain new or modified systems. This investment is returned many times over by the enthusiastic support most of our new systems receive from management." Discuss.

14.4 "We spent a lot of money hiring clerks to prepare special reports for us before we found out that many of these reports were available from our system. Apparently my predecessor didn't request copies when the system was implemented originally." Comment.

14.5 Excerpt from a programmer's standards manual: "Each programmer is responsible for testing the programs they have written. The project leader is responsible for testing the system in its entirety." Evaluate this statement.

14.6 "Desk checking is a waste of my time. I would rather let the computer test my programs." Discuss the pro's and con's of this statement.

14.7 "I don't care how much testing a programmer performs on a program, the first time they try real data, they receive a surprise." Comment.

14.8 "The costs associated with performing corrective maintenance on an operating system correlates with whether or not the system was tested using controlled data." Discuss the implications of this statement.

14.9 "The file conversion was going along smoothly until we discovered one of the special programs we wrote for the conversion was putting garbage into part of the record. We had to rerun the entire 18 hours of processing, although the error occurred in the last two hours or so." Discuss.

14.10 "We never completely finish installing a system." Evaluate.

14.11 Follow-up activities are seldom found in an installation plan. What reasons might there be for not planning follow-up?

14.12 What is a test deck? What is its purpose? What conditions are checked with a test deck?

14.13 "One really important advantage to this new computer is that it requires no reprogramming to process your existing programs." Comment.

14.14 "Never implement a new system without a period of parallel operations with the old system." Discuss the rationale behind this statement.

14.15 "They have been implementing the new sales reporting system for three years now." What reason might have prompted this statement?

14.16 "We will not be able to implement the new payroll system for three more months. Although all the reporting programs have been tested, we still have to write the data collection programs." How might this situation have been avoided, at least in part?

EXERCISES **14.1** Select a systems design that you prepared, for an exercise or problem, in an earlier chapter in this text and prepare a presentation for your classmates explaining your design. Have each student prepare a critique of your presentation. Analyze the critiques and submit a two or three page evaluation of your presentation.

14.2 Select a relatively easy operation (e.g. putting a ball point pen together, tying your shoe, construction of a paper airplane, etc.). Prepare a formal write-up describing this operation step by step from beginning to end. Select three fellow students in your class. Give one student your formal instructions and ask him to perform the activity. Instruct the second student verbally as to how the operation is to be performed. Let the third student read your formal instructions and assist him verbally as required. Prepare a brief report analyzing your results with each student.

14.3 Analyze the following situations. Which approach to systems conversion would you probably recommend for each? Explain fully your recommendation.

(1) Implementing a check deposit system utilizing OLRT (online real time) devices into a bank with 40 area branches.
(2) Implementing an inventory control system for 50,000 items at two warehouses.
(3) Implementing a centralized order entry system servicing 40 sales offices.
(4) Implementing a sales statistics system to be accessed by CRT devices
(5) Implementing a computer based lottery system, with 250 ticket offices and remote batch entry.
(6) Implementing a computer based accounts receivable system where a manual system existed previously.
(7) Implementing an integrated system that includes, order entry, inventory control, accounts receivable, sales statistics, and product forecasting, into a multiple plant organization with sales of more than $100,000,000.

PROBLEMS   **14.1** An employee time card contains the following data:

Field	Length	Comment
1. Employee number	6	(1) Must be numeric. (2) Table of valid employee numbers available.
2. Department worked in	2	(1) Must be numeric. (2) Table of valid department numbers available.
3. Regular hours worked	1	(1) Must be numeric. (2) Must be 8 or less.
4. Overtime hours worked	2	(1) Must be numeric. (2) Valid only if regular hours $= 8$. (3) Must be $1 - 16$.
5. Total hours worked	2	(1) Must be numeric. (2) Must equal $3 + 4$.

This time card is punched daily and submitted to the computer for processing. Only time cards with all valid data are accepted for input. An edit is performed on the data fields to check their validity at the time of input.

Your assignment is to construct a test deck with each input record to test that the edit is functioning correctly for each separate control. How many data records are required in the test deck?

14.2 Leather Furniture, Inc. is converting a manual accounts receivable system into a computer based system. The present manual system has the following characteristics: (1) a copy of all invoices and credits issued is placed in a folder for each customer; (2) when a remittance is received, it is matched to an open document and then placed in a file called "current closed" which in turn is purged every six months; (3) a "permanent closed" file is maintained for a period of seven years; (4) each month the "open file" is tallied and dated by a clerk; (5) the "current closed" is accessed periodically at the request of the credit manager or a customer; and, (6) the "permanent closed" file is accessed only rarely.

The new system is to contain three files: (1) a customer master, (2) an open item, and (3) a closed item. The first two files will be stored on magnetic disk, while the third file will be stored on magnetic tape.

Assume you were responsible for the conversion of the old system to the new system. Please answer the following questions:

(1) What type of systems conversion is required?
(2) What approach to systems conversion would you recommend?
(3) What special clerical procedures might be required during systems conversion?
(4) What type of special programming would be required for the systems conversion?
(5) How would you control or ensure that the systems conversion was successful?
(6) What critical timing considerations would have to be determined?

BIBLIOGRAPHY   Kanter, *Management Guide to Computer Systems Selection and Use,* Englewood Cliffs, N.J.: Prentice-Hall, Inc., 1970.

Li, *Accounting, Computers, Management Information Systems,* New York: McGraw-Hill Book Co., 1968.

Murdick and Ross, *Information Systems for Modern Management,* Englewood Cliffs, N.J.: Prentice-Hall, Inc., 1971.

15 Management Consider- ations of the Information System

15.1 Introduction

We conclude Part III by providing some suggestions concerning the proper management of the information system. The specific objectives of this chapter are:

1. To discuss general management activities relative to the information system.
2. To discuss techniques used to manage the data center.
3. To discuss techniques used to manage systems and programming work.
4. To provide guidelines for the development of more maintainable systems.
5. To present methods used to audit systems.
6. To discuss insights into people's problems, people's needs, and managing change.

15.2 General Management Activities

The purpose of this text has been to analyze and discuss the many aspects of information systems.

We have discussed the role of the information system as the primary interface between the management system and the operations system within the organization. However, the information system is itself a large, complex resource which requires managing. In this section, we briefly discuss general management activities which should be established to ensure effective management of the information system. These activities are: (1) establishment of a master plan; (2) selection, training, and assignment of personnel; (3) delineation of responsibilities; (4) establishment of procedures and performance standards; (5) establishment of internal control; and (6) establishment of user request procedures and billing.

Establishment of a Master Plan

For an information system to function effectively, it must be guided by a master plan rather than a piecemeal or "brush fire" approach. A master plan effects an overall framework of objectives for the total information system and states general guidelines as to how to achieve these objectives. The benefits derived from establishing a master plan for the total information system are the same as those derived from establishing a master plan for other endeavors. These benefits are: (1) it provides a long-range plan that facilitates the smooth transition and implementation of subsequent applications; (2) it provides a sense of direction and reduces confusion; (3) it decreases uncertainty; (4) it establishes benchmarks; (5) it gives a means for controlling activities and projects; (6) it unifies and coordinates manpower and other resources; (7) it helps ensure a uniform basis for determining priorities and a sequence of systems development; and (8) it reduces the number of isolated, noncompatible subsystems which might otherwise be developed, operated, and maintained.

Selection, Training, and Assignment of Personnel

As in any other part of the organization, the effectiveness and operational success of the in-

formation system is a function of the quality of personnel hired to work in the system. Without proper selection and training of personnel, it is difficult, if not impossible, to develop a viable information system. It is, therefore, the responsibility of the management of the information system to select capable personnel, assign them to the designated tasks, monitor their performance, and establish a training program for new employees, and for updating the training of all employees. Alternatives that can provide training to information systems personnel include using established institutions of formal education such as, universities and colleges, special trade schools, professional seminars and conferences, inhouse training programs, and, of course, special assignments which provide on the job learning experiences. The requirements for training personnel vary considerably, from that of clerical persons responsible for extremely routine work, to that of the systems analyst who must deal with uncertainty, change, and generalities.

. . . the systems analyst must tactfully determine what the executive's information requirements actually are, rather than accept what he says they are.

The things that the systems analyst brings to the conference with the executive are a general knowledge of how work is done (this allows him to put himself in the executive's place as the process is described) and a knowledge of computer capabilities, which allows him to offer the executive results that he never would have thought to ask for.[1]

In the past many managements have looked to their programming staffs as a source of systems analysts. However, whereas the systems analyst deals with uncertainty, change, and generalities, programmers deal with certainty and specifics. Such a divergence does not necessarily mean that a programmer is precluded from becoming a systems analyst, or vice versa. There have been numerous instances where persons have had the ability to adapt quite readily to different tasks, when properly trained. However, it should be noted that such transitions may be more the exception than the rule.

It is the responsibility of information system management to evaluate new or old personnel for vacancies and to effect an appropriate matching of tasks with aptitudes. There are a number of aptitude tests and review procedures available to management, many developed by computer manufacturers, which can be used as inputs into the evaluation process. Otherwise, without proper training and evaluation, it often happens that the wrong employee is selected for the job. This results in having an employee not only illsuited for his or her job, but also one who is unhappy and unmotivated in their work.

Delineation of Responsibilities

One of the ways management exercises control in any organization is in establishing the role each person will play. This involves a clear delineation of responsibilities, and the related appropriate authorities for each person in the organization. Within the information system, the following categories of responsibilities are applicable:

1. *Systems Work.* As we have discussed throughout the text, this function is responsible for analyzing and defining the informational requirements related to the organization, the evaluation of present techniques and procedures in processing data, and the design and development of improved methods to satisfy identified informational requirements. Ultimately, it is the responsibility of the systems analyst to translate specific aspects of the systems design into program specifications which are implemented by the programmer.

2. *Programming.* Translating program specifications into a medium which can be executed by a computer is the responsibility of the programming function. Additionally, the programmer must communicate to the data processing operating personnel the instruc-

tions necessary to implement his or her programs for execution on a routine basis.

3. *Data Center.* The data center encompasses three functions:

a. General operations: this area includes data preparation activities, clerical work, equipment maintenance, and operations of computer equipment, which includes control of the job stream and maximum utilization of available resources, in light of schedules and priorities.

b. Data base: this area of responsibility deals with storage and control of all data files which are contained in the data base. This function as discussed in Part II, is handled by the Data Base Administrator.

c. Security: in addition to these other areas of responsibility, some large and complex information systems may require a security group whose job it is to see to it that those security controls, discussed elsewhere in this text, are established and adhered to.

Establishment of Procedures and Performance Standards

Written procedures are another method used for effective communication and management. These procedures help management to communicate to various personnel what it expects them to do, how it expects them to do it, when it expects it to be done, and by whom it is to be done.

To further support the control function of management, it is essential that performance standards be established in conjunction with each procedure identified. Performance standards include four distinct aspects: (1) quantity, (2) quality, (3) time, and (4) cost. Performance standards must be set for both personnel and equipment.

Establishment of Internal Control

Internal control has been defined by the Committee on Auditing Procedure of the American Institute of Certified Public Accountants as follows:

Internal control comprises the plan of organization and all of the coordinate methods and measures adopted within a business to safeguard its assets, check the accuracy and reliability of accounting data, promote operational efficiency, and encourage adherence to prescribed managerial policies.[2]

This definition of internal control can be applied to information systems to ensure protection against theft, fraud, misrepresentation, or inaccuracies. Most of the controls, such as input controls, programming controls, and so forth, have already been discussed. Management of the information system can also increase the integrity and control of the system by effecting separation of duties, the underlying principle of internal control. With this principle, one person's work is a check on another's, and although this method does not eliminate the possibility that two or more people will misrepresent through collusion, the likelihood of dishonesty and malfeasance is greatly reduced.

In a typical information system, there is a natural separation of duties; it is up to management to see that these duties remain separate. As stated earlier, these functional areas are: (1) system analysis, (2) programming, and (3) data center operations. There is a separation between those who analyze and design systems, those who prepare the programs, those who operate the equipment, and those who control the files and general operations. Systems analysts and programmers should not be involved with equipment operations; by the same token, operators should not be allowed to develop or change programs. Completed programs, files, documents, and so forth should be controlled by a data base administrator who is engaged in no other activity. Any items from the library should be issued to others only upon proper authorization. If there is a security group, then this group would be responsible for general usage of, and access to, the system.

One should, however, understand that in smaller systems, part or all of these functions are handled by the same person. Establishment of effective internal control in these systems is difficult, if not impossible. In these instances, management must rely upon periodic and aperiodic audits performed by independent auditors.

Establishment of User Request Procedures and Pricing

Financial management of the information system is accomplished by budgets which become part of the master plan. Moreover, there should be a rigid system for approval and implementation of user requests. To serve the user departments best, there should be one person in each department designated as the point of contact for the systems analyst. This point of contact person acts as a liaison between their department and the systems analyst. This method does not preclude the systems analyst from interviewing other personnel, but it does mean that major communications will flow through these two people, resulting in a more efficient and coordinated systems effort.

In our view, the information system can be managed more effectively under a budget and, in turn, by billing user departments for services rendered. With this method, excellent cost control is established for both user departments and the information system, in that all work must be cost/effective. A billing policy for information system services should have the following three main elements: (1) a data collection mechanism, (2) a formula for allocating the cost of resources to users, and (3) established rates for each information system resource.[3]

15.3 Managing the Data Center

The data center is a popular term used to describe a place where all of the activities directly

[2] *Internal Control,* Committee on Auditing Procedure, American Institute of Certified Public Accountants, 1949, p. 6; and reaffirmed in *Auditing Standards and Procedures,* Committee on Auditing Procedure Statement No. 33, American Institute of Certified Public Accountants, 1063. p. 27.

[3] For a good article on billing procedures, see: Philip G. Bookman, "Make Your User Pay the Price," *Computer Decisions,* September, 1972, pp. 28–31.

involved in the operations of the information system are performed. Most of the activities (discussed earlier) are repetitive, routine tasks which are easily measured and controlled. In this section, we will discuss some performance standards by which productivity is measured.

These performance standards are set up and calculated on the basis of such items as: (1) number of hours spent running equipment for production; (2) number of hours spent working with equipment without production, e.g., correcting errors, recycling jobs, card jams, setup time, and so forth; (3) number of hours idle for both equipment and operators; (4) quality of production; (5) quantity of production; and (6) cost of production.

From the following study by Schroeder, one may infer that setting proper performance standards, measuring actual performance against standards, and taking corrective action is a significant responsibility of management.

Of the total available machine hours (three shifts, 30 days per month = 720 hours) the average computer in the study performs productive work only 48% of the time. Productive work is defined as the time equipment is used to process production runs and testing, without regard for how effectively the computing power of the machine is being used at any one time. . . .

. . . .

A comparison of productive time with total hours that a computing center is manned and operated is most revealing. This comparison indicates that 25% of costs are wasted due to idleness, reruns, machine maintenance and down time.

. . . .

It is readily apparent management should evaluate the productivity ratios of the computer installation before authorizing multiple shifts and new equipment. During the time the computers are manned but idle, the company is paying for both rental and payroll.

. . . .

On the average, the companies in the study are incurring these annual losses due to idle time and reruns:

Size of Computer Installation	Annual Costs Idle Time	Due to Reruns
Small	$ 30,000	$ 2,000
Medium	$ 84,000	$18,000
Large	$280,000	$94,000

These costs represent inadequate management in the truest sense and result from such factors as: inadequate instructions for computer operators, absence of internal controls and improper or nonexistent computer scheduling.[4]

The utilization of performance standards for equipment and operators provides a basis for scheduling work, spotting units which need to be replaced or repaired, and evaluating operator performance. There are an almost unlimited number of calculations one can perform in making evaluations in this area. We will illustrate some of these calculations below. It should be noted that such measurements are only guidelines and would thus need modification and extension in a real application.

1. *Variance Analysis.* The following brief example shows how standards should be set and variances from them computed. It is the responsibility of management to determine, if such variances are significant and if so, the proper action to be taken.

Standard process cost per hour	$36.00
Actual process cost per hour	$38.80
Actual quantity processed	10 master files
Standard time to process one master file	1/2 hour
Actual time to process one master file	1/4 hour

$$Cost\ Variance = (Standard\ Cost - Actual\ Cost) \times Actual\ Hours$$
$$= (36.00 - 38.80) \times 2.5$$
$$= \$7.00\ UNFAVORABLE\ VARIANCE$$

Efficiency Variance = (Standard Time − Actual
Time) × Standard Cost
= (5.0 − 2.5) × 36.00
= $90.00 FAVORABLE
VARIANCE

The reason for using performance standards is to isolate areas of responsibility for control purposes. The main questions in deciding whether any variances from standards should be calculated are: (1) what does the variance actually indicate? and (2) what will the supervisor use it for? If the variance does not measure anything significant, and/or the variance is not used for some specific control purpose, then it should not be calculated. Elaborate reporting systems and long lists of variances will be of little consequence to supervisors if they cannot and do not use such analysis for investigative purposes and corrective action.

2. *Indices.* There are also indices which management can use that may help in making proper evaluations. Examples of some of these indices are:

$$\text{Capacity Index} = \frac{\text{Number Hours Actual}}{\text{Number Hours Assigned}}$$

$$\text{Equipment Rate Per Hour} = \frac{\text{Media Volume}}{\text{Meter Time}}$$

$$\text{Actual Rate Per Hour} = \frac{\text{Media Volume}}{\text{Actual Time}}$$

$$\text{Percent Meter to Actual Time} = \frac{\text{Meter Time}}{\text{Actual Time}}$$

$$\text{Quality of Production} = \frac{\text{Number of Recycles}}{\text{Volume of Production}}$$

or

$$= \frac{\text{Number of Errors}}{\text{Volume of Production}}$$

Time of Production

$$= \frac{\text{Actual Throughput Time}}{\text{Standard Throughput Time}}$$

In the above discussion about performance standards, there are many items that can be measured which pertain to utilization of equipment, and the activities of operators. However, there are three possible shortcomings with this kind of evaluation. These are:

1. Employees tend to optimize those items that are being measured and evaluated instead of working on a basis of coordinated throughput.

2. As the level of tasks become more important, the more difficult it is to objectively measure those more significant aspects of these tasks. Some area could have good utilization ratios and favorable performance variances, but still not be accomplishing good throughput and satisfying overall user requirements.

3. Performance statistics and reports are costly to prepare.

15.4 Managing Systems Work and Programming Development

Understanding the management of the systems and programming functions requires a somewhat different analysis than the approach used for analyzing the management of the data center. Unlike the operations of the data center, and most other activities in an organization that are generally continuous or repetitive by nature, the development cycle of systems and programming can be viewed as having relatively specific start and stop points. In addition to being definable, the development of systems and programming requires many diverse talents and tasks.

Below, we indicate some methods by which management can better plan for and control these talents and activities involved in systems and programming work.

Estimating Project Efforts

Once the analyst determines the activities and tasks appropriate for the project effort he or she must further identify how much time is required to conduct each one. For example, it might be estimated that 30 interviews will be required during fact finding. In most organizations, there are few engineered standards available for use in estimating the time requirement for systems activities. Consequently, the analyst relies on past experience in order to develop most time requirements. The following illustrates this approach to estimating time:

2 hrs. — Prepare for interview
2 hrs. — Conduct interview
1 hr. — Document interview
1 hr. — Follow up interview
<u>2 hrs.</u> — Analyze interview
8 hrs. — Total time per interview

8 hrs. × 30 interviews
= 240 hrs. for interviewing

As in the above illustration, it is suggested that a task, such as interviewing, be broken down into basic subtasks. This subdividing of tasks allows an analyst, even a relatively inexperienced one, to arrive at a reasonable expectation for planning purposes.

The PERT method (see Appendix A) of estimating expected time to complete an activity lends reliability to an estimate by combining the experience of several persons in a statistical method. For example, a number of proposed activities are presented to several analysts, possibly including the supervisor analyst. Each analyst prepares three estimates for every activity: optimistic, most likely, and pessimistic. These estimates are tabulated and averaged for a final optimistic (O), most likely (M), and pessimistic (P) estimate. The final three estimates are then combined in a weighted average, using the following formula, by which the expected time (t_e) to complete a particular activity is computed.

$$t_e = \frac{O + 4M + P}{6}$$

This method uses the knowledgeable subjective experience of the analysts who mentally take into consideration all constraints, and contingencies, of the present situation. It provides a fairly objective method of estimating time (or cost) for anything activity oriented, and is especially applicable to estimating systems and programming work.

Another key to establishing good estimates for future work is to keep performance information of past work. For example, if performance

Type of Program Activities	Simple	Average	Complex
Design logic	10%	25%	32%
Code	15%	20%	30%
Test	40%	35%	28%
Document	35%	20%	10%

FIGURE 15.1. Matrix illustrating the proportion of time spent on each activity for different types of programs.

information has been compiled for some time on a programming group using COBOL, then estimates for future programming efforts can be extrapolated fairly accurately. Using programming as an example, this information should be structured in such a way that it is applicable to special types of programs, and those activities involved in programming development. These designations are summarized in Figure 15.1. The listed percentages indicate the proportion of time required for each activity. These measurements are only for illustrative purposes and are subject to vary in practice.

If the total number of hours needed to develop a program is 200 manhours on the average, then 50 manhours will be spent on the design of program logic, 40 manhours on coding, 70 manhours on testing, and 40 manhours on documentation. These figures are averages and would have to be adjusted in accordance with the programmer's experience.

Also, these figures must be continuously updated as new routines and packages are developed and implemented in the programming effort. Moreover, the use of different approaches to the programming task itself can substantially reduce time estimates. For example, it is often possible for programmers to use decision tables, especially the extended entry type, right in the programs. This approach has an increasing payoff as the logic becomes more complex. Estimates, by users and researchers, have indicated that the overall productivity, for both analyst and programmers in developing and maintaining COBOL — based systems, has been at least double what it would have been without the use of decision tables.[5]

Scheduling the Project Effort

Once the overall project time estimates have been established and schedules prepared, individual resources must be allocated to meet this schedule. The nature of systems work and programming efforts requires careful scheduling in order to be utilized effectively. A number of special charting and network techniques based on timing estimates, have been devised that can assist information systems management in scheduling and controlling a systems development project.

The Gantt chart and its variations are excellent tools for scheduling less complicated or minimum time-constraint projects. Projects having a high level of complexity and/or severe scheduling requirements can benefit from the use of a network system such as CPM or PERT. It is estimated today that more than 200 varia-

tions of network systems are available and utilized for the planning and control of project efforts. Many of these systems are available for processing with a computer. In this section we will provide a brief introduction to these special charting techniques.

1. *Gantt Charts.* The Gantt chart is a variation of the bar charting technique. It is used to measure the performance of an activity versus time criteria. It is an excellent planning, scheduling, and controlling tool, but does not provide the kind of information that is often required in complex projects. Figure 15.2, illustrates the use of a Gantt chart in a systems development project effort.

Time is represented across the horizontal axis and the various developmental activities are represented across the vertical axis. In our illustration we have included a mechanism for updating performance on the chart. Note, however, that any dependencies among activities is not readily apparent from viewing the chart. For many systems projects, however, the Gantt chart provides all the planning, scheduling, and controlling information that is required.

---

[5] "That Maintenance 'Iceberg'." *EDP Analyzer,* October, 1972, p. 3. Used with permission.

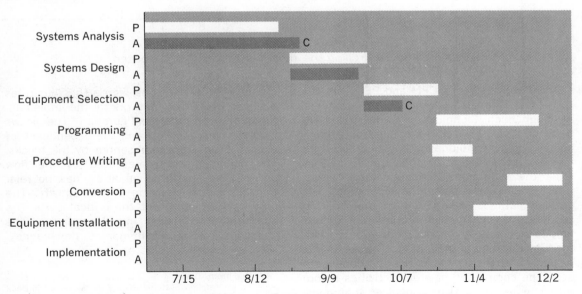

FIGURE 15.2. A variation of the Gantt chart used for planning, scheduling, and controlling the development of a system.
P = Plan; A = Actual; C = Complete.

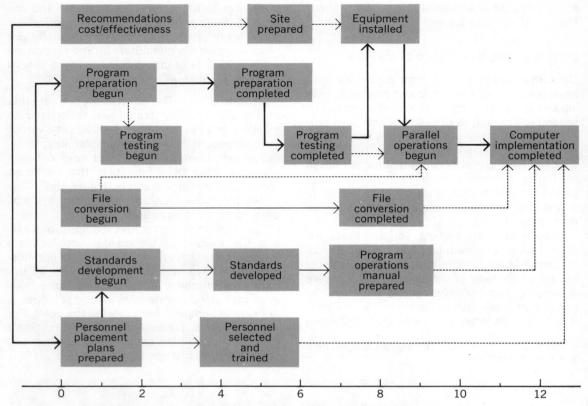

FIGURE 15.3. A PERT/CPM network used for planning, scheduling, and controlling the implementation of a computer cconfiguration.

2. *Network Systems.* CPM and PERT are the two most widely known network systems. Although each technique was developed independently with its own emphasis and terminology, both techniques are concerned with events and activities. Events are defined as either the beginning or completion of activities, whereas activities represent time durations. The critical path is identified as the specific sequence of events which requires the longest time to complete, and can thus be equated with the total duration of the project. This technique recognizes that many activities are dependent upon the completion of other activities before they can begin. It also recognizes that many activities are relatively independent of the completion of other activities. Figure 15.3 illustrates a simple PERT/CPM network for the implementation of a computer configuration.[6] The arrows indicate both the flow and the dependency of events. Events are represented by the blocks. The activities are represented by the flow arrows. The length of an arrow has no relationship to the duration of the activity. The broad arrows represent the critical path. The line arrows represent interdependency. The dashed arrows represent noninterdependency.

[6] Adapted from: David H. Li, *Accounting, Computers, Management Information Systems* (New York: McGraw-Hill Book Company, 1968.) p. 155. Used with permission of McGraw-Hill Book Company.

Need for Continuous Planning and Controlling

The most often used illustration of planning and controlling involves the construction of some concrete object. Control is effected in part by counting or observing what has been constructed and reporting this against what was planned. This reporting activity, combined with direct supervision, generally provides an adequate level of control. For example, a brick-layer lays 3000 bricks in a given period. The plan calls for laying 12,000 bricks to complete the job. With regard to the total number of bricks, the job is 1/4 completed.

While the development of systems also provides some observable outputs (e.g., interview report, design proposal, programs and procedures), there remain long periods of time where it is difficult to measure or assess progress, since much of the effort is characterized by logical and mental commitments. During these time periods, the analyst in charge of, or responsible for, the project effort, experiences a feeling of little or no control over the final outcome. One suggestion for minimizing this feeling of no control is to implement continuous planning. The following examples illustrate this technique.

Jim Smith provides his management with an estimate of 100 hours to identify and define the sales department's information requirements concerning export sales. His plan includes the following tasks and anticipated times for each task:

1. Interview the Vice President of Marketing, manager of export sales, and two export sales representatives   32 hours
2. Review present reports   20 hours
3. Review existing reporting system   30 hours
4. Document findings   <u>18 hours</u>
           Total   100 hours

His efforts the first day on the job indicate that the existing reporting is fairly extensive. After spending six hours on the job, he reports to his management that he will have to spend 40 more hours in review of existing reports. This last piece of information, 40 hours required, allows the following analysis to be made:

Review reports — initial plan — 20 hours
Current status — 6 hours expended/40 hours remaining
Project progress — 26 hours late

Thus, after only one day of effort, it is apparent that the project is going to be completed about 3 days later than planned. After spending two more days reviewing reports, Jim reports the following:

	Original Hours Planned	Actual Hours Worked	Estimated Remaining Hours
Review reports	20	19	16
Review reporting system	30	0	50

At this time, it is apparent to all concerned that the overall project is significantly underestimated. Consequently, before Jim expends further efforts, his management is made aware of, first, the potential lateness and related expenses which could be expected, and, second, that if Jim is going to complete this assignment, any future plans for his time will have to be postponed. Moreover, Jim's management is continually in control of the project progress and can cancel the project if necessary, or provide additional support to Jim.

Had Jim merely reported that he had expended 19 hours on the project, his management might have concluded that this equated to his completing 19% of the planned work. As a result, Jim could have gone much further into the project without anyone, including himself, being aware of the increasing probability of lateness and excessive expense being incurred.

Because of the extensive amount of judgement which goes into developing systems development plans, this concept of continual planning is of great importance to the systems analyst. A second example, involving a programming effort, further illustrates the type of control continuous planning provides.

Bob Malcom is assigned an average program

which is estimated to require 150 hours to implement. The plan provides the following tasks and related times for each task.

Design program logic		45 hours
Code program		31 hours
Test program		60 hours
Document program		14 hours
	Total	150 hours

After reviewing the program and developing a general flowchart, Bob begins to code. At the end of the first day he reports the following:

	Planned	Actual	Remaining
Design program logic	45	6	0
Code program	31	2	24
Test program	60	0	40
Document program	14	0	8
Totals	150	8	72

At this point, again, both Bob and his supervisor are in a position to reassess the project plan and progress. Quite possibly Bob is confused and, therefore, misunderstands what is required. Or perhaps, on the other hand, Bob is familiar with this particular area and does not need to reinvent all of the required program logic. Or lastly, the complexity of the program might have been overestimated.

Regardless of the cause of the variation, both Bob and his supervisor are able to determine the effect of this program on the overall project effort. If Bob is in error, his problem is brought to light quickly for corrective action. If Bob is correct, the project leader has obtained some additional flexibility to utilize Bob's time in other project efforts.

The efforts of systems analysts and programmers are extremely difficult activities to exert control over. Direct supervision usually results in little value on a short term basis as compared to the cost of this control. However, combined with the concept of continuous planning, supervision can provide a viable means of control.

15.5 Managing Maintenance

One of the major goals of information system management is to develop a system with a high degree of maintainability. More maintainable systems are actually those requiring less attention, and fewer modifications and changes, but which, at the same time, are easier to change when maintenance *is* required. This section analyzes how more maintainable systems might be achieved and managed.

Causes of Maintenance Work

Following are some of the causes why programs, data files, documentation, and general procedures must be changed in an existing system.

1. *Emergency Maintenance.* Emergency maintenance is directed at resolving a malfunction in the system. This maintenance is the most urgent in nature and usually calls for immediate attention. Normally, the cause is incomplete testing. However, surprisingly, a system, program, etc., may run for months and never encounter a major malfunction when suddenly, for no apparent reason, it requires attention. Although this type of activity is normally associated with programming, oftentimes the system's malfunction is identified by an information user. At this time, the analyst, programmer, etc., must determine if the malfunction is in a computer program or a system input. The ability to rapidly diagnose a malfunction and to provide a remedy is of considerable value to the organization.

2. *Routine Maintenance.* Routine maintenance activities are required to keep systems performance relevant as it reflects the environment within and around the organization. This activity may take the form of rewriting manual procedures, conducting training sessions, altering information report formats and contents, and defining new processing logic for computer procedures. For example, a new tax law may require a change in the calculation of net pay, or that a new report be produced from

the system, or the adoption of a new accounting depreciation method, or compensation method for salesmen, etc., all of which might require revisions to the existing system.

3. *Special Reporting Requests.* Periodic requests from tactical and strategic management for information not scheduled for routine production from a system, are usually termed special reporting requests. The analyst must first define what is being requested; second, what is required to produce the information; and finally, the most efficient way to produce the information based on available resources. While many of these special requests can be satisfied directly by a user via a generalized data base management system, often the analyst assists in preparing the necessary parameters for the request. Even in an online environment, a user may be unfamiliar with the total data base available to them. Examples of special requests might include a special analysis of pay rates during labor/management bargaining sessions, a special report on selected products during a sales promotion, a special analysis of a particular vendor's delivery performance, or any other special analysis utilizing management science models.

4. *Systems Improvements.* When a new system is implemented, users may suggest additional improvements to the system at that time. In short, many users' information requirements are subject to a tremendous rate of change. To accommodate these changing requirements, an analyst must first define what is needed, decide how it can best be met with the existing data base, and develop the necessary manual and computer procedures to satisfy these requirements. The approach utilized by the analyst in this activity differs only in duration when compared to the development of a system.

Problems of Maintenance

With the above causes it is little wonder that existing systems are subject to almost continual change. Unfortunately, these maintenance causes can result in a number of problems, which are:[7]

1. *Cost.* Changing existing application systems can be quite costly, requiring, in some instances, one-half of an organization's systems costs. Many organizations have adopted the principle of setting a budget for maintenance activities and then doing just the highest priority jobs that can be accomplished within that budget.

2. *Personnel Morale.* Personnel working in the information system, especially programmers, often object to the amount of maintenance work they are asked to do. They do not want to spend up to one-half of their time maintaining or trying to patch up systems designed and implemented years ago. In some organizations, programmers are rotated from one project group to another on a one to three year cycle. This policy of rotation has a number of advantages. First, it means new assignments for the programmer, even if much of the work might be classified as maintenance. Second, such a policy provides backup because the experience base of the personnel is increased, making the information system more flexible for further change. Third, rotation brings fresh outlooks, increasing the chance of better ideas being proposed. And, fourth, evaluation of personnel becomes more objective by comparing the performance of two or more persons on the same job, and by evaluating the performance of a person under several project leaders.

3. *Failures.* Maintenance programming reputedly has a history of causing more catastrophic failures than the original development programming. If the maintenance programmer is not familiar with the program and/or if the documentation is poor, it is possible that some changes made will result in serious failures. For the first problem, obviously it behooves management to assign complex maintenance problems to the most knowledgeable people. For the second, it is the responsibility of man-

---

[7] Summarized from: "That Maintenance 'Iceberg'," *op. cit.,* pp. 4–8. Used with permission.

agement to see to it that all programs are properly documented, because documentation is actually the information about a program necessary to change it. Probably the best way to document is to have the documentation in the code rather than in a typewritten document removed from the program.

4. *Extra Training Costs.* To maintain older application systems using outdated programming languages and equipment necessitates extra training for new persons who will be working on such systems.

5. *Unmanageable Conditions.* Management may find itself faced with a complex and unwieldy problem; a problem that was not fully appreciated as it developed, or one that was inherited from predecessor management. This situation develops from such things as: (1) thousands of programs rambling in design, (2) little documentation, (3) variety of hardware/software configurations resulting in incompatible operations, and (4) use of outdated equipment and procedures.

In such a situation, information system management can just barely keep user departments satisfied. There are few, if any, manhours available, and no budget available, to really clean up the situation. In a case like this, the severe problems of maintenance (and dissatisfied users) will continue indefinitely.

Procedures to Achieve More Maintainable Systems

It can readily be seen that uncontrolled maintenance is a serious problem. What is needed is a plan of action that increases the maintainability of systems. Such systems, are those which have been developed according to standards and procedures that will both reduce the need for maintenance as well as make any necessary maintenance easier to perform. There are six major aspects which lead to more maintainable systems:[8]

1. *Designing for Change.* This aspect encompasses a variety of procedures, some of which are:

[8] *Ibid.,* pp. 8–14.

a. Standard data definitions: The trend toward the integrated generalized data base management system is supporting the push for standard data definitions. Many organizations now have redundant and inconsistent data definitions. These inconsistent data definitions are found in procedure manuals, in source program documentation, in data files, and so forth, all of which add to the problem of maintenance. So the use of standard data definitions will provide a real step toward more maintainable systems.

b. Standard program languages: The use of a standard language such as COBOL will make maintenance easier.

c. Standard set of configuration resources: Standards should be developed and enforced on the use of resources (such as core space) that a program can use, peripherals that a program can use, and so forth.

d. Modular design of programs: As with the maintenance of appliances (e.g., TV sets) where a repairman can determine which module is causing trouble and quickly replace it, the maintenance programmer can also change modules of a program much easier than trying to deal with the total program.

e. Use of decision tables: Decision tables support modular program design. They make program logic clear to the maintenance programmer. Also, there are decision table preprocessors[9] which provide a means for automatically converting decision tables into source code, thus reducing the chance for error.

f. Use of generalized design: Generalized design attempts to identify those aspects of a system that are most likely to change, and then to design the programs to accept this change.

g. Documentation standards: System, program, and operation documentation is needed so that all the information needed for operating and maintaining a particular application is available. Since documentation is so essential, it is imperative that procedures be established and enforced for producing the documentation and keeping it current.

[9] See: R. N. Dean, "A Comparison of Decision Tables Against Conventional COBOL as a Programming Tool for Commercial Applications," *Software World,* Spring, 1971, pp. 26–30. Also see: "COBOL Aid Packages," *EDP Analyzer,* May, 1972.

2. *Design Changes.* Even when programs are designed to facilitate change, maintenance programmers need other tools to aid them in making and testing the changes. One tool that is needed is cross reference listings of commonly used resources such as subroutines, files, records, and so forth. For example, when a change is to be made to a subroutine, the maintenance programmer wants to know all of the programs that use that subroutine. Two of the main sources of maintenance work are the input validation programs and the report preparation programs. Input is changed to accommodate new or changed source documents. Output is changed to provide new report formats and/or new report contents, as well as ad hoc reports.

3. *Configuration Policies.* The total configuration of an installation is subject to almost continual change. Maintenance requirements will be eased if the information system adheres to the policy of interchangeability (plug-compatibility), when making these configuration changes. If a noninterchangeable change is made in the configuration, then some or all of the programs will not run. A great deal of maintenance work is, therefore, necessary to make these programs run on this new noncompatible equipment.

4. *Control and Audit.* Several types of administrative controls should be established by management to make sure that the policies and procedures designed to reduce maintenance requirements are in fact being followed. These are as follows:

a. Formal change procedure: Make sure that all changes are evaluated and authorized, and that the source programs and documentation are kept up to date. Emergency maintenance, such as when a production program abnormally terminates, must be performed immediately. But as soon as possible, put any program changes through a formal review and change process.

b. Use of librarian package: Both source and object programs should be stored under control of a librarian package, and source decks should be eliminated.

c. Use of enforcement aids: Preprocessors for source code can include an enforcement mechanism, for flagging violations of some installation standards.

d. Audit of documentation system: Not only must an adequate system be set up for creating and maintaining the necessary documentation, its use must be enforced. One way of checking to see that this documentation is being used properly is through aperiodic audits. The documentation system should be checked all the way through, from creation of documentation to its retention in backup storage. These surprise audits might be performed by the company's internal auditors.

5. *Organizing for Maintenance.* The question is: should maintenance be performed in the development groups, or in separate maintenance programming groups? Some thoughts:

a. Arguments for combined development and maintenance: If both development and maintenance are performed in the same group, then the user departments will have one point of contact with the information system personnel who can effect change. User departments often do not know if a job will be classified as development or maintenance since large revisions or system improvements are often treated as development. Further, the analysts and programmers who developed the application systems originally have the best knowledge of those systems, and can best assess the full impact of changes. Some systems are so critical and complex that maintenance must be handled by the most capable and, in many instances, the most capable people are the ones who developed the systems in the first place.

b. Arguments for separate maintenance: Separate maintenance tends to force better documentation, formal turnover procedures, and formal change procedures. Maintenance programmers can learn a great deal about the total organization because they are involved in some systems work, as well as in programming. Senior maintenance programmers may be promoted to development project leaders, since they have a good knowledge of documentation requirements, standards, operations, and so forth.

6. *Converting to More Maintainable Systems.* Management should convert to a more maintainable system using the procedures as described above as new systems are developed or as existing systems undergo major revisions. Then rather than having a combined maintenance/development group, it is probably advisable to transfer the maintenance responsibility to a separate group staffed for this type of work.

15.6 Auditing Considerations

Auditing is not only a legitimate form of systems work, but it directly affects the way systems work is performed. Consequently, the systems analyst should be aware of the different types of audits that the information system is subjected to, and the general approach taken by auditors, particularly when a computer is the heart of the system.

It is, however, the ultimate responsibility of management to see to it that the information system maintains a high degree of integrity. Therefore, all information systems should be audited both periodically and aperiodically. The general purpose of the audit is to detect inadequacies in the system and pinpoint defective operating procedures.

Types of Audits

There are a number of types of audits which can be performed in the information system, each with its own particular objectives. All, however, are performed to ensure the integrity and operational efficiency of the system.

1. *Post Implementation Audit.* The basic purpose of this audit is to identify what actually occurred, versus what was projected, during the development phase. In a large information system, a systems analyst may perform the post implementation audit. However, the audit should not be performed by any analyst who was involved with the analysis, design, development, and implementation of the system. In many organizations, a management consulting group is commissioned to perform the post implementation audit, in order to ensure that a high degree of objectivity prevails.

From the perspective of the systems operations, this audit should determine that manual procedures are formally documented, that all computer programs are properly documented, all operating personnel are trained, and that the level of accuracy and reliability of information outputs is acceptable to the users. With regard to developmental projections, the actual cost spent during each phase should be compared to the projected costs. Likewise, actual developmental schedules should be compared to previously projected schedules.

Depending on the size and magnitude of the system implemented, the post implementation audit should not be conducted until the system has been operating for six months or more. This delay factor is intended to eliminate or minimize any learning curve effects on the system, which might unduly distort the auditor's findings.

2. *Routine Operational Audit.* In a large information system, the routine operational audit is performed by a specially designated control group within the system itself, possibly by personnel from the security group. In a smaller information system, the routine operational audit may be performed by personnel from some group, say systems analysts or maintenance programmers, in addition to their other activities. In either case, the primary purpose of this audit is to determine how well operations are adhering to established control procedures (see Chapter 13) and to provide assurance that the system is operating as designed. This audit involves such tasks as comparing output totals to input totals; reviewing console logs and error registers; verifying that input, processing, and output schedules are being met; and comparing actual procedures against standard procedures.

3. *Financial Audit.* The financial audit is a unique function of independent accountants. The primary purpose of this audit is to examine the organization's financial statements and express an opinion as to their fairness, their conformity with generally accepted accounting

principles, and the consistency with which the accounting principles have been applied from year to year. Since one of the major outputs of the information system are the financial statements, this type of audit serves as an excellent control over general operations of the system.

   . . . If the CPA firm that performs the annual audit does not detect the inadequacies, and if serious losses result, the CPA firm can be sued by stockholders. If the CPA firm does detect the inadequacies, it will probably feel compelled to qualify the company's financial statements by noting such inadequacies in the statements. If such qualifications are made, and if there is not sufficient time to correct the control system and insure the integrity of the records, the company will be faced with the embarrassment of the notes in the annual statement.[10]

4. *Systems Audit.* Another service to top management is in the area of the systems audit. A systems audit generally involves review and evaluation of the following: (1) overall systems logic and design; (2) programming logic, operating system, compilers; (3) computer configuration design and selection methods; (4) computer operation and utilization; (5) systems backup and contingency plans; (6) security and procedure controls; and (7) documentation.

  In summary, the post implementation audit simply answers the question posed by management: "Does the system do what the development people said it would do within projected schedule and cost?" The routine operational audit aids supervisors in ensuring that day-to-day operations meet standard operating procedures. Although CPA auditors are primarily concerned with satisfying themselves to the extent necessary to express an opinion on the financial statements, they may also be commissioned to perform many functions relative to a systems audit. During the course of the financial audit, the auditor may develop helpful comments and suggestions on improving the effec-

tiveness and the efficiency of policies, procedures, and controls which pertain to the information system. In recent times, the most significant advance in the role played by the auditor is this extension from the traditional financial audit. Often, the auditor is charged with a broader responsibility encompassing many aspects of the systems audit.

Auditing Techniques

The principal techniques used by an auditor in performing any type of audit are:

  1. *Observation.* With this technique, the auditor surveys and takes notice of various aspects of the system to ascertain the effectiveness of operations for the purpose of establishing the scope of the audit. In other words, by observation the auditor can get a fairly good idea as to the audit procedures to be followed, and the extent to which they must be applied, to result in an adequate audit. For example, an auditor may note that there is a lack of separation of duties which may indicate inadequate internal controls. In this case, the auditor undertakes more extensive and intensive examinations than would have otherwise been necessary with a proper system of internal control. The auditor may also: (1) acclimate to the system, by reviewing the organizational chart of the system, (2) review and study manuals, and (3) review and study documentation.

  2. *Inspection.* The auditor examines closely such items as documentation, program changes, and various operations. For example, an aspect of inspection is test-checking, i.e., the auditor may test the adequacy of programming controls by actually running a program with a number of contrived, fictitious data (test deck) to see what happens under predetermined conditions. A test of sales involves the comparison of customer order data, bills of lading and other shipping documents, invoices, and accounts receivable. The auditor may also inspect (1) hardware controls, (2) data base and security controls, and (3) post implementation evaluation reports.

  3. *Sampling.* Auditors can save a great deal

---

[10] "Computer Security: Backup and Recovery Methods," *EDP Analyzer,* January, 1972, p. 11. Used with permission.

of time in their work, and still maintain a high level of confidence that the audit has been effective, by using statistical sampling techniques in selecting those items to be tested. For example, an auditor may randomly select ten programs out of N and test each one for optimum record blocking. The results of the test would indicate whether or not other samples should be tested.

4. *Confirmation.* The auditor, in many instances, needs to corroborate, especially from third parties, the existence of certain items. For example, accounts receivable requests, controlled by the auditor, are sent to customers outside the organization. Types of confirmation requests used are: (1) positive and (2) negative. The positive request calls for a direct reply to the auditor, confirming the balance shown on the confirmation request or reporting any differences or exceptions. The negative confirmation request provides that the auditor be notified only in the event the customer does not agree with the amount shown on the request.

5. *Comparison.* Here, the auditor examines two or more items to ascertain variances, if any. Obviously, in performing the post implementation audit, the auditor is primarily comparing stated costs, schedules, and performance with actual costs, schedules, and performance. The objective in making comparisons are to determine and report to management the reasons for significant variations.

6. *Inquiry.* Although the auditing techniques discussed above include an element of inquiry, this technique is especially effective to the auditor in searching out facts that are not readily evident in records of the system; such as, commitments, contingencies, or future plans. The auditor can learn of these additional facts only through specific inquiry of management and other personnel.

Computer Auditing Approaches

In a computer based information system the auditor must make a determination as to how he or she will validate that the processing done on the computer is correct. There are two approaches to testing the processing logic of the computer: (1) auditing around the computer and (2) auditing through the computer.[11]

1. *Auditing around the Computer.* In earlier times, the typical auditor, being unfamiliar with computer technology, programming, and other techniques used in electronic data processing, developed audit procedures to include review of input documents and output reports only. With this approach, the basic assumption is that if the input data are correct, and if the output is properly handled, then the processing function itself must be correct.

For example, the auditor selects source documents to be tested (e.g., employees' time cards), traces them through computer printouts (e.g., payroll accounts), and then reverses the order by tracing from summary accounts through computer printouts to source documents. The rationale behind this approach is that if source documents are properly reflected in the master files and in turn the master files are properly supported by source documents, then the processing functions of the computer (e.g., the black box) must be performing correctly: Therefore, there is no need to review or test computer programs or computer operations. These steps are completely bypassed as if the computer printouts were prepared manually, hence the term auditing around the computer. This approach is illustrated in Figure 15.4.

2. *Auditing through the Computer.* As limitations of the above approach became more significant, as audit trails began to disappear with more sophisticated applications (e.g., the monitoring method), and as auditors became more knowledgeable in computer operations, auditing procedures also changed. Transactions began to be tested through the computer. With this approach, the auditor verifies the effectiveness of control procedures over computer

---

[11] For auditing computer systems, see: Robert J. Thierauf, *Data Processing for Business and Management* (New York: John Wiley & Sons, Inc., 1973), Chapter 16; and David H. Li, *Accounting, Computers, Management Information Systems* (New York: McGraw-Hill Book Company, 1968), pp. 296–310.

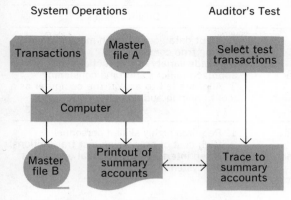

FIGURE 15.4. Test of transactions around the computer.

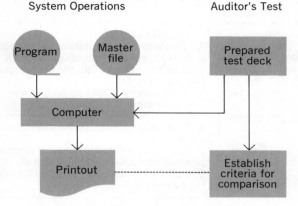

FIGURE 15.5. Test of transactions through the computer.

operations and computer programs, and the correctness of internal processing. One of the key tools in this approach is a prefabricated test deck which is designed by the auditor. It consists of a series of simulated transactions used to check the comprehensiveness and generality of a program, and also discloses any weaknesses in various controls and programmed checks.

For example, there are three possible conditions which can exist concerning FICA in a payroll program: no FICA withholding, full FICA withholding, and limited FICA withholding. Transactions in the test deck should check all three conditions and thus the comprehensiveness or generality of the program.

Other conditions which should be tested are:

1. Out of sequence conditions;
2. Processing with wrong files;
3. Out of limit conditions;
4. Invalid unit of measure;
5. Invalid dates, account codes, and field relationships;
6. Numeric data where alphabetic data should be or vice versa; and
7. Loss of the negative sign where a number is in fact negative, etc.

Computer audit programs, especially generalized ones, are another key tool. These programs perform specified audit routines such as: (1)

selecting and printing audit samples for such things as accounts receivable confirmations (example given later); (2) testing footings and extensions; and (3) retrieving, manipulating, totaling, and comparing any data records within the data base.

In some instances the auditor might write their own program or use the client's personnel to do so. However, more auditors are using generalized computer audit programs, such as Haskins & Sells Auditape. Other, similar, audit packages are Audassist, Audipak, and Cars 2. These packages not only help to test a number of conditions, but they assist the auditor by allowing the computer to make the calculations, comparisons, and audit functions which, in the past, have been tedious and time consuming.

The rationale of the through the computer approach is that if computer programs are effective, the output from various tests will bear this out, and if they are deficient, the output will highlight these shortcomings. This approach is illustrated in Figure 15.5.

Summary Comparison of Both Computer Auditing Approaches

Figure 15.6, is a matrix which gives the advantages and disadvantages of both approaches. It should be pointed out, however, that many au-

Approaches	Advantages	Disadvantages
Around the Computer	1. Logic is plausible. 2. Simple to use and is familiar to auditors. 3. Lessens need for specialized training. 4. Does not interfere with the normal operations of the system. 5. Applicable for audits of fairly small, simplistic systems.	1. Input data goes through many changes, limiting true comparisons. 2. A wide variety of transactions makes this approach tedious and time consuming. 3. Auditors fail to exploit the computer as a tool to help in auditing chores.
Through the Computer	1. Applicable for larger, more sophisticated systems. 2. Gives a more detailed review of computer processing programs and procedures. 3. Utilizes the computer as a tool for performing auditing functions.	1. Requires highly skilled personnel. 2. High cost of processing test transactions. 3. Often interferes with normal operations of the system.

FIGURE 15.6.   Advantages and disadvantages of auditing approaches.

ditors use a combination of both approaches for effective auditing procedures.

Example of Exploiting the Computer as an Auditing Tool

An early feeling among some auditors was that a computer based system is more difficult to audit than a manual system because of the "mysterious" operations of the computer and because much of the interim data is stored in machine-readable form. Such reasoning is based more on a lack of understanding of the computer than on reality.

First, the computer is merely another data processing tool that helps to facilitate the tedious operations required for routine data processing work and information analysis. The computer must be told what to do step-by-step by a program which is written by a human. The computer can neither think nor create. If the computer prints a check for vendor XYZ in the amount of $100,000, either legally or illegally, one must remember that it had to be furnished the necessary input, it had to be given the necessary instructions, and it had to have available on the printer the necessary check form.

Secondly, there are real advantages to auditing a computer based system as compared to auditing other types of systems:

1. The computer requires far more rigidity, systemization, and uniformity in handling data than that which can be accommodated by less mechanized systems. One has to be precise in his or her work before the computer will perform its work.

2. Once systems procedures are set up and validated, the auditor can be relatively sure, by making proper tests, that all data are being processed in accordance with these procedures.

3. The internal reliability of the computer is, by far, greater than that of less mechanized systems. This reliability is due to solid state, transistorized, circuitry coupled with many built-in checks (e.g., parity checks, echo checks).

4. Numerous control checks can be written into the programs wherein the computer acts as its own auditing system.

5. The computer can also be used to run audit programs as shown in Figure 15.7, an example of preparing accounts receivable confirmation requests.

15.7 Managing Change

Many systems analysts, as well as managements, make the mistake of assuming that information systems development is controlled only by technical, economic, and schedule constraints. There *is* a fourth constraint, operation,

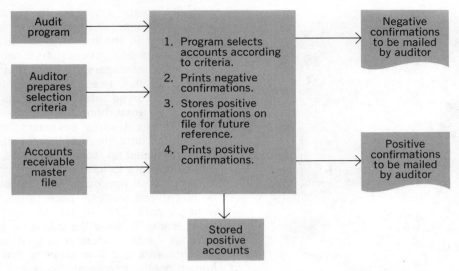

FIGURE 15.7. Example of how the computer, along with an audit program, can be used to assist the auditor with auditing functions.

that deals mainly with the people element in the organization. In the long run, operation often has a greater impact on systems development than the other three constraints combined. Much of the current literature related to the field of information systems, reflects a concern that a preoccupation with technology and techniques have replaced the systems analyst's ability to deal effectively with people. While the dramatic and rapid developments in technology require an inordinate amount of attention from the analyst, these developments have also resulted in a greater need to pay attention to the human element of systems work.

The major result of the systems analyst's work is change, and many of the users and/or personnel in an organization cannot deal effectively with the changes which they are being asked to accept. This problem is more acute in the areas of the organization that traditionally performed many of the operations now done automatically by the information system. Moreover, these problems are found at each level of the organization.

People basically resist change, especially social change. The problems of change have been explored in *Future Shock* by Alvin Toffler.[12] He is concerned not so much with the direction of change, but with the rate of change. Rapid changes have a very unstabilizing effect on people and these effects are manifested in a variety of unusual behavior patterns. These include increased anxiety, depression, alienation, physical illness, apathy, withdrawal, and violence. Undue stress is caused in people by the difference between the rate at which life is changing and the rate at which people can adapt to these changes.

According to Toffler, the reason an increased rate of change is upsetting to people is because people are reared with "durational expectations." People come to expect how long one waits until something happens, or how long something will take. Technology is accelerating the rate of change and since people cannot cope with an increasing rate of change they are upset. Moreover, people's relationship with each other, with places, with things, with organizations, and with values are becoming ephemeral. One solution to managing change, ac-

[12] Alvin Toffler, *Future Shock,* (New York: Random House, Inc., 1970). Used with permission.

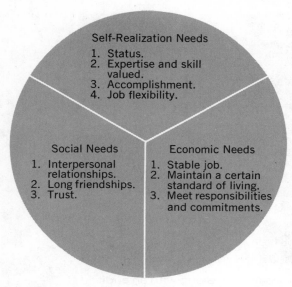

FIGURE 15.8. Human needs.

cording to Toffler, is to hold firm to some aspects of life and not let them change, and, if possible, introduce change into other aspects of life in some managed fashion.

In any event, the analyst and management must be aware of human behavior and understand the range of human needs and emotions, both normal and neurotic. Some of the basic needs of all people are shown in Figure 15.8. If systems analysts ignore the existence of these needs of people, they are in fact ignoring the existence of factors which, in the final analysis, determines whether or not a systems endeavor is accepted or rejected by the people who use it, or are affected by it.

There are at least three approaches that can be used to avoid resistance to systems work. These are: the bulldozer approach, the participation approach, and the objectives approach.

Bulldozer Approach. This approach is authoritarian in essence. The advocates of the information system changes force them through regardless of the outcome. Some successful information systems have been developed utilizing this approach. Normally, however, the results from such an approach

probably create a greater resistance toward any subsequent changes that might need to be made in the future. Such an approach causes users and general personnel, and possibly many managers, to feel that they are being controlled, used, and manipulated. Personnel are forced into becoming automatons. Feelings of frustration, alienation, and insecurity increases, thereby decreasing motivation, cooperation, and interest. In general, although it is still used in some instances, this approach appears to have little to recommend it.

Participation Approach. Most people want to be recognized and gain acceptance. They also want to participate in any changes that are being made. To allow the people to participate provides better understanding of information systems work and also reduces fear of losing human needs. People are more apt to accept the changes and support the system if they have a part in its development. It gives the participants a chance to go through a catharsis or blowing off steam process. Moreover, it provides a means by which the analyst can receive helpful suggestions. If this is the case, the analyst must remember to give credit where credit is due.

With this approach, it is emphasized that merely allowing people to participate in systems changes will not necessarily deter their resistance to proposed changes. This is especially true if the systems analyst pays lip service to involving people in systems changes to make them think they are really participating. Most people will recognize such tactics as a fraud and this can result in serious repercussions. Conversely, if systems analysts are conscientious in their efforts to have people participate in the systems effort, they can better understand specific human needs and design the system to be compatible with them.

Objectives Approach. This approach places the analyst more in the role of a teacher so that the people in the organization are to be fully apprised of what the systems objectives are. This approach uses some of the basic ideas in the participation approach, but the major developmental tasks are handled by the analyst. Most of the users are interested in, and are motivated by, those objectives which are consistent with their own goals, activities, and needs. The objectives, therefore, must be acceptable and compatible to those who must react to change.

Early in the systems analysis stage the analyst starts dealing with needs, and problems of resistance. At each step during systems development, the analyst gathers information about specific human needs, recognizes these as constraints, and creates the design of a system where the objectives are in line with human needs. At the same time, the analyst must clearly communicate to the users and others how the systems objectives will save effort and time; how it will increase efficiency, increase sales, and promote better relations with customers; and how the user will receive more specific, better tailored information. Change, using this approach, will be achieved to the degree that the analyst makes the user understand the need for the change, and how the change will specifically aid the user.

With the participation or objectives approach, a good system of human to human communications must be maintained. From the project management viewpoint, the status meeting is the primary vehicle for verbal communications. The status meeting is an excellent way to brief not only the project team members, but also various interested members of management as a whole, and users specifically. The following guidelines are recommended to the analyst to help ensure that any type of meeting is a productive activity.

1. Planning a Meeting
   a. Define the purpose of the meeting.
   b. Prepare a list of participants.
   c. Prepare an agenda and time schedule.
   d. Secure a meeting place which is conducive to both the participants and the subject.
   e. Notify the desired participants.
   f. Arrange for any special materials required in the meeting, e.g., flip charts, video equipment.

2. Conducting the Meeting
   a. State the purpose of the meeting.
   b. Welcome the participants.
   c. Describe the procedure which will be used at the meeting.
   d. Proceed from subject to subject in accordance with the agenda and time schedule.
   e. Defer any new problems or disagreements to another session.
   f. End the meeting promptly as scheduled to allow participants to make other time commitments.

3. Following up the Meeting
   a. Prepare a report which highlights major subjects, commitments, unresolved problems, etc.
   b. Send the meeting report to all participants and any who were excused.

SUMMARY

General management activities include: (1) the establishment of, and adherence to, a master plan for the information system; (2) selection, training, and assignment of personnel; (3) definition and description of each employee's responsibilities and duties; (4) establishment of procedures and performance standards; (5) establishment of internal control; and (6) the preparation and establishment of budgets, user request procedures, and pricing techniques.

Data center activities are routine in nature, and performance can usually be easily measured and controlled. On the other hand, since systems and programming work are more creative in nature, they are difficult to manage. However, with the use of appropriate time estimates and control techniques, management's effectiveness in planning, scheduling, and controlling these activities can be enhanced considerably.

Causes of systems maintenance are: (1) emergency maintenance, (2) routine maintenance, (3) special reporting requests, and (4) systems improvements. One of the major goals of management is to develop a highly maintainable system. This objective can be accomplished by: (1) designing for change, (2) design changes, (3) the establishment of standard configuration policies, (4) the enforcement of maintenance policies through control and audit procedures, (5) the organization of programmers and systems analysts for maintenance work, and (6) converting to more maintainable systems.

Auditing procedures are performed to ensure that management objectives are being met and that the integrity of the system is maximized. Types of audits include: (1) post implementation audit, (2) routine operational audit, (3) financial audit, and (4) systems audit. Many auditors, especially independent CPA auditors, are extending their traditional financial audits to include many aspects of the systems audit. Auditing techniques include: (1) observation, (2) inspection, (3) sampling, (4) confirmation, (5) comparison, and (6) inquiry. Approaches used to audit the computer operation of the information system include: (1) auditing around the computer, and (2) auditing through the computer.

In performing effective systems work and ensuring that changes in the system are accepted by the personnel of the organization, both the systems analyst and the management of the information system must be aware of human needs, and see to it that all systems designs are compatible with these needs. If the technical potential of information systems are to be realized, the various factors arising from people problems must be satisfied first.

REVIEW QUESTIONS

15.1 List and discuss the general management activities relative to the information system.

15.2 Discuss the methods used in measuring the performance of the data center. Give examples.

15.3 Why are performance measurements for the data center significantly different from those used in systems and programming work?

15.4 How might decision tables decrease the time required to write programs?

15.5 Why are more maintainable systems a major objective of management? Discuss fully.

15.6 List and discuss the causes of maintenance work. Give at least one example (of your own) of these causes.

15.7 List and discuss problems of maintenance. Discuss fully.

15.8 Why do you think most people dislike maintenance work?

15.9 List and fully discuss the procedures for achieving more maintainable systems.

15.10 Define modular design of programs.

15.11 Should maintenance be performed in the development groups, or in separate maintenance groups?

15.12 List and discuss the types of audits.

15.13 Why should the post implementation audit be delayed until several months after the implementation of a system?

15.14 List and give at least one example of auditing techniques.

15.15 Define internal control. Give a complete example of internal control.

15.16 List and discuss computer auditing approaches. Give advantages and disadvantages of each approach.

15.17 There are three approaches that can be used by the systems analyst to avoid resistance to change. List and discuss these approaches. Which do you recommend?

15.18 The planning of any complex systems project does not run in sequential blocks of time. Plans for these systems projects must be projected in networks that reflect not only the operation of overlapping tasks, but the interrelationships of these tasks. What technique do you suggest to help plan for this kind of project?

QUESTIONS FOR DISCUSSION

15.1 "Better scheduling of operations can modify workloads to provide better turnaround services to users. For example, the operations group can fit short CPU-time jobs (less than five minutes, with a small amount of input/output) into time slots in the schedule." Comment on this statement.

15.2 "The efforts of systems analysts and programmers are extremely difficult activities to exert control over." Discuss this statement.

15.3 How can one differentiate between some maintenance work, such as "systems improvements," and new development work?

15.4 "We wrote all our programs in LOGELNUM, the language promoted by the vendor we acquired our computer from. Now, we are planning on changing to another vendor but we are in a real bind because LOGELNUM is not compatible with the proposed new equipment." Comment on the several ramifications applicable to this statement.

15.5 Compare and contrast systems work performed by a systems analyst, and the auditing function performed by an auditor. Discuss fully.

15.6 "During the course of the financial audit, the auditor may develop helpful comments and suggestions on improving the effectiveness and the efficiency of policies, procedures, and controls which pertain to information systems. In recent times, the most significant advance in the role played by the auditor is in this extension from the traditional financial audit." Discuss.

15.7 "Many systems analysts, as well as managements, make the mistake of assuming that information systems development is controlled by technical, economic, and schedule constraints. There is a fourth constraint which might be more severe." What is this fourth constraint? Discuss fully.

15.8 Is technological development a boon or curse to mankind?

15.9 "The only way you can evaluate analysts and programmers is that they either get the job done or they don't." Discuss.

15.10 "Systems analysis involves a great deal of research and consequently cannot be managed effectively." Evaluate.

15.11 "Our programmers operate the computer themselves during testing periods." Discuss.

15.12 "For two years the systems department worked on the payroll system. When they finally got it completed, management refused to accept it." Discuss the possibilities for this situation actually occurring.

15.13 "All of our project managers are former analysts. We select our analysts from our programming staff and for the most part, all of our programmers are former computer operators." Discuss the advantages and disadvantages from this approach to personnel selection.

15.14 It has been estimated that almost 30% of a systems analyst's time is spent in administrative functions of some sort. Evaluate this comment.

15.15 "The manager of systems development is a tough negotiator. When he disagrees with the users, he does it his way or not at all." Discuss fully.

EXERCISES   **15.1** J. Caldwell, H. Custer, and H. Mann, have given the following time estimates respectively, to complete the cost/effectiveness analysis on some software packages:

Optimistic:	9 Days	6 Days	7 Days
Most likely:	14 Days	12 Days	14 Days
Pessimistic:	20 Days	18 Days	19 Days

As the chief systems analyst, compute the expected time to complete this project.

15.2 Using Figure 15.1, how long will it take to code a 300 manhour program (average)? How many manhours will it take to test this program?

15.3 Past experience has shown that a particular type program has an expected time of completion equal to 200 manhours. H. Wilson is assigned to prepare this program. The plan provides the following tasks and related times for each task.

Design program logic	50 Manhours
Code program	40 Manhours
Test program	70 Manhours
Document program	40 Manhours

After reviewing the program and developing a general (macro) flowchart, Wilson begins to code. At the end of several days, Wilson reports the following:

	Planned	Actual	Remaining
Design program logic	50	20	0
Code program	40	4	27
Test program	70	0	15
Document program	40	0	12

You are the chief programmer. What is your reaction to Wilson's revised plan?

15.4 You and your colleagues have done extensive research to determine the feasibility of acquiring computer equipment, to be housed in your school, for hands on use by students 24 hours per day, seven days a week. You are now ready to call a meeting of representative students, faculty, the dean, and president of the university. Prepare a complete agenda for this proposed meeting.

15.5 You have just accepted a position as Manager of Information Systems. Some of the major criticisms voiced by users are: (1) programming and systems project deadlines are seldom (if ever) met, and (2) projects in progress are scrapped and restarted when programmers or systems analysts leave.

How do you propose to meet this criticism?

15.6 Obtain from the library a series of journals related to data processing and information systems. From the articles and advertisements contained therein prepare a report discussing the types of equipment which promise "plug to plug compatibility."

Suggestions for reference: *Data Management, Automation, Datamation, Infosystems, Data Processor, Computer Decisions,* and *Computerworld.*

15.7 You have been put in charge of planning for, and scheduling, the establishment of terminal facilities at your school for faculty and students. The following times (in months) for each activity have been estimated.

	Activity	Optimistic	Most Likely	Pessimistic
1,2	Prepare site for terminals.	2	3	5
1,3	Order and receive terminals.	1	4	7
1,4	Order and receive supplies.	1	2	2
2,3	Install telecommunications.	2	3	4
2,6	Train consultants.	2	3	6
3,4	Test and correct equipment.	1	2	3
3,6	Seminars and faculty training.	3	4	6
4,5	Train programmers.	3	5	7
5,6	Write program packages.	6	12	18

Construct a network for each activity and compute the expected times, then compute the earliest and latest times and identify the critical path. Discuss the benefits of a network technique, such as PERT, for planning, scheduling, and controlling.

PROBLEMS   **15.1** Monitoring is the collection of statistics and actual performance parameters of an operating, live system. There are three goals of monitoring, as identified by Carlson: (1) save money, (2) understand the system better, and (3) indicate future developments and trends that will lead to better service and lower cost. Therefore, monitoring is implemented to measure a system's efficiency much as a time-study efficiency expert monitors an entire operation in a manufacturing plant.

Prepare a report on monitoring. To get started, read: Bell, "Choose Your Tools to Check Your Computer," *Computer Decisions,* November, 1972; Canning, "Savings from Performance Monitoring," *EDP Analyzer,* September, 1972; Carlson, "How to Save Money with Computer Monitoring," *Proceedings of the ACM Annual Conference,* Boston, 1972; and Lucas, "Performance Evaluation and Monitoring," *Computing Surveys,* September, 1971.

15.2 Refer to exercise 13.5 for a brief description of a state lottery system. Several months after this lottery system was implemented, the Director of the Lottery, R. Flippo, sent a request to the systems department for the following information to be provided:

(1) A monthly report of lottery tickets sold, by terminal, that would show the number of tickets sold for each terminal for each of the preceding 12 months.

(2) A report showing the number of winning tickets sold by each terminal for each of the last 12 months.

An archival file has been maintained which contains the following data:

> Sequence no.
> Lottery no.
> Series
> Area
> Territory
> Terminal code
> Won/loss indicator

Your assignment is to prepare the programming specifications to meet this special reporting request.

15.3 Interview a practicing systems analyst or auditor. Ascertain the problems he or she normally encounters in performing an audit. Prepare a report of your findings.

15.4 Conduct a post implementation audit of some system in your school or a local business. Prepare a report of your findings, highlighting the discrepancies between any projections and actual results.

15.5 The Giant S Manufacturing Corporation leases a small computer configuration for $12,000 a month. This payment includes machine usage for up to 176 hours per month and all hardware maintenance. Each metered hour of computer usage in excess of this base (176 hours per month) incurs a charge equal to 10% of the hourly rate for a base hour. The cost of operating personnel for the computer has been calculated at $9.50 per hour. Historically, the corporation has realized .8 of a computer usage hour for each operating personnel hour reported. Supply costs are estimated at $1100 per month. Lastly, the data processing center is assessed a monthly charge of $900 for use of building, utilities, and management fees, etc. The Manager of Data Processing, Sandra Widener, estimates that 300 hours per month will be metered during the next year.

(1) Calculate the budget for the Giant S Manufacturing Corporation's data processing center for the next year.
(2) Calculate the monthly budget.
(3) Calculate the expected cost per operating hour.

Betty Larance, the Manager of Systems and Programming for the Giant S Manufacturing Corporation, is in the process of completing an investigation for computerizing a manual Accounts Payable system. Thus far the following statistics have been determined: (1) $14,000 annually in clerical cost savings can be realized if the computer is utilized, (2) 25 meter hours per month will be required if the computer is utilized, (3) supply costs will not differ significantly whether the computer is used or not.

Based on these statistics as well as the economics you calculated in the first portion of this problem, determine the following:
(1) The cost of using the computer for processing Accounts Payable, based on the budgeted hourly cost.
(2) The actual cost which would be incurred by Giant S if Accounts Payable was processed on the computer.
(3) What would be your recommendation, based solely on the economics that you have determined?

BIBLIOGRAPHY   *Auditing Standards and Procedures,* Committee on Auditing Procedure Statement No. 33, New York: American Institute of Certified Public Accountants, 1963.

Bookman, "Make Your User Pay the Price," *Computer Decisions,* September, 1972.

Burke, "Selecting a Systems Analyst," *Business Automation,* July, 1969.

"COBOL Aid Packages," *EDP Analyzer,* May, 1972.

Dean, "A Comparison of Decision Tables Against Conventional COBOL as a Programming Tool for Commercial Applications," *Software World,* Spring, 1971.

Duvall, "Rules for Investigating Cost Variances," *Management Science,* June, 1967.

Dyckman, "The Investigation of Cost Variances," *Journal of Accounting Research,* Autumn, 1969.

Li, *Accounting, Computers, Management Information Systems,* New York: McGraw-Hill Book Co., 1968.

Rothery, *Installing and Managing a Computer,* New York: Brandon/Systems Press, Inc., 1968.

"Savings From Performance Monitoring," *EDP Analyzer,* September, 1972.

Schiff and Lewin, "The Impact of People on Budgets," *The Accounting Review,* April, 1970.

Schroeder, "The Real Part Time Computer," *Business Automation,* January, 1971.

Study Group on Computer Control and Audit Guidelines, Toronto, Canada: The Canadian Institute of Chartered Accountants, 1971.

"That Maintenance 'Iceberg'," *EDP Analyzer,* October, 1972.

Thierauf, *Data Processing for Business and Management,* New York: John Wiley & Sons, Inc., 1973.

Toffler, *Future Shock,* New York: Random House, Inc., 1970.

Vroom, V., *Some Personality Determinants of the Effects of Participation,* Englewood Cliffs, N.J.: Prentice-Hall, Inc., 1960.

Vroom, V., *Work and Motivation,* New York: John Wiley & Sons, Inc., 1964.

Wolfe, "A New Look at Programming Aptitudes," *Business Automation,* August, 1970.

IV

Appendices

Introduction
to Appendices

In the beginning of this text, it was stated that three basic components are required in modern information systems. These components are: (1) logico-mathematical models; (2) data processing methods, especially the computer and its related technology; and (3) systems analysis.

Therefore, three appendices are presented which treat the specific elements of these components. The text part of this book has dealt with information system concepts and practice. These three appendices provide the underlying techniques which give efficacy to this theory and practice.

Appendix A
Logico-Mathematical Models

Introduction

Many informational needs of an organization can be met by establishing a common data base and from it providing timely reports or online responses to the users, via remote terminals such as CRTs. An information system is also comprised of a number of information subsystems such as traditional accounting, inventory control, process control and production scheduling, shipping and transportation, sales analysis, and so on. The total information system is management oriented; thus, in addition to being a data processing center, it also uses logico-mathematical models to aid management in its planning, controlling, and decision making functions. In addition to developing reports and systems for historical record keeping and to satisfy business and governmental requirements, it is also the responsibility of the information systems analyst to select, test, and implement these models in order to provide alternative, predictive, optimizing, and performance information.

A systems analyst therefore needs to have a working knowledge of the various logico-mathematical models to provide maximum quality information to management and others. In this appendix several models, which over the years have proven to be valuable in converting raw data elements into meaningful information, are presented.

Traditional Accounting Models

The traditional accounting function, in addition to handling routine data processing activities, also provides a great deal of information to both internal and external constituents. Much of the information provided by this function is historical, and is stated in terms of money. However, traditional accounting also provides information which is performance oriented. In the following subsections most of the models used by traditional accountants are presented.[1]

Accounting reports derived from models aid management (as well as others) in:

1. Planning, because reporting information on past periods helps the user to make predictions about future events.
2. Controlling, because budgets and standards are set, and performances are measured against these budgets and standards.
3. Decision making, because the reporting of possible outcomes based on alternative inputs allows the decision maker to select the best alternatives.

The accounting function also acts as an overall control device for external constituents such as stockholders because it provides performance measurement via position statements, earnings statements, and fund statements, which together help to indicate how management is doing. It also helps asset control (e.g., cash, securities, receivables, and so on) by promoting efficiency and internal control,

which reduces loss through error or fraud. Moreover, it limits needless expenditures by establishing a decentralized system of budgets.

Bookkeeping Model

The bookkeeping model is an equation which sets up a procedure for classifying, recording, and reporting financial transactions of an organization. It can be stated as:

Assets (A_t) = Liabilities (L_t)
$\qquad$ + Contributed Capital (CC_t)
$\qquad\qquad$ + Retained Earnings (RE_t)

Each category represents some financial amount at some point in time. All transactions are classified and recorded in such a way that the total assets equal the sum of liabilities, contributed capital, and retained earnings.

Retained earnings at some point in time (usually stated at the end of an accounting period) is the algebraic sum of the retained earnings of the previous period, RE_{t-1}, the earnings for the period, $E_{t-1/t}$ and the dividends declared during the period, D. This equation is stated as:

$$RE_t = RE_{t-1} + E_{t-1/t} - D$$

Earnings are determined by matching the inputs, for the period, with the outputs, for the period. In business organizations the inputs are measured in terms of sales revenue, (R), and the outputs are measured in terms of expenses (EXP) required to generate this revenue. Income tax (TAX), is not recognized as an expense, per se, but as a social cost of doing business. The equation for earnings is stated as:

$$E_{t-1/t} = R_{t-1/t} - EXP_{t-1/t} - TAX_{t-1/t}$$

Accounts

Accounts are set up which represent each category in the above equations. These accounts are merely a place to receive transactional data, and to show increases or decreases where, at certain periods, the current amount balance of an item is available. All accounts can be algebraically summed, in accordance with the pro-

---

[1] For a tutorial treatment of these models, we refer you to: Paul E. Fertig, Donald F. Istvan, and Homer J. Mottice, *Using Accounting Information: An Introduction,* Second Edition, (New York: Harcourt Brace Jovanovich, Inc., 1971). Robert N. Anthony, *Management Accounting,* Fourth Edition (Homewood Illinois: Richard D. Irwin, Inc., 1970). Charles T. Horngren, *Cost Accounting: A Managerial Emphasis,* Second Edition, (Englewood Cliffs, N.J.: Prentice-Hall, Inc., 1967).

cedures dictated by the equations, to provide financial statements whenever needed.

These accounts take a variety of forms, depending on whether they are recorded on paper for manual data processing methods, or recorded on punched cards, magnetic tape, magnetic disk, etc. for computer processing. The basic procedures in classifying, recording, and reporting are the same whatever data processing method is used.

The essential features of an account can be shown in the form of a classical T-account, as follows:

DEBIT | CREDIT

The rules of recording are as follows:

1. *Debits* increase asset items, and decrease liabilities, contributed capital, and retained earnings.
2. *Credits* decrease asset items, and increase liabilities, contributed capital, and retained earnings.

Retained earnings represent the "meter" for earnings, i.e., revenue increases retained earnings, therefore a credit increases a revenue account. Conversely, an expense decreases retained earnings, so a debit increases an expense account.

Accounting data can also be structured in the form of an *m* by *n* matrix with the following general notation:

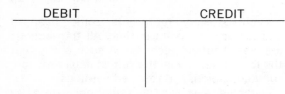

$$A = \begin{bmatrix} a_{11} & a_{12} & \cdots & a_{1n} \\ a_{21} & a_{22} & \cdots & a_{2n} \\ \cdot & \cdot & & \cdot \\ \cdot & \cdot & & \cdot \\ \cdot & \cdot & & \cdot \\ a_{m1} & a_{m2} & \cdots & a_{mn} \end{bmatrix}$$

Such a matrix is usually represented by the following abbreviation

$$A = (a_{ij}) \qquad i = 1, 2, \ldots, m$$
$$j = 1, 2, \ldots, n$$

where i = rows and j = columns.

An accounting matrix, using sixteen common accounts, is shown in Figure A.1. Notice that the increases and decreases in the accounts work the same as previously explained and that a current balance can be determined at any time. For example, look at Sales, a revenue account. It obviously has a credit balance (unless there were sales returns, which would be another account) and that balance is $90,000. But how were the sales made, cash or credit? Looking at the Cash and Accounts Receivable accounts, under the Sales account, one can readily determine that $30,000 of the sales were for cash and $60,000 were for credit.

Cost-Volume-Profit Model

Costs react on the basis of activity, time, or a combination thereof. We can categorize costs into four basic behavior patterns, which are:

1. *Variable cost behavior.* These costs react in direct proportion to changes in activity.
2. *Nonvariable cost behavior.* These costs remain the same no matter what the level of activity, as these costs are strictly a function of time.
3. *Semi-variable cost behavior.* These costs are basically nonvariable at low volumes of activity, but at higher volumes of activity they tend to exhibit characteristics of variable costs.
4. *Semi-fixed cost behavior.* These costs are nonvariable over some period of time but change to a new level at the end of the relevant time period. For example, this year's rent is $12,000, next year it will be $18,000.

In knowing cost behavior, we can simulate those profits which might be obtained with changes in volume (activity). This simulated activity can be illustrated in a profitgraph[2], as shown in Figure A.2. In this graph, for simplicity, we delineate only two categories of cost—variable and nonvariable.

Figure A.2 shows the relationship between cost and profit at various volume levels. The measure of volume can be number of units produced and sold, or it can be sales revenue. At lower volumes, a loss is expected; at higher volumes a profit is expected; somewhere in

[2] Anthony, *op. cit.,* pp. 461–466.

	01	02	03	04	05	06	07	08	09	10	11	12	13	14	15	16	17	18	19
CREDITS / DEBITS	CASH	RE	INV	PR	PE	AD	AP	CS	RE	S	COGS	WAGE	DEP	RENT	OTH	DIV	BEG DR	Σ DR	END DR
01 CASH		10000						400000		30000								440000	266000
02 ACCOUNTS RECEIVABLE										60000								60000	50000
03 INVENTORY							150000											150000	150000
04 PREPAID RENT	12000																	12000	12000
05 PLANT AND EQUIPMENT	75000						25000											100000	100000
06 ACCUMULATED DEPRECIATION																			
07 ACCOUNTS PAYABLE	65000																	65000	0
08 CAPITAL STOCK																			
09 RETAINED EARNINGS																			
10 SALES																			
11 COST OF GOODS SOLD																			
12 WAGES EXPENSE	22000																	22000	22000
13 DEPRECIATION EXPENSE																			
14 RENT EXPENSE																			
15 OTHER EXPENSE							8000											8000	8000
16 DIVIDENDS																			
17 BEGINNING CREDIT BALANCE																			
18 Σ CREDIT TOTALS THIS PERIOD	174000	10000					183000	400000		90000									
19 ENDING CREDIT BALANCES	0	0					118000	400000		90000									

FIGURE A.1. The accounting matrix.

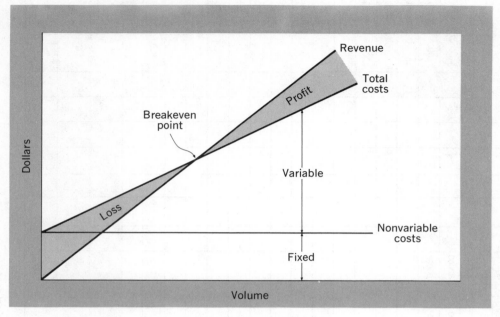

FIGURE A.2. Profitgraph.

between a breakeven point exists where cost equals revenue.

The cost-volume-profit relationship provides a useful way for simulating the profit factors of any organization. The factors which increase profit are:

1. Increased selling price per unit.
2. Decreased variable cost per unit.
3. Decreased nonvariable cost.
4. Increased volume.

A typical question from management may be: What would the profit picture look like if we decreased selling price by 5%, variable cost remained constant, decreased nonvariable cost by 8%, and increased volume of sales by 20%? A variety of questions such as this, proposed by management, could generate information which could effectively enhance planning and decision making.

Budget and Performance Analysis Models

A budget is a plan of action, expressed in quantitative terms, which covers some specific time period. The key concept of a budget is to structure it in terms that equate to the responsibility of those who are charged with its execution. In this way, the budget is used not only as a planning device but also as a control device. Budgets are of three types:[3]

1. An operating budget which shows planned operations for the forthcoming period.
2. A cash budget which shows the anticipated sources and uses of cash.
3. A capital budget which shows for planned changes in a variety of resources in addition to cash.

The budgeting process involves a planning-control-planning life cycle, which is described as follows:

1. Planning which entails selecting objectives and means for their obtainment.
2. Controlling encompasses two activities:
   a. translate objectives into units of output and determine specific inputs to generate outputs.

[3] Ibid., p. 491.

b. comparison of actual operations with budgeted operations.

3. Planning at this stage uses performance reports for evaluating past operations for planning future operations.

Budgets can also be viewed as being prepared for different levels in an organization. Typically, budgets may relate to four levels: (1) entire organization (master budget), (2) division, (3) department, and (4) subunit. For example, a typical performance report is structured as follows:

	Budgeted	Actual	Variance*
Material	XX	XX	XU
Labor	XX	XX	XF
Other	XX	XX	XU

* U: Unfavorable; F: Favorable.

Budget is a macro concept whereas standards are a micro concept. For example, the standard cost per labor hour may be $5. The budget for 20,000 manhours would show a total labor cost of $100,000. The standard itself is a predetermined estimate of what performance should be under stated conditions. In preparing performance information based on standards, we can use three models:

Quantity Variance = (Actual Quantity
－ Standard Quantity)
× Standard Cost

Cost Variance = (Actual Cost － Standard
Cost) × Actual Quantity

Total Variance = Quantity Variance + Cost
Variance

Payoff Graph Analysis Model

The payoff graph is another tool that can be effectively used by the analyst to enhance the information received by management. Payoff

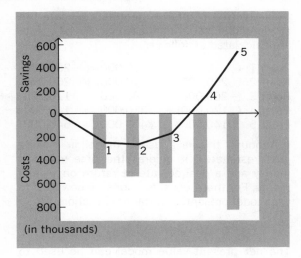

FIGURE A.3. Payoff analysis graph comparing the proposed system to the present system.

analysis is a simple, straightforward technique which can be used by analysts to compare costs and savings of alternative systems. For example, examine the set of figures given in the table below.

These figures represent the costs of both systems and the resulting savings (or dis-savings) when compared to each other. Figure A.3 depicts a payoff analysis graph which, in a meaningful manner, makes this comparison.

The present system's costs are represented by the cross-hatched areas. Savings are calculated by subtracting the proposed system's costs from the present system's costs. The savings are:

YEAR 1: 450,000 － 700,000 ＝ －250,000
YEAR 2: 500,000 － 510,000 ＝ －10,000
YEAR 3: 570,000 － 480,000 ＝   90,000
YEAR 4: 720,000 － 410,000 ＝ 310,000
YEAR 5: 810,000 － 410,000 ＝ 400,000

	Year 1	Year 2	Year 3	Year 4	Year 5
Costs:					
Semi–automatic (Present System)	$450,000	$500,000	$570,000	$720,000	$810,000
Automatic (Proposed System)	$700,000	$510,000	$480,000	$410,000	$410,000
Savings:	($250,000)	($ 10,000)	$ 90,000	$310,000	$400,000

The plotted points in the graph indicate the accumulated net annual savings. These points are calculated as follows:

Point 1:   0   + (−250,000) = −250,000
Point 2: (−250,000) + (−10,000) = −260,000
Point 3: (−260,000) +   90,000 = −170,000
Point 4: (−170,000) +   310,000 = 140,000
Point 5:   140,000 +   400,000 = 540,000

Although this is a useful model in making gross estimates, it ignores the time value of money and a desired rate of return on investments. For these considerations we now turn to the model presented in the next section.

Net Present Value Model

The net present value model can be used to help management make decisions about investment proposals if such a proposal can be reduced to monetary amounts. Stated simply, neglecting nonmonetary considerations, an investment proposal is accepted if the present value of its earnings or cost savings equals or exceeds the amount of the investment required at some selected rate of return.

For example, suppose that management is thinking of purchasing a computer system for $380,000. The useful life of the computer is five years. The cost savings for the first year is $30,000, for the next three years $100,000, and for the last year $80,000. The minimum desired rate of return is 10%. Neglecting other quantitative or qualitative considerations, should management purchase the computer?

In the example below, the net present value of − $77,050 means the investment has not earned what it should at a minimum desired rate of return of 10%. Therefore, the investment is undesirable. If the present value were positive or zero, the investment would be desirable because its return either exceeds or meets the desired minimum. However, this simplistic problem assumes that there are no other investment projects competing for a finite amount of investment funds.

Additional Models

In addition to some of the basic, traditional accounting models presented above there are others which also help managements in their planning, controlling, and decision making. In many organizations, the function of management is performed on an intuitive basis. That is, no systematic effort is made to define and measure variables affecting the organization. There are, however, a number of logico-mathematical

	Present Value of $1 Discounted at 10%	Present Value	Cost Savings Streams					
			0	1	2	3	4	5
Annual Cost Savings:								
	.909	$ 27,270	$30,000					
	.826	82,600		$100,000				
	.751	75,100			$100,000			
	.683	68,300				$100,000		
	.621	49,680					$80,000	
Present Value of Future Cost Savings		$ 302,950						
Initial Investment	1.000	−380,000	$380,000					
Net Present Value		$− 77,050						

models which help to systematize and quantify certain variables in a manner where management can make more knowledgeable decisions. In this section, we discuss some of these models.[4]

Contribution-By-Value Analysis Model

A very simple, but quite effective, logical model that can be used in almost any kind of performance analysis is termed contribution-by-value analysis (also called ABC analysis). This analysis is based on Pareto's Law, which when roughly interpreted is: an empirical relationship describing the number of objects X whose contribution is Y in the form $X = AY^{-(1 \pm \alpha)}$.[5]

Pareto's Law shows an empirical relationship describing the number of persons X whose income is Y where $0 \leqslant Y \leqslant \infty$ and A is a constant. The expression $X = AY^{-(1+\alpha)}$ is used to designate any frequency distribution whether related to income or not, that is, the variable Y may be measured from an arbitrary value. The coefficient α is called the Pareto Index and indicates the degree of concentration of incomes or any other measurements.

To explain in laymen's terms, Pareto's Law states that in most situations a relatively small percentage of certain objects contribute a relatively high percentage of output. For instance, it can be shown that in most areas approximately 15–30% of the population contributes 70–90% of the tax revenue. Or, for example, that 20% of the employees in an office do 80% of the work. Many systems analysts find that when inventory items are plotted on a cumulative percentage graph, in order of descending value, Pareto's relationship usually exists. Relative to such a phenomenon, one frequently hears a rule of thumb quoted as: 20% of the items in inventory account for 80% of the sales. Such an analysis is quite effective in that it reveals very clearly the performance of any situation analyzed. For inventory analysis, the contribution-by-value analysis can be applied to sales by customer, by salesman, by product item, by territory, by warehouse, and so on.

An example on contribution-by-value analysis relative to sales by warehouses is discussed and illustrated in Figure A.4.

To prepare the analysis, the following steps are taken.

1. Dollar annual sales are calculated for each warehouse by multiplying sales price times quantity sold for each product and computing a grand total for all products in each warehouse.

2. All warehouses are arranged by dollar annual sales in descending sequence.

3. A list is printed from these ranked warehouses. Included in this report is such information as warehouse number, warehouse count, percent of total, annual sales of each warehouse, cumulative sales, and percent of total contribution. The relevant points of this report are:

a. The top 10% of the warehouses account for 81.20% of the dollar sales. In other words, a mere five out of fifty warehouses account for over four-fifths of the sales of the entire business or close to $6.83 million annually.

b. The upper 20% of the warehouses account for 88.30% of the sales. An additional 10% increase in the number of warehouses increased sales by 7.10%.

c. The upper 50% of the warehouses account for 96% of the sales.

d. The upper 74% of the warehouses account for 99.20% of the sales. Conversely, the lower 26% of the warehouses account for only .80% of the sales.

The information from the report is plotted to assist management in visualizing the relationships between number of warehouses and their relative contribution to sales volume. A plot of the results of this analysis, with the percentage of cumulative annual sales on the vertical axis, and the percentage of warehouses on the horizontal axis, appears in Figure A.5.

The contribution-by-value analysis shows that

---

[4] For an in depth treatment of a variety of models, refer to: H. Bierman, C. P. Bonini, L. E. Fouraker, and R. Jaedicke, *Quantitative Analysis for Business Decisions,* Revised Edition, (Homewood, Illinois: Richard D. Irwin, Inc., 1965). Howard Raiffa, *Decision Analysis,* (Reading, Massachusetts: Addison-Wesley, 1968).

[5] C. Jay Slaybaugh, "Pareto's Law and Modern Management," *Management Services,* March–April, 1967.

Warehouse Number	Warehouse Count	Number of Warehouses Percent of Total	Annual Sales	Cumulative Sales	Cumulative Percent of Total Contribution
1	1	2.00	4,331,927.34	4,331,927.34	56.00
2	2	4.00	1,331,521.32	5,663,448.66	73.20
41	3	6.00	271,765.00	5,935,213.66	76.70
3	4	8.00	189,880.05	6,125,093.71	79.10
50	5	10.00	157,450.05	6,282,543.76	81.20
94	6	12.00	145,175.00	6,427,717.76	83.10
45	7	14.00	123,044.65	6,550,762.41	84.60
14	8	16.00	98,355.30	6,649,117.71	85.90
48	9	18.00	94,579.75	6,743,697.46	87.10
43	10	20.00	86,769.56	6,830,467.02	88.30
42	11	22.00	75,180.12	6,905,647.14	89.20
25	12	24.00	68,287.65	6,973,934.79	90.10
67	13	26.00	66,245.20	7,040,179.99	91.00
26	14	28.00	60,040.40	7,100,220.39	91.80
64	15	30.00	58,352.45	7,158,572.84	92.50
38	16	32.00	42,587.50	7,201,160.34	93.10
39	17	34.00	36,915.80	7,238,076.14	93.50
15	18	36.00	35,601.80	7,273,677.94	94.00
29	19	38.00	32,322.60	7,306,000.54	94.40
36	20	40.00	29,919.65	7,335,920.19	94.80
4	21	42.00	29,322.25	7,365,242.44	95.20
24	22	44.00	29,184.10	7,394,426.54	95.60
19	23	46.00	28,548.05	7,422,974.59	95.90
57	24	48.00	27,129.90	7,450,104.49	96.30
95	25	50.00	24,260.13	7,474,364.62	96.60
62	26	52.00	23,088.10	7,497,452.72	96.90
47	27	54.00	23,379.75	7,520,832.47	97.20
16	28	56.00	22,110.39	7,542,942.86	97.50
17	29	58.00	19,293.90	7,562,236.76	97.70
66	30	60.00	18,705.50	7,580,942.26	98.00
71	31	62.00	17,925.20	7,598,876.46	98.20
46	32	64.00	15,764.25	7,614,631.71	98.40
58	33	66.00	14,306.00	7,628,937.71	98.60
18	34	68.00	13,304.20	7,642,241.91	98.80
35	35	70.00	12,741.70	7,654,983.61	98.90
28	36	72.00	11,347.80	7,666,331.41	99.10
65	37	74.00	10,164.25	7,676,495.66	99.20
34	38	76.00	10,087.15	7,686,582.81	99.30
61	39	78.00	9,422.20	7,696,005.01	99.50
27	40	80.00	6,463.10	7,702,468.11	99.50
91	41	82.00	6,196.60	7,708,664.61	99.60
54	42	84.00	5,592.55	7,714,257.16	99.70
55	43	86.00	4,507.80	7,718,764.96	99.70
5	44	88.00	4,049.70	7,722,814.66	99.80
70	45	90.00	3,356.00	7,726,170.96	99.80
37	46	92.00	3,262.10	7,729,433.06	99.90
60	47	94.00	2,402.35	7,731,835.41	99.90
49	48	96.00	1,694.50	7,733,529.91	99.90
23	49	98.00	558.35	7,734,088.26	99.90
68	50	100.00	252.50	7,734,340.76	100.00

FIGURE A.4. Contribution-by-warehouse sales report.

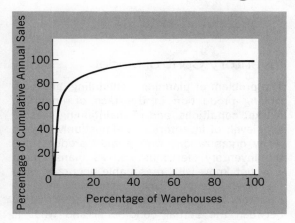

FIGURE A.5. Graphic representation of the contribution-by-warehouse sales report.

the company is operating several warehouses which are probably not necessary for efficient and streamlined operations. However surprising the above relationships are on first exposure, they will probably be found in any organization no matter what the situation. It should also be noted that the discernment of such relationships provide management with valuable information even though the contribution-by-value analysis model is, itself, simplistic.

Forecast Models

Good forecasts are vital to the success of every organization. The sales forecast, for example, is a key function in planning and controlling inventory systems. Inventory management, production, and procurement generally are geared to the sales activity that transpires in the subsequent period. The sales forecast is the basic information for production, inventory, procurement, and employment plans. Even though there are inherent errors in any forecasting model, an organization that bases its operations on intuitive decision making is ignoring the possibilities for a more efficient operation.

The Least Squares Model

As an extrapolative forecast model, the least squares technique uses historical data exclusively. When a model of this type is used, two

basic assumptions must be made: that the recent level of quantity will continue and that the recent rate of change will remain about the same. The least squares line approximating the set of points (X_1, Y_1), (X_2, Y_2), . . . , (X_n, Y_n) has the equation

$$Y = a_0 + a_1 X$$

where the constants a_0 and a_1 are determined by solving simultaneously the equations

$$\Sigma Y = a_0 N + a_1 \Sigma X$$
$$\Sigma XY = a_0 \Sigma X + a_1 \Sigma X^2$$

which are called the normal equations for the least squares line. Here, X is the independent variable and Y is the dependent variable. The constants, a_0 and a_1, of the above formulas can be found from the formulas

$$a_0 = \frac{(\Sigma X^2)(\Sigma Y) - (\Sigma XY)(\Sigma X)}{N\Sigma X^2 - (\Sigma X)^2}$$

$$a_1 = \frac{N\Sigma XY - (\Sigma Y)(\Sigma X)}{N\Sigma X^2 - (\Sigma X)^2}$$

The least squares line passes through the point $(\bar{X}, \bar{Y})$, called the centroid or center of gravity of the data.

Suppose the value of X represents time, such as months, and the value of Y represents quantities of products sold each month. The value of Y can be extrapolated according to some value of X. In other words, if the independent variable X is time, the data show the values of Y at various times in the future.

Since Y is estimated from X, $\hat{Y}$ represents the value of Y for given values of X as estimated from the least squares regression line of

$$Y = a_0 + a_1 X$$

From this a measure of the scatter about the regression line of X on Y is supplied by the quantity

$$S_{Y.X} = \sqrt{\frac{(Y - \hat{Y})^2}{N}}$$

which is called the standard error of the estimate of Y on X.[6]

[6] The above discussion of the least squares method represents a summarization of several comprehensive textbooks. For example, see: Samuel B. Richmond, *Statistical Analysis* (New York: The Ronald Press Company, 1964), Chapters 2, 7, 18, and 19.

The Exponential Smoothing Model

Exponential smoothing is similar to a moving average; however, where applicable, exponential smoothing is normally chosen as a forecasting method for two reasons, which are:

1. With the moving average all data in the series are weighted equally. In other words, recent data are given the same weight as older data.
2. Forecasting by the moving average method requires that a great deal of data be maintained.

Actually, exponential smoothing is nothing more or less than a form of weighted moving average. All that is needed to use the exponential smoothing model is a smoothing constant, the current forecast, and a new observation.

The computational procedure of exponential smoothing is shown by the following formula:

New Average = Old Average
+ α(New Demand − Old Average)

where α designates a smoothing constant between 0 and 1.

The new average represents the forecast of demand for the subsequent forecast interval. The old average is the new average of the preceding forecast interval, and the new demand is the actual demand for the present period.

By controlling the weight of the most recent data, α simultaneously determines the average age of the data included in the estimate of the average. The value chosen for the smoothing constant can be such that the estimate is very stable, or reacts very quickly. For example, $\alpha = 0.5$ would give a greater weight to the new data than $\alpha = 0.1$. Regardless of the value of α, the weighting of data follows what is called an exponential curve; therefore, the name exponential smoothing.

One of the crucial questions which arises when one uses exponential smoothing is the size of the smoothing constant that should be used. Conceptually, the answer is simple. There should be enough weight to give the system stability, but it should be small enough so that real

(not random) changes in the level of demand will be recognized.

Inventory Control Model

The problem of planning, scheduling, and controlling production in the face of uncertain market conditions, and of maintaining reasonable levels of inventories, is almost universal. In many organizations with a wide product line, the inventory clerks as well as management may not know with reasonable accuracy what the levels are, and an investigation into the inventory will often indicate a wide variation between the actual conditions, and what is thought to be the inventory. When an inventory item is overstocked, the error may not become evident for a long time, or not at all. When an item is understocked and a stock-out occurs, customer goodwill is reduced. Any organization with inventory problems, therefore, needs an inventory management system that accomplishes two things: (1) it makes certain that approximately all items are available in the correct quantity when they are needed, and (2) it prevents an increase of inventory beyond proper limits. Proper inventory management assures that an adequate supply of inventory items be maintained and requires an optimum balance between shortage and overstock. Too many shortages decrease customer service level. Conversely, an overstock of items ties up working capital that can be used more profitably elsewhere.

Replenishment, Lead Time, and Safety Stock

There are two approaches to replenishing inventories. The first is shown in Figure A.6, and is termed a periodic system wherein an order is placed on a specific date. The disadvantage of this method is that there is a risk of stock-outs. The second approach illustrated in Figure A.7, is termed reorder point system in that an order is placed when the inventory level of an item reaches a predetermined level L_{RE}.

The time T in the periodic method is always the same, whereas T in the reorder point

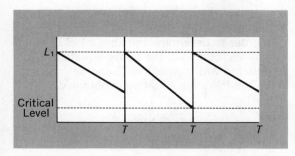

FIGURE A.6. Periodic replenishment system.

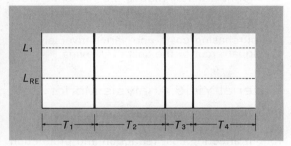

FIGURE A.7. Reorder point replenishment system.

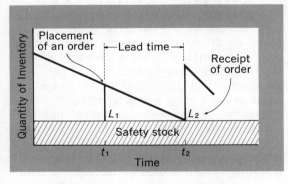

FIGURE A.8. Illustration of lead time and safety stock.

method is unequal. The method more often used is the second method which consists of placing a constant order quantity when the inventory level reaches the reorder level. The reorder level is computed as follows:

Reorder Level =
    Lead Time × Forecast of Demand
                          + Safety Stock

The lead time t_1 to t_2 is that time interval between placement of an order and receipt of that order. In Figure A.7, it was assumed that lead time was zero. Such an assumption is normally not realistic. Lead time would probably be similar to that shown in Figure A.8. The safety stock allows for a margin of error in estimating lead time or demand.

The Problem of How Much to Order

There are many different methods of determining how much to order. The best known model used in this area is the classic EOQ (economic order quantity) model. This model reveals to the inventory clerk how much to buy (or order) when a reorder point is reached.

The order quantity chosen will incur certain costs. Two different sets of cost factors are considered. If a greater or lesser quantity is ordered, some costs will increase, while others decrease. Among those costs which increase are interest, obsolescence, risk, and storage, while the set of decreasing costs includes such items as freight and procurement costs. These costs can be lumped into two categories: (1) cost to purchase and (2) cost to carry inventory. The goal is to balance the opposing costs in order to obtain the minimum total. For an illustration, see Figure A.9. The graph illustrates two facts:

1. As orders are placed more frequently, purchasing costs increase.
2. As orders are placed more frequently, carrying costs decrease because the cycle stock (cycle stock is one-half the order quantity) is less.

The total operating cost is the sum of purchasing and carrying costs, and Figure A.9 shows that it is lowest when these two are equal. Notice that there is a relevant range of choices between *A* and *B* where the resultant total cost is not greatly affected by slight deviations from the best ordering frequency.

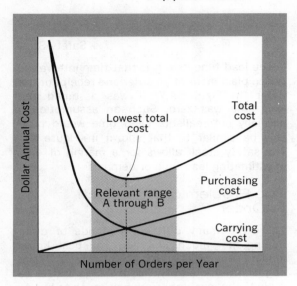

FIGURE A.9. Total inventory costs versus ordering frequency.

The literature normally handles the cost of purchasing as a constant amount for each order placed, and the cost of carrying is lumped into one percentage figure which is represented by P. Let Y designate the expected yearly demand in physical units (determined from the forecast model), let Q be the economic lot size in physical units, C be the unit cost, and S be the cost of purchasing involved in making one order in dollars. Then total annual variable costs (TVC) are expressed as follows:[7]

$$TVC = \frac{QC}{2} P + \frac{Y}{Q} S$$

In the absence of safety allowances, inventories vary from Q to 0. The average values of inventory is therefore $QC/2$ if the new order quantity replenishes stock at the time the inventory is depleted. The $QC/2$ times P represents the annual carrying cost. Y/Q represents the number of times a year that orders are

[7] For example, see: Thomson M. Whitin, *The Theory of Inventory Management* (Princeton, N.J.: Princeton University Press, 1957), pp. 32–34. Martin K. Starr and David W. Miller, *Inventory Control: Theory and Practice* (Englewood Cliffs, N.J.: Prentice-Hall, Inc., 1962).

placed. Therefore, $(Y/Q)S$ represents the total annual purchasing costs.

In order to determine the amount of Q which minimizes total cost, the above equation is differentiated with respect to Q and set equal to zero. The following equation is obtained:

$$\frac{PC}{2} - \frac{YS}{Q^2} = 0$$

which results in the solution:

$$Q = \sqrt{\frac{2YS}{PC}}$$

This formula states that Q, the economic order quantity, varies directly with the square root of the forecasted demand and the square root of the purchasing costs and varies inversely with the square root of the cost of carrying.

Material Yield Analysis Model

In a number of industries, particularly of the process type, material yield plays a significant role in effecting cost reduction and production improvement. Material yield standards are generally set for various types of raw material. In most cases the yield standards are based on laboratory tests or company records. A substantial cost reduction is achieved through the improvement of the yield of good products based on proper procurement and production efforts. A variance analysis program pointing out and evaluating causes of low yield aids management in minimizing of shrinkage and waste in purchasing and production. If, for example, the procurement personnel purchase defective raw material, an excess of shrinkage will occur during preparation of this material for processing. Consequently, a yield analysis and reporting system should be installed to determine the degree of shrinkage or waste.

Standards for material usage during the production phase are of paramount importance to top management. The plant manager and top management personnel need to have feedback which will enable them to detect and measure losses of raw produce during the production process. Not only do the reports of material

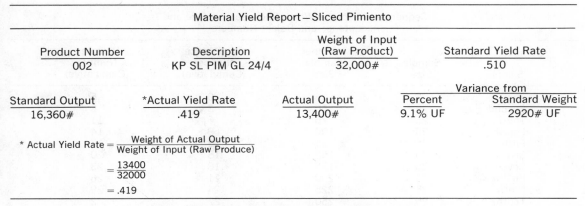

Material Yield Report—Sliced Pimiento

Product Number	Description	Weight of Input (Raw Product)	Standard Yield Rate
002	KP SL PIM GL 24/4	32,000#	.510

Standard Output	*Actual Yield Rate	Actual Output	Variance from Percent	Variance from Standard Weight
16,360#	.419	13,400#	9.1% UF	2920# UF

$$* \text{ Actual Yield Rate} = \frac{\text{Weight of Actual Output}}{\text{Weight of Input (Raw Produce)}}$$

$$= \frac{13400}{32000}$$

$$= .419$$

FIGURE A.10.   Yield analysis report.

yield disseminate information to responsible persons, but they ensure a significant degree of control of the processing function.

The basic question is whether the standard amount of raw material is used to obtain a given output of the finished product. The difficulty here is that computation of variances is delayed until the production process is completed. However, at the Yummy Company, production is run where a number of batches comprise sub-batches of an overall batch.

An example of yield information reporting is shown in Figure A.10.

The yield analysis report of Figure A.10 does not tell why there is an unfavorable variance in the yield of this particular batch of pimiento. It does, however, give feedback to the plant manager, the manager of procurement, the president, and other responsible persons that particular phases in the processing function may be faulty. A retracing of the overall process must be set into motion in order to isolate the cause of the unfavorable variances and take necessary corrective action.

Quality Control Analysis and Reporting

Every organization, large or small, faces the problem of attaining and maintaining satisfactory quality of their output. First, the quality attributes must be identified. Next, accurate standard measurements must be set. Finally, the allowable departures from such standard measurements must be determined. Moreover, satisfactory quality must be obtained at a reasonable and competitive cost level.

Product quality variation arises out of the variables which constitute a given process. The following are basic:

1. The raw materials which enter a process themselves vary in form and composition.
2. The production process itself varies and the resulting output may be below satisfactory quality.

The obvious objectives, therefore, are to reduce the amount of defective raw materials going into production and to eliminate defective finished products. These objectives are never fully possible, but a reduction in the number of defectives in the total operation must be sought.

Statistical sampling and control tables can be used effectively in implementing quality control in organizations. A simple table for this purpose is shown in Figure A.11.

The table indicates that if in the first sample of 25 from some population (batch or lot), there are 5 or more defectives then that population being tested is rejected. If there are more than 0 and less than 5 defectives, then another sample of 25 is taken. In this next sample if the

Sequence of Samples Which Show Sample Size and
Acceptance and Reject Numbers

Sample	Sample Size	Combined Sample Size	Acceptance Number (Cumulative)	Rejected Number (Cumulative)
First	25	25	0	5
Second	25	50	3	8
Third	25	75	6	11
Fourth	25	100	9	14
Fifth	25	125	12	17
Sixth	25	150	15	20
Seventh	25	175	18	23
Eighth	25	200	21	26
Ninth	25	225	24	29
Tenth	25	250	27	32

FIGURE A.11. A table of acceptance and rejection numbers.

cumulative total of defectives is 3 or less the population is accepted. If the number of defectives is greater than 3 but less than 8, another sample is taken. If the cumulative total of defectives at the second sample is 8 or more, the population is rejected, and so on.

Network Model

PERT[8] is an example of a network model used for planning and controlling projects with well defined activities and events. PERT is based on a network composed of activities that take time to accomplish. Between the activities are instantaneous events, which designate the completion of each activity. Probably a better interpretation indicates that events represent a start or finish of the activities.

The activities are placed on a network and are represented by arrows. Generally, the arrows or activities flow from left to right. There are four rules to follow when placing an activity on the network. They are:

1. A determination must be made to see if any activities logically precede the activity that is under consideration.

2. A determination must be made to see if any activities are logically concurrent with the activity under consideration.

3. A determination must be made to spot activities which are logically subsequent to the activity under consideration.

4. Events must be clearly defined relative to their beginning and end.

Expected Time

The activity time must be estimated by someone knowledgeable about particular processes such as foremen, plant managers, etc. There are three time estimates furnished, which are:

1. *Most Likely Time.* What time would you expect to complete this particular activity?

2. *Optimistic Time.* If everything progresses normally the first time and there are no difficulties, how much time will it take to complete this particular activity? In other words, what is the minimum possible time in which this particular task or activity can be completed?

3. *Pessimistic Time.* What is the longest time this particular activity or task has ever taken?

The goal in getting three subjective time estimates is to use them to calculate a single weighted average or mean time. This average or mean time is called the expected time of the activity. Briefly, the three time estimates are

[8] For full treatment of PERT, refer to: Russell D. Archibald and Richard L. Villoria, *Network-Based Management Systems (PERT/CPM).* (New York: John Wiley and Sons, Inc., 1967). Harry F. Evarts, *Introduction to PERT,* (Boston: Allyn and Bacon, Inc., 1964).

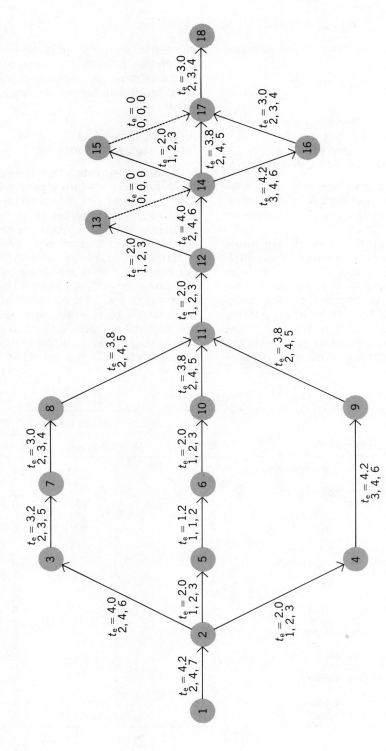

FIGURE A.12. Network for okra/tomatoes/corn batch project.

related to the expected time by the following formula:

$$t_e = \frac{O + 4M + P}{6}$$

where O = optimistic time estimate
 M = most likely time estimate
 P = pessimistic time estimate
 t_e = expected time (weighted average)

The network for a batch-project of okra/tomatoes/corn is shown in Figure A.12. The activities and time estimates are listed below in Table A.1.

Critical events on the network are those which have zero slack time. Slack time equals the latest event time less the earliest event time. The latest event time is the latest time that an event can be completed without disrupting the project. Earliest event time is the earliest time that an event can occur. A line connecting these critical events represents the critical path. An increase or decrease in time along this path will increase or decrease the completion date by the same amount. Figure A.13 illustrates the critical path (represented by the broader line) for our okra/tomatoes/corn example.

Probability and Statistical Models

Many data elements which become input into various models are future oriented or they basically represent an unknown quantity. Consequently, estimates must be made. These estimates are often made in the form of a probability distribution and merely represent a formalization of an estimator's judgment. For example, "what will sales revenue be for the next quarter?" is a typical question an analyst might ask. The estimator states a range of possibilities together with an estimate of the probability each will occur. The sum of these possibilities multiplied by the applicable probability equals the expected value of the

TABLE A.I

| Activity | Description | Time in Days | | | |
		Optimistic	Most Likely	Pessimistic	t_e
1,2	Unloading/testing raw produce	2	4	7	4.2
2,3	Washing okra	2	4	6	4.0
2,4	Washing/stemming tomatoes	1	2	3	2.0
2,5	Loading can racks	1	2	3	2.0
3,7	Cutting okra	2	3	5	3.2
4,9	Blanching tomatoes	3	4	6	4.2
5,6	Mixing device changeover	1	1	2	1.2
6,10	Preparation of corn for mixing	1	2	3	2.0
7,8	Preparation of okra for mixing	2	3	4	3.0
8,11	Loading of okra	2	4	5	3.8
9,11	Loading of tomatoes	2	4	5	3.8
10,11	Loading of corn	2	4	5	3.8
11,12	Canning process	1	2	3	2.0
12,13	Quality control–testing	1	2	3	2.0
12,14	Pressure cooker process	2	4	6	4.0
13,14	Dummy	0	0	0	0
14,15	Quality control–testing	1	2	3	2.0
14,16	Cool bath process	3	4	6	4.2
14,17	Warehouse preparation	2	4	5	3.8
15,17	Dummy	0	0	0	0
16,17	Stacking in warehouse	2	3	4	3.0
17,18	Cleanup and retooling	2	3	4	3.0

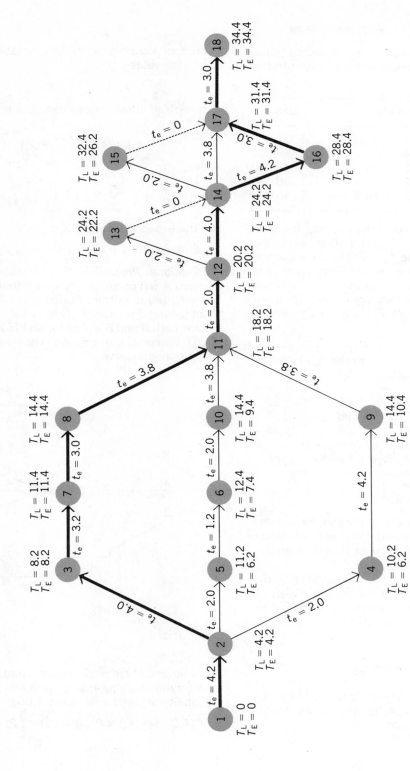

FIGURE A.13. Network showing earliest and latest times. Legend: ⟶ represents critical path.

probability distribution. The expected value of sales for the next quarter is computed as follows:

Sales	Probability	Amount
$100,000	.1	$ 10,000
120,000	.4	48,000
160,000	.3	48,000
200,000	.2	40,000
	Expected Value	$146,000

Many managers rather than stating these estimates in a normal distribution as shown above, often choose to make their estimates based on optimistic, most likely, and pessimistic conditions. For example, an estimate on the number of employees needed for a particular job can be formulated and computed as follows:

Condition	Amount	Proba-bility	Expected Value
Optimistic	200	.03	60
Most Likely	250	.05	125
Pessimistic	420	.02	84
	Expected Number of Employees Needed		269

Probability Concepts

The following concepts of probability and random variables represent the basic knowledge that a systems analyst must have in formulating successful models.

Probability of an Event. The probability that an event E will occur is the ratio between the number, n, of cases in which E occurs and the total number, N, of the elementary cases, all equally likely,

$$P(E) = \frac{n}{N}$$

where the assumption of equally likely outcomes describe such processes as tossing coins, rolling a die, and so on.

Random Variable. A random variable, X, assumes the values

$$X_1, X_2, \ldots, X_n$$

with each of these values having a probability of

$$P(X_1), P(X_2), \ldots, P(X_n)$$

where

$$\sum_{i=1}^{n} P(X_i) = 1$$

and the expected value of X is

$$E(X) = X_1 P(X_1) + X_2 P(X_2) + \cdots + X_n P(X_n)$$

Conditional Probability. The probability that an event A will occur, if it is known that event B has occurred is written: $P(A/B)$.

Compound Probability. This is the probability that both A and B will occur and is written: $P(A, B)$. Compound events are shown in a tree diagram model below.

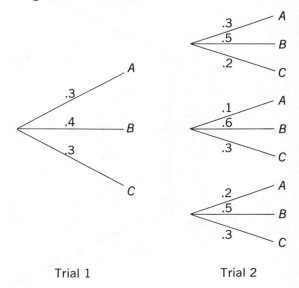

Trial 1   Trial 2

The probability of a compound event is determined by multiplying branch probabilities. The probability of compound event $A_1 C_2$ is:

$$P(A_1 C_2) = P(A_1) \times P(C_2) = (.3) \times (.2) = .06$$

Total Probability. This is the probability that A alone, B alone, or A and B together will occur and is written:

$$P(A + B)$$

Cumulative Probability. This is the process of accumulating the values of $P(X)$ which results in the cumulative probability function,

$$P(\chi) = P(X \leqslant \chi) = \sum_{x_1 \leqslant \chi} P(\chi_i)$$

where the function,

$$P(X > \chi) = (1 - P)(X \leqslant \chi)$$

is the complementary contribution.

Customer Demand χ	Probability of χ
3	.1
4	.2
5	.3
6	.2
7	.2
	1.0

P (number of units sold $\leqslant 5$) $= P$ (number of units sold $= 5$) $+ P$ (number of units sold $= 4$) $+ P$ (number of units sold $= 3$) $= .3 + .2 + .1 = .6$.

Markov Chain Processes. In this process the result of each trial is dependent upon the result of the immediately preceding trial, and only on that result. For each trial there is a finite number of outcomes. A probability is assigned to the outcome, C, for any trial, given that outcome B immediately preceded it. These probabilities are called transition probabilities, where

$$P = \begin{bmatrix} P_{11} & P_{12} & P_{13} \\ P_{21} & P_{22} & P_{23} \\ P_{31} & P_{32} & P_{33} \end{bmatrix}$$

and an illustration of an experiment with three outcomes A, B, and C is given by the matrix:

$$P = \begin{matrix} & \begin{matrix} A & B & C \end{matrix} \\ \begin{matrix} A \\ B \\ C \end{matrix} & \begin{bmatrix} .5 & .3 & .2 \\ .0 & .4 & .6 \\ .1 & .5 & .4 \end{bmatrix} \end{matrix}$$

The stochastic matrix illustrates the probability of going to successive outcomes, given that the trial begins at A or B or C. For example, the probability of going from outcome A to outcome B is .3.

The Poisson Distribution. This distribution is used quite effectively in queuing problems where a service utility has a number of arrivals and departures in a continuous time period. Also this distribution is applicable in building a model to determine the probability of n number of defects in a continuous process.

The Poisson distribution is stated as

$$P = \frac{a^n}{n!} e^{-\alpha}$$

Statistical Concepts

Statistical concepts represent additional methods of manipulating data to provide information. Some of these basic concepts are indicated here.

Histogram. This is a table showing the number of individual observations falling within each interval or class; this number is called the frequency. Before constructing a histogram, the following must be defined:

1. the limits of the group studies,
2. the data or characteristics measured for each individual,
3. the conditions under which the measurements were made.

Mean. Given a population consisting of N individuals, if f_i is the frequency of the variate χ_i, the mean, $\overline{\chi}$, is given by the formula:

$$\overline{\chi} = \frac{1}{N} \sum_{i=1}^{k} f_i \chi_i$$

where k is the number of classes and

$$N = \sum_{i=1}^{k} f_i$$

Mean of the Means. If m measurements are taken in populations of the same nature:

$$\overline{\overline{\chi}} = \frac{n_1 \overline{\chi}_1 + n_2 \overline{\chi}_2 + \cdots + n_m \overline{\chi}_m}{N}$$

Mode. The mode is the value of χ_i for which f_i is greatest.

Median. The median is the value of χ_i (or lying between two consecutive χ_i) for which

$$cum\ f = \frac{1}{2}\ N$$

Two Measures of Dispersion. The standard deviation, or mean square deviation:

$$\sigma\chi = \sqrt{\frac{1}{N}\sum_{i=1}^{k} f_i(\chi_i - \bar{\chi})^2}$$

σ = standard deviation
χ = observations
$\bar{\chi}$ = mean

and the variance is $(\sigma\chi)^2$.

Random Sample. A sample from a population is considered to be drawn at random if the trials that produced the sample are independent, and if the probability distribution function of the random variable connected with each trial remains unchanged throughout the trials.[9]

Basic Queuing Models

Many types of problems encountered in any organization are described by the buildup of queues of some input to a service facility. The queues result from stochastic phenomena. In all cases, inputs arrive at a facility for processing and the time of arrival of individual inputs at the service facility is random as is the time of processing. The randomness of one or more parameters in a queue system is responsible for the uncertainties associated with it. In all organizations, the queuing phenomena is ever present. In production, machines are idle or overburdened. Patients wait for hours in hospitals. Trucks wait in long lines at loading docks. At times inventories are excessive; at other times, there are too many stockouts. And so it goes. Management must strike a balance between costs of idleness and costs of overburdened service facilities. Consequently, management must know something about the activity and length of a queue, the demand on the service activity, the capacity of the service facility

to handle the random demand, and the time spent waiting in the queue plus the time in the service facility.

There are four basic structures of queuing situations which describe the general conditions of a service facility. The simplest situation is where arriving units from a single queue are to be serviced by a single service facility; for example, a car in a car wash. This structure is called a single-channel, single-phase condition. A simple assembly line has a number of service facilities in series or tandem and represents the single-channel, multiple-phase conditions. If the number of service facilities is increased (two or more car washes), but still draws on one queue, this is represented by a multiple-channel, single-phase condition. Finally, the last structure is a multiple-channel, multiple-phase condition which might be illustrated by two or more parallel production lines.[10] These structures are illustrated in Figure A.14.

Simulation Models

In a probabilistic model some dimensions are known, while the value of others are based on phenomena of a stochastic nature. The randomness of one or more parameters in a system is responsible for the uncertainties which exist. There are random machine breakdowns, customer demand, labor strikes, competitor price changes, and so on. Normal and Poisson distributions are used in building most probabilistic simulation models.

Simulation models help to organize disjointed data and activities, and illustrates interrelationships previously unknown. The perception of combinational aspects of a complex problem and their affect on a system can in many instances be handled only by a model. For example, the problem of smog control is amenable to simulation techniques. A complete understanding of the problem involves the interrelationship of climate, the molecular behavior of gasses, the chemistry of engine exhaust, the number of vehicles, the geographic layout of the city (including the location of the homes,

[9] Arnold Kaufmann, *Methods and Models of Operations Research* (Englewood Cliffs, N.J.: Prentice-Hall, Inc., 1963), p. 246–248.

[10] Elwood S. Buffa, *Operations Management,* (New York: John Wiley and Sons, Inc., 1968), pp. 320–321.

(a) Single channel, single phase condition.

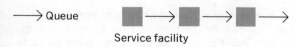

(b) Single channel, multiple phase condition.

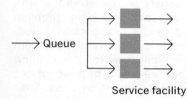

(c) Multiple channel, single phase condition.

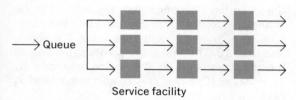

(d) Multiple channel, multiple phase condition.

FIGURE A.14. Four basic structures of queuing conditions.

work places, and highway arteries), the availability of alternate means of transportation, the speed of traffic and the timing of traffic lights, the incomes of the population, the chemistry and biology of the lungs and blood stream, problems of microbes and virus growth under chemical, light, and temperature conditions produced by smog—among other problems.[11]

The above smog control problem can be attacked through the use of simulation. Decision makers can see more clearly the aspects of the problem and how they interrelate. By so doing,

[11] Alfred Kuhn, *The Study of Society: A Unified Approach,* (Homewood, Illinois: Richard D. Irwin, Inc., and The Dorsey Press, 1963), p. 4.

the information produced by the model can aid the decision maker in choosing between a number of alternative courses of action.

Linear Programming Model

As in other problem areas, the systems analyst should be able to recognize those kinds of problems in the organization that are adaptable to linear programming analysis. It is the duty of the information systems analyst to recognize the problem, define the problem, and construct a model to solve the problem. Linear programming is an important development in management science methodology. The purpose of linear programming is to provide a method of optimizing the allocation of scarce resources to competing demands.

Generally speaking, methods for solving optimization problems—that is, problems which attempt to maximize or minimize a given function subject to a set of limitations or constraints—have been available for over a century. However during World War II, a different type of optimization problem was being considered. The U.S. Air Force was primarily concerned with these new optimization problems, hence referred to as programming problems; however, they have since found applications in other fields such as industrial operations.

Following is a list of kinds of problems which have been solved by linear programming methods. These are the kinds of problems that the systems analyst would encounter in most organizations; however, this list is not exhaustive and indicates only a few examples.

1. Allocation of energy sources in electrical power generation.

2. Determining optimal mix of food products for beef cattle production.

3. Adapting production to variable and seasonal sales.

4. Allocation of limited raw materials and production facilities to the production of a multiple product line.

5. Optimum multiple plant and warehouse location.

The viewpoint that the analyst should take is to concentrate on the definition of the problem and formulation of the model and leave the technical intricacies and solution of the model to the technical staff of the information system. The technical staff would include, among others, mathematicians, OR specialists, and application programmers.

Two major assumptions are required in using linear programming techniques: linearity and certainty. Linearity means all the relationships involve variables of the first degree and can be illustrated graphically by straight lines. Certainty requires that the value of all variables must be known and that all variables are non-negative.[12]

An example of the general form in which a linear programming problem may take on, follows:

maximize $\quad p_1x_1 + p_2x_2 + \cdots + p_nx_n$

subject to $\quad a_{11}x_1 + a_{12}x_2 + \cdots + a_{1n}x_n \leqslant b_1$

$\qquad\qquad a_{21}x_1 + a_{22}x_2 + \cdots + a_{2n}x_n \leqslant b_2$

$$\qquad\qquad\qquad\cdot\qquad\qquad\cdot\qquad\qquad\qquad\cdot$$
$$\qquad\qquad\qquad\cdot\qquad\qquad\cdot\qquad\qquad\qquad\cdot$$
$$\qquad\qquad\qquad\cdot\qquad\qquad\cdot\qquad\qquad\qquad\cdot$$

$\qquad\qquad a_{n1}x_1 + a_{n2}x_2 + \cdots + a_{2n}x_n \leqslant b_n$

The p_i's in the objective function may refer to profit contributions to the given products x_1, $x_2, \ldots, x_n$. On the other hand, the a_{ij}'s may refer to the required amounts of manufacturing material, for the given products, which are in limited supply according to $b_1, b_2, \ldots, b_n$. The linear programming problem would then be to maximize the profit contribution subject to the given limitations on manufacturing material.

Let us consider a simple graphical example of a linear programming problem, as follows:

maximize $\quad 3x_1 + 2x_2$

subject to $\quad 2x_1 + 3x_2 \leqslant 10$

$\qquad\qquad 3x_1 + \ x_2 \leqslant 6$

$\qquad\qquad\ x_1 \qquad\quad \geqslant 0$

$\qquad\qquad\qquad\ x_2 \geqslant 0$

Consider the x_1x_2 coordinate system. Any point (x_1, x_2) can be plotted in this system. For example see Figure A.15. All points lying on or to the right of the x_2 axis satisfy the constraint that $x_1 \geqslant 0$. Similarly, all points lying on or above the x_1 axis satisfy the constraint $x_2 \geqslant 0$. Therefore a feasible solution to the problem must be contained in the first section (quadrant) of the coordinate system. Now let us consider the other two constraints. If we allow equality to hold then we would have equations for straight lines and any point on these lines would satisfy the equations. Refer to Figure A.16. Observe also, that any point (x_1, x_2) in the first quadrant which lies on or below one of the given lines satisfies that inequality. For example, the point (1,2) substituted into the equation $2x_1 + 3x_2 = 10$ yields the value 7 which is less than 10. Therefore, the points satisfying all the constraints lie in the region bounded by $2x_1 + 3x_2 = 10$, $3x_1 + x_2 = 6$, and the x_1 and x_2 axes.

We must now find the point in the region which maximizes the objective function, $3x_1 + 2x_2$. Allowing this function to take on different

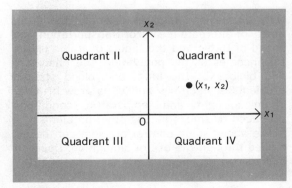

FIGURE A.15. The x_1, x_2 coordinate system.

[12] For detailed analysis of linear programming models, refer to: C. Almon, *Matrix Methods in Economics*, (Reading, Massachusetts: Addison-Wesley Publishing Company, 1967); A. Charnes, W. W. Cooper and A. Henderson, *An Introduction to Linear Programming*, (New York: John Wiley and Sons, Inc., 1953); S. I. Gass, *Linear Programming*, (New York: McGraw-Hill Book Company, 1958); G. Hadley, *Linear Algebra*, (Reading, Massachusetts: Addison-Wesley Publishing Company, 1961); and R. Stansbury Stockton, *Introduction to Linear Programming*, (Boston: Allyn and Bacon, Inc., 1963).

	D_1	D_2	D_3	*Contribution Margin
P_1	20 minutes	12 minutes	26 minutes	8.00
P_2	15 minutes	20 minutes	13 minutes	10.00

* Contribution Margin = Sales Price − Variable Cost

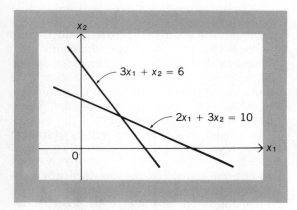

FIGURE A.16. Graphical example of constraints in a linear programming problem.

values produces straight lines which are parallel. We must then find the line which gives the objective function its greatest value and at the same time has at least one point in the constrained region. Let us give $3x_1 + 2x_2$ the value 6 and plot this line in the x_1x_2 coordinate system. See Figure A.17. This line has many points within the constrained region, but it should be obvious that there exist parallel lines above this line which give the objective function a greater value and still have at least one point within the constrained region. In fact, the line which gives the objective function its greatest value and still contains at least one point within the given region is the line passing through the point of intersection of the two lines $2x_1 + 3x_2 = 10$, and $3x_1 + x_2 = 6$. Solving these two equations simultaneously, we find $x_1 = 8/7$ and $x_2 = 18/7$. It is these two values which, when substituted into the ob-

jective function, give it its maximum value of $60/7$.

For a "real world" application of the linear programming model, assume a company manufactures two products, P_1 and P_2, which are processed by three departments. The products can be processed in any order. Pertinent data are shown in the table above.

The number of minutes each department will be available for operation during the month are as follows:

12,600 minutes for D_1
14,400 minutes for D_2
13,000 minutes for D_3

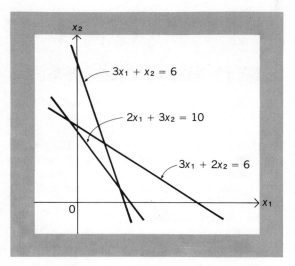

FIGURE A.17. Graphical example of objective function taking on one of many values.

Corner	Product P_1	Product P_2	(Objective Function) Total Contribution Margin
a 0,0	0	0	$Z = \$8.00(0) + \$10.00(0) = \$0.00$
b 500,0	500	0	$Z = \$8.00(120) + \$10.00(0) = \$4,000.00$
c 250,510	250	510	$Z = \$8.00(250) + \$10.00(510) = \$7,100.00$
d 150,640	150	640	$^*Z = \$8.00(150) + \$10.00(640) = \$7,600.00$
e 0,720	0	720	$Z = \$8.00(0) + \$10.00(720) = \$7,200.00$

* Optimum solution.

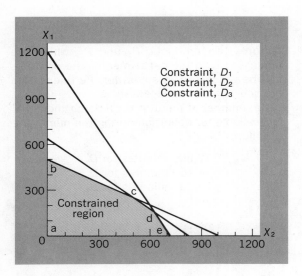

FIGURE A.18. Graphical solution.

The question to answer is, how much of Product P_1 and Product P_2 should be produced to maximize total contribution margin? The objective function, therefore, is $Z = 8X_1 + 10X_2$, where X_1 is the number of units of product P_1, and X_2 is the number of units of P_2. Then: $Z = 8X_1 + 10X_2$ the function to be maximized with the conditions $X_1 \geqslant 0$, $X_2 \geqslant 0$.

The constraints are:

$$20X_1 + 15X_2 \leqslant 12,600 \text{ for department } D_1$$
$$12X_1 + 20X_2 \leqslant 14,400 \text{ for department } D_2$$
$$26X_1 + 13X_2 \leqslant 13,000 \text{ for department } D_3$$

There is an infinite number of feasible solutions; among them is one or more for which Z is

maximum. The graph in Figure A.18 illustrates a graphical solution of the above problem.

The area enclosed by abcde includes all feasible solutions to the production problem. The maximum solution can be found by computing the values at each corner of the polygon. These computations are made in the table above.

The maximum Z is represented by a straight line for a particular value of Z equal to $7600. Since the coefficients $8 and $10 are invariant, this line will remain parallel to itself when the value of Z is changed. The maximum will always correspond to one of the extreme points of the constrained region which is furthest from the point of origin. Therefore, the further this line moves from the origin, the greater the value of Z, and vice versa.

Probably the most important single development in the solution of linear programming problems took place in the late 1940's when George Dantzig devised the Simplex Method. Consider for a moment the graphical example of a linear programming problem treated above. Note that a line drawn between any two points in the constrained area lies entirely within that area. This fact holds for any linear programming problem in which a feasible solution exists and the constrained region is said to be convex. Also note that an optimal point for the objective function will be at one of the corners of the convex region. The Simplex Method gives us a procedure for moving step by step from a given corner (extreme point) to an optimal corner (extreme point).[13]

[13] G. Hadley, *op. cit.*

BIBLIOGRAPHY   Almon, *Matrix Methods in Economics,* Reading, Mass.: Addison-Wesley Publishing Co., 1967.

Anthony, *Management Accounting,* Fourth Edition, Homewood, Illinois: Richard D. Irwin, Inc., 1970.

Archibald and Villoria, *Network-Based Management Systems (PERT/CPM),* New York: John Wiley & Sons, Inc., 1967.

Bierman, Bonini, Fouraker, and Jaedicke, *Quantitative Analysis for Business Decisions,* Revised Edition, Homewood, Illinois: Richard D. Irwin, Inc., 1965.

Brown, *Smoothing, Forecasting, and Production of Discrete Time Series,* Englewood Cliffs, N.J.: Prentice-Hall, Inc., 1963.

Buffa, *Operations Management,* New York: John Wiley & Sons, Inc., 1968.

Burch, "Computer Application of Contribution Analysis," *Journal of Systems Management,* August, 1970.

Charnes, Cooper, and Henderson, *An Introduction to Linear Programming,* New York: John Wiley & Sons, Inc., 1953.

Dutton and Starbuck, *Computer Simulation of Human Behavior,* New York: John Wiley & Sons, Inc., 1971.

Evarts, *Introduction to PERT,* Boston: Allyn and Bacon, Inc., 1964.

Fertig, Istvan, and Mottice, *Using Accounting Information: An Introduction,* Second Edition, New York: Harcourt Brace Jovanovich, Inc., 1971.

Gass, *Linear Programming,* New York: McGraw-Hill Book Co., 1958.

Hadley, *Linear Algebra,* Reading, Mass.: Addison-Wesley Publishing Co., 1961.

Horngren, *Cost Accounting: A Managerial Emphasis,* Second Edition, Englewood Cliffs, N.J.: Prentice-Hall, Inc., 1967.

Kaufmann, *Methods and Models of Operations Research,* Englewood Cliffs, N.J.: Prentice-Hall, Inc., 1963.

Kuhn, *The Study of Society: A Unified Approach,* Homewood, Illinois: Richard D. Irwin, Inc., and The Dorsey Press, 1963.

Maisel and Gnugnoli, *Simulation of Discrete Stochastic Systems,* Chicago: Science Research Associates, Inc., 1972.

Martin, *Computer Modeling and Simulation,* New York: John Wiley & Sons, Inc., 1968.

Raiffa, *Decision Analysis,* Reading, Mass.: Addison-Wesley Publishing Co., 1968.

Richmond, *Statistical Analysis,* New York: The Ronald Press Co., 1964.

Schrader, Malcom, and Willingham, *Financial Accounting: An Input/Output Approach,* Homewood, Illinois: Richard D. Irwin, Inc., 1970.

Slaybaugh, "Pareto's Law and Modern Management," *Management Services,* March–April, 1967.

Starr and Miller, *Inventory Control: Theory and Practice,* Englewood Cliffs, N.J.: Prentice-Hall, Inc., 1962.

Whitin, *The Theory of Inventory Management,* Princeton, N.J.: Princeton University Press, 1957.

Appendix B
The Compute
and Related
Technology

Introduction

The computer and related technology can be divided into three major sections, which are: (1) the central processor, (2) devices peripheral to the central processor, and (3) data communication devices which connect peripheral devices to the central processor. The aim of this appendix is twofold: (1) to increase your knowledge about these three sections, and (2) to review some of the newer approaches used to increase the processing power of computer based information systems.

The Central Processor

The heart of any computer configuration is the central processing unit, or CPU. First, we will analyze the central processor and then present a few techniques which help to increase its processing power.

Overview of the Central Processor

The central processor is really the "computer" in a computer configuration and all computer configurations perform five basic functions, which are:

1. *Input.* The data to be operated upon and the instructions as to the method of operation are made available to the central processing unit in a form it can utilize via input media.

2. *Primary Storage.* From the input media, data and instructions are entered into the main storage section of the central processor. Other storage media (e.g., magnetic tape, magnetic disk) are considered auxiliary to primary storage.

3. *Arithmetic-Logic.* The processor manipulates the data in accordance with the algorithm of instructions. These manipulations are performed in the arithmetic-logic section, one operation at a time, with intermediate results being placed back into primary storage. The arithmetic-logic section performs addition, subtraction, multiplication, division, and certain logical operations such as comparing the magnitude of two numbers.

4. *Controls.* Controls are required inside a computer system to: (1) tell the input media what data to enter into primary storage and when to enter it; (2) tell the primary storage section where to place these data; (3) tell the arithmetic-logic section what operations to perform, where the data are to be found, and where to place the results; (4) tell what file devices to access and what data to access; and (5) tell what output media the final results are written on.

5. *Output.* This function refers to the output of the results of the data processed within the central processor. This final result is written on any one or a combination of the various output media.

A schematic of a computer system, emphasizing the central processor, is illustrated in Figure B.1. All digital computers, regardless of

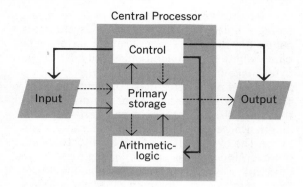

FIGURE B.1. General diagram of a central processor. Legend: ----→ Data flow; —→ Instruction flow; —→ Control flow.

size, speed, and details of operation, follow this same basic logical structure.

Size of the Central Processor

When manufacturers state the size of their processor, it is the size of the primary storage that they are referring to. Size of a processor's primary storage helps to determine the maximum size of programs and the amount of data available for processing at any one time. Each primary storage location has an address, analogous to a set of mailboxes in a post office, each having a unique number which identifies a particular storage location. The address identifies the location for both storing and accessing data. Storage capacity is expressed in terms of the number of addressable storage locations within the primary storage unit. It is, therefore, necessary to know the manner in which a particular manufacturer designates its primary storage before a logical comparison can be made. Although all data are represented as binary digits or bits, the smallest addressable location in main storage differs from one computer to another. Depending on the design of the computer, each addressable location is a character or the beginning of a computer word. These storage locations may be designated as follows:

1. *Byte-Addressable Combination.* The basic storage unit of some computer systems is called the byte. The byte is made up of eight binary digits and an additional parity digit. Two bytes make up a half word. Four bytes make up a word, and eight bytes make up a double word. The primary storage addresses are designed so that both fixed-word-length and variable-word-length words can be used in the same computer. The byte itself is a fixed binary structure; however, these bytes can be strung together in different ways to provide variable-length or fixed-length words. The main aspect to note in a byte-addressable system is that it is flexible in the sense that each byte is addressable when each byte can represent two numbers or one character. Flexibility results from the ability to string together bytes in a way to make half-words, words, and double-words. A computer with 64K (where K, or kilo means thousands) locations of storage has 64,000 bytes, each of which is addressable by the programmer.

2. *Character-Addressable.* In a character-addressable system, it may require a six-bit set (not including control bits) to encode a character. If the number 47 is in storage, the 4 will take up one storage location having an address; the 7 is in another contiguous storage location with a separate address. An 8 bit byte would provide greater storage than a six-bit character because two decimal digits may be packed in a byte. All character-addressable computers are variable-word-length computers.

3. *Word-Addressable.* A computer word consists of an ordered set of bits which may be fixed-length or variable-length, depending on the computer. However, computers which are designated as word addressable are fixed word-length computers. Common word sizes for fixed-word-length computers are 24, 30, 32, 36, 48, 54, and 64 bit words. As pointed out in item 2 above, the variable-word-length computer is normally designated as a character-addressable machine and has an address for each set of bits which can encode one character.

The basic differences between fixed-word-length and variable–word–length are discussed here.

1. *Fixed-Word-Length.* Each data item is stored in a separate word. If the data item does not fill the word, some storage space is wasted, i.e., the unused space is filled with zeros or blanks. In some word-addressable computers, several data items can be packed into a single fixed-word-length by using proper programming instructions, but such work requires extra time. In a fixed-word-length computer, the amount of data in a word is moved as a unit. These type computers perform arithmetic operations in parallel where all positions of the digits to be processed, including carrier, are added at the same time, in one step. Most large-scale, scientific-oriented computers use this type of addressing because of its greater computational power.

2. *Variable-Word-Length.* Character-addressable computers use variable-word-length addressing. Since variable-word-length computers operate on characters rather than words, such terminology is a misnomer; however, it is common terminology used throughout the computer industry and we will not change it here. Each word can contain a variable number of characters. Such a group of characters can be accessed by specifying a word mark bit (a special control bit) which designates the starting location for the group of characters. Many administrative oriented computers are variable-word-length machines. The need in administrative data processing is fast input/output with relatively small demands for internal processing. Variable-word-length computers meet these needs much better than word-addressable machines, and at less cost. Byte-addressable computers combine the advantages of both character-addressable and word addressable computers.

Speed of the Processor

Other aspects to consider when evaluating primary storage are: access and cycle time. These aspects are discussed here.[1]

[1] Gordon B. Davis, *Computer Data Processing* (New York: McGraw-Hill Book Company 1969) p. 150. Used with permission of McGraw-Hill Book Company.

1. *Access Time.* Access time refers to the time it takes for the control section to locate instructions and data for processing. It represents the time interval between initiating a transfer of data to or from storage and the instant when this transfer is completed. This time interval varies from one computer to another. In most primary storage devices, access time is measured in microseconds (one-millionth of a second); however, some large-scale computers access time is measured in nanoseconds (one-billionth of a second).

2. *Cycle Time.* A computer performs its operations on a cycle basis. The computer operates on pulses per length of time like a clock. The computer during a cycle of time is either in the instruction cycle or the execution cycle. An instruction is obtained from a main storage location and transferred to the arithmetic-logic unit where the instruction is in the operation code specifying what is to be done (op-code) and the address of the data or device to be operated upon (operand). The computer then moves into the execution cycle, during which time the decoded instruction is executed using data in the locations specified by the instruction. When the execution cycle is completed, the computer automatically goes back into the instruction cycle, retrieving another instruction from main storage for the next instruction and moves on into the execution cycle again, and so on.

The amount of data that can be accessed in one cycle depends on the computer design, and is expressed in bytes, characters, or words. For example, Model X may have a slower basic access time than Model Y, but Model X may access four bytes at a time whereas Model Y accesses two bytes. Therefore, two factors combine which result in effective access time: the amount of data accessed during each cycle and the number of microseconds (or nanoseconds) required per cycle.

Size of storage used is normally based on cost, and cost of storage in turn is based on speed, i.e., as access speed increases, the cost per bit stored also increases. This speed mismatch and cost variation between various storage media has caused a number of processor configuration innovations manifested in different storage hierarchy systems. For example, a hierarchy of storage might consist of a very high-speed (nanosecond range) semiconductor storage; medium-speed (microsecond range) core storage; and large, slow-speed (millisecond range) magnetic disk or drum. The hierarchy of storage concept can be illustrated by the virtual storage and buffer storage techniques which are discussed in the following sections.

Virtual Storage Technique

The basic idea behind virtual storage is the dynamic linking of primary storage of the processor and auxiliary storage so that to each user (several may be using the system concurrently) it appears that he or she has at his or her disposal a very large primary storage, usually measured in megabytes. Parts of a program or data associated with it may be broken up and scattered both in primary storage and magnetic disk or drum, thus giving the "virtual" affect of a much larger primary storage to the programmer.[2] This technique is illustrated in Figure B.2.

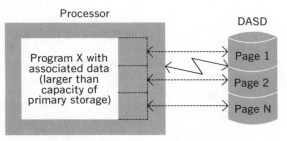

FIGURE B.2. Illustration of virtual storage.

Normally only the instructions and data necessary for immediate processing will be located

[2] Robert Haavind, "A User's Guide to System Evolution," *Computer Decisions,* June, 1971, pp. 26–30. Used with permission.

in primary storage in the form of "pages" which are transferred between primary storage and slower auxiliary (DASD) storage automatically.[3] With this approach, jobs are loaded into partitions or regions of a very large auxiliary storage space. During processing, small blocks or pages of instructions and data are transferred between auxiliary storage and processor storage according to the momentary needs of each job.[4]

The application versatility of the virtual storage technique can be illustrated in the following summary points:[5]

1. The limited amount of available primary storage space has been a barrier to applications. From a programmer's viewpoint, virtual storage allows him or her to write a much larger program without worrying if it fits the confines of primary storage. In many applications, it is not unusual for a program to run over 200K. Many conventional processors were unable to hold a program of this size; consequently, a great deal of time and cost was spent segmenting the program where it could be used in multiple job steps. In the past, as high as 20% or more of programming productivity went into trying to get programs to fit primary storage.

2. Virtual storage will have a noticeable effect on the flexibility provided systems analysts and programmers in the design of new applications. The availability of such a large address space creates an entirely new environment in which to plan program modules and job runs. There are no basic changes in the approach to the actual programming or operations as such. Although addresses in virtual code may specify locations far outside the limits of primary storage, all such virtual addresses will be referenced automatically by means of dynamic address translation handled by the computer's operating system. Since the task of managing primary storage and of transferring pages between primary storage and auxiliary storage is performed by the operating system, all of these functions are said to be "transparent" to the programmer, i.e., he or she need not be concerned with them.

3. An online teleprocessing application that faces a varying message volume will not need a large dedicated space in processor storage. Such a terminal oriented, event driven application may be supported for longer hours, perhaps into the second shift, since background jobs will use almost all resources when the top-priority application does not need them.

4. A data base application, which would otherwise be handled on a once-a-day batch basis because of its extensive storage requirements, may be put online to terminals for at least a few hours a day.

5. A high priority job can usually be started immediately without disrupting any long-running jobs with extensive storage space. In many cases, this may result in a significant improvement in turnaround time for urgent jobs. For example, in a configuration, at the same time, there could be a resident writer, resident teleprocessing program, a region reserved for "hot" jobs, and two or more batch regions large enough for the running of large jobs.

Buffer Storage Technique

This technique, also called cache memory, utilizes a limited capacity but very fast semiconductor storage combined with less expensive, slower, large capacity core storage to give the overall effect of a faster primary storage. This technique requires careful look-ahead procedures as a program progresses to get the correct data into semiconductor storage when it is required.[6] The buffer storage technique is illustrated in Figure B.3.

It is the function of the buffer to fetch frequently used instructions and data to be used by the arithmetic-logic part of the central processor. In most cases, these instructions and data will be available at the buffer rate of N bytes in nanoseconds, rather than the slower primary storage rate. This technique actually

[3] *Ibid.*

[4] "Key to Enhanced Application Development," *Data Processor,* September, 1972, pp. 2–9. Used with permission.

[5] *Ibid.*

[6] Haavind, *op. cit.,* p. 26.

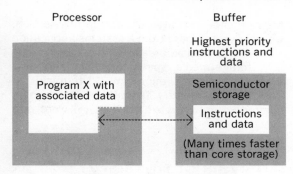

Processor   Buffer

Highest priority instructions and data

Program X with associated data

Semiconductor storage

Instructions and data

(Many times faster than core storage)

FIGURE B.3. Illustration of buffer storage.

operates in a fashion where the buffer is analogous to the intermediate storage concept which is based on the theory that adjacent bytes in primary storage will usually be used at the same time. If the required data are in the buffer, they are transferred to the arithmetic-logic unit at buffer speed. If the required data are not in the buffer then they are obtained from primary storage. However, according to studies conducted by IBM, the required data are in the buffer approximately 90% of the time. As with the virtual storage technique, the buffer storage technique provides increased performance without adding new responsibilities for the programmer, i.e., the operation of buffer storage is "transparent" to the programmer.

Solid-State Storage

The expanding use of multiprogramming and complexity of computer applications have resulted in a growing need for larger capacity, high speed primary processor storage. Although the virtual storage and buffer storage techniques relieve some of this growing need by providing dynamic allocation of primary storage, normal application growth will probably still result in an increasing demand for more primary processor storage as well.[7]

Adding primary storage modules to the processor is made easier through the use of large-scale integration (LSI). This technique provides

[7] "New Compact Main Storage Technology," *op. cit.* p. 9.

an accumulation of many (100 or more) switching circuits on a single chip of semiconductor. Through a series of processes, which include photolithography, chemical etching and diffusion, a micro-miniature pattern of circuits with transistors and conductors is created along the surface of a silicon chip. The more circuits on a chip, the more bits of data it can store.[8]

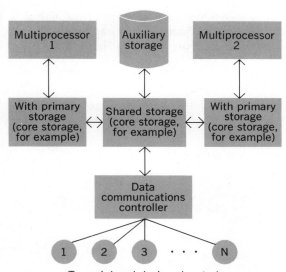

Multiprocessor 1   Auxiliary storage   Multiprocessor 2

With primary storage (core storage, for example)   Shared storage (core storage, for example)   With primary storage (core storage, for example)

Data communications controller

1   2   3   · · ·   N

To peripheral devices located throughout organization.

FIGURE B.4. Illustration of a multiprocessing configuration.

Multiprocessors

It should be recognized by the reader that a computer configuration in many applications, operates with more than one processor unit (multiprocessing). There are endless ways in which one can configure a total computer system, but for one typical illustration of a multiprocessing system, refer to Figure B.4.

The system above, for an example, could be used as a redundant backup system where each processor is equipped with its own dedi-

[8] *Ibid.*

cated core memory and also shares common partitioned storage which can access the data base files and is also connected to various peripherals. The partitioned core storage configuration allows either processor to operate the entire system in event the other processor fails.

Types of Storage

We will conclude this section by presenting a summary classification of storage media.[9] This classification is presented in Figure B.5.

Name of Storage Media	Primary Storage	Online Auxiliary Storage	Offline Auxiliary Storage
Bubble*	X		
LSI	X		
Semiconductor	X		
Magnetic Core	X	X	
Thin Films	X		
Plated Wire	X		
Magnetic Drum	X	X	
Magnetic Disks	X	X	X
Magnetic Cards/Strips		X	X
Magnetic Tape			X
Punched Paper Tape			X
Punched Cards			X

* Experimental, see: Gerald Lapidus, "The Domain of Magnetic Bubbles," *Spectrum*, September, 1972, pp. 58–62.

FIGURE B.5. Types of storage media.

Devices and Applications Peripheral to the CPU

In Figure B.6 we present a general schematic of devices peripheral to the computer. For a good text treatment of these items we refer you to the reference indicated below.[10] In this section, we will present more from a systems application viewpoint five basic areas: (1) aspects of auxiliary storage media, specifically magnetic tape, magnetic disk, and microfilm; (2) terminal devices; (3) data entry techniques; (4) remote computing networks (RCN); and (5) word processing.

Analysis of Auxiliary Storage Devices

Primary storage is very expensive and can only be used economically to hold several programs (by multiprogramming and partitioning methods), and data which the computer is presently processing. Primary storage with the capacity to hold anything beyond this would probably be cost prohibitive. Auxiliary storage devices are used to store other programs and data which are made available to the computer when needed. Popular storage devices which transfer data or instructions rapidly between primary storage and an input/output drive unit are: magnetic tape, magnetic disk, magnetic drum, and magnetic strips (data cells). Each of these devices has operating characteristics which are basically the same.[11] Computer output microfilm (COM) can also be considered as auxiliary storage. We will treat, in this section, three of these devices, namely: (1) magnetic tape, (2) magnetic disk, and (3) COM.

Magnetic Tape

Magnetic tape is a very popular medium for storage of voluminous amounts of data. It is a sequential medium and is widely used in batch processing environments.

Physical Characteristics

Data are recorded on 7, 8, 9, or 10 channel tape in the form of magnetized spots. Tape widths

[9] For detailed discussions, see: Donald H. Sanders, *Computers in Business: An Introduction,* Second Edition, (New York: McGraw-Hill Book Company, 1972); C. Gordon Bell and Allen Newell, *Computer Structures* (New York: McGraw-Hill Book Company, 1971); Herbert Sobel, *Introduction to Digital Computer Design.* (Reading, Mass.: Addison-Wesley Publishing Co., Inc., 1971)

[10] Sanders, *op. cit.* Used with permission of McGraw-Hill Book Company.
[11] Gene Dippel and William C. House, *Information Systems,* (Glenview, Illinois: Scott Foresman & Company, 1969), p. 233.

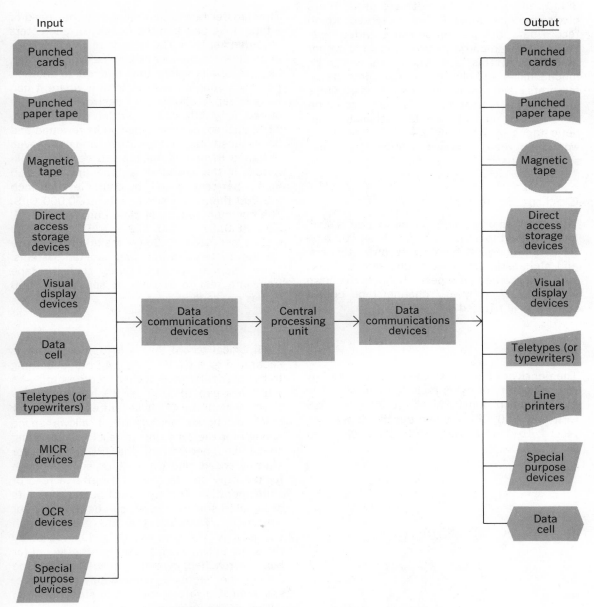

FIGURE B.6. The computer and its peripherals.

are normally 1/2 inch, although some tapes are 3/4, 1, and 3 inches in width are used. There are some new tapes being marketed which record data in a fashion similar to video tape, i.e., data are recorded across the tape rather than along it. This technique allows bits to be much smaller and closer together. Some manufacturers claim that packing density is 40 times greater than regular tape. Further discussion will be based on 7 channel tape. Usually, magnetic tapes of 2400–3600 feet in length are wound on reels; however, shorter tapes are sometimes used.

Coding Scheme

The recording of data on magnetic tape is similar in concept to a tape recorder. Magnetic tape for data processing, however, records numbers, and alphabetic and special characters. These data are recorded on tape in channels as shown in Figure B.7. Only a 7 channel tape coding scheme is illustrated.

Density

The density of magnetic tape is represented by the characters or bytes recorded per inch. The most common density sizes are 200 CPI, 556 CPI, and 800 CPI. Higher density tapes can record 1511 CPI, 1600 CPI, 3200 CPI, and 6250 CPI.

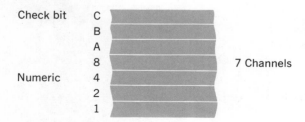

FIGURE B.7 Magnetic tape using BCD coding.

Transfer Rate

The transfer rate is determined by the speed of a tape drive unit and the density of characters recorded per inch. The tape drive unit functions in much the same way as a home tape recorder, i.e., the tape is wound from one reel to another, passing through a read-write unit where it can be read repeatedly without destroying the data stored. New data can be written over old data, when desired, and the tape can be rewound and backspaced. Some tape drive units are even designed to permit the tape to be read backwards. If the speed of a tape unit is 112.5 inches per second and the characters per inch are 800 then the transfer rate is 90,000 CPS. The common speeds of tape units are: 18.75, 22.5, 36.0, 37.5, 75.0, 112.5, 125.0, and 200.0 inches per second. Some manufacturers use vacuum systems rather than capstan systems. These vacuum systems literally suck the tape from one reel to another at speeds of 1000 inches per second.

Blocking Records

Each logical record that is written on a tape is separated by a blank (1/2″, 3/4″, etc. according to the particular tape system) referred to as an interblock gap (IBG). The IBG has three purposes, which are: (1) it separates a record (or block discussed below), (2) it allows space enough for the tape unit to reach its operating speed, i.e., one-half of the IBG is used for starting speed, and (3) it allows space enough for the tape unit to decelerate after a read or write operation. The tape must be moving at its designated speed before it can be read from or written on. Therefore the IBG gives enough space to get the tape moving at full speed. By the same token, when the end of the record (or block) is reached, in reading or writing, the tape cannot be stopped immediately; therefore, space must also be provided to stop the tape.

The IBG contains no data. For example, if a recording density is 556 CPI, this means that a 1/2″ IBG could hold 278 characters of data. Or looking at it another way, approximately the data found in seven 80-column cards

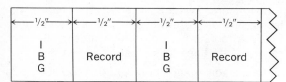

FIGURE B.8. Unblocked records.

I B G	Logical Record 1	Logical Record 2	Logical Record 3	Logical Record 4	Logical Record 5	I B G

FIGURE B.9. Blocked records with a blocking factor of 5.

could be stored in two 1/2" IBG's. The records in a tape with each record separated by an IBG are shown in Figure B.8. The records contain 278 characters and are unblocked.

Tape economy is realized by combining the records into a block of records by a blocking factor of N, where N equals the number of records within each block. The block itself becomes a physical group of characters separated by IBG's and the data records within the block become a logical record. A block is therefore said to be a tape-recording concept, whereas a record within the block is a logical record, or a data processing concept. Figure B.9 represents blocked records with a blocking factor of 5.

The concept of transfer rate as pointed out in earlier discussion is a little misleading because as can be seen with the discussion thus far, as a tape unit reads blocks of logical records, it stops each time it comes to an IBG. Consequently, when blocks are being read or written, a certain amount of time is spent at each IBG. The total amount of time required to read or write a given number of blocks is equal to the sum of the time spent reading or writing the data plus the time spent starting and stopping at the IBG's. To realize the effect that start/stop time has on reading and writing speeds, consider the following example:

Tape density = 800 CPI
Tape unit speed = 75.0 inches per second
Therefore, stated transfer rate = 60,000 CPS

Number of blocks on tape = 8000
Blocking factor = 5 where each record contains 30 characters; therefore, each block contains 150 characters or a total of 1,200,000 characters.
Number of IBG's = 8000
Size of IBG = 3/4"
Time to pass over IBG = .010 second
Therefore,
Total start/stop time = 8000 × .010
= 80 seconds
Total time for reading data = 1,200,000 ÷ 60,000
= 20 seconds
Therefore,
Total time to read all records = 80 + 20
= 100 seconds
Effective transfer rate = 1,200,000 ÷ 100
= 12,000 CPS

Consequently, it takes 80 seconds to start and stop the tape, and only 20 seconds to read the data. There is a waste of tape space and of processing time. To reduce this waste more records should be placed in a block. If the blocking factor is 20, then the number of IBG's would be reduced to 2000 instead of 8000. The total time to read the records is 20 seconds for reading data plus 20 seconds (2,000 × .010) or 40 seconds. When an installation has thousands of tape reels, reducing wasted space becomes quite significant. The reduction in wasted space results in:

1. *Less Cost for Tape.* Typical costs for tape reels are between $15 and $100. If a system has 1000 tapes with a cost of $80,000 and the space can be reduced 50% then a cost savings of $40,000 can be effected.

2. *Saves Time.* Reduction of wait-time of the processing unit resulting either from tapes being moved from the tape units and/or space in the tape itself. Obviously, an increased blocking factor increases I/O speeds.

3. *Saves Storage.* In older systems that have not had proper data management, increasing number of applications, combined with increasing stringent requirements for data retention,

have resulted in a squeeze on available storage space. In some instances, this squeeze has caused an expenditure for a new wing of the tape library. The principle of large blocking factors can be applied to many older systems on two levels: (1) The software system should be investigated to ascertain if the largest possible blocking factor is being used by every program. This would be particularly applicable in those installations that have upgraded their central processor storage capacity. (2) The re-blocking of archival files should be done to contain the highest blocking factor that the hardware can handle. It is often found that multiple reel tape files can be reduced to a single reel. The recompilation of source programs to increase blocking factors, the necessary de-blocking and file extraction run, and the re-blocking of tapes are methods that use computer time, but the time lost on this fairly infrequent procedure would be more than balanced by the overall cost savings. Incidentally, physical space occupied by tapes can be reduced by writing short files on small reels, which are then stored on special racks to maximize the space savings.

Advantages/Disadvantages of Magnetic Tape

The advantages are listed as follows:

1. They have a much faster transfer rate than cards.
2. A tape record can have any number of characters (within limits), where cards are limited to 80 columns.
3. Tapes play an important role and remain unchallenged for backup storage and for low-cost, high-capacity applications requiring only sequential access.
4. They require less storage space than other media such as cards.
5. They are erasable and can be used over again for many different applications.
6. Tape manufacturers offer a wide range of specifications to meet particular applications.
7. Relatively speaking, tapes are inexpensive where one cent can buy enough tape capacity to store tens of thousands of characters.

8. In card systems, there is a chance of losing one or more records from a file. A tape file is a monolithic unit which means that no record of the file can be lost.

The disadvantages of magnetic tape are:

1. Since tape is a sequential medium, the access of a particular record is made only after all records preceding it have been read. It is, therefore, not applicable for jobs which require rapid, direct access to specific records.
2. Each reel of tape is indistinguishable from the next which means, for control purposes, all tapes must contain an external label as well as an internal label.
3. Since the tape is also continuous in design, a clerk can not physically remove, insert, or change a record without reading from the original and rewriting it with the change to another tape.
4. The magnetized spots are unreadable by humans. A printout of the tape is required to read or verify tape data.
5. The temperature, humidity, and dust content of the tape environment must be tightly controlled. Particles of dust on a tape can cause improper processing. Temperature and humidity conditions that fall outside of prescribed ranges can cause peculiar and mysterious results from processing.

Magnetic Disk

Magnetic disks have now become the medium of choice for service as auxiliary storage. Computer vendors in the past offered only magnetic tapes and magnetic drums for secondary storage. After a while they began to offer more and more computer models which could handle disk operations, while still offering magnetic tapes, but decreasing their offerings of magnetic drums. Now, all digital computers can handle magnetic disk processing. The price per character or byte stored continues to decrease for magnetic disks as well as other media. The direct access capability of disks gives the systems analyst far more options and flexibility in designing systems. Online inquiry capability of large files is an example.

Physical Characteristics

There are several models of magnetic disks which come in different sizes, some as stationary devices, others in the form of removable disk packs. A magnetic disk file is made up of a stack of rotating metal disks on which records are stored. Direct access of any record can be made without having to read through a sequence of other, irrelevant records. This direct capability also allows random entry of transactional data and random inquiry into the file from a user. The different disk models range from 5 to 100 disks measuring from 1 1/2 to 3 feet in diameter. The IBM 2316 disk pack (removable) is used to illustrate physical characteristics of magnetic disks. A schematic of it is illustrated in Figure B.10.

The illustration below represents a six disk unit of which ten of the twelve surfaces are used for recording data. Each surface is divided into 200 tracks which are analogous to flattened, circular sections of magnetic tape. Each track has a capacity of 3625 bytes. A positioning of the read-write mechanism stations ten read-write heads where each head is on a separate track which forms a vertical cylinder of ten tracks. Since each surface consists of 200 tracks, we can see that the disk pack is composed of 200 concentric cylinders. In Figure B.10, the read-write heads are positioned over the tracks which make up cylinder 013.

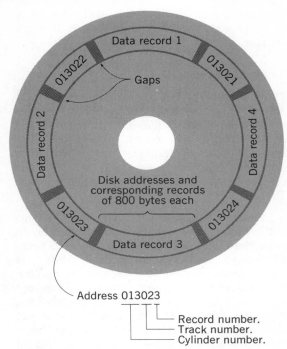

FIGURE B.11. Four 800 byte records stored on disk showing an address for each record.

Read Addressing

In Figure B.11, we have four 800 byte records stored on cylinder 013, track 02. These records, although not shown, are coded using EBCDIC. Each record within the track is numbered sequentially. Therefore, each record is preceded by a small address record which contains the address of the record following this address in a clockwise manner.

With these addresses, it is possible to directly access any desired record stored on the disk. Note that records are separated by gaps, similar to an IBG in magnetic tape. Since the addresses and gaps require a portion of the track, it is therefore impossible to store a full 3625 bytes of data on a track when more than one record per track is stored. As the number of records per track increases, the number of gaps and addresses increase, causing the capacity for data per track to decrease. For example, if

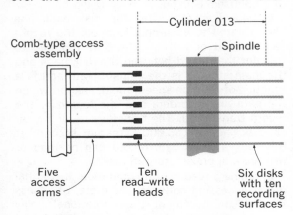

FIGURE B.10. Side view of a disk pack.

the record size is 80 bytes, then the track capacity would be 25 records for a total track capacity of 2000 bytes of data.

Transfer Rate

The disk pack rotates on a spindle clockwise at an operating speed of 2400 RPM (there are other models with different speeds) as the access mechanism moves in and out. The speed with which data are read or written is dependent upon these two factors plus read/write head selection and data transfer. These factors are discussed below:

1. *Access Mechanism Movement Time.* This is the time it takes for the access assembly to move the read-write heads to a specified cylinder (called Seek Time or Access Time). The access movement time is based on the number of cylinders the read-write heads move across to reach the one specified and the speed of the mechanism itself. The movement rate is not uniform because the mechanism is electromechanical and does not move at constant speed (notice the movement of the player arm of a record; the naked eye can detect a somewhat irregular movement). For a movement of one cylinder, minimum time is 25 msec; across all 200 cylinders, maximum is 135 msec. See Figure B.12. The average movement speed over the entire pack is 75 msec. If the read-write heads are already at their proper position during access, there is no need to move them; therefore, the access movement time is zero. On some disk systems the read-write heads are fixed in position over each track which eliminates seek time consideration.

2. *Read-Write Head Selection.* After the access mechanism has been properly positioned on the specified cylinder, the head that is to read or write is switched on. This switching takes place at 186,000 miles per second, the speed of electricity, which means that such a time delay in negligible; therefore, it is disregarded when determining amount of time to directly access and read a record on a disk pack.

3. *Rotational Delay.* Before data are read or

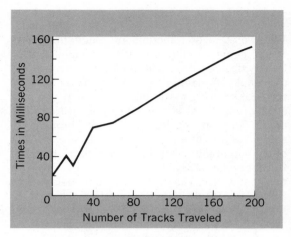

FIGURE B.12. Disk pack access time chart.

written the proper location on the track must rotate to the read-write heads. The time spent in rotating to a proper alignment of the read-write heads with the specified location is called rotational delay. For the IBM 2316 disk pack, a full rotation requires 25 msec. If, after positioning the access mechanism over the desired track, the desired record has just passed, then the rotational delay is 25 msec. If, on the other hand, the desired record has just reached the read-write head, the rotational delay is zero. Normally, for timing calculations, average rotational delay of 12.5 msec. is used.

4. *Data Transfer.* After the disk pack has been rotated to its proper location, the record can be read or written. The time required to transfer the record between the disk pack and the main storage is the transfer rate and is a function of rotation speed, the density at which the data are recorded, and the length of the record transferred. The transfer rate of a typical disk pack is 156,000 bytes per second. At this rate, a 3625 byte record can be read or written in approximately 23 msec.

In timing a read or write operation, the actual direct accessing consists, therefore, of access mechanism movement time, rotational delay (using average time), and data transfer rate. The total time for a complete processing job requires, in addition, the consideration of additional factors such as program processing time, access method processing time, and control program time. The following is, however, a summary of timing for the disk system only:

A record which is to be read, updated, and written, contains 356 bytes. The access mechanism is positioned in the first cylinder and the specific record sought is the fourth one on the second track of the fiftieth cylinder. How long will it take to perform this I/O job? An access time chart is illustrated in Figure B.12, and the timing summary of this problem is shown in Table B.I.

Simplified Example of Rating Disk Speeds

The following two examples are based on the IBM 3330 Disk Storage System as compared to its older 2314 Disk Storage System:

	2314	3330
Access Time	60.0 ms. average	30.0 ms. average
Rotation Time	12.5 ms. average	8.4 ms. average
Transfer Rate (KB/sec)	312	806

Using these figures a 1000 character READ would require:

	2314	3330
Access Time	60.0	30.0
Rotation Time	12.5	8.4
Read	3.2	1.2
	75.7 ms.	39.6 ms.

Advantages/Disadvantages of Magnetic Disk

The advantages are as follows:

1. A disk file may be organized sequentially and processed like a magnetic tape in addition

TABLE B.1. Timing Summary

Reading Time:		
Access mechanism movement (approx.)	70.0 ms.	
Rotational delay (average)	12.5 ms.	
Data transfer	2.0 ms.	
Subtotal		84.5 ms.
Writing Time:		
Access mechanism movement	0.0 ms.	
Rotational delay (average)	12.5 ms.	
Data transfer	2.0 ms.	
Subtotal		14.5 ms.
Total time for job (excluding program processing time, access method processing time, control program time, and verification* time).		99.0 ms.

* After a record is written on a disk, it is normally verified by comparing it with the source data input. Such verification is accomplished by an instruction in the program. For verification the record must rotate all the way around to the read-write head. This rotation time is 25 ms.

to indexed sequential and direct access organization.

2. All transactions can be processed as they occur which keeps the system current.

3. All inquiries are handled on a quick response basis.

4. Multiple and interrelated files may be stored in a way which permits a transaction to be processed against all pertinent files simultaneously.

The disadvantages are as follows:

1. Magnetic disk is still more expensive than magnetic tape (10 to 1 ratio of raw cost per character stored). However, falling prices and improved recording densities have given real bargains to users of magnetic disks (and tapes, too, as far as costs are concerned).

2. For many applications, sequential batch processing is just as acceptable and effective as using disk.

3. In accounting work, there is a need for a clearly discernible audit trail. In updating a file on a magnetic disk, the record is read, updated, and written at the same location thus destroying the original contents. If there is no provision

for error detection and file reconstruction, costly errors may go undetected.

4. Disk operations require more sophisticated hardware, operating systems, and highly skilled technicians than do tape operations.

5. As a last disadvantage, if a system has fixed disk modules and the system goes down there is no way to process the data. However, with removable disk packs, processing can be performed on another system assuming compatability.

Hybrid Systems

The two media, magnetic tape and disk, are complementary with tapes providing cheaper storage and disks giving fast access. In many situations, the answer to data base development is in a hybrid system. Disks are used for controlling response time and for virtual storage concepts and the tape used for massive storage. Such a mix makes large data bases practicable.

Also, the development of automated tape libraries affect the future use of tapes. Automated tape libraries put the tape reels "online" by physically delivering tapes, in a matter of seconds, from the library to the operator for mounting on the drive unit. Such a system significantly increases the productivity and throughput of the entire system.

Computer Output Microfilm (COM)

COM provides another medium for storing large amounts of data. This approach is shown in Figure B.13. Data output from the central processor is read into a microfilm recorder which is connected to a film developer. The final microfilm output is in two basic forms: (1) microfiche and (2) roll film. Either one can be viewed directly through special CRT type readers.[12]

Advantages of COM are:

1. Although COM is generally considered as a replacement for data on paper, in many situa-

[12] For further information, see: Richard G. Canning, "Computer Output to Microfilm," *EDP Analyzer,* June, 1970, pp. 1–14.

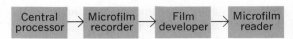

FIGURE B.13. Illustration of processes involved in producing COM.

tions it can be considered as a magnetic tape replacement.

2. Quite applicable for archival files (five or more years) because magnetic tape is not made for long-term storage of data, whereas microfilm is. The tape deteriorates over a long period of nonuse and, in addition, the recorded magnetic signals must be insulated from possible damage from environmental conditions such as radiation, heat, humidity, and random signals from electrical fixtures.

3. It significantly reduces the need for storage space because it reduces the paper explosion.

4. Information is available directly from storage in human readable form with the aid of a microfilm reader.

5. Relatively inexpensive.

The major disadvantages are:

1. It is a poor application wherein records within the file require continuous updating.

2. Most searching methods must be performed by hand.

Summary Characteristics of Auxiliary Storage Devices

We have discussed in detail the three popular auxiliary storage devices—magnetic tape, disk, and COM. A summary of the important characteristics of all storage devices is shown in Figure B.14.

In seeking the best mix of devices, the high-speed devices such as magnetic tape, magnetic disk, and data cells are generally the best for quick processing of large quantities of data. In archival files where minimum physical size and high data storage capacity are important, microfilm and data cell devices may be the best choice; on the other hand, action information which pertains to a particular process and has

Auxiliary Storage Media	Online	Offline	Type of Access		
			Sequential (reversible)	Sequential (nonreversible)	Direct
Paper document		X			
Punched card	X	X		X	
Punched paper tape	X	X		X	
MICR on paper		X		X	
Ledger card (with magnetic strip)		X		X	
Optical character (on paper)		X		X	
Microfilm	X	X	X	X	
Magnetic tape	X	X	X	X	
Magnetic disks	X	X		X	X
Data cells	X	X	X		X
Magnetic drum	X	X			X

FIGURE B.14.   Summary characteristics of auxiliary storage devices.

only temporary significance may be handled best by magnetic disk. Applications which require voluminous amounts of data processed on a periodic basis requiring little, if any, inquiry capability is handled best by magnetic tape.

At the slower and lower cost end of the spectrum are punched cards and punched paper tape. It is quite difficult to make a sensible comparison between these two media and other media listed above, because of the great difference in cost, transfer rate, storage capacity, and so on. However, the decision, as to which of the two to select often depends on how the data are to be organized. Paper tape is preferable when files are organized sequentially and there is no need for insertions, modifications, or deletions. On the other hand, punched cards are preferable when the unit-record concept is to be used, i.e., the punched card serves as a record where each card is designed to contain data about a certain transaction. Each record is then stored in a tray which serves as the file. Each record can be separately updated, modified, deleted, or shifted to other positions in the file. The ledger cards with magnetic strips are based on the unit record concept except the machine-readable part of the card is recorded on a magnetic strip which increases the transfer rate.

The high cost of data preparation and input is creating a push toward the use of the source document as the computer input. In dealing with character recognition, there are two aspects: (1) the data on a document is read directly from the page into the computer such as a test scoring sheet with optical marks, and (2) special type characters are printed in magnetic ink and are sensed magnetically and similarly read into the computer such as checks with magnetic ink character recognition (MICR).

The first aspect deals with optical recognition of either a mark or a character. Optical-mark readers are online to the computer and can read up to 2000 documents per hour. They operate on the basis of sensing a mark in a specific location in the document. Applications for this device are: test scoring, surveys, order entry, inventory control, insurance questionaires, and payroll. The optical character recognition (OCR) device reads special characters, which include: the alphabet, the ten decimal digits, and special signs. OCR characters can be printed by computer printers, accounting machines, cash registers, and typewriters. Some OCR equipment is available to read hand-printed characters. However, the characters have to be written precisely. This equipment is expensive and would not be feasible unless the data volume were in the neighborhood of

10,000–20,000 documents per day. Also, the documents processed would have to be of standard form such as sales slips.

Magnetic ink character recognition (MICR) is used primarily by the banking institutions for check processing such as sorting and routing them to the appropriate banks. The MICR characters are preprinted on the checks and are composed of the ten decimal digits and four special characters. The characters are read by a device with a sensing mechanism. This device looks similar to a card sorter and can be used either offline or online. It can process checks at a rate of 750–1800 per minute.

A considerable number of different devices, covering a wide range of speeds and capacities, is currently available from a great number of manufacturers. It is not the intention here to make a fine comparison of the various devices, since specific technical information about them is available from either the vendor or special services. During the final stages of systems work, the systems analyst becomes deeply involved in making comparisons between competitive equipment, and he or she will at that time need specifications of devices from each vendor.

Terminal Devices

Terminals actually represent devices which are used to get the data into the system and the information from the system. Terminals are fundamental to an online system. Terminal hardware will vary with the needs of the different users throughout the organization. Terminals vary from simple teletypewriters to card readers, high-speed printers, CRTs, magnetic tape units, and so on. The distance of the terminal from the central processor has no effect on its function. Move a magnetic tape unit to a plant 500 miles from the central processor, add a communication data control unit, connect it to a communication channel, and it becomes a remote job entry (RJE) terminal. Hook up a CRT to the data base and one has an interrogative terminal, and so on.

The total computer system can be configured in a variety of ways. Systems design and terminal selection is a more complicated problem today than ever before.

If the Sixties can be said to have experienced a computer explosion, perhaps the largest piece of fallout from the explosion is not the number of computers in existence but rather the realization that you don't have to be sitting in a computer room to be able to use the computer. You can share your central processor with remote locations. Or you can rent a piece of somebody else's remote computer. Further, you can actually operate on a transaction as it takes place. Data processing has been combined with communications to put the power of the computer almost everywhere.

But to take advantage of this power, whether you are in the room next to the computer or in another city, you need a terminal—a data entry and reception station with communications capabilities.[13]

In this section, we will devote our discussion primarily to two types of terminals: (1) telephone terminals and (2) intelligent terminals.

Telephone Terminals

The Touch-Tone® (sometimes used with the Picturephone®)* is an example of a low-speed terminal in the sense that it can handle effectively only low volumes of data. This telephone can be used for voice or data communications which provides an additional dimension as a terminal to the central processor. It can be used to update files, retrieve response information either by voice answer-back or printout or visual display on other devices. Two examples of its use are: (1) Such a system can help to maintain up-to-the-minute status on a multiplicity of inventory items during their transit through the logistics system, a dispatcher from

[13] D. H. Surgan, "Terminals: On-Line and Off, Conversational and Batch," *Control Engineering,* February, 1970. p. 96. Used with permission.

* Touch–Tone and Picturephone are registered trademarks of the Bell System.

a plant transmits shipping information such as load location, size, content, and shipping priority by a simple numeric code to the organization's warehouse, the warehouseman receives this information via a teletypewriter which enables him to prepare available space, coordinate loading and unloading facilities with maximum efficiency; and (2) It can provide credit status on credit card customers. Clerks type in an access code to the central processor, the customer's account number, and the amount of the purchase. By voice answerback, heard only by the clerk, the central processor either approves the transaction or instructs the clerk to call the credit department for further instructions. The computer has a 32-word recorded "vocabulary" which makes possible as many as 48 different types of responses, depending upon the transaction. Sixty Touch-Tone telephones in a system can handle as many as 720 inquiries per hour. A similar system to this could be used as an order entry system in conjunction with reporting inventory availability to incoming calls from customers and/or salesmen.

Intelligent Terminal

An intelligent terminal incorporates a processing capability usually in the form of a minicomputer. This minicomputer has the capability to perform operations on the data it handles in addition to transmitting it to a central processor. To discuss intelligent terminals, we will divide this section into two parts: (1) definition of minicomputers and (2) applications of the intelligent terminal concept.

Definition of Minicomputers

Minicomputers have three basic characteristics, which are: (1) physically small; (2) relatively inexpensive; and (3) stored program with at least 4K words of primary storage where word lengths vary from 8 to 24 bits, the most common being 12 and 16 bits.[14]

[14] "Elusive Mini Defies Definition, and That's a Sign of Its Growth," *Computerworld*, Supplement, August 30, 1972, p. 1. Used with permission. Copyright by *Computerworld*, Newton, Massachusetts 02160.

There are three basic uses of a minicomputer: (1) as a data communications control device (we discuss this use in the data communications section), (2) as a general purpose computer system with a variety of peripheral devices and software wherein it functions as a full capacity computer system in its own right, and (3) as an intelligent terminal.

Applications of Intelligent Terminals

Intelligent terminals are used to: (1) extend the power of the central computer and (2) accept data at its origin and perform some level of processing. Many of the intelligent terminals include minicomputers which can be used for different purposes based on how they are configured and programmed. For instance, by using one set of peripherals and programs, a remote job entry (RJE) system is developed, and by using a different set of peripherals and programs a data entry system such as a remote key-to-disk system is created.

With the advent of lower costs and greater availability of computers and data communication systems, the use of RJE systems have become cost/effective for small users who cannot economically justify their own data processing systems. Also, this RJE technique is applicable to the distributed information systems approach with a large organization wherein different plants or divisions have their own subsystems which in turn are connected to other subsystems or a central processor.

Also, intelligent terminals are used to provide a form of backup for the central computer. With nonintelligent terminals connected to the main processor, if this processor breaks down, the terminals are disabled and for all practicable purposes the entire system is down. Transactions cannot be entered and processed. At most, transactions might be captured on paper tape or magnetic tape for later transmission to the computer. With an intelligent terminal, it is feasible for the terminal to accept transactions and perform some of the processing when the main computer is down or the data communications system is disrupted. This capability is one of the main reasons why banks and retail stores have selected intelligent terminals. Sales transactions in a store, or savings transactions in a financial institution, can still be recorded at the terminal for processing and later transmission if necessary, even though the central computer is down.[15]

Another reason for using the intelligent terminal is that it can relieve the central processor of some of the processing workload. This situation helps to reduce an overload on the central processor, allowing the system to get along with a smaller central processor than would otherwise be the case.[16]

Data Entry Techniques

More than half the cost of using computers in many organizations is incurred in the capture and conversion of data for computer processing. Probably no other aspect of computer application offers more potential for cost savings than does this one area. The preparation of data for computer processing is truly the big bottleneck in the entire system and, as a result, it substantially decreases throughput. Newer computers are faster and more powerful than ever before; consequently, the input bottleneck can cause gross underutilization of the computer. The general aim of the systems analyst is to accelerate the conversion of data because no computer can function faster than the slowest element in the system.

In this section on data entry techniques, we will direct our attention to three main areas: (1) keyboard-to-storage, (2) point of sale (POS), and (3) optical character recognition (OCR).

Keyboard-to-Storage

The keyboard-to-storage technique consists of several keyboards (CRT) connected to a minicomputer or programmed controller which collects the data input, verifies it, provides various

other functions, and writes it on tape or disk for processing. Some of the functions that this kind of data entry system perform are:

1. Keyed in data are input to an edit program to filter out errors.
2. CRT input terminals provide sight verification for the operator and if an error is made backspacing and deletion allows the operator to quickly correct the error.
3. Program is in the system which provides productivity statistics for monitoring and checking operators' efficiency.
4. Provides automatic preparation of check digits and batch totals.
5. Makes certain reasonableness and relevancy checks.
6. Allows true modular input of data because it merges blocks of data in proper sequence for further processing.

The typical key-to-storage system is referred to as key-to-tape (sometimes called key-to-disk) system. It consists of a low-cost minicomputer; direct access intermediate storage usually, magnetic disk; and magnetic tape for final output. Most manufacturers of these systems offer 8–64 CRT Keystations per system. Studies indicate that at the present cost levels, disregarding any other benefits, a system has to replace ten to fourteen keypunches before a key-to-tape system is cost/effective. With falling prices, in the near future, the same basic system may be cost/effective at a five or six keypunch level. A key-to-tape system is shown in Figure B.15.

An online data entry system works basically the same way except the data flows directly into the central processor. For an example, refer to Figure B.16.

Advantages/Disadvantages of Key-to-Storage Systems

The advantages are listed as follows:[17]

1. Editing, formatting, combining input data, and dumping data from system's storage to

[15] "Intelligent Terminals," *EDP Analyzer*, April, 1972, p. 7. Used with permission.

[16] *Ibid.*

[17] "Three Key-to-Disk Experiences," *Data Dynamics*, August/September, 1971, pp. 17–22.

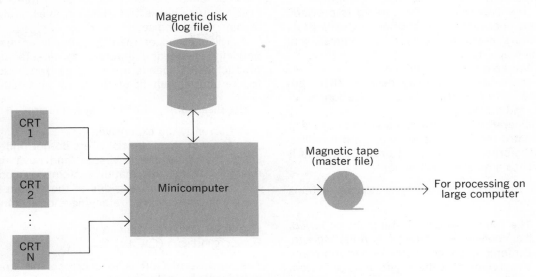

FIGURE B.15. Illustration of key-to-tape system.

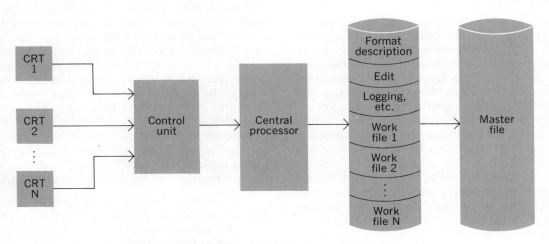

FIGURE B.16. Illustration of online entry system.

the master file are basic functions all of which are automatically handled by the computer.

2. The supervisor of the system is provided various operational statistics on such things as operators' performance, work in progress, and work completed.

3. Variable costs are reduced.

4. Increases productivity because there are no delays for card feeding, duplication, skipping, and stacking.

5. Operators' acceptance is good because it eliminates menial tasks such as card handling and the creation and use of drum cards and it furnishes a quieter environment.

The disadvantages of key-to-storage systems are:

1. The source document still must be keyed, i.e., it cannot be read directly into file storage.

2. Buffered keypunch/verifiers perform many of the functions that the key-to-storage system performs.

3. Practically everyone understands the keypunch and the ubiquitous punched card.

Point of Sale (POS)

Point of sale systems provide a method by which vital data are captured at the point of sale as occurs in department stores, supermarkets, and large discount stores. However, the same technique is applicable to other user categories where it is important to capture data at the time of an event or transaction. For example, in a production control system, a POS system can capture data and report production information in the time frame where it is still valid.

This technique uses either hand-held "wand" readers or stationary sensors which capture price, stock, and other data from merchandise tags or tickets which contain either optical or magnetic characters. All of these readers in the organization are linked either to a central processor or an intelligent terminal. The main advantages are:

1. Provides large-scale data collection and online capabilities.

2. A large department store sells thousands of items at many different locations. There must be quick identification of such items as credit status checks and trends in sales of high fashion merchandise.

3. The method of reading optically or magnetically encoded characters on tickets and product items speeds up the sales transaction to the mutual benefit of the buyer and seller.

The disadvantages of POS systems are:

1. Currently too expensive.

2. Many of the potential users do not understand the value of the system and have not related it to the information systems concept.

3. Requires major revisions to the system in a number of areas, e.g., retagging and recoding.

Optical Character Recognition (OCR)

The purpose of OCR is to decrease the input bottleneck by reducing the number of keying operations and errors in transcription. Ideally, OCR equipment will read any document and transmit the data to a computer, thus eliminating any intermediate data preparation tasks. "Although machines are available that read handwritten numbers, the automatic reading of handwritten script is still some years in the future."[18] Most OCR devices being used in organizations are designed to read machine-printed characters and handmade marks. In order to reduce the problem of unique type fonts, a study was conducted by USASCII of a standard character set called OCR-A which includes both upper-case and lower-case characters. A general flow of data using OCR devices is shown in Figure B.17.

The advantages of OCR are listed as follows:

1. Since data conversion is handled photographically, data errors are decreased.

2. Increases throughput.

3. Reduces paper pollution.

The disadvantages are as follows:

1. Unsettled technology.

2. Standardization problems in type fonts and document inputs.

[18] Sanders, *op. cit.,* p. 183.

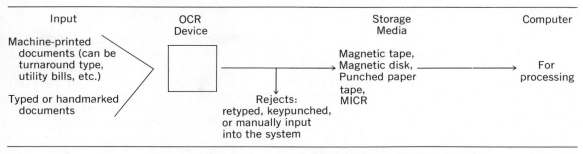

Input	OCR Device		Storage Media	Computer

Machine-printed documents (can be turnaround type, utility bills, etc.)

Typed or handmarked documents

Rejects: retyped, keypunched, or manually input into the system

Magnetic tape, Magnetic disk, Punched paper tape, MICR

For processing

FIGURE B.17.   Illustration of OCR application.

3. Because of increased sensitivity to document conditions, smudges, creased documents, dirt, and poor quality paper can cause many rejects.

4. OCR devices with low prices have correspondingly low throughput and reading vocabulary usually limited to one font. Devices with the capability to read a great number of type fonts are very expensive.

5. The installation of OCR equipment usually requires complete forms redesign.

Remote Computing Networks (RCN)

In the future, it has been projected[19] that most organizations will no longer have computers. Dr. Feeney does not foresee the demise of the computer industry, but the rise of the computer utility will cause many organizations to give up their in-house computers in favor of local terminals connected to centralized high performance computers that will serve an entire region of the country.

Analogous to such an idea is the electric utility where every user has appliances, using different amounts of power, but almost nobody has their own power generator. It is also projected that large data files will not be maintained locally either. These projections border on fulfillment with the advent of remote computing networks which are discussed below.

The remote computing network, the son of timesharing and maybe the father of computer utilities, is characterized by multiple users, remote terminals, and a central processor(s). The old timesharing systems are primarily scientific oriented where their major forte is providing access to extraordinary computational power. In an information system context, if you remember, there are additional demands, namely: volume, time, and complexity. RCN provide not only exceptional computational power but also accommodate the other three systems demands. By combining reliable data communications systems, computing, and massive storage, the RCN vendors are providing new levels of service for most vital information needs of multi-location organizations.

Classes of RCN

Approximately two dozen companies offer some form of national network service, and these fall into two general classes.[20]

1. *Star Configuration.* This class is the most widely used with communication channels from all users feeding into a single computer complex, often through a series of multiplexers and data concentrators.

2. *Ring Configuration.* This class uses several CPUs in several locations with two or more network paths uniting them. This configuration is basically distributive in nature and, thus, provides a build-up of redundancy which may increase its reliability.

[19] Dr. George Feeney, "A Three-Stage Theory of Evolution for the Sharing of Computer Power," *Computer Decisions,* November, 1971, pp. 42–45. Used with permission.

[20] T/S Vendors Supporting Users' Communication Needs," *Computerworld,* Supplement, June 28, 1972, p. 13. Used with permission. Copyright by *Computerworld,* Newton, Massachusetts 02160.

Advantages/Disadvantages of RCN

The advantages are listed as follows:[21]

1. Whatever the configuration approach, the RCN provides needed data communications services to users who can afford their own computers, but not their own networks.
2. Data communications have a high degree of reliability. For example, General Electric provides satellite transmission between America and Europe, but has also laid a trans-Atlantic cable for backup. Tymshare has developed and installed 22 specifically designed minicomputers to ensure good communications along the 40,000 miles of leased telephone lines that make up its ring network.
3. The systems permit access to data bases, either private or public.
4. A number of programs are made available to users on a national basis.
5. Users are provided with the ability to design and operate multi-level information systems.
6. The system provides the coordination, development, and maintenance of programs for large groups of users.
7. The users are charged only for the time they are connected to the system plus the utilization of mass storage.
8. The users are provided with large machine and data file storage capability at a fraction of the cost of an equivalent system they might purchase or lease on their own.

The disadvantages of an RCN are:

1. The software packages may not be customized enough to meet specific demands of certain users.
2. System reliability may present a problem with some vendors.
3. These systems are not very applicable to organizations where the demands are primarily that of routine administrative data processing such as payrolls, billings, etc.

[21] *Ibid.*, pp. 13–14.

Word Processing

One of the major problems in organizations is that of written communications. This area is peripheral to normal information systems work and can be substantially improved by thorough systems analysis.

Definition of Word Processing

Word processing is a method of producing written communications and copying at top speed, with the greatest accuracy, combined use of proper procedures, automated business equipment, and trained personnel. Two kinds of business equipment play key roles in WP, which are: (1) dictating machines and (2) automatic typewriters which may also be connected to auxiliary storage. Dictating speeds the formulating of communications and automatic typewriters speed their production.[22]

The main advantage to using dictating equipment in a WP operation is that it increases both executive and secretarial productivity. The main benefit of automatic or power typing is that it multiplies the productivity of the typist. The basic advantage of automatic typing is the retrieval of keystrokes. As information is typed, it is recorded on magnetic disk, magnetic tape, punched cards, or punched paper tape. An operator types three or four times faster because the operator types at rough draft speed, correcting mistakes merely by backspacing and striking over. Playing back, or automatically typing the contents of a tape or card, is seven to ten times faster than manual typing. Net savings average 30–50%.[23]

Application of Word Processing

There are five basic applications of WP. These are:[24]

[22] "Word Processing: The New Approach to Internal Profit," *Modern Office Procedures*, August, 1972, pp. 36–37. Used with permission.

[23] *Ibid.*

[24] *Ibid.* For further information about WP, refer to: "Ways to Put Word Processing to Work," *Modern Office Procedures*, August, 1972, pp. 38–39. "What Goes Into a Word Processing Workstation," *Modern Office Procedures*, August, 1972, pp. 40–44.

1. Straight repetitive communications, such as the form letter. Here the message does not vary from letter to letter or document to document.

2. Combined repetitive and variable typing, where standard paragraphs are used from document to document. Here the originator may combine stored paragraphs to form a message, or may use standard stored paragraphs plus dictated paragraphs that apply in specific cases. Another use: financial reports, where headings and tabulations remain fixed but figures change from period to period.

3. Transcription typing. Here the WP operator keyboards from the transcriber. The job is handled in one of two ways, depending on the procedure chosen: (a) to type for a finished document on first transcription, and store on tape or card in case there are corrections; (b) the first WP operator keyboards only rough drafts. The storage media and the draft then go to a second operator who proofs, corrects, and plays back the finished product.

4. Text preparation, editing, and revision such as in long reports, contracts, proposals, or material for publication. Here the original material is keyboarded into the word processor. The draft goes back to the originator for review and correction. He or she marks changes and sends the draft back to the WP operator, who automatically plays back all stored correct copy at 100–175 words a minute, stopping only to keyboard in the author's revisions.

5. Composition. This application involves a composing typewriter that uses a variety of type fonts to produce camera-ready copy for printed material.

Data Communications

Data communications systems transmit data between peripherals and the central processor and, thus, allow people and equipment to be geographically dispersed rather than being at one central location. In computer based information systems, nearly all of the information produced must be disseminated to a variety of users, some many miles away. This transmission load is increasing each year and is making the interdependency of computers and data communications systems even more apparent. Data communications control systems, equipment, and services have, cumulatively, become possibly the fastest growing area of information systems activity. "Full consideration of its role and implementation must be given in the early planning stages if you are to have any chance of turning up a successful system."[25]

Typical applications which require design, selection, and implementation of data communications systems are as follows:

1. *Timesharing.* This application allows a number of remote users to gain access to the computational services of a central computer system. Data flow is in both directions (interactive), i.e., the terminal is both sending and receiving.

2. *Computer Job Load Sharing.* This application permits the interconnection of two or more computers, e.g., distributive systems.

3. *Remote Job Entry (RJE).* This application entails the linkage of the central large computer with two or more small computers in separate locations which are equipped with high-speed printers, card read-punches, and magnetic disk and tape. The purpose of RJE is to transmit voluminous amounts of data to a central processor for further processing.

4. *Interrogation.* This application requires the implementation of an online inquiry system using such terminal devices as CRTs and teletypewriters to gain access to the data base to make inquiries and receive specific responses. Also, similar to RJE, the user may also update records within certain integrated files.

The four major areas of data communications systems are:

1. *Communication Channels.* These channels provide a path for electrical transmission between two or more points. These channels are also called circuits, lines, or links.

2. *Modems.* The term modem represents a

---

[25] Dr. L. Carey, "Data Communications," *Data Management,* September, 1971, pp. 58–60.

contraction of modulator-demodulator. These devices modulate and demodulate signals transmitted over communication channels.

3. *Multiplexers and Concentrators.* A multiplexer is a device which combines or merges (multiplexs) several separate data signals onto a single signal for transmission over a channel. A concentrator is similar to a multiplexer except the idea of contention is introduced into the system.

4. *Programmable Communication Processors.* These devices are computers (usually minicomputers) and serve a supporting role in the overall communications system. They perform two basic functions in the system: (1) message switching and (2) front-end processing.

Communication Channels

Communication channels are comprised of one or a combination of the following: (1) telegraph lines, (2) telephone lines, (3) radio links, (4) coaxial cable, (5) microwave, (6) satellite, and (7) experimental laser beam and helical waveguides. Depending on the terminal equipment and the application required, the channels can be arranged for operation in one or more of the three basic transmission modes:

1. *Simplex.* Transmission is made in one direction only.

2. *Half-duplex.* Transmission can be in both directions, but not at the same time.

3. *Full-duplex.* Transmission can be made in both directions at the same time.

Data Transmission

Data are transmitted over a wire line (or microwave system) by an electrical signal which is comprised of three elements: (1) amplitude-strength of the signal, (2) phase-duration of signal, and (3) frequency-number of times a wave form is repeated during a specified time interval. These elements are illustrated in Figure B.18.

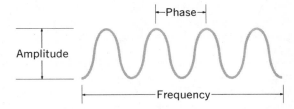

FIGURE B.18. Schematic of wave form.

These signals can be used to transmit binary numbers. As you already know, the binary numbering system can be used to represent all alphabetic characters, numeric characters, and special characters. When the binary numbering system is used to represent characters, a pulse for a defined time interval represents a 1-bit, and no pulse is used to represent a 0-bit. The pulse or no pulse is based on the amplitude, phase, and frequency of the signal which is termed the "state."

Data transmission is of two general types: (1) asynchronous and (2) synchronous. Asychronous transmission is the slower rate such as in telegraph communication. Signal elements are transmitted to indicate the start and stop of each character. Three common asynchronous codes are:

1. *Baudot.* A 5-level code with 32 (2^5) possible combinations. With the use of a shift code (shift from a code for numbers to code for alphabetics and special characters), it is possible to code 62 combinations. The term, baud, is used for measurement, e.g., baud per second, means one pulse or code element per second. This coding method uses five bits for the character plus a start and stop bit.

2. *Binary Coded Decimal.* The BCD method is similar to the Baudot method. It has, however, a 6-level code and has been discussed earlier in the section dealing with magnetic tape.

3. *American Standard Code for Information Interchange.* This code, termed ASCII, uses seven or eight character bits, plus two or three bits for starting and stopping.

All start and stop bits are normally stripped out of the data stream along with control characters by the communications modem prior to entering it into the central processor.

Synchronous transmission is normally used where the transmission rate exceeds 2000 bits per second. The synchronous data transmission requires the receiving terminal to be synchronized bit-for-bit with the sending terminal which eliminates the need for start and stop bits, consequently improving the efficiency of data transmission. However, this system requires a clocking mechanism at both the sending and receiving ends.

Grade of Channels

The above discussion represented the directional flow of data and types of transmission and codes used. Another very important consideration is the grade of the channel. Channels are graded on speed of transmission which is directly proportional to bandwidth. For example, telegraph lines are narrow-band, telephone lines are voice-band, and coaxial cable or mircowave are broad-band. The bandwidth of a channel is measured by a unit called a Hertz (Hz) which means cycles per second. From empirical studies, it has been shown that the band-width of a channel should be approximately twice the number of bits to be transmitted per second. For example, if one is to transmit data at 1200 bits per second (bps), then a channel with a bandwidth of 2400 Hz is required. However, the simplest way to classify communication channels are:[26] (1) low-speed, (2) medium-speed, and (3) high-speed.

Low-Speed Channels

This grade is narrow-band and was originally developed for use with teletypewriters (TTYs). It transmits data in the range of 45, 75, 110, 150, and 300 bits per second. AT & T developed the TWX (Teletypewriter Exchange Service) which consisted of a network of channels and teletypewriters that covered the United States and

Canada. This service has been sold to Western Union but will continue over the Bell System network for the next several years. This system will eventually be integrated with Western Union's TELEX system.

Data can be transmitted via the teletypewriter online, or paper tape can be prepared offline and transmitted during slack periods. These systems normally use 5-channel (Baudot) code, but, at higher speeds, they also have available the 8-channel ASCII Code.

With the TWX system, each customer is assigned a TWX number which is listed in a nationwide TWX directory. Any user can transmit data to another user by dialing the central operator, who makes the connection. This method is called a "switched" service which means that a connection is made by dialing and is disconnected at the end of transmission. A "dedicated" line, on the other hand, is a line that remains connected between its terminal points for the duration of the lease.

A usage charge is based on the airline distance between two stations and the connect time between the two stations for switched lines. For dedicated lines, a charge is made monthly.

Medium-Speed Channels

This grade is voice-band and is provided by the Bell System and the independent telephone companies. These voice-band channels are used for voice and data communications, interchangeably. Their typical transmission rate is 300–9600 bits per second. There are three types of services available:[27] (1) private line, (2) the dial-up network, and (3) WATS.

1. *Private Lines.* The major difference in this system and a dial-up system is that the channel remains connected for the duration of the lease, the routing can be chosen, and the line can be electrically conditioned so that the transmission rate can be increased. Private lines are leased on a monthly basis with unlim-

[26] Fonnie H. Reagan, Jr., "A Manager's Guide to Phone and Services," *Computer Decisions,* November, 1971, pp. 36–39. Used with permission.

[27] Karl I. Nordling, "Analysis of Common Carrier Tariff Rates," *Datamation,* May 1, 1971, pp. 28–35. Reprinted with permission of *Datamation*®, Copyright 1971 by Technical Publishing Company, Greenwich, Connecticut 06830.

ited usage and the rate is a function of airline miles from point to point.

Conditioning refers to the process by which the phone company maintains the quality of a specific, privately leased line to a certain standard of permissible error rate. Such conditioning adjusts the frequency and phase response characteristics of the channel to meet closer tolerance specifications.

An additional type of private line service of interest to the systems analyst is the foreign exchange line (FX line). This service in effect connects a user to an exchange other than his or her own, thus allowing toll-free calling to telephones served by that exchange; however, channel conditioning is not available.

2. *Dial-up or Public Switched Network.* The dial-up or public switched network is currently the most commonly used method of transmitting data. The channel is available as long as the connection is made, and payment varies according to mileage, time of day or night, and duration of connect time. The rate approximates the rate for a normal voice telephone call. The average speed of transmission is generally from 2000 to 2400 bits per second.

Since each dial-up connection may involve a unique combination of channels, the telephone company does not guarantee the characteristics of the dial-up channels. Consequently, to achieve high transmission rates (2000–2400 bps) on a dial-up network, the required conditioning must be performed within the modem. Such a modem rapidly determines the channel characteristics and compensates for them at the start of the connection and then continuously adapts to any changes during connect time.

3. *Wide Area Telephone Service* (*WATS*). WATS is a pricing arrangement for users of large volume data (and voice) transmission over long distances. WATS offers two billing plans: (1) a full period service, and (2) a measured time service. Under full period service, the subscriber may use the channel as much as he or she wishes in the geographical area for which he subscribes at a flat monthly rate. Under measured time service, the basic monthly rate

covers the first ten hours of use per month for calls to Data-Phones (or telephones) within the subscribed service area. An additional charge per hour of actual use is levied beyond the first ten hours; however, the tariff which governs this service is extremely complicated and a full explanation is beyond the scope of this text. There is, however, a formula which will help indicate the proper choice between the unlimited and the measured WATS. This formula is:

$$C = F + R(H)$$

where,

$C =$ Cost in dollars per month,
$F =$ Flat rate for first ten hours of measured plan,
$R =$ Rate of charge used after ten hours for the measured plan, and
$H =$ Hours of usage beyond first ten hours.

The break-even point can be calculated by setting C equal to the monthly charge of the unlimited method and solving for H.

Comparison of Different Medium-Speed Services

Services are available in a variety of specific forms and with a very complicated rate structure. It is nearly impossible to state before hand what type of service will be optimum for a given application. However, we present, below, some general guidelines which should help the systems analyst perform at least a first level analysis.

1. *Dial-up vs. Private.* For most systems analysts, configuring a data network involves complex tradeoffs. One set of considerations involves the choice of dial-up channels versus private channels. The foremost consideration usually is cost. While private line rates are usually based on airline mileage from point to point, long distance dial-up costs are figured on a timed or message unit basis depending on often complicated tariffs. In some instances, costs of using dial-up services can be reduced by using WATS.

Other considerations in choosing between

dial-up or private lines are related to throughput and geography. If users of the system transmit data from changing point locations versus fixed points, then dial-up channels must be used. Such a system would contain a broadly mixed base with dispersion in both geographic area and terminal population.

In systems where response time is important, a 15–20 second connect delay required by a dial-up channel can be prohibitive. For example in typical reservation systems and other systems where transactions have to be processed immediately, the private line is usually required.

Higher transmission speeds and high data volume make the dial-up lines over long distances very costly. In remote job entry (RJE) applications when data are sent in the opposite direction dial-up lines can be a problem unless the equipment has a reverse channel (full-duplex) capability.

Private channels are usually cleaner than dial-up channels because of conditioning. Maximum transmission rates on different types of channels depend very much on the type of channel available. Normally, users can reach a top data rate of 3000–4800 bits per second on dial-up channels while private channels usually can support rates from 7200 to 9600 bits per second. There are exceptions to these rates.

Most data transmission users begin with dial-up channels until their data volume and needs are fully determined. Later, as higher data rates and increased volume become important, a private channel network may have advantages.[28]

2. *Normal Dial-up vs. WATS.*[29] The comparison between dial-up and WATS is based on data volume level and data distribution. If transmission is made up of many simultaneous calls, WATS is inefficient. If calls can be sequential, and monthly volume exceeds 50–70 hours, full period, WATS is typically more economical than dial-up service. Measured WATS is significantly

more economical than dial-up only when traffic is made up of mostly short calls.

In general, private channels are intended for high transmission rate, quick response, and high volume traffic among relatively few points. Dial-up service is best suited for low volume random traffic. The break-even point between leasing a channel and using a dial-up channel is a function of distance and average length of connect time. WATS, a pricing arrangement, is intended for high volume traffic between one fixed point and many, widely distributed, other points.

Studies have shown that a dial-up service is more economical than private channel for 50–80 hours per month levels of usage and that WATS is not much more expensive than private channels, and yet offers network-wide access capability while private channel service is limited to a few points. Such comparison is based on the assumption that data rates and quality on dial-up lines are comparable to those on private lines. With new high speed modems for dial-up use, now becoming available, this is a realistic assumption.[30] However, a constraint on dial-up channel service is that the user is not assured of making the same connection each time he or she dials which means that a 4800 bits per second transmission rate may work one time and fail on the next attempt because of automatic re-routing by the telephone company. A summary table of advantages and disadvantages of private and dial-up channels is presented in Figure B.19.

High-Speed Channels

Where data are to be transmitted at high speeds and very high volumes, then a broadband service should be used. Both the Bell System and Western Union offer leased broadband services. These broad-band lines comprise a group of channels of voice grade. Each channel when properly arranged can carry voice, computer data, or facsimile signals. Two

---

[28] Based on: "Users Must Consider Dial-Up and Private Lines," *Computerworld*, Supplement, July 26, 1972, p. 16. Used with permission. Copyright by *Computerworld*, Newton, Massachusetts 02160.

[29] Based on: Nordling, *op. cit.*

[30] *Ibid.*

Service	Advantages	Disadvantages
Private Channel	1. Full-duplex. 2. Free from busy signals. 3. Fast response. 4. Fixed charge, unlimited use. 5. Conditioning available for better data quality and higher transmission rates.	1. Higher cost as volume demands decrease. 2. Fixed points of connection.
Dial-up Channel	1. Portability; user can connect with any point where there is a telephone. 2. User pays only for the time he uses the channel.	1. Half-duplex. 2. Maximum speeds of 4800 bps requiring synchronous transmission (a rate of less than 4800, however, may be quite adequate for many systems). 3. Often the channels are noisy, causing incorrect data transmission. 4. Requires elaborate and time-consuming error-checking devices. 5. Often impossible to get a connection because of busy channels.

FIGURE B.19. Advantages and disadvantages of private channel versus dial-up channel.

classes of services (formerly called TELPAK) are offered.

1. *Type 5700 Line.* Has a base capacity of 60 voice grade channels and a maximum equivalent bandwidth of 240 kHz (Kilo-hertz).

2. *Type 5800 Line.* Has a capacity of 240 voice grade channels and a maximum equivalent bandwidths of 1,000 kHz.

This service is quite flexible because it can be used as a single broad-band channel for fast and voluminous data transmission or as several individual lower-speed channels. In certain cases, a user group with similar needs may share a line, whereas on an individual basis, they could not afford such a service. A flat monthly rate is charged for this service, regardless of the volume of data transmitted. This rate is based on the number of channels, total capacity, and distance between transmission points.

Some companies have found it more economical and efficient to develop and use their own private-line microwave systems. Oil companies, in particular, have made use of microwave communication. Other broad-band transmission services with capacity up to 230,000 bps (bits per second) are available only to United States government agencies.

Projections about satellite data transmission is that the user will connect the computer to a satellite transmission system in the same way that a dial-up user now connects to a telephone system. These systems will use several differing technologies including cables, microwave, and time-division multiplexing. The carrier that provides satellite channels will have to provide the user with the same transparency he or she presently receives with other data communication systems, which means that software and hardware will remain basically the same. It is also projected that users will go to satellite transmission in the future for two reasons: (1) the greater available bandwidth and the superior quality of the circuits will make them much more desirable than present telephone facilities, and (2) it will provide inexpensive digital transmission facilities.[31]

[31] Summarized from: "Satellite Data Too Costly?," *Computerworld,* June 21, 1972, p. 13. Used with permission. Copyright by *Computerworld,* Newton, Massachusetts 02160.

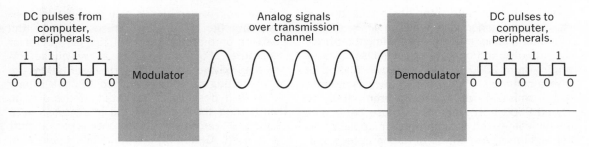

FIGURE B.20. Illustration of modulation-demodulation.

Modems

Modem is an acronym for *mo*dulator-*dem*odulator and is also known as a data set. Modems are used to handle the data stream from a peripheral device to the central processor or vice versa through the common carrier network. The modem can operate in simplex, half-duplex, or full-duplex mode.

Modem Operation

Telephone channels were developed for voice transmission which is analog. In communication applications involving digital data, the modulator portion of a modem converts digital dc pulses, representing binary 1's and 0's, by the computer or peripheral equipment, to an analog, wave-like signal acceptable for transmission over analog telephone channels. The demodulator reverses this process, converting the analog telephone signal back into a pulse train acceptable to the peripheral or computer at the other end. For example, see Figure B.20. If a modem was not used to convert/reconvert data signals, and the computer or peripheral was directly connected to the telephone channel, the signal would be degraded and the data made unintelligible by the electrical characteristics of the channel.[32]

Modem Types

Modems can be categorized into two broad types: (1) those handling asynchronous data, and (2) those handling synchronous data. Asynchronous modems are usually associated with keyboard entry terminal devices such as CRTs and TTYs. Synchronous modems are used with continuous data sources such as punched paper tape readers, magnetic tape, and magnetic disk.[33]

Asynchronous data are transmitted one character at a time, and are typically produced by low-speed peripherals. Synchronous transmission, on the other hand, makes use of an internal clocking device within the modem. Once the start bits have been sensed by the receiving equipment and the system put into synch and the clock started, data transmission proceeds character by character but without intervening start and stop bits used in asynchronous transmission.[34]

Asynchronous transmission is advantageous when transmission is irregular such as caused by changes in an operator's keying rate. These modems are less expensive than synchronous modems, but they do not utilize the channels as efficiently. Acoustic couplers are a special type of asynchronous modem which are not directly wired to the transmission channel, i.e., the modem is connected accoustically to the channel via a telephone handset. While their transmission rate is somewhat limited (600 bps range, maximum), these devices do offer the user the advantage of low cost and portability. All asynchronous modems are generally low-

[32] John A. Murphy, "Modems and Multiplexers—A Primer," *Modern Data,* December, 1971, pp. 47–48. Used with permission.

[33] *Ibid.*

[34] Robert Toombs, "Considering Telecommunications? Select the Right Modem," *Computer Decisions,* July, 1971, pp. 16–18. Used with permission.

speed, with maximum rates of up to 1800 bps using a conditioned leased channel.[35]

Medium-speed modems are almost entirely synchronous, and operate at transmission rates ranging from 2000 to 4800 bps over dial-up or private channels. Higher speed devices operate at transmission rates ranging from 4800 to around 9600 bps. Modems in these categories are typically used for multiplexer applications and higher speed peripheral to computer applications which we will discuss later in this appendix.[36]

Modulation Techniques

There are four basic modulation techniques: (1) on-off signal, (2) frequency modulation, (3) amplitude, and (4) phase modulation. These techniques are utilized by modems to transmit the analog equivalents of binary 1's and 0's.

1. *On-Off Signal.* A signal pulse of constant amplitude and frequency is turned "on" for a certain time interval to represent a binary 1 and is turned "off" to represent a binary 0.

2. *Frequency Modulation* (*FM*). The most popular form of frequency modulation is known as Frequency Shift Keying (FSK). With this technique, signals of two different frequencies are transmitted to represent binary 1 or binary 0. For example, if the carrier frequency is operating at 1500 Hz, it may be modulated ±500 Hz to represent binary 1 and binary 0, respectively. This modulation technique allows transmission rates of 1800 bps, or less.

3. *Amplitude Modulation* (*AM*). The amplitude of a constant frequency signal is varied to different levels to represent the binary 1's and 0's, and in some cases, start and stop signals. Both AM and FM are suitable for data transmission. FM, however, has a noise advantage over AM, but AM allows more efficient use of the available bandwidth.[37]

4. *Phase Modulation* (*PM*). These kinds of modems are generally described in terms of the number of phase shifts generated, and operate at speeds of 2000 bps and above. In this tech-

nique, the transmitted signal is shifted a certain number of degrees in response to the pattern of bits coming from the peripheral or computer. For example, in a two-phase PM modem, if the analog signal generated by the transmitting modem is shifted 180°, a binary 1 (or 0 if desired) is indicated. If there is no shift, then the signal will be interpreted as a series of zeroes (or ones) until such a shift is sensed. Generally, PM modems operate in four and eight phases, permitting up to twice or three times the data to be sent over the line in the same bandwidth.[38]

Multiplexers and Concentrators

The basic aim of using multiplexers or concentrators is to permit connection of more peripherals to the central processor using fewer channels. Their use, therefore, is not a technological decision but an economical one. "More users are considering a multiplexer when it comes to optimizing their networks. 'There's only one justification for multiplexing and that's saving money.' The more miles, the fewer channels are required in order to make multiplexing feasible."[39]

Multiplexer

When a number of low-speed and/or low-activity remote terminals are connected online to the central processor, it is desirable to provide some method of allowing access for each of the slow or infrequently used terminals to the central processor. A voice-band grade channel capacity ranges from 300 to 9600 bits per second according to type of service and line conditioning. However, many of the most widely used remote terminals operate at speeds between 45 and 300 bits per second, with 100–150 bits per second being typical. Where there are a number

---

[35] *Ibid.*
[36] *Ibid.*
[37] *Ibid.*

[38] *Ibid.*
[39] "Multiplexing Costs Based on Volume and Distance," *Computerworld,* Supplement, July 26, 1972, p. 5. Used with permission. Copyright by *Computerworld,* Newton, Massachusetts 02160.

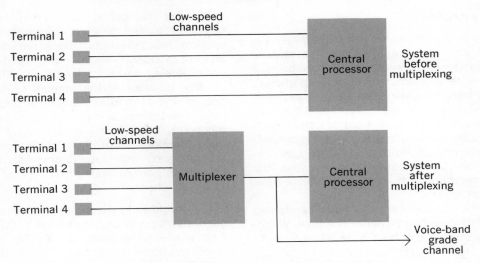

FIGURE B.21. Communication system before and after multiplexing.

of such terminals in one or more areas outside the toll-free zone of the central processor, the common carrier tariff structure makes it economically attractive to operate a group of such terminals through one voice-band grade channel instead of connecting them separately to the central processor via a number of narrow-band grade channels. In most situations of this type, multiplexing will reduce the cost of the communication network by allowing one voice-band grade channel to substitute for many sub-voice (slow-speed, telegraph) channels that might otherwise be poorly utilized. Figure B.21 illustrates a communication system before and after multiplexing.

As shown in the example above, the multiplexer accepts inputs from several terminal sources, combines these inputs, and then transmits the combined input over one channel, and at the other end (not shown) a similar unit again separates the discrete data inputs for further processing.

Two basic techniques are used to multiplex data: (1) frequency division multiplexing (FDM), and (2) time division multiplexing (TDM). In FDM, the digital pulse signal from each terminal is converted by a modem into an analog signal having a frequency unique to the individual terminal. Each separate signal is allocated its own portion of the frequency band available. All the signals are electrically combined and then transmitted over the line. The receiving end of a FDM device demultiplexes the individual signals by using a set of filters, each designed to "hear" a particular tone. The tone is then demodulated by a modem back into a digital pulse signal.[40]

The TDM approach uses transmitting capability according to available time elements. Digital inputs from each terminal are continuously sampled, one by one, for a fixed time period. The sampling time per input corresponds to the time expended to designate a bit (bit-interleaved TDM) or a byte/character (byte-interleaved TDM) by the terminal signal. The bit or byte signal so sampled is time compressed and placed into a time slot in the TDM output signal.[41]

FDM is probably better where the system has a number of low-speed terminals, geographically dispersed with less than sixteen channels. If the transmission rate is 2400 bits per second or more, and/or a great many channels are used, then the system should use TDM.

[40] Murphy, *op. cit.,* p. 48.
[41] *Ibid.*

Concentrator

A concentrator differs from a multiplexer because it employs contention into the system. For example, a concentrator accommodates X number of terminals but allows only a portion of them to transmit their data over the available lines. There may be twelve terminals but only six channels. All terminals must contend for the channels and those which do not make connection are busied out. With a multiplexer, all terminals can be accommodated because the basic assumption is that all terminals are used 100% of the time.

The concentrator works as a normal switching device that polls one terminal at a time. Whenever a channel is idle, the first terminal ready to send or receive gets control of one of the channels and retains it for the duration of its transaction. The concentrator then continues to poll the other channels in sequence until another terminal is ready to transmit. Each terminal has a code address by which it identifies itself when it requests transmission and to which it responds when addressed by the central processor. Whenever any terminal is engaged in a transaction with the central processor, the voice-band grade channel is unavailable to the other terminals for sending or receiving, i.e., the other terminals are "busied out" by the active ones. If several transactions occur simultaneously, each terminal must wait its turn on a FIFO (first in, first out) basis.

The cost savings in using a multiplexer are based on combining the data while the cost savings using a concentrator are based on the amount of data traffic in the system. In effect, the use of a concentrator is based on the assumption that all of the terminals will not be in contention for the available facilities at any one time.

Programmable Communications Processors

As long as the total number of peripherals, local and remote, and the amount of data transmitted are maintained at a certain level, the computer control program (in residence) can execute the interrupts, move the data into and out of storage, and perform the necessary housekeeping without significant throughput penalty. However, if the number of terminals and volume of data increase to a point, computer throughput is significantly reduced. At this point, it may be more economical to move these functions out of the computer mainframe and into a communications processor.[42] These processors perform some, if not all, of the following functions:

1. Housekeeping—the handling of message queues and priorities, processing of addresses, data requests, message blocks, file management, and updating the executive on peripheral activity.
2. Error checking and retransmission requests to prevent incomplete messages from reaching the host processor.
3. Code translation into the "native" code of the host CPU.
4. Preprocessing and editing.
5. Communications analysis processing—error analysis, the gathering of traffic statistics, and so forth.
6. Establishing and acknowledging the required channel connections including automatic dialing, if this is a feature of the system.
7. Verifying successful completition of the message, or detecting line breaks and either calling for or executing remedial action.
8. Disconnecting after a completed message, to permit polling to resume.
9. Assembling the serial bit stream into a bit-parallel buffered message.
10. Routing messages to and from required memory locations and notifying the software as required.

The major advantage of moving these functions from the central processor (host computer) to a communications processor is economic. With a large number of terminals or

[42] "Smart Users 'Deemphasize' Host," *Computerworld*, Supplement, July 27, 1972, p. 10. Used with permission. Copyright by *Computerworld* Newton, Massachusetts 02160.

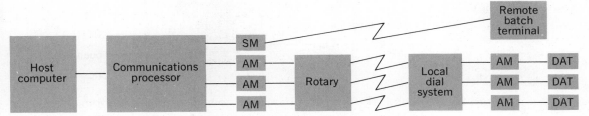

FIGURE B.22. Computer system with multiple communications ports served by a communications processor. SM: synchronous modem, AM: asychronous modem. DAT: dial-up terminal.

communications lines, as much as half the processing time of the host computer (even a large one) can be spent in input-output processing and line control. A separate, specialized computer can perform the same functions with fewer steps and simpler software, reducing direct processor time costs, programming costs, and debugging time. The lease or purchase price of the communications processor is often one or two orders of magnitude lower than that of the main computer; if it can assume work which formerly occupied half the main computer's time, it can obviously be economically justified. In Figure B.22, a typical configuration is illustrated.[43]

The increased use of programmable communications processors can be directly attributed to the current proliferation of low-cost flexible minicomputers, and also to the developments in integrated circuit technology that have enabled digital computers to be manufactured at greatly reduced costs.[44] The application of programmable communications processors are described below.

Message-Switching

In message-switching, the communications processor acts principally as a data traffic director. It normally does not perform any data processing activities (there are exceptions) beyond

handling the message itself.[45] In most systems a terminal transmits (or "talks") only to the host computer, but with a message-switching system, a terminal can talk directly to another terminal by going through the message-switching processor. This processor then, becomes the central exchange in a fully interconnected communications network.[46]

The message-switching computer itself can perform many of the functions of a front-end processor (which we will discuss next), including error checking and correcting, code conversion, preprocessing and editing, and other functions previously listed in this section. In addition, it constantly monitors data traffic on the channels, directing messages through the most efficient and least costly route. It can compensate for channels going down and reroute data traffic accordingly.[47]

Front–End

The front-end processor takes over most, if not all of communications functions from the host CPU. Channels from various terminals and remote concentrators end at the front-end processor, and this processor in turn transmits "clean" data to the host computer. It performs all of the functions previously listed at the beginning of this section. A typical front-end

[43] R. L. Aronson, "Data Links and Networks Devices and Techniques," *Control Engineering*, February, 1970, pp. 105–116. Used with permission.

[44] "All about Programmable Communication Processors," *Datapro70*, January, 1971, Supplement.

[45] *Ibid.*

[46] "Minicomputers Role in Data Communications," *Computerworld*, Supplement, July 26, 1972, p. 14. Used with permission. Copyright by *Computerworld*, Newton, Massachusetts. 02160.

[47] *Ibid.*

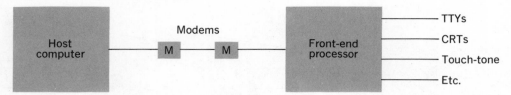

Figure B.23. A typical front-end processor communications system.

processor communications system is illustrated in Figure B.23.

Reasons for Using Programmable Communications Processors

Programmable communications processors are enjoying increased popularity in various parts of data communications systems because they are demonstrating themselves to be more cost/effective.[48] General reasons which contribute to this cost/effective edge include the following:

1. A large host processor is designed to work optimally when it can function continuously, executing a full set of program instructions on a given application before branching to another. Interruptions and delays caused by handling data communications traffic causes discontinuity of operations by the main processor and consumes large amounts of primary storage which, in turn, reduces productivity and throughput.

2. The communications processor presents a standard I/O interface so that programmers do not have to constantly adapt software to terminals.[49]

3. It adds flexibility to the total system by having the capability to adapt to changing requirements. For example, it can easily accommodate, without major modification, new terminals, more channels, and new devices with different characteristics.[50]

4. A group of processors can very readily support a distributed system. They can be programmed to perform varying amounts of productive processing and can share portions of the overall processing load with other processors in the system, including the central processor.[51]

5. When programmable communications processors are not involved in their principal data communications tasks, they can often be used as stand-alone data processing systems. Simple media conversion tasks, such as card-to-tape and tape-to-print, can be valuable by-products from these otherwise communications-oriented processors.[52] They can also act as a backup to the host computer, thus increasing system reliability.

Typical Front-End Configurations

Basically, any computer configuration is a data processing system, and what that configuration comprises, may vary from a small batch processing configuration with minimal capabilities to a large configuration with a complex mix of peripherals. Always, however, the main purpose of all computer configurations is to support the information system design in accordance with what is needed and what is economically feasible. There are probably hundreds of different variables to front-end configurations,[53] but ac-

---

[48] "All about Programmable Communication Processors," *op. cit.*

[49] "Minicomputers Role in Data Communications," *op. cit.*

[50] *Ibid.*

[51] "All about Programmable Communication Processors," *op. cit.*

[52] *Ibid.*

[53] Based on: "Front-end Uses Tied to Mainframe Applications," *Computerworld,* Supplement, July 26, 1972, pp. 14–15. Used with permission. Copyright by *Computerworld,* Newton, Massachusetts 02160.

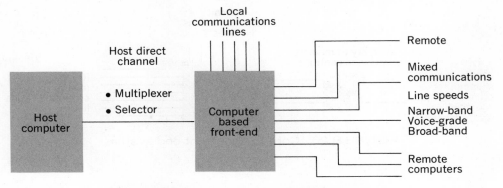

FIGURE B.24. Plug-compatible front-end.

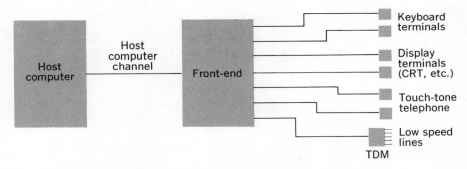

FIGURE B.25. Plug-compatible processor with TDMs.

cording to John Gould, Director of Data Communications at Interdata, Inc., there are basically five ways to connect a front-end processor to a host computer(s).

Plug-for-Plug Replacements

The plug-for-plug replacement system connects physically and electrically to the standard host computer channel as though it were a standard peripheral. The value of the plug-compatible front-end, shown in Figure B.24, becomes much more important if the user takes advantage of its power to perform some of the functions that might otherwise be done by the host computer. (These functions have been listed earlier in this section.)

In the plug-compatible processor with TDMs, as shown in Figure B.25, the front-end performs the demultiplexing function directly from the multiplexed medium-speed port. The major advantage to the use of a plug-compatible processor is in its flexibility and resulting system cost savings. The programmable nature of the front-end allows the direct connection of asynchronous TDMs, thus reducing the number of adaptors and halving the TDM costs.

This system also allows connection of devices which would not normally be supported by the host hardware or software. For example, computer-based message concentrators, noncompatible host computers, nonsupported terminals, and TDM equipment can all be made acceptable to the host computer complex by appropriate front-end software.

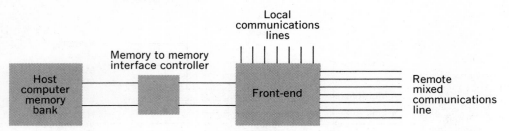

FIGURE B.26.   Core-to-core front-end system.

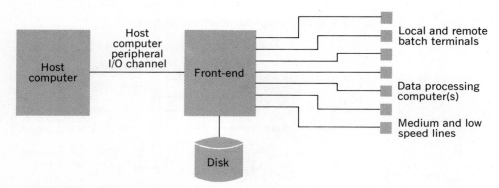

FIGURE B.27.   Illustration of psuedo-device system where the front-end imitates I/O peripherals.

Core-to-Core System

A core-to-core system, illustrated in Figure B.26, is generally reserved for larger systems where fast core cycle time transfer speeds are required. This same approach is used for connecting low-speed peripherals such as card readers and line printers to a high-speed processor.

This approach is generally restricted to computers of the same manufacturer since they are direct primary storage interfaces. In cases where the machines are from different manufacturers, there is generally a substantial black-box engineering requirement for matching internal format and signaling requirements. This type of system should not be more than 500–1000 feet from the primary storage of the host computer.

Pseudo-Device System

This approach includes a pseudo-device interface wherein the software of the communications front-end imitates the operation of a standard peripheral device such as a magnetic tape, disk, or drum subsystem. This system is shown in Figure B.27.

The pseudo-device system has the communications front-end responding to the host computer as a series of magnetic tape units. The obvious advantage is that of software compatibility. This system becomes more and more attractive when coupled with a host computer that has a sophisticated operating system.

Data Link System

The use of a data communications link between

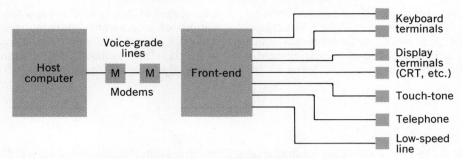

FIGURE B.28. Data link processor connection system.

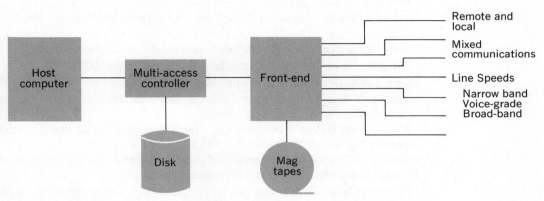

FIGURE B.29. Inter-computer peripheral system providing an intermediate storage configuration.

the host computer and the front-end is illustrated in Figure B.28.

In general, the data link will be accomplished through common-carrier facilities using modems and other communications hardware to effect the connection. In certain cases, when the front-end and the host are in the same room (approximately 1000 feet from each other), both the front-end and host limited distance line adapters may be used in place of the normal common-carrier link. This is generally less expensive and improves the overall system reliability. The data link approach is probably the "cleanest" interface between multicomputer systems, especially where several manufacturers are involved. The connection generally involves standard off-the-shelf data com-

munications interfaces from each vendor. At the same time, the data link method is probably the most expensive since it involves communications equipment at all ports and probably a good deal of redundancy.

Inter-Computer Peripherals System

The inter-computer peripherals method refers to the use of a multi-access, random storage device such as magnetic disk or drum for transferring data from the front-end to the host computer. This approach is illustrated in Figure B.29.

The storage device is dual-accessed and is the only connection between the processors.

Each system interrogates fixed control areas on the device for information transfer instructions, or a high-speed processor-to-processor interrupt line is added to provide the inter-computer instructions and command path. Some of the advantages of this type of system are the elimination of redundant storage, since either system can achieve very high transfer rates when data are available, and it can be supported by standard operating system software.

BIBLIOGRAPHY

"All About Programmable Communication Processors," *Datapro 70,* Supplement, January, 1971.

Aronson, "Data Links and Networks Devices and Techniques," *Control Engineering,* February, 1970.

Bell and Newell, *Computer Structures,* New York: McGraw-Hill Book Co., 1971.

Carey, "Data Communications," *Data Management,* September, 1971.

"Computer Output to Microfilm," *EDP Analyzer,* June, 1970.

Davis, *Computer Data Processing,* New York: McGraw-Hill Book Co., 1969.

Dippel and House, *Information Systems,* Glenview, Illinois: Scott Foresman & Co., 1969.

"Elusive Mini Defies Definition, and That's a Sign of Its Growth," *Computerworld,* Supplement, August 30, 1972.

Feeney, "A Three-stage Theory of Evolution for the Sharing of Computer Power," *Computer Decisions,* November, 1971.

"Front-end Uses Tied to Mainframe Applications," *Computerworld,* Supplement, July 26, 1972.

Haavind, "A User's Guide to System Evolution," *Computer Decisions,* June, 1971.

"Intelligent Terminals," *EDP Analyzer,* April, 1972.

"Key to Enhanced Application Development," *Data Processor,* September, 1972.

Lapidus, "The Domain of Magnetic Bubbles," *Spectrum,* September, 1972.

Laurie, *Modern Computer Concepts,* Cincinnati: South Western Publishing Co., 1970.

Martin, J., *Telecommunications and the Computer,* Englewood Cliffs, N.J.: Prentice-Hall, Inc., 1969.

Martin, J., *Systems Analysis for Data Transmission,* Englewood Cliffs, N.J.: Prentice-Hall, Inc., 1972.

"Minicomputers Role in Data Communications," *Computerworld,* Supplement, July 26, 1972.

"Multiplexing Costs Based on Volume and Distance," *Computerworld,* Supplement, July 26, 1972.

Murphy, "Modems and Multiplexors—A Primer," *Modern Data,* December, 1971.

Nordling, "Analysis of Common Carrier Tariff Rates," *Datamation,* April 15, 1971.

Reagan, F., "A Manager's Guide to Phone and Services," *Computer Decisions,* November, 1971.

Reagan, F., and Totaro, "Take the Data Communications Load Off Your System," *Computer Decisions,* February, 1972.

Sanders, *Computers In Business: An Introduction,* Second Edition, New York: McGraw-Hill Book Co., 1972.

"Satellite Data Too Costly?" *Computerworld,* June 21, 1972.

"Smart Users 'Deemphasize' Host," *Computerworld,* Supplement, July 27, 1972.

Sobel, *Introduction to Digital Computer Design,* Reading, Mass.: Addison-Wesley Publishing Co., Inc., 1971.

Surgan, "Terminals: On-Line and Off Conversational and Batch," *Control Engineering,* February, 1970.

"The Emerging Computer Networks," *EDP Analyzer,* January, 1973.

"The Mini-Computer's Quiet Revolution," *EDP Analyzer,* December, 1972.

"Three Key-to-Disk Experiences," *Data Dynamics,* August/September, 1971.

Toombs, "Considering Telecommunications? Select the Right Modem," *Computer Decisions,* July, 1971.

"T/S Vendors Supporting Users' Communication Needs," *Computerworld,* Supplement, June 28, 1972.

"Users Must Consider Dial-Up and Private Lines," *Computerworld,* Supplement, June 26, 1972.

"Ways to Put Processing to Work," *Modern Office Procedures,* August, 1972.

"What Goes Into a Word Processing Workstation," *Modern Office Procedures,* August, 1972.

"Word Processing: The New Approach to Internal Profit," *Modern Office Procedures,* August, 1972.

Appendix C Tools and Techniques of the Information Systems Analyst

Introduction

In each phase of the information system's development process the systems analyst relies on specific tools or techniques for accomplishing his or her goals and objectives. Like any good craftsman, some analysts rely more heavily on one tool or technique to serve them. In most systems endeavors, however, the systems analyst requires many forms of assistance.

The tools and techniques presented in this appendix do not represent an exhaustive list of what is available or what is utilized. It does, however, identify the major tools and techniques used by systems analysts in developing information systems.

The Interview

Within an organization, interviewing is the most significant and productive fact finding technique available to the analyst. Simply stated, the interview is a face-to-face exchange of information. It is a communication channel between the analyst and the organization. Interviewing is used to gain information concerning what is required and how these requirements can be met. The interview can be used to gain support or understanding from the user for a new idea or method. Moreover, the interview provides an excellent opportunity for the analyst to establish rapport with user personnel which is essential throughout the study.

Interviewing is conducted at all levels of operations within the organization from the president or chief operating officer to the mail clerk or the maintenance engineer. Consequently, the interview proceedings can vary from highly formal to somewhat casual. Even the locations where interviewing is conducted are subject to wide variations such as the operating floor of the plant or in an executive suite. The success of interviewing is dependent on how well the analyst is able to adjust to these environmental variables. This adjustment is further complicated by the qualities possessed or lacking in the analyst. These qualities include his or her previous education and experience, as well as his or her basic abilities to communicate with all levels of personnel.

Preparing to Interview

1. Identify the proposed interviewee's position within the organization, basic job responsibilities, activities, etc. (Research).

2. Prepare a preliminary general structure of the questions to be asked and documents required (Organization).

3. Set a time limit and agenda for the interview (Psychology).

4. Choose a location for the interview which will be most conducive to setting the interviewee at ease (Psychology).

5. Arrange for an appointment ahead of time (Planning).

Conducting the Interview

1. Explain the purpose and scope of the study as fully as possible (Honesty).

2. Explain your role as the analyst and the expected role of the interviewee (Impartial).

3. Ask specific questions which allow for a quantitative response (Factual).

4. Avoid questions that require biased opinions, subjectivity and the like (Skill).

5. Avoid buzz words and meaningless jargon (Clarity).

6. Be courteous and polite and avoid making value judgments (Objective).

7. Maintain control of the interview using discrimination in ending ramblings and tangent comments (Control).

8. Listen attentively to what is said; guard against anticipating answers (Communication).

9. Question the obvious and that which is vague (Comprehension).

10. At the end of the interview, summarize the main points of the session, thank the respondent and indicate that if there are any further questions you will return (Courtesy).

Following Up the Interview

1. Formally write up the findings from the interview (Documentation).

2. Return a copy of these findings to the respondent asking for verification, corrections or additions (Professional).

3. File the interview results for future reference and analysis (Documentation).

Note taking is a traditional and acceptable method for the analyst to record the points made in an interview. Similar to taking notes during a lecture in school, the analyst must guard against excessive note taking and thus losing the ideas being presented. The use of voice recorders in place of taking notes is becoming a widespread practice. While voice recorders eliminate the problems associated with taking notes, the presence of a voice recording machine may make the interviewee unnecessarily nervous and overcautious in answering questions. Common sense is usually the best guide to the analyst when choosing between fact recording techniques.

Although the analyst is cautioned to concentrate on matters that can be discussed objectively and even quantitatively in an interview, it is important to note that careful interviewing often reveals certain attitudes and covert reasons for things being what they are or are not. As such, the interview can provide a wealth of facts unavailable to the analyst through any other fact finding technique.

The Questionnaire

The questionnaire is another tool which can be used at various times by the systems analyst in the systems development process. The use of the questionnaire in systems work can be: (1) to obtain a consensus, (2) to identify a direction or area for in depth study, (3) to do a post implementation audit, and (4) to identify specific but varying requirements.

Use of the Questionnaire in Systems Analysis

As a fact finding tool, the questionnaire is a somewhat restricted channel of communication and should be utilized with great care. The analysts must identify what it is that they desire to know, structure the questions which will result in the answers to these needs, and prepare and submit the questionnaire to the individual who is to complete it. Unlike the interview, the analyst has no immediate opportunity to readdress comments which are vague or unclear. Moreover, the analyst cannot follow up tangent comments that might well lead to additional facts or ideas.

The use of the questionnaire in the systems analysis should be limited to only those situations that the analyst cannot query in person. Additionally, when an analyst feels that a questionnaire is in order, he or she may well rethink his or her needs to determine if the information is truly of importance or whether the requirement could not be met utilizing still another fact finding technique.

A good rule of thumb when considering the use of a questionnaire is: if an individual can be interviewed, he or she should be interviewed.

The questionnaire can be utilized best as a fact finding tool: (1) when the recipient is physically removed from the analyst and travel is prohibited for either person, (2) there are many potential recipients (e.g. a sales force), and (3) when the information is being used to verify similar information gathered from other sources.

The reasons for recommending a limited use of the questionnaire in the systems analysis are numerous: (1) it is extremely difficult to structure meaningful questions without anticipating a certain response, (2) the inability for immediate follow-up and redirect tends to limit the real value of this type of communication, and (3) it appears to be human nature to assign low priorities and importance to "blanket" style documents, especially questionnaires.

Guidelines for Constructing a Questionnaire

When the analyst decides to make use of a questionnaire there are a few, but important guidelines he or she should follow. The structure and content of a questionnaire should include:

1. An explanation of the purpose, use, security and disposition of the responses.
2. Detailed instructions as to how to complete the questions.
3. A time limit or deadline for returning the document.
4. Positive and concise questions.
5. The questions should be formulated with consideration as to whether the answers will be tabulated mechanically or manually.
6. The space provided for the response should be sufficient to answer the question. (Remember, the space provided for a response is not only a physical contraint but a psychological constraint as well.)

Observation

Another technique available to the analyst during fact finding is to observe people in the act of executing their job. Observation as a fact finding technique has widespread acceptance by all scientists. Sociologists, psychologists and industrial engineers utilize this technique extensively for studying people in groups and organizational activities. The purpose of observation is multifold. Its use allows the analyst to determine what is being done, how it is being done, who does it, when it is done, how long it takes, where it is done, and why it is done.

Types of Observation

The systems analyst can observe in either of three basic ways. First, the analyst may observe a person or activity without awareness by the observee and without any interaction by the analyst. This alternative is probably of little importance in systems analysis as it is nearly impossible to achieve the necessary conditions. Secondly, the analyst can observe an operation without any interactions but with the party being observed fully aware of the analyst's observation. Lastly, the analyst can observe and interact with the persons being observed. This interaction can be simply questioning a specific task, asking for an explanation and so forth.

Observation can be used to verify what was revealed in an interview or as a preliminary to interviewing. Observation is also a valuable technique for gathering facts representing relationships. Observation tends to be more meaningful at the technical level of data processing where tasks can be more easily quantified. Technical activities include tasks related to data collection, accumulation and transformation. Decision making activities do not lend themselves to observation as easily. Decision making activities can best be understood through the process of interviewing and other fact finding techniques.

To maximize the results obtainable from observation, there are a number of guidelines the analyst should follow.

Preparing for Observation

1. Identify and define what it is that is going to be observed.

2. Estimate the length of time this observation will require.
3. Secure the proper management approvals to conduct the observation.
4. Explain to the parties being observed what it is you will be doing and why.

Conducting the Observation

1. Familiarize yourself with the physical surroundings and components in the immediate area of observation.
2. Periodically note the time while observing.
3. Note what is observed as specifically as possible. Generalities and vague descriptions are to be avoided.
4. If you are interacting with the persons being observed, refrain from making qualitative or value judgment oriented comments.
5. Observe proper courtesy and safety regulations.

Following Up the Observation

1. Formally document and organize your notes, impressions, etc.
2. Review your findings and conclusions with the person observed, immediate supervisor and, perhaps, another systems analyst.

The benefits to be derived from skillful observation are many. As the analyst gains experience, however, he or she will become more selective as to what and when he or she observes. Observation is often quite time consuming and thus expensive. Moreover, people in general do not like to be observed. It is strongly recommended that when observation is used, it should be used in conjunction with other fact finding techniques in order to maximize its effectiveness, particularly with less experienced analysts.

Sampling and Document Gathering

Two additional techniques available to the analyst particularly during his or her fact finding endeavors are: sampling and document gathering. Both of these techniques are oriented to the paperwork stored throughout the organization. Moreover, both techniques can provide a source of information unavailable via any other fact finding approach.

Sampling

Sampling is a statistical approach to arriving at an understanding. Sampling is founded in the theory of statistics and laws of probability. The value of sampling is directed to problems which would involve a tremendous amount of detail work of collecting and accumulating data to provide a given piece of information; or, to operations which are unmeasurable. For example, if an analyst desired to know how long it would take to process 10,000 customer orders in the shipping room, he or she might measure the time it would take to process 40 or 50 customer orders and, based on this sample, calculate the expected time period for 10,000 orders.

40 orders require T time

$\dfrac{T}{40}$ = time per order

$10,000 \times \dfrac{T}{40}$ = time for 10,000 orders

Another practical example of sampling is illustrated in the following example.

"How many purchase orders required a Vice President's signature of approval last year?," asked the Manager of Purchasing to Joe Dee, Systems Analyst. "Well," replied Joe, "the policy states that any P.O. greater then $10,000 requires V.P. approval. I checked the P.O. 'dead' file for last year and found that we have 13 ½ drawers filled with P.O.'s. I asked Mary, the file clerk, if she kept any records concerning approvals or dollar amounts on P.O.'s and she said she did not. She said there was no particular organization to the 'dead' file. I knew you needed some idea of how many V.P. approvals there were, so I took a little sample.

I measured the drawers and found that the file space was about two feet in length. That told me I had 27 feet of P.O.'s and 30 minutes to figure out how many had V.P. stamps. I took about 4 inches of paper out of one of the drawers and fingered through the documents. I noted seven 'big' ones. I figured if there was no special handling involved with V.P. P.O.'s that would be about 21 to a foot; 21 times 27 feet is about 560–570 Purchase Orders with Vice President signatures."

The Purchasing Manager thanked Joe for his help and proceeded to call the President. "Jim, we don't keep records concerning executive signatures required on P.O.'s but a sampling the systems boys made on the closed file indicates about 600 a year are required."

The above example is of course hypothetical and may raise a number of questions concerning its validity, both in actually occurring and as to the sampling done. However, large transactional files such as Purchase Orders, Customer Orders, Invoices and the like, do exist in most organizations. And surprisingly, in this day and age, statistics similar to that requested by the Purchasing Manager are not available. While Joe may have used more scientific methods to attain his number (certainly we can question the size and representation of the sample), systems analysts often use rules of thumb to arrive at this type of information.

The point is, whether you use rules of thumb or classical algorithms, the technique of sampling can provide valuable facts and insights during the systems analysis phase.

Sampling is also an effective technique for projecting resource requirements. It is again not unusual for an analyst to measure a certain activity on a limited basis and then project the resources required to perform this function for a full blown system.

Document Gathering

Collecting exhibits of source documents, worksheets, reports, etc., is another way for the analyst to gather information during the systems analysis. From these exhibits or sample documents, the analyst can gain an understanding of what is presently done, how it is structured, what is not available and, perhaps, get a "feel" for what is considered important. When an analyst is conducting an interview or an observation, if the analyst has a copy of the documents involved, efforts in gathering facts will be enhanced. Moreover, a working knowledge of user documents on the part of the analyst increases the likelihood of smoother communications between the analyst and the user personnel.

Charting

Charting is the technique which pictorially represents some dimension of an organization or an organizational activity. Of all the tools and techniques utilized by systems personnel, charting is the one technique most closely identified with systems efforts. Indeed, charting is not only an important fact finding technique but it is also a valuable technique for performing analysis, synthesis, communication, and documentation. Quite obviously a tool with many uses will be favored over single purpose tools.

There are many different types of charts utilized by the systems analyst. This multiplicity of charting results no doubt because there are few aspects of an organization or organization information processing activities which do not lend

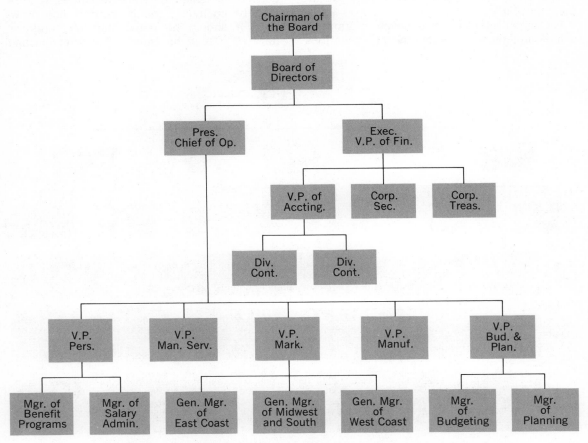

FIGURE C.1. A typical organization chart of upper management in a medium size corporation.

themselves to being represented by some type of chart. We can quickly identify three broad classifications of charting used by the systems analyst: Organization Charts, Physical Layout Charts and Flowcharts.

Organization Charts

Figure C.1 represents a typical organizational chart of the management of a medium sized company.

In most large organizations, the analyst can usually secure a copy of the official organization chart. Many times, however, the organizational chart is nonexistent or outdated. In the latter cases, the analyst must construct the organization chart himself.

The organization chart provides information concerning reporting relationships, quantities of resources, interrelationships, and levels of authority and responsibility.

Oftentimes during fact findings, the analyst will prepare a brief narrative which is coded to the organization charts. Figure C.2 provides an example of this combined usage of narrative and organizational charts.

The brief annotation relative to each decision making level provides not only the function of each manager but also an overall insight into the role that they play in the organization. For instance, the function and responsibility of the sales manager is to hire, fire and establish training programs for salesmen; set specific quotas for each salesmen; and make a breakdown of the sales force and resources by territory, by customer, and by product line. However, it should be noted that Mr. Andrews devotes 50% of his time to the selection and

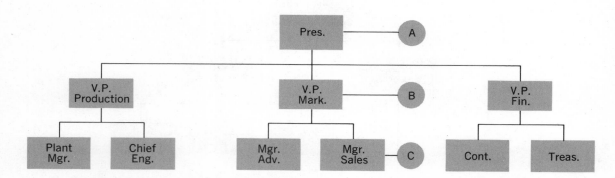

FIGURE C.2. The analyst can combine the narrative with the organization chart to achieve greater understanding and clarity.

	New Products	New Markets	Training	Salary and Commission
President	A			A
Vice-President Marketing	A	A		A
General Manager Sales	C	A	A	AP
Regional Manager Sales	C	P	AP	C
Manager Product Planning	PC	P		
Vice President Personnel				A
Manager Supply and Transportation	O	O		
Manager Product Engineering	APC			
Manager Manufacturing	O			
Salesmen	O	O	PO	
Manager Research and Development	P			
Controller				PC
Manager Information Systems	O	O	O	PO

FIGURE C.3. An illustration of a linear organization chart of some of the marketing functions. Legend: A: Approval; C: Control; P: Planning; O: Operation.

training of salesmen and nearly all of the remainder of the time he devotes to analyzing salesmen's performance. This additional insight into each decision maker's function and responsibility will be of great value to the analyst later when he or she is determining user requirements, and still later when he or she is designing the data base.

The traditional organization charts we have been discussing are often ineffectual for portraying the complex structures of modern organizations. This is true even when a narrative is attached to the organization chart. Traditional box charts depict the organization from the point of view of formal reporting relationships. At best this portrayal reflects the organization at one point in time and treats the organization structure as though it were static. In reality, however, the organization is a dynamic entity. Additionally, the modern trend to minimize the rigid boundaries of hierarchical structures encourages a great deal of responsibility sharing. To better depict this aspect of shared responsibility or interfunctional relationships, the analyst can develop what is termed a linear organization chart (LOC). Figure C.3 illustrates a linear organization chart reflecting various marketing functions in a medium size corporation.

In our example, the activity pertaining to the development and usage of a new product line is a multi-function responsibility. The President, Vice-President Marketing, and the Manager of Production Engineering all share in the approval process. Planning is the responsibility of the Manager of Research and Development, Manager of Product Planning, and Manager of Product Engineering. Control is exercised by the General Manager of Sales, Manager of Product Planning, and the various Regional Sales Managers. Operations responsibility is shared by various levels of marketing personnel in ad-

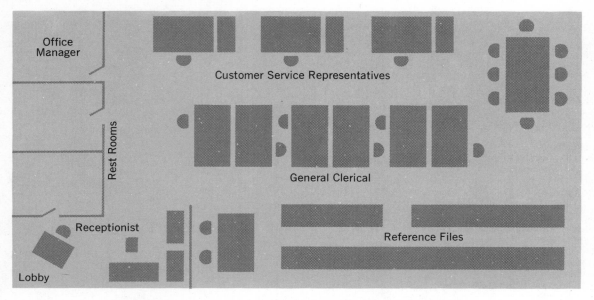

FIGURE C.4. An example of a typical office layout chart.

Physical Layout Charts

A second classification of charting reflects the physical environment which concerns the analyst. Figure C.4 represents a typical office layout. Figure C.5 shows the layout of computer components in a data processing installation. Understanding the physical environment in which an activity is executed provides information concerning space and resources available. Additionally, the analyst can gain insights into why specific tasks are performed the way they are, as well as possible physical changes which might have an impact on the organization's information requirements.

Flowcharting

Perhaps the most important of all charting techniques to the analyst is the flowchart. A flowchart is a set of symbols representing an activity. Flowcharts are widely used in systems work because they can graphically represent the interrelationships among elements in a

dition to supply and transportation, manufacturing, etc.

In order to construct an LOC the analyst must delineate three basic elements: (1) the decision makers, (2) the business activities, and (3) the degree of responsibility each decision maker has for each business activity.

The advantages to constructing an LOC include: (1) graphically representing the organization, (2) the necessity to develop an in-depth understanding by the analyst before charting, (3) displaying redundancies, and (4) reflecting lack of responsibility or potential bottlenecks. Disadvantages to constructing an LOC include: (1) not as readily understood, (2) longer construction time, and (3) increased development costs.

The organization chart is of immense value to the analyst in understanding the make-up of the levels of management, and ascertaining the span of control and chain of command. In short, the organization chart depicts the role of each manager in the decision making hierarchy.

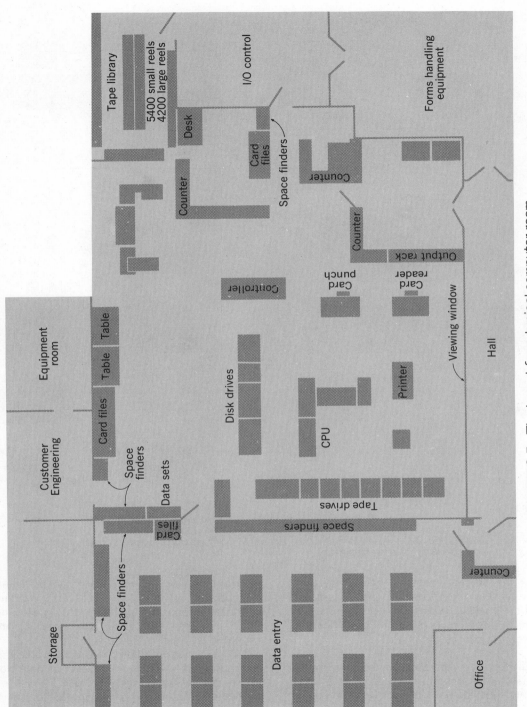

FIGURE C.5. The layout for a typical computer room.

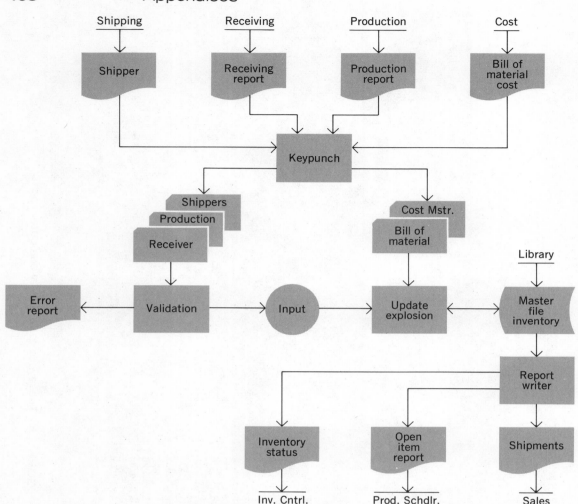

FIGURE C.6. An illustration of an inventory control system flowchart prepared for management.

system to varying degrees of detail. Consequently, flowcharts can be used in problem definition, analysis, synthesis, communications, and documentation. Three broad classifications of flowcharts can be distinguished.

1. The *Systems Flowchart* as its name implies is a chart which depicts the system as a whole with only subsystems or major elements shown. Figure C.6 is a systems flowchart prepared for general management which portrays an inventory control system. Figure C.7 is a systems flowchart prepared for computer personnel which portrays the same inventory control system illustrated in Figure C.6.

2. The *Procedural Flowchart* is a graphic representation of a specific operation or data flow within the system. Figures C.8–C.11 are examples of different ways procedural flowcharts can be drawn. The first three examples all por-

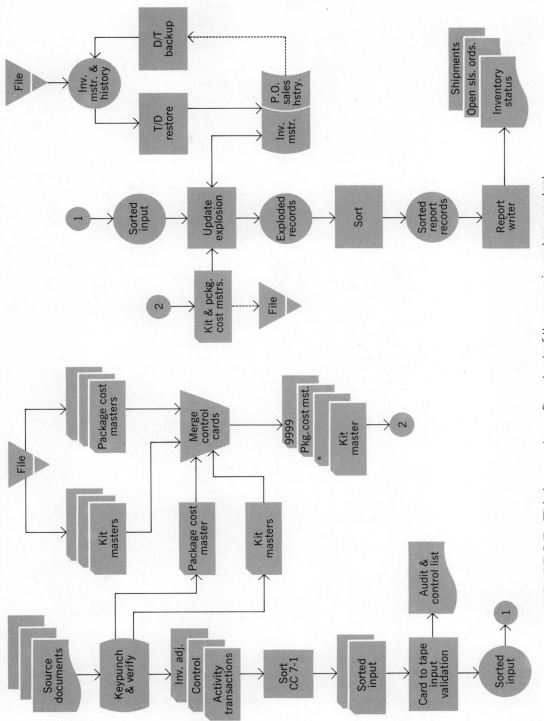

FIGURE C.7. This is a systems flowchart of the same inventory control system depicted in the previous figure. However, it was developed for use by computer operators and programmers.

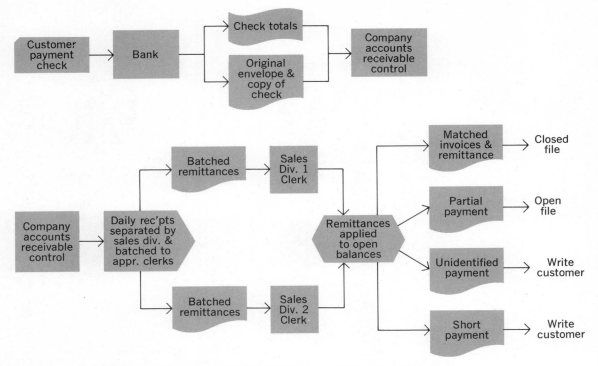

FIGURE C.8. A representation, in broad terms of how a customer payment is processed and what resultant actions occur. Additional charting may or may not be necessary in order for the analyst to understand this activity.

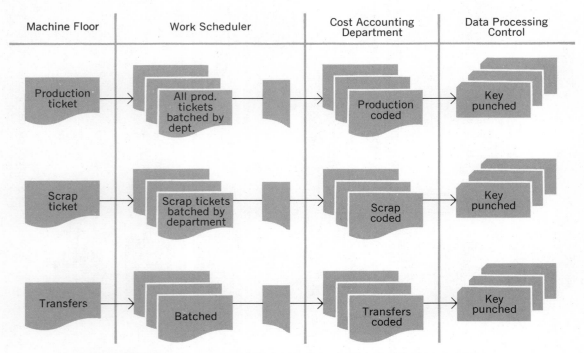

FIGURE C.9. A hypothetical flow of operations data through the organization to data processing.

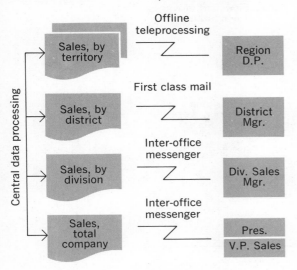

FIGURE C.10. An illustration of the flow of specific levels of sales information throughout the organization.

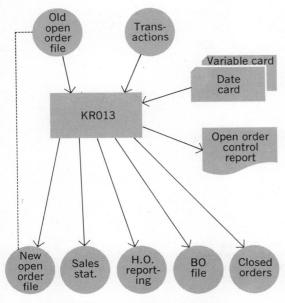

FIGURE C.11. A portrayal of one computer program as a procedure.

tray paper flow within a system. The fourth exhibit focuses on a computer program as a specific procedure.

3. The *Logic Flowchart* is the most specific of all the flowcharts. The intent of this type of flowchart is to provide an in-depth analysis of a given set of logical or arithmetical processing steps. The logic flowchart is of particular value when the sequencing of events is essential. Figure C.12 illustrates the calculations to be performed for Net Pay, a typical problem in a payroll system. Figure C.13 depicts the considerations which a programmer must be cognizant of at the end of processing a program having three input files.

The Template

Within the flowcharting examples presented in this section, there have been a variety of symbols used to represent certain logical or processing operations. These symbols are used by many systems personnel for a number of reasons: (1) the symbols have specific connotations attached to them, (2) these connotations are standard among computer and technical persons, and (3) these symbols can be drawn quickly through the use of a template. Figure C.14 illustrates an extensive list of special symbols used in flowcharting.

A template is usually constructed from tinted plastic; however, it may be constructed from any hard surface material. The special symbols noted in Figure C.14 are precut into the template. Thus, these symbols may be drawn on paper by simply tracing with a pencil or pen around the edges of the symbol cutout. Templates exist for office and computer layout charting as well.

While it is not necessary to use special symbols when flowcharting, the use of symbols can enhance the viewer's understanding. This is particularly true when the viewer is a computer or technically oriented individual. When the chart is intended for use in communicating with general management or nontechnical personnel, the analyst is advised to utilize few special purpose symbols. The use of technical symbols can serve as a psychological barrier to

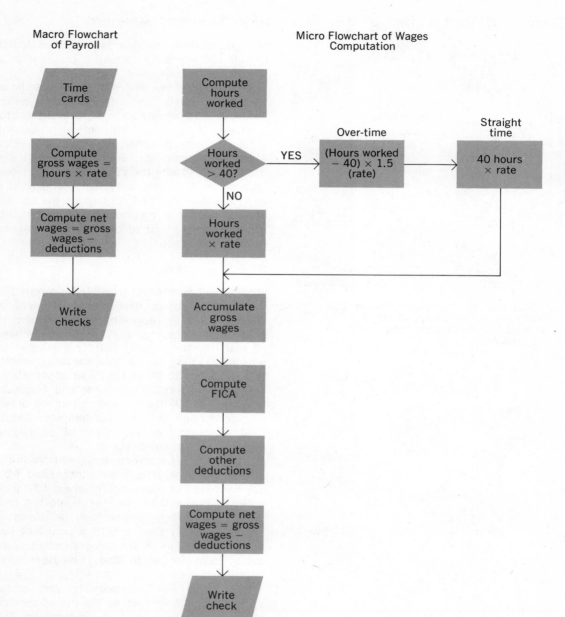

FIGURE C.12. This illustration shows the calculations required to produce Net Pay. The left half of the example is a macro chart; the right half of the chart shows more detail and is called a micro flowchart.

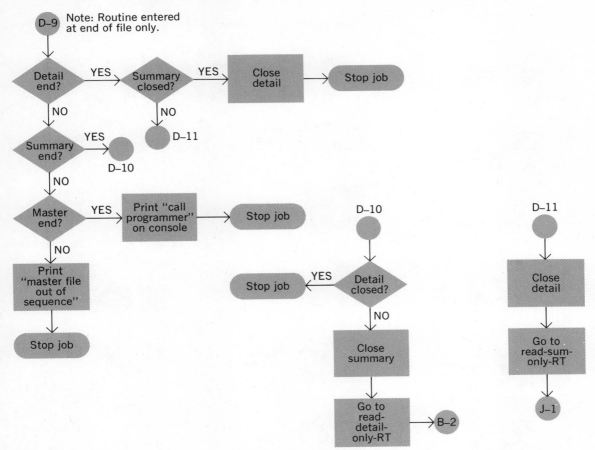

FIGURE C.13. This is an example of flowcharting detail decision logic. This particular situation reflects the logic process a programmer or analyst must identify in order to properly close a computer program having three input files.

effective communications with nontechnically oriented persons.

Other Charting Techniques

There are many other charting techniques with which many of us are familiar but which are not necessarily associated with systems work *per se.* This general familiarity with these charts results in their usage being helpful particularly in communicating with management and nontechnical personnel. Moreover, these charting techniques can be utilized in problem definition, analysis and control endeavors. One classification of these charts includes: (1) Line Charts, (2) Bar Charts, (3) Pie Charts, and (4) Pictorial Charts. Figure C.15 illustrates each of these four types of charts. Figure C.16 lists the advantages and disadvantages of each charting technique. A second classification of charts generally familiar to management and other business professionals is associated with scheduling and control activities. The more popular charts in these classifications include: (1) Pro-

Summary of Flowchart Symbols

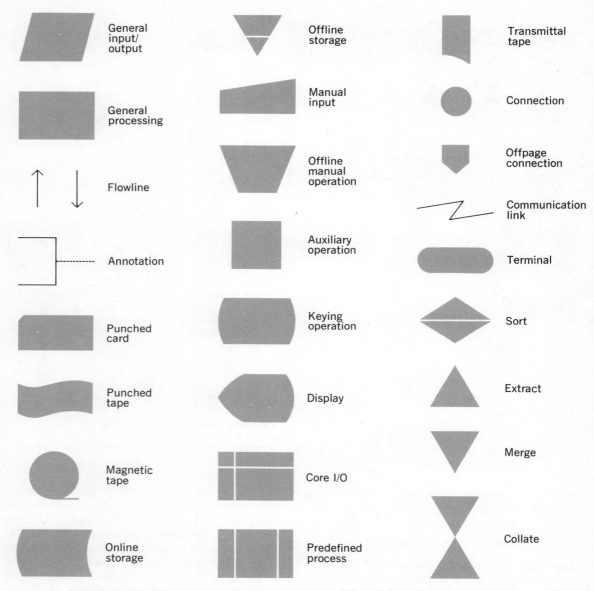

FIGURE C.14. Each of these flowcharting symbols has a special meaning to assist the viewer in understanding the flowchart.

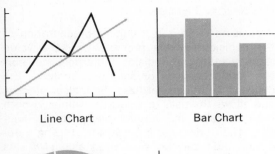

Line Chart　　　　　Bar Chart

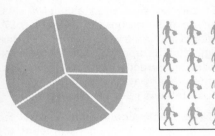

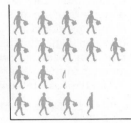

Pie Chart　　　　　Pictorial Chart

FIGURE C.15. Four of the more universally known charting techniques which the systems analyst can use particularly for improving communications with nontechnical personnel.

gram Evaluation and Review Technique (PERT), (2) Critical Path Method (CPM), and (3) Gantt Charts. These charts were discussed in Part III PERT was discussed further in Appendix A.

Guidelines for Charting

While it may appear that charting is a relatively simple task, the novice analyst will find that early attempts at charting, particularly flow-charting, can be frustrating, time consuming and complicated. Even with experienced analysts, first attempts to chart an organization or activity are considered drafts and are quickly redrawn. The usefulness that charts can provide, however, makes them a necessary tool in the analyst's repertoire.

The following set of guidelines are provided to assist the analyst to gain maximum usefulness from charting attempts.

1. The first attempt at constructing a chart should be free hand.

2. If the chart is for the analyst's use only, a formal chart need not be drawn.

3. If a chart is not readily understandable to the viewer, the chart should be either simplified or redrawn as two or more charts.

4. The symbols used in a chart should aid the viewer and not hamper his or her understanding.

Line Charts	Bar Charts	Pie Charts	Pictorial Charts
Advantages			
1) Shows time and magnitude of relationships well.	1) Good for comparisons.	1) Good for monetary comparisons.	1) Very easily understood.
2) Can show many points.	2) Emphasizes one point.	2) Good for part vs. whole comparison.	2) Easily constructed.
3) Degree of accuracy adjustable.	3) Accurate.	3) Very easily understood.	
4) Easily read.	4) Easily read.		
Disadvantages			
1) Limited to less than four lines without adding complexity.	1) Limited to one point.	1) Limited usage.	1) Limited usage.
2) Limited to two dimensions per flow.	2) Spacing can mislead.	2) Limited precision.	2) Limited precision.
3) Spacing can mislead.		3) Tends to oversimplify.	3) Tends to oversimplify.

FIGURE C.16. Advantages and disadvantages of four types of common charting techniques.

5. Charts which are to be used as permanent documentation should be keyed to brief narratives or computer programs as appropriate.

6. Charts used in management presentation should minimize symbolism.

7. Charts should be large enough so that all members of the audience can read them.

Decision Tables and Matrices

Very early in our formal education we are introduced to tables and their usage as a technique for representing varied and complex subjects. These same techniques can be valuable to systems analysts for problem definition, analysis, synthesis, procedure and programs development, communications and documentations. A relatively recent development in this area is called decision tables.

Decision Tables

A decision table is a tabular representation of the decision making process. Unlike a value table or matrix, a decision table does not portray static answers or solutions. Instead, the decision table standardizes the logical process and allows the user to insert the values in both the conditions and actions related to the decision. The underlying premise for utilizing a decision table can be structured as an—*if* this occurs, *then* do this—proposition. Figure C.17 illustrates a decision table which represents the decision logic that is applied to a given paycheck in order to correctly post that paycheck amount to the proper payroll register.

The decision table is read as follows:

Rule 1. If the check code is equal to L, K, F, G, I, R, E, P or D, post that check amount to Register X.

Rule 2. If the check code is equal to B and the division code is not equal to 24, post that check amount to Register Y.

						Register Posting Logic							
IF:	1	2	3	4	5	6	7	8	9	10	11	12	13
Check code = L, K, F, G, I, R, E, P, or D	Y	N	N	N	N	N	N	N	N	N	N	N	E
Check code = B	N	Y	Y	N	N	N	N	N	N	N	N	N	L
Check code = C	N	N	N	Y	Y	N	N	N	N	N	N	N	S
Check code = A	N	N	N	N	N	Y	Y	Y	Y	Y	Y	Y	E
Company code = A						Y	Y	N	N	N			
Company code = B			N	Y	N				Y	Y			
Company code = H			N								Y	N	
Company code = N, P, or B			N										
Pay class = J						Y	N						
Pay class = T									Y	N			
Division code = 24		N	Y					Y	N	N			
THEN:													
Post register X	X		X	X		X		X	X		X		
Post register Y		X			X		X			X		X	
Go to bad check code													X

FIGURE C.17. Decision tables are techniques which assist the analyst to understand and communicate complex logic. This decision table represents the logical process applied to posting pay checks to registers.

Rule 3. If the check code equals B and the division code equals 24 and the company code is not equal to N, P, B, or H post that check amount to Register X.

Each rule is applied to the situation that the table users are confronted with until they have made a match of conditions and can take one of the specified actions. If they have a situation which does not match the table condition entries, there is either an error in the table or another table exists which must be used for that decision process.

Structure of a Decision Table

Figure C.18 is a conceptual model of a decision table. The upper half of the table contains the decision conditions, which are expressed in areas called stubs and entries. Condition stubs are those criteria the decision maker wishes to apply to his or her decision. In order to incorporate these criteria into a decision table, they must be phrased to follow the word *IF*.

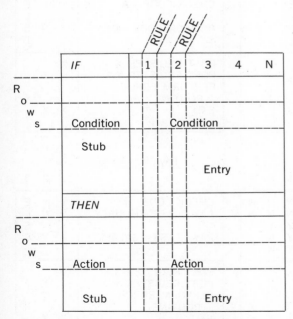

FIGURE C.18.   A conceptual model of a decision table.

The lower half of the table contains the actions which are to be taken when the specified conditions are satisfied. Actions are also indicated as stubs and entries. In order to incorporate actions into the table, they must be structured to follow the term *THEN*.

Combining the conditions with the actions results in: *IF* (these conditions exist), *THEN* (perform these actions).

Single condition decisions do not require decision tables for communication or understanding. Thus, the table allows for multiple conditions. Conditions are listed vertically along the upper left side of the table which is called the stub and are read as—*IF* (condition 1) *AND* (condition 2) *AND* (condition N) *THEN* action 1, action 2, action N.

Again, one alternative in a decision process may not require all conditions nor demand all actions to be taken. Selectivity is accomplished by choosing the correct rule to meet the decision requirements. Rules are numbered horizontally across the top of the decision table and are applied as *OR*. For example, "My situation can match Rule 1 *OR* Rule 2 *OR* Rule *N*." Any given decision which is appropriate to the decision table can apply to one rule only.

The proper rule is determined by examining the condition entries for each rule one at a time until a rule is identified which matches the conditions in the decision being applied to the table. Condition entries may contain one of three symbols; Y, N or –. If Y is present in the condition entry then that condition must exist in the situation facing the decision maker. If *N* is present in that condition entry then that condition must not exist in the situation confronting the decision maker. If neither Y nor N are present, the entry should have a – ; often times the entry is left empty. A –, or empty condition entry, indicates that the condition does not apply to the situation the decision maker is concerned about.

When all of the condition entries included in the table are evaluated and the proper rule is identified, the table user then performs all of the actions indicated by an *X* in the action entry portion of the table to achieve his solution.

Reexamining Figure C.18 and the explanation provided for the figure, the reader should now be able to follow all of the remaining rules in that table.

Decision Table Vocabulary

A set of standard linkage terms has been developed for use with decision tables since complex decision processes cannot always be reflected in one decision table. The four most common terms are:

GO TO — This is an action stub term which tells the table user where to go for further processing.

ELSE — This is a general rule which must always be the last rule in the table when used. The ELSE option is used where a set of rules require either the same actions or further examination before they may be matched. The action stub entry for the ELSE rule is usually a GO TO.

PERFORM — This term links the table users to another table and when that table has been executed, the users must return to the table where they were instructed to PERFORM.

EXIT — This action entry term is always used with the PERFORM term and is the signal to return to the table where they were instructed to PERFORM.

Figure C.19 is an example of decision tables where special linkage terms are used.

Check Code Table

	1	2	3	4	5
CHECK CODE = L,K,F,G,I,R,E,P, or D	Y	N	N	N	E
CHECK CODE = B, M or Y	-	Y	N	N	L
CHECK CODE = C	-	-	-	N	S
CHECK CODE = A	-	-	-	Y	E
POST REGISTER X	X				
POST REGISTER Y		X			
GO TO COMPANY CODE TABLE			X		
GO TO DIVISION CODE TABLE				X	
PERFORM ERROR ROUTINE					X
EXIT	X	X			

Division Code Table

	1	2	3
CHECK CODE = A	Y	Y	E
			L
DIVISION CODE = 01	Y	N	S
			E
POST REGISTER X	X		
POST REGISTER Y		X	
PERFORM ERROR ROUTINE			X
EXIT	X	X	

Company Code Table

	1	2	3	4	5	6	7
CHECK CODE = B	Y	Y	N	N	N	N	N
CHECK CODE = M	N	N	Y	Y	N	N	N
CHECK CODE = Y	N	N	N	N	Y	Y	N
COMPANY CODE = A	N	N	Y	N	Y	N	
COMPANY CODE = B or C	Y	N	-	Y	N		
POST REGISTER X	X				X		
POST REGISTER Y		X		X			
GO TO PAY CLASS TABLE			X				
PERFORM ERROR ROUTINE		X				X	
EXIT	X	X		X	X		

Pay Class Table

	1	2	3
CHECK CODE = M	Y	Y	E
PAY CLASS = HOURLY	Y	N	L
			S
PAY CLASS = SALARY	-	Y	E
POST REGISTER X	X		
POST REGISTER Y		X	
PERFORM ERROR ROUTINE			X
EXIT	X	X	

FIGURE C.19. An example of linking decision tables.

Types of Decision Tables

Up to this point we have been discussing one type of decision table known as a limited entry table. A limited entry table is so called because the conditions or actions required are contained within the appropriate stubs; and, symbols are used in the entry sections (e.g. Conditions = Y, N or –; Actions = X or Blank) to relate to specific rules. This type of table is the most widely used in practice.

A second type of decision table is known as an extended entry table. Both the stub and the entry sections of any specific condition must be considered together in order to decide if a condition is applicable to a given rule. This type of table is applicable in describing problems with few variables which may have many different values. In addition, it may save space. Figure C.20 is an example of a decision table in the limited entry format and in the extended entry format.

Limited Entry

	1	2	3	4
Approved Credit	N	Y	Y	Y
Order qty. 0–25 gallons		Y		
Order qty. 26–55 gallons			Y	
Order qty. 56 or more gallons				Y
Reject Order	X			
Release Order		X	X	X
5% Discount			X	
10% Discount				X

Extended Entry

	1	2	3	4
Approved Credit	N	Y	Y	Y
Quantity Ordered		0–25	26–55	≥56
% Discount		0	5	10
Release Order		X	X	X
Reject Order	X			

FIGURE C.20. Examples of the use of a limited entry table and an extended entry table.

Constructing Decision Tables

When an analyst identifies an opportunity for constructing a decision table, the following guidelines should be followed:

1. Limit the decision process or objective of the decision table with firm boundaries.

2. List all the conditions which must be addressed before a decision can be executed.

3. List all the activities which must be accomplished based on the exact nature of the decision.

4. Identify and define the values of all conditions and actions.

5. Classify and consolidate like conditions and actions.

6. A decision table can have only one entry point into the table.

7. A decision table may have many exits from the table.

8. Only one rule in a table may be satisfied by a situation (this may be the *ELSE* rule).

9. Rules may be considered in any order. (It is often helpful in reading the decision table if conditions are grouped or sequenced.)

10. Actions must be executed in the order written.

11. If there are two conditions, one of which is the negative of the other, eliminate one of the conditions.

12. If with the exception of one condition, two rules have the same condition entries, and if for that one condition one rule has a Y entry and the other an N entry, the rules may be combined with that one condition becoming indifferent.

13. Each rule in the final table must have at least one condition entry different than any other rule.

14. In a limited entry table, before rule consolidation, the number of rules should equal 2^N where N = the sum of the conditions.

15. Test each rule in the table as well as the table as a whole for completeness, accuracy, and proper format.

The construction of meaningful decision tables is an iterative process. Few other analytical tools or techniques result in as complete an understanding as do decision tables. Moreover, as a communication and documentative aid, decision tables not only help understanding but they often eliminate the possibility of misunderstanding. Figures C.21–C.24 provide a detail explanation of how a decision table is developed from a narrative.

Matrices, Arrays and Value Tables

Matrices, Arrays, and Value Tables are all terms which refer to similar techniques whose prime purpose is to order or arrange data. The earliest such technique most of us remember is our addition and multiplication tables. Later, we were

---

Unfilled Order File Reporting
 Each record on the unfilled order file must be examined and classified as either a Closed order, Back order, In-Process order, Current order, or a Future order. Any record which has the order quantity equal to the shipped quantity is considered closed. Any record having a to-be-shipped date earlier than the report date is a back-order. A record with the to-be-shipped date equal to the report date is treated as in-process. Any record with a to-be-shipped date more than seven days later than the report date is a future order. All other records are considered current, except any record with net dollars less than zero which are called closed.

FIGURE C.21.   An example of a complex procedure in narrative form.

Unfilled Order File Reporting
 Each record on the unfilled order file must be examined and classified as either a Closed Order, Back order, In-Process order, Current order, or a Future order. Any record which has the order quantity equal to the shipped quantity is considered closed. Any record having a to-be-shipped date earlier than the report date is a back-order. A record with the to-be-shipped date equal to the report date is treated as in-process. Any record with a to-be-shipped date more than seven days later than the report date is a future order. All other records are considered current, except any record with net dollars less than zero which are called closed.

FIGURE C.22.   An illustration of the analyst identifying IF-THEN relationships by underlining conditions once and actions twice.

Conditions	Actions
The order quantity equal to the shipped quantity	closed
A to-be-shipped date earlier than the report date	backorder
The to-be-shipped date equal to the report date	in-process
A to-be-shipped date more than seven days later	future
Any record with net dollars less than zero	closed
All other records	current

FIGURE C.23.   The conditions and actions are all listed. Redundancies and ambiguities are eliminated.

IF	1	2	3	4	5	6
Net $ < 0	Y	N	N	N	N	N
Order Qty = Shipped Qty		Y	N	N	N	N
TBS Date = Rep Date			Y	N	N	N
TBS < Rep Date				Y	N	N
TBS > Rep Date + 7					Y	N
THEN						
Closed Order	X	X				
Back Order				X		
In-Process			X			
Current						X
Future					X	

FIGURE C.24.   There is small chance that an unfilled order file record would be misclassified using the decision table.

	Customer Statements	Aged Trial Balance	Open Item Ledger	Dunning Letters	Account Analysis
Trigger					
Code in customer master record	X			X	
Transactions	X			X	X
Request		X	X		X
Content					
Customer name	X	X	X	X	X
Customer address	X	X	X	X	X
Account number	X	X	X	X	X
Document number	X		X	X	X
Document date	X		X	X	X
Document amount	X		X	X	X
Cust. document number	X		X	X	X
Cust. document date	X		X	X	X
Cust. document amount	X		X	X	X
Account total dollars	X	X	X	X	X
Date due	X	X		X	X
Special message				X	
Sequence					
By customer	X	X	X	X	X
document	X		X	X	X

FIGURE C.25.　An illustration of the use of a matrix for analyzing, documenting or communicating related logical elements.

introduced to still more uses of this technique in math, science, history, geography and so forth. In each case a matrix was used to provide (1) easy reference to a value related to certain conditions or (2) to help foster understanding of a complex subject by reflecting one or more important relationships contained therein.

This same technique is valuable in systems efforts for analysis, communication and documentation. Figure C.25 illustrates the various data elements which might be contained in a data base from which a number of Accounts Receivable/Credit Reports are extracted.

BIBLIOGRAPHY

Chapin, *Flowcharts,* Philadelphia: Auerbach Publishers, 1971.

"Decision Tables, A Systems Analysis and Documentation Technique," *IBM Data Processing Techniques,* White Plains, N.Y.,: IBM Technical Publications Department, 1962.

DeMasi, *An Introduction To Business Systems Analysis,* Reading, Mass.: Addison-Wesley Publishing Co., 1969.

McDaniel, *Applications of Decision Tables—A Reader,* Princeton, N.J.: Brandon/Systems Press, 1970.

Glossary

Access

User Access to the computer system is available to a user who has been issued a user number/code and/or job card.

Controlled Access to the computer system is limited according to the user's specific needs.

Applications Programmer Person who writes computer programs for nonprogrammers. An applications programmer should be familiar with the discipline he programs in, such as psychology, electrical engineering, etc.

Bundling Degree to which a computer manufacturer supports its customers with hardware engineers, software packages, programs, and system conversion advice.

Codes

Numerical String of decimal digits, usually of a given length, with each combination representing a unique item. They are easily adaptable to computer processing, but are hard to remember if manually processed.

Alphabetic String of letters which is used exactly as a numerical code except that they are usually easier to remember when processed manually.

Alphanumeric String of letters and decimal digits.

Sequential Each item to be coded is given a single decimal number beginning with one (1) and running through to the number of items to be coded.

Block Related items are assigned to a range or block of numbers (letters can also be used), in order to make the coding scheme more effective.

Mnemonic Alphabetic or alphanumeric codes that are used in manual systems to aid the users' memory.

483

Phonetic   Alphanumeric code which attempts to show the name of the item to be coded in an abbreviated form.

Compatibility   Degree in which hardware and software of one model computer can be interchanged with hardware and software of another model computer.

Control Totals   Critical values derived from raw data are compared at each step of processing to be certain that nothing has been lost during that step.

Costs

By Type:

Direct Costs   Those costs that can be easily identified with the proposed system.

Indirect Costs   Overhead costs such as rent, taxes, and any cost that cannot be easily identified with the proposed system.

By Behavior:

Variable Costs   These costs vary directly with respect to changes in the level of activity of the system.

Nonvariable Costs   Although these costs may vary from time to time, the changes are not related to the level of activity of the system.

By Function:

Development Costs   Initial costs of a new procedure, system, or piece of equipment are referred to as development costs.

Operational Costs   Costs that are required to maintain a given level of operations are classified as operational costs.

Maintenance Costs   Repair costs, both parts and labor, are considered maintenance costs.

By Time:

Recurring Costs   Costs that are repeated at regular intervals.

Nonrecurring Costs   Costs that will end after a given period of time.

Data   Refers to raw facts that alone have little or no meaning, but as a group allow for meaningful relationships to be drawn from it.

Data Association

Chains and Pointers:

Simple Chains   Allows for easy access to those records related by the values in a pre-determined field.

Ring Structure   Similar to a simple chain, except that it utilizes a closed loop (i.e., the last record will point back to the first record).

Directories   Table that specifies the addresses of all records pertinent to a given attribute.

Data Base Primary collection of data in an organization which its information system relies on.

Data Base Administration Arbitrator of conflicting user needs; his or her functions also include organizing, monitoring, and re-organizing the data base system.

Data Description Language Provides an interface between the data base and user programs.

Data Independence Provides for different programs to access the same set of data.

Data Manipulation Language Acts as an interface between the data base and the nonprogrammer user; hence the user can manipulate the data base without the need to write a program.

Data Processing

Centralized All data processing is done in one place; either internal or external to the organization.

Decentralized Each department or unit of the organization performs its own data processing function.

Data Processing Methods Four basic methods for data processing are generally accepted. These are manual electromechanical, punched card, and computer.

Decision Making

Programmed Well-defined problems that allow for automatic decision making under the given conditions.

Nonprogrammed Problem areas that cannot be defined in such a way as to allow for automatic or programmed decision making.

Strategic Level of Long range future-oriented decisions and hence usually are highly speculative.

Tactical Level of Although decision making at this level is short run, there is still considerable uncertainty, and therefore is not suited for programmed decision rules.

Technical Level of Emphasizes programmed decision rules; decisions made at this level tend to be highly deterministic.

Deterministic A system is deterministic when the results of a given action can be predicted with complete certainty.

Dump A backup copy of the data base stored on a less expensive storage medium (i.e., a disk dump to magnetic tape).

Duplication Check Hardware capability that checks for an erroneous transfer of data.

Echo Check Hardware capability that allows the CPU to determine if a particular peripheral device is currently available.

Error Log All errors encountered during processing are maintained in a separate file so that they can be corrected and reprocessed at a later time.

External Method of Providing Information Information originating external to a given organization is made available to management at the strategic decision making level.

Feasibility Analysis

Technical Feasibility Determination of whether existing technology would permit development and implementation of the proposed system.

Economical Feasibility Comparison of the expected benefits and expected costs of the proposed system.

Operational Feasibility If the proposed system will require changes in the organization's operating procedures or personnel, then this should be noted in the Operational Feasibility Analysis.

Schedule Feasibility Expected date of completion of the proposed system, usually including a PERT or similar chart.

Feedback Results of past decisions or actions are used to help make future decisions.

Field Smallest data element in the data base, usually located in the same relative position in a given record.

File Collection of logically related records is called a file.

File Organization and Selection

Update Fields and/or records in an existing file are modified and a new, updated, file is created.

Size File size can be a critical factor when determining such things as file medium cost and speed.

Interrogation Without updating the file, specific data from a record can be retrieved for processing.

Activity Measure of the proportion of records processed by an updating run.

Volatility Frequency in which modifications are made to a file in a given time interval; a file's volatility increases as the number of modifications per unit time increases.

Response Time Amount of time required to interrogate a file.

Files

By Content:

Master Files Contain somewhat permanent, historical, statistical, or identification type of data. The master file could also be termed the Current Status file.

Transaction File Contains new records or modifications to old records and are used to update the master file.

Index File Analogous to a card file in a library, an index file is used to identify the location of specific records in another file.

Table File Contains tables of data referenced often for use while processing another file, but rarely updated itself.

Summary File Data extracted from one file during a given run, may be stored in a summary file for further processing at a later time. Also called a working file.

Archival File Contain noncurrent data and can in fact be past period master files.

Backup File Used only if a current master file is destroyed, to recreate the current status of records.

By Mode of Processing:

Input Data that is to be updated during a given run is called input data.

Output Data that has been processed and used to create an updated file is output.

Overlay When updating a file, if instead of creating a separate new master file, updated values replace the old values in the original file. Only a direct access storage device will allow this mode of processing.

By Organization:

Sequential All records appear in the file in some pre-determined sequence, and they must be processed one at a time beginning with the first one. Updating a sequential file means the creation of an entirely new file.

Direct Allows the record in question to be accessed immediately without referencing other records in the file. Also called random.

Filtering Method of Providing Information By limiting the level of detail of the data, a decision maker may not find himself bogged down with more than he or she can handle, and hence may make better, quicker decisions.

Final Systems Design Report Report which management uses to make a final decision as to whether the proposed system will be implemented.

General Systems Design Proposal Specifies at a general level, how the proposed system will be effective.

Heuristic Algorithm that bases future actions on results from past actions.

Information Data that has been processed to obtain specific results of relationships is called information. It increases knowledge of the recipient.

Interface Any person or device that acts as a translator from one mode of communication to another.

Interrogative Method of Providing Information The idea behind this method is for the user to submit his inquiry to an access device or interface and the information will be returned in a relevant time period.

Lists Sequential collection of records where contiguous records are related only by their position.

Magnetic Disk Direct access storage device whereby magnetizable tracks on a rotating disk are used to store data.

Magnetic Drum Direct access storage device whereby magnetizable tracks on a rotating drum are used to store data.

Magnetic Tape Sequential storage medium whereby magnetizable spots on a variable length piece of tape are used to store data.

Maintainability Mean time to repair a malfunctioning element is usually referred to as a measure of the system's maintainability.

Maintenance
Preventive Precautionary measures taken to help avoid equipment breakdown.
Emergency Whatever is necessary to repair an existing malfunctioning element of the system.

Model Representation of something else; it can be very useful in predicting the outcome of taking a particular action without actually having to take the action.

Modeling Method of Providing Information A model is used to provide probabilistic information usually to tactical level decision makers.

Modularity Allows for the addition of faster or more extensive equipment to an existing configuration without the need to replace the entire system.

Monitoring Method of Providing Information The proportion of relevant information supplied to a decision maker can be increased by generating records only when extreme variances are determined, or when cut-and-dry decisions are made automatically.

Network Structures Allows the file designer to structure the data logically in the file where the storage and access algorithm can start with any record in the file and traverse the file in a multidirectional manner.

Optimization Deals with maximizing satisfaction while minimizing costs.

Parity Check Used to help spot erroneous transmissions of data between storage devices.

Probabilistic Outcome of a particular event cannot be determined with certainty.

Punched Card Sequential storage medium whereby holes punched in predesignated areas are used by the computer to determine the data.

Record   Set of logically related fields form a record.

Record Relationships

Fixed-Fixed   Number and size of logical records within each physical record is constant throughout the file.

Fixed-Variable   Length of the logical records in the file varies, but there are a constant number of records per block.

Variable-Fixed   Length of the logical records is constant; however, the number of logical records per block is variable.

Variable-Variable   Length of both the logical and physical records in the file is variable.

Reliability   Measure of the failure rate of the electronic circuitry.

Scientific Method   Method utilizing the following steps: Observation, Formulation of a Model, Testing the Model, and Application or Implementation.

Searching Sorted Codes

Sequential Search   Beginning with the first record of a file, each record is tested until the correct one is located. If there are N records in the file, on the average the search will require $N/2$ tests.

Binary Search   The fact that the records in the file are in sorted order, allows the programmer to check the middle record in the file and eliminate half the records in the file immediately. The remaining records in the file are searched the same way until the correct record is located, or in the case where the record being searched for does not exist in the file, the entire file is eliminated.

Sequence Check   Specific ordered field in each record of a file is checked to prevent incorrect processing.

Sorting   Various techniques are used to order the records in a file with respect to the contents of a particular field of each record; thereafter records can be more readily accessed from the file.

System

Open Loop   Any system which either does not incorporate feedback or does not take advantage of feedback that exists.

Closed Loop   Any system designed to operate using some type of feedback mechanism.

Integrated   Relies on a common data base for the entire organization.

Distributed   Each department maintains its own data base and processing procedures for its own needs but still provides for particular information to flow throughout the entire organization.

System Conversion Approaches

Direct Conversion   Occurs when the old system is completely abandoned upon implementation of the new system.

Parallel Conversion Procedure in which the old system is gradually discontinued while the new system is gradually put into full-scale implementation.

Modular Conversion Procedure in which the new system is implemented in small steps or pieces.

Phase-in Conversion Procedure in which parts of the new system techniques are interfaced in order to operate with the old system; thereafter those parts of the old system still remaining are replaced with the new system completing the conversion process.

Systems Analysis Completion Report After completing a study on the system in question, the systems analyst submits his final analysis report. The contents of this report range from a description of the present system to preliminary designs of a new or proposed system, possibly including cost estimates.

Systems Approach Involves the attainment of specific organizational goals through the implementation of coordinated activities and operations.

Systems Design Phase which attempts to determine the best of several methods for implementing the proposed system.

Test Data Inputs to the new system which conform to the format of the actual data that will be used when the system is implemented, but which allows the analyst to determine whether completion of the new system is proceeding satisfactorily.

Threshold of Detail Concept which deals with the level of detail necessary for any given level of management.

Timesharing System that allows a communication link to exist simultaneously between the computer and a varied number of users.

Transmission Security Safeguard against the illegal monitoring and/or destroying of data—by various methods such as wiretapping—passed through communication lines.

Tree Structure Logical pictorial diagram relating all the components of an organization in a hierarchical manner.

Verification Analysis of coded data input to the system to determine errors made during the coding process.

Index

Abacus, 4
ABC analysis technique, 399–401
Accessibility, information quality, 34
Access time, 421
Accounting, bookkeeping model, 393–395
  chart of accounts, 166–167
Accounting machine (see Data, processing methods)
Accounts payable system, 260–262
Accounts receivable system, 81–83, 269–272, 470, 481
Accuracy, information quality, 34
Acquisition, computer financial consideration, 286–296
Active tapping, 321–322
American Bankers Association, 162
Analysis, frameworks, 238–241
  techniques, 241–242
  (see also Systems analysis)
Analyst (see Systems analyst)
Appropriateness, information quality, 34
Archival file, 181
Arithmetic proof, control, 311
Arranging, data operation, 26–27
ASCII, 442
Asynchronous transmission, 442, 447
Audit, auditing, 374–378
  auditors, 329
  audit trail, 312
  computer aids, 377
Automatic notification, design method, 116–117
Auxiliary storage, 424, 434

Babbage, Charles, 4
Babylonian, 4–5
Backup files, 181, 313–315
Bar chart, 473–475
Batch totals, 309
Baud, 442
Baudot, 442
BCD, 442
Benchmark, 283
Billing system, 81–83, 265
Bill of Material, 218–222
Binary search, 213–214
Block code, 160–161
Blocking, 426–428
Budget model, 396–398
Buffer storage, 422–423
Bundling, 286
Byte, 420

Calculating, data operation, 26–27
Capturing, data operation, 26–27
Cause-effect analysis, 47
Census Bureau, 124
Chains/pointers, 204–209
Change, systems development, 378–381
Channels, 441–446
Charting, 463–476
Chart of accounts, 166–167
  (see also Accounting)
Check digit, 164–166, 309
Circular list, 199–200, 206–207
Clarity, information quality, 34
Classifying, data operation, 26–27, 157–158
Clerical errors, 307–309
Closed-loop system, 52
CODASYL Committee, 139, 140, 141, 145

Coding, 158–169
Communicating/disseminating, data operation, 26–27
Communication, data, 441–456
  network, 82–84, 89
  process, 59–60
  systems development, 242–245
Compatibility, 285, 350
Comprehensiveness, information quality, 34
Computational demand, 29–30
Computer, 7–9, 27–29, 73–74, 418–424
  (see also Minicomputers)
Computer Output Microfilm (COM), 432
Concentrator, 443, 448–450
Contracts, 286–288
Contribution-by-value analysis, 399–401
Controlling, management function, 51–52
Controls, 307–318, 362–363
Conversion, 349–354
  (see also Implementation)
Cost, effectiveness, 10–11, 30–36, 290–296
  marginal, 35
  model, 394–396
  opportunity, 11
  systems development, 290–296
  systems operating, 30–36
CPM, 366–368, 406–409, 473–475
Credit system, 81–83, 115, 269–272
Crossfooting, 311
CRT, 436
  (see also Terminals)

Cryptology, cryptanalysis, cryptograph, 321–322
Customer codes, 167
Cycle time, 421

Data, association, 203–209
  base, 80–83, 88–89, 133–148, 218–222, 269–272, 312–315, 352, 353
  collection methods, 265, 309–310
  communications, 441–456
  definition, 23
  directories, 207–209, 214–216
  entry methods, 436–439
  files, 179–190, 199–201
  operations, 26–27, 258–259
  processing methods, 27–31, 258
  structure, 199–203
Data base (see Data)
Data base administrator, 144, 146
Data base management, 136–140, 143
Data cells, 432–433
Data Description Language (DDL), 145–146
Data Manipulation Language (DML), 145–146
Dearden, John, 87
Debugging, 331
Decentralized data processing, 76–77
Decimal code, 162–163
Decision level analysis, 238
Decision making, 6–8, 52–56, 111, 115–116, 269–272, 463–466
Design, communicating, 268, 296, 297
  data files, 186–190
  information system, 74–92, 110–125, 256–269, 278–282
  optimum system, 261–264
Deterministic—probabilistic analysis, 48–49
Dewey Decimal Classification, 157, 162–163
Direct access, 182–184, 216–218
Direct Access Storage Device (DASD), 135–136, 178, 428–433
Disaster recovery, 323–324

Disseminating/communicating, data operation, 26–27
Distributed system, 79, 87–89
Distribution frequency analysis, 218
Documentation (see Procedures)
Document gathering, 461–463
DUN's number, 167–168
Duplex, 442

Echo check, 318
Economic feasibility, 244
Economic Order Point (EOP), 402–404
Economic Order Quantity (EOQ), 219, 402–404
EDP, 75–77
Effect-delay analysis, 47–48
Effectiveness (see Cost, effectiveness)
Electromechanical data processing method, 27–29
Engineering system, 218–222
Equipment checks, 316–318
Error log, 312
Estimating, 365–370
Exponential smoothing, 402
External information, 123–125
External method, 123–125

Facet code, 162
Facilities Management (FM), 75–76
Fact finding tools, 458–481
Fayol, Henri, 6
Feasibility, 243–245
Federal Drug Administration (FDA), 168
Feedback, 51–52
Feeney, George, 439
File management, 139–143
File Management Language (FML), 145–146
Files, 135–136, 175–190
Filtering method, 111–114
Flexibility, information quality, 34
Flores, Ivan, 215
Flowchart, 466–472
Forecast models, 401–402
Formal information, 73
Forms, 309, 324–328
Freedom from bias, information quality, 34
Future Shock, 379

Gantt chart, 367, 473–475
Gantt, H. L., 6
Gathering facts (see Systems analysis)
Gould, John, 453

Hall, D. M., 50
Hash total, 309, 312
Hertz (Hz), 443
History file, 181
Hollerith code, 177
Hollerith, Herman, 4

Implementation, data base, 143–147
  system, 344–356
  (see also Conversion)
Index file, 181
Index-sequential file, 182–183
Information, definition, 23–26
  flow analysis, 238–239
  value, 30–36
  (see also Information system; System)
Information requirements, 5–6, 258
Information system, approaches, 74–90
  definition, 71–72
  examples, 81–83, 92–100, 265, 269–272
  management, 360–382
  objectives, 72–73
Input file, 181–182
Integrated system, 79–87, 91–92
Intelligent terminals, 435–436
  (see also Terminals)
Interchange sorting technique, 211
Internal sorting, 209–211
Interrogative method, 120–123
Interview, 458–460
Inventory control system, 265, 402–404, 468–470
Inverted list, 200–201
Investigation (see Systems analysis)

Jacquard, Joseph, 4
Job Control Language (JCL), 331
Justification, 278–297

Key disk, 436–438
Keypunch (see Punched card data processing)
Key tape, 436–438

Large Scale Integration (LSI), 422–423
Lead time (*see* Inventory control system)
Leased telephone lines (*see* Channels; WATS)
Leibniz, Gottfried, 4
Legal systems, 96–99
Life cycle, 13
Limit checks, 311
Linear Organization Charts (LOC), 465–466
Linear programming, 413
Line chart, 473–475
Lists, 199–201
  (*see also* Data, files; Files)
Logical file, 135–136

Magnetic, disk, 178, 428–432
  tape, 177–178, 313–315, 424–428
  (*see also* Media)
Maintainability, 285–286
Maintenance, 370–374
Make or buy decision, 267–268
Management function, 50–56
Management science, 6–7
Manager, information system, 83–85, 89–90
Manual data processing method, 27–29
Marginal cost, 35
Mass media, 4
Master file, 181
Master plan, 361
Material yield analysis, 404–405
Media, 4, 8, 175–190
Member record, 199–203
Merging, 211–213
MICR, 433–434
Minicomputers, 435, 450–456
MIS, 71
  (*see also* Information system)
Mnemonic codes, 163
Models, conceptual, 261
  definition, 6, 7
  examples, 396–416
  formal information system, 60–62
  process, 117–120
Modems, 441, 444, 447–448
Modularity, 285
Modular system, 264–265

Monitoring, design method, 114–117
Monolithic system, 264
MTBF, 285
MTTR, 286
Multiplexor, 442, 448–450
Multiprocessors, 423–424

Napier, John, 4
National Drug Code (NDC), 168
National Health Related Items Code (NHRIC), 168
Neighborhood locatability, 215
Net present value analysis, 398
Network, association model, 202–203
  computer, 439–440
  planning and scheduling, 406–409, 473–475
  (*see also* CPM; Data, structure; PERT; Remote Computing Network)
Numbering systems (*see* Coding)

Observation, 460–461
OCR, 325, 433–434, 438–439
Off-line storage (*see* Media)
OLRT (*see* On-line systems)
On-line systems, 8, 269–272, 437
Open-loop system, 52
Operational feasibility, 244–245
Operations Research (OR) (*see* Management science)
Opportunity cost, 11
Optimization, 9
Optimum systems design, 261–264
Order entry system, 81–83, 121–123
Organization, charting, 463–466
  (*see* System)
Output controls, 315
Output file, 181–182
Overlay file, 181–182
Owner record, 199–203

Parametric user, 144–146
Pareto's Law, 399–401
Parity check, 316
Partitioned sequential file, 182–184
Parts structure, 219
  (*see also* Bill of Material)

Pascal, Blaise, 4
Passive tapping, 321–322
Payoff analysis, 397–398
Payroll system, 472
Performance analysis, 364–365, 396, 398
Performance standards, 330–331
Personnel, systems, 361–362
PERT, 366–368, 406–409, 473–475
Phonetic code, 163–164
Physical files, 135–136
Pictorial chart, 473–475
Picturephone, 434
Pie chart, 473–475
Planning, 50
Plug-to-plug compatible, 350
Pointer/chains, 204–209
Point of Sale (POS), 159, 309, 438
Preventative maintenance, 315–316
Prime division, 217
Principles, systems design, 259–266
Printing press, 4
Procedures, 328–330, 362
Production scheduling system, 121
Program, art, 330–331
  controls, 311–312
  modifications, 322–323
  programmer, 144–147, 361
  specifications, 330–335
Program decision making, 53
Programmable Communications Processor, 450–452
  (*see* Minicomputer)
Project planning, 367–370
Pseudo-device, 454
Punched card data processing, 27–29, 176–177
Punched tape, 176
Purchase, financial considerations, 286–290
Purchasing system, 116

Quality control analysis, 405–406
Quantifiable, information quality, 34
Questionnaire, 460

Reasonableness check, 311
Recording media (*see* Media)

Records, 177, 179–180
Reliability, 285
Remote Computing Network
    (RCN), 439–440
Remote terminals, 321
    (see also Terminals)
Rent acquisition considerations,
    286–290
Report file, 181
Reproducing, data operation,
    26–27
Response time, 186–188
Resources, 258
Retreiving, data operation, 26–27
Ring structure, 206–207
RJE, 434–435, 441
    (see also Terminals)

Sales reporting system, 265, 471
Sampling, 462
Schedule feasibility, 245
Schroedor, W. J., 364
Scientific method, 7
Searching techniques, 213–216
Security, 318–324
Sequential, check, control, 312
    code, 160
    files, 182
    search, 213
Service bureau, 75–76
Simplex, 442
Simulation, 283–284, 346
Smith, Adam, 157
Societal systems, 99–100
Sorting, 209–213
Soundex, 163–164
Source Data Automation (SDA),
    309, 325
Sources of facts, 235–238
Storage media, 176–178
    (see also Media)
Storing, data operation, 26–27

Strategic decision making, 55–59
Suboptimization, 79
Summarizing, data operation,
    26–27
Summary file, 181
Synchronous transmission, 442,
    447
System, classifications, 46–50
    conceptual model, 261
    definition, 46
    goal, 260–261
    life cycle, 12–13
    requirements, 258, 278–282
    (see also Information system)
Systems analysis, alternatives,
    245
    completion report, 242–243
    information systems, 11–12,
    231–246
    problem solving, 10–11
    proposal to conduct, 234–235
Systems analyst, 13–16, 361
Systems approach, 9–10
Systems concept, 9–10
    (see also Systems approach)

Table file, 181
Tactical decision making, 55–57
Tailoring, systems design ap-
    proaches, 110–125, 281
Tapping, 321–322
Taylor, Fredrick, 6
Technical decision making, 55–59
Technical feasibility, 244
Teletypwriter — TWX, 443
    (see also Terminals)
TELEX, 443
TELPAK, 445–446
Template, 471–474
Terminals, 434–436
Test deck, 375–377
Testing, 331, 347–349

Third party lease, 286–290
Threshold of detail, 111
Time, 29–30
Timeliness, information quality, 34
Timesharing, 75–76, 441
Toffler, Alvin, 379
Touch tone, 434
Training, 345–347
Transaction file, 181
Transformation techniques,
    216–218
Tree structure (see Data, struc-
    ture; Network)
Trigger, 116

Unit record (see Media; Punched
    card data processing)
Universal Product Code (UPC),
    168–169
User, data base, 144–147
    (see also Systems analysis)

Value (see Cost, effectiveness)
Variance reporting, 114–115
Vendor, evaluation, 283–286
    proposals, 282–283
    support, 286
Verify, data operation, 26–27, 309
    information quality, 34
Virtual storage, 421–422
Volatility, 186, 187
Volume, 29–30

Wagner, H. M., 6
WATS, 445
Where-used, data association con-
    cept, 221–222
Word processing, 440–441
Work file, 181

ZIP code, 160–161